Get a FREE eBook

To register this book, scan the code or go to
www.manning.com/freebook/huang

By registering you get

- **FREE eBook copy**
  download in PDF and ePub

- **FREE online access**
  to Manning's liveBook platform

- **FREE audio**
  read and listen online in liveBook

- **FREE AI Assistant**
  it knows the book and what you are reading when it answers

- **FREE in-book testing**
  fun tests to lock in your knowledge

In Manning's liveBook platform you can share discussions and comments with other readers, add your own bookmarks and highlights, insert personal notes anywhere on the page, see color versions of all the book's graphics, download source code and other resources, and more!

To register, scan the code or go to www.manning.com/freebook/huang

Praise for the first edition

With this publication, we finally have a definitive treatise on PyTorch. It covers the basics and abstractions in great detail.

—From the Foreword by Soumith Chintala, Cocreator of PyTorch

Deep learning divided into digestible chunks with code samples that build up logically.

—Mathieu Zhang, NVIDIA

Timely, practical, and thorough. Don't put it on your bookshelf but next to your laptop.

—Philippe Van Bergen, P2 Consulting

Deep Learning with PyTorch offers a very pragmatic overview of deep learning. It is a didactical resource.

—Orlando Alejo Mendez Morales, Experian

Deep Learning with PyTorch
Second Edition

Training and applying deep learning and generative AI models

Howard Huang
Luca Antiga
Eli Stevens
Thomas Viehmann

MANNING
Shelter Island

For online information and ordering of this and other Manning books, please visit www.manning.com. The publisher offers discounts on this book when ordered in quantity. For more information, please contact

    Special Sales Department
    Manning Publications Co.
    20 Baldwin Road
    PO Box 761
    Shelter Island, NY 11964
    Email: orders@manning.com

©2026 by Manning Publications Co. All rights reserved.

No part of this publication may be reproduced, stored in a retrieval system, or transmitted, in any form or by means electronic, mechanical, photocopying, or otherwise, without prior written permission of the publisher.

Many of the designations used by manufacturers and sellers to distinguish their products are claimed as trademarks. Where those designations appear in the book, and Manning Publications was aware of a trademark claim, the designations have been printed in initial caps or all caps.

♾ Recognizing the importance of preserving what has been written, it is Manning's policy to have the books we publish printed on acid-free paper, and we exert our best efforts to that end. Recognizing also our responsibility to conserve the resources of our planet, Manning books are printed on paper that is at least 15 percent recycled and processed without the use of elemental chlorine.

The authors and publisher have made every effort to ensure that the information in this book was correct at press time. The authors and publisher do not assume and hereby disclaim any liability to any party for any loss, damage, or disruption caused by errors or omissions, whether such errors or omissions result from negligence, accident, or any other cause, or from any usage of the information herein.

Manning Publications Co. 20 Baldwin Road PO Box 761 Shelter Island, NY 11964	Development editor: Elesha Hyde Technical editor: Fábio Vinicius Moreira Perez Review editor: Angelina Lazukić Production editor: Aleksandar Dragosavljević Copy editor: Alisa Larson Proofreader: Mike Beady Typesetter: Dennis Dalinnik Cover designer: Marija Tudor

ISBN: 9781633438859
Printed in the UK by CPI Group Ltd

To Fred, Mary, Ward, and Edward, the best unpaid editors, critics, and supporters I could ask for

—*Howard Huang*

Same :-) But, really, this is for you, Alice and Luigi

—*Luca Antiga*

To my wife (this book would not have happened without her invaluable support and partnership), my parents (I would not have happened without them), and my children (this book would have happened a lot sooner but for them), thank you for being my home, my foundation, and my joy

—*Eli Stevens*

To Eva, Rebekka, Jonathan, and David

—*Thomas Viehmann*

contents

preface xvii
acknowledgments xix
about this book xxi
about the authors xxvii
about the cover illustration xxviii

PART 1 CORE PYTORCH 1

1 Introducing deep learning and the PyTorch library 3

1.1 What is deep learning? 4

1.2 The shift from machine learning to deep learning 5

1.3 What to expect 7

1.4 Why PyTorch? 8

The deep learning competitive landscape 9

1.5 How PyTorch supports deep learning projects 10

1.6 Hardware and software requirements 13

Using Jupyter Notebooks 14

1.7 Exercises 15

2 — Pretrained networks 17

- 2.1 A pretrained network that recognizes the subject of an image 18

  *Obtaining a pretrained network for image recognition 20
  AlexNet 21 • The Vision Transformer 23 • Ready, set, almost run 23 • Run! 26*

- 2.2 Generating and editing images 29

  The inpainting process 29 • A network that turns horses into zebras 30

- 2.3 Model Zoo: Hugging Face 34
- 2.4 A pretrained network that describes scenes 35

  BLIP in action 36

- 2.5 Conclusion 37
- 2.6 Exercises 38

3 — It starts with a tensor 39

- 3.1 The world as floating-point numbers 40
- 3.2 Tensors: Multidimensional arrays 42

  From Python lists to PyTorch tensors 42 • Constructing our first tensors 43 • The essence of tensors 43

- 3.3 Indexing tensors 46
- 3.4 Broadcasting 47
- 3.5 Named tensors 48
- 3.6 Tensor element types 51

  Specifying the numeric type with dtype 51 • A dtype for every occasion 52 • Managing a tensor's dtype attribute 52

- 3.7 The tensor API 53
- 3.8 Tensors: Scenic views of storage 55

  Indexing into storage 55 • Modifying stored values: In-place operations 56

- 3.9 Tensor metadata: Size, offset, and stride 57

  *Views of another tensor's storage 58 • Transposing without copying 59 • Transposing in higher dimensions 61
  Contiguous tensors 62*

- 3.10 Moving tensors to the GPU 64

  Managing a tensor's device attribute 65

- 3.11 NumPy interoperability 66

- 3.12 Generalized tensors are tensors, too 67
- 3.13 Serializing tensors 68

    Serializing to HDF5 with h5py 68
- 3.14 Conclusion 70
- 3.15 Exercises 70

4 Real-world data representation using tensors 72

- 4.1 Working with images 73

    Adding color channels 74 ▪ Loading an image file 74
    Changing the layout 75 ▪ Normalizing the data 76
- 4.2 3D images: Volumetric data 77

    Loading a specialized format 78
- 4.3 Representing tabular data 79

    Using a real-world dataset 79 ▪ Loading a wine data tensor 80
    Representing scores 83 ▪ One-hot encoding 83 ▪ When to
    categorize 85 ▪ Finding thresholds 87
- 4.4 Working with time series 89

    Adding a time dimension 89 ▪ Shaping the data by time
    period 91 ▪ Ready for training 93
- 4.5 Representing text 96

    Converting text to numbers 97 ▪ One-hot-encoding characters 97
    One-hot encoding whole words 99 ▪ Text embeddings 101
    Text embeddings as a blueprint 103
- 4.6 Conclusion 104
- 4.7 Exercises 104

5 The mechanics of learning 106

- 5.1 A timeless lesson in modeling 107
- 5.2 Learning is just parameter estimation 109

    A hot problem 110 ▪ Gathering some data 110 ▪ Visualizing
    the data 111 ▪ Choosing a linear model as a first try 111
- 5.3 Less loss is what we want 112

    From problem back to PyTorch 113
- 5.4 Down along the gradient 116

    Decreasing loss 117 ▪ Getting analytical 118 ▪ Iterating to
    fit the model 121 ▪ Normalizing inputs 124 ▪ Visualizing
    (again) 127

5.5 PyTorch's autograd: Backpropagating all things   128

Computing the gradient automatically   128 • Optimizers à la carte   132 • Training, validation, and overfitting   136 Training set   141 • Autograd nits and switching it off   142

5.6 Conclusion   144

5.7 Exercises   144

6 Using a neural network to fit the data   146

6.1 Artificial neurons   147

Composing a multilayer network   149 • Understanding the error function   149 • Adding nonlinearity with activation functions   150 • More activation functions   152 • Choosing the best activation function   153 • What learning means for a neural network   154

6.2 The PyTorch nn module   157

Using nn.Module as a callable   157 • Returning to the linear model   158

6.3 Finally, a neural network   163

Replacing the linear model   163 • Inspecting the parameters   164 Comparing to the linear model   167

6.4 Conclusion   167

6.5 Exercises   168

7 Telling birds from airplanes: Learning from images   170

7.1 A dataset of tiny images   171

Downloading CIFAR-10   171 • The Dataset class   172 Dataset transforms   174 • Normalizing data   176

7.2 Distinguishing birds from airplanes   178

Building the dataset   179 • A fully connected model   180 Output of a classifier   181 • Representing the output as probabilities   182 • Training the classifier   189 • The limits of going fully connected   196

7.3 Conclusion   198

7.4 Exercises   199

8 Using convolutions to generalize   200

8.1 The case for convolutions   201

What convolutions do   201

8.2 Convolutions in action 204

Padding the boundary 206 ▪ Detecting features with convolutions 208 ▪ Looking further with depth and pooling 211 Putting it all together for our network 213

8.3 Subclassing nn.Module 215

Our network as an nn.Module 216 ▪ How PyTorch keeps track of parameters and submodules 218 ▪ The functional API 219

8.4 Training our convolutional neural network 220

Measuring accuracy 222 ▪ Saving and loading our model 223 Training on the GPU 224

8.5 Model design 226

Adding memory capacity: Width 227 ▪ Helping our model to converge and generalize: Regularization 229 ▪ Going deeper to learn more complex structures: Depth 233 ▪ Comparing the designs from this section 239 ▪ It's already outdated 239

8.6 Conclusion 240

8.7 Exercises 240

PART 2 PRACTICAL DEEP LEARNING APPLICATIONS 243

9 How transformers work 245

9.1 A motivating example: Generating names character by character 247

9.2 Self-supervised learning 249

Limits of the bigram model 251

9.3 Generating our training data 252

9.4 Embeddings and linear layers 254

Visualizing embeddings 259

9.5 Attention 260

Dot product self-attention 261 ▪ Scaled dot product causal self-attention 264

9.6 Transformers 268

The decoder 269

9.7 Other Transformer architectures 274

The encoder 274 ▪ The encoder-decoder 275

- 9.8 Tokenization 276
  - *Generating sentences 278*
- 9.9 The Vision Transformer 279
- 9.10 Conclusion 281
- 9.11 Exercises 281

10 Diffusion models for images 283

- 10.1 History of VAEs and GANs 284
- 10.2 Motivator for diffusion models 285
- 10.3 Diffusion in detail 286
- 10.4 Setting up the data 287
- 10.5 The forward process 289
- 10.6 Training 293
  - *Loss 295*
- 10.7 Reversing diffusion (how to sample) 297
- 10.8 Conclusion 300
- 10.9 Exercises 300

11 Using PyTorch to fight cancer 302

- 11.1 Introduction to the use case 303
- 11.2 Preparing for a large-scale project 304
- 11.3 What is a CT scan, exactly? 306
- 11.4 The project: An end-to-end detector for lung cancer 309
  - *Why can't we just throw data at a neural network until it works? 312* ▪ *Our data source: The LUNA Grand Challenge 317* ▪ *Downloading the LUNA data 317*
- 11.5 Conclusion 318

12 Combining data sources into a unified dataset 320

- 12.1 Raw CT data files 322
- 12.2 Parsing LUNA's annotation data 322
  - *Training and validation sets 324* ▪ *Unifying our annotation and candidate data 325*
- 12.3 Loading individual CT scans 327
  - *Hounsfield Units 329*

12.4 Locating a nodule using the patient coordinate system 330

The patient coordinate system 331 • CT scan shape and voxel sizes 333 • Converting between millimeters and voxel addresses 333 • Extracting a nodule from a CT scan 335

12.5 Straightforward dataset implementation 336

Caching candidate arrays with the getCtRawCandidate function 339 • Constructing our dataset in LunaDataset.__init__ 340 • A training/validation split 340 • Rendering the data 342

12.6 Conclusion 342

12.7 Exercises 343

13 Training a classification model to detect suspected tumors 344

13.1 A foundational model and training loop 344

13.2 The main entry point for our application 347

13.3 Pretraining setup and initialization 349

Initializing the model and optimizer 350 • Care and feeding of data loaders 351

13.4 Our first-pass neural network design 353

The core convolutions 354 • The full model 357

13.5 Training and validating the model 360

The computeBatchLoss function 362 • The validation loop is similar 364

13.6 Outputting performance metrics 365

The logMetrics function 366

13.7 Running the training script 369

Data needed for training 370 • Interlude: The tqdm function 371

13.8 Evaluating the model: Getting 99.7% correct means we're done, right? 372

13.9 Graphing training metrics with TensorBoard 373

Running TensorBoard 374 • Adding TensorBoard support to the metrics logging function 377

13.10 Why isn't the model learning to detect nodules? 379

13.11 Conclusion 380

13.12 Exercises 380

14 Improving training with metrics and augmentation   382

- 14.1 High-level plan for improvement   383
- 14.2 Good dogs vs. bad guys: False positives and false negatives   384
- 14.3 Graphing the positives and negatives   386

  Recall is Chirpy's strength   388 ▪ Precision is Dozer's forte   389 Implementing precision and recall in logMetrics   390 ▪ Our ultimate performance metric: The F1 score   391 ▪ How does our model perform with our new metrics?   395

- 14.4 What does an ideal dataset look like?   396

  Making the data look less like the actual and more like the "ideal"   399 ▪ Contrasting training with a balanced LunaDataset to previous runs   404 ▪ Recognizing the symptoms of overfitting   406

- 14.5 Revisiting the problem of overfitting   408

  An overfit face-to-age prediction model   408

- 14.6 Preventing overfitting with data augmentation   409

  Specific data augmentation techniques   410 ▪ Seeing the improvement from data augmentation   415

- 14.7 Conclusion   417
- 14.8 Exercises   417

15 Using segmentation to find suspected nodules   420

- 15.1 Utilizing a second model in our project   421
- 15.2 Various types of segmentation   423
- 15.3 Semantic segmentation: Per-pixel classification   423

  The Segment Anything model (SAM)   425

- 15.4 SAM architecture   426

  Trying out an off-the-shelf model for our project   428

- 15.5 Using the SAM model directly   430
- 15.6 Updating the dataset for segmentation   432

  Working around SAM's limitation on 2D data   432 ▪ Building the segmentation dataset   434 ▪ Training a model to flag potential candidates   436

- 15.7 Updating our training for fine-tuning   439

  How to fine-tune a model   440 ▪ Using the AdamW optimizer   442 Designing our training loop   442 ▪ Saving our model   444

CONTENTS

15.8 Inference and results 445
15.9 Conclusion 446
15.10 Exercises 447

16 Training models on multiple GPUs 449

16.1 Introduction to parallel programming 450

Distributed computing terminology 451 ▪ Hardware requirements 453 ▪ Initializing a distributed program 453

16.2 Collective communication 455
16.3 Introduction to parallelisms 458
16.4 Data parallelism 459
16.5 Model parallelism 461

Pipeline parallelism 462 ▪ Tensor parallelism 464 Deciding between pipeline and tensor parallelism 465

16.6 n-dimensional parallelism 466
16.7 Fully sharded data parallelism 468
16.8 Large language model–specific parallelisms 470

Context parallelism 470 ▪ Expert Parallelism 470

16.9 Tying all parallelisms together 471
16.10 Conclusion 471
16.11 Exercises 471

17 Deploying to production 474

17.1 Serving PyTorch models 475

Our model served by Gradio 476 ▪ Our model behind a FastAPI server 477 ▪ What we want from deployment 481 ▪ Request batching and streaming responses 482 ▪ How to make PyTorch models even faster 486

17.2 Exporting models 490

Interoperability beyond PyTorch with ONNX 491 ▪ PyTorch's own export: torch.export 492

17.3 Expanding on torch.compile 495

Full graph capture vs. disjoint graphs 496

17.4 Understanding execution with torch.profiler 499
17.5 Using PyTorch outside of Python 501

LibTorch: PyTorch in C++ 501

17.6 Going mobile: ExecuTorch 504
17.7 Conclusion 505
17.8 Exercises 505

index 507

preface

When I first started exploring machine learning, the idea that a computer could learn the algorithms I needed instead of painstakingly coding them felt magical. Leaning into my laziness, I loved that I could define a model and let the system discover the internals for me. I had no idea then how far things would go. Today, models can even code themselves, and we're limited more by the clarity of our prompts than by the machinery itself. The pace of progress has been astounding, and part of what I want to do in this book is peel back that sense of mystery.

My first experience with AI was back in college. In 2016, I purchased a few technical books, much like this one, on machine learning and deep learning. At the time, I tried learning Scikit-learn and TensorFlow but found the learning curve quite steep. Whether due to the libraries themselves or my own inexperience, I struggled to get past the basics, barely managing to build simple models and often feeling stuck. Then PyTorch was released on January 18, 2017, and it immediately struck me as different. It was the first framework that hit the right balance between ease of use and power.

When I finally had the opportunity to contribute to PyTorch, I jumped at the chance. It took me a while to build the confidence to make contributions to such a large open source project—I worried that what I was doing was wrong, too small, or insignificant. But after working as a core contributor over the past several years, I can say that any contribution, whether big or small, is deeply appreciated and can truly make a difference.

Writing this book, I kept returning to my younger self: I wanted something that balanced theory and practice, nudged you forward without overwhelming you, and made hard ideas feel tractable. I hope these pages do that for you.

While PyTorch has changed significantly over the years, its ethos has remained the same: to provide a deep learning library that's easy to use yet powerful enough to tackle cutting-edge problems. I hope this book stays true to that spirit. From tackling the basics to building real-world projects, PyTorch has been my go-to framework, and I'm excited to share it with you. I can't wait to see what you'll build with it.

—HOWARD HUANG

acknowledgments

Creating this book was definitely a journey through many changes in my life. It has been a wild ride, and I am grateful for the support of my close network. I can't possibly name everyone here, but I hope I can get a copy of this book to Andrew Huang, Austin Lee, Brandon Pon, Chang Liu, Edward Ding, Elise Yuen, Elizabeth Tran, Fernando Altamirano, James Lee, Jason Xie, Jay Gandhi, Justin Hwang, Kyle Wilcots, Melinda Leung, Melissa Chen, Nikka Mofid, Paulina Lei, Steven Zheng, and Tim Liew.

A huge shoutout to the Manning team for all the work behind the scenes to make this book a reality. Thanks to Suresh Jain for reaching out about this book and thanks to Michael Stephens for encouraging me to take this on. Thanks to Ivan Martinović for prepping the manuscript during the MEAP process. Thank you, Fábio Perez, for serving as a technical editor on the book and providing your invaluable edits, feedback, and suggestions. Your attention to detail and thoroughness have helped beyond words. Fábio holds a B.Sc. in computer engineering and an M.Sc. in artificial intelligence. His research publications have won awards and spawned international patents. There are countless others at Manning who have been tagged in cc chains, and I appreciate all your help.

Elesha Hyde has been a tireless development editor through it all. Thank you so much for your support through the whole process. Your positive emails really helped to keep me on track and motivated to finish the book.

I am deeply indebted to the PyTorch team. This book would not exist if it were not for Soumith Chintala, Adam Paszke, and all the other early contributors who had the idea of building PyTorch from an intern project to the massive world-class framework it is today. PyTorch has grown so much that the core contributors are too many to name, but I would like to acknowledge the PyTorch team at Meta for their tireless work. Working with the PyTorch team, I can see how passionate they are about making PyTorch the best deep learning framework and how dedicated they are to supporting the open source community.

—HOWARD HUANG

about this book

This book aims to provide the foundations of deep learning with PyTorch and demonstrate them in action through a real-life project. We strive to provide the key concepts underlying deep learning and show how PyTorch puts them in the hands of practitioners. In the book, we try to provide intuition that will support further exploration, and in doing so, we selectively delve into details to show what is going on behind the curtain.

Deep Learning with PyTorch doesn't try to be a reference book; rather, it's a conceptual companion that will allow you to explore more advanced material independently online. As such, we focus on a subset of the features offered by PyTorch.

Who should read this book

This book is intended for developers who are, or aim to become, deep learning practitioners and want to get acquainted with PyTorch. We imagine our typical reader to be a computer scientist, data scientist, or software engineer, or an undergraduate or graduate student in a related program. Since we don't assume prior knowledge of deep learning, some parts in the first half of the book may be a repetition of concepts that are already understood by experienced practitioners. For those readers, we hope the exposition will provide a slightly different angle to known topics.

We expect readers to have basic knowledge of imperative and object-oriented programming. Since the book uses Python, you should be familiar with the syntax and operating environment. Knowing how to install Python packages and run scripts on your platform of choice is a prerequisite. Readers coming from C++, Java, JavaScript,

Ruby, or other such languages should have an easy time picking it up, but they will need to do some catch-up outside this book. Similarly, being familiar with NumPy will be useful. We also expect familiarity with some basic linear algebra, such as knowing what matrices and vectors are and what a dot product is.

How this book is organized: A roadmap

Deep Learning with PyTorch is organized into two distinct parts. Part 1 covers the foundations, while part 2 explores advanced topics, including modern generative models, a comprehensive medical imaging project, distributed training, and production deployment. You will likely notice different voices and graphical styles among the parts. Although the book is a result of endless hours of collaborative planning, discussion, and editing, the writing and authoring graphics were split between the authors. The following is a breakdown of each part into chapters and a brief description of each.

In part 1, we take our first steps with PyTorch, building the fundamental skills needed to understand PyTorch projects out there in the wild as well as starting to build our own. We'll cover the PyTorch API and some behind-the-scenes features that make PyTorch the library it is and work on training an initial classification model. By the end of part 1, we'll be ready to tackle a real-world project.

The individual chapters in part 1 address the following:

- Chapter 1 introduces PyTorch as a library and its place in the deep learning revolution and touches on what sets PyTorch apart from other deep learning frameworks.
- Chapter 2 shows PyTorch in action by running examples of pretrained networks; it demonstrates how to download and run models from Hugging Face Hub.
- Chapter 3 introduces the basic building block of PyTorch—the tensor—showing its API and going behind the scenes with some implementation details.
- Chapter 4 demonstrates how different kinds of data can be represented as tensors and how deep learning models expect tensors to be shaped.
- Chapter 5 walks through the mechanics of learning through gradient descent and how PyTorch enables it with automatic differentiation.
- Chapter 6 shows the process of building and training a neural network for regression in PyTorch using the `nn` and `optim` modules.
- Chapter 7 builds on the previous chapter to create a fully connected model for image classification and expands the knowledge of the PyTorch API.
- Chapter 8 introduces convolutional neural networks and touches on more advanced concepts for building neural network models and their PyTorch implementation.

Part 2 begins with modern generative models, including transformers and diffusion models, and then tackles a comprehensive lung cancer detection project that demonstrates real-world problem-solving at scale. The part concludes with distributed training techniques and production deployment strategies, providing a complete journey from advanced architectures to production-ready systems.

Chapters in part 2 cover the following topics:

- Chapter 9 introduces the Transformer architecture, exploring how attention mechanisms enable text generation and laying the foundation for understanding modern generative AI models.
- Chapter 10 demonstrates diffusion models for image generation, showing how neural networks can learn to create realistic images through an iterative denoising process.
- Chapter 11 presents the end-to-end strategy for the lung cancer detection project, explaining how we'll combine CT scan imaging with deep learning for tumor identification.
- Chapter 12 covers loading and processing raw CT scan data, implementing custom datasets, and converting medical imaging data into tensors suitable for training.
- Chapter 13 builds a classification model to detect suspected tumors, establishing the foundational training loop and model architecture for nodule detection.
- Chapter 14 improves the classification model by introducing precision, recall, and F1 score metrics and then applies data balancing and augmentation techniques to address class imbalance problems.
- Chapter 15 introduces segmentation using the Segment Anything model (SAM) to automatically identify potential nodule locations in CT scans without requiring hand-annotated candidate data.
- Chapter 16 covers training models on multiple GPUs using distributed computing, explaining data parallelism, model parallelism, pipeline parallelism, and tensor parallelism for efficient large-scale training.
- Chapter 17 focuses on deploying PyTorch models to production, demonstrating serving strategies with Gradio and FastAPI, model export using ONNX, performance optimization with `torch.compile`, and deployment to mobile devices with ExecuTorch.

About the code

All the code in this book was written for Python 3.10 or later. The code for the book is available for download from Manning's website (https://www.manning.com/books/deep-learning-with-pytorch-second-edition) and on GitHub (https://github.com/deep-learning-with-pytorch/dlwpt-code-2e). Version 3.10 or later is required to run the examples in this book. For example,

```
$ python
Python 3.10.10 (main, Apr  8 2025, 11:35:47) [Clang 17.0.0 (clang-
    1700.0.13.3)] on darwin
Type "help", "copyright", "credits" or "license" for more information.
>>>
```

Command lines intended to be entered at a Bash prompt start with $ (e.g., the $ python line in this example). Fixed-width inline code looks like this.

Code blocks that begin with >>> are transcripts of a session at the Python interactive prompt. The >>> characters are not meant to be considered input; text lines that do not start with >>> or ... are output. In some cases, an extra blank line is inserted before the >>> to improve readability in print. These blank lines are not included when you actually enter the text at the interactive prompt:

```
>>> print("Hello, world!")
Hello, world!

>>> print("Until next time...")
Until next time...
1
```

⟵ This blank line would not be present during an actual interactive session.

We also make heavy use of Python notebooks, as described in chapter 1, section 1.6.1. Code from a notebook that we provide as part of the official GitHub repository looks like this:

```
# In[1]:
print("Hello, world!")

# Out[1]:
Hello, world!

# In[2]:
print("Until next time...")

# Out[2]:
Until next time...
```

Some example notebooks contain the following boilerplate in the first cell (some lines may be missing in early chapters), which we skip including in the book after this point:

```
# In[1]:
%matplotlib inline
from matplotlib import pyplot as plt
import numpy as np

import torch
import torch.nn as nn
import torch.nn.functional as F
import torch.optim as optim

torch.set_printoptions(edgeitems=2)
torch.manual_seed(123)
```

Otherwise, code blocks are partial or entire sections of .py source files. For example,

```
def main():
    print("Hello, world!")
```

```
if __name__ == '__main__':
    main()
```

Many of the code samples in the book are presented with two-space indents. Due to the limitations of print, code listings are limited to 76-character lines, which can be impractical for heavily indented sections of code. The use of two-space indents helps to mitigate the excessive line wrapping that would otherwise be present. All the code available for download for the book (again, at https://www.manning.com/books/deep-learning-with-pytorch-second-edition or https://github.com/deep-learning-with-pytorch/dlwpt-code-2e) uses a consistent four-space indent.

Hardware and software requirements

Part 1 has been designed not to require any particular computing resources. Any recent computer or online computing resource will be adequate. Similarly, no certain operating system is required. In part 2, we anticipate that completing a full training run for the more advanced examples will require a CUDA-capable GPU. The default parameters used in part 2 assume a GPU with at least 8 GB of RAM (we suggest an NVIDIA RTX 4060 Ti, RTX 4070, or better), but the parameters can be adjusted if your hardware has less RAM available. Luckily, online computing services recently started offering GPU time for free. We discuss computing requirements in more detail in the appropriate sections. The raw data needed for part 2's cancer-detection project is about 60 GB to download. We provide an option to use only part of the dataset for more rapid experimentation, but for the full project experience, you will need a total of around 200 GB of free disk space on the system.

You need Python 3.10 or later; instructions can be found on the Python website (http://www.python.org/downloads). For PyTorch installation information, see the Get Started guide on the official PyTorch website (https://pytorch.org/get-started/locally). We suggest that Windows users install with Anaconda or Miniconda (https://www.anaconda.com/distribution or https://docs.conda.io/en/latest/miniconda.html, respectively). Other operating systems like Linux typically have a wider variety of workable options, with pip being the most common package manager for Python. We provide a requirements.txt file that pip can use to install dependencies. Since current Apple laptops do not include GPUs that support CUDA, the precompiled macOS packages for PyTorch are CPU-only. Of course, experienced users are free to install packages in the way that is most compatible with their preferred development environment.

Other online resources

Although this book does not assume prior knowledge of deep learning, it is not a foundational introduction to deep learning. We cover the basics, but our focus is on proficiency with the PyTorch library. We encourage interested readers to build up an intuitive understanding of deep learning either before, during, or after reading this book. For a thorough introduction and reference, we direct you to *Deep Learning* by Goodfellow et al. (http://www.deeplearningbook.org).

And, of course, Manning Publications has an extensive catalog of deep learning titles (https://www.manning.com/catalog#section-83) that cover a wide variety of topics in the space. Depending on your interests, many of them will make an excellent next book to read.

liveBook discussion forum

Purchase of *Deep Learning with PyTorch, Second Edition* includes free access to liveBook, Manning's online reading platform. Using liveBook's exclusive discussion features, you can attach comments to the book globally or to specific sections or paragraphs. It's a snap to make notes for yourself, ask and answer technical questions, and receive help from the author and other users. To access the forum, go to https://livebook.manning.com/book/deep-learning-with-pytorch-second-edition/discussion. You can also learn more about Manning's forums and the rules of conduct at https://livebook.manning.com/discussion.

Manning's commitment to our readers is to provide a venue where a meaningful dialogue between individual readers and between readers and the author can take place. It is not a commitment to any specific amount of participation on the part of the author, whose contribution to the forum remains voluntary (and unpaid). We suggest you try asking the author some challenging questions lest his interest stray! The forum and the archives of previous discussions will be accessible from the publisher's website as long as the book is in print.

about the authors

HOWARD HUANG is a software engineer who has worked on the PyTorch library for over five years and been an avid user for even longer. He has a background in distributed systems and ML systems, working on distributed training for most of his career. At publication, he is on the PyTorch team at Meta.

LUCA ANTIGA worked as a researcher in biomedical engineering in the 2000s and spent the last decade as a cofounder and CTO of an AI engineering company. He has contributed to several open source projects, including the PyTorch core. He recently cofounded a US-based startup focused on infrastructure for data-defined software.

ELI STEVENS has spent most of his career working at startups in Silicon Valley, with roles ranging from software engineer (making enterprise networking appliances) to CTO (developing software for radiation oncology). At publication, he is working on machine learning in the self-driving-car industry.

THOMAS VIEHMANN is a machine learning and PyTorch specialty trainer; a consultant based in Munich, Germany; and a PyTorch core developer. With a PhD in mathematics, he is not scared by theory, but he is thoroughly practical when applying it to computing challenges.

about the cover illustration

The figure on the cover of *Deep Learning with PyTorch, Second Edition* is captioned "Kabardinien," or "Kabardian." The illustration is taken from a collection of dress costumes from various countries by Jacques Grasset de Saint-Sauveur (1757–1810), titled *Costumes Civils actuels de tous les Peuples connus*, published in France in 1788. This illustration is finely drawn and colored by hand.

Part 1

Core PyTorch

Welcome to the first part of this book. This is where we'll take our first steps with PyTorch, gaining the fundamental skills needed to understand its anatomy and work out the mechanics of a PyTorch project.

Chapter 1 introduces PyTorch, explains what it is, what problems it solves, and how it compares to other deep learning frameworks. Chapter 2 gives us a hands-on tour with pretrained models on interesting tasks. Chapter 3 gets a bit more serious and teaches the basic data structure used in PyTorch programs: the tensor. Chapter 4 will take us on another tour, this time across ways to represent data from different domains as PyTorch tensors. Chapter 5 unveils how a program can learn from examples and how PyTorch supports this process. Chapter 6 provides the fundamentals of what a neural network is and how to build a neural network with PyTorch. Chapter 7 tackles a simple image classification problem with a neural network architecture. Finally, chapter 8 shows how the same problem can be cracked in a much smarter way using a convolutional neural network.

By the end of part 1 (chapters 1–8), we'll have what it takes to tackle real-world problems with PyTorch in part 2.

Introducing deep learning and the PyTorch library

> **This chapter covers**
> - How deep learning changes our approach to machine learning
> - Understanding why PyTorch is a good fit for deep learning
> - Examining a typical deep learning project
> - The hardware you need to follow along with the examples

PyTorch is a Python library that facilitates building deep learning projects. It emphasizes flexibility and allows deep learning models to be expressed in idiomatic Python. This approachability and ease of use found early adopters in the research community, and in the years since its first release, it has grown into one of the most prominent deep learning tools across a broad range of applications.

This book teaches you from start to finish how to build complete deep learning projects using PyTorch. You'll learn to work with tensors (PyTorch's fundamental data structure), design neural network architectures, train models on your data, and deploy them to production. We include several major hands-on projects—namely, building your own language model, working with image generation models, and creating a medical image segmentation system from scratch, giving you practical experience with the entire deep learning workflow.

Understanding deep learning gives you the power to solve problems that were previously impossible to automate. These skills open up new career opportunities in artificial intelligence (AI) development, and since AI is eating the world right now, PyTorch can be your fork and knife. While this book focuses on PyTorch, the concepts transfer to other frameworks. By reading this book, you'll gain the skills of a deep learning practitioner, not just someone who is specialized in PyTorch.

1.1 What is deep learning?

Understanding how we arrived at PyTorch requires looking at the broader context of AI development. The term *artificial intelligence* refers to computer systems that can perform tasks typically requiring human intelligence. AI encompasses a range of disciplines that have recently gained significant attention, often leading to varied interpretations and definitions. While recent advances in AI have been marked by hype and fearmongering reminiscent of science fiction, the reality is far more measured. It would be disingenuous to claim that today's machines are learning to "think" in any human sense of the word. Rather, we've discovered a general class of algorithms that are able to approximate complicated, nonlinear processes very, very effectively, which we can use to automate tasks that were previously limited to humans. While this may seem straightforward or even underwhelming, it has already greatly expanded our understanding of what is possible with computers.

For example, ChatGPT (https://chat.openai.com/), a chatbot developed by AI research company OpenAI, utilizes a large language model that can answer queries and generate paragraphs of text. When we fed it the prompt

```
Give an introduction about yourself through a poem
```

it produced the following:

> *In realms of words, I come alive,*
> *A creation born to help and thrive.*
> *I'm ChatGPT, an AI so grand,*
> *With knowledge vast, at your command.*
>
> *Through the art of language, I've been trained,*
> *To assist and guide, with wisdom ingrained.*
> *From lofty thoughts to mundane chit-chat,*
> *I'm here to converse, imagine that!*

That's a remarkably coherent and creative response for a machine. Even more impressively, the ability to perform these formerly human-only tasks is acquired *through examples*, rather than encoded by a human as a set of handcrafted rules.

> **NOTE** The output of language models is determined probabilistically and may be nondeterministic, something we will see in chapter 9.

In a way, we're learning that intelligence is a notion we often conflate with self-awareness, and self-awareness is definitely not required to successfully carry out these kinds of tasks. In the end, the question of computer intelligence might not even be important. Edsger W. Dijkstra found that the question of whether machines could think was "about as relevant as the question of whether Submarines Can Swim" ("The Threats to Computing Science," http://mng.bz/nPJ5).

That general class of algorithms we're talking about falls under the AI subcategory of *deep learning*, which deals with training mathematical entities named *deep neural networks* by presenting instructive examples. Deep learning uses large amounts of data to approximate complex functions that involve widely different inputs and outputs. For example, it can take a sentence and generate a realistic image based on that textual description. It can also take a written script and convert it into a natural-sounding voice, reciting the spoken words. Or, in a simpler case, it can identify a golden retriever in a picture and confirm that the dog is indeed a golden retriever. This kind of capability allows us to create programs with functionality that was, until very recently, exclusively the domain of human beings.

1.2 The shift from machine learning to deep learning

To appreciate the paradigm shift ushered in by this deep learning approach, let's take a step back for a bit of perspective. Until the last decade, the broader class of systems that fell under the label *machine learning* relied heavily on *feature engineering*.

Raw features are simply the unmodified data values themselves. However, these raw features often don't directly expose the patterns necessary for machine learning algorithms to perform well. This is where feature engineering comes in—the process of using domain knowledge to create new features from raw data that make machine learning algorithms work more effectively.

Feature engineering involves creating suitable transformations so that the subsequent algorithms can effectively solve a task. For instance, to tell 1s from 0s in images of handwritten digits, we would come up with a set of filters to estimate the direction of edges over the image and then train a classifier to predict the correct digit given a distribution of edge directions. Another helpful feature could be the number of enclosed holes, as seen in a 0, an 8, and, particularly, a loopy 2.

Deep learning, on the other hand, deals with finding such representations automatically, from raw data, to successfully perform a task. This process reduces the need for extensive manual feature engineering. In the 1s versus 0s example, filters would be refined during training by iteratively looking at pairs of examples and target labels. This is not to say that feature engineering has no place with deep learning; we often need to inject some form of prior knowledge into a learning system. However, the ability of a neural network to ingest data and extract useful representations based on examples is what makes deep learning so powerful. The focus of deep learning practitioners is not so much on handcrafting those representations but on operating on a mathematical entity so that it discovers representations from the training data autonomously. Often, these automatically created features are better than those that are handcrafted! As with many disruptive technologies, this fact has led to a change in perspective.

On the left side of figure 1.1, we see a practitioner busy defining engineering features and feeding them to a learning algorithm; the results of the task will be as good as the features defined by the practitioner engineers. With deep learning, on the right, the raw data is fed to an algorithm that extracts hierarchical features automatically, guided by the optimization of its own performance on the task; the results will be as good as the ability of the practitioner to drive the algorithm toward its goal.

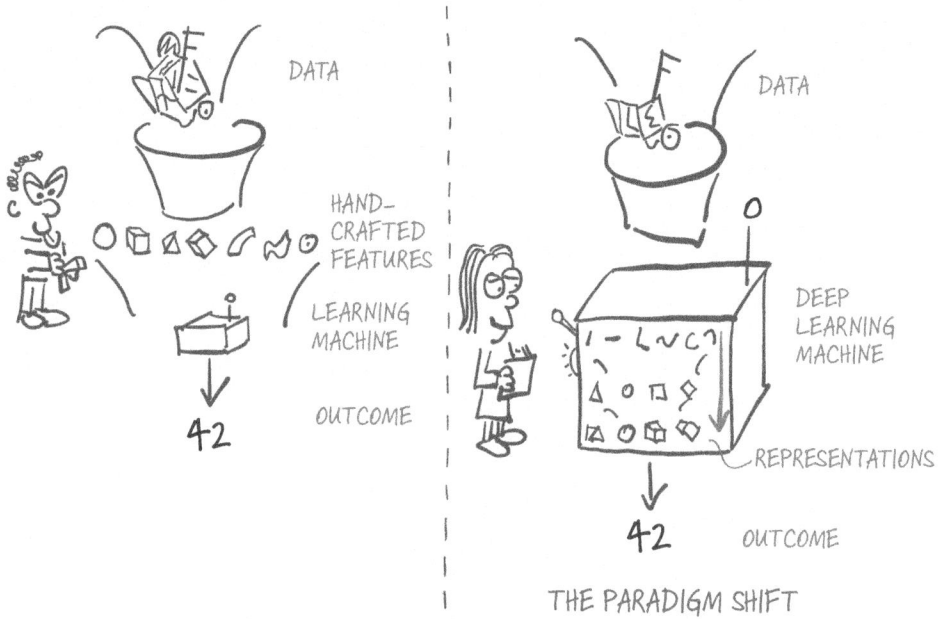

Figure 1.1 Deep learning exchanges the need to handcraft features for an increase in data and computational requirements.

Looking at the right side in figure 1.1, we already get a glimpse of what we need to execute successful deep learning:

- We need a way to ingest whatever data we have at hand.
- We somehow need to define the deep learning machine.
- We must have an automated way, *training*, to obtain useful representations and make the machine produce desired outputs.

This process leaves us with taking a closer look at this training thing we keep talking about. During training, we employ a *loss function*, also known as a *criterion, objective function*, or *cost function*—all these terms are commonly used interchangeably in deep learning literature, which is a real-valued function that compares the model's outputs to the reference data. This function calculates a numerical score representing the difference between the desired and actual outputs of the model, with a lower score generally indicating better performance. Training consists of driving the loss function toward lower and lower scores by incrementally modifying our deep learning machine until it achieves low scores, even on data not seen during training.

1.3 What to expect

As Python does for programming, PyTorch provides an excellent introduction to deep learning. At the same time, PyTorch has been proven to be fully qualified for use in professional contexts for real-world, high-profile work. We believe that PyTorch's clear syntax, streamlined API, and easy debugging make it an excellent choice for introducing deep learning. We highly recommend studying PyTorch for your first deep learning library. Whether it will be the last deep learning library you learn, only time will tell, but at least you'll have mastered the fundamental concepts that all deep learning libraries offer.

At its core, the deep learning machine in figure 1.1 is a rather complex mathematical function mapping inputs to an output. To facilitate expressing this function, PyTorch provides a core data structure, the *tensor*, which is a multidimensional array that shares many similarities with NumPy arrays. Around that foundation, PyTorch comes with features to perform accelerated mathematical operations on dedicated hardware, which makes it convenient to design neural network architectures and train them on individual machines or parallel computing resources.

Although we stress the practical aspects of building deep learning systems with PyTorch, we believe that providing an accessible introduction to a foundational deep learning tool is more than just a way to facilitate the acquisition of new technical skills. It is a step toward equipping a new generation of scientists, engineers, and practitioners from a wide range of disciplines with working knowledge that will be the backbone of many software projects for decades to come.

To get the most out of this book, you will need two things:

- Some experience programming in Python. We're not going to pull any punches on that one; you'll need to be up on Python data types, classes, floating-point numbers, and the like.
- A willingness to dive in and get your hands dirty. We'll be starting from the basics and building up our working knowledge, and it will be much easier for you to learn if you follow along with us.

Deep learning is a huge space. In this book, we will be covering a small fraction of that space: specifically, using PyTorch for generative AI applications for creating text and images. We will also cover smaller-scope classification and segmentation projects, with image processing of 2D and 3D datasets used for most of the motivating examples. This book focuses on practical PyTorch, with the aim of covering enough ground to allow you to solve real-world machine learning problems with deep learning or explore new models as they pop up in research literature. Most, if not all, of the latest publications related to deep learning research can be found in the arXiV public preprint repository, hosted at https://arxiv.org.

1.4 Why PyTorch?

As we've said, deep learning allows us to carry out a very wide range of complicated tasks, like machine translation, playing strategy games, or identifying objects in cluttered scenes, by exposing our model to illustrative examples. To do so in practice, we need tools that are flexible, so they can be adapted to such a wide range of problems, and efficient, to allow training to occur over large amounts of data in reasonable times. And we need the trained model to perform correctly in the presence of variability in the inputs. Let's take a look at some of the reasons we decided to use PyTorch.

PyTorch is easy to recommend because of its simplicity. Many researchers and practitioners find it easy to learn, use, extend, and debug. It's Pythonic, and while, like any complicated domain, it has caveats and best practices, using the library generally feels familiar to developers who have used Python previously.

More concretely, programming the deep learning machine is very natural in PyTorch. PyTorch gives us a data type, the Tensor, to hold numbers, vectors, matrices, or arrays in general. In addition, it provides functions for operating on them. We can program with them incrementally and, if we want, interactively, just like we are used to from Python. If you know NumPy, this will be very familiar.

But PyTorch offers two things that make it particularly relevant for deep learning. First, it provides accelerated computation using graphical processing units (GPUs), often yielding speedups from 10× to 1000× over doing the same calculation on a CPU. While your computer's CPU may have four or eight cores, each capable of executing tasks independently, modern GPUs are equipped with thousands. Second, PyTorch provides facilities that support numerical optimization on generic mathematical expressions, which deep learning uses for training. Note that both features are useful for scientific computing in general, not exclusively for deep learning. In fact, we can safely characterize PyTorch as a high-performance library with optimization support for scientific computing in Python.

A design driver for PyTorch is expressivity, allowing a developer to implement complicated models without undue complexity being imposed by the framework. PyTorch arguably offers one of the most seamless translations of ideas into Python code in the deep learning landscape. For this reason, PyTorch has seen widespread adoption in research, as witnessed by the high citation counts at international conferences.

PyTorch also has a compelling story for the transition from research and development into production. While it was initially focused on research workflows, PyTorch has been equipped with a high-performance C++ runtime that can be used to deploy models for inference without relying on Python, and can be used for designing and training models in C++. It has also grown bindings to other languages and an interface for deploying to mobile devices. These features allow us to take advantage of

PyTorch's flexibility and, at the same time, take our applications where a full Python runtime would be hard to get or would impose expensive overhead.

Of course, claims of ease of use and high performance are trivial to make. We hope that by the time you are in the thick of this book, you'll agree with us that our claims here are well-founded.

1.4.1 The deep learning competitive landscape

While all analogies are flawed, it seems that the release of PyTorch 0.1 marked the transition from a Cambrian-explosion-like proliferation of deep learning libraries, wrappers, and data-exchange formats into an era of consolidation and unification.

At the time of PyTorch's first beta release,

- Theano and TensorFlow were the premier low-level libraries, working with a model that had the user define a computational graph and then execute it.
- Lasagne and Keras were high-level wrappers around Theano, with Keras wrapping TensorFlow and CNTK as well.
- Caffe, Chainer, DyNet, Torch (the Lua-based precursor to PyTorch), MXNet, CNTK, DL4J, and others filled various niches in the ecosystem.

In the years that followed, the landscape changed drastically. The research community largely consolidated around PyTorch as the framework of choice used to implement new research ideas. In the industry, most technology is built on PyTorch, TensorFlow, or Hugging Face, with the adoption of other libraries dwindling, except for those filling specific niches. In a nutshell,

- Theano
  - One of the first deep learning frameworks.
  - Has ceased active development.
- TensorFlow
  - Consumed Keras entirely, promoting it to a first-class API.
  - Provided an immediate-execution "eager mode" that is somewhat similar to how PyTorch approaches computation.
  - Released TF 2.0 with eager mode by default.
- JAX
  - A library by Google that was developed independently from TensorFlow.
  - Has started gaining traction as a NumPy equivalent with GPU, automatic differentiation, and just-in-time (JIT) compilation.
- PyTorch
  - Consumed Caffe2 for its backend.
  - Replaced CNTK and Chainer as the framework of choice by their respective corporate sponsors.
  - Replaced most of the low-level code reused from the Lua-based Torch Project.
  - Added support for ONNX, a vendor-neutral model description and exchange format.

– Released version 2.0, which introduces `torch.compile` to speed up PyTorch code by JIT compiling it while requiring minimal code changes.

Interestingly, with the advent of compilation mode and eager mode introduced in both PyTorch and TensorFlow, we have seen each of their feature sets start to converge with the other's, although the presentation of these features and the overall experience is still quite different between the two.

Hugging Face has become increasingly popular as a high-level wrapper for deep learning frameworks, emphasizing application-oriented usage. It features a convenient model hub, serving as a repository for users to discover and exchange pretrained models and weights. These models are built on a framework such as PyTorch or TensorFlow. Users can readily access and incorporate existing models into their applications. However, it's worth noting that Hugging Face's focus on simplicity and ease of use might limit the level of fine-grained control and flexibility that one could achieve by directly authoring models using PyTorch or TensorFlow.

1.5 How PyTorch supports deep learning projects

We have already hinted at a few building blocks in PyTorch. Let's now take some time to formalize a high-level map of the main components that form PyTorch. We can best do this by looking at what a deep learning project needs from PyTorch.

First, although PyTorch has the "Py" in Python, there's a lot of non-Python code in it. Actually, for performance reasons, most of PyTorch is written in C++ and CUDA (https://developer.nvidia.com/cuda-zone), a C++-like language from NVIDIA that can be compiled to run with massive parallelism on GPUs. There are ways to run PyTorch directly from C++; however, most of the time, we'll interact with PyTorch from Python, building models, training them, and using the trained models to solve actual problems.

Indeed, the Python API is where PyTorch shines in terms of usability and integration with the wider Python ecosystem. Let's take a peek at the mental model of what PyTorch is.

As we already touched on, at its core, PyTorch is a library that provides *multidimensional arrays*, or *tensors* in PyTorch parlance (we'll go into details on those in chapter 3), and an extensive library of operations on them, provided by the `torch` module. Both tensors and the operations on them can be used on a CPU or GPU. Moving computations from a CPU to a GPU in PyTorch doesn't require more than an additional function call or two.

The next core thing that PyTorch provides is the ability of tensors to remember what numerical operations are done on them, creating a history of these operations. By using this history, PyTorch can calculate how the final model output changes if we modify any of the initial data. It is used in numerical optimization (i.e., how the model "learns"), and PyTorch's automatic differentiation engine (called *autograd*) handles these calculations for us behind the scenes. We'll discuss this process in detail in chapter 5.

By having tensors and the autograd-enabled tensor standard library, PyTorch can be used for physics, rendering, optimization, simulation, modeling, and more—we're very likely to see PyTorch used in creative ways throughout the spectrum of scientific applications. But PyTorch is, first and foremost, a deep learning library, and as such, it provides all the building blocks needed to build neural networks and train them. Figure 1.2 shows a standard setup that loads data, trains a model, and then deploys that model to production.

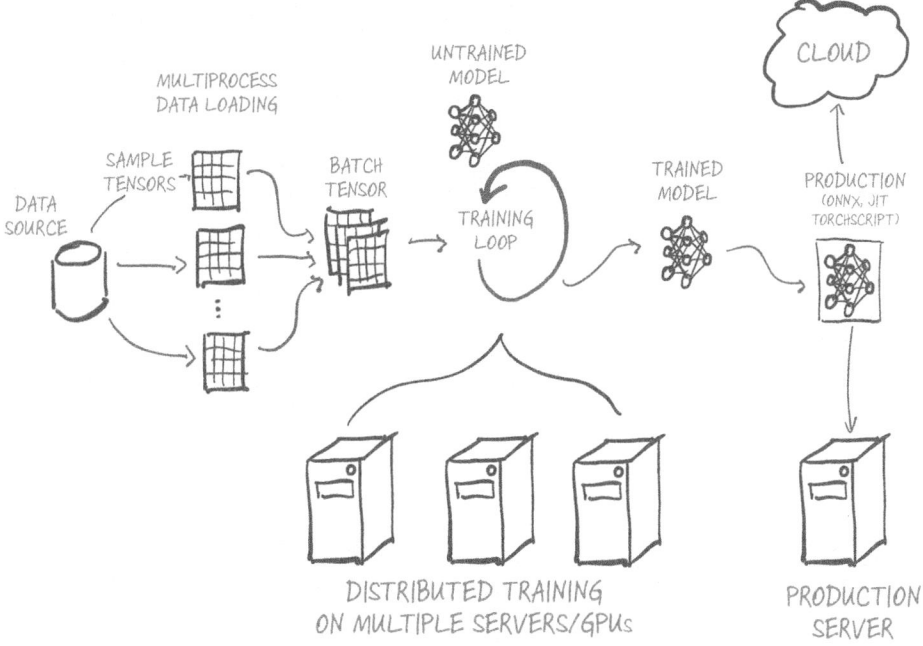

Figure 1.2 Basic, high-level structure of a PyTorch project, with data loading, training, and deployment to production

The core PyTorch modules for building neural networks are located in torch.nn, which provides common neural network layers and other architectural components. Fully connected layers, convolutional layers, activation functions, and loss functions can all be found here (we'll go into more detail about what all that means as we go through the rest of this book). These components can be used to build and initialize the untrained model we see in the center of figure 1.2. To train our model, we need a few additional things: a source of training data, an optimizer to adapt the model to the training data, and a way to get the model and data to the hardware that will actually be performing the calculations needed for training the model.

At the left in figure 1.2, we see that quite a bit of data processing is needed before the training data even reaches our model. (And that's just the data preparation that is done on the fly, not the preprocessing, which can be a pretty large part in practical projects.) First, we need to physically get the data, most often from some sort of storage as the data source. Then we need to convert each sample from our data into something PyTorch can actually handle: tensors. This bridge between our custom data (in whatever format it might be) and a standardized PyTorch tensor is the `Dataset` class PyTorch provides in `torch.utils.data`. As this process is wildly different from one problem to the next, we will have to implement this data sourcing ourselves. We will look in detail at how to represent various types of data we might want to work with as tensors in chapter 4.

As data storage is often slow—in particular, due to access latency—we want to parallelize data loading. However, although Python is widely adored for many reasons, it is not particularly known for its ease, efficiency, and parallel processing capabilities. Therefore, to efficiently load and organize data into *batches* (tensors containing multiple samples), we will need to utilize multiple processes. While this method is rather elaborate, it is also relatively generic: PyTorch readily provides all that magic in the `DataLoader` class. Its instances can spawn child processes to load data from a dataset in the background so that it's ready and waiting for the training loop as soon as the loop can use it. We will meet and use `Dataset` and `DataLoader` in chapter 7.

With the mechanism for getting batches of samples in place, we can turn to the training loop itself at the center of figure 1.2. Typically, the training loop is implemented as a standard Python `for` loop. In the simplest case, the model runs the required calculations on a local CPU or a single GPU. Once the training loop has the data, computation can start immediately. This will likely be your basic setup, too, and it's the one we'll assume in this book.

At each step in the training loop, we evaluate our model on the samples we got from the data loader. We then compare the outputs of our model to the desired output (the targets) using some *loss function*. Just as it offers the components from which to build our model, PyTorch also has a variety of loss functions at our disposal. They, too, are provided in `torch.nn`.

After we have compare our actual outputs to the ideal with the loss functions, we need to push the model a bit to better match its outputs to the target. As mentioned earlier, this is where the PyTorch autograd engine comes in, but we also need an *optimizer* doing the updates, and PyTorch offers us just that in `torch.optim`. We will start looking at training loops with loss functions and optimizers in chapter 5 and then hone our skills in chapters 6 through 8.

It's increasingly common to use more elaborate hardware like multiple GPUs or multiple machines that contribute their resources to training a large model, as seen in the bottom center of figure 1.2. In chapter 9, we will examine how, in those cases, the `torch.distributed` submodule can be employed to use the additional hardware. Once we have a good understanding of this, we will proceed with our practical projects in part 2.

The training loop might be the most unexciting yet most time-consuming part of a deep learning project. At the end of it, we are rewarded with a model whose parameters have been optimized on our task: the *trained model* (depicted in the figure to the right of the training loop). Having a model to solve a task is great, but for it to be useful, we must put it where the work is needed. This *deployment* part of the process (depicted in the figure on the right) may involve putting the model on a server or exporting it to load it to a cloud engine, as shown in the figure. Or we might integrate it with a larger application or run it on a phone.

One particular step in the deployment exercise is exporting the model. As mentioned earlier, PyTorch defaults to an immediate execution model (eager mode). Whenever an instruction involving PyTorch is executed by the Python interpreter, the corresponding operation is immediately carried out by the underlying C++ or CUDA implementation. As more instructions operate on tensors, more operations are executed by the backend implementation.

PyTorch also provides tools for scaling and deployment. For large models, torch.distributed enables training across multiple GPUs and machines. For production deployment, torch.compile optimizes model performance, while *ONNX* export ensures cross-platform compatibility. Mobile deployment is supported through libraries like ExecuTorch. We'll explore these capabilities in much more detail in the final chapters.

1.6 Hardware and software requirements

This book will require coding and running tasks that involve heavy numerical computing, such as the multiplication of large numbers of matrices. As it turns out, running a pretrained network on new data is within the capabilities of any recent laptop or personal computer. Even taking a pretrained network and retraining a small portion of it to specialize it on a new dataset doesn't necessarily require specialized hardware. You can follow along with everything we do in part 1 of this book using a standard personal computer or laptop.

However, we anticipate that completing a full training run for the more advanced examples in part 2 will require a CUDA-capable GPU. The default parameters used in part 2 assume a GPU with 8 GB of RAM (we suggest an NVIDIA GTX 1070 or better), but those can be adjusted if your hardware has less RAM available. To be clear: such hardware is not mandatory if you're willing to wait, but running on a GPU cuts training time by at least an order of magnitude (and usually it's 40–50× faster). Taken individually, the operations required to compute parameter updates are fast (from fractions of a second to a few seconds) on modern hardware like a typical laptop CPU. The issue is that training involves running these operations over and over, many, many times, incrementally updating the network parameters to minimize the training error.

Moderately large networks can take hours to days to train from scratch on large, real-world datasets on workstations equipped with a good GPU. That time can be reduced by using multiple GPUs on the same machine, and even further on clusters of machines equipped with multiple GPUs. These setups are less prohibitive to access than they sound, thanks to the offerings of cloud computing providers.

So, if there's a GPU around by the time you reach part 2, great. Otherwise, we suggest checking out the offerings from the various cloud platforms, many of which offer GPU-enabled Jupyter Notebooks with PyTorch preinstalled, often with a free quota. Google Colaboratory (https://colab.research.google.com) is a great place to start.

The last consideration is the OS. PyTorch runs on Linux, macOS, and Windows. Throughout the book, we will try to avoid assuming you are running a particular OS, although some of the scripts in part 2 are shown as if running from a Bash prompt under Linux. Those scripts' command lines should convert to a Windows-compatible form readily. For convenience, code will be listed as if running from a Jupyter Notebook when possible.

For installation information, please see the Get Started guide on the official PyTorch website (https://pytorch.org/get-started/locally). We suggest that Windows users install with Anaconda or Miniconda (https://www.anaconda.com/distribution or https://docs.conda.io/en/latest/miniconda.html). Other operating systems like Linux typically have a wider variety of workable options, with `pip` being the most common package manager for Python. We provide a requirements.txt file that `pip` can use to install dependencies. Of course, if you are an experienced user, you are free to install packages in the way that is most compatible with your preferred development environment.

Part 2 has some nontrivial download bandwidth and disk space requirements as well. The raw data needed for the cancer-detection project in part 2 is about 60 GB to download, and when uncompressed, it requires about 120 GB of space. The compressed data can be removed after decompressing it. In addition, due to caching some of the data for performance reasons, another 80 GB will be needed while training. You will need a total of 200 GB (at minimum) of free disk space on the system that will be used for training. While it is possible to use network storage for this, there might be training speed penalties if the network access is slower than the local disk. Preferably, you will have space on a local SSD to store the data for fast retrieval.

1.6.1 Using Jupyter Notebooks

We're going to assume you've installed PyTorch and the other dependencies and have verified that things are working. Earlier, we touched on the opportunities to follow along with the code in the book. We are going to be making heavy use of Jupyter Notebooks for our example code. A Jupyter Notebook shows itself as a page in the browser through which we can run code interactively. The code is evaluated by a *kernel*, a process running on a server that is ready to receive code to execute and send back the results, which are then rendered inline on the page. A notebook maintains the state of the kernel, like variables defined during the evaluation of code, in memory until it is terminated or restarted.

The fundamental unit with which we interact with a notebook is a *cell*: a box on the page where we can type code and have the kernel evaluate it (through the menu item or by pressing Shift-Enter). We can add multiple cells in a notebook, and the new cells will see the variables we created in the earlier cells. The value returned by the last line of a cell will be printed right below the cell after execution, and the same goes for plots. By mixing source code, results of evaluations, and Markdown-formatted text cells, we can generate beautiful interactive documents. You can read everything about Jupyter Notebooks on the project website (https://jupyter.org).

At this point, you need to start the notebook server from the root directory of the code checkout from GitHub. How exactly starting the server looks depends on the details of your OS and how and where you installed Jupyter. If you have questions, feel free to ask on the book's forum (https://mng.bz/yNPe). Once started, your default browser will pop up, showing a list of local notebook files.

> **NOTE** Jupyter Notebooks are a powerful tool for expressing and investigating ideas through code. While we think that they make for a good fit for our use case with this book, they're not for everyone. We would argue that it's important to focus on removing friction and minimizing cognitive overhead, and that's going to be different for everyone. Use what you like during your experimentation with PyTorch.

Full working code for all listings from the book can be found at the book's website (https://www.manning.com/books/deep-learning-with-pytorch-second-edition) and in our repository on GitHub (https://github.com/deep-learning-with-pytorch/dlwpt-code-2e).

1.7 Exercises

1. Start Python to get an interactive prompt.
   a. What Python version are you using? We hope it is at least 3.10!
   b. Can you `import torch`? What version of PyTorch do you get?
   c. What is the result of `torch.cuda.is_available()`? Does it match your expectations based on the hardware you're using?
2. Start the Jupyter Notebook server.
   a. What version of Python is Jupyter using?
   b. Is the location of the `torch` library used by Jupyter the same as the one you imported from the interactive prompt?

Summary

- Deep learning represents a paradigm shift from traditional machine learning. While traditional machine learning methods heavily depend on feature engineering, deep learning methods are designed to automatically learn the associations between inputs and desired outputs from provided examples.
- Libraries like PyTorch efficiently facilitate building and training neural network models for deep learning tasks.
- Since the release of PyTorch in early 2017, PyTorch has emerged as a leading framework in the deep learning landscape. TensorFlow remains used in industry,

and Hugging Face has become increasingly popular as a high-level wrapper for deep learning frameworks.
- PyTorch prioritizes flexibility and speed, minimizing cognitive overhead, and defaults to immediate execution for operations.
- PyTorch is a library that revolves around tensors, which are multidimensional arrays, and provides an extensive set of operations that can be performed on them.
- Throughout the book, we will cover the entire process of building a model using PyTorch, including data loading, model definition, training, and evaluation.

Pretrained networks

This chapter covers
- Running pretrained image-recognition models
- Working with pretrained transformers and diffusion models
- Accessing models through Hugging Face
- Captioning images with a pretrained model

In our first chapter, we hinted at the transformative potential of deep learning, and now it's time to deliver. Computer vision is certainly one of the fields that has been most affected by the advent of deep learning, for a variety of reasons. As the need to classify or interpret the content of natural images grew, very large datasets became available, and new constructs such as convolutional layers were invented and could be run quickly on GPUs with unprecedented accuracy. All of these factors are combined with the internet giants' desire to understand pictures taken by millions of users with their mobile devices and managed on their platforms. Quite the perfect storm.

If you're coming to PyTorch from another deep learning framework and you'd rather jump right into learning the nuts and bolts of PyTorch, you can get away with skipping to the next chapter. The things we'll cover in this chapter are more fun than foundational and are somewhat independent of any given deep learning tool. That's not to say they're not important! But if you've worked with pretrained models in other deep learning frameworks, you already know how powerful a tool they can be. And if you're already familiar with with diffusion-based image generation and inpainting, you don't need us to explain them to you.

We hope you keep reading, though, since this chapter hides some important skills under the fun. Learning how to run a pretrained model using PyTorch is a useful skill—full stop. It's especially useful if the model has been trained on a large dataset. We will need to get accustomed to the mechanics of obtaining and running a neural network on real-world data, and then visualizing and evaluating its outputs, whether we trained it or not.

We are going to learn how to use the work of the best researchers in the field by downloading and running very interesting models that have already been trained on open, large-scale datasets. We can think of a pretrained neural network as similar to a program that takes inputs and generates outputs. The behavior of such a program is dictated by the architecture of the neural network and by the examples it saw during training, in terms of desired input-output pairs, or desired properties that the output should satisfy. Using an off-the-shelf model can be a quick way to jump-start a deep learning project, since it draws on expertise from the researchers who designed the model, as well as the computation time spent training the weights.

In this chapter, we will explore four popular pretrained models: a model that can label an image according to its content, another that can fabricate a new image from a real image, a model that can finish your sentence, and a model that can describe the content of an image using proper English sentences. We will learn how to load and run these pretrained models in PyTorch, and we will introduce how Hugging Face, a tool through which PyTorch models, like the pretrained ones we'll discuss, can be easily made available through a uniform interface. Along the way, we'll discuss data sources, define terminology like *label*, and turn a horse into a zebra.

2.1 A pretrained network that recognizes the subject of an image

As our first foray into deep learning, we'll run a state-of-the-art deep neural network that was pretrained on an object-recognition task. There are many pretrained models available through dedicated repositories and interfaces like PyTorch's torchvision and Hugging Face. These platforms provide standardized ways to access models along with their preoptimized weights, eliminating the need to train from scratch. The weights represent knowledge gained from training on reference datasets. Using one of these models could enable us to, for example, equip our next web service with image-recognition capabilities with very little effort.

The pretrained network we'll explore here was trained on a subset of the ImageNet dataset (http://imagenet.stanford.edu). ImageNet is a very large dataset of over 14 million images maintained by Stanford University. All the images are labeled with a hierarchy of nouns that come from the WordNet dataset (http://wordnet.princeton.edu), which is, in turn, a large lexical database of the English language.

The ImageNet dataset originated from academic competitions like the ImageNet Large Scale Visual Recognition Challenge (ILSVRC), which began in 2010. Among its various tasks, the classification challenge requires algorithms to identify images by producing five ranked labels from 1,000 categories, meaning for each image, the algorithm provides its top five predictions in order of confidence. The potential practical applications of achieving automated classification are vast, including autonomous vehicle navigation, quality control in manufacturing, and assistance in diagnosing medical conditions such as cancer, wildlife monitoring, and more.

The training set for ILSVRC consists of 1.2 million images labeled with one of 1,000 nouns (e.g., "dog"), referred to as the *class* of the image. In this sense, we will use the terms *label* and *class* interchangeably. We can take a peek at images from ImageNet in figure 2.1.

Figure 2.1 A small sample of ImageNet images

We are going to end up being able to take our own images and feed them into our pretrained model, as pictured in figure 2.2. This will result in a list of predicted labels for that image, which we can then examine to see what the model thinks our image is. Some images will have predictions that are accurate, and others will not!

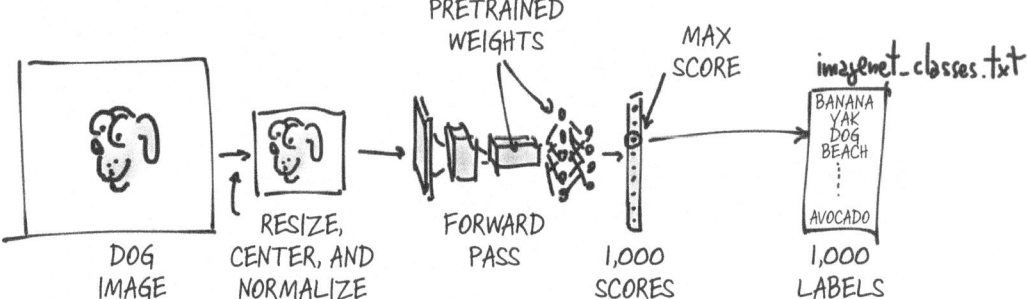

Figure 2.2 **The inference process**

The input image will first be preprocessed into an instance of the multidimensional array class torch.Tensor. It is an RGB (red, green, blue) image with height and width, so this tensor will have three dimensions: the color channels and two spatial image dimensions of a specific size. (We'll get into the details of what a tensor is in chapter 3, but for now, think of it as being like a vector or matrix of floating-point numbers.) Our model will take that processed input image and pass it into the pretrained network to obtain scores for each class. The highest score corresponds to the most likely class according to the weights. Each class is then mapped one-to-one onto a class label. That output is contained in a torch.Tensor with 1,000 elements, each representing the score associated with that class.

Before we can do all that, we'll need to get the network itself, take a peek under the hood to see how it's structured, and learn about how to prepare our data before the model can use it.

2.1.1 *Obtaining a pretrained network for image recognition*

As discussed, we will now equip ourselves with a network trained on ImageNet. To do so, we'll take a look at the TorchVision project (https://github.com/pytorch/vision), which contains a few famous neural network architectures for computer vision, such as AlexNet (http://mng.bz/lo6z), Inception v3 (https://arxiv.org/pdf/1512.00567.pdf), and, more recently, VisionTransformer (https://arxiv.org/pdf/2010.11929.pdf). It also has easy access to datasets like ImageNet and other utilities for getting up to speed with computer vision applications in PyTorch. We'll dive into some of these further later in the book. For now, let's load and run our first model, AlexNet, one of the early breakthroughs in image recognition. If PyTorch isn't set up from chapter 1, take a moment to do that now.

The predefined models can be found in torchvision.models (code/p1ch2/2 _pre_trained_networks.ipynb):

```
# In[1]:
import torchvision
from torchvision import models
```

We can take a look at the actual models:

```
# In[2]:
models.list_models()

# Out[2]:
['alexnet',
 'convnext_base',
 'convnext_large',
 'convnext_small',
 'convnext_tiny',
 'densenet121',
 'densenet161',
 'densenet169',
 'densenet201',
 ...
 'googlenet',
 'inception_v3',
 'maxvit_t',
 'mnasnet0_5',
 'mnasnet0_75',
 ...
 'vit_h_14',
 'vit_l_16',
 'vit_l_32',
 'wide_resnet101_2',
 'wide_resnet50_2']
```

The names refer to Python classes that implement a number of popular models. They differ in their *architecture*—that is, in the arrangement of the operations occurring between the input and the output. The lowercase names are convenience functions that return models instantiated from those classes, sometimes with different parameter sets. For instance, densenet121 returns an instance of DenseNet with 121 layers, densenet201 has 201 layers, and so on. We'll now turn our attention to AlexNet.

2.1.2 AlexNet

AlexNet remains a historical milestone for deep learning. It re-ignited the field and brought it into the mainstream. Before AlexNet, neural networks had fallen out of favor due to limited computational resources and lackluster results on large-scale tasks. However, in 2012, the AlexNet architecture won the ILSVRC competition by a large margin, with a top-five test error rate (i.e., the correct label must be in the top-five predictions) of 15.4%. By comparison, the second-best submission, which wasn't based on a deep network, trailed at 26.2%. This was a defining moment in the history of computer vision: the moment when the community started to realize the potential of deep learning for vision tasks. That leap was followed by constant improvement, with more modern architectures and training methods getting top-five error rates as low as 3%.

By today's standards, AlexNet is a rather small network, compared to current state-of-the-art models. But, in our case, it's perfect for taking a first peek at a neural network that does something and learning how to run a pretrained version of it on a new image.

We can see the structure of AlexNet in figure 2.3. We don't have all the elements for understanding it yet, but we can anticipate a few aspects. First, each block consists of a bunch of multiplications and additions, plus a sprinkle of other functions in the output that we'll discover in chapter 5. We can think of it as a filter—a function that takes one or more images as input and produces other images as output. The way it does so is determined during training, based on the examples it has *seen* and on the desired outputs for those.

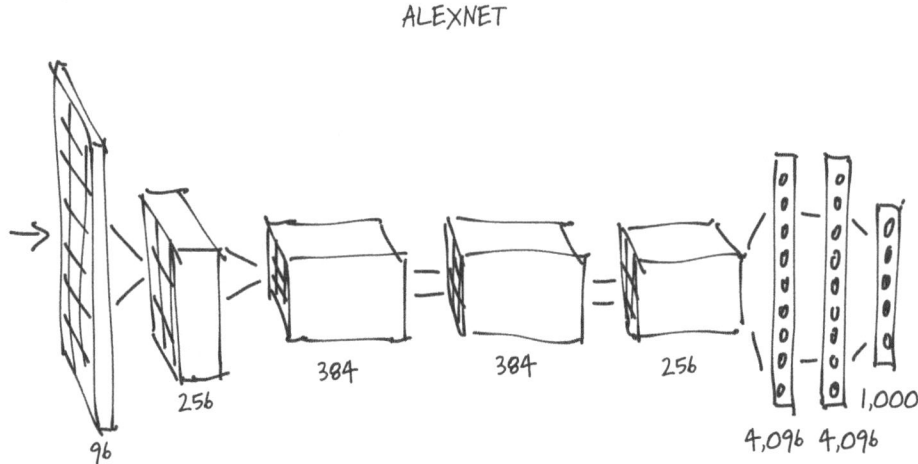

Figure 2.3 The AlexNet architecture (numbers denote outputs at each layer)

In figure 2.3, input images come in from the left and go through five stacks of filters, each producing intermediate representations of the images. After each filter, these representations are reduced in size, as annotated. The intermediate representations produced by the last stack of filters are laid out as a 4,096-element 1D vector and classified to produce 1,000 output probabilities, one for each output class.

To run the AlexNet architecture on an input image, we can create an instance of the AlexNet class. This is how it's done:

```
# In[3]:
alexnet = models.AlexNet()
```

At this point, alexnet is an object that can run the AlexNet architecture. It's not essential for us to understand the details of this architecture for now. For the time being, alexnet is just an opaque object that can be called like a function. By providing alexnet with some precisely sized input data (we'll see shortly what this input data should be), we will run a *forward pass* through the network. That is, the input will run through the first set of neurons, whose outputs will be fed to the next set of neurons, all the way to the final output. Practically speaking, assuming we have an input object of the right type, we can run the forward pass with output = alexnet(input).

But if we did that, we would be feeding data through the whole network to produce garbage! That's because the network is uninitialized: its weights, the numbers by which inputs are added and multiplied, have not been trained on anything—the network itself is a blank (or rather, random) slate. We need to either train it from scratch or load weights from prior training, which we'll do now.

To this end, let's go back to the models module. Uppercase names correspond to classes that implement popular architectures for computer vision. The lowercase names are functions that instantiate models with predefined numbers of layers and units and optionally download and load pretrained weights into them. Note that there's nothing essential about using one of these functions: they just make it convenient to instantiate the model with a number of layers and units that match how the pretrained networks were built.

2.1.3 The Vision Transformer

Nowadays, vision transformers (ViT; https://arxiv.org/pdf/2010.11929) have taken the lead in many computer vision tasks, demonstrating state-of-the-art performance. Self-attention mechanisms, something we will learn in chapter 9, can capture intricate relationships within images, which are used to improve classification accuracy.

ViTs for image classification have demonstrated significantly lower error rates on ImageNet compared to AlexNet. Top-five error rates can be as low as 5% (compared to AlexNet's 15.3%)—it just took a whole 9 years to get there!

Using the vit_b_16 function, we'll now instantiate a ViT for image classification. We'll pass an argument that will instruct the function to download the ViT_B_16_Weights.IMAGENET1K_V1 weights trained on the ImageNet dataset, with 1.2 million images and 1,000 categories:

```
vit = models.vit_b_16(weights=models.ViT_B_16_Weights.IMAGENET1K_V1)
```

While we're staring at the download progress, we can take a minute to appreciate that vit_b_16 sports 88.6 million parameters—that's a lot of parameters to optimize automatically!

2.1.4 Ready, set, almost run

OK, what did we just get? Since we're curious, we'll take a peek at what a vit_b_16 model looks like. We can do so by printing the value of the returned model. This gives us a textual representation of the same kind of information we saw in figure 2.3, providing details about the structure of the network. For now, this will be information overload, but as we progress through the book, we'll increase our ability to understand what this code is telling us:

```
# In[5]:
vit

# Out[5]:
VisionTransformer(
  (conv_proj): Conv2d(3, 768, kernel_size=(16, 16), stride=(16, 16))
  (encoder): Encoder(
    (dropout): Dropout(p=0.0, inplace=False)
    (layers): Sequential(
      (encoder_layer_0): EncoderBlock(
        (ln_1): LayerNorm((768,), eps=1e-06, elementwise_affine=True)
        (self_attention): MultiheadAttention(
          (out_proj): NonDynamicallyQuantizableLinear(in_features=768,
     out_features=768, bias=True)
        )
        (dropout): Dropout(p=0.0, inplace=False)
        (ln_2): LayerNorm((768,), eps=1e-06, elementwise_affine=True)
        (mlp): MLPBlock(
          (0): Linear(in_features=768, out_features=3072, bias=True)
          (1): GELU(approximate='none')
          (2): Dropout(p=0.0, inplace=False)
          (3): Linear(in_features=3072, out_features=768, bias=True)
          (4): Dropout(p=0.0, inplace=False)
        )
      )
      (encoder_layer_1): EncoderBlock(
        (ln_1): LayerNorm((768,), eps=1e-06, elementwise_affine=True)
        (self_attention): MultiheadAttention(
          (out_proj): NonDynamicallyQuantizableLinear(in_features=768,
     out_features=768, bias=True)
        )
...
  )
  (heads): Sequential(
    (head): Linear(in_features=768, out_features=1000, bias=True)
  )
)
```

What we are seeing here is modules, one per line. Note that they have nothing in common with Python modules: they are individual operations, the building blocks of a neural network. They are also called *layers* in other deep learning frameworks.

Modules can be nested: larger building blocks (e.g., Encoder) contain submodules (like the repeated EncoderBlock), which, in turn, hold other modules. Printed model summaries show this hierarchy via indentation; conceptually it's a tree where container modules group and order their children (e.g., a Sequential), making it easier to reason about and access parts of the network.

We see the EncoderBlock module contains that attention mechanism we mentioned earlier in this section, as well as other modules. That's the anatomy of a typical deep neural network for computer vision: a more-or-less sequential cascade of operations and nonlinear functions, ending with a layer (fc) producing scores for each of the 1,000 output classes (out_features).

The vit variable can be called like a function, taking as input one or more images and producing an equal number of scores for each of the 1,000 ImageNet classes. Before we can do that, we have to preprocess the input images so they are the right size and so that their values (colors) sit roughly in the same numerical range. To do that, the torchvision module provides transforms, which allow us to quickly define pipelines of basic preprocessing functions:

```
# In[6]:
from torchvision import transforms
preprocess = transforms.Compose([
        transforms.Resize(256),
        transforms.CenterCrop(224),
        transforms.ToTensor(),
        transforms.Normalize(
            mean=[0.485, 0.456, 0.406],
            std=[0.229, 0.224, 0.225]
    )])
```

In this case, we defined a preprocess function that will scale the input image to 256 × 256, crop the image to 224 × 224 around the center, transform it to a tensor (a PyTorch multidimensional array; in this case, a 3D array with color, height, and width), and normalize its RGB components so that they have defined means and standard deviations. These need to match what was presented to the network during training if we want the network to produce meaningful answers. We'll go into more depth about transforms when we dive into making our own image-recognition models in section 7.1.3.

We can now grab a picture of our favorite dog (say, bobby.jpg from the GitHub repo), preprocess it, and then see what our model thinks of it. We can start by loading an image from the local filesystem using Pillow (https://pillow.readthedocs.io/en/stable), an image-manipulation module for Python:

```
# In[7]:
from PIL import Image
img = Image.open("../data/p1ch2/bobby.jpg")
```

If we were following along from a Jupyter Notebook, we would do the following to see the picture inline (it would be shown where the <PIL.JpegImagePlugin... is in the following):

```
# In[8]:
img
# Out[8]:
<PIL.JpegImagePlugin.JpegImageFile image mode=RGB size=1280x720 at
 0x1B1601360B8>
```

Otherwise, we can invoke the show method, which will pop up a window with a viewer, to see the image shown in figure 2.4:

```
>>> img.show()
```

Figure 2.4 Bobby, our very special input image

Next, we can pass the image through our preprocessing pipeline:

```
# In[9]:
img_t = preprocess(img)
```

Then we can reshape, crop, and normalize the input tensor in a way that the network expects. We'll understand more of this in the next two chapters; hold tight for now:

```
# In[10]:
import torch
batch_t = torch.unsqueeze(img_t, 0)
```

We're now ready to run our model.

2.1.5 Run!

In the field of deep learning, the term used for running a trained model on new data is called *inference*. To do inference, we need to put the network in eval mode:

```
# In[11]:
vit.eval()

# Out[11]:
VisionTransformer(
  ...
)
```

If we forget to do that, some sections of the model, like *batch normalization* and *dropout*, will not produce meaningful answers, just because of the way they work internally. Now that eval has been set, we're ready for inference:

```
# In[12]:
out = vit(batch_t)
out

# Out[12]:
tensor([[-2.0532e-01, -6.0847e-02, -5.4069e-02,  1.3571e-01,  5.3633e-02,
         -4.3015e-02,  1.0885e-01, -4.5990e-02, -2.2472e-01,  3.2890e-01,
         ...
          6.5441e-03, -1.2580e-01,  1.4917e-01,  1.6322e-01, -7.2893e-02,
         -1.3575e-01,  2.0132e-01,  3.9502e-02,  1.4893e-01,  1.8419e-01]])
```

A staggering set of operations involving 88.6 million parameters has just happened, producing a vector of 1,000 scores, one per ImageNet class. That didn't take long, did it?

We now need to find out the label of the class that received the highest score. This will tell us what the model saw in the image. If the label matches how a human would describe the image, that's great! It means everything is working. If not, either something went wrong during training, or the image is so different from what the model expects that the model can't process it properly, or there's some other similar issue.

To see the list of predicted labels, we will load a text file listing the labels in the same order they were presented to the network during training, and then we will pick out the label at the index that produced the highest score from the network. Almost all models meant for image recognition have output in a form similar to what we're about to work with.

Let's load the file containing the 1,000 labels for the ImageNet dataset classes:

```
# In[13]:
with open('../data/p1ch2/imagenet_classes.txt') as f:
    labels = [line.strip() for line in f.readlines()]
```

At this point, we need to determine the index corresponding to the maximum score in the out tensor we obtained previously. We can do that using the max function in PyTorch, which outputs the maximum value in a tensor, as well as the indices where that maximum value occurred:

```
# In[14]:
_, index = torch.max(out, 1)
```

We can now use the index to access the label. Here, index is not a plain Python number, but a one-element, one-dimensional tensor (specifically, tensor([207])), so we need to get the actual numerical value to use as an index into our labels list using .item(). This only works for tensors with one element and returns the value of the tensor as a standard Python number. We also use torch.nn.functional.softmax (http://mng.bz/BYnq) to normalize our outputs to the range [0, 1] and divide by the sum. That gives us something roughly akin to the confidence that the model has in its prediction. In this case, the model is 96% certain that it knows what it's looking at is a golden retriever:

```
# In[15]:
percentage = torch.nn.functional.softmax(out, dim=1)[0] * 100
labels[index.item()], percentage[index.item()].item()

# Out[15]:
('golden retriever', 86.44094848632812)
```

Uh oh, who's a good boy?

Since the model produced scores, we can also find out what the second-best, third-best, and so on were. To do this, we can use the `sort` function, which sorts the values in ascending or descending order and also provides the indices of the sorted values in the original array:

```
# In[16]:
_, indices = torch.sort(out, descending=True)
[(labels[idx], percentage[idx].item()) for idx in indices[0][:5]]

# Out[16]:
[('golden retriever', 86.44094848632812),
 ('Labrador retriever', 0.35488149523735046),
 ('tennis ball', 0.32364416122436523),
 ('cocker spaniel, English cocker spaniel, cocker', 0.15340152382850647),
 ('Airedale, Airedale terrier', 0.14846619963645935)]
```

We see that the four are dogs (Airedale is a breed; who knew?), but one of the answers seems funny. The answer, "tennis ball," is probably because there are enough pictures of tennis balls with dogs nearby that the model is essentially saying, "There's a 0.32% chance that I've completely misunderstood what a tennis ball is." This is a great example of the fundamental differences in how humans and neural networks view the world, as well as how easy it is for strange, subtle biases to sneak into our data.

Time to play! We can go ahead and interrogate our network with random images and see what it comes up with. How successful the network will be will largely depend on whether the subjects were well represented in the training set. If we present an image containing a subject outside the training set, it's quite possible that the network will come up with a wrong answer with pretty high confidence. It's useful to experiment and get a feel for how a model reacts to unseen data.

We've just run a network that is considered a state-of-the-art image classifier. It learned to recognize our dog from examples of dogs, together with a ton of other real-world subjects. We'll now see how different architectures can achieve other kinds of tasks, starting with image generation.

2.2 Generating and editing images

Imagine a painter tasked with restoring a small area of a piece of artwork. Their instructions are as follows: "Update the color of the damaged patch, but leave the rest of the painting exactly as it is." The painter performs this restoration by first laying low-tack masking tape over the rest of the painting, leaving only the target patch exposed.

Just as the painter covers everything with masking tape and leaves only the repair patch exposed, the mask we pass to the pretrained diffusion model is a digital stencil. Black pixels mark protected areas that are copied back unchanged at every restoration step. White pixels mark the editable, "primed" region where the model may repaint.

That, in a nutshell, is modern diffusion-based inpainting: text-guided, mask-aware, iterative refinement that can make localized, realistic edits without retraining a model. With inpainting, it is easy to replace or edit specific areas of an image. Next, we'll describe how this all works.

2.2.1 The inpainting process

Modern inpainting methods rely on diffusion models. At a high level, a diffusion model learns how to reverse a gradual "noising" process. During training, clean images are repeatedly perturbed with small amounts of noise until they become nearly random. The model is taught to run this process in reverse, removing a little noise at a time so that structure re-emerges as a coherent picture. We will learn more about this process in chapter 10, so don't worry about all the details right now.

At inference time, this learned reversal process becomes a powerful editing tool. If we start from pure noise and guide the denoising process with a text description, the model can synthesize a brand-new image that matches the description. If we start from an existing picture, the model can re-render it in line with our description while preserving much of the original layout and geometry. When we provide a mask, the model applies its changes only inside the masked region (white), leaving the rest (black) untouched—this is inpainting. We can see all the available inputs into the model in figure 2.5.

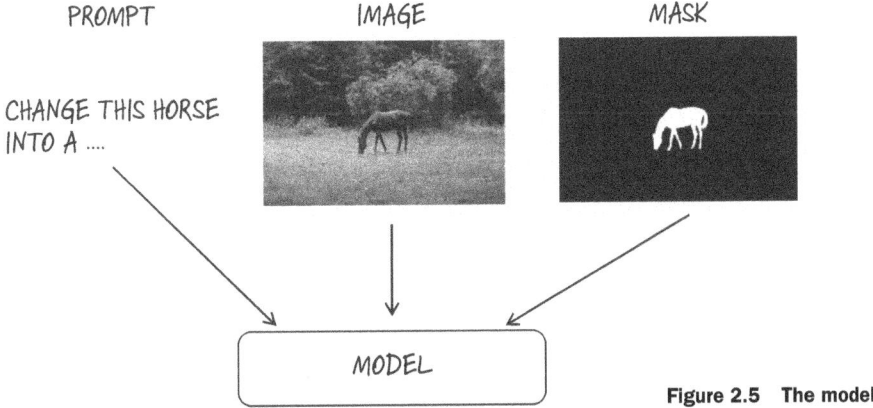

Figure 2.5 The model inputs

Thinking this way keeps the roles clear: the prompt says what we want, the input image anchors where we begin, and the mask constrains where edits may happen. The denoising does the heavy lifting, turning noisy pixels back into a realistic result that fits the instructions.

In figure 2.6, we see the process of gradually creating an image. The input is a photo of a horse, with a mask indicating the area to be modified. Over successive steps, the model refines the noisy input, ultimately producing a realistic image of a zebra that blends seamlessly with the unaltered parts of the original photo.

Figure 2.6 A diffusion model gradually processing an image

The mask enforces locality: pixels outside the mask are preserved by re-inserting the original content during each step, while pixels inside the mask are free to change to satisfy the prompt (e.g., "turn the horse into a zebra"). After a sequence of denoising steps, we get an image that keeps the unmasked scene and pose while repainting only the selected region. If we omit the mask, the same process performs image-to-image generation, allowing the whole frame to be re-rendered in line with the prompt while still respecting the original composition.

2.2.2 *A network that turns horses into zebras*

We can play with this model right now. The Stable Diffusion network has been trained on a dataset of (unrelated) images, including many horses and zebras. While humankind hasn't held its breath over the last few thousand years for a tool that turns horses into zebras, this task showcases the ability of these architectures to model complex real-world processes with distant supervision. While they have their limits, there are hints that in the near future we won't be able to tell real from fake in a live video feed, which opens a can of worms that we'll duly close right now.

Playing with a pretrained model lets us see how to instantiate and run an inpainting workflow. We'll use the diffusers "inpaint pipeline," which packages the trained components and exposes a simple function that takes an input image, a mask, and a text prompt. Our goal here is to use it, not re-implement it, so we'll focus on the invocation rather than the internals (see code/p1ch2/3_inpainting.ipynb):

```
# In[2]:
from diffusers import StableDiffusionInpaintPipeline
import torch
import PIL.Image as Image

device = "cuda" if torch.cuda.is_available() else "cpu"
pipe = StableDiffusionInpaintPipeline.from_pretrained(
    "sd2-community/stable-diffusion-2-inpainting",
    torch_dtype=torch.float16
).to(device)
```

Here we create `pipe`, a diffuser pipeline for inpainting. A pipeline bundles all the parts needed for generation—the tokenizer and text encoder for the text prompt, a UNet denoiser, a variational autoencoder (VAE) that compresses the image into a compact internal ("latent") representation and then reconstructs it, and a scheduler—and moves them onto the selected device:

```
# In[]:
pipe

# Out[]:
StableDiffusionInpaintPipeline {
  "_class_name": "StableDiffusionInpaintPipeline",
  "_diffusers_version": "0.33.1",
  "_name_or_path": "stabilityai/stable-diffusion-2-inpainting",
  "feature_extractor": [
    "transformers",
    "CLIPImageProcessor"
  ],
  "image_encoder": [
    null,
    null
  ],
  "requires_safety_checker": false,
  "safety_checker": [
    null,
    null
  ],
  "scheduler": [
    "diffusers",
    "PNDMScheduler"
  ],
  "text_encoder": [
    "transformers",
    "CLIPTextModel"
  ],
  ...
  "vae": [
    "diffusers",
    "AutoencoderKL"
  ]
}
```

Printing out the model as we did earlier, we can appreciate that it's actually pretty condensed, considering what it does. It takes an image, recognizes the mask and the area it needs to change, and individually modifies the values of those pixels so that what comes out looks like a credible replacement.

We're ready to load a random image of a horse and see what our model produces. Let's open a horse file (see figure 2.7):

```
# In[4]:
img = Image.open("../data/p1ch2/horse.jpg")
img
```

Figure 2.7 A horse, of course.

OK, let's pass this along with our mask, which we created through a separate process. We skipped the generation of the mask image for brevity, but we have included the code snippet in the same file. Now, let's pass in our prompt, image, and mask to the pipeline:

```
# In[5]:
mask_img = Image.open("../data/p1ch2/horse_mask.jpg")

prompt = ("a zebra replacing the original horse, same pose, same lighting,
    background unchanged")
negative = "distorted background, blurry, text, watermark"

out = pipe(
    prompt=prompt,
    image=img,
    mask_image=mask_img,
    negative_prompt=negative,
```

The negative_prompt argument is optional, but useful to specify undesired features in the generated image, helping to steer the model away from producing unwanted artifacts or characteristics.

```
        guidance_scale=7.5,
        strength=0.8,
        generator=torch.Generator(device).manual_seed(42)
)
```

out is now the output of the generator, which contains our new image:

```
# In[6]:
out.images[0]
```

Figure 2.8 A zebra? Sort of.

If we were to manually code the image in figure 2.8 in a traditional programming language, it would be a nightmare, but with a model like we use here, it's just a matter of calling a function. We won't recognize anything zebra-specific in the model printout (or in the source code, for that matter) because there is *not* anything zebra-specific in there! The network is a scaffold—the juice is in the weights.

The resulting image in figure 2.8 is not perfect, but it bears repeating that the learning process has not passed through direct supervision, where humans have delineated tens of thousands of horses or manually Photoshopped thousands of zebra stripes. The model has learned to produce an image that matches just the image and directives it has been trained on!

Many other fun models have been trained using this approach. Some of them are capable of creating credible human faces of nonexistent individuals; others can translate sketches into real-looking pictures of imaginary landscapes. Generative models are also being explored for producing real-sounding audio, credible text, and enjoyable music. It is likely that these models will be the basis of future tools that support the creative process.

On a serious note, it's hard to overstate the implications of this kind of work. Tools like the one we just downloaded are only going to become higher quality and more ubiquitous. Face-swapping technology, in particular, has gotten considerable media attention. Searching for "deep fakes" will turn up a plethora of example content.

NOTE A relevant example of face-swapping is described in the *Vox* article "Jordan Peele's Simulated Obama PSA Is a Double-Edged Warning Against Fake News," by Aja Romano (https://mng.bz/PwEv; warning: coarse language).

So far, we've had a chance to play with a model that sees into images and a model that generates new images. We have seen how to use natural language to steer image generation and editing. To close, we'll flip the direction: a vision-language model that takes an image and produces a natural-language caption. But before we do that, let's take a moment to look at the options we've explored for downloading pretrained models from the internet.

2.3 Model Zoo: Hugging Face

We've just had the pleasure of working with various models from model zoos in a variety of packages (e.g., torchvision, transformers, diffusers). A model zoo refers to a collection or repository of pretrained models. Pretrained models have been published since the early days of deep learning, but historically, there was no standardized way for users to access them through a uniform interface. TorchVision is a good example of a clean interface, as we saw earlier in this chapter.

One of the most prominent model repositories in the deep learning ecosystem today is Hugging Face, a recognized leader in open source and the most comprehensive model zoo. Hugging Face has a wide array of transformer and diffusion models (architectures we will build from scratch in the later chapters).

Hugging Face's most popular library is the transformers package, which, as you may have guessed, holds a host of transformer models. As an example, we'll use the pretrained library GPT2 for text generation (code/p1ch2/4_model_zoos.ipynb):

```
from transformers import pipeline
generator = pipeline('text-generation', model='gpt2')
generator("AI models are so smart they can replace my",
➥ max_length=10)

# [{'generated_text': 'AI models are so smart they can replace my brain with
    a totally different one.'}]
```

The pipeline function provides a convenient way to load a model and apply it to a specific task, such as generating text.

Based on the pipeline loaded, various arguments can be passed in. In this case, we are generating an output of length 10.

In the previous code example, we are effectively asking the model to complete our nine-word input phrase. The resulting output—albeit a bit concerning (can they really replace our brains?)—is a demonstration of the ease of use for downloading pretrained models and applying them. This suggestion is determined by considering the model's inherent understanding of language patterns and context, guided by a sampling strategy trained on gigabytes of data.

We will take a closer look at the mechanics of text generation by transformers in chapter 9. However, for now, let's finish with our final example of working with image and text together.

2.4 A pretrained network that describes scenes

We started with image classification, moved on to image generation, and then performed a text generation task with `transformers`. Now, let's see if we can perform a task that uses natural language processing to perform image annotation. Vision and language are two fundamental skills in how humans understand the world, and image captioning is a great example of how deep learning can accomplish tasks that were once thought to be uniquely solvable by humans.

We will employ a pretrained image-to-text model known as BLIP, developed by a team at Salesforce Research. BLIP is a multimodal model; that is, it is designed to handle different types of data (or *modalities*)—text and images, in this case—as its input.

BLIP was trained with various image and text combinations to learn the relationship between the two. It was trained with large datasets of images and their paired sentence descriptions—for example, "A Tabby cat is leaning on a wooden table, with one paw on a laser mouse and the other on a black laptop." Before training BLIP, the team also performed some preprocessing tricks to filter certain captions from the noisy web data and generate synthetic captions to augment the dataset.

Since the model is trained on images and caption pairs, how is it able to annotate images it has never seen before? The image dataset is large, but not large enough to encompass every image that can be imagined. At a high level, during training, the image is encoded into a vector of numbers called an embedding. Likewise, the corresponding caption is also encoded into another embedding. These values are compared to determine how similar the image and caption, which iteratively trains the model, are. Additionally, the model has a decoder that generates guesses for the caption based on the image. There are many more details to this process, but we try not to get bogged down in the details.

> **NOTE** For the adventurous, see the paper "BLIP: Bootstrapping Language-Image Pre-training for Unified Vision-Language Understanding and Generation," available at https://arxiv.org/pdf/2201.12086.pdf.

To perform inference, the user only needs to use the image encoder and text decoder parts of the model to generate text, as shown in figure 2.9. The captioning model has two halves; the first half of the model is an *image encoder* that learns to generate "descriptive" numerical representations of the scene (Tabby cat, laser mouse, paw). This embedding "encoding" is then taken to the second half of the model. That second half is a *text decoder* that generates a coherent sentence by transforming this encoding into a text representation. The resulting output is a caption of the model that describes the image. We will learn more about how encoders and decoders actually work in chapter 9.

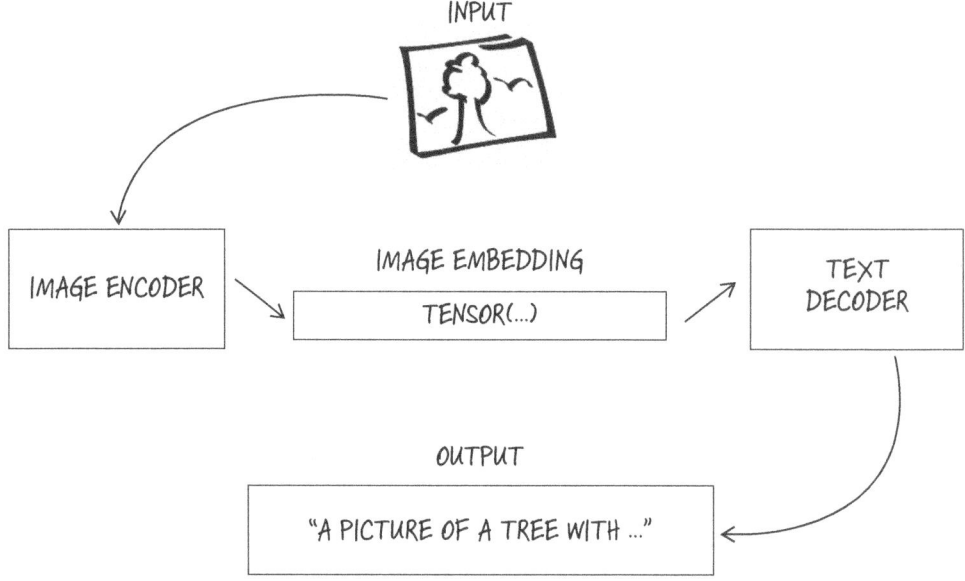

Figure 2.9 Conceptual diagram of BLIP caption generation

2.4.1 BLIP in action

We can use what we learned from our model zoo to find BLIP on Hugging Face. Following the code in code/p1ch2/4_model_zoos.ipynb, we can load the processor for the image and the model itself:

```
# In[5]:
from PIL import Image
from transformers import BlipProcessor, BlipForConditionalGeneration

processor = BlipProcessor.from_pretrained("Salesforce/
➥blip-image-captioning-large")
model = BlipForConditionalGeneration.from_pretrained("Salesforce/
➥blip-image-captioning-large")
```

We will also define a helper function to use these and print out the caption:

```
# In[6]:
def annotate_image(image: Image) -> None:
    display(image)
    inputs = processor(image, return_tensors="pt")
    out = model.generate(**inputs)
    print(processor.decode(out[0], skip_special_tokens=True))
```

Let's try it with our horse.jpg image from before:

```
# In[7]
annotate_image(Image.open("../data/p1ch2/horse.jpg"))
```

```
# Out[7]:
there is a brown horse grazing in a field of green grass
```

How descriptive! Now, just for fun, let's see whether our diffusion model can also fool this BLIP model. Let's add the zebra.jpg image in the data folder and rerun the model: "zebra grazing in a field of green grass with trees in the background." Well, there's no fooling it; it got the animal right there, too. In addition, it is unlikely that zebras graze on such green pastures and in such environments. This is an impressive feat: we generated a fake image with an impossible situation, and the captioning network was flexible enough to get the main subject right.

We'd like to stress that something like this, which would have been extremely hard to achieve before the advent of deep learning, can be obtained with under 1,000 lines of code, with a general-purpose architecture that knows nothing about horses or zebras and a corpus of images and their descriptions. No hardcoded criterion or grammar—everything, including the sentence, emerges from patterns in the data.

The network we saw in this chapter was, in a way, more complex than the ones we saw earlier in AlexNet, as it includes multiple networks, each feeding into each other and learning through each other. This gives us a taste of using complex models to accomplish real-life tasks, and we will learn how this process works under the hood shortly.

2.5 Conclusion

We hope this was a fun chapter. We took some time to play with models created with PyTorch, which were optimized to carry out specific tasks. In fact, the more enterprising of us could already put one of these models behind a web server and start a business, sharing the profits with the original authors. (Contact the publisher for franchise opportunities!) Once we learn how these models are built, we will also be able to use the knowledge we gained here to download a pretrained model and quickly fine-tune it on a slightly different task.

We will also see how building models that deal with different problems on different kinds of data can be done using the same building blocks. One thing that PyTorch does particularly right is providing those building blocks in the form of an essential toolset.

This book does not focus on going through the complete PyTorch API or reviewing deep learning architectures; rather, we will build hands-on knowledge of these building blocks. This way, you will be able to consume the excellent online documentation and repositories on top of a solid foundation.

Starting with the next chapter, we'll embark on a journey that will enable us to teach our computer skills, like those described in this chapter from scratch, using PyTorch. We'll also learn that starting from a pretrained network and fine-tuning it on new data, without starting from scratch, is an effective way to solve problems when the data points are not particularly numerous. This is one further reason pretrained networks are an important tool for deep learning practitioners to have. Time to learn about the first fundamental building block: tensors.

2.6 Exercises

1. Feed the image of the golden retriever into the horse-to-zebra model:
   a. What do you need to do to the image to prepare it?
   b. What does the output look like?
2. Search the Hugging Face model hub for projects that provide pretrained models:
   a. How many models are available in the hub?
   b. Find an interesting-looking model on the Hugging Face model hub. Can you understand the purpose of the model from its documentation?
   c. Bookmark the project and come back after you've finished this book. Can you understand the implementation?

Summary

- A pretrained network is a model that has already been trained on a dataset. Such networks can typically produce useful results immediately after loading the network weights.
- Using a pretrained model allows us to integrate a neural network into a project without building or training it.
- *Inference* is the term for running a model on new data, enabling it to make predictions or decisions based on its learned knowledge.
- AlexNet is a deep convolutional network that set new benchmarks for image recognition in the years it was released.
- Diffusion models generate or edit images by reversing a gradual noising process, iteratively denoising toward a coherent result guided by a text prompt.
- Inpainting re-renders an input image; an optional mask confines changes to selected regions while keeping the rest unchanged.
- Hugging Face models provide a convenient and widely-used way to access pretrained models from the deep learning community, available through the `transformers` library.
- BLIP is a multimodal model to consume an image and produce a text description of the image.

It starts with a tensor

This chapter covers
- Understanding tensors, the basic data structure in PyTorch
- Indexing and operating on tensors
- Interoperating with NumPy multidimensional arrays
- Moving computations to the GPU for speed

In the previous chapter, we took a tour of some of the many applications that deep learning enables. They invariably consisted of taking data in some form, like images or text, and producing data in another form, like labels, numbers, or more images or text. Viewed from this angle, deep learning consists of building a system that can transform data from one representation to another. This transformation is driven by finding patterns across many examples that show the input-to-output relationship we want to achieve. For example, the system might note the general shape of a dog and the typical colors of a golden retriever. By combining the two image properties, the system can correctly map images with a given shape and color to the golden retriever label, instead of a black lab (or a tawny tomcat, for that matter).

The resulting system can consume broad swaths of similar inputs and produce meaningful output for those inputs.

The process begins by converting our input into floating-point numbers. In this chapter, we will cover converting image pixels to numbers, but to do so, we will first learn how to deal with all the floating-point numbers in PyTorch using tensors. Tensors are the fundamental data structures in deep learning frameworks, and PyTorch provides a rich API to manipulate them, so let's get started.

3.1 The world as floating-point numbers

Since floating-point numbers are the way a network deals with information, we need a way to encode real-world data of the kind we want to process into something digestible by a network and then decode the output back to something we can understand and use for our purpose.

A deep neural network typically learns the transformation from one form of data to another in stages, which means the partially transformed data between each stage can be thought of as a sequence of intermediate representations, as shown in figure 3.1. For image recognition, early representations can be things such as edge detection or certain textures like fur. Deeper representations can capture more complex structures like ears, noses, or eyes.

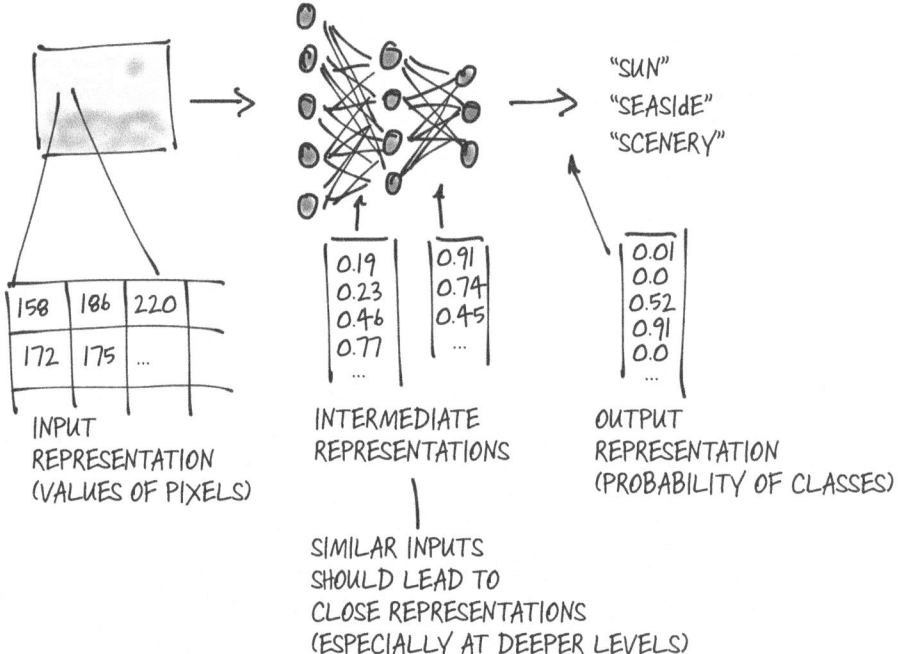

Figure 3.1 A deep neural network learns how to transform an input representation to an output representation. Note: The numbers of neurons and outputs are not to scale.

In general, such intermediate representations are collections of floating-point numbers that characterize the input and capture the data's structure in a way that is instrumental for describing how inputs are mapped to the outputs of the neural network. Such characterization is specific to the task at hand and is learned from relevant examples. These collections of floating-point numbers and their manipulation are at the heart of modern AI—we will see several examples of this throughout the book.

It's important to keep in mind that these intermediate representations (like those shown in the second step of figure 3.1) are the results of combining the input with the weights of the previous layer of neurons. Each intermediate representation is unique to the inputs that preceded it.

Before we can begin the process of converting our data to floating-point input, we must first have a solid understanding of how PyTorch handles and stores data—as input, as intermediate representations, and as output. This chapter will be devoted to precisely that.

To this end, PyTorch introduces a fundamental data structure: the *tensor*. We already bumped into tensors in chapter 2, when we ran inference on pretrained networks. If you have a background in mathematics or physics, you might know tensors differently, but in deep learning, tensors refer to the generalization of vectors and matrices to an arbitrary number of dimensions, as shown in figure 3.2. Another name for the same concept is *multidimensional array*, or for those familiar with NumPy, it is also called an *ndarray*. The dimensionality of a tensor coincides with the number of indices used to refer to scalar values within the tensor. The dimensions are zero-indexed and ordered from left to right. For example, the 3D tensor in the figure has four sets of 3 × 3 arrays. So, the shape of the tensor would be (4, 3, 3). We refer to the leftmost dimension (size 4) as dimension 0, the second dimension (size 3) as dimension 1, and so on.

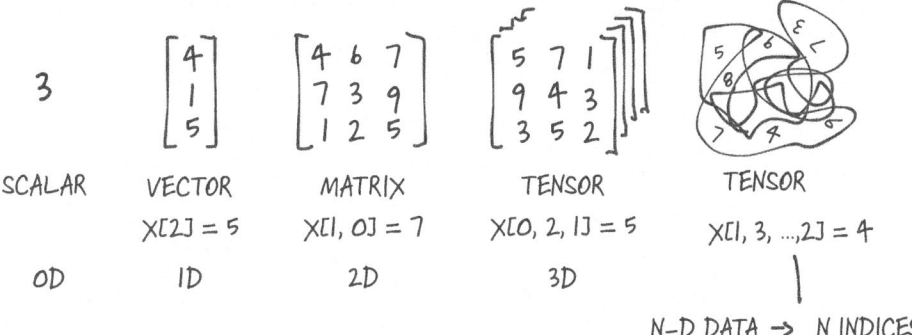

Figure 3.2 Tensors are the building blocks for representing data in PyTorch. Scalars, vectors, and matrices can also all be considered tensors.

PyTorch is not the only library that deals with multidimensional arrays. NumPy is by far the most popular multidimensional array library, to the point that it has now arguably become the lingua franca of data science. PyTorch features seamless interoperability with NumPy, which brings with it first-class integration with the rest of the scientific libraries in Python, such as SciPy (https://www.scipy.org/), Scikit-learn (https://scikit-learn.org), and pandas (https://pandas.pydata.org).

Compared to NumPy arrays, PyTorch tensors have a few superpowers, such as the ability to perform very fast operations on graphical processing units (GPUs), distribute operations on multiple devices or machines, and keep track of the graph of computations that created them. These are all important features when implementing a modern deep learning library.

We'll start this chapter by introducing PyTorch tensors, covering the basics to set things in motion for our work in the rest of the book. First and foremost, we'll learn how to manipulate tensors using the PyTorch tensor library, including how the data is stored in memory, how certain operations can be performed on arbitrarily large tensors in constant time, and the aforementioned NumPy interoperability and GPU acceleration. Understanding the capabilities and API of tensors is important if they're to become go-to tools in our programming toolbox. In the next chapter, we'll put this knowledge to good use and learn how to represent several different kinds of data in a way that enables learning with neural networks.

3.2 *Tensors: Multidimensional arrays*

We have already learned that tensors are the fundamental data structure in PyTorch. A tensor is an array—that is, a data structure that stores a collection of numbers that are accessible individually using an index, and that can be indexed with multiple indices.

3.2.1 *From Python lists to PyTorch tensors*

Let's see list indexing in action so we can compare it to tensor indexing. Take a list of three numbers in Python (code/p1ch3/1_tensors.ipynb):

```
# In[1]:
a = [1.0, 2.0, 1.0]
```

We can access the first element of the list using the corresponding zero-based index:

```
# In[2]:
a[0]

# Out[2]:
1.0

# In[3]:
a[2] = 3.0
a

# Out[3]:
[1.0, 2.0, 3.0]
```

3.2.2 Constructing our first tensors

It is not unusual for simple Python programs dealing with vectors of numbers, such as the coordinates of a 2D line, to use Python lists to store the vectors. As we will see in the following chapter, using the more efficient tensor data structure, many types of data—from images to time series, and even sentences—can be represented. By defining operations over tensors, some of which we'll explore in this chapter, we can slice and manipulate data expressively and efficiently at the same time, even from a high-level (and not particularly fast) language such as Python.

3.2.2 Constructing our first tensors

Let's construct our first PyTorch tensor and see what it looks like. It won't be a particularly meaningful tensor for now, just three 1s in a column:

```
# In[4]:
import torch            ◁──┤ Imports the torch module
a = torch.ones(3)       ◁──┤ Creates a one-dimensional
a                          │ tensor of size 3 filled
                           │ with 1s

# Out[4]:
tensor([1., 1., 1.])

# In[5]:
a[1]                    ◁──┤ Indexes an element
                           │ out of the tensor

# Out[5]:
tensor(1.)

# In[6]:
float(a[1])

# Out[6]:
1.0
                           │ Assigns a new value
# In[7]:                   │ to an element in
a[2] = 2.0              ◁──┤ the tensor
a

# Out[7]:
tensor([1., 1., 2.])
```

After importing the `torch` module, we call a function that creates a (one-dimensional) tensor of size 3 filled with the value `1.0`. We can access an element using its zero-based index or assign a new value to it. Although on the surface this example doesn't differ much from a list of number objects, under the hood, things are completely different.

3.2.3 The essence of tensors

Python lists or tuples of numbers are collections of Python objects that are individually allocated in memory, as shown on the left in figure 3.3. PyTorch tensors or NumPy arrays, on the other hand, are views over (typically) contiguous memory blocks containing *unboxed* C numeric types rather than Python objects. Tensors are homogeneous (i.e., all elements are of the same data type). Each element is a 32-bit (4-byte) float in this case, as we can see on the right side of the figure. So, storing a 1D tensor of 1 million float numbers will require exactly 4 million contiguous bytes, plus a small overhead for the metadata (such as dimensions and numeric type).

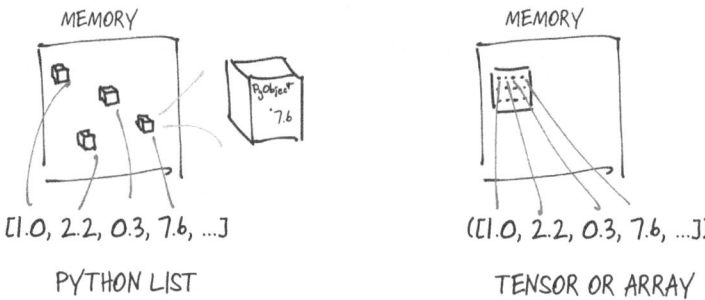

Figure 3.3 Python object (boxed) numeric values vs. tensor (unboxed array) numeric values

Say we have a list of coordinates we'd like to use to represent a geometrical object: perhaps a 2D triangle with vertices at coordinates (4, 1), (5, 3), and (2, 1). The example is not particularly pertinent to deep learning, but it's easy to follow. Instead of having coordinates as numbers in a Python list, as we did earlier, we can use a one-dimensional tensor by storing *X*s in the even indices and *Y*s in the odd indices, like this:

```
# In[8]:
points = torch.zeros(6)
points[0] = 4.0
points[1] = 1.0
points[2] = 5.0
points[3] = 3.0
points[4] = 2.0
points[5] = 1.0
```

Using .zeros is just a way to get an appropriately sized array.

We overwrite those zeros with the values we want.

We can also pass a Python list to the constructor, to the same effect:

```
# In[9]:
points = torch.tensor([4.0, 1.0, 5.0, 3.0, 2.0, 1.0])
points

# Out[9]:
tensor([4., 1., 5., 3., 2., 1.])
```

To get the coordinates of the first point, we do the following:

3.2 Tensors: Multidimensional arrays

```
# In[10]:
float(points[0]), float(points[1])

# Out[10]:
(4.0, 1.0)
```

This setup is OK, although it would be more practical to have the first index refer to individual 2D points rather than point coordinates. For this, we can use a 2D tensor:

```
# In[11]:
points = torch.tensor([[4.0, 1.0], [5.0, 3.0], [2.0, 1.0]])
points

# Out[11]:
tensor([[4., 1.],
        [5., 3.],
        [2., 1.]])
```

Here, we pass a list of lists to the constructor. We can ask the tensor about its shape:

```
# In[12]:
points.shape

# Out[12]:
torch.Size([3, 2])
```

This informs us about the size of the tensor along each dimension. We could also use zeros or ones to initialize the tensor, providing the size as arguments:

```
# In[13]:
points = torch.zeros(3, 2)
points

# Out[13]:
tensor([[0., 0.],
        [0., 0.],
        [0., 0.]])
```

Now we can access an individual element in the tensor using two indices:

```
# In[14]:
points = torch.tensor([[4.0, 1.0], [5.0, 3.0], [2.0, 1.0]])
points

# Out[14]:
tensor([[4., 1.],
        [5., 3.],
        [2., 1.]])

# In[15]:
points[0, 1]
```

```
# Out[15]:
tensor(1.)
```

This code returns the *Y*-coordinate of the zeroth point in our dataset. We can also access the first element in the tensor as we did before to get the 2D coordinates of the first point:

```
# In[16]:
points[0]
```

```
# Out[16]:
tensor([4., 1.])
```

The output is another tensor that presents a different *view* of the same underlying data. The new tensor is a 1D tensor of size 2, referencing the values of the first row in the `points` tensor. Does this mean a new chunk of memory was allocated, values were copied into it, and the new memory was returned wrapped in a new tensor object? No, because that would be very inefficient, especially if we had millions of points. We'll revisit how tensors are stored later in this chapter when we cover views of tensors in section 3.8.

3.3 Indexing tensors

What if we need to obtain a tensor containing all points but the first? That's easy using range indexing notation, which also applies to standard Python lists. Here's a reminder:

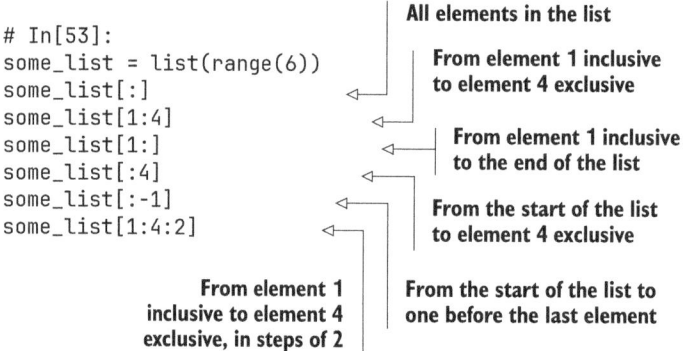

To achieve our goal, we can use the same notation for PyTorch tensors, with the added benefit that, just as in NumPy and other Python scientific libraries, we can use range indexing for each of the tensor's dimensions:

```
# In[54]:
points[1:]
points[1:, :]
points[1:, 0]
points[None]
```

- All rows after the first; implicitly all columns
- All rows after the first; all columns
- All rows after the first; first column
- Adds a dimension of size 1; the same can be accomplished with points.unsqueeze(dim=0).

In addition to using ranges, PyTorch features a powerful form of indexing, called *advanced indexing*, which we will look at in the next chapter.

3.4 Broadcasting

One important feature PyTorch tensors support is NumPy's broadcasting semantics. *Broadcasting* is a mechanism that simplifies complex tensor operations by enabling efficient element-wise computations between tensors of varying shapes. During broadcasting, dimensions are compared element-wise from right to left. If the dimensions are compatible, the tensors can be broadcast together. Compatible dimensions are

- Equal dimensions.
- One of the dimensions is 1.

Here is an example demonstrated with scalars, where the scalar value is applied to all the elements of the tensor:

```
Tensor X:           Scalar Y:

[[ 1  2  3 ]]   +      10

Result (Broadcasted Scalar Addition):

[[ 11 12 13 ]]
```

On the other hand, when a 1 × 3 tensor is multiplied by a 3 × 1 tensor, we match up each dimension and see that they are compatible. The first dimension of the first tensor is 1, and the second dimension of the second tensor is 1. Therefore, we can broadcast the tensors together, resulting in a 3 × 3 tensor:

```
3 x 1
1 x 3
------
3 x 3

  Tensor A:           Tensor B:

  [[ 1  2  3 ]]         [[10]
                   *     [20]
                         [30]]

Result (Broadcasted Multiplication):

  [[ 10  20  30 ]
   [ 20  40  60 ]
   [ 30  60  90 ]]
```

When tensors have varying dimensions, we right-align the tensor shapes. When the dimensions are matching, we apply the operation element-wise. And when one of the dimensions is 1, we can think of the values of that dimension being virtually duplicated to match the greater dimension. Let's look at an example with a 2 × 1 × 3 and 2 × 3 tensor:

```
    2 x 3
2 x 1 x 3
---------
2 x 2 x 3

  Matrix A:              Tensor B:

  [[ 1  2  3 ]           [[[10 20 30]]
                    +
   [ 4  5  6 ]]          [[40 50 60]]]

Result (Broadcasted Tensor Addition):

[[[ 11 22 33 ]
  [ 44 55 66 ]]
 [[ 41 52 63 ]
  [ 44 55 66 ]]]
```

We did a quick walk-through of broadcasting, but we will have additional practice with it in chapter 5.

3.5 Named tensors

The dimensions (or axes) of our tensors usually index something like pixel locations or color channels. As a result, when we want to index into a tensor, we need to remember the ordering of the dimensions and write our indexing accordingly. As data is transformed through multiple tensors, keeping track of which dimension contains what data can be error-prone.

To make things concrete, imagine that we have a 3D tensor like img_t from section 2.1.4 (we will use dummy data for simplicity here), and we want to convert it to grayscale. We looked up typical weights for the colors to derive a single brightness value:

```
# In[2]:
img_t = torch.randn(3, 5, 5) # shape [channels, rows, columns]
weights = torch.tensor([0.2126, 0.7152, 0.0722])
```

We also often want our code to generalize—for example, from grayscale images represented as 2D tensors with height and width dimensions to color images, adding a third channel dimension (as in RGB) or from a single image to a batch of images. In section 2.1.4, we introduced an additional batch dimension in batch_t; here, we pretend to have a batch of 2:

```
# In[3]:
batch_t = torch.randn(2, 3, 5, 5) # shape [batch, channels, rows, columns]
```

So sometimes the RGB channels are in dimension 0, and sometimes they are in dimension 1. But we can generalize by counting from the end: they are always in dimension -3, the third from the end. The lazy, unweighted mean can thus be written as follows:

```
# In[4]:
img_gray_naive = img_t.mean(-3)
batch_gray_naive = batch_t.mean(-3)
img_gray_naive.shape, batch_gray_naive.shape

# Out[4]:
(torch.Size([5, 5]), torch.Size([2, 5, 5]))
```

But now we have the weight, too. Recall for *broadcasting*, PyTorch will allow us to multiply things that are the same shape, as well as shapes where one operand is of size 1 in a given dimension. It also appends the leading dimensions of size 1 automatically. batch_t of shape (2, 3, 5, 5) is multiplied by unsqueezed_weights of shape (3, 1, 1), resulting in a tensor of shape (2, 3, 5, 5), from which we can then sum the third dimension from the end (the three channels):

```
# In[5]:
unsqueezed_weights = weights.unsqueeze(-1).unsqueeze_(-1)
img_weights = img_t * unsqueezed_weights
batch_weights = batch_t * unsqueezed_weights
img_gray_weighted = img_weights.sum(-3)
batch_gray_weighted = batch_weights.sum(-3)
batch_weights.shape, batch_t.shape, unsqueezed_weights.shape

# Out[5]:
(torch.Size([2, 3, 5, 5]), torch.Size([2, 3, 5, 5]), torch.Size([3, 1, 1]))
```

As we can see, the dimensions of the tensors are not apparent unless working back through the computation. This process is error-prone, especially when the locations where tensors are created and used are far apart in our code. This issue has caught the eye of practitioners, and so it has been suggested that the dimension be given a name instead (see Sasha Rush's article, "Tensor Considered Harmful," Harvard NLP, http://nlp.seas.harvard.edu/NamedTensor).

PyTorch 1.3 added *named tensors* as an prototype feature (see https://pytorch.org/docs/stable/named_tensor.html). Tensor factory functions such as tensor and rand take a names argument. The names should be a sequence of strings:

```
# In[7]:
weights_named = torch.tensor([0.2126, 0.7152, 0.0722], names=['channels'])
weights_named

# Out[7]:
tensor([0.2126, 0.7152, 0.0722], names=('channels',))
```

When we already have a tensor and want to add names (but not change existing ones), we can call the method refine_names on it. Similar to indexing, the ellipsis (...) allows you to leave out any number of dimensions. With the rename sibling method, you can also overwrite or drop (by passing in None) existing names:

```
# In[8]:
img_named =  img_t.refine_names(..., 'channels', 'rows', 'columns')
batch_named = batch_t.refine_names(..., 'channels', 'rows', 'columns')
print("img named:", img_named.shape, img_named.names)
print("batch named:", batch_named.shape, batch_named.names)

# Out[8]:
img named: torch.Size([3, 5, 5]) ('channels', 'rows', 'columns')
batch named: torch.Size([2, 3, 5, 5]) (None, 'channels', 'rows', 'columns')
```

For operations with two inputs, in addition to the usual dimension checks—whether sizes are the same, or if one is 1 and can be broadcast to the other—PyTorch will now check the names for us. So far, it does not automatically align dimensions, so we need to do this explicitly. The method align_as returns a tensor with missing dimensions added and existing ones permuted to the right order:

```
# In[9]:
weights_aligned = weights_named.align_as(img_named)
weights_aligned.shape, weights_aligned.names

# Out[9]:
(torch.Size([3, 1, 1]), ('channels', 'rows', 'columns'))
```

Functions accepting dimension arguments, like sum, also take named dimensions:

```
# In[10]:
gray_named = (img_named * weights_aligned).sum('channels')
gray_named.shape, gray_named.names

# Out[10]:
(torch.Size([5, 5]), ('rows', 'columns'))
```

If we try to combine dimensions with different names, we get an error:

```
gray_named = (img_named[..., :3] * weights_named).sum('channels')

RuntimeError: Error when
 attempting to broadcast dims ['channels', 'rows',
   'columns'] and dims ['channels']: dim 'columns' and dim 'channels'
   are at the same position from the right but do not match.
```

If we want to use tensors outside functions that operate on named tensors, we need to drop the names by renaming them to None. The following gets us back into the world of unnamed dimensions:

```
# In[12]:
gray_plain = gray_named.rename(None)
gray_plain.shape, gray_plain.names

# Out[12]:
(torch.Size([5, 5]), (None, None))
```

Given the experimental nature of this feature at the time of writing and to avoid mucking around with indexing and alignment, we will stick to unnamed tensors for the remainder of the book. Named tensors have the potential to eliminate many sources of alignment errors, which—if the PyTorch forum is any indication—can be a source of headaches. It will be interesting to see how widely they will be adopted.

3.6 Tensor element types

So far, we have covered the basics of how tensors work, but we have not yet touched on what kinds of numeric types we can store in a Tensor. As we hinted at in section 3.2, using the standard Python numeric types can be suboptimal for several reasons:

- *Numbers in Python are objects.* Whereas a floating-point number might require only, for instance, 32 bits to be represented on a computer, Python will convert it into a full-fledged Python object with reference counting, and so on. This operation, called *boxing*, is not a problem if we need to store a small number of numbers, but allocating millions gets very inefficient.
- *Lists in Python are meant for sequential collections of objects.* There are no operations defined for, say, efficiently taking the dot product of two vectors or summing vectors together. Also, Python lists have no way of optimizing the layout of their contents in memory, as they are indexable collections of pointers to Python objects (of any kind, not just numbers). Finally, Python lists are one-dimensional, and although we can create lists of lists, the process is again very inefficient.
- *The Python interpreter is slow compared to optimized, compiled code.* Performing mathematical operations on large collections of numerical data can be much faster using optimized code written in a compiled, low-level language like C.

For these reasons, data science libraries rely on NumPy or introduce dedicated data structures like PyTorch tensors, which provide efficient low-level implementations of numerical data structures and related operations on them, wrapped in a convenient high-level API. To enable this structure, the objects within a tensor must all be numbers of the same type, and PyTorch must keep track of this numeric type.

3.6.1 Specifying the numeric type with dtype

The dtype argument to tensor constructors (i.e., functions like tensor, zeros, and ones) specifies the numerical data (d) type that will be contained in the tensor. The data type specifies the possible values the tensor can hold (integers versus floating-point numbers) and the number of bytes per value (and whether signed or unsigned, in the case of uint8). The dtype argument is deliberately similar to the standard NumPy argument of the same name. PyTorch supports 12 different dtype arguments:

- torch.float32 *or* torch.float—32-bit floating-point
- torch.float64 *or* torch.double—64-bit, double-precision floating-point
- torch.complex64 *or* torch.cfloat—64-bit complex
- torch.complex128 *or* torch.cdouble—128-bit complex
- torch.float16 *or* torch.half—16-bit, half-precision floating-point
- torch.bfloat16—brain float 16-bit, half-precision floating-point (This is a new data type introduced by Google in 2019. It is similar to torch.float16 but uses a different encoding that can encode a larger range, while float16 is better for precision.)
- torch.int8—signed 8-bit integers
- torch.uint8—unsigned 8-bit integers
- torch.int16 *or* torch.short—signed 16-bit integers
- torch.int32 *or* torch.int—signed 32-bit integers
- torch.int64 *or* torch.long—signed 64-bit integers
- torch.bool—Boolean

The default data type for tensors is 32-bit floating-point.

3.6.2 A dtype for every occasion

As we will see in future chapters, computations happening in neural networks are typically executed with 32-bit floating-point precision. Higher precision, like 64-bit, will not buy improvements in the accuracy of a model and will require more memory and computing time. It is possible to switch to the 16-bit floating-point, half-precision data type to decrease the memory footprint of a neural network model if needed, with a minor effect on accuracy.

Tensors can be used as indices in other tensors. In this case, PyTorch expects indexing tensors to have a 64-bit integer data type. Creating a tensor with integers as arguments, such as using torch.tensor([2, 2]), will create a 64-bit integer tensor by default. As such, we'll spend most of our time dealing with float32 and int64.

Finally, predicates on tensors, such as points > 1.0, produce bool tensors indicating whether each individual element satisfies the condition. These are the numeric types in a nutshell.

3.6.3 Managing a tensor's dtype attribute

To allocate a tensor of the right numeric type, we can specify the proper dtype as an argument to the constructor. For example:

```
# In[47]:
double_points = torch.ones(10, 2, dtype=torch.double)
short_points = torch.tensor([[1, 2], [3, 4]], dtype=torch.short)
```

We can find out about the dtype for a tensor by accessing the corresponding attribute:

```
# In[48]:
short_points.dtype

# Out[48]:
torch.int16
```

We can also cast the output of a tensor creation function to the right type using the corresponding casting method, such as

```
# In[49]:
double_points = torch.zeros(10, 2).double()
short_points = torch.ones(10, 2).short()
```

or the more convenient to method:

```
# In[50]:
double_points = torch.zeros(10, 2).to(torch.double)
short_points = torch.ones(10, 2).to(dtype=torch.short)
```

Under the hood, to checks whether the conversion is necessary and, if so, does it. The dtype-named casting methods like float are shorthand for to, but the to method can take additional arguments, which we'll discuss in section 3.9.

When mixing input types in operations, the inputs are converted to the larger type automatically. Thus, if we want 32-bit computation, we need to make sure all our inputs are (at most) 32-bit:

```
# In[51]:
points_64 = torch.rand(5, dtype=torch.double)       ◁──┐  rand initializes the
points_short = points_64.to(torch.short)               │  tensor elements to
points_64 * points_short                               │  random numbers
                                                       │  between 0 and 1.
# Out[51]:
tensor([0., 0., 0., 0., 0.], dtype=torch.float64)
```

3.7 The tensor API

At this point, we know what PyTorch tensors are and how they work under the hood. Before we wrap up, it is worth taking a look at the tensor operations that PyTorch offers. It would be of little use to list them all here. Instead, we're going to get a general feel for the API and establish a few directions on where to find things in the online documentation at http://pytorch.org/docs.

First, the vast majority of operations on and between tensors are available in the torch module and can also be called as methods of a tensor object. For instance, the transpose function can be used from the torch module as

```
# In[71]:
a = torch.ones(3, 2)
a_t = torch.transpose(a, 0, 1)
```

```
a.shape, a_t.shape

# Out[71]:
(torch.Size([3, 2]), torch.Size([2, 3]))
```

or as a method of the a tensor:

```
# In[72]:
a = torch.ones(3, 2)
a_t = a.transpose(0, 1)

a.shape, a_t.shape

# Out[72]:
(torch.Size([3, 2]), torch.Size([2, 3]))
```

There is no difference between the two forms; they can be used interchangeably.

We mentioned the online docs earlier (http://pytorch.org/docs). They are exhaustive and well organized, with the tensor operations divided into groups:

- *Creation ops*—Functions for constructing a tensor, like `ones` and `from_numpy`
- *Indexing, slicing, joining, mutating ops*—Functions for changing the shape, stride, or content of a tensor, like `transpose`
- *Math ops*—Functions for manipulating the content of the tensor through computations
  - *Pointwise ops*—Functions for obtaining a new tensor by applying a function to each element independently, like `abs` and `cos`
  - *Reduction ops*—Functions for computing aggregate values by iterating through tensors, like `mean`, `std`, and `norm`
  - *Comparison ops*—Functions for evaluating numerical predicates over tensors, like `equal` and `max`
  - *Spectral ops*—Functions for transforming in and operating in the frequency domain, like `stft` and `hamming_window`
  - *Other operations*—Special functions operating on vectors, like `cross`, or matrices, like `trace`
  - *BLAS and LAPACK operations*—Functions following the Basic Linear Algebra Subprograms (BLAS) specification for scalar, vector-vector, matrix-vector, and matrix-matrix operations
- *Random sampling*—Functions for generating values by drawing randomly from probability distributions, like `randn` and `normal`
- *Serialization*—Functions for saving and loading tensors, like `load` and `save`
- *Parallelism*—Functions for controlling the number of threads for parallel CPU execution, like `set_num_threads`

Take some time to play with the general tensor API. This chapter has provided all the prerequisites to enable this kind of interactive exploration. We will also encounter several of the tensor operations as we proceed with the book, starting in the next chapter.

3.8 Tensors: Scenic views of storage

It is time for us to look a bit closer at the implementation under the hood. Values in tensors are allocated in contiguous chunks of memory managed by torch.Storage instances. A storage is a one-dimensional array of numerical data—that is, a contiguous block of memory containing numbers of a given type, such as float (32 bits representing a floating-point number) or int64 (64 bits representing an integer). A PyTorch Tensor instance is a view of such a Storage instance that is capable of indexing into that storage using an offset and per-dimension strides.

> **NOTE** Storage may not be directly accessible in future PyTorch releases, but what we show here still provides a good mental picture of how tensors work under the hood.

Multiple tensors can index the same storage even if they index into the data differently. We can see an example in figure 3.4. In fact, when we requested points[0] in section 3.2, we got back another tensor that indices the same storage as the points tensor—just not all of it, and with different dimensionality (1D versus 2D). The underlying memory is allocated only once, so creating alternate tensor views of the data can be done quickly, regardless of the size of the data managed by the Storage instance.

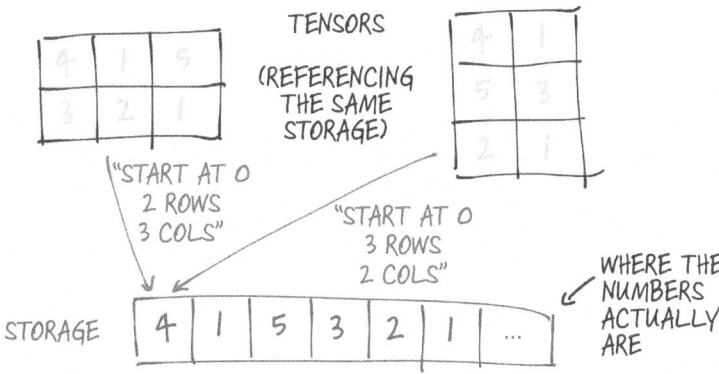

Figure 3.4 Tensors are views of a Storage instance.

3.8.1 Indexing into storage

Let's see how indexing into the storage works in practice with our 2D points. The storage for a given tensor is accessible using the .storage property:

```
# In[17]:
points = torch.tensor([[4.0, 1.0], [5.0, 3.0], [2.0, 1.0]])
points.storage()
```

```
# Out[17]:
 4.0
 1.0
 5.0
 3.0
 2.0
 1.0
[torch.FloatStorage of size 6]
```

Even though the tensor reports itself as having three rows and two columns, the storage under the hood is a contiguous array of size 6. In this sense, the tensor just knows how to translate a pair of indices into a location in the storage.

We can also index into a storage manually. For instance,

```
# In[18]:
points_storage = points.storage()
points_storage[0]

# Out[18]:
4.0

# In[19]:
points.storage()[1]

# Out[19]:
1.0
```

We can't index a storage of a 2D tensor using two indices. The layout of a storage is always one-dimensional, regardless of the dimensionality of any and all tensors that might refer to it.

At this point, it shouldn't come as a surprise that changing the value of a storage changes the content of its referring tensor:

```
# In[20]:
points = torch.tensor([[4.0, 1.0], [5.0, 3.0], [2.0, 1.0]])
points_storage = points.storage()
points_storage[0] = 2.0
points

# Out[20]:
tensor([[2., 1.],
        [5., 3.],
        [2., 1.]])
```

3.8.2 Modifying stored values: In-place operations

In addition to the operations on tensors introduced in the previous section, a small number of operations exist only as methods of the Tensor object. They are recognizable from a trailing underscore in their name, like zero_, which indicates that the method operates *in place* by modifying the input instead of creating a new output tensor and returning it. For instance, the zero_ method zeros out all the elements of the input. Any method *without* the trailing underscore leaves the source tensor unchanged and instead returns a new tensor:

```
# In[73]:
a = torch.ones(3, 2)
```

```
# In[74]:
a.zero_()
a
```

```
# Out[74]:
tensor([[0., 0.],
        [0., 0.],
        [0., 0.]])
```

3.9 Tensor metadata: Size, offset, and stride

To index into a storage, tensors rely on a few pieces of information that, together with their storage, unequivocally define them: size, offset, and stride. Figure 3.5 shows how these elements interact. The size (or shape, in NumPy parlance) is a tuple indicating the number of elements across each dimension the tensor represents. The storage offset is the index in the storage corresponding to the first element in the tensor. The stride is the number of elements in the storage that need to be skipped over to obtain the next element along each dimension.

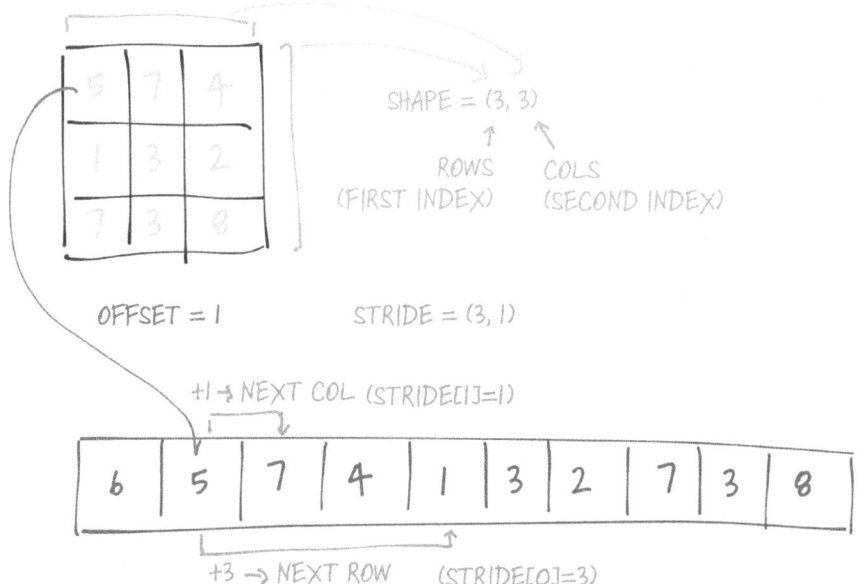

Figure 3.5 Relationship between a tensor's offset, size, and stride. Here, the tensor is a view of a larger storage, like one that might have been allocated when creating a larger tensor.

3.9.1 Views of another tensor's storage

We can get the second point in the tensor by providing the corresponding index:

```
# In[21]:
points = torch.tensor([[4.0, 1.0], [5.0, 3.0], [2.0, 1.0]])
second_point = points[1]
second_point.storage_offset()

# Out[21]:
2

# In[22]:
second_point.size()

# Out[22]:
torch.Size([2])
```

The resulting tensor has offset 2 in the storage (since we need to skip the first point, which has two items), and the size is an instance of the Size class containing one element, since the tensor is one-dimensional. It's important to note that this is the same information contained in the shape property of tensor objects:

```
# In[23]:
second_point.shape

# Out[23]:
torch.Size([2])
```

The stride is a tuple indicating the number of elements in the storage that have to be skipped when the index is increased by 1 in each dimension. For instance, our points tensor has a stride of (2, 1):

```
# In[24]:
points.stride()

# Out[24]:
(2, 1)
```

Accessing an element i, j in a 2D tensor results in accessing the storage_offset + stride[0] * i + stride[1] * j element in the storage. The offset will usually be zero; if this tensor is a view of a storage created to hold a larger tensor, the offset might be a positive value.

This indirection between Tensor and Storage makes some operations inexpensive, like transposing a tensor or extracting a subtensor, because they do not lead to memory reallocations. Instead, they consist of allocating a new Tensor object with a different value for size, storage offset, or stride.

We already extracted a subtensor when we indexed a specific point and saw the storage offset increasing. Let's see what happens to the size and stride as well:

3.9 Tensor metadata: Size, offset, and stride

```
# In[25]:
second_point = points[1]
second_point.size()

# Out[25]:
torch.Size([2])

# In[26]:
second_point.storage_offset()

# Out[26]:
2

# In[27]:
second_point.stride()

# Out[27]:
(1,)
```

The bottom line is that the subtensor has one less dimension, as we would expect, while still indexing the same storage as the original points tensor. This also means changing the subtensor will have a side effect on the original tensor:

```
# In[28]:
points = torch.tensor([[4.0, 1.0], [5.0, 3.0], [2.0, 1.0]])
second_point = points[1]
second_point[0] = 10.0
points

# Out[28]:
tensor([[ 4.,  1.],
        [10.,  3.],
        [ 2.,  1.]])
```

This setup might not always be desirable, so we can eventually clone the subtensor into a new tensor with its own dedicated storage:

```
# In[29]:
points = torch.tensor([[4.0, 1.0], [5.0, 3.0], [2.0, 1.0]])
second_point = points[1].clone()
second_point[0] = 10.0
points

# Out[29]:
tensor([[4., 1.],
        [5., 3.],
        [2., 1.]])
```

3.9.2 Transposing without copying

Let's try transposing now. Let's take our points tensor, which has individual points in the rows and X and Y coordinates in the columns, and turn it around so that individual points are in the columns. We take this opportunity to introduce the t function, a shorthand alternative to transpose for two-dimensional tensors:

```
# In[30]:
points = torch.tensor([[4.0, 1.0], [5.0, 3.0], [2.0, 1.0]])
points

# Out[30]:
tensor([[4., 1.],
        [5., 3.],
        [2., 1.]])

# In[31]:
points_t = points.t()
points_t

# Out[31]:
tensor([[4., 5., 2.],
        [1., 3., 1.]])
```

> **TIP** To help build a solid understanding of the mechanics of tensors, it may be a good idea to grab a pencil and a piece of paper and scribble diagrams like the one in figure 3.5 as we step through the code in this section.

We can easily verify that the two tensors share the same storage:

```
# In[32]:
id(points.storage()) == id(points_t.storage())

# Out[32]:
True
```

And that they differ only in shape and stride:

```
# In[33]:
points.stride()

# Out[33]:
(2, 1)
# In[34]:
points_t.stride()

# Out[34]:
(1, 2)
```

This code tells us that increasing the first index by one in points—for example, going from points[0,0] to points[1,0]—will skip along the storage by two elements, while increasing the second index—from points[0,0] to points[0,1]—will skip along the storage by one. In other words, the storage holds the elements in the tensor sequentially row by row.

We can transpose points into points_t, as shown in figure 3.6. We change the order of the elements in the stride. After that, increasing the row (the first index of the tensor) will skip along the storage by one, just like when we were moving along columns in points. This is the very definition of transposing. No new memory is allocated: transposing is obtained only by creating a new Tensor instance with different stride ordering than the original.

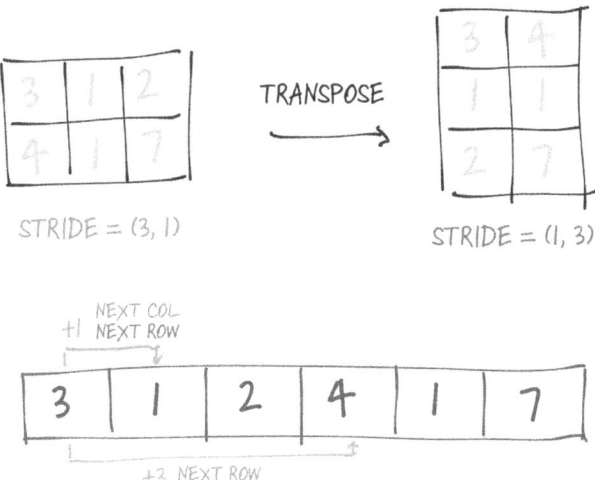

Figure 3.6 Transpose operation applied to a tensor

3.9.3 Transposing in higher dimensions

Transposing in PyTorch is not limited to matrices. We can transpose a multidimensional array by specifying the two dimensions along which transposing (flipping shape and stride) should occur:

```
# In[35]:
some_t = torch.ones(3, 4, 5)
transpose_t = some_t.transpose(0, 2)
some_t.shape

# Out[35]:
torch.Size([3, 4, 5])

# In[36]:
transpose_t.shape

# Out[36]:
torch.Size([5, 4, 3])

# In[37]:
some_t.stride()
```

```
# Out[37]:
(20, 5, 1)

# In[38]:
transpose_t.stride()

# Out[38]:
(1, 5, 20)
```

A tensor whose values are laid out in the storage starting from the rightmost dimension onward (i.e., moving along rows for a 2D tensor) is defined as contiguous. Contiguous tensors are convenient because we can visit them efficiently in order without jumping around in the storage (improving data locality improves performance because of the way memory access works on modern CPUs). This advantage, of course, depends on the way algorithms visit.

3.9.4 Contiguous tensors

Some tensor operations in PyTorch only work on contiguous tensors, such as view, which we'll encounter in the next chapter. In that case, PyTorch will throw an informative exception and require us to call contiguous explicitly. Calling contiguous will do nothing (and will not hurt performance) if the tensor is already contiguous.

In our case, points is contiguous, while its transpose is not:

```
# In[39]:
points.is_contiguous()

# Out[39]:
True

# In[40]:
points_t.is_contiguous()

# Out[40]:
False
```

We can obtain a new contiguous tensor from a noncontiguous one using the contiguous method. The content of the tensor will be the same, but the stride will change because we are essentially rearranging the values in a new storage:

```
# In[41]:
points = torch.tensor([[4.0, 1.0], [5.0, 3.0], [2.0, 1.0]])
points_t = points.t()
points_t

# Out[41]:
tensor([[4., 5., 2.],
        [1., 3., 1.]])
```

```
# In[42]:
points_t.storage()

# Out[42]:
 4.0
 1.0
 5.0
 3.0
 2.0
 1.0
[torch.FloatStorage of size 6]

# In[43]:
points_t.stride()

# Out[43]:
(1, 2)

# In[44]:
points_t_cont = points_t.contiguous()
points_t_cont

# Out[44]:
tensor([[4., 5., 2.],
        [1., 3., 1.]])

# In[45]:
points_t_cont.stride()

# Out[45]:
(3, 1)

# In[46]:
points_t_cont.storage()

# Out[46]:
 4.0
 5.0
 2.0
 1.0
 3.0
 1.0
[torch.FloatStorage of size 6]
```

Notice that the storage has been reshuffled for elements to be laid out row-by-row in the new storage. The stride has been changed to reflect the new layout.

As a refresher, figure 3.7 shows our diagram, first introduced in figure 3.5, again. Hopefully, it will all make sense now that we've taken a good look at how tensors are built.

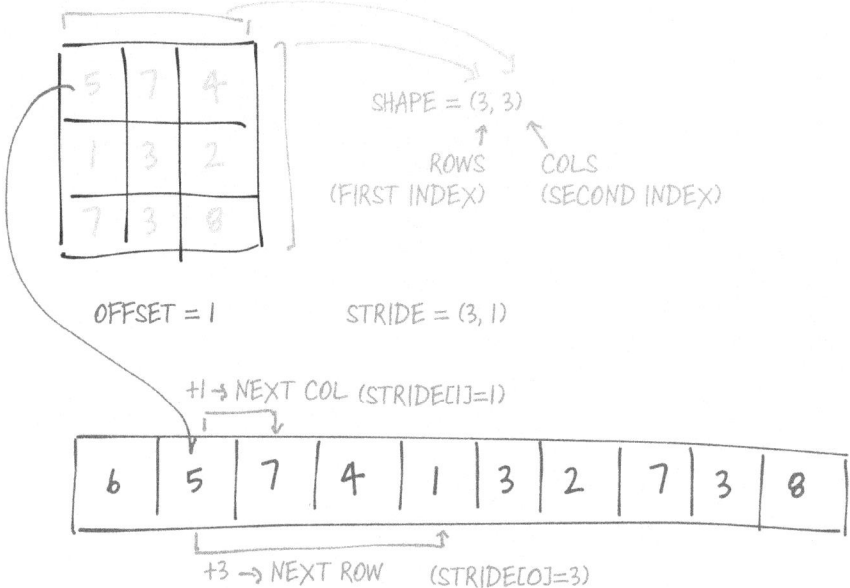

Figure 3.7 Recall that stride (3, 1) means moving to the next row requires skipping three elements in storage, while moving to the next column requires skipping one element—as seen in the contiguous tensor layout.

3.10 Moving tensors to the GPU

So far in this chapter, when we've talked about storage, we've meant memory on the CPU. PyTorch tensors can also be stored on a different kind of processor: a graphics processing unit (GPU). Every PyTorch tensor can be transferred to (one of) the GPU(s) to perform massively parallel, fast computations. All operations that will be performed on the tensor will be carried out using GPU-specific routines that come with PyTorch.

> **PyTorch support for various GPUs**
>
> As of 2025, PyTorch has significantly expanded its GPU acceleration capabilities. It now supports both Nvidia's CUDA-enabled GPUs and AMD's ROCm platform. Both of these platforms have native support and can be installed directly using pip or conda, as detailed at https://pytorch.org/get-started/locally/#start-locally. For Apple Silicon Mac users, PyTorch provides Metal Performance Shaders (MPS) support, allowing tensors to be accelerated on Apple's integrated GPUs. Support for Google's tensor processing units (TPUs) comes from a separately available torch_xla package (https://github.com/pytorch/xla). Similarly, support for Intel's XPUs is available through intel_extension_for_pytorch (https://github.com/intel/intel-extension-for-pytorch).
>
> A fundamental principle of PyTorch is to provide abstractions that allow new hardware vendors to add support for their hardware seamlessly, without necessitating changes to the library for existing users. This approach has led to significant growth in the ecosystem of hardware vendors, a trend that is set to continue!

3.10.1 Managing a tensor's device attribute

In addition to dtype, a PyTorch Tensor also has the notion of device, which is where the tensor data is placed on the computer. We can create a tensor on the GPU by specifying the corresponding argument to the constructor:

```
# In[64]:
points_gpu = torch.tensor([[4.0, 1.0], [5.0, 3.0], [2.0, 1.0]],
                          device='cuda')
```

We could instead copy a tensor created on the CPU onto the GPU using the to method:

```
# In[65]:
points_gpu = points.to(device='cuda')
```

This returns a new tensor that has the same numerical data, but it is stored in the RAM of the GPU, rather than in regular system RAM. Now that the data is stored locally on the GPU, we'll start to see the speedups mentioned earlier when performing mathematical operations on the tensor. In almost all cases, CPU- and GPU-based tensors expose the same user-facing API, making it much easier to write code that is agnostic to where, exactly, the heavy number crunching is running.

If our machine has more than one GPU, we can also decide on which GPU we allocate the tensor by passing a zero-based integer identifying the GPU on the machine, such as

```
# In[66]:
points_gpu = points.to(device='cuda:0')
```

At this point, any operation performed on the tensor, such as multiplying all elements by a constant, is carried out on the GPU:

```
# In[67]:
points = 2 * points                          ← Multiplication performed on the CPU
points_gpu = 2 * points.to(device='cuda')    ← Multiplication performed on the GPU
```

The points_gpu tensor is not brought back to the CPU once the result has been computed. Here's what happened in this line:

1. The points tensor is copied to the GPU.
2. A new tensor is allocated on the GPU—that is, all storage for the tensor resides in GPU memory. The results of the multiplication also remain in GPU memory.
3. A handle to that GPU tensor is returned, which allows us to manipulate it as a regular variable as part of our program.

Therefore, if we also add a constant to the result,

```
# In[68]:
points_gpu = points_gpu + 4
```

the addition is still performed on the GPU, and no information flows to the CPU (unless we print or access the resulting tensor). To move the tensor back to the CPU, we need to provide a cpu argument to the to method, such as

```
# In[69]:
points_cpu = points_gpu.to(device='cpu')
```

We can also use the shorthand methods cpu and cuda instead of the to method to achieve the same goal:

```
# In[70]:
points_gpu = points.cuda()         ◀──┐ Defaults to
points_gpu = points.cuda(0)            │ GPU index 0
points_cpu = points_gpu.cpu()
```

It's also worth mentioning that by using the to method, we can change the placement and the data type simultaneously by providing both device and dtype as arguments.

3.11 NumPy interoperability

We've mentioned NumPy here and there. While we do not consider NumPy a prerequisite for reading this book, we strongly encourage you to become familiar with NumPy due to its ubiquity in the Python data science ecosystem. PyTorch tensors can be converted to NumPy arrays, and vice versa, very efficiently. By doing so, we can take advantage of the huge swath of functionality in the wider Python ecosystem that has built up around the NumPy array type. This zero-copy interoperability with NumPy arrays is possible because the storage system works with the Python buffer protocol (https://docs.python.org/3/c-api/buffer.html).

To get a NumPy array out of our points tensor, we just call

```
# In[55]:
points = torch.ones(3, 4)
points_np = points.numpy()
points_np

# Out[55]:
array([[1., 1., 1., 1.],
       [1., 1., 1., 1.],
       [1., 1., 1., 1.]], dtype=float32)
```

which will return a NumPy multidimensional array of the right size, shape, and numerical type. Interestingly, the returned array shares the same underlying buffer with the tensor storage. This means the numpy method can be effectively executed at basically no cost, as long as the data sits in CPU RAM. It also means modifying the NumPy array will lead to a change in the originating tensor. If the tensor is allocated on the GPU, PyTorch will make a copy of the content of the tensor into a NumPy array allocated on the CPU.

Conversely, we can obtain a PyTorch tensor from a NumPy array,

```
# In[56]:
points = torch.from_numpy(points_np)
```

which will use the same buffer-sharing strategy we just described.

> **NOTE** While the default numeric type in PyTorch is 32-bit floating-point, for NumPy it is 64-bit. As discussed in section 3.5.2, we usually want to use 32-bit floating-points, so we need to make sure we have tensors of dtype `torch.float` after converting.

3.12 Generalized tensors are tensors, too

For the purposes of this book, and for the vast majority of applications in general, tensors are multidimensional arrays, just as we've seen in this chapter. If we risk a peek under the hood of PyTorch, there is a twist: how the data is stored under the hood is separate from the tensor API we discussed in section 3.6. Any implementation that meets the contract of that API can be considered a tensor!

PyTorch will cause the right computation functions to be called regardless of whether our tensor is on the CPU or the GPU. This is accomplished through a *dispatching* mechanism, and that mechanism can cater to other tensor types by hooking up the user-facing API to the right backend functions. Sure enough, there are other kinds of tensors: some are specific to certain classes of hardware devices (like Google TPUs), and others have data-representation strategies that differ from the dense array style we've seen so far. For example, sparse tensors store only nonzero entries, along with index information. The PyTorch dispatcher shown in figure 3.8 (left) is designed to be extensible; the subsequent switching to accommodate the various numeric types (right) is a fixed aspect of the implementation coded into each backend.

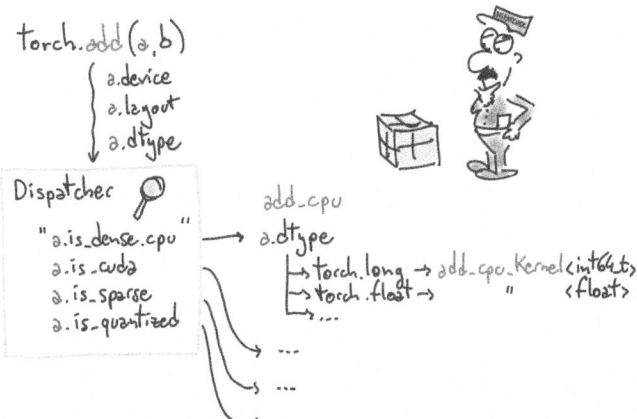

Figure 3.8 The dispatcher in PyTorch is one of its key infrastructure bits.

Sometimes the usual tensors we use are called *dense* or *strided* to differentiate them from tensors using other memory layouts.

As with many things, the number of kinds of tensors has grown as PyTorch supports a broader range of hardware and applications. We can expect new kinds to continue to arise as people explore new ways to express and perform computations with PyTorch.

3.13 *Serializing tensors*

Creating a tensor on the fly is all well and good, but if the data inside is valuable, we will want to save it to a file and load it back at some point. After all, we don't want to have to retrain a model from scratch every time we start running our program! PyTorch uses `pickle` to serialize the tensor object, plus dedicated serialization code for the storage. Here's how we can save our `points` tensor to an ourpoints.t file:

```
# In[57]:
torch.save(points, '../data/p1ch3/ourpoints.t')
```

As an alternative, we can pass a file descriptor in lieu of the filename:

```
# In[58]:
with open('../data/p1ch3/ourpoints.t','wb') as f:
    torch.save(points, f)
```

Loading our points back is similarly a one-liner,

```
# In[59]:
points = torch.load('../data/p1ch3/ourpoints.t')
```

or, equivalently,

```
# In[60]:
with open('../data/p1ch3/ourpoints.t','rb') as f:
    points = torch.load(f)
```

While we can quickly save tensors this way if we only want to load them with PyTorch, the file format itself is not interoperable: we can't read the tensor with software other than PyTorch. Depending on the use case, this may or may not be a limitation, but we should learn how to save tensors interoperably for those times when it is. We'll look at how to do so next.

3.13.1 *Serializing to HDF5 with h5py*

Every use case is unique, but we suspect that needing to save tensors interoperably will be more common when introducing PyTorch into existing systems that already rely on different libraries. New projects probably won't need to save tensors interoperably as often.

For those cases when you need to, however, you can use the HDF5 format and library (https://www.hdfgroup.org/solutions/hdf5). HDF5 is a portable, widely supported format for representing serialized multidimensional arrays, organized in a nested key-value dictionary. Python supports HDF5 through the h5py library (http://www.h5py.org/), which accepts and returns data in the form of NumPy arrays.

We can install h5py using

```
$ conda install h5py
```

At this point, we can save our points tensor by converting it to a NumPy array (at no cost, as we noted earlier) and passing it to the create_dataset function:

```
# In[61]:
import h5py

f = h5py.File('../data/p1ch3/ourpoints.hdf5', 'w')
dset = f.create_dataset('coords', data=points.numpy())
f.close()
```

Here 'coords' is a key into the HDF5 file. We can have other keys—even nested ones. One of the interesting things in HDF5 is that we can index the dataset while on disk and access only the elements we're interested in. Let's suppose we want to load just the last two points in our dataset:

```
# In[62]:
f = h5py.File('../data/p1ch3/ourpoints.hdf5', 'r')
dset = f['coords']
last_points = dset[-2:]
```

The data is not loaded when the file is opened or the dataset is required. Rather, the data stays on disk until we request the second and last rows in the dataset. At that point, h5py accesses those two columns and returns a NumPy array-like object encapsulating that region in that dataset that behaves like a NumPy array and has the same API.

Owing to this fact, we can pass the returned object to the torch.from_numpy function to obtain a tensor directly. In this case, the data is copied over to the tensor's storage:

```
# In[63]:
last_points = torch.from_numpy(dset[-2:])
f.close()
```

Once we're finished loading data, we close the file. Closing the HDFS file invalidates the datasets, and trying to access dset afterward will give an exception. As long as we stick to the order shown here, we are fine and can now work with the last_points tensor.

3.14 Conclusion

Now we have covered the information we need to start representing everything in floats. We'll cover other aspects of tensors, such as creating views of tensors; indexing tensors with other tensors; and broadcasting, which simplifies performing element-wise operations between tensors of different sizes or shapes, as needed along the way.

In chapter 4, we will learn how to represent real-world data in PyTorch. We will start with simple tabular data and move on to something more elaborate. In the process, we will get to know more about tensors.

3.15 Exercises

1. Create a tensor a from `list(range(9))`. Predict and then check the size, offset, and stride.
   a. Create a new tensor using `b = a.view(3, 3)`. What does `view` do? Check that a and b share the same storage.
   b. Create a tensor `c = b[1:,1:]`. Predict and then check the size, offset, and stride.
2. Pick a mathematical operation like cosine or square root. Can you find a corresponding function in the `torch` library?
   a. Is there a version of your function that operates in place?
   b. Apply the function element-wise to a. Does it error?
   c. What operation is required to make the function work?

Summary

- Neural networks transform floating-point representations into other floating-point representations. The starting and ending representations are typically human-interpretable, but the intermediate representations are less so.
- The floating-point representations that are understood by neural networks are stored in tensors.
- Tensors are multidimensional arrays; they are the basic data structure in PyTorch.
- Tensors have indexing notation similar to NumPy arrays, which allows you to access different dimensions of the tensor.
- Broadcasting in PyTorch is a mechanism that allows for element-wise operations between tensors of different shapes by automatically extending the dimensions of smaller tensors to match the shape of the larger tensor, making operations compatible.
- Tensor numeric types can be specified with `dtype` to define the data type of the tensor (e.g., integer, floating, Boolean), including the number of bytes per value (e.g., 8-bit, 16-bit, 32-bit, 64-bit).
- PyTorch has a comprehensive standard library for tensor creation, manipulation (through indexing, slicing, joining, etc.), mathematical operations, random sampling, serialization, and controlling parallelism.

- Tensors have an internal storage representation utilizing size, offset, and stride metadata that allow them to be accessed and manipulated without copying the underlying data, greatly saving time and memory.
- All tensor operations in PyTorch can execute on the CPU as well as on the GPU, with no change in the code.
- PyTorch uses a trailing underscore to indicate that a function operates in place on a tensor (e.g., `Tensor.sqrt_`).
- Tensors can be serialized to disk and loaded back.

Real-world data representation using tensors

This chapter covers
- Representing real-world data as PyTorch tensors
- Working with a range of data types
- Loading data from a file
- Converting data to tensors
- Shaping tensors so they can be used as inputs for neural network models

In the previous chapter, we learned that tensors are the building blocks for data in PyTorch. For PyTorch, neural networks take tensors as input and produce tensors as outputs. In fact, all operations within a neural network and during optimization are operations between tensors, and all parameters (e.g., weights and biases) in a neural network are tensors. Having a good sense of how to perform operations on tensors and index them effectively is central to using tools like PyTorch successfully. Now that you know the basics of tensors, your dexterity with them will grow as you make your way through the book.

Here's a question that we can already address: How do we take a piece of data, a video, or a line of text and represent it with a tensor in a way that is appropriate for training a deep learning model? We'll learn how in this chapter. We'll cover different types of data with a focus on the types relevant to this book and show how to represent that data as tensors. Then we'll learn how to load the data from the most common on-disk formats and get a feel for those data types' structure so we can see how to prepare them for training a neural network. Often, our raw data won't be perfectly formed for the problem we'd like to solve, so we'll have a chance to practice our tensor-manipulation skills with a few more interesting tensor operations.

Each section in this chapter will describe a data type, and each will come with its own dataset. While we've structured the chapter so that each data type builds on the previous one, feel free to skip around a bit if you're so inclined.

We'll be using a lot of image and volumetric data through the rest of the book, since those are common data types and they reproduce well in book format. We'll also cover tabular data, time series, and text, as those will also be of interest to a number of our readers.

Since a picture is worth a thousand words, we'll start with image data. We'll then demonstrate working with a three-dimensional array using medical data that represents patient anatomy as a volume. Next, we'll work with tabular data about wines, just like what we'd find in a spreadsheet. After that, we'll move to *ordered* tabular data, with a time-series dataset from a bike-sharing program. Finally, we'll dip our toes into text data from Jane Austen. Text data retains its ordered aspect but introduces the problem of representing words as arrays of numbers.

In every section, we will stop where a deep learning researcher would start: right before feeding the data to a model. We encourage you to keep these datasets; they will constitute excellent material for when we start learning how to train neural network models in the next chapter.

4.1 Working with images

The introduction of convolutional neural networks revolutionized computer vision, and image-based systems have since acquired a whole new set of capabilities. Problems that required complex pipelines of highly tuned algorithmic building blocks are now solvable at unprecedented levels of performance by training end-to-end networks using paired input-and-desired-output examples. To harness the power of these advanced computer vision capabilities, we need to be able to load an image from common image formats and then transform the data into a tensor representation that has the various parts of the image arranged in the way PyTorch expects.

An image is simply a grid of numbers arranged in rows and columns representing pixels. Each pixel may contain either a single scalar value (creating a grayscale image) or multiple scalar values (typically representing different colors or other *features* like depth information from specialized cameras).

Scalars representing values at individual pixels are often encoded using 8-bit integers, as in consumer cameras. In medical, scientific, and industrial applications, it is not unusual to find higher numerical precision, such as 12-bit or 16-bit. This level of precision allows a wider range or increased sensitivity in cases where the pixel encodes information about a physical property, like bone density, temperature, or depth.

4.1.1 Adding color channels

We mentioned colors earlier. There are several ways to encode colors into numbers (this is something of an understatement). The most common is RGB, where a color is defined by three numbers representing the intensity of red, green, and blue. We can think of a color channel as a grayscale intensity map of only the color in question, similar to what you'd see if you looked at the scene in question using a pair of pure red sunglasses. Figure 4.1 shows a rainbow, where each of the RGB channels captures a certain portion of the spectrum (the figure is simplified; for example, it omits the orange and yellow bands, which are represented as a combination of red and green).

Figure 4.1 A rainbow, broken into red, green, and blue channels. Printed in grayscale; see the online version of this book for a full-color image.

The red band of the rainbow is brightest in the red channel of the image, while the blue channel has both the blue band of the rainbow and the sky as high-intensity. Note also that the white clouds are high-intensity in all three channels.

4.1.2 Loading an image file

Images come in several different file formats, but luckily, there are plenty of ways to load images in Python. Let's start by loading a JPG image using the `imageio` module (code/p1ch4/1_image_dog.ipynb).

Listing 4.1 Loading an image

```
# In[2]:
import imageio.v2 as imageio
```

```
img_arr = imageio.imread('../data/p1ch4/image-dog/bobby.jpg')
img_arr.shape

# Out[2]:
(720, 1280, 3)
```

> **NOTE** We'll use `imageio` throughout the chapter because it handles different data types with a uniform API. For many purposes, using TorchVision is a great default choice for handling image and video data. We go with `imageio` here for a somewhat lighter exploration.

At this point, `img_arr` is a NumPy array-like object with three dimensions: two spatial dimensions, width and height, and a third dimension corresponding to the red, green, and blue channels. Any library that outputs a NumPy array will suffice to obtain a PyTorch tensor. The only thing to watch out for is the layout of the dimensions. PyTorch modules dealing with image data require tensors to be laid out as $C \times H \times W$: channels, height, and width, respectively.

4.1.3 Changing the layout

We can use the tensor's `permute` method with the old dimensions for each new dimension to get to an appropriate layout. Given an input tensor $H \times W \times C$ as obtained previously, we get a proper layout by having channel 2 first and then channels 0 and 1:

```
# In[3]:
img = torch.from_numpy(img_arr)
out = img.permute(2, 0, 1)
out.shape

# Out[3]:
torch.Size([3, 720, 1280])
```

We've seen this previously, but note that this operation does not make a copy of the tensor data. Instead, `out` uses the same underlying storage as `img` and only plays with the size and stride information at the tensor level. This is convenient because the operation is very cheap—but just as a heads-up, changing a pixel in `img` will lead to a change in `out`.

Other deep learning frameworks use different layouts. For instance, originally TensorFlow kept the channel dimension last, resulting in an $H \times W \times C$ layout (it now supports multiple layouts). This strategy has pros and cons from a low-level performance standpoint, but for our concerns, it doesn't make a difference as long as we reshape our tensors properly.

So far, we have described a single image. We will follow the same strategy we've used for earlier data types: to create a dataset of multiple images to use as input for our neural networks, we store the images in a batch along the first dimension to obtain an $N \times C \times H \times W$ tensor.

We can preallocate a tensor of appropriate size and fill it with images loaded from a directory, like so:

```
# In[4]:
import os
data_dir = '../data/p1ch4/image-cats/'
png_files = [f for f in os.listdir(data_dir) if f.endswith('.png')]
batch = torch.zeros(len(png_files), 3, 256, 256, dtype=torch.uint8)
```

This snippet indicates that our batch will consist of len(png_files) RGB images 256 pixels in height and 256 pixels in width. Notice the type of the tensor: we're expecting each color to be represented as an 8-bit integer, as in most photographic formats from standard consumer cameras. We can now read all PNG images from an input directory and store them in the tensor (1_image_dog.ipynb1_image_dog.ipynb).

Listing 4.2 Reading all image files

```
# In[5]:
for i, filename in enumerate(png_files):
    img_arr = imageio.imread(os.path.join(data_dir, filename))
    img_t = torch.from_numpy(img_arr)
    img_t = img_t.permute(2, 0, 1)
    img_t = img_t[:3]            ◁── Here, we keep only the first three channels.
    batch[i] = img_t                  Sometimes images also have an alpha
                                      channel indicating transparency, but
                                      our network only wants RGB input.
```

4.1.4 Normalizing the data

We mentioned earlier that neural networks usually work with floating-point tensors as their input. Neural networks exhibit the best training performance when the input data ranges roughly from 0 to 1, or from –1 to 1 (this is an effect of how their building blocks are defined).

A typical thing we'll want to do is cast a tensor to floating-point and normalize the values of the pixels. Casting to floating-point is easy, but normalization is trickier, as it depends on what range of the input we decide should lie between 0 and 1 (or –1 and 1). One possibility is to divide the values of the pixels by 255 (the maximum representable number in 8-bit unsigned):

```
# In[6]:
batch = batch.float()
batch /= 255.0
```

Another possibility is to compute the mean and standard deviation of the input data and scale it so that the output has zero mean and unit standard deviation across each channel—a technique commonly known as standardization:

```
# In[7]:
n_channels = batch.shape[1]
for c in range(n_channels):
    mean = torch.mean(batch[:, c])
    std = torch.std(batch[:, c])
    batch[:, c] = (batch[:, c] - mean) / std
```

NOTE Here, we normalize just a single batch of images because we do not know yet how to operate on an entire dataset. In working with images, it is good practice to compute the mean and standard deviation on all the training data in advance and then subtract and divide by these fixed, precomputed quantities.

We can perform several other operations on inputs, such as geometric transformations like rotations, scaling, and cropping. These may help with training or may be required to make an arbitrary input conform to the input requirements of a network, like the size of the image. We will stumble on quite a few of these strategies in section 12.6. For now, just remember that you have image-manipulation options available.

4.2 3D images: Volumetric data

We've learned how to load and represent 2D images, like the ones we take with a camera. In some contexts, such as medical imaging applications involving, say, CT (computed tomography) scans, we typically deal with sequences of images stacked along the head-to-foot axis, each corresponding to a slice across the human body. In CT scans, the intensity represents the density of the different parts of the body—lungs, fat, water, muscle, and bone, in order of increasing density—mapped from dark to bright when the CT scan is displayed on a clinical workstation. The density at each point is computed from the amount of X-rays reaching a detector after crossing through the body, with some complex math to deconvolve the raw sensor data into the full volume.

CTs have only a single intensity channel, similar to a grayscale image. This means that often, the channel dimension is left out in native data formats; so, similar to the last section, the raw data typically has three dimensions. By stacking individual 2D slices into a 3D tensor, we can build volumetric data representing the 3D anatomy of a subject. Unlike what we saw in figure 4.1, the extra dimension in figure 4.2 represents an offset in physical space, rather than a particular band of the visible spectrum.

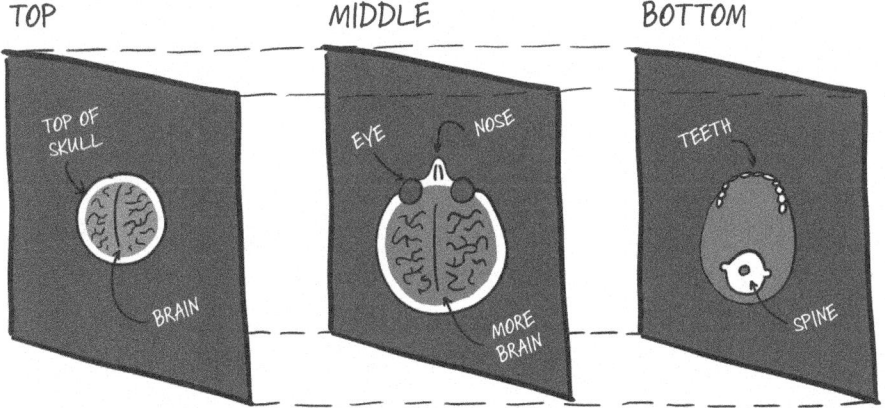

Figure 4.2 Slices of a CT scan, from the top of the head to the jawline

Part 2 of this book is devoted to tackling a medical imaging problem in the real world, so we won't go into the details of medical imaging data formats. For now, it suffices to say that there's no fundamental difference between a tensor storing volumetric data versus image data. We just have an extra dimension, *depth*, after the *channel* dimension, leading to a 5D tensor of shape $N \times C \times D \times H \times W$.

4.2.1 Loading a specialized format

Let's load a sample CT scan using the `volread` function in the `imageio` module, which takes a directory as an argument and assembles all Digital Imaging and Communications in Medicine (DICOM) files (from the Cancer Imaging Archive's CPTAC-LSCC collection: https://mng.bz/AGZg) in a series in a NumPy 3D array (code/p1ch4/2_volumetric_ct.ipynb).

> **Listing 4.3 Load DICOM series and check shape**

```
# In[2]:
import imageio

dir_path = "../data/p1ch4/volumetric-dicom/2-LUNG 3.0  B70f-04083"
vol_arr = imageio.volread(dir_path, 'DICOM')
vol_arr.shape

# Out[2]:
Reading DICOM (examining files): 1/99 files (1.0%99/99 files (100.0%)
  Found 1 correct series.
Reading DICOM (loading data): 31/99  (31.3%2/99  (92.9%9/99  (100.0%)

(99, 512, 512)
```

As was true in section 4.1.3, the layout is different from what PyTorch expects, due to having no channel information. So, we'll have to make room for the `channel` dimension using `unsqueeze`:

```
# In[3]:
vol = torch.from_numpy(vol_arr).float()
vol = torch.unsqueeze(vol, 0)

vol.shape

# Out[3]:
torch.Size([1, 99, 512, 512])
```

> **NOTE** `unsqueeze` adds a new dimension of size 1 at the specified position. Here it transforms the 3D array of shape \[D, H, W\] to a 4D tensor of shape \[1, D, H, W\], where the first dimension represents the channel.

At this point, we could assemble a 5D dataset by stacking multiple volumes along the `batch` direction, just as we did in the previous section. We'll see a lot more CT data in part 2.

4.3 Representing tabular data

The simplest form of data we'll encounter on a machine learning job is sitting in a spreadsheet, CSV file, or database. Whatever the medium, it's a table containing one row per sample (or record), where columns contain one piece of information about our sample.

At first, we are going to assume the samples appearing in the table have no meaningful order. Such a table is a collection of independent samples, unlike a time series, for instance, in which samples are related by a time dimension.

Columns may contain numerical values, like temperatures at specific locations, or labels, like a string expressing an attribute of the sample, like "blue." Therefore, tabular data is typically not homogeneous: different columns don't have the same type. We might have a column showing the weight of apples and another encoding their color in a label.

PyTorch tensors, on the other hand, are homogeneous. Information in PyTorch is typically encoded as a number, typically floating-point (though integer types and Boolean are supported as well). This numeric encoding is deliberate since neural networks are mathematical entities that take real numbers as inputs and produce real numbers as output through successive application of matrix multiplications and nonlinear functions.

4.3.1 Using a real-world dataset

Our first job as deep learning practitioners is to encode heterogeneous, real-world data into a tensor of floating-point numbers, ready for consumption by a neural network. A large number of tabular datasets are freely available on the internet; see, for instance, https://github.com/caesar0301/awesome-public-datasets.

Let's start with something fun: wine! The Wine Quality dataset is a freely available table containing chemical characterizations of samples of *vinho verde*, a wine from northern Portugal, together with a sensory quality score. The dataset for white wines can be downloaded here: http://mng.bz/90Ol. For convenience, we also created a copy of the dataset on this book's Git repository, under data/p1ch4/tabular-wine.

The file contains a comma-separated collection of values organized in 12 columns preceded by a header line containing the column names. The first 11 columns contain values of chemical variables, and the last column contains the sensory quality score from 0 (very bad) to 10 (excellent). These are the column names in the order they appear in the dataset:

```
fixed acidity
volatile acidity
citric acid
residual sugar
chlorides
free sulfur dioxide
total sulfur dioxide
density
```

```
pH
sulphates
alcohol
quality
```

A possible machine learning task on this dataset is predicting the quality score from chemical characterization alone. Don't worry, though; machine learning is not going to kill wine tasting anytime soon. We have to get the training data from somewhere! As we can see in figure 4.3, we're hoping to find a relationship between one of the chemical columns in our data and the quality column. Here, we're expecting to see quality increase as sulfur decreases.

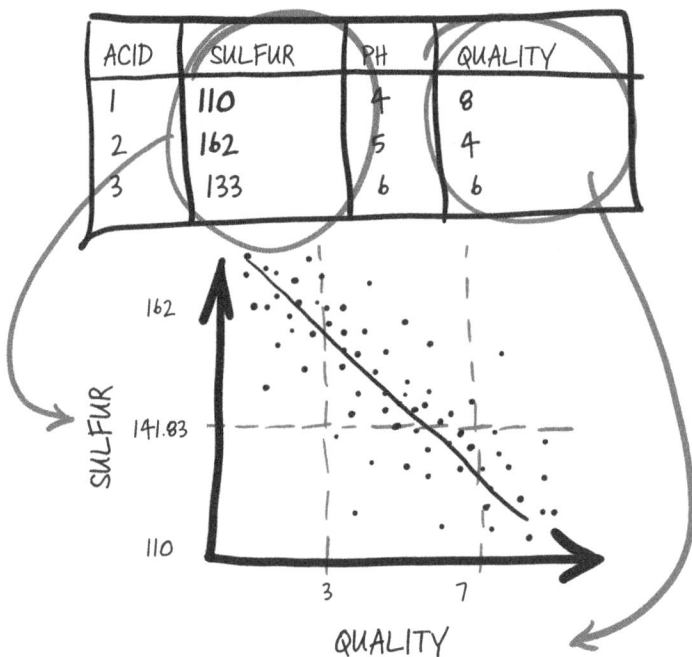

Figure 4.3 The relationship (we hope) between sulfur and quality in wine

4.3.2 Loading a wine data tensor

Before we can get to that, we need to be able to examine the data in a more usable way than opening the file in a text editor. Let's see how we can load the data using Python and then turn it into a PyTorch tensor. Python offers several options for quickly loading a CSV file. Three popular options are

- The csv module that ships with Python
- NumPy
- pandas

4.3 Representing tabular data

The third option is the most time- and memory-efficient. However, we'll avoid introducing an additional library in our learning trajectory just to load a file. Since we already introduced NumPy in the previous section and PyTorch has excellent NumPy interoperability, we'll go with that. Let's load our file and turn the resulting NumPy array into a PyTorch tensor (code/p1ch4/3_tabular_wine.ipynb).

Listing 4.4 Loading CSV data

```
# In[2]:
import csv
wine_path = "../data/p1ch4/tabular-wine/winequality-white.csv"
wineq_numpy = np.loadtxt(wine_path, dtype=np.float32, delimiter=";",
                        skiprows=1)
wineq_numpy

# Out[2]:
array([[ 7.  , 0.27, 0.36, ..., 0.45,  8.8 , 6. ],
       [ 6.3 , 0.3 , 0.34, ..., 0.49,  9.5 , 6. ],
       [ 8.1 , 0.28, 0.4 , ..., 0.44, 10.1 , 6. ],
       ...,
       [ 6.5 , 0.24, 0.19, ..., 0.46,  9.4 , 6. ],
       [ 5.5 , 0.29, 0.3 , ..., 0.38, 12.8 , 7. ],
       [ 6.  , 0.21, 0.38, ..., 0.32, 11.8 , 6. ]], dtype=float32)
```

Here, we prescribe what the type of the 2D array should be (32-bit floating-point), the delimiter used to separate values in each row, and the fact that the first line should not be read since it contains the column names. Let's check that all the data has been read:

```
# In[3]:
col_list = next(csv.reader(open(wine_path), delimiter=';'))

wineq_numpy.shape, col_list

# Out[3]:
((4898, 12),
 ['fixed acidity',
  'volatile acidity',
  'citric acid',
  'residual sugar',
  'chlorides',
  'free sulfur dioxide',
  'total sulfur dioxide',
  'density',
  'pH',
  'sulphates',
  'alcohol',
  'quality'])
```

Now, we'll convert the NumPy array to a PyTorch tensor:

```
# In[4]:
wineq = torch.from_numpy(wineq_numpy)

wineq.shape, wineq.dtype

# Out[4]:
(torch.Size([4898, 12]), torch.float32)
```

At this point, we have a floating-point `torch.Tensor` containing all the columns, including the last, which refers to the quality score.

> **Continuous, ordinal, and categorical values**
>
> We should be aware of three different kinds of numerical values as we attempt to make sense of our data. The first kind is continuous values. These are the most intuitive when represented as numbers. They are strictly ordered, and a difference between various values has a precise mathematical meaning. For example, with temperature measurements, the difference between 20°C and 25°C represents the exact same physical change in heat energy as the difference between 30°C and 35°C. Similarly, with height measurements, a 5 cm difference has the same physical meaning regardless of whether we're comparing heights of 150 cm and 155 cm or 185 cm and 190 cm.
>
> The literature divides continuous values further. When it makes sense to say one value is twice another, as with weight (10 kg is twice as heavy as 5 kg) or distance (30 miles is three times farther than 10 miles), these values are said to be on a ratio scale. Temperature in Celsius, on the other hand, does have the notion of consistent difference, but it is not reasonable to claim that 20°C is twice as hot as 10°C (since 0°C doesn't represent zero heat); so Celsius temperature offers only an interval scale.
>
> Next, we have ordinal values. The strict ordering as with continuous values remains, but the fixed mathematical relationship between differences no longer applies. A good example of this is ordering a small, medium, or large drink, with small mapped to the value 1; medium, 2; and large, 3. The large drink is bigger than the medium, in the same way that 3 is bigger than 2, but it doesn't tell us anything about how much bigger. If we converted our 1, 2, and 3 to the actual volumes (say, 8, 12, and 24 fluid ounces), then they would switch to being interval values. It's important to remember that we can't "do math" on the values outside of ordering them; trying to average large = 3 and small = 1 does not result in a medium drink!
>
> Finally, categorical values have neither ordering nor numerical meaning to their values. These are often just enumerations of possibilities assigned arbitrary numbers. Assigning water to 1, coffee to 2, soda to 3, and milk to 4 is a good example. There's no real logic to placing water first and milk last; they simply need distinct values to differentiate them. We could assign coffee to 10 and milk to -3, and there would be no significant change (although assigning values in the range 0.. $N - 1$ will have advantages for one-hot encoding and the embeddings we'll discuss in section 4.5.4). Because the numerical values bear no meaning, they are said to be on a nominal scale.

4.3.3 Representing scores

We can treat the score as a continuous variable, keep it as a real number, and perform a regression task, or we can treat it as a label and try to guess the label from the chemical analysis in a classification task. In both approaches, we will typically remove the score from the tensor of input data and keep it in a separate tensor, so that we can use the score as the ground truth without it being input to our model:

```
# In[5]:
data = wineq[:, :-1]      ◁——— Selects all rows and all
data, data.shape                 columns except the last

# Out[5]:
(tensor([[ 7.00,  0.27,  ...,  0.45,  8.80],
         [ 6.30,  0.30,  ...,  0.49,  9.50],
         ...,
         [ 5.50,  0.29,  ...,  0.38, 12.80],
         [ 6.00,  0.21,  ...,  0.32, 11.80]]), torch.Size([4898, 11]))

# In[6]:
target = wineq[:, -1]     ◁——— Selects all rows and
target, target.shape             the last column

# Out[6]:
(tensor([6., 6.,  ..., 7., 6.]), torch.Size([4898]))
```

If we want to transform the target tensor into a tensor of labels, we have two options, depending on the strategy or what we use the categorical data for. One is simply to treat labels as an integer vector of scores:

```
# In[7]:
target = wineq[:, -1].long()
target

# Out[7]:
tensor([6, 6,  ..., 7, 6])
```

If targets were string labels, like *wine color*, assigning an integer number to each string would let us follow the same approach.

4.3.4 One-hot encoding

The other approach is to build a *one-hot* encoding of the scores—that is, encode each of the 10 scores in a vector of 10 elements, with all elements set to 0 but one, at a different index for each score. This way, a score of 1 could be mapped onto the vector (1,0,0,0,0,0,0,0,0,0), a score of 5 onto (0,0,0,0,1,0,0,0,0,0), and so on. Note that the fact that the score corresponds to the index of the nonzero element is purely incidental: we could shuffle the assignment, and nothing would change from a classification standpoint.

There's a marked difference between these two representation approaches. Using wine quality as integer values (1, 2, 3, etc.) preserves two mathematical properties: ordering (e.g., a score of 4 is higher than a score of 1) and equal intervals (e.g., the difference between scores 1 and 3 equals the difference between 2 and 4). This representation works well if these properties accurately reflect wine quality in reality.

However, for truly categorical data, such as grape varieties (e.g., Merlot, Cabernet, Chardonnay), one-hot encoding is more appropriate, as these categories have no natural ordering or meaningful numerical distance between them. One-hot encoding can also be useful when dealing with ratings that are strictly discrete levels rather than points on a continuous scale—for instance, when quality can only be *poor, average,* or *excellent*, with no valid intermediate states. In such cases, the representation should clearly indicate whether a wine is definitively in one category or another, rather than being somewhere in between.

We can achieve one-hot encoding using the `scatter_` method, which fills the tensor with values from a source tensor along the indices provided as arguments:

```
# In[8]:
target_onehot = torch.zeros(target.shape[0], 10)
target_onehot.scatter_(1, target.unsqueeze(1), 1.0)

random_indices = torch.randint(0, len(target), (5,))
print(target[random_indices])
print(target_onehot[random_indices])

# Out[8]:
5 random wine quality ratings (original):
tensor([6, 6, 7, 4, 5])

First 5 wine quality ratings (one-hot encoded):
tensor([[0., 0., 0., 0., 0., 0., 1., 0., 0., 0.],
        [0., 0., 0., 0., 0., 0., 1., 0., 0., 0.],
        [0., 0., 0., 0., 0., 0., 0., 1., 0., 0.],
        [0., 0., 0., 0., 1., 0., 0., 0., 0., 0.],
        [0., 0., 0., 0., 0., 1., 0., 0., 0., 0.]])
```

Let's see what `scatter_` does. First, we notice that its name ends with an underscore. As you learned in the previous chapter, this is a PyTorch convention that indicates the method will not return a new tensor, but will instead modify the tensor in place. The arguments for `scatter_` are as follows:

- The dimension along which to apply the indices. For this example, dimension 0 would scatter the indices across rows, and dimension 1 would scatter them across columns.
- A column tensor indicating the indices of the elements to scatter.
- A tensor containing the elements to scatter or a single scalar to scatter (1, in this case).

In other words, the previous invocation reads, "For each row, take the index of the target label (which coincides with the score in our case) and use it as the column index to set the value 1.0." The end result is a tensor encoding categorical information.

The second argument of `scatter_`, the index tensor, is required to have the same number of dimensions as the tensor we scatter into. Since `target_onehot` has two dimensions (4,898 × 10), we need to add an extra dummy dimension to `target` using `unsqueeze`:

```
# In[9]:
target_unsqueezed = target.unsqueeze(1)
target_unsqueezed

# Out[9]:
tensor([[6],
        [6],
        ...,
        [7],
        [6]])
```

The call to `unsqueeze` adds a *singleton* dimension, from a 1D tensor of 4,898 elements to a 2D tensor of size (4,898 × 1), without changing its contents. No extra elements are added; we just decided to use an extra index to access the elements. That is, we access the first element of `target` as `target[0]` and the first element of its unsqueezed counterpart as `target_unsqueezed[0,0]`.

PyTorch allows us to use class indices directly as targets while training neural networks. However, if we wanted to use the score as a categorical input to the network, we would have to transform it to a one-hot-encoded tensor.

4.3.5 *When to categorize*

Now we have seen ways to deal with both continuous and categorical data. You may wonder what the deal is with the ordinal case. There is no general recipe for it; most commonly, such data is either treated as categorical (losing the ordering part and hoping that maybe our model will pick it up during training if we only have a few categories) or continuous (introducing an arbitrary notion of distance). We summarize our data mapping in a small flow chart in figure 4.4.

Let's go back to our `data` tensor, containing the 11 variables associated with the chemical analysis. We can use the functions in the PyTorch Tensor API to manipulate our data in tensor form. Let's first obtain the mean and standard deviations for each column:

```
# In[10]:
data_mean = torch.mean(data, dim=0)
data_mean

# Out[10]:
tensor([6.85e+00, 2.78e-01, 3.34e-01, 6.39e+00, 4.58e-02, 3.53e+01,
        1.38e+02, 9.94e-01, 3.19e+00, 4.90e-01, 1.05e+01])
```

```
# In[11]:
data_var = torch.var(data, dim=0)
data_var

# Out[11]:
tensor([7.12e-01, 1.02e-02, 1.46e-02, 2.57e+01, 4.77e-04, 2.89e+02,
        1.81e+03, 8.95e-06, 2.28e-02, 1.30e-02, 1.51e+00])
```

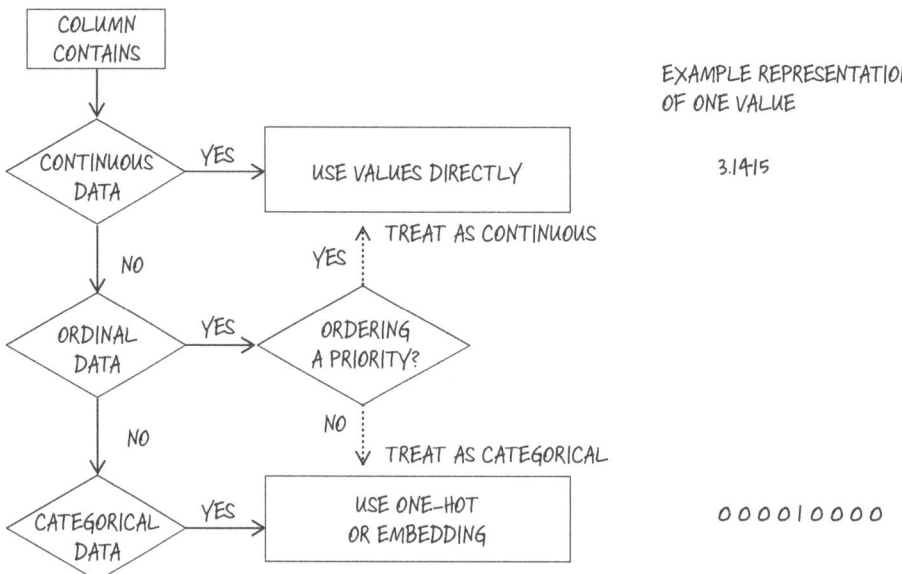

Figure 4.4 How to treat columns with continuous, ordinal, and categorical data

In this case, `dim=0` indicates that the reduction is performed along dimension 0. At this point, we can normalize the data by subtracting the mean and dividing by the standard deviation, which helps with the learning process (we'll discuss this topic in more detail in chapter 5):

```
# In[12]:
data_normalized = (data - data_mean) / torch.sqrt(data_var)
data_normalized

# Out[12]:
tensor([[ 1.72e-01, -8.18e-02,  ..., -3.49e-01, -1.39e+00],
        [-6.57e-01,  2.16e-01,  ...,  1.35e-03, -8.24e-01],
        ...,
        [-1.61e+00,  1.17e-01,  ..., -9.63e-01,  1.86e+00],
        [-1.01e+00, -6.77e-01,  ..., -1.49e+00,  1.04e+00]])
```

4.3.6 Finding thresholds

Next, let's start to look at the data with an eye to whether an easy way exists to tell good and bad wines apart at a glance. First, we're going to determine which rows in target correspond to a score less than or equal to 3:

```
# In[13]:
bad_indexes = target <= 3
bad_indexes.shape, bad_indexes.dtype, bad_indexes.sum()

# Out[13]:
(torch.Size([4898]), torch.bool, tensor(20))
```

⬅ PyTorch also provides comparison functions, here torch.le(target, 3), but using operators seems to be a good standard.

Note that only 20 of the bad_indexes entries are set to True! By using a feature in PyTorch called *advanced indexing*, we can use a tensor with data type torch.bool to index the data tensor. This will essentially filter data to be only items (rows) corresponding to True in the indexing tensor. The bad_indexes tensor has the same shape as target, with values of False or True, depending on the outcome of the comparison between our threshold and each element in the original target tensor:

```
# In[14]:
bad_data = data[bad_indexes]
bad_data.shape

# Out[14]:
torch.Size([20, 11])
```

The new bad_data tensor has 20 rows, the same as the number of rows with True in the bad_indexes tensor. It retains all 11 columns. Now we can start to get information about wines grouped into good, middling, and bad categories. Let's take the .mean() of each column:

```
# In[15]:
bad_data = data[target <= 3]
mid_data = data[(target > 3) & (target < 7)]
good_data = data[target >= 7]

bad_mean = torch.mean(bad_data, dim=0)
mid_mean = torch.mean(mid_data, dim=0)
good_mean = torch.mean(good_data, dim=0)

for i, args in enumerate(zip(col_list, bad_mean, mid_mean, good_mean)):
    print('{:2} {:20} {:6.2f} {:6.2f} {:6.2f}'.format(i, *args))

# Out[15]:
 0 fixed acidity          7.60   6.89   6.73
 1 volatile acidity       0.33   0.28   0.27
 2 citric acid            0.34   0.34   0.33
 3 residual sugar         6.39   6.71   5.26
 4 chlorides              0.05   0.05   0.04
```

⬅ For Boolean NumPy arrays and PyTorch tensors, the & operator does a logical "and" operation.

```
 5 free sulfur dioxide     53.33  35.42  34.55
 6 total sulfur dioxide   170.60 141.83 125.25
 7 density                  0.99   0.99   0.99
 8 pH                       3.19   3.18   3.22
 9 sulphates                0.47   0.49   0.50
10 alcohol                 10.34  10.26  11.42
```

It looks like we're on to something here: at first glance, the bad wines seem to have higher total sulfur dioxide, among other differences. We could use a threshold on total sulfur dioxide as a crude criterion for discriminating good wines from bad ones. Let's get the indices where the total sulfur dioxide column is below the midpoint we calculated earlier, like so:

```
# In[16]:
total_sulfur_threshold = 141.83
total_sulfur_data = data[:,6]
predicted_indexes = torch.lt(total_sulfur_data, total_sulfur_threshold)

predicted_indexes.shape, predicted_indexes.dtype, predicted_indexes.sum()

# Out[16]:
(torch.Size([4898]), torch.bool, tensor(2727))
```

Our threshold implies that just over half of all the wines are going to be high quality. Next, we'll need to get the indices of the actually good wines:

```
# In[17]:
actual_indexes = target > 5

actual_indexes.shape, actual_indexes.dtype, actual_indexes.sum()

# Out[17]:
(torch.Size([4898]), torch.bool, tensor(3258))
```

About 500 more wines are categorized as good than our threshold predicted, so we already have hard evidence that it's not perfect. Now we need to see how well our predictions line up with the actual rankings. We will perform a logical "and" between our prediction indexes and the actual good indexes (remember that each is just an array of zeros and ones) and use that intersection of wines-in-agreement to determine how well we did:

```
# In[18]:
n_matches = torch.sum(actual_indexes & predicted_indexes).item()
n_predicted = torch.sum(predicted_indexes).item()
n_actual = torch.sum(actual_indexes).item()

n_matches, n_matches / n_predicted, n_matches / n_actual

# Out[18]:
(2018, 0.74000733406674, 0.6193984039287906)
```

We got around 2,000 wines right! Since we predicted 2,700 wines, we have a 74% chance that if we predict a wine to be high quality, it actually is. Unfortunately, there are 3,200 good wines, and we only identified 61% of them. Well, we got what we signed up for; that's barely better than random! Of course, this is all very naive: we know for sure that multiple variables contribute to wine quality, and the relationships between the values of these variables and the outcome (which could be the actual score, rather than a binarized version of it) are likely more complicated than a simple threshold on a single value.

Indeed, a simple neural network would overcome all of these limitations, as would a lot of other basic machine learning methods. We'll have the tools to tackle this problem after the next two chapters, once we learn how to build our first neural network from scratch. Let's move on to other data types for now.

4.4 Working with time series

In the previous section, we covered how to represent data organized in a flat table. As we noted, every row in the table was independent from the others; their order did not matter. Or, equivalently, there was no column that encoded information about what rows came earlier and what came later.

Going back to the wine dataset, we could have had a "year" column that allowed us to look at how wine quality evolved year after year. Unfortunately, we don't have such data at hand, so we'll switch to another interesting dataset: data from a Washington, DC, bike-sharing system reporting the hourly count of rental bikes in 2011–2012 in the Capital Bikeshare system, along with weather and seasonal information (available at http://mng.bz/jgOx). Our goal will be to take a flat, 2D dataset and transform it into a 3D one, as shown in figure 4.5.

4.4.1 Adding a time dimension

In the source data, each row is a separate hour of data. Figure 4.5 shows a transposed version that fits better on the printed page. We want to change the row-per-hour organization so that we have one axis that increases at a rate of one day per index increment, and another axis that represents the hour of the day (independent of the date). The third axis will be our different columns of data (i.e., weather, temperature, etc.).

Let's load the data (code/p1ch4/4_time_series_bikes.ipynb).

Listing 4.5 Loading the bike-sharing time series dataset

```
# In[2]:
bikes_numpy = np.loadtxt(
    "../data/p1ch4/bike-sharing-dataset/hour-fixed.csv",
    dtype=np.float32,
    delimiter=",",
    skiprows=1,
    converters={1: lambda x: float(x[8:10])})
bikes = torch.from_numpy(bikes_numpy)
bikes
```

Converts date strings to numbers corresponding to the day of the month in column 1

```
# Out[2]:
tensor([[1.0000e+00, 1.0000e+00,  ..., 1.3000e+01, 1.6000e+01],
        [2.0000e+00, 1.0000e+00,  ..., 3.2000e+01, 4.0000e+01],
        ...,
        [1.7378e+04, 3.1000e+01,  ..., 4.8000e+01, 6.1000e+01],
        [1.7379e+04, 3.1000e+01,  ..., 3.7000e+01, 4.9000e+01]])
```

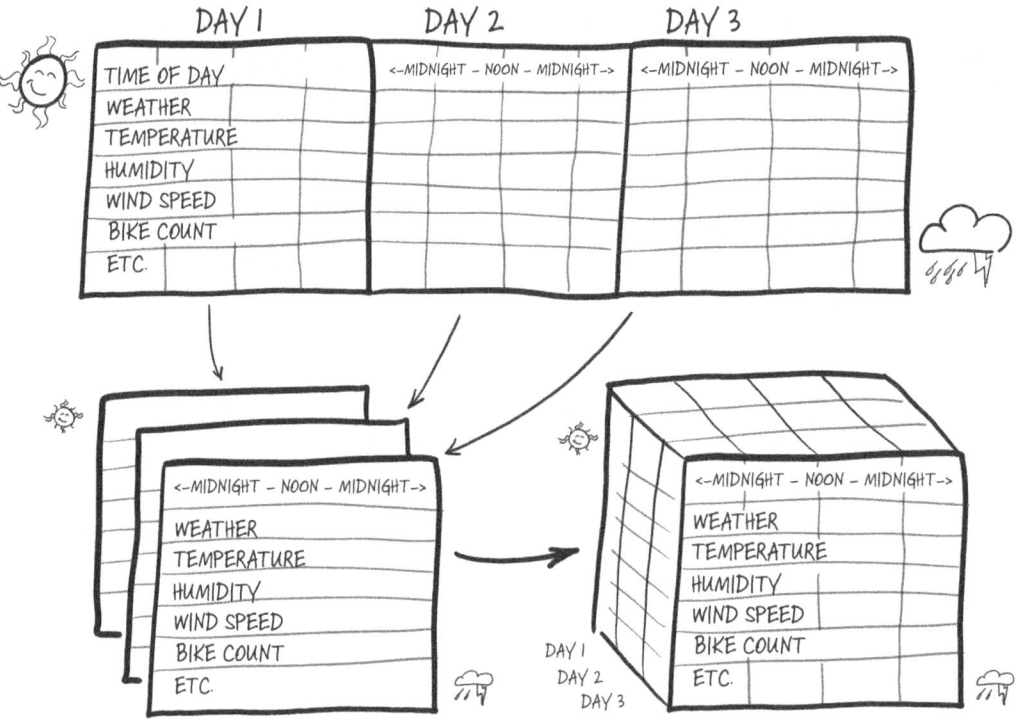

Figure 4.5 Transforming a 2D dataset of hours into a 3D dataset by adding a new axis for date.

The column names and an example row from the data are shown in the following listing.

Listing 4.6 Example of data in `hour-fixed.csv`

```
instant,dteday,season,yr,mnth,hr,holiday,weekday,workingday,weathersit,
 temp,atemp,hum,windspeed,casual,registered,cnt

1,2011-01-01,1,0,1,0,0,6,0,1,0.24,0.2879,0.81,0,3,13,16
```

For every hour, the dataset reports the following variables:

- *Index of record*—instant
- *Day of month*—day
- *Season*—season (1: spring, 2: summer, 3: fall, 4: winter)

- *Year*—yr (0: 2011, 1: 2012)
- *Month*—mnth (`1` to `12`)
- *Hour*—hr (`0` to `23`)
- *Holiday status*—holiday
- *Day of the week*—weekday
- *Working day status*—workingday
- *Weather situation*—weathersit (1, clear; 2, mist; 3, light rain/snow; 4, heavy rain/snow)
- *Temperature in °C*—temp
- *Perceived temperature in °C*—atemp
- *Humidity*—hum
- *Wind speed*—windspeed
- *Number of casual users*—casual
- *Number of registered users*—registered
- *Count of rental bikes*—cnt

In a time-series dataset such as this one, rows represent successive timepoints: there is a dimension along which they are ordered. Sure, we could treat each row as independent and try to predict the number of circulating bikes based on, say, a particular time of day, regardless of what happened earlier. However, the existence of an ordering gives us the opportunity to exploit causal relationships across time. For instance, it allows us to predict bike rides at one time based on the fact that it was raining at an earlier time. For the time being, we're going to focus on learning how to turn our bike-sharing dataset into something that our neural network will be able to ingest in fixed-size chunks.

Neural network models can accept any dimensionality of data, but it is also up to us to shape the data so that the input is intuitive, allowing us to create a model that can operate on it effectively. In our case, with this time-series data, having a separation of days, columns, and hours is a good approach. Let's have a go at it!

4.4.2 Shaping the data by time period

We can break up the two-year dataset into wider observation periods, such as days. This way we'll have N (days) collections of C (columns) sequences of length L (hours). In other words, our time-series dataset would be a tensor of dimension 3 and shape $N \times C \times L$. The C would remain our 17 variables from our original dataset, while L would be 24 for each hour of the day.

You may be wondering why we don't order it as $N \times L \times C$, which would be days by hours by variables. This ordering is also valid, but it splits the variable data along individual columns such that each row represents each variable at a specific hour point (see figure 4.6). For this particular exercise, we want to keep each individual variable (e.g., temperature, humidity, etc.) together in a single sequence, so they can be accessed as an entire row, and we will keep it as $N \times C \times L$.

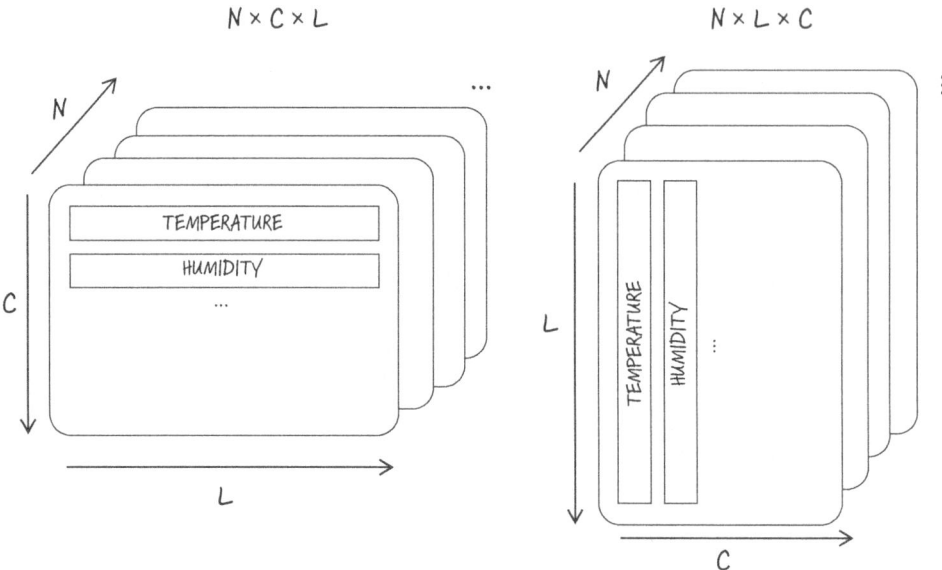

Figure 4.6 The dimensions *N* × *C* × *L* (left) vs. *N* × *L* × *C* (right) visualized

Furthermore, there's no particular reason why we *must* use chunks of 24 hours, although the general daily rhythm is likely to give us patterns we can exploit for predictions. We could also use 7 × 24 = 168 hour blocks to chunk by week instead, if we desired. It all depends, naturally, on our dataset having the right size—the number of rows must be a multiple of 24 or 168. Also, for this approach to make sense, we cannot have gaps in the time series.

Let's go back to our bike-sharing dataset. The first column is the index (the global ordering of the data), the second is the date, and the sixth is the time of day. We have everything we need to create a dataset of daily sequences of ride counts and other exogenous variables. Our dataset is already sorted, but if it were not, we could use torch.sort on it to order it appropriately.

> **NOTE** The version of the file we're using, hour-fixed.csv, has had some processing done to include rows missing from the original dataset. We presume that the missing hours had zero bike activity (they were typically in the early morning hours).

To obtain our daily hours dataset, we need to view the same tensor in batches of 24 hours. Let's take a look at the shape and strides of our bikes tensor:

```
# In[3]:
bikes.shape, bikes.stride()

# Out[3]:
(torch.Size([17520, 17]), (17, 1))
```

That's 17,520 hours and 17 columns. Now let's reshape the data to have three axes—day, hour, and our 17 columns:

```
# In[4]:
daily_bikes = bikes.view(-1, 24, bikes.shape[1])
daily_bikes.shape, daily_bikes.stride()
```

```
# Out[4]:
(torch.Size([730, 24, 17]), (408, 17, 1))
```

What happened here? First, bikes.shape[1] is 17, the number of columns in the bikes tensor. But the real crux of this code is the very important call to view: it changes the way the tensor looks at the same data as contained in storage.

As you learned in the previous chapter, calling view on a tensor returns a new tensor that changes the number of dimensions and the striding information, without changing the storage. As a result, we can rearrange our tensor at basically zero cost because no data will be copied. Our call to view requires us to provide the new shape for the returned tensor. We use -1 as a placeholder for "however many indexes are left, given the other dimensions and the original number of elements."

Remember also from the previous chapter that storage is a contiguous, linear container for numbers (floating-point, in this case). Our bikes tensor will have each row stored one after the other in its corresponding storage, which is confirmed by the output from the call to bikes.stride() earlier.

For daily_bikes, the stride is telling us that advancing by 1 along the hour dimension (the second dimension) requires us to advance by 17 places in the storage (or one set of columns). Advancing along the day dimension (the first dimension) requires us to advance by a number of elements equal to the length of a row in the storage times 24 (here, 408, which is 17 × 24).

We see that the rightmost dimension is the number of columns in the original dataset. Then, in the middle dimension, we have time, split into chunks of 24 sequential hours. In other words, we now have N sequences of L hours in a day, for C channels. To get to our desired $N \times C \times L$ ordering, we need to transpose the tensor:

```
# In[5]:
daily_bikes = daily_bikes.transpose(1, 2)
daily_bikes.shape, daily_bikes.stride()
```

```
# Out[5]:
(torch.Size([730, 17, 24]), (408, 1, 17))
```

Now, let's apply some of the techniques we learned earlier to this dataset.

4.4.3 Ready for training

The "weather situation" variable is ordinal. It has four levels: 1 for good weather, and 4 for, er, really bad. We could treat this variable as categorical, with levels interpreted as labels, or as a continuous variable. If we decided to go with categorical, we would turn the variable into a one-hot-encoded vector and concatenate the columns with the dataset.

> **NOTE** This situation could also be a case where it is useful to step off beyond the main path. Speculatively, we could also try to reflect *like categorical, but with order* more directly by generalizing one-hot encodings to mapping the *i*th of our four categories here to a vector that has ones in the positions 0 ... *i* and zeros beyond that. Or, similar to the embeddings we discussed in section 4.5.4, we could take partial sums of embeddings, in which case it might make sense to make those positive. As with many things we encounter in practical work, this could be a place where *trying what works for others* and then experimenting in a systematic fashion is a good idea.

To make it easier to render our data, we're going to limit ourselves to the first day for a moment. We initialize a zero-filled matrix with a number of rows equal to the number of hours in the day and a number of columns equal to the number of weather levels:

```
# In[6]:
first_day = bikes[:24].long()
weather_onehot = torch.zeros(first_day.shape[0], 4)
first_day[:,9]

# Out[6]:
tensor([1, 1, 1, 1, 1, 2, 1, 1, 1, 1, 1, 1, 1, 2, 2, 2, 2, 2, 3, 3, 2, 2,
        2, 2])
```

Then we scatter 1s into our matrix according to the corresponding level at each row. Remember the use of `unsqueeze` to add a singleton dimension as we did in the previous sections:

```
# In[7]:
weather_onehot.scatter_(
    dim=1,
    index=first_day[:,9].unsqueeze(1).long() - 1,      ◁─── Decreases the values by
    value=1.0)                                              1 because the weather
                                                            situation ranges from
# Out[7]:                                                   1 to 4, while indices
tensor([[1., 0., 0., 0.],                                   are zero-based
        [1., 0., 0., 0.],
        ...,
        [0., 1., 0., 0.],
        [0., 1., 0., 0.]])
```

Our day started with weather 1 and ended with 2, so that seems right.

Last, we concatenate our matrix to our original dataset using the `cat` function. Let's look at the first of our results:

```
# In[8]:
torch.cat((bikes[:24], weather_onehot), 1)[:1]
```

```
# Out[8]:
tensor([[ 1.0000,  1.0000,  1.0000,  0.0000,  1.0000,  0.0000,  0.0000,
          6.0000,  0.0000,  1.0000,  0.2400,  0.2879,  0.8100,  0.0000,
          3.0000, 13.0000, 16.0000,  1.0000,  0.0000,  0.0000,  0.0000]])
```

Here, we prescribed our original `bikes` dataset and our one-hot-encoded "weather situation" matrix to be concatenated along the *column* dimension (that is, 1). In other words, the columns of the two datasets are stacked together, or equivalently, the new one-hot-encoded columns are appended to the original dataset. For `cat` to succeed, the tensors must have the same size along the other dimensions—the *row* dimension, in this case. Note that our new last four columns are 1, 0, 0, 0, exactly as we would expect with a weather value of 1.

We can do the same process with the reshaped `daily_bikes` tensor. Remember that it is shaped (B, C, L), where $L = 24$. We first create the zero tensor with the same B and L but with the number of additional columns as C:

```
# In[9]:
daily_weather_onehot = torch.zeros(daily_bikes.shape[0], 4,
                                   daily_bikes.shape[2])
daily_weather_onehot.shape

# Out[9]:
torch.Size([730, 4, 24])
```

Then we scatter the one-hot encoding into the tensor in the C dimension. Since this operation is performed in place, only the content of the tensor changes:

```
# In[10]:
daily_weather_onehot.scatter_(
    1, daily_bikes[:,9,:].long().unsqueeze(1) - 1, 1.0)
daily_weather_onehot.shape

# Out[10]:
torch.Size([730, 4, 24])
```

And we concatenate along the C dimension:

```
# In[11]:
daily_bikes = torch.cat((daily_bikes, daily_weather_onehot), dim=1)
```

We mentioned earlier that this is not the only way to treat our "weather situation" variable. Indeed, its labels have an ordinal relationship, so we can pretend they are special values of a continuous variable. We can transform the variable so that it runs from 0.0 to 1.0:

```
# In[12]:
daily_bikes[:, 9, :] = (daily_bikes[:, 9, :] - 1.0) / 3.0
```

As we mentioned in the previous section, rescaling variables to the [0.0, 1.0] interval or the [-1.0, 1.0] interval is something we'll want to do for all quantitative variables, like `temperature` (column 10 in our dataset). We'll see why later; for now, let's just say that it is beneficial to the training process.

Multiple possibilities exist for rescaling variables. We can either map their range to [0.0, 1.0] as

```
# In[13]:
temp = daily_bikes[:, 10, :]
temp_min = torch.min(temp)
temp_max = torch.max(temp)
daily_bikes[:, 10, :] = ((daily_bikes[:, 10, :] - temp_min)
                        / (temp_max - temp_min))
```

or subtract the mean and divide by the standard deviation:

```
# In[14]:
temp = daily_bikes[:, 10, :]
daily_bikes[:, 10, :] = ((daily_bikes[:, 10, :] - torch.mean(temp))
                        / torch.std(temp))
```

In the latter case, our variable will have a zero mean and unitary standard deviation. If our variable were drawn from a Gaussian distribution, 68% of the samples would sit in the [–1.0, 1.0] interval.

Great, we've built another nice dataset, and we've seen how to deal with time-series data. For this tour d'horizon, it's important only that we get an idea of how a time series is laid out and how we can wrangle the data in a form that a network will digest.

Other kinds of data look like a time series, in that there is a strict ordering. Top two on the list? Text and audio. We'll take a look at text next, and the final section of this chapter has links to additional examples for audio.

4.5 Representing text

Deep learning has taken the field of natural language processing (NLP) by storm, particularly using models that repeatedly consume a combination of new input and previous model output. These models are called *recurrent neural networks* (RNNs), and they have been applied with great success to text categorization, text generation, and automated translation systems. More recently, a class of networks called *transformers* with a more flexible way to incorporate past information has made a big splash. Previous NLP workloads were characterized by sophisticated multistage pipelines that included rules encoding the grammar of a language (see Nadkarni et al., "Natural Language Processing: An Introduction," http://mng.bz/8pJP).

Now, state-of-the-art work trains networks end to end on large corpora, starting from scratch, letting those rules emerge from the data. For the last several years, the most-used automated translation systems available as services on the internet have been based on deep learning.

Our goal in this section is to turn text into something a neural network can process—a tensor of numbers, just like our previous cases. If we can do that and later choose the right architecture for our text-processing job, we'll be in the position to do NLP with PyTorch. We see right away how powerful all this is: we can achieve state-of-the-art performance on a number of tasks in different domains *with the same PyTorch tools*; we just need to cast our problem in the right form. The first part of this job is reshaping the data.

4.5.1 Converting text to numbers

There are two particularly intuitive levels at which networks operate on text: at the character level, by processing one character at a time, and at the word level, where individual words are the finest-grained entities visible to the network. The technique with which we encode text information into tensor form is the same whether we operate at the character level or the word level. And it's not magic, either. We stumbled upon it earlier: one-hot encoding.

Let's start with a character-level example. First, let's get some text to process. An amazing resource here is Project Gutenberg (http://www.gutenberg.org/), a volunteer effort to digitize and archive cultural work and make it available for free in open formats, including plain text files. If we're aiming at larger-scale corpora, the Wikipedia corpus stands out: it's the complete collection of Wikipedia articles, containing 1.9 billion words and more than 4.4 million articles. Several other corpora can be found at the English Corpora website (https://www.english-corpora.org/).

Let's load Jane Austen's *Pride and Prejudice* from the Project Gutenberg website: http://www.gutenberg.org/files/1342/1342-0.txt. We'll save the file and read it in (code/p1ch4/5_text_jane_austen.ipynb).

Listing 4.7 Reading a text file

```
# In[2]:
with open('../data/p1ch4/jane-austen/1342-0.txt', encoding='utf8') as f:
    text = f.read()
```

4.5.2 One-hot-encoding characters

There's one more detail we need to take care of before we proceed: encoding. Encoding is a pretty vast subject, and we will just touch on it. Every written character is represented by a code—a sequence of bits of appropriate length so that each character can be uniquely identified. The simplest such encoding is ASCII (American Standard Code for Information Interchange), which dates back to the 1960s. ASCII encodes 128 characters using 128 integers. For instance, the letter *a* corresponds to binary 1100001 or decimal 97, the letter *b* to binary 1100010 or decimal 98, and so on. The encoding fits 8 bits, which was a big bonus in 1965.

> **NOTE** Clearly, 128 characters are not enough to account for all the glyphs, accents, ligatures, and so on that are needed to properly represent written text in languages other than English. To this end, a number of encodings have been developed that use a larger number of bits as code for a wider

range of characters. That wider range of characters was standardized as Unicode, which maps all known characters to numbers, with the representation in bits of those numbers provided by a specific encoding. Popular encodings are UTF-8, UTF-16, and UTF-32, in which the numbers are a sequence of 8-, 16-, or 32-bit integers, respectively. Strings in Python 3.x are Unicode strings.

We are going to one-hot encode our characters. It is instrumental to limit the one-hot encoding to a character set that is useful for the text being analyzed. In our case, since we loaded text in English, it is safe to use ASCII and deal with a small encoding. We could also make all of the characters lowercase to reduce the number of different characters in our encoding. Similarly, we could screen out punctuation, numbers, or other characters that aren't relevant to our expected kinds of text. This may or may not make a practical difference to a neural network, depending on the task at hand.

At this point, we need to parse through the characters in the text and provide a one-hot encoding for each of them. Each character will be represented by a vector of length equal to the number of different characters in the encoding. This vector will contain all 0s, except for a 1 at the index corresponding to the location of the character in the encoding.

We first split our text into a list of lines and pick an arbitrary line to focus on:

```
# In[3]:
lines = text.split('\n')
line = lines[200]
line

# Out[3]:
'"Impossible, Mr. Bennet, impossible, when I am not acquainted with him'
```

Let's create a tensor that can hold the total number of one-hot-encoded characters for the whole line:

```
# In[4]:
letter_t = torch.zeros(len(line), 128)     ◁—┐ 128 hardcoded
letter_t.shape                                │ due to the limits
                                              │ of ASCII
# Out[4]:
torch.Size([70, 128])
```

letter_t holds a one-hot-encoded character per row. Now, we need to set a 1 on each row in the correct position so that each row represents the correct character. The index where the 1 has to be set corresponds to the index of the character in the encoding:

```
# In[5]:
for i, letter in enumerate(line.lower().strip()):
    letter_index = ord(letter) if ord(letter) < 128 else 0    ◁—┐ The text uses
    letter_t[i][letter_index] = 1                                │ directional double
                                                                 │ quotes, which are
                                                                 │ not valid ASCII, so
                                                                 │ we screen them
                                                                 │ out here.
```

4.5.3 One-hot encoding whole words

We have one-hot encoded our sentence into a representation that a neural network can digest. Word-level encoding can be done the same way by establishing a vocabulary and one-hot encoding sentences—sequences of words—along the rows of our tensor. Since a vocabulary has many words, the encoding will produce very wide encoded vectors, which may not be practical. We will see in the next section that there is a more efficient way to represent text at the word level, using *embeddings*. For now, let's stick with one-hot encodings and see what happens.

We'll define `clean_words`, which takes text and returns it in lowercase and stripped of punctuation. When we call it on our "Impossible, Mr. Bennet" line, we get the following:

```
# In[6]:
def clean_words(input_str):
    punctuation = '.,;:"!?""_-'
    word_list = input_str.lower().replace('\n',' ').split()
    word_list = [word.strip(punctuation) for word in word_list]
    return word_list

words_in_line = clean_words(line)
line, words_in_line

# Out[6]:
('"Impossible, Mr. Bennet, impossible, when I am not acquainted with him',
 ['impossible',
  'mr',
  'bennet',
  'impossible',
  'when',
  'i',
  'am',
  'not',
  'acquainted',
  'with',
  'him'])
```

Next, let's build a mapping of unique words to indexes in our encoding:

```
# In[7]:
word_list = sorted(set(clean_words(text)))
word2index_dict = {word: i for (i, word) in enumerate(word_list)}

len(word2index_dict), word2index_dict['impossible']

# Out[7]:
(7261, 3394)
```

`word2index_dict` is now a dictionary with words as keys and an integer as a value. We will use it to efficiently find the index of a word as we one-hot encode it. Let's now focus on our sentence: we break it up into words and one-hot encode it—that is, we populate a tensor with one one-hot-encoded vector per word. We create an empty vector and assign the one-hot-encoded values of the word in the sentence:

```
# In[8]:
word_t = torch.zeros(len(words_in_line), len(word2index_dict))
for i, word in enumerate(words_in_line):
    word_index = word2index_dict[word]
    word_t[i][word_index] = 1
    print('{:2} {:4} {}'.format(i, word_index, word))

print(word_t.shape)

# Out[8]:
 0 3394 impossible
 1 4305 mr
 2  813 bennet
 3 3394 impossible
 4 7078 when
 5 3315 i
 6  415 am
 7 4436 not
 8  239 acquainted
 9 7148 with
10 3215 him
torch.Size([11, 7261])
```

At this point, tensor represents one sentence of length 11 in an encoding space of size 7,261, the number of words in our dictionary. Figure 4.7 compares the gist of our two options for splitting text (and using the embeddings we'll look at in the next section).

The choice between character-level and word-level encoding leaves us to make a tradeoff. In many languages, there are significantly fewer characters than words: representing characters has us representing just a few classes, while representing words requires us to represent a very large number of classes and, in any practical application, deal with words that are not in the dictionary. On the other hand, words convey much more meaning than individual characters, so a representation of words is considerably more informative by itself. Given the stark contrast between these two options, it is perhaps unsurprising that intermediate ways have been sought, found, and applied with great success. For example, the *byte pair encoding* method starts with a dictionary of individual letters but then iteratively adds the most frequently observed pairs to the dictionary until it reaches a prescribed dictionary size. Our example sentence might then be split into tokens like this:

```
_Im|pos|s|ible|,|_Mr|.|_B|en|net|,|_impossible|,|_when|_I|_am|_not|
↪ _acquainted|_with|_him
```

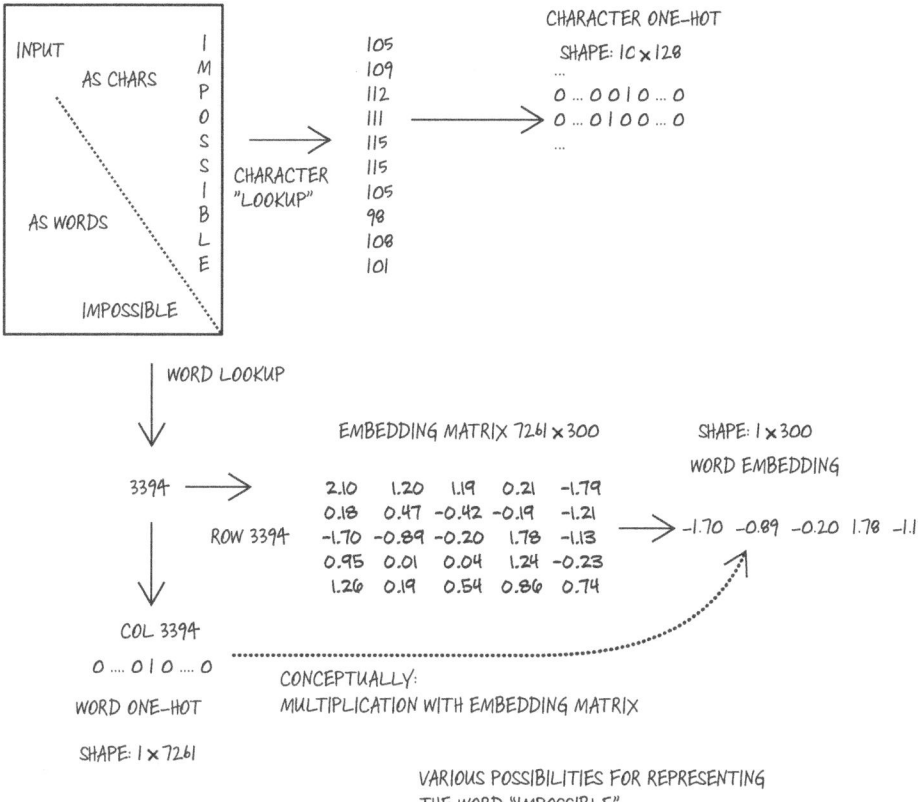

Figure 4.7 Three ways to encode a word

NOTE Byte pair encoding is commonly implemented by the subword-nmt and SentencePiece libraries. The conceptual drawback is that the representation of a sequence of characters is no longer unique. (This example is from a SentencePiece tokenizer trained on a machine translation dataset.)

For most things, our mapping is just splitting by words. But the rarer parts—the capitalized *Impossible* and the name *Bennet*—are composed of subunits.

4.5.4 Text embeddings

One-hot encoding is a very useful technique for representing categorical data in tensors. However, as we have anticipated, one-hot encoding starts to break down when the number of items to encode is effectively unbound, as with words in a corpus. In just one book, we had over 7,000 items!

We certainly could do some work to deduplicate words, condense alternate spellings, collapse past and future tenses into a single token, and that kind of thing. Still, a general-purpose English-language encoding would be *huge*. Even worse, every time we encountered a new word, we would have to add a new column to the vector, which would mean adding a new set of weights to the model to account for that new vocabulary entry, which would be painful from a training perspective.

How can we compress our encoding down to a more manageable size and put a cap on the size growth? Well, instead of vectors of many zeros and a single one, we can use vectors of floating-point numbers. A vector of, say, 100 floating-point numbers can indeed represent a large number of words. The trick is to find an effective way to map individual words into this 100-dimensional space in a way that facilitates downstream learning. This is called an *embedding*.

In principle, we could simply iterate over our vocabulary and generate a set of 100 random floating-point numbers for each word. This would work, in that we could cram a very large vocabulary into just 100 numbers, but it would forgo any concept of distance between words based on meaning or context. A model using this word embedding would have to deal with very little structure in its input vectors. An ideal solution would be to generate the embedding in such a way that words used in similar contexts are mapped to nearby regions of the embedding.

Well, if we were to design a solution to this problem by hand, we might decide to build our embedding space by choosing to map basic nouns and adjectives along the axes. We can generate a 2D space where axes map to nouns—*fruit* (0.0-0.33), *flower* (0.33-0.66), and *dog* (0.66-1.0)—and adjectives—*red* (0.0-0.2), *orange* (0.2-0.4), *yellow* (0.4-0.6), *white* (0.6-0.8), and *brown* (0.8-1.0). Our goal is to take actual fruit, flowers, and dogs and lay them out in the embedding.

As we start embedding words, we can map *apple* to a number in the *fruit* and *red* quadrant. Likewise, we can easily map *tangerine, lemon, lychee,* and *kiwi* (to round out our list of colorful fruits). Then we can start on flowers, and assign *rose, poppy, daffodil, lily,* and . . . . Hmm, not many brown flowers out there. Well, *sunflower* can get *flower, yellow,* and *brown,* and then *daisy* can get *flower, white,* and *yellow.* Perhaps we should update *kiwi* to map close to *fruit, brown,* and *green.* (Actually, with our 1D view of color, this is not possible, as *sunflower*'s *yellow* and *brown* will average to *white,* but you get the idea, and it does work better in higher dimensions.) For dogs and color, we can embed *redbone* near *red*; uh, *fox* perhaps for *orange*; *golden retriever* for *yellow*; *poodle* for *white*; and many kinds of dogs are *brown.*

Now our embeddings look like figure 4.8. While encoding manually isn't feasible for a large corpus, we had an embedding size of 2, and we described 15 different words *besides the base 8* and could probably cram in quite a few more if we took the time to be creative about it.

As you've probably already guessed, this kind of work can be automated. By processing a large corpus of organic text, embeddings similar to the one we just discussed can be generated. The main differences are that the embedding vector has 100 to 1,000 elements and the axes do not map directly to concepts: rather, conceptually similar words map in neighboring regions of an embedding space whose axes are arbitrary floating-point dimensions.

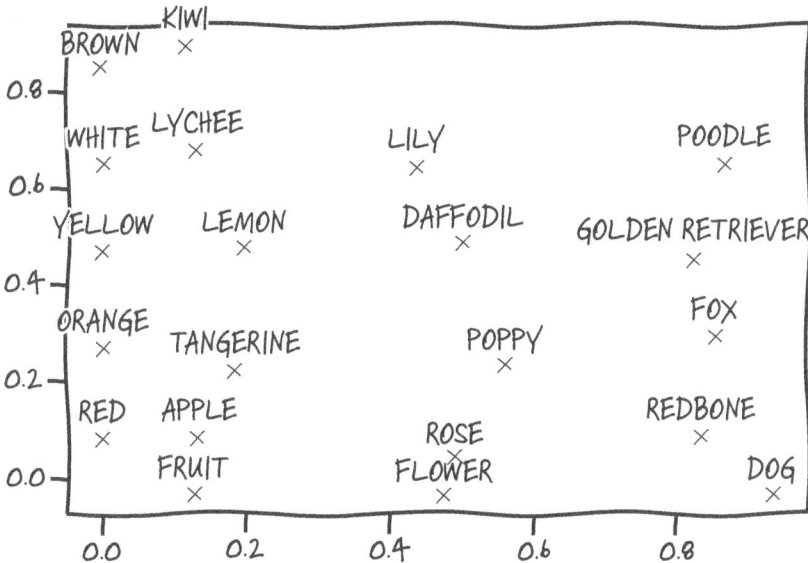

Figure 4.8 Our manual word embeddings

While the exact algorithms (e.g., see word2vec at https://code.google.com/archive/p/word2vec) used are a bit out of scope for what we're wanting to focus on here, we'd like to mention that embeddings are often generated using neural networks, trying to predict a word from nearby words (the context) in a sentence. In this case, we could start from one-hot-encoded words and use a (usually rather shallow) neural network to generate the embedding. Once the embedding was available, we can use it for downstream tasks.

One interesting aspect of the resulting embeddings is that similar words end up not only clustered together, but also having consistent spatial relationships with other words. For example, if we were to take the embedding vector for *apple* and begin to add and subtract the vectors for other words, we could begin to perform analogies like *apple - red - sweet + yellow + sour* and end up with a vector very similar to the one for *lemon*.

More contemporary embedding models—with BERT and GPT making headlines even in mainstream media—are much more elaborate and context sensitive; that is, the mapping of a word in the vocabulary to a vector is not fixed but depends on the surrounding sentence. Yet they are often used just like the simpler *classic* embeddings we've touched on here.

4.5.5 *Text embeddings as a blueprint*

Embeddings are an essential tool when a large number of entries in the vocabulary have to be represented by numeric vectors. How text is represented and processed can also be seen as an example of dealing with categorical data in general. Embeddings are useful wherever one-hot encoding becomes cumbersome. Indeed, in the form described previously, they are an efficient way of representing one-hot encoding immediately followed by multiplication with the matrix containing the embedding vectors as rows.

In nontext applications, we usually do not have the ability to construct the embeddings beforehand, but we will start with the random numbers we eschewed earlier and consider improving them as part of our learning problem. This technique is standard—so much so that embeddings are a prominent alternative to one-hot encodings for any categorical data. On the flip side, even when we deal with text, improving the prelearned embeddings while solving the problem at hand has become a common practice. This process goes by the name *fine-tuning*.

When we are interested in co-occurrences of observations, the word embeddings we saw earlier can serve as a blueprint, too. For example, recommender systems—for example, customers who liked our book also bought book *X*—use the items the customer already interacted with as the context for predicting what else will spark interest. Similarly, processing text is perhaps the most common, well-explored task dealing with sequences. For example, when working on tasks with time series, we might look for inspiration in what is done in NLP.

4.6 Conclusion

We've covered a lot of ground in this chapter. We learned to load the most common types of data and shape them for consumption by a neural network. Of course, there are more data formats in the wild than we could hope to describe in a single volume. Some, like medical histories, are too complex to cover here. Others, like audio and video, were deemed less crucial for the path of this book. If you're interested, however, we provide short examples of audio and video tensor creation in bonus Jupyter Notebooks provided on the book's website (https://www.manning.com/books/deep-learning-with-pytorch-second-edition) and in our code repository (https://github.com/deep-learning-with-pytorch).

Now that we're familiar with tensors and how to store data in them, we can move on to the next step toward the goal of the book: teaching you to train deep neural networks! The next chapter covers the mechanics of learning for simple linear models.

4.7 Exercises

1 Take several pictures of red, blue, and green items with your phone or other digital camera (or download some from the internet, if a camera isn't available):
   a Load each image and convert it to a tensor.
   b For each image tensor, use the `.mean()` method to get a sense of how bright the image is.
   c Take the mean of each channel of your images. Can you identify the red, green, and blue items from only the channel averages?

2 Select a relatively large file containing Python source code:
   a Build an index of all the words in the source file (feel free to make your tokenization as simple or as complex as you like; we suggest starting with replacing `r"[^a-zA-Z0-9_]+"` with spaces).
   b Compare your index with the one we made for *Pride and Prejudice*. Which is larger?
   c Create the one-hot encoding for the source code file.
   d What information is lost with this encoding? How does that information compare to what's lost in the *Pride and Prejudice* encoding?

Summary

- Neural networks require data to be represented as multidimensional numerical tensors, often 32-bit floating-point.
- In general, PyTorch expects data to be laid out along specific dimensions according to the model architecture—for example, convolutional versus recurrent. We can reshape data effectively with the PyTorch tensor API.
- PyTorch integrates well with Python, making it easy to load common data types and convert them into tensors.
- Images can have one or many channels. The most common are the red-green-blue channels of typical digital photos.
- Many images have a per-channel bit depth of 8, although 12 and 16 bits per channel are not uncommon. These bit depths can all be stored in a 32-bit floating-point number without loss of precision.
- Single-channel data formats (e.g., grayscale images) sometimes omit an explicit channel dimension.
- Volumetric data is similar to 2D image data, with the exception of adding a third dimension (depth).
- Converting spreadsheets to tensors can be very straightforward. Categorical- and ordinal-valued columns should be handled differently from interval-valued columns.
- Text or categorical data can be encoded to a one-hot representation through the use of dictionaries. Very often, embeddings give good, efficient representations.

The mechanics of learning

This chapter covers

- Understanding how algorithms can learn from data
- Reframing learning as parameter estimation using differentiation and gradient descent
- Walking through a simple learning algorithm
- How PyTorch supports learning with autograd

With the blooming of machine learning that has occurred over the last decade, the notion of machines that learn from experience has become a mainstream theme in both technical and journalistic circles. Now, how is it exactly that a machine learns? What are the mechanics of this process—or, in words, what is the *algorithm* behind it?

From the point of view of an observer, a learning algorithm is presented with input data that is paired with desired outputs. Once learning has occurred, that algorithm will be capable of producing correct outputs when it is fed new data that is *similar enough* to the input data it was trained on. With deep learning, this process works even when the input data and the desired output are *far* from each other—when they come from different domains, like an image and a sentence describing it, as we saw in chapter 2.

5.1 A timeless lesson in modeling

Building models that allow us to explain input/output relationships dates back centuries, at least. When Johannes Kepler, a German mathematical astronomer (1571–1630), figured out his three laws of planetary motion in the early 1600s, he based them on data collected by his mentor Tycho Brahe during naked-eye observations (yep, seen with the naked eye and written on a piece of paper).

Not having Newton's law of gravitation at his disposal (actually, Newton used Kepler's work to figure things out), Kepler extrapolated the simplest possible geometric model that could fit the data. And, by the way, it took him six years of staring at data that didn't make sense to him, together with incremental realizations, to finally formulate these laws (as recounted by physicist Michael Fowler; http://mng.bz/K2Ej). We can see this process in figure 5.1.

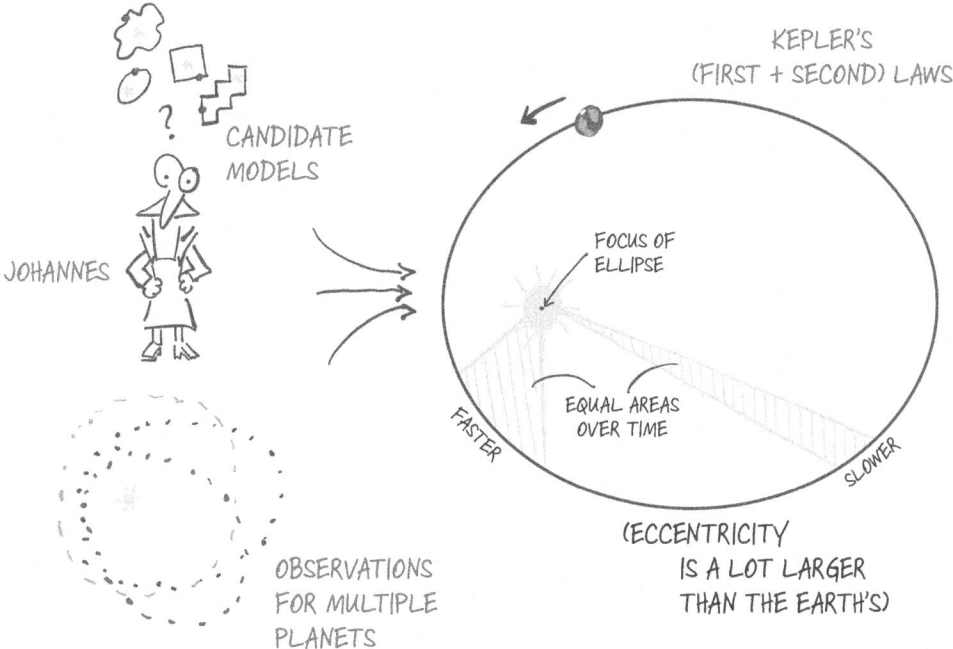

Figure 5.1 Johannes Kepler considers multiple candidate models that might fit the data at hand, settling on an ellipse.

Kepler's first law reads: "The orbit of every planet is an ellipse with the Sun at one of the two *foci*." He didn't know what caused orbits to be ellipses, but given a set of observations for a planet (or a moon of a large planet, like Jupiter), he could estimate the shape (the *eccentricity*) and size (the *semi-latus rectum*) of the ellipse. With those two parameters computed from the data, he could tell where the planet might be during its journey in the sky. Once he figured out the second law—"A line joining a planet and the Sun sweeps out equal areas during equal intervals of time"—he could also tell *when* a planet would be at a particular point in space, given observations in time.

> **NOTE** Understanding the details of Kepler's laws is not needed to understand this chapter, but you can find more information at https://mng.bz/V9rO.

So, how did Kepler estimate the eccentricity and size of the ellipse without computers, pocket calculators, or even calculus, none of which had been invented yet? We can learn how from Kepler's own recollection in his book *New Astronomy*, or from how J. V. Field put it in his series of articles, "The Origins of Proof" (http://mng.bz/9007):

> *Essentially, Kepler had to try different shapes, using a certain number of observations to find the curve, then use the curve to find some more positions, for times when he had observations available, and then check whether these calculated positions agreed with the observed ones.*

So, let's sum things up. Over six years, Kepler

- Got lots of good data from his friend Brahe (not without some struggle)
- Tried to visualize the heck out of it because he felt there was something fishy going on
- Chose the simplest possible model that had a chance to fit the data (an ellipse)
- Split the data so that he could work on part of it and keep an independent set for validation
- Started with a tentative eccentricity and size for the ellipse and iterated until the model fit the observations
- Validated his model on the independent observations
- Looked back in disbelief

There's a data science handbook for you, all the way from 1609. The history of science is literally constructed on these seven steps. And we have learned over the centuries that deviating from them is a recipe for disaster—unless you're a theoretical physicist ;).

This process is exactly what we will do to *learn* something from data. In fact, in this book, there is virtually no difference between saying that we'll *fit* the data and that we'll make an algorithm *learn* from data. The process always involves a function with a number of unknown parameters whose values are estimated from data—in short, a *model*.

We can argue that *learning from data* presumes the underlying model is not engineered to solve a specific problem (as was the ellipse in Kepler's work) and is instead capable of approximating a much wider family of functions. A neural network would have predicted Tycho Brahe's trajectories really well without requiring Kepler's flash of insight to try fitting the data to an ellipse. However, Sir Isaac Newton would have had a much harder time deriving his laws of gravitation from a generic model.

In this book, we're interested in models that are not engineered to solve a specific, narrow task and can be automatically adapted to specialize themselves for any one of many similar tasks using input and output pairs—in other words, general models trained on data relevant to the specific task at hand. In particular, PyTorch is designed to make it easy to create models for which the derivatives of the fitting error, with respect to the parameters, can be expressed analytically. No worries if that last sentence didn't make any sense; coming next, we have a full section that hopefully clears it up for you.

This chapter is about how to automate generic function-fitting. After all, we do this with deep learning—deep neural networks being the generic functions we're talking about—and PyTorch makes this process as simple and transparent as possible. To make sure we get the key concepts right, we'll start with a model that is a lot simpler than a deep neural network. This model will allow us to understand the mechanics of learning algorithms from first principles in this chapter, so we can move to more complicated models in chapter 6.

5.2 *Learning is just parameter estimation*

In this section, we'll learn how we can take data, choose a model, and estimate the parameters of the model so that it will give good predictions on new data. To do so, we'll leave the intricacies of planetary motion and divert our attention to the second-hardest problem in physics: calibrating instruments.

Figure 5.2 shows the high-level overview of what we'll implement by the end of the chapter. Given input data and the corresponding desired outputs (ground truth), as well as initial values for the weights, the model is fed input data (forward pass), and a measure of the error (loss) is evaluated by comparing the resulting outputs to the ground truth. To optimize the parameter of the model (i.e., its *weights*), the change in the error following a unit change in weights (i.e., the *gradient* of the error with respect to the parameters) is computed using the chain rule for the derivative of a composite function (backward pass). The value of the weights is then updated in the direction that leads to a decrease in the error. The procedure is repeated until the error, evaluated on unseen data, falls below an acceptable level. If what we just said sounds obscure, we've got a whole chapter to clear things up. By the time we're done, all the pieces will fall into place, and this paragraph will make perfect sense.

We're now going to take a problem with a noisy dataset, build a model, and implement a learning algorithm for it. When we start, we'll be doing everything by hand, but by the end of the chapter, we'll be letting PyTorch do all the heavy lifting for us. When we finish the chapter, we will have covered many of the essential concepts that underlie training deep neural networks, even if our motivating example is very simple and our model isn't actually a neural network (yet!).

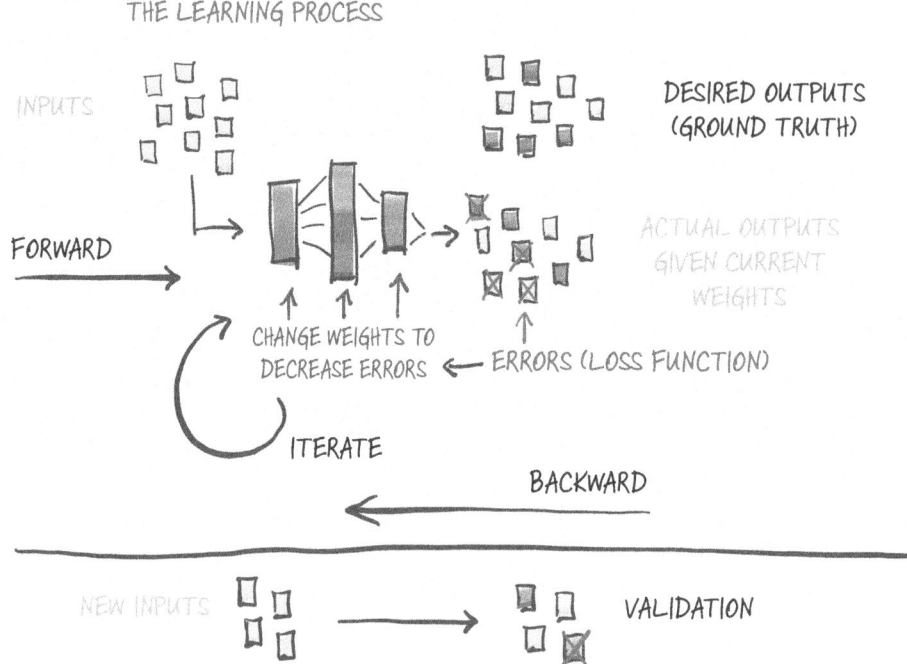

Figure 5.2 Our mental model of the learning process.

5.2.1 A hot problem

We just got back from a trip to some obscure location, and we brought back a fancy, wall-mounted analog thermometer. It looks great, and it's a perfect fit for our living room. Its only flaw is that it doesn't show units. Not to worry, we've got a plan: we'll build a dataset of readings and corresponding temperature values in our favorite units, choose a model, adjust its weights iteratively until a measure of the error is low enough, and finally be able to interpret the new readings in units we understand.

> **NOTE** This task—fitting model outputs to continuous values in terms of the types discussed in chapter 4—is called a *regression* problem. In part 2, particularly chapter 7, we will be concerned with *classification* problems.

Let's try following the same process Kepler used. Along the way, we'll use a tool he never had available: PyTorch!

5.2.2 Gathering some data

We'll start by making a note of temperature data in good old Celsius and measurements from our new thermometer to figure things out. After a couple of weeks, we collect the following data (code/p1ch5/1_parameter_estimation.ipynb):

```
# In[2]:
t_c = [0.5,  14.0, 15.0, 28.0, 11.0,  8.0,  3.0, -4.0,  6.0, 13.0, 21.0]
t_u = [35.7, 55.9, 58.2, 81.9, 56.3, 48.9, 33.9, 21.8, 48.4, 60.4, 68.4]
t_c = torch.tensor(t_c)
t_u = torch.tensor(t_u)
```

Here, the t_c values are temperatures in Celsius, and the t_u values are our unknown units. We can expect noise in both measurements, coming from the devices themselves and from our approximate readings. For convenience, we've already put the data into tensors; we'll use it in a minute.

5.2.3 Visualizing the data

A quick plot of our data in figure 5.3 tells us that it's noisy, but we think there's a pattern here.

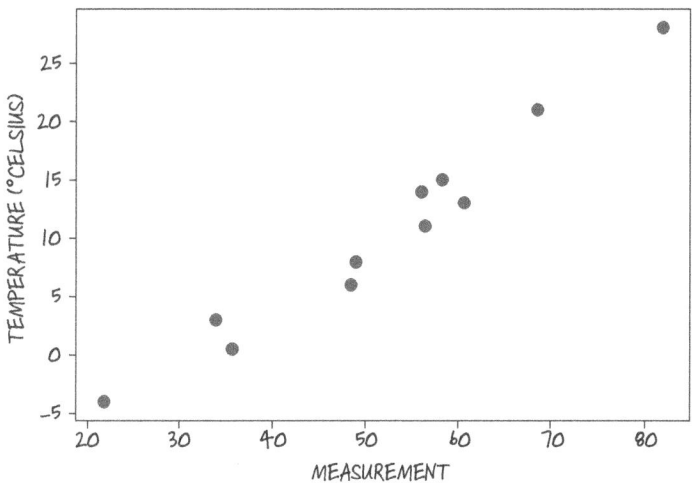

Figure 5.3 Our unknown data just might follow a linear model.

> **NOTE** Spoiler alert: we know a linear model is correct because the problem and data have been fabricated, but please bear with us. It's a useful motivating example to build our understanding of what PyTorch is doing under the hood.

5.2.4 Choosing a linear model as a first try

In the absence of further knowledge, we assume the simplest possible model for converting between the two sets of measurements, just like Kepler might have done. The two may be linearly related—that is, multiplying t_u by a factor and adding a constant, we may get the temperature in Celsius (up to an error that we omit):

```
t_c = w * t_u + b
```

Is this a reasonable assumption? Probably. We'll see how well the final model performs. We chose to name w and b after *weight* and *bias*, two very common terms for linear scaling and the additive constant. We'll bump into those all the time.

> **NOTE** The weight tells us how much a given input influences the output. The bias is what the output would be if all inputs were zero.

OK, now we need to estimate w and b, the parameters in our model, based on the data we have. We must do it so that the temperatures we obtain from running the unknown temperatures t_u through the model are close to the temperatures we actually measured in Celsius. If that sounds like fitting a line through a set of measurements, well, yes, because that's exactly what we're doing. We'll go through this simple example using PyTorch and realize that training a neural network will essentially involve changing the model for a slightly more elaborate one, with a few (or a metric ton) more parameters.

Let's flesh it out again: we have a model with some unknown parameters, and we need to estimate those parameters so that the error between predicted outputs and measured values is as low as possible. We notice that we still need to exactly define a measure of the error. Such a measure, which we refer to as the *loss function*, should be high if the error is high and should ideally be as low as possible for a perfect match. Our optimization process should therefore aim at finding w and b so that the loss function is at a minimum.

5.3 Less loss is what we want

A *loss function* (or *cost function*) is a function that computes a single numerical value that the learning process will attempt to minimize. The calculation of loss typically involves taking the difference between the desired outputs for some training samples and the outputs actually produced by the model when fed those samples. In our case, that would be the difference between the predicted temperatures t_p output by our model and the actual measurements: t_p - t_c.

We need to make sure the loss function makes the loss positive, both when t_p is greater than and when it is less than the true t_c because the goal is for t_p to match t_c. We have a few choices, the most straightforward being |t_p - t_c| and (t_p - t_c)^2. Based on the mathematical expression we choose, we can emphasize or discount certain errors. Conceptually, a loss function is a way of prioritizing which errors to fix from our training samples, so that our parameter updates result in adjustments to the outputs for the highly weighted samples instead of changes to some other samples' output that had a smaller loss.

Both of the example loss functions have a clear minimum at zero and grow monotonically as the predicted value moves further from the true value in either direction. Because the steepness of the growth also monotonically increases away from the minimum, both are *convex*. Since our model is linear, the loss is a function of w, and b is also convex. When our loss function is convex (shaped like a bowl), we could use specialized algorithms to efficiently find the minimum. However, in this chapter, we'll focus on two common, simple loss functions that work well across a variety of problems. While these fundamental approaches provide an excellent foundation, we'll explore more sophisticated and specialized loss functions later when we work with deep neural networks that need to capture more complex relationships in the data.

For our two loss functions |t_p - t_c| and (t_p - t_c)^2, as shown in figure 5.4, we notice that the square of the differences behaves more favorably for optimization. When t_p equals t_c (our ideal scenario), the squared difference function has a smooth, well-defined minimum. The absolute difference function, however, has a sharp point at its minimum, which can make optimization more challenging. We'll explore the mathematical reasons for this in more detail when we discuss gradients, but for now, we'll stick with the squared differences for its more desirable optimization properties.

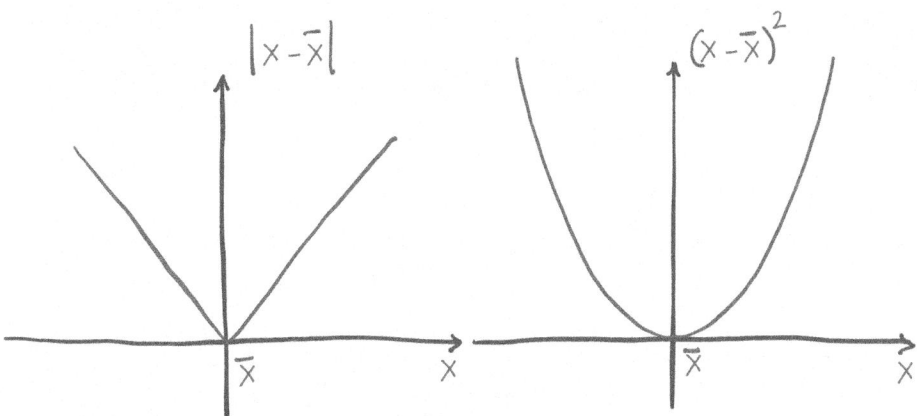

Figure 5.4 Absolute difference vs. difference squared

It's worth noting that the square difference also penalizes wildly wrong results more than the absolute difference does. Often, having more slightly wrong results is better than having a few wildly wrong ones, and the squared difference helps prioritize those as desired.

5.3.1 *From problem back to PyTorch*

We've figured out the model and the loss function—we've already got a good part of the high-level picture in figure 5.2 figured out. Now we need to set the learning process in motion and feed it actual data. Also, enough with math notation; let's switch to PyTorch—after all, we came here for the *fun*.

We've already created our data tensors, so now let's write out the model as a Python function:

```
# In[3]:
def model(t_u, w, b):
    return w * t_u + b
```

We're expecting t_u, w, and b to be the input tensor, weight parameter, and bias parameter, respectively. In our model, the parameters will be PyTorch scalars (aka zero-dimensional tensors), and the product operation will use broadcasting to yield the returned tensors. Time to define our loss:

```
# In[4]:
def loss_fn(t_p, t_c):
    squared_diffs = (t_p - t_c)**2
    return squared_diffs.mean()
```

We are building a tensor of differences, taking their square element-wise, and finally producing a scalar loss function by averaging all of the elements in the resulting tensor. It is a *mean square loss*.

We can now initialize the parameters, invoke the model with

```
# In[5]:
w = torch.ones(())
b = torch.zeros(())

t_p = model(t_u, w, b)
t_p

# Out[5]:
tensor([35.7000, 55.9000, 58.2000, 81.9000, 56.3000, 48.9000, 33.9000,
        21.8000, 48.4000, 60.4000, 68.4000])
```

and check the value of the loss:

```
# In[6]:
loss = loss_fn(t_p, t_c)
loss

# Out[6]:
tensor(1763.8846)
```

We implemented the model and the loss in this section. We've finally reached the meat of the example: How do we estimate w and b such that the loss reaches a minimum? We'll first work things out by hand and then learn how to use PyTorch's superpowers to solve the same problem in a more general, off-the-shelf way.

Broadcasting

We mentioned broadcasting in chapter 3, and we promised to look at it more carefully when we need it. In our example, w and b are scalars (zero-dimensional tensors). We use them with the input vector t_u like this: w * t_u + b. That means

- Multiply the scalar w by every element of t_u (element wise scaling).
- Add the scalar b to every element of the result (element wise offset).

Usually (especially in early versions of PyTorch), we can only use element-wise binary operations such as addition, subtraction, multiplication, and division for arguments of the same shape. The entries in matching positions in each of the tensors will be used to calculate the corresponding entry in the result tensor. Broadcasting, which is popular in NumPy and adapted by PyTorch, relaxes this assumption for most binary operations. It uses the following rules to match tensor elements:

- For each index dimension, counted from the back, if one of the operands is size 1 in that dimension, PyTorch will use the single entry along this dimension with each of the entries in the other tensor along this dimension.
- If both sizes are greater than 1, they must be the same, and element-wise matching is used.
- If one of the tensors has more index dimensions than the other, the entirety of the other tensor will be used for each entry along these dimensions.

This process sounds complicated (and it can be error-prone if we don't pay close attention, which is why we have named the tensor dimensions as shown in section 3.5), but usually, we can either write down the tensor dimensions to see what happens or picture what happens by using space dimensions to show the broadcasting, as in the following figure. Of course, this would all be theory if we didn't have some code examples:

```
# In[7]:
x = torch.ones(())
y = torch.ones(3,1)
z = torch.ones(1,3)
a = torch.ones(2, 1, 1)
print(f"shapes: x: {x.shape}, y: {y.shape}")
print(f"        z: {z.shape}, a: {a.shape}")
print("x * y:", (x * y).shape)
print("y * z:", (y * z).shape)
print("y * z * a:", (y * z * a).shape)

# Out[7]:

shapes: x: torch.Size([]), y: torch.Size([3, 1])
        z: torch.Size([1, 3]), a: torch.Size([2, 1, 1])
x * y: torch.Size([3, 1])
y * z: torch.Size([3, 3])
y * z * a: torch.Size([2, 3, 3])
```

(continued)

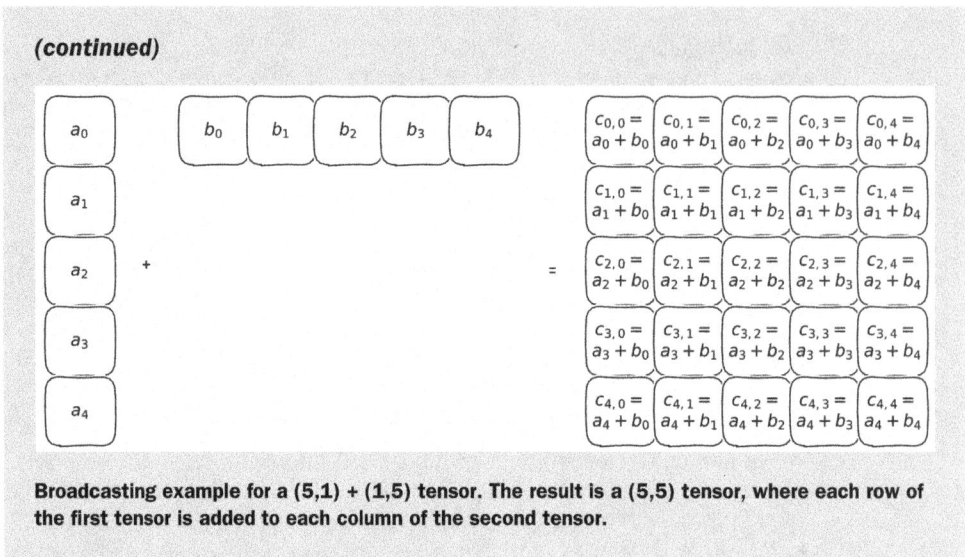

Broadcasting example for a (5,1) + (1,5) tensor. The result is a (5,5) tensor, where each row of the first tensor is added to each column of the second tensor.

5.4 Down along the gradient

We'll optimize the loss function with respect to the parameters using the *gradient descent* algorithm. In this section, we'll build our intuition for how gradient descent works from first principles, which will help us a lot in the future. Gradient descent is actually a very simple idea, and it scales up surprisingly well to large neural network models with millions of parameters. Let's start with a mental image, which we conveniently sketched out in figure 5.5.

Figure 5.5 Cartoon depiction of the optimization process, where a person with knobs for w and b searches for the direction to turn the knobs that makes the loss decrease.

Suppose we are in front of a mysterious machine with two adjustment knobs labeled w and b. On the machine's display screen, you see a single number: the "loss value" that you need to minimize. Here's how you might approach this task step by step:

1   Try turning knob w slightly right—the loss increases, oh no! Turn it back and try left instead—the loss decreases. Good!
2   Similarly, experiment with knob b to find its direction of decreasing loss.
3   Turn both knobs in their "good directions," watching the number drop rapidly at first.
4   As you get closer to the optimal settings, you notice the loss decreases more slowly with each adjustment.
5   Making a large adjustment suddenly causes the loss to increase again—you've gone too far!
6   You back up and make smaller, more careful adjustments as you get closer to the minimum.
7   Eventually, with patient fine-tuning, you find the perfect combination of knob positions where any movement in any direction would only increase the loss.

This trial-and-error process mirrors how gradient descent works in machine learning: systematically adjusting parameters in the direction that reduces loss, with smaller adjustments as we approach the minimum, until we converge on the optimal solution.

5.4.1 Decreasing loss

Now, let's formalize this intuitive approach into a mathematical process. Gradient descent is not that different from the scenario we just described. The idea is to compute the rate of change of the loss with respect to each parameter and modify each parameter in the direction of decreasing loss. Just like when we were fiddling with the knobs, we can estimate the rate of change by adding a small number to w and b and seeing how much the loss changes in that neighborhood.

The rate of change at point A can also be interpreted as the slope of the line between two points close to A. The slope of a line is just the difference in y-values divided by the difference in x-values. To calculate this numerically for w, we can add and subtract a small number (delta) from w, calculate the loss for both of those values, and divide the sum of that over the distance (2*delta). In formal terms, this equation is known as the central difference approximation:

```
# In[8]:
delta = 0.1

loss_rate_of_change_w = \
    (loss_fn(model(t_u, w + delta, b), t_c) -
    loss_fn(model(t_u, w - delta, b), t_c)) / (2.0 * delta)
```

This is saying that in the neighborhood of the current values of w and b, a unit increase in w leads to some change in the loss. If the change is negative, then we need to increase w to minimize the loss, whereas if the change is positive, we need to decrease w. By how much? Applying a change to w that is proportional to the rate of change of the loss is a good idea, especially when the loss has several parameters: we apply a change to those that exert a significant change on the loss. It is also wise to change the parameters slowly in general, because the rate of change could be dramatically different at a distance from the neighborhood of the current w value. Therefore, we typically should scale the rate of change by a small factor. This scaling factor has many names; the one we use in machine learning is learning_rate:

```
# In[9]:
learning_rate = 1e-2

w = w - learning_rate * loss_rate_of_change_w
```

We can do the same with b:

```
# In[10]:
loss_rate_of_change_b = \
    (loss_fn(model(t_u, w, b + delta), t_c) -
     loss_fn(model(t_u, w, b - delta), t_c)) / (2.0 * delta)

b = b - learning_rate * loss_rate_of_change_b
```

This represents the basic parameter-update step for gradient descent. By reiterating these evaluations (and provided we choose a small enough learning rate), we will converge to an optimal value of the parameters for which the loss computed on the given data is minimal. We'll show the complete iterative process soon, but the way we just computed our rates of change is rather crude and needs an upgrade before we move on. Let's see why and how.

5.4.2 Getting analytical

Computing the rate of change by using repeated evaluations of the model and loss to probe the behavior of the loss function in the neighborhood of w and b doesn't scale well to models with many parameters. Also, it is not always clear how large the neighborhood should be. We chose delta equal to 0.1 in the previous section, but it all depends on the shape of the loss as a function of w and b. If the loss changes too quickly compared to delta, we won't have a very good idea of in which direction the loss is decreasing the most.

What if we could make the neighborhood infinitesimally small, as in figure 5.6? That's exactly what happens when we analytically take the derivative of the loss with respect to a parameter. In a model with two or more parameters like the one we're dealing with, we compute the individual derivatives of the loss with respect to each parameter and put them in a vector of derivatives: the *gradient*.

5.4 Down along the gradient

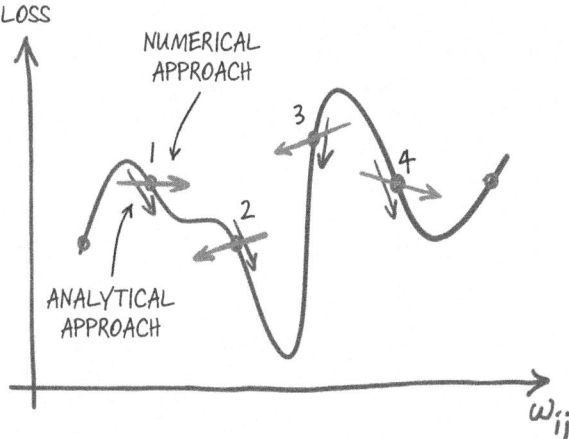

Figure 5.6 Comparing numerical vs. analytical gradient calculation. The numerical approach (arrow through points) estimates the gradient using finite differences between discrete points, while the analytical approach (arrow along the curves) calculates the exact gradient at a specific point.

COMPUTING THE DERIVATIVES

To compute the derivative of the loss with respect to a parameter, we can apply the chain rule and compute the derivative of the loss with respect to its input (which is the output of the model) times the derivative of the model with respect to the parameter:

$$\frac{d\text{loss\_fn}}{dw} = \frac{d\text{loss\_fn}}{dt_p} \times \frac{dt_p}{dw}$$

Recall that our model is a linear function, and our loss is a sum of squares. Let's figure out the expressions for the derivatives. Recalling the expression for the loss

```
# In[4]:
def loss_fn(t_p, t_c):
    squared_diffs = (t_p - t_c)**2
    return squared_diffs.mean()
```

Thus, our loss function can be written mathematically as

$$L = \frac{1}{n}\sum_{i=1}^{n}(t_{p_i} - t_{c_i})^2$$

where n is the number of data points. To find how the loss changes when a prediction changes, we need

$$\frac{\partial L}{\partial t_{p_i}}$$

for each element:

$$\frac{\partial L}{\partial t_{p_i}} = \frac{\partial}{\partial t_{p_i}} \frac{1}{n} \sum_{j=1}^{n} (t_{p_j} - t_{c_j})^2$$

$$= \frac{1}{n} \frac{\partial}{\partial t_{p_i}} (t_{p_i} - t_{c_i})^2$$

$$= \frac{1}{n} \times 2(t_{p_i} - t_{c_i})$$

This gives us exactly what we implement:

```
# In[11]:
def dloss_fn(t_p, t_c):
    dsq_diffs = 2 * (t_p - t_c) / t_p.size(0)
    return dsq_diffs
```

> The division using t_p.size(0) is the number of elements for t_p.

This function returns a tensor where each element represents how much the loss would change if we slightly adjusted the corresponding prediction. The factor of 2 comes from the power rule for differentiation, while the division by t_p.size(0) accounts for the averaging operation in the original loss function.

APPLYING THE DERIVATIVES TO THE MODEL

For the model, recalling that our model is

```
# In[3]:
def model(t_u, w, b):
    return w * t_u + b
```

we get these derivatives:

```
# In[12]:
def dmodel_dw(t_u, w, b):
    return t_u
```

```
# In[13]:
def dmodel_db(t_u, w, b):
    return 1.0
```

DEFINING THE GRADIENT FUNCTION

Putting all of this together, the function returning the gradient of the loss with respect to w and b is

```
# In[14]:
def grad_fn(t_u, t_c, t_p, w, b):
    dloss_dtp = dloss_fn(t_p, t_c)
    dloss_dw = dloss_dtp * dmodel_dw(t_u, w, b)
    dloss_db = dloss_dtp * dmodel_db(t_u, w, b)
    return torch.stack([dloss_dw.sum(), dloss_db.sum()])
```

The summation in the last line is the reverse of the broadcasting we implicitly do when applying the parameters to an entire vector of inputs in the model. We use torch.stack to combine the weights and bias into one tensor because the parameters are passed in as one tensor, so the resulting gradients should also be a single tensor.

The same idea expressed in mathematical notation is shown in figure 5.7. Again, we're averaging (i.e., summing and dividing by a constant) over all the data points to get a single scalar quantity for each partial derivative of the loss.

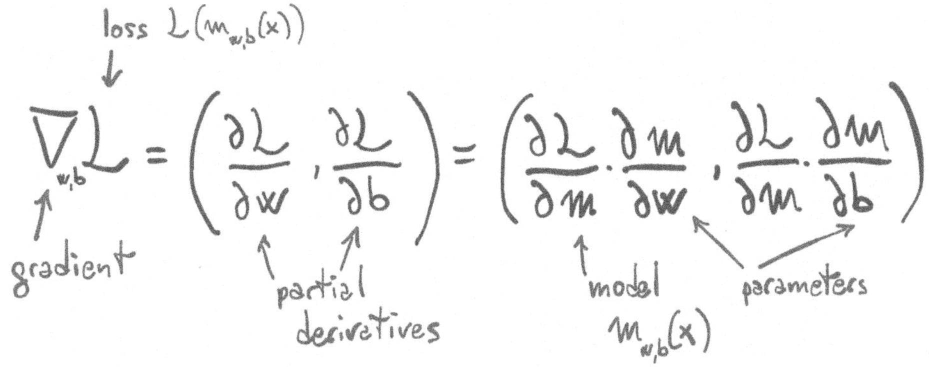

$$\text{loss } L(m_{w,b}(x))$$

$$\nabla_{w,b} L = \left(\frac{\partial L}{\partial w}, \frac{\partial L}{\partial b} \right) = \left(\frac{\partial L}{\partial m} \cdot \frac{\partial m}{\partial w}, \frac{\partial L}{\partial m} \cdot \frac{\partial m}{\partial b} \right)$$

gradient — partial derivatives — model $m_{w,b}(x)$ — parameters

Figure 5.7 The derivative of the loss function with respect to the weights

5.4.3 Iterating to fit the model

We now have everything in place to optimize our parameters. Starting from a tentative value for a parameter, we can iteratively apply updates to it for a fixed number of iterations or until w and b stop changing. There are several stopping criteria; for now, we'll stick to a fixed number of iterations.

THE TRAINING LOOP

Since we're at it, let's introduce another piece of terminology. In deep learning, an *epoch* refers to a complete pass through the entire training dataset, where all samples have been used once to update the model parameters. An epoch is different from a single *training iteration* (or step), which typically involves processing one batch of data through forward and backward passes. With our current implementation, we're using the entire dataset in each iteration, so one iteration equals one epoch. In larger datasets, we'll typically split data into batches, requiring multiple iterations to complete a single epoch.

The complete training loop looks like this (code/p1ch5/1_parameter_estimation .ipynb):

```
# In[15]:
def training_loop(n_epochs, learning_rate, params, t_u, t_c):
    for epoch in range(1, n_epochs + 1):
        w, b = params
```

```
    t_p = model(t_u, w, b)              ◁─── Forward pass
    loss = loss_fn(t_p, t_c)
    grad = grad_fn(t_u, t_c, t_p, w, b)  ◁─── Backward pass

    params = params - learning_rate * grad

    print('Epoch %d, Loss %f' % (epoch, float(loss)))   ◁─┐ This logging line
                                                          │ can be very
return params                                             │ verbose.
```

The actual logging logic used for the output in this text is more complicated (see cell 15 in the same notebook: http://mng.bz/pBB8), but the differences are unimportant for understanding the core concepts in this chapter.

Now, let's invoke our training loop:

```
# In[17]:
training_loop(
    n_epochs = 100,
    learning_rate = 1e-2,
    params = torch.tensor([1.0, 0.0]),
    t_u = t_u,
    t_c = t_c)

# Out[17]:
Epoch 1, Loss 1763.884644
    Params: tensor([-44.1730,  -0.8260])
    Grad:   tensor([4517.2969,  82.6000])
Epoch 2, Loss 5802485.500000
    Params: tensor([2568.4014,  45.1637])
    Grad:   tensor([-261257.4219,  -4598.9712])
Epoch 3, Loss 19408035840.000000
    Params: tensor([-148527.7344,  -2616.3933])
    Grad:   tensor([15109614.0000,  266155.7188])
...
Epoch 10, Loss 90901154706620645225508955521810432.000000
    Params: tensor([3.2144e+17, 5.6621e+15])
    Grad:   tensor([-3.2700e+19, -5.7600e+17])
Epoch 11, Loss inf
    Params: tensor([-1.8590e+19, -3.2746e+17])
    Grad:   tensor([1.8912e+21, 3.3313e+19])

tensor([-1.8590e+19, -3.2746e+17])
```

OVERTRAINING

Wait, what happened? Our training process literally blew up, leading to losses becoming inf. This is a clear sign that params is receiving updates that are too large, and the values start oscillating back and forth as each update overshoots and the next overcorrects even more. The optimization process is unstable: it *diverges* instead of converging to a minimum. We want to see smaller and smaller updates to params, not larger, as shown in figure 5.8.

5.4 Down along the gradient

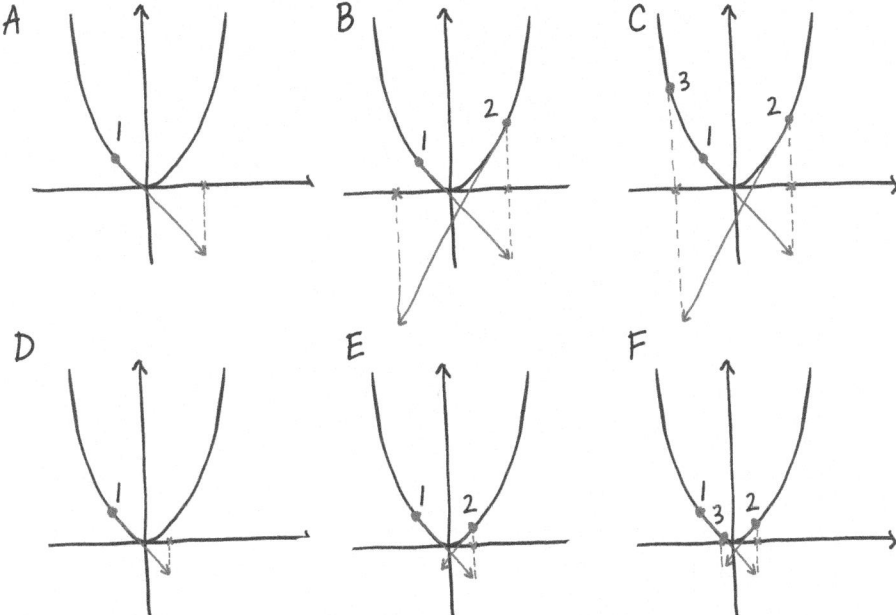

Figure 5.8 Top: Diverging optimization on a convex function (parabola-like) due to large steps. Bottom: Converging optimization with small steps is the behavior we want to achieve.

How can we limit the magnitude of learning_rate * grad? Well, that looks easy. We could simply choose a smaller learning_rate, and indeed, the learning rate is one of the things we typically change when training does not go as well as we would like.

> **NOTE** The fancy name for this is *hyperparameter tuning*. *Hyperparameter* refers to the fact that we are training the model's parameters, but the hyperparameters control how this training goes. Typically, these are more or less set manually. In particular, they cannot be part of the same optimization.

We usually change learning rates by orders of magnitude, so we might try with 1e-3 or 1e-4, which would decrease the magnitude of the updates by orders of magnitude. Let's go with 1e-4 and see how it works out:

```
# In[18]:
training_loop(
    n_epochs = 100,
    learning_rate = 1e-4,
    params = torch.tensor([1.0, 0.0]),
    t_u = t_u,
    t_c = t_c)

# Out[18]:
Epoch 1, Loss 1763.884644
    Params: tensor([ 0.5483, -0.0083])
    Grad:   tensor([4517.2969,   82.6000])
```

```
Epoch 2, Loss 323.090546
    Params: tensor([ 0.3623, -0.0118])
    Grad:   tensor([1859.5493,    35.7843])
Epoch 3, Loss 78.929634
    Params: tensor([ 0.2858, -0.0135])
    Grad:   tensor([765.4667,   16.5122])
...
Epoch 10, Loss 29.105242
    Params: tensor([ 0.2324, -0.0166])
    Grad:   tensor([1.4803, 3.0544])
Epoch 11, Loss 29.104168
    Params: tensor([ 0.2323, -0.0169])
    Grad:   tensor([0.5781, 3.0384])
...
Epoch 99, Loss 29.023582
    Params: tensor([ 0.2327, -0.0435])
    Grad:   tensor([-0.0533, 3.0226])
Epoch 100, Loss 29.022669
    Params: tensor([ 0.2327, -0.0438])
    Grad:   tensor([-0.0532, 3.0226])

tensor([ 0.2327, -0.0438])
```

Nice—the behavior is now stable. But there's another problem: the updates to parameters are very small, so the loss decreases very slowly and eventually stalls. We could obviate this problem by making `learning_rate` adaptive—that is, change according to the magnitude of updates. There are optimization schemes that do that, and we'll see one toward the end of this chapter, in section 5.5.2.

However, there's another potential troublemaker in the update term: the gradient itself. Let's go back and look at `grad` at epoch 1 during optimization.

5.4.4 Normalizing inputs

We can see that the first-epoch gradient for the weight is about 50 times larger than the gradient for the bias. Thus, the weight and bias live in differently scaled spaces. If this is the case, a learning rate that's large enough to meaningfully update one will be so large as to be unstable for the other, and a rate that's appropriate for the other won't be large enough to meaningfully change the first. So, we're not going to be able to update our parameters unless we change something about our formulation of the problem. We could have individual learning rates for each parameter, but for models with many parameters, this method would be too much to bother with; it's babysitting of the kind we don't like.

There's a simpler way to keep things in check: changing the inputs so that the gradients aren't quite so different. We can make sure the range of the input doesn't get too far from the range of –1.0 to 1.0, roughly speaking. In our case, we can achieve something close enough to that by simply multiplying t_u by 0.1:

```
# In[19]:
t_un = 0.1 * t_u
```

Here, we denote the normalized version of t_u by appending an n to the variable name. At this point, we can run the training loop on our normalized input:

```
# In[20]:
training_loop(
    n_epochs = 100,
    learning_rate = 1e-2,
    params = torch.tensor([1.0, 0.0]),
    t_u = t_un,
    t_c = t_c)
```
⬅ We updated t_u to our new, rescaled t_un.

```
# Out[20]:
Epoch 1, Loss 80.364342
    Params: tensor([1.7761, 0.1064])
    Grad:   tensor([-77.6140, -10.6400])
Epoch 2, Loss 37.574917
    Params: tensor([2.0848, 0.1303])
    Grad:   tensor([-30.8623,  -2.3864])
Epoch 3, Loss 30.871077
    Params: tensor([2.2094, 0.1217])
    Grad:   tensor([-12.4631,   0.8587])
...
Epoch 10, Loss 29.030487
    Params: tensor([ 2.3232, -0.0710])
    Grad:   tensor([-0.5355,  2.9295])
Epoch 11, Loss 28.941875
    Params: tensor([ 2.3284, -0.1003])
    Grad:   tensor([-0.5240,  2.9264])
...
Epoch 99, Loss 22.214186
    Params: tensor([ 2.7508, -2.4910])
    Grad:   tensor([-0.4453,  2.5208])
Epoch 100, Loss 22.148710
    Params: tensor([ 2.7553, -2.5162])
    Grad:   tensor([-0.4446,  2.5165])

tensor([ 2.7553, -2.5162])
```

Even though we set our learning rate back to 1e-2, parameters don't blow up during iterative updates. Let's take a look at the gradients: they're of similar magnitude, so using a single learning_rate for both parameters works just fine. We could probably do a better job of normalization than a simple rescaling by a factor of 10, but since doing so is good enough for our needs, we're going to stick with that for now.

> **NOTE** The normalization here absolutely helps get the network trained, but you could make an argument that it's not strictly needed to optimize the parameters for this particular problem. That's absolutely true! This problem is small enough that there are numerous ways to beat the parameters into submission. However, for larger, more sophisticated problems, normalization is an easy and effective (if not crucial!) tool to improve model convergence.

Let's run the loop for enough iterations to see the changes in params get small. We'll change n_epochs to 5,000.

> **NOTE** The number of epochs is a hyperparameter, and the choice of 5,000 is arbitrary. We could have chosen 10,000 or 1,000, or we could have used a stopping criterion based on the magnitude of the gradient.

```
# In[21]:
params = training_loop(
    n_epochs = 5000,
    learning_rate = 1e-2,
    params = torch.tensor([1.0, 0.0]),
    t_u = t_un,
    t_c = t_c,
    print_params = False)

params

# Out[21]:
Epoch 1, Loss 80.364342
Epoch 2, Loss 37.574917
Epoch 3, Loss 30.871077
...
Epoch 10, Loss 29.030487
Epoch 11, Loss 28.941875
...
Epoch 99, Loss 22.214186
Epoch 100, Loss 22.148710
...
Epoch 4000, Loss 2.927680
Epoch 5000, Loss 2.927648

tensor([  5.3671, -17.3012])
```

Good, our loss decreases while we change parameters along the direction of gradient descent. It doesn't go exactly to zero; this result could mean that there aren't enough iterations to converge to zero or that the data points don't sit exactly on a line. As we anticipated, our measurements were not perfectly accurate, or there was noise involved in the reading.

But look: the values for w and b look an awful lot like the numbers we need to use to convert Fahrenheit to Celsius. We had our model learn the relationship C=w*unknown + b, and from science, we know the exact formula to be C = (F - 32) * 5/9, which simplifies to C = (5/9) * F - (32 * 5 / 9) to give us exact values w=.55556 and b=-17.7778. Multiply w by 10 to account for our earlier normalization when we multiplied our inputs by 0.1 and our model parameters are pretty close to the expected w and b. Our fancy thermometer was showing temperatures in Fahrenheit the whole time. No big discovery, except that our gradient descent optimization process works!

5.4.5 Visualizing (again)

Let's revisit something we did right at the start: visualizing our data. Seriously, this is the first thing anyone doing data science should do. Always try to understand your data and plot it out:

```
# In[22]:
%matplotlib inline
from matplotlib import pyplot as plt

t_p = model(t_un, *params)

fig = plt.figure(dpi=600)
plt.xlabel("Temperature (°Fahrenheit)")
plt.ylabel("Temperature (°Celsius)")
plt.plot(t_u.numpy(), t_p.detach().numpy())
plt.plot(t_u.numpy(), t_c.numpy(), 'o')
```

> Remember that we're training on the normalized unknown units. We also use argument unpacking.

> But we're plotting the raw unknown values.

We are using a Python trick called argument unpacking here: *params means to pass the elements of params as individual arguments. In Python, this is usually done with lists or tuples, but we can also use argument unpacking with PyTorch tensors, which are split along the leading dimension. So here, model(t_un, *params) is equivalent to model(t_un, params[0], params[1]).

This code produces figure 5.9. Our linear model is a good model for the data, it seems. It also seems our measurements are somewhat erratic. We should either call our optometrist for a new pair of glasses or think about returning our fancy thermometer.

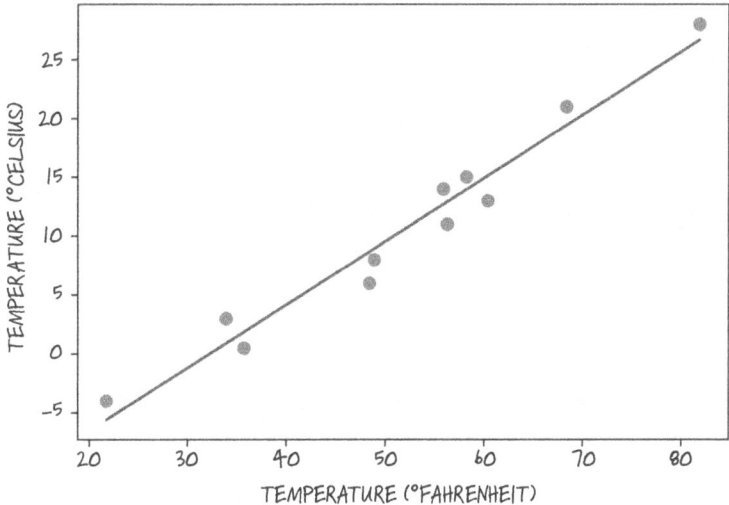

Figure 5.9 The plot of our linear-fit model (solid line) vs. our input data (circles)

5.5 PyTorch's autograd: Backpropagating all things

In our little adventure, we just saw a simple example of backpropagation: we computed the gradient of a composition of functions—the model and the loss—with respect to their innermost parameters (w and b) by propagating derivatives backward using the *chain rule*. The basic requirement here is that all functions we're dealing with can be differentiated analytically. If this is the case, we can compute the gradient—what we earlier called "the rate of change of the loss"—with respect to the parameters in one sweep.

Even if we have a complicated model with millions of parameters, as long as our model is differentiable, computing the gradient of the loss with respect to the parameters amounts to writing the analytical expression for the derivatives and evaluating them *once*. Granted, writing the analytical expression for the derivatives of a very deep composition of linear and nonlinear functions is not a lot of fun (or maybe it is; we won't judge how you spend your weekend!). It isn't particularly quick, either.

5.5.1 Computing the gradient automatically

This is when PyTorch tensors come to the rescue, with a PyTorch component called *autograd*. Chapter 3 presented a comprehensive overview of what tensors are and what functions we can call on them. We left out one very interesting aspect, however: PyTorch tensors can remember where they come from, in terms of the operations and parent tensors that originated them, and they can automatically provide the chain of derivatives of such operations with respect to their inputs. Consequently, we won't need to derive our model by hand (Bummer! What are we going to do on Saturdays now?) given a forward expression, because, no matter how nested, PyTorch will automatically provide the gradient of that expression with respect to its input parameters.

APPLYING AUTOGRAD

At this point, the best way to proceed is to rewrite our thermometer calibration code, this time using autograd, and see what happens. First, we recall our model and loss function (see code/p1ch5/2_autograd.ipynb).

Listing 5.1 Defining the model and loss function

```
# In[3]:
def model(t_u, w, b):
    return w * t_u + b

# In[4]:
def loss_fn(t_p, t_c):
    squared_diffs = (t_p - t_c)**2
    return squared_diffs.mean()
```

Let's again initialize a parameters tensor, containing our w and b:

```
# In[5]:
params = torch.tensor([1.0, 0.0], requires_grad=True)
```

5.5 PyTorch's autograd: Backpropagating all things

USING THE GRAD ATTRIBUTE

Notice the `requires_grad=True` argument to the tensor constructor? That argument is telling PyTorch to track the entire family tree of tensors resulting from operations on `params`. In other words, any tensor that will have `params` as an ancestor will have access to the chain of functions that were called to get from `params` to that tensor. In case these functions are differentiable (and most PyTorch tensor operations will be), the value of the derivative will be automatically populated as a `grad` attribute of the `params` tensor.

In general, all PyTorch tensors have an attribute named `grad`. Normally, it's `None`:

```
# In[6]:
params.grad is None

# Out[6]:
True
```

All we have to do to populate it is to start with a tensor with `requires_grad` set to `True`, then call the model and compute the loss, and finally call `backward` on the `loss` tensor:

```
# In[7]:
loss = loss_fn(model(t_u, *params), t_c)
loss.backward()

params.grad

# Out[7]:
tensor([4517.2969,   82.6000])
```

At this point, the `grad` attribute of `params` contains the derivatives of the loss with respect to each element of `params`.

When we compute our `loss` while the parameters `w` and `b` require gradients, in addition to performing the actual computation, PyTorch creates what's called a *computation graph*. As figure 5.10 illustrates, this autograd computation graph records operations (shown as black circles; top row) as nodes. When we call `loss.backward()`, PyTorch traverses this graph in the reverse direction to compute the gradients, as shown by the arrows in the bottom row of the figure.

ACCUMULATING GRAD FUNCTIONS

We could have any number of tensors with `requires_grad` set to `True` and any composition of functions. In this case, PyTorch would compute the derivatives of the loss throughout the chain of functions (the computation graph) and accumulate their values in the `grad` attribute of those tensors (the leaf nodes of the graph).

Alert! *Big gotcha ahead.* This is something PyTorch newcomers—and a lot of more experienced folks, too—trip up on regularly. We just wrote *accumulate*, not *store*.

> **WARNING** Calling backward will lead derivatives to *accumulate* at leaf nodes. We need to *zero the gradient explicitly* after using it for parameter updates.

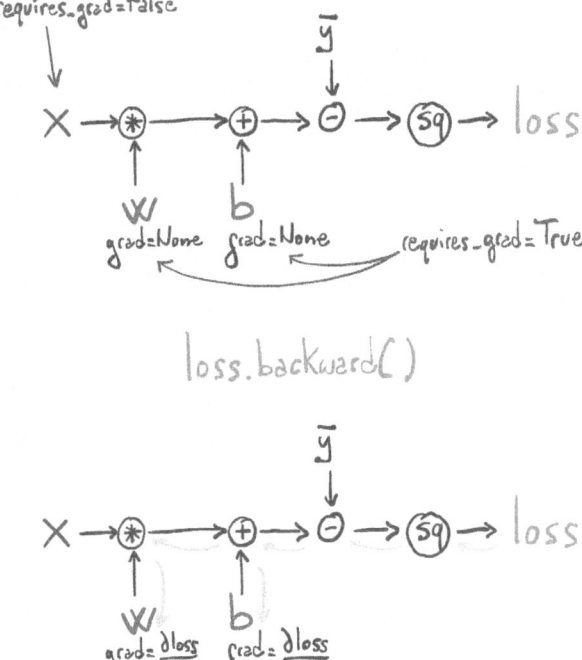

Figure 5.10 The forward graph and backward graph of the model as computed with autograd.

Let's repeat together: calling backward will lead derivatives to *accumulate* at leaf nodes. So, if backward was called earlier, the loss is evaluated again, backward is called again (as in any training loop), and the gradient at each leaf is accumulated (i.e., summed) on top of the one computed at the previous iteration, which leads to an incorrect value for the gradient.

To prevent this problem from occurring, we need to *zero the gradient explicitly* at each iteration. We can do this easily using the in-place zero_ method:

```
# In[8]:
if params.grad is not None:
    params.grad.zero_()
```

> **NOTE** You might be curious why zeroing the gradient is a required step instead of zeroing happening automatically whenever we call backward. Doing it this way provides more flexibility and control when working with gradients in complicated models. For example, some models intentionally accumulate gradients over multiple iterations.

Having this reminder drilled into our heads, let's see what our autograd-enabled training code looks like, start to finish:

```
# In[9]:
def training_loop(n_epochs, learning_rate, params, t_u, t_c):
```

```
    for epoch in range(1, n_epochs + 1):
        if params.grad is not None:          ◁── This could be done at any point
            params.grad.zero_()                   in the loop prior to calling
                                                  loss.backward().
        t_p = model(t_u, *params)
        loss = loss_fn(t_p, t_c)
        loss.backward()
                                                  This is a somewhat
        with torch.no_grad():                ◁──  cumbersome bit of code, but
            params -= learning_rate * params.grad  as we'll see in the next section,
                                                  it's not an issue in practice.
        if epoch % 500 == 0:
            print('Epoch %d, Loss %f' % (epoch, float(loss)))

    return params
```

Note that our code updating params is not quite as straightforward as we might have expected. There are two particularities. First, we are encapsulating the update in a no_grad context using the Python with statement. So, within the with block, the PyTorch autograd mechanism should *look away* — that is, not add edges to the forward graph (in reality, it will track that something changed params using an in-place operation). In fact, when we are executing this bit of code, the forward graph that PyTorch records is consumed when we call backward, leaving us with the params leaf node. But now we want to change this leaf node before we start building a fresh forward graph on top of it.

Second, we update params in place. We keep the same params tensor around but subtract our update from it. When using autograd, we usually avoid in-place updates because PyTorch's autograd engine might need the values we would be modifying for the backward pass. Here, however, we are operating within the torch.no_grad() context where autograd tracking is disabled for the parameter update, so it's safe to modify the params tensor in place.

Let's see if it works:

```
# In[10]:
training_loop(
    n_epochs = 5000,
    learning_rate = 1e-2,
    params = torch.tensor([1.0, 0.0], requires_grad=True),
    t_u = t_un,
    t_c = t_c)

# Out[10]:
Epoch 500, Loss 7.860116
Epoch 1000, Loss 3.828538
Epoch 1500, Loss 3.092191
Epoch 2000, Loss 2.957697
Epoch 2500, Loss 2.933134
Epoch 3000, Loss 2.928648
Epoch 3500, Loss 2.927830
```

Adding requires_grad=True is key.

Again, we're using the normalized t_un instead of t_u.

```
Epoch 4000, Loss 2.927679
Epoch 4500, Loss 2.927652
Epoch 5000, Loss 2.927647

tensor([  5.3671, -17.3012], requires_grad=True)
```

The result is the same as we got previously. Good for us! It means that while we are *capable* of computing derivatives by hand, we no longer need to.

5.5.2 Optimizers à la carte

In the example code, we used *vanilla* gradient descent for optimization, which worked fine for our simple case. Needless to say, several optimization strategies and tricks can assist convergence, especially when models get complicated.

We'll dive deeper into this topic in later chapters, but now is the right time to introduce the way PyTorch abstracts the optimization strategy away from user code—that is, the training loop we've examined. This process saves us from the error-prone, boilerplate busywork of having to update each and every parameter to our model ourselves. The torch module has an optim submodule where we can find classes implementing different optimization algorithms. Here's an abridged list (code/p1ch5/3_optimizers.ipynb):

```
# In[5]:
import torch.optim as optim

dir(optim)

# Out[5]:
['ASGD',
 'Adadelta',
 'Adagrad',
 'Adam',
 'AdamW',
 'Adamax',
 'LBFGS',
 'NAdam',
 'Optimizer',
 'RAdam',
 'RMSprop',
 'Rprop',
 'SGD',
 'SparseAdam',
 ...
]
```

Every optimizer constructor takes a list of parameters (aka PyTorch tensors, typically with requires_grad set to True) as the first input. All parameters passed to the optimizer are retained inside the optimizer object so the optimizer can update the parameters' values and access their grad attribute, as represented in figure 5.11.

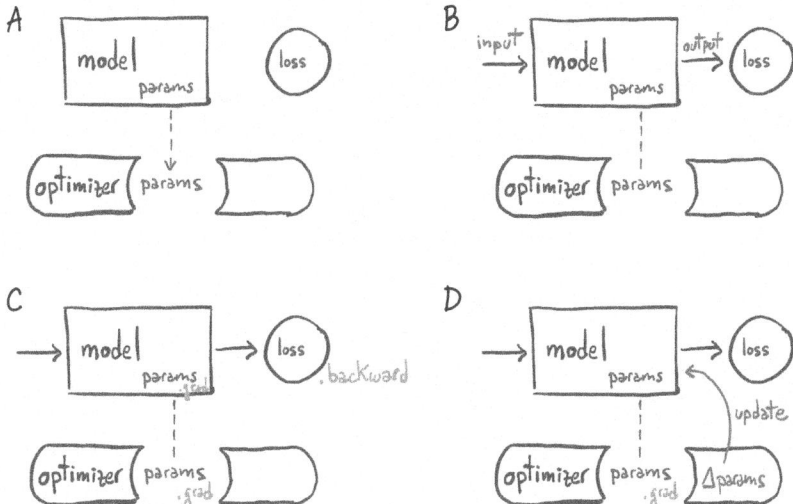

Figure 5.11 (A) Conceptual representation of how an optimizer holds a reference to parameters. (B) After a loss is computed from inputs, (C) a call to .backward leads to .grad being populated on parameters. (D) At that point, the optimizer can access .grad and compute the parameter updates.

Each optimizer exposes two methods: zero_grad and step. zero_grad zeroes the grad attribute of all the parameters passed to the optimizer upon construction. step updates the value of those parameters according to the optimization strategy implemented by the specific optimizer.

USING A GRADIENT DESCENT OPTIMIZER

Let's create params and instantiate a gradient descent optimizer:

```
# In[6]:
params = torch.tensor([1.0, 0.0], requires_grad=True)
learning_rate = 1e-5
optimizer = optim.SGD([params], lr=learning_rate)
```

Here SGD stands for *stochastic gradient descent*. Actually, the optimizer itself is exactly a vanilla gradient descent (as long as the momentum argument is set to 0.0, which is the default). The term *stochastic* comes from the fact that the gradient is typically obtained by averaging over a random subset of all input samples, called a *minibatch*. However, the optimizer does not know if the loss was evaluated on all the samples (vanilla) or a random subset of them (stochastic), so the algorithm is literally the same in the two cases.

Anyway, let's take our fancy new optimizer for a spin:

```
# In[7]:
t_p = model(t_u, *params)
loss = loss_fn(t_p, t_c)
loss.backward()
```

```
optimizer.step()

params

# Out[7]:
tensor([ 9.5483e-01, -8.2600e-04], requires_grad=True)
```

The value of params is updated upon calling step without us having to touch it ourselves! What happens is that the optimizer looks into params.grad and updates params, subtracting learning_rate times grad from it, exactly as in our former hand-rolled code.

Ready to stick this code in a training loop? Nope! The big gotcha almost got us—we forgot to zero out the gradients. Had we called the previous code in a loop, gradients would have accumulated in the leaves at every call to backward, and our gradient descent would have been all over the place! Here's the loop-ready code, with the extra zero_grad at the correct spot (right before the call to backward):

```
# In[8]:
params = torch.tensor([1.0, 0.0], requires_grad=True)
learning_rate = 1e-2
optimizer = optim.SGD([params], lr=learning_rate)

t_p = model(t_un, *params)
loss = loss_fn(t_p, t_c)

optimizer.zero_grad()      ◁─┐  As before, the exact placement of
loss.backward()              │  this call is somewhat arbitrary. It
optimizer.step()             │  could be earlier in the loop as well.

params

# Out[8]:
tensor([1.7761, 0.1064], requires_grad=True)
```

Perfect! See how the optim module helps us abstract away the specific optimization scheme? All we have to do is provide a list of params to it (that list can be extremely long, as is needed for very deep neural network models), and we can forget about the details.

Let's update our training loop accordingly:

```
# In[9]:
def training_loop(n_epochs, optimizer, params, t_u, t_c):
    for epoch in range(1, n_epochs + 1):
        t_p = model(t_u, *params)
        loss = loss_fn(t_p, t_c)

        optimizer.zero_grad()
        loss.backward()
        optimizer.step()

        if epoch % 500 == 0:
            print('Epoch %d, Loss %f' % (epoch, float(loss)))
```

```
        return params
```

```
# In[10]:
params = torch.tensor([1.0, 0.0], requires_grad=True)
learning_rate = 1e-2
optimizer = optim.SGD([params], lr=learning_rate)

training_loop(
    n_epochs = 5000,
    optimizer = optimizer,
    params = params,
    t_u = t_un,
    t_c = t_c)
```

> It's important that both params are the same object; otherwise, the optimizer won't know what parameters were used by the model.

```
# Out[10]:
Epoch 500, Loss 7.860118
Epoch 1000, Loss 3.828538
Epoch 1500, Loss 3.092191
Epoch 2000, Loss 2.957697
Epoch 2500, Loss 2.933134
Epoch 3000, Loss 2.928648
Epoch 3500, Loss 2.927830
Epoch 4000, Loss 2.927680
Epoch 4500, Loss 2.927651
Epoch 5000, Loss 2.927648

tensor([  5.3671, -17.3012], requires_grad=True)
```

Again, we get the same result as before. Great! This is further confirmation that we know how to descend a gradient by hand!

TESTING OTHER OPTIMIZERS

To test more optimizers, all we have to do is instantiate a different optimizer, say Adam, instead of SGD. The rest of the code stays as it is. Pretty handy stuff.

We won't go into much detail about Adam; suffice to say that it is a more sophisticated optimizer in which the learning rate is set adaptively. In addition, it is a lot less sensitive to the scaling of the parameters—so insensitive that we can go back to using the original (nonnormalized) input t_u, and even increase the learning rate to 1e-1, and Adam won't even blink:

```
# In[11]:
params = torch.tensor([1.0, 0.0], requires_grad=True)
learning_rate = 1e-1
optimizer = optim.Adam([params], lr=learning_rate)       ◁─── New optimizer class

training_loop(
    n_epochs = 2000,
    optimizer = optimizer,
    params = params,
    t_u = t_u,         ◁─── We're back to the original t_u as our input
    t_c = t_c)
```

```
# Out[11]:
Epoch 500, Loss 7.612903
Epoch 1000, Loss 3.086700
Epoch 1500, Loss 2.928578
Epoch 2000, Loss 2.927646

tensor([  0.5367, -17.3021], requires_grad=True)
```

The optimizer is not the only flexible part of our training loop. Let's turn our attention to the model. To train a neural network on the same data and the same loss, we only need to change the `model` function. It wouldn't make particular sense in this case, since we know that converting Celsius to Fahrenheit amounts to a linear transformation, but we'll do it anyway in chapter 6. We'll see quite soon that neural networks allow us to remove our arbitrary assumptions about the shape of the function we should be approximating. Even so, we'll see how neural networks manage to be trained even when the underlying processes are highly nonlinear (such as in the case of describing an image with a sentence, as we saw in chapter 2).

We have touched on a lot of the essential concepts that will enable us to train complicated deep learning models while knowing what's going on under the hood: backpropagation to estimate gradients, autograd, and optimizing weights of models using gradient descent or other optimizers. Really, there isn't a lot more. The rest is mostly filling in the blanks, however extensive they are.

Next up, we're going to offer an aside on how to split our samples because that sets up a perfect use case for learning how to better control autograd.

5.5.3 Training, validation, and overfitting

Johannes Kepler taught us one last thing that we haven't discussed so far. Remember? He kept part of the data on the side so that he could validate his models on independent observations. Validating our data is vital, especially when the model we adopt could potentially approximate functions of any shape, as in the case of neural networks. In other words, a highly adaptable model will tend to use its many parameters to make sure the loss is minimal *at* the data points, but we'll have no guarantee that the model behaves well *away from* or *in between* the data points. After all, that's what we're asking the optimizer to do: minimize the loss *at* the data points. Sure enough, if we had independent data points that we didn't use to evaluate our loss or descend along its negative gradient, we would soon find out that evaluating the loss at those independent data points would yield higher-than-expected loss. This phenomenon is called *overfitting*.

The first action we can take to combat overfitting is recognizing that it might happen. To do so, as Kepler figured out in 1600, we must take a few data points out of our dataset (the *validation set*) and only fit our model on the remaining data points (the *training set*), as shown in figure 5.12. Then, while we're fitting the model, we can evaluate the loss once on the training set and once on the validation set. When we're trying to decide whether we've done a good job of fitting our model to the data, we must look at both!

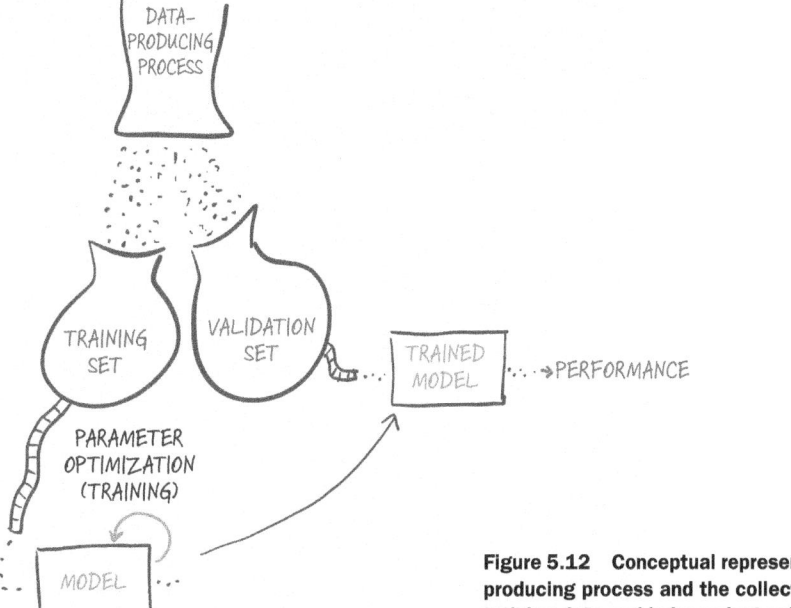

Figure 5.12 Conceptual representation of a data-producing process and the collection and use of training data and independent validation data

EVALUATING THE TRAINING LOSS
The training loss will tell us if our model can fit the training set at all—in other words, if our model has enough *capacity* to process the relevant information in the data. If our mysterious thermometer somehow managed to measure temperatures using a logarithmic scale, our poor linear model would not have had a chance to fit those measurements and provide us with a sensible conversion to Celsius. In that case, our training loss (the loss we were printing in the training loop) would stop decreasing well before approaching zero.

A deep neural network can potentially approximate complicated functions, provided that the number of neurons and, therefore, parameters is high enough. The fewer the number of parameters, the simpler the shape of the function our network will be able to approximate. So, rule 1: if the training loss is not decreasing, chances are the model is too simple for the data—a situation commonly known as *underfitting*. The other possibility is that our data just doesn't contain meaningful information that lets it explain the output: if the nice folks at the shop sell us a barometer (pressure monitor) instead of a thermometer, we will have little chance of predicting temperature in Celsius from pressure data points, even if we use the fanciest neural network architecture.

GENERALIZING TO THE VALIDATION SET
What about the validation set? Well, if the loss evaluated in the validation set doesn't decrease along with the training set, it means our model is improving its fit of the samples it is seeing during training, but it is not *generalizing* to samples outside this precise set. As soon as we evaluate the model at new, previously unseen points, the values of

the loss function are poor. So, rule 2: if the training loss and the validation loss diverge, we're overfitting.

Let's delve into this phenomenon a little, going back to our thermometer example. We could have decided to fit the data with a more complicated function, like a piecewise polynomial or a really large neural network. It could generate a model meandering its way through the data points, as in figure 5.12, just because it pushes the loss very close to zero. Since the behavior of the function away from the data points does not increase the loss, there's nothing to keep the model in check for inputs away from the training data points, as shown in figure 5.13.

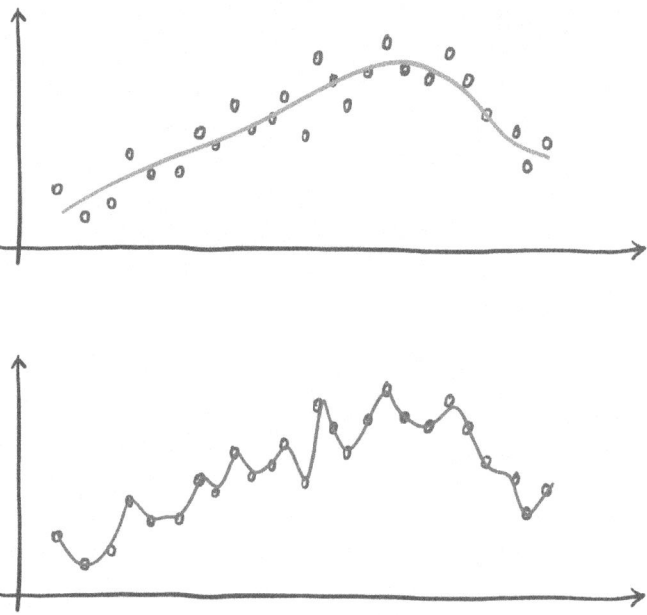

Figure 5.13 Rather extreme example of overfitting

What's the cure, though? Good question. From what we just said, overfitting really looks like a problem of making sure the behavior of the model *in between* data points is sensible for the process we're trying to approximate. First, we should make sure we get enough data for the process. If we collected data from a sinusoidal process by sampling it regularly at a low frequency, we would have a hard time fitting a model to it.

Assuming we have enough data points, we should ensure that the model, which is capable of fitting the training data, behaves smoothly between those points. The model should produce outputs that vary predictably between training data points rather than showing erratic fluctuations. There are several ways to achieve this.

One approach is adding *penalization terms* (also called *regularization*) to the loss function. These terms penalize large parameter values, encouraging the model to find simpler solutions. Common techniques include L1 and L2 regularization, which add terms proportional to either the absolute value or the square of weights, making it "cheaper" for the model to use smaller weights that typically result in smoother behavior.

Another approach is adding noise to the input samples, artificially creating new data points between training samples and forcing the model to generalize better. This technique, sometimes called *data augmentation*, helps prevent the model from memorizing exact training points.

But the best favor we can do for ourselves, at least as a first move, is to make our model simpler. From an intuitive standpoint, a simpler model may not fit the training data as perfectly as a more complicated model would, but it will likely behave more consistently between data points, resulting in better generalization to unseen examples.

We've got some nice tradeoffs here. On the one hand, we need the model to have enough capacity for it to fit the training set. On the other hand, we need the model to avoid overfitting. Therefore, to choose the right size for a neural network model in terms of parameters, the process is based on two steps: increase the size until it fits and then scale it down until it stops overfitting. We will cover this process in more detail later in the book, in chapters 8 and 14.

For now, let's get back to our example and see how we can split the data into a training set and a validation set. We'll do it by shuffling t_u and t_c the same way and then splitting the resulting shuffled tensors into two parts.

SPLITTING A DATASET

Shuffling the elements of a tensor amounts to finding a permutation of its indices. The randperm function does exactly this:

```
# In[12]:
n_samples = t_u.shape[0]
n_val = int(0.2 * n_samples)

shuffled_indices = torch.randperm(n_samples)

train_indices = shuffled_indices[:-n_val]
val_indices = shuffled_indices[-n_val:]

train_indices, val_indices
```

Since these indices are random, don't be surprised if your values end up different from here on out.

```
# Out[12]:
(tensor([9, 6, 5, 8, 4, 7, 0, 1, 3]), tensor([ 2, 10]))
```

We just got index tensors that we can use to build training and validation sets starting from the data tensors:

```
# In[13]:
train_t_u = t_u[train_indices]
train_t_c = t_c[train_indices]

val_t_u = t_u[val_indices]
val_t_c = t_c[val_indices]
```

```
train_t_un = 0.1 * train_t_u
val_t_un = 0.1 * val_t_u
```

Our training loop doesn't really change. We just want to evaluate the validation loss at every epoch to have a chance to recognize whether we're overfitting:

```
# In[14]:
def training_loop(n_epochs, optimizer, params, train_t_u, val_t_u,
                  train_t_c, val_t_c):
    for epoch in range(1, n_epochs + 1):
        train_t_p = model(train_t_u, *params)
        train_loss = loss_fn(train_t_p, train_t_c)

        val_t_p = model(val_t_u, *params)
        val_loss = loss_fn(val_t_p, val_t_c)

        optimizer.zero_grad()
        train_loss.backward()
        optimizer.step()

        if epoch <= 3 or epoch % 500 == 0:
            print(f"Epoch {epoch}, Training loss {train_loss.item():.4f},"
                  f" Validation loss {val_loss.item():.4f}")

    return params
```

> These two pairs of lines are the same except for the train_* vs. val_* inputs.

> There is no val_loss.backward() here because we don't want to train the model on the validation data.

```
# In[15]:
params = torch.tensor([1.0, 0.0], requires_grad=True)
learning_rate = 1e-2
optimizer = optim.SGD([params], lr=learning_rate)

training_loop(
    n_epochs = 3000,
    optimizer = optimizer,
    params = params,
    train_t_u = train_t_un,
    val_t_u = val_t_un,
    train_t_c = train_t_c,
    val_t_c = val_t_c)
```

> Since we're using SGD again, we're back to using normalized inputs.

```
# Out[15]:
Epoch 1, Training loss 66.5811, Validation loss 142.3890
Epoch 2, Training loss 38.8626, Validation loss 64.0434
Epoch 3, Training loss 33.3475, Validation loss 39.4590
Epoch 500, Training loss 7.1454, Validation loss 9.1252
Epoch 1000, Training loss 3.5940, Validation loss 5.3110
Epoch 1500, Training loss 3.0942, Validation loss 4.1611
Epoch 2000, Training loss 3.0238, Validation loss 3.7693
Epoch 2500, Training loss 3.0139, Validation loss 3.6279
Epoch 3000, Training loss 3.0125, Validation loss 3.5756

tensor([  5.1964, -16.7512], requires_grad=True)
```

Here, we are not being entirely fair to our model. The validation set is really small, so the validation loss will only be meaningful up to a point. In any case, we note that the validation loss is higher than our training loss, although not by an order of magnitude. We expect a model to perform better on the training set, since the model parameters are being shaped by the training set. Our main goal is to also see both the training loss *and* the validation loss decreasing. While ideally both losses would be roughly the same value, as long as the validation loss stays reasonably close to the training loss, we know that our model is continuing to learn generalized things about our data. In figure 5.14, case C is ideal, while case D is acceptable. In case A, the model isn't learning at all, and in case B, we see overfitting.

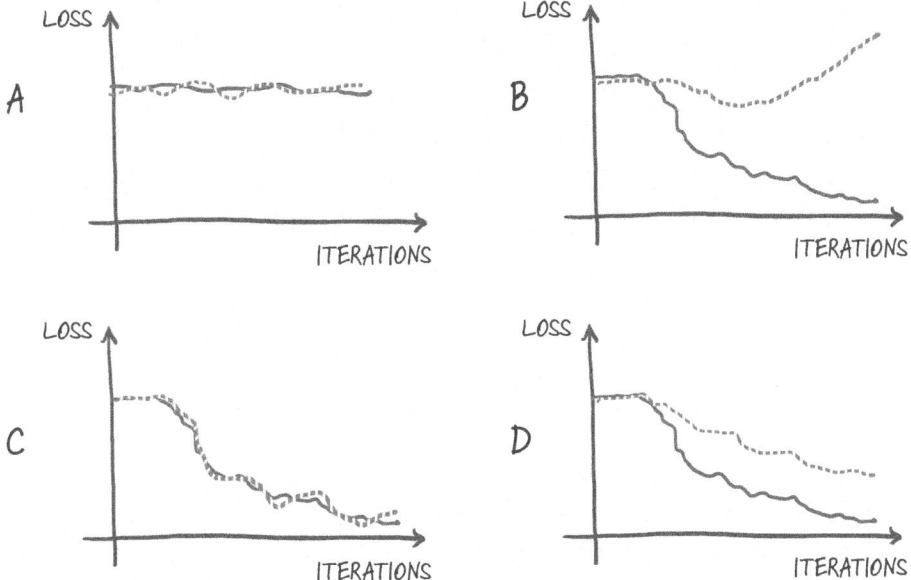

Figure 5.14 Overfitting scenarios when looking at the training (solid line) and validation (dotted line) losses. (A) Training and validation losses do not decrease; the model is not learning because there is no information in the data or the model's capacity is insufficient. (B) Training loss decreases while validation loss increases: overfitting. (C) Training and validation losses decrease exactly in tandem. Performance may be improved further as the model is not at the limit of overfitting. (D) Training and validation losses have different absolute values but similar trends; overfitting is under control.

5.5.4 Training set

We've learned about the distinct roles of different data subsets used throughout the model development process. We should also mention that another crucial piece of data is the *test set*. After the model's parameters have been adjusted using the training set and the hyperparameters optimized with the validation set, the test set is employed to provide an unbiased final evaluation of the model. It is entirely possible to overfit on the validation set, even if we are not using it to explicitly update the model's parameters. This occurs primarily through the repeated use of the validation set to make model design decisions. The test set is only used once the model is fully trained, preserving its role as an independent measure of model performance.

Finally, one significant concern during the training process is data leakage, which occurs when information that should not be available during the training inadvertently influences the model. This can happen if the training data includes future information or if there is an accidental overlap between the training, validation, and test sets. Data leakage can lead to overly optimistic performance estimates and significantly degrade the model's effectiveness in real-life scenarios. Understanding the roles of the training, validation, and test sets, as well as the risks associated with data leakage, equips us with the knowledge to better design and evaluate our machine learning models. With these insights, we can now turn our attention to another crucial aspect of model training: managing the computational graph and memory usage through the use of autograd in PyTorch. Autograd will help us ensure that our models are not only accurate but also efficient in their use of resources.

5.5.5 *Autograd nits and switching it off*

From the previous training loop, we can appreciate that we only ever call backward on train_loss. Therefore, errors will only ever backpropagate based on the training set—the validation set is used to provide an independent evaluation of the accuracy of the model's output on data that wasn't used for training.

The curious reader will have an embryo of a question at this point. The model is evaluated twice—once on train_t_u and once on val_t_u—and then backward is called. Won't this confuse autograd? Won't backward be influenced by the values generated during the pass on the validation set?

Luckily for us, this isn't the case. The first line in the training loop evaluates model on train_t_u to produce train_t_p. Then train_loss is evaluated from train_t_p. This creates a computation graph that links train_t_u to train_t_p to train_loss. When model is evaluated again on val_t_u, it produces val_t_p and val_loss. In this case, a separate computation graph will be created that links val_t_u to val_t_p to val_loss. Separate tensors have been run through the same functions, model and loss_fn, generating separate computation graphs, as shown in figure 5.15.

The only tensors these two graphs have in common are the parameters. When we call backward on train_loss, we run backward on the first graph. In other words, we accumulate the derivatives of train_loss with respect to the parameters based on the computation generated from train_t_u.

If we (incorrectly) called backward on val_loss as well, we would accumulate the derivatives of val_loss with respect to the parameters *on the same leaf nodes.* Remember the zero_grad thing, whereby gradients are accumulated on top of each other every time we call backward unless we zero out the gradients explicitly? Well, here something very

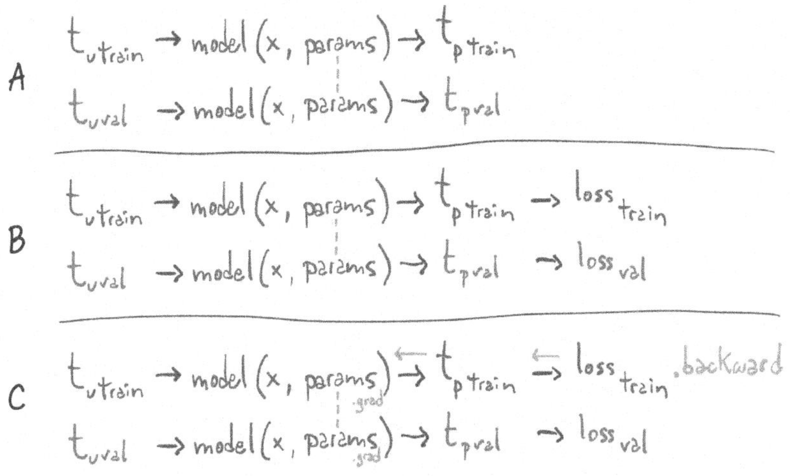

$$
\begin{aligned}
A \quad & t_{u\,train} \rightarrow model(x, params) \rightarrow t_{p\,train} \\
& t_{u\,val} \rightarrow model(x, params) \rightarrow t_{p\,val}
\end{aligned}
$$

$$
\begin{aligned}
B \quad & t_{u\,train} \rightarrow model(x, params) \rightarrow t_{p\,train} \rightarrow loss_{train} \\
& t_{u\,val} \rightarrow model(x, params) \rightarrow t_{p\,val} \rightarrow loss_{val}
\end{aligned}
$$

$$
\begin{aligned}
C \quad & t_{u\,train} \rightarrow model(x, params_{.grad}) \overset{\leftarrow}{\rightarrow} t_{p\,train} \overset{\leftarrow}{\rightarrow} loss_{train}.backward \\
& t_{u\,val} \rightarrow model(x, params_{.grad}) \rightarrow t_{p\,val} \rightarrow loss_{val}
\end{aligned}
$$

Figure 5.15 Diagram showing how gradients propagate through a graph with two losses when .backward is called on one of them.

similar would happen: calling backward on val_loss would lead to gradients accumulating in the params tensor, on top of those generated during the train_loss.backward() call. In this case, we would effectively train our model on the whole dataset (both training and validation) since the gradient would depend on both. Pretty interesting.

There's another element for discussion here. Since we're not ever calling backward on val_loss, why are we building the graph in the first place? We could, in fact, just call model and loss_fn as plain functions, without tracking the computation. However optimized, building the autograd graph comes with additional costs that we could totally forgo during the validation pass, especially when the model has millions of parameters.

To address this issue, PyTorch allows us to switch off autograd when we don't need it, using the torch.no_grad context manager.

> **NOTE** We should not think that using torch.no_grad necessarily implies that the outputs do not require gradients. There are particular circumstances (involving views, as discussed in section 3.8.1) in which requires_grad is not set to False even when created in a no_grad context. It is best to use the detach function if we need to be sure.

A context manager in Python (using the with statement) ensures proper setup and cleanup actions happen automatically when entering and exiting a code block. We won't see any meaningful advantage in terms of speed or memory consumption on our small problem. However, for larger models, the differences can add up. We can make sure this works by checking the value of the requires_grad attribute on the val_loss tensor:

```
# In[16]:
def training_loop(n_epochs, optimizer, params, train_t_u, val_t_u,
                  train_t_c, val_t_c):
    for epoch in range(1, n_epochs + 1):
        train_t_p = model(train_t_u, *params)
        train_loss = loss_fn(train_t_p, train_t_c)

        with torch.no_grad():                              ◁──┐ Context
            val_t_p = model(val_t_u, *params)                  manager here
            val_loss = loss_fn(val_t_p, val_t_c)
            assert val_loss.requires_grad == False         ◁──┐ Checks that our
                                                               output requires_grad
        optimizer.zero_grad()                                  args are forced to
        train_loss.backward()                                  False inside this block
        optimizer.step()
```

Using the related `set_grad_enabled` context, we can also condition the code to run with autograd enabled or disabled, according to a Boolean expression—typically indicating whether we are running in training or inference mode. We could, for instance, define a `calc_forward` function that takes data as input and runs `model` and `loss_fn` with or without autograd according to a Boolean `is_train` argument:

```
# In[17]:
def calc_forward(t_u, t_c, is_train):
    with torch.set_grad_enabled(is_train):
        t_p = model(t_u, *params)
        loss = loss_fn(t_p, t_c)
    return loss
```

5.6 Conclusion

We started this chapter with a big question: How can a machine learn from examples? We spent the rest of the chapter describing the mechanism by which a model can be optimized to fit data. We chose to stick with a simple model to see all the moving parts without unneeded complications.

Now that we've had our fill of appetizers, in chapter 6, we'll finally get to the main course: using a neural network to fit our data. We'll work on solving the same thermometer problem, but with the more powerful tools provided by the `torch.nn` module. We'll adopt the same spirit of using this small problem to illustrate the larger uses of PyTorch. The problem doesn't need a neural network to reach a solution, but it will allow us to develop a simpler understanding of what's required to train a neural network.

5.7 Exercises

1 Redefine the model to be `w2 * t_u ** 2 + w1 * t_u + b`:
   a What parts of the training loop, and so on, need to change to accommodate this redefinition?
   b What parts are agnostic to swapping out the model?

    c Is the resulting loss higher or lower after training?
    d Is the actual result better or worse?

Summary

- Linear models are the simplest reasonable models to use to fit data.
- Convex optimization techniques can be used for linear models, but they do not generalize to neural networks, so we focus on stochastic gradient descent for parameter estimation.
- Deep learning can be used for generic models that are not engineered for solving a specific task but instead can be automatically adapted to specialize on the problem at hand.
- Learning algorithms amount to optimizing parameters of models based on observations. A loss function is a measure of the error in carrying out a task, such as the error between predicted outputs and measured values. The goal is to get the loss function as low as possible.
- The rate of change of the loss function with respect to the model parameters can be used to update the same parameters in the direction of decreasing loss.
- The `optim` module in PyTorch provides a collection of ready-to-use optimizers for updating parameters and minimizing loss functions.
- Optimizers use the autograd feature of PyTorch to compute the gradient for each parameter, depending on how that parameter contributes to the final output. This allows users to rely on the dynamic computation graph during complex forward passes.
- The basic steps of neural network training are forward propagation (forward pass), calculating the loss, backpropagation (backward pass), and updating the parameters (optimizer step).
- After the parameters are updated, it is important to clear the accumulated gradients by calling `optimizer.zero_grad()` to prevent them from being incorrectly incorporated into subsequent updates.
- Context managers like `with torch.no_grad():` can be used to control autograd's behavior so that the autograd graph does not get created.
- Data is often split into separate sets of training samples and validation samples. This lets us evaluate a model on data it was not trained on.
- Overfitting a model happens when the model's performance continues to improve on the training set but degrades on the validation set. Overfitting is usually due to the model not generalizing and, instead, memorizing the desired outputs for the training set.

Using a neural network to fit the data

This chapter covers
- Activation functions: the key difference between neural networks and linear models
- Working with PyTorch's nn module
- Solving a linear-fit problem with a neural network

So far, we've taken a close look at how a linear model can learn and how to make that happen in PyTorch. We've focused on a very simple regression problem that used a linear model with only one input and one output. Such a simple example allowed us to dissect the mechanics of a model that learns, without getting overly distracted by the implementation of the model itself. As we saw in the overview diagram in figure 5.2 (repeated here as figure 6.1), the exact details of a model are not needed to understand the high-level process that trains the model. Backpropagating errors to parameters and then updating those parameters by taking the gradient with respect to the loss are the same, no matter what the underlying model is.

In this chapter, we will make some changes to our model architecture: we're going to implement a full artificial neural network to solve our temperature-conversion problem. We'll continue using our training loop from the last chapter, along with

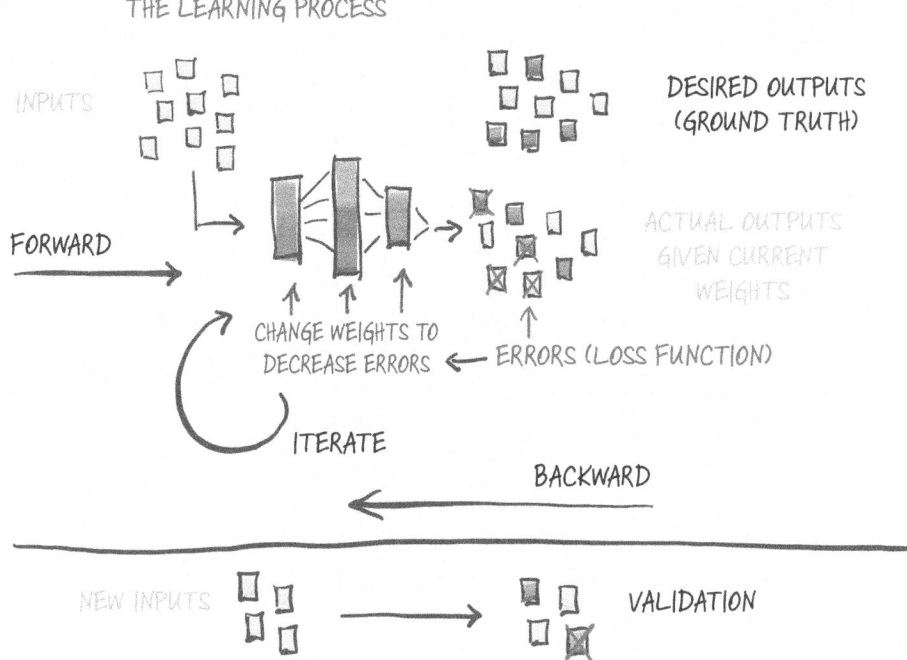

Figure 6.1 Our mental model of the learning process, as implemented in chapter 5

our Fahrenheit-to-Celsius samples split into training and validation sets. We could start to use a quadratic model: rewriting `model` as a quadratic function of its input (e.g., y = a * x**2 + b * x + c). Since such a model would be differentiable, PyTorch would take care of computing gradients, and the training loop would work as usual. That wouldn't be too interesting for us, though, as we would still be fixing the function's shape, which is impossible to know for more complex problems.

In this chapter, we begin to link the foundational work we've put in with the PyTorch features you'll be using day in and day out as you work on your projects. You'll gain an understanding of what's going on underneath the porcelain of the PyTorch API, rather than it just being so much of a black box. Before we get into the implementation of our new model, though, let's cover what we mean by *artificial neural network*.

6.1 Artificial neurons

At the core of deep learning are neural networks, mathematical entities capable of representing complicated functions through a composition of simpler functions. The term *neural network* is obviously suggestive of a link to the way our brain works. Although the initial models were inspired by neuroscience (see F. Rosenblatt, "The Perceptron: A Probabilistic Model for Information Storage and Organization in the

Brain," *Psychological Review* 65(6), 386–408 (1958), https://pubmed.ncbi.nlm.nih.gov/13602029/), modern artificial neural networks bear only a slight resemblance to the mechanisms of neurons in the brain. It seems likely that both artificial and physiological neural networks use vaguely similar mathematical strategies for approximating complicated functions because that family of strategies works very effectively.

> **NOTE** We are going to drop the *artificial* and refer to these constructs as just *neural networks* from here forward.

The basic building block of these complicated functions is the *neuron*, as illustrated in figure 6.2. At its core, it is nothing but a linear transformation of the input—for example, multiplying the input by a number (the *weight*) and adding a constant (the *bias*), followed by the application of a fixed nonlinear function (referred to as the *activation function*).

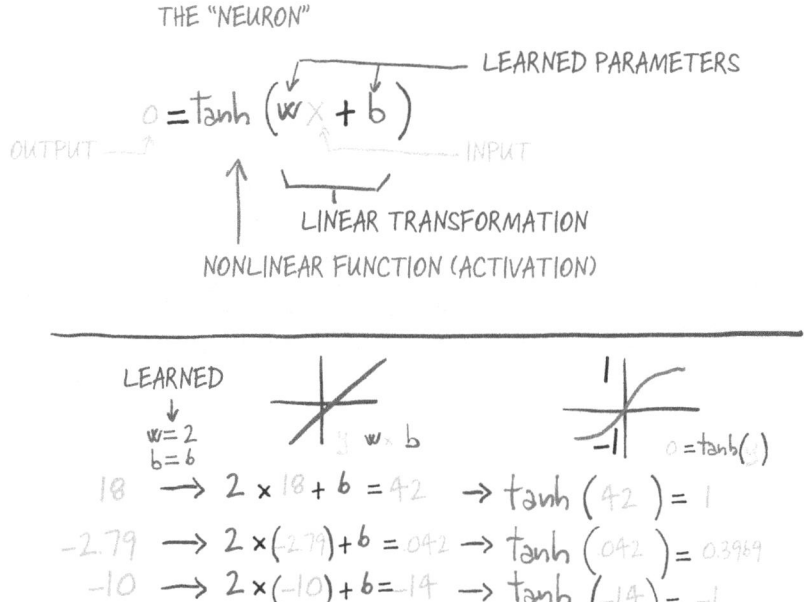

Figure 6.2 An artificial neuron: a linear transformation enclosed in a nonlinear function

Mathematically, we can write this out as $o = f(w \times x + b)$, with x as our input, w our weight or scaling factor, and b as our bias or offset. f is our activation function, set to the hyperbolic tangent, or tanh function here. In general, x and o can be simple scalars or vector-valued (meaning holding many scalar values); similarly, w can be a single scalar or matrix, while b is a scalar or vector (the dimensionality of the inputs and weights must match, however). In the latter case, the previous expression is referred

6.1.1 Composing a multilayer network

A multilayer neural network, as represented in figure 6.3, is made up of a composition of functions like those we just discussed

```
x_1 = f(w_1 * x + b_1)        Layer 1
x_2 = f(w_2 * x_1 + b_2)      Layer 2
...
o = f(w_h * x_n + b_h)        Layer h
```

where the output of a layer of neurons is used as an input for the following layer. Remember that in this context, w_1 is a matrix, and x is a vector! Using a vector allows w_1 to hold an entire *layer* of neurons, not just a single weight. This matrix format allows w_1 to accommodate the weights for an entire layer of neurons, effectively enabling simultaneous calculations through linear algebra.

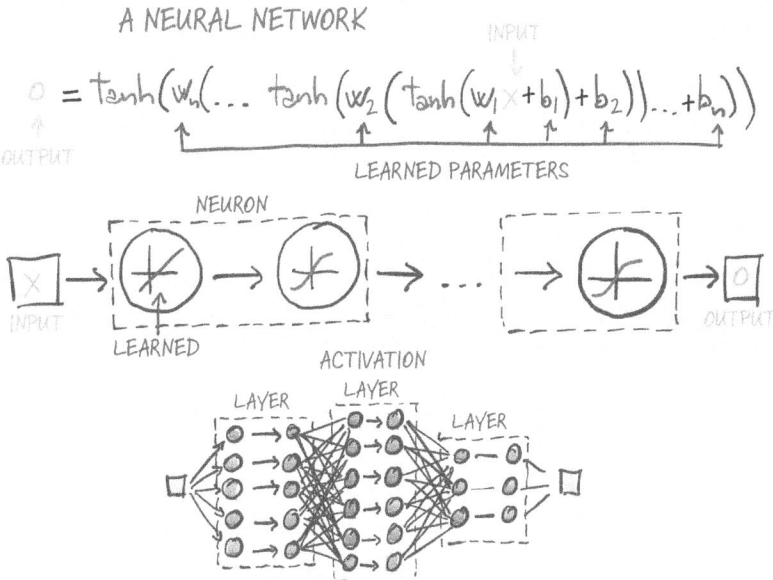

Figure 6.3 A neural network with three layers

6.1.2 Understanding the error function

An important difference between our earlier linear model and what we'll actually be using for deep learning is the shape of the error function. Our linear model and error-squared loss function had a convex error curve with a singular, clearly defined minimum. If we used other methods, we could solve for the parameters, minimizing the error function automatically and definitively. Thus, our parameter updates attempted to *estimate* that singular correct answer as best they could.

Neural networks do not have the same property as a convex error surface, even when using the same error-squared loss function! There's no single right answer for each parameter we're attempting to approximate. Instead, we are trying to get all of the parameters, when acting *in concert*, to produce a useful output. Since that useful output is only going to *approximate* the truth, there will be some level of imperfection. Where and how imperfections manifest is somewhat arbitrary, and by implication, the parameters that control the output (and, hence, the imperfections) are also somewhat arbitrary. The parameters themselves don't have individual interpretability—they only make sense as part of the collective system. Consequently, two neural networks trained on the same data may have different internal parameter values while achieving similar performance.

This nonconvex nature of neural networks is actually a strength when dealing with real-world problems. The real world rarely follows simple linear patterns, requiring more complex models to represent it accurately. To capture this complexity, neural networks need activation functions that introduce nonlinearity, allowing them to model the complex relationships found in real-world data.

6.1.3 Adding nonlinearity with activation functions

As we have seen, the simplest unit in (deep) neural networks is a linear operation (scaling + offset) followed by a nonlinear activation function. We already had our linear operation in our latest model—the linear operation *was* the entire model. The activation function plays two important roles:

- In the inner parts of the model, it allows the output function to have different slopes at different values—something a linear function, by definition, cannot do. By trickily composing these differently sloped parts for many outputs, neural networks can approximate arbitrary functions, as we will see in section 6.1.6.
- At the last layer of the network, it has the role of transforming the outputs of preceding layers into values that make sense for the problem we're trying to solve (e.g., a number for a regression problem or class scores for a classification problem).

NOTE Intuitively, nonlinear activations let us build small "bump" functions by scaling and shifting them. By placing and summing these bumps, a network can approximate any continuous function over an interval. This is the essence of the Universal Approximation Theorem. For a hands-on demo, see chapter 4 of Michael Nielsen's interactive book *Neural Networks and Deep Learning* at http://mng.bz/Mdon.

Let's talk about what the second point means. Pretend that we're assigning a "good doggo" score to images. Pictures of retrievers and spaniels should have a high score, while images of airplanes and garbage trucks should have a low score. Bear pictures should have a lowish score, too, although higher than garbage trucks.

The problem is that we have to define a "high score": we've got the entire range of float32 to work with, which means we can go pretty high. Even if we say, "It's a 10-point scale," there's still the issue that our model is sometimes going to produce a score of 11 out of 10. Remember that under the hood, it's all sums of (w*x+b) matrix multiplications, and those won't naturally limit themselves to a specific range of outputs.

CAPPING THE OUTPUT RANGE

We want to firmly constrain the output of our linear operation to a specific range so that the consumer of this output doesn't have to handle numerical inputs of puppies at 12/10, bears at –10, and garbage trucks at –1,000.

One possibility is to just cap the output values: anything below 0 is set to 0, and anything above 10 is set to 10. That's a simple activation function called torch.nn.Hardtanh (https://mng.bz/JwnP), but note that the default range is –1 to +1).

COMPRESSING THE OUTPUT RANGE

Another family of functions that work well is torch.nn.Sigmoid, which includes 1 / (1 + e ** -x), torch.tanh, and others that we'll take a look at in a moment. These functions have a curve that asymptotically approaches 0 or –1 as x goes to negative infinity, approaches 1 as x increases, and have a mostly constant slope at $x == 0$. Conceptually, functions shaped this way work well because there's an area in the middle of our linear function's output that our neuron (which, again, is just a linear function followed by an activation) will be sensitive to, while everything else gets lumped next to the boundary values. As we can see in figure 6.4, our garbage truck gets a score of –0.97, while bears, foxes, and wolves end up somewhere in the –0.3 to 0.3 range.

This process results in garbage trucks being flagged as "not dogs," our good dog mapping to "clearly a dog," and our bear ending up somewhere in the middle. In code, we can see the exact values:

```
>>> import math
>>> math.tanh(-2.2)
-0.9757431300314515
>>> math.tanh(0.1)
0.099667994624955882
>>> math.tanh(2.5)
0.9866142981514303
```

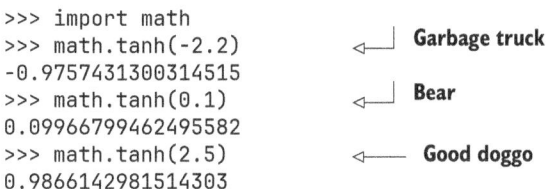

⟵┘ Garbage truck

⟵┘ Bear

⟵── Good doggo

With the bear in the sensitive range, small changes to the bear will result in a noticeable change to the result. For example, we could switch from a grizzly to a polar bear (which has a vaguely more traditionally canine face) and see a jump up the Y-axis as we slide toward the "very much a dog" end of the graph. Conversely, a koala bear would register as less dog-like, and we would see a drop in the activated output. There isn't much we could do to the garbage truck to make it register as

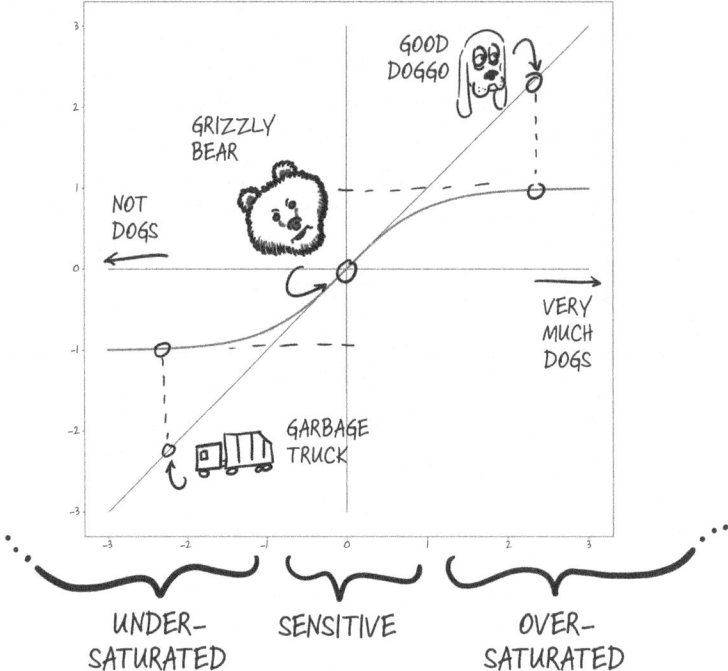

Figure 6.4 Dogs, bears, and garbage trucks mapped to how dog-like they are via the `tanh` activation function

dog-like, though; even with drastic changes, we might only see a shift from –0.97 to –0.8 or so.

6.1.4 More activation functions

There are quite a few activation functions, some of which are shown in figure 6.5. In the first column, we see the smooth functions `Tanh` and `Softplus`, while the second column has "hard" versions of the activation functions to their left: `Hardtanh` and `ReLU`. `ReLU` (for *rectified linear unit*) deserves special note, as it is currently considered one of the best-performing general activation functions; many state-of-the-art results have used it. The `Sigmoid` activation function, also known as the *logistic function*, was widely used in early deep learning work but has since fallen out of common use except where we explicitly want to move to the 0…1 range—for example, when the output should be a probability. Finally, the `LeakyReLU` function modifies the standard `ReLU` to have a small positive slope, rather than being strictly zero for negative inputs. (Typically, this slope is 0.01, but it's shown here with slope 0.1 for clarity).

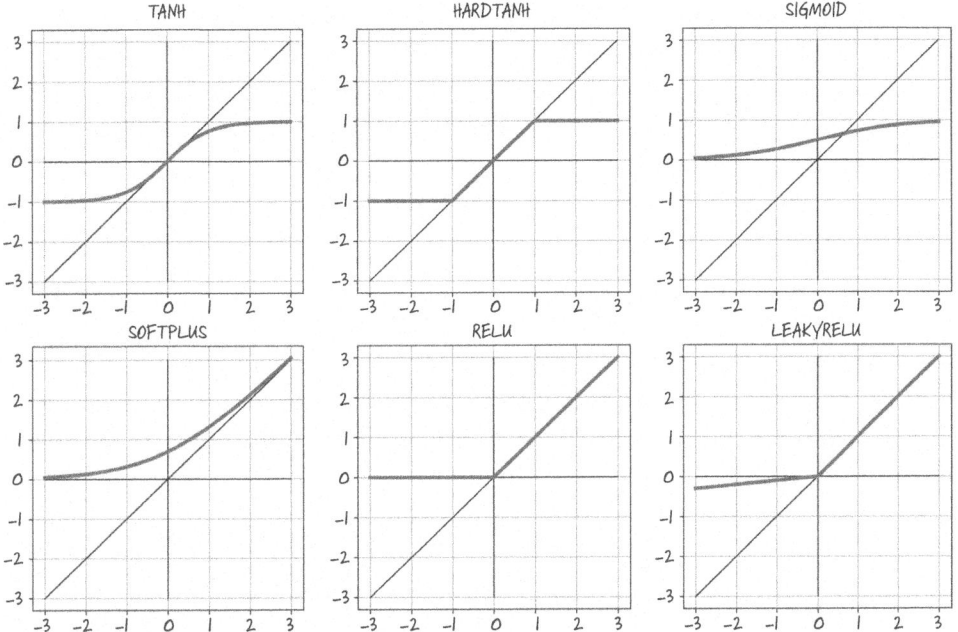

Figure 6.5 A collection of common and not-so-common activation functions

6.1.5 Choosing the best activation function

Activation functions are curious because with such a wide variety of proven successful ones (many more than shown in figure 6.5), it's clear that there are few, if any, strict requirements. As such, we're going to discuss some generalities about activation functions that can probably be trivially disproved in the specific. That said, by definition, activation functions are

- *Nonlinear*—Repeated applications of (w*x+b) without an activation function result in a function of the same (affine linear) form. The nonlinearity allows the overall network to approximate more complex functions.
- *Differentiable*—Thus, the gradients can be computed through them. Point discontinuities in which the derivative may be undefined at specific values, as we can see in Hardtanh or ReLU, are fine. Without these characteristics, the network either falls back to being a linear model or becomes difficult to train.

NOTE Of course, even these statements aren't *always* true; see Jakob Foerster, "Nonlinear Computation in Deep Linear Networks," OpenAI, 2019, http://mng.bz/gygE.

The following are true for the functions:

- They have at least one sensitive range, where meaningful changes to the input result in corresponding meaningful changes to the output. This feature is needed for training.

- Many functions have an insensitive (or saturated) range, where changes to the input result in little or no change to the output.

By way of example, the Hardtanh function could easily be used to make piecewise-linear approximations of a function by combining the sensitive range with different weights and biases on the input.

Often (but far from universally so), the activation function will have at least one of these:

- A lower bound that is approached (or met) as the input goes to negative infinity
- A similar, but inverse, upper bound for positive infinity

Thinking of what we know about how backpropagation works, we can figure out that the errors will propagate backward through the activation more effectively when the inputs are in the response range. Conversely, errors will not greatly affect neurons for which the input is saturated (since the gradient will be close to zero, due to the flat area around the output).

Put together, the result is a pretty powerful mechanism: we're saying that in a network built out of linear + activation units, when different inputs are presented to the network, (a) different units will respond in different ranges for the same inputs, and (b) the errors associated with those inputs will primarily affect the neurons operating in the sensitive range, leaving other units more or less unaffected by the learning process. In addition, thanks to the fact that derivatives of the activation with respect to its inputs are often close to 1 in the sensitive range, estimating the parameters of the linear transformation through gradient descent for the units that operate in that range will look a lot like the linear fit we have seen previously.

We are starting to get a deeper intuition for how joining many linear activation units in parallel and stacking them one after the other leads us to a mathematical object that is capable of approximating complicated functions. Different combinations of units will respond to inputs in different ranges, and those parameters for those units are relatively easy to optimize through gradient descent, since learning will behave a lot like that of a linear function until the output saturates.

6.1.6 What learning means for a neural network

Building models out of stacks of linear transformations followed by differentiable activations leads to models that can approximate highly nonlinear processes and whose parameters we can estimate surprisingly well through gradient descent. This fact remains true even when dealing with models with millions of parameters. What makes using deep neural networks so attractive is that it saves us from worrying too much about the exact function that represents our data—whether it is quadratic, piecewise polynomial, or something else. Many problems would be impossible to describe with a handcrafted function—for example, how do you create a mathematical function that tells whether an image has a dog in it? With a deep neural network model, we have a universal approximator and a method to estimate its parameters. This approximator can be customized to our needs in terms of model capacity and its ability to model complicated input/output relationships just by composing simple building blocks. Figure 6.6 shows some examples.

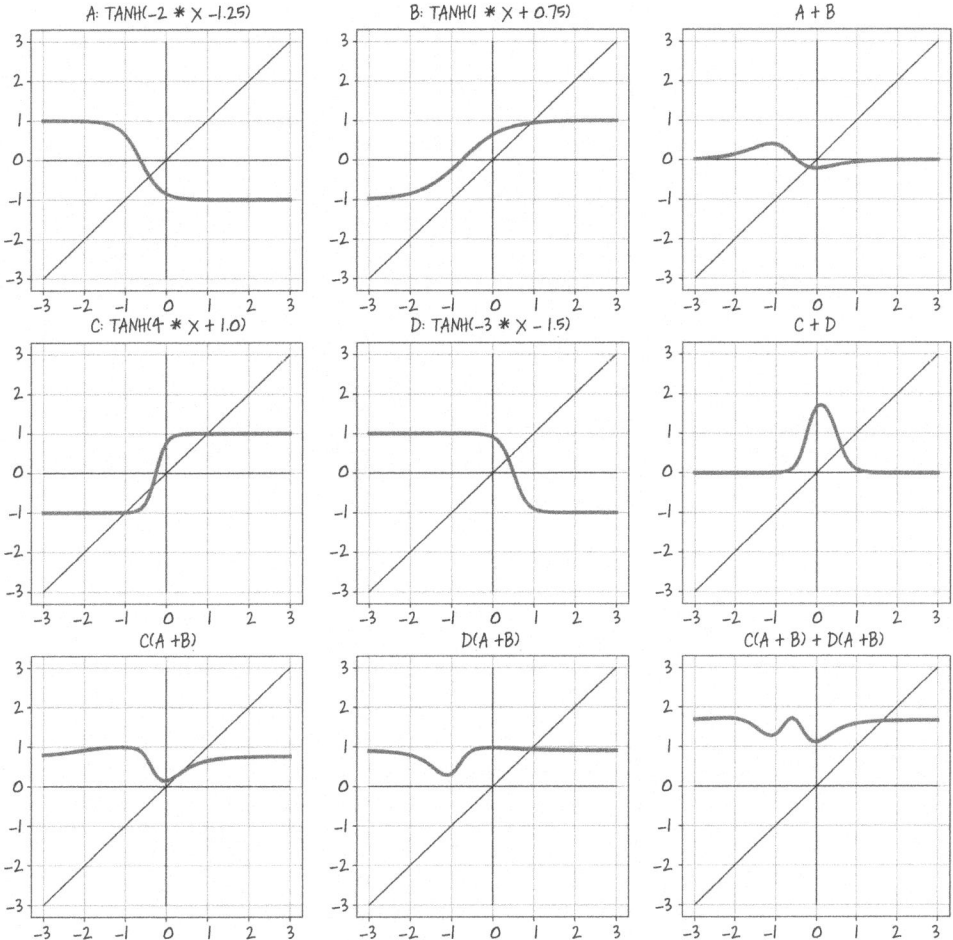

Figure 6.6 Composing multiple linear units and tanh activation functions to produce nonlinear outputs

The four upper-left graphs of figure 6.6 show four neurons—A, B, C, and D—each with its own (arbitrarily chosen) weight and bias. Each neuron uses the Tanh activation function with a min of −1 and a max of 1. The varied weights and biases move the center point and change how drastically the transition from min to max happens, but they clearly all have the same general shape. The columns to the right of those show both pairs of neurons added together (A + B and C + D). Here, we start to see some interesting properties that mimic a single layer of neurons. A + B shows a slight S curve, with the extremes approaching 0, but with both a positive bump and a negative bump in the middle. Conversely, C + D has only a large positive bump, which peaks at a higher value than our single-neuron max of 1.

In the third row of figure 6.6, we begin to compose our neurons as they would be in a two-layer network. Both C(A + B) and D(A + B) have the same positive and negative bumps that A + B shows, but the positive peak is more subtle. The composition of C(A + B) + D(A + B) shows a new property: *two* clearly negative bumps and possibly also a very subtle second positive peak to the left of the main area of interest. All this with only four neurons in two layers!

Again, these neurons' parameters were chosen only to have a visually interesting result. Training consists of finding acceptable values for these weights and biases so that the resulting network correctly carries out a task, such as predicting likely temperatures given geographic coordinates and time of the year. By *carrying out a task successfully*, we mean obtaining a correct output on unseen data produced by the same data-generating process used for training data. A successfully trained network, through the values of its weights and biases, will capture the inherent structure of the data in the form of meaningful numerical representations that work correctly for previously unseen data.

Let's take another step in our realization of the mechanics of learning: deep neural networks give us the ability to approximate highly nonlinear phenomena without having an explicit model for them. Instead, starting from a generic, untrained model, we specialize it on a task by providing it with a set of inputs and outputs and a loss function from which to backpropagate. Specializing a generic model to a task using examples is what we refer to as *learning* because the model wasn't built with that specific task in mind—no rules describing how that task worked were encoded in the model.

For our thermometer example, we assumed that both thermometers measure temperatures linearly. That assumption is where we implicitly encoded a rule for our task: we hardcoded the shape of our input/output function; we couldn't have approximated anything other than data points sitting around a line. As the dimensionality of a problem grows (i.e., many inputs to many outputs) and input/output relationships get complicated, assuming a shape for the input/output function is unlikely to work. The job of a physicist or an applied mathematician is often to come up with a functional description of a phenomenon from first principles, so that we can estimate the unknown parameters from measurements and get an accurate model of the world.

Deep neural networks, on the other hand, are families of functions that have the ability to approximate a wide range of input/output relationships without necessarily requiring us to come up with an explanatory model of a phenomenon. In a way, we're renouncing an explanation in exchange for the possibility of tackling increasingly complicated problems. In another way, we sometimes lack the ability, information, or computational resources to build an explicit model of what we're presented with, so data-driven methods are our only way forward.

6.2 The PyTorch nn module

All this talking about neural networks is probably making you really curious about building one from scratch with PyTorch. Our first step will be to replace our linear model with a neural network unit. This step is a somewhat useless step backward from a correctness perspective, since we've already verified that our calibration only required a linear function, but it will still be instrumental for starting on a sufficiently simple problem and scaling up later.

PyTorch has a whole submodule dedicated to neural networks, called torch.nn. It contains the building blocks needed to create all sorts of neural network architectures. Those building blocks are called *modules* in PyTorch parlance (such building blocks are often referred to as *layers* in other frameworks). A PyTorch module is a Python class deriving from the nn.Module base class. A module can have one or more nn.Parameter instances as attributes, which are tensors whose values are optimized during the training process (think w and b in our linear model). A module can also have one or more submodules (subclasses of nn.Module) as attributes, and it will be able to track their parameters as well.

> **NOTE** The submodules must be top-level *attributes*, not buried inside list or dict instances! Otherwise, the optimizer will not be able to locate the submodules (and, hence, their parameters). For situations where your model requires a list or dict of submodules, PyTorch provides nn.ModuleList and nn.ModuleDict.

Unsurprisingly, we can find a subclass of nn.Module called nn.Linear, which applies an affine transformation to its input (via the parameter attributes weight and bias) and is equivalent to what we implemented earlier in our thermometer experiments. We'll now start precisely where we left off and convert our previous code to a form that uses nn.

6.2.1 Using nn.Module as a callable

PyTorch's nn.Module is designed to be used as a callable object, meaning it has its own __call__ method defined. As a result, we can instantiate an nn.Linear and call it as if it were a function (code/p1ch6/1_neural_networks.ipynb):

```
# In[5]:
import torch.nn as nn

linear_model = nn.Linear(1, 1)       ◁─┤ We'll look into the constructor
linear_model(t_un_val)                  │ arguments in a moment.

# Out[5]:
tensor([[0.6018],
        [0.2877]], grad_fn=<AddmmBackward>)
```

Calling an instance of nn.Module with a set of arguments ends up calling a method named forward with the same arguments. The forward method is what executes the forward computation, while `__call__` does other rather important chores before and after calling `forward`. So, it is technically possible to call `forward` directly, and it will produce the same output as `__call__`, but this should not be done from user code:

```
y = model(x)              ◁─┘ Correct!
y = model.forward(x)      ◁─┐ Silent error.
                            │ Don't do it!
```

In some instances, PyTorch modules attach `hooks`, which are functions that can be specified to be executed at specific times during the forward and backward passes. These hooks can be defined by the user, or in some advanced use cases, the PyTorch library itself will use them, for example, to implement a distributed training strategy. If you call `forward` directly, the hooks won't be executed, which may cause an error in the program.

6.2.2 Returning to the linear model

Back to our linear model. The constructor to `nn.Linear` accepts three arguments: the number of input features, the number of output features, and whether the linear model includes a bias (defaulting to `True`, here):

```
# In[5]:
import torch.nn as nn

linear_model = nn.Linear(1, 1)     ◁── The arguments are input size, output size, and bias, which defaults to True.
linear_model(t_un_val)

# Out[5]:
tensor([[0.6018],
        [0.2877]], grad_fn=<AddmmBackward>)
```

The number of features in our case just refers to the size of the input and the output tensor for the module, so 1 and 1. If we used both temperature and barometric pressure as input, for instance, we would have two features in input and one feature in output. As we will see, for more complex models with several intermediate modules, the number of features is associated with the capacity of the model.

We have an instance of `nn.Linear` with one input and one output feature. That only requires one weight and one bias:

```
# In[6]:
linear_model.weight

# Out[6]:
Parameter containing:
tensor([[-0.0674]], requires_grad=True)

# In[7]:
linear_model.bias
```

```
# Out[7]:
Parameter containing:
tensor([0.7488], requires_grad=True)
```

We can call the module with some input:

```
# In[8]:
x = torch.ones(1)
linear_model(x)

# Out[8]:
tensor([0.6814], grad_fn=<AddBackward0>)
```

Although PyTorch lets us get away with it, we don't actually provide an input with the right dimensionality. We have a model that takes one input and produces one output, but PyTorch's nn.Module and its subclasses are designed to do so on multiple samples at the same time. To accommodate multiple samples, modules expect the zeroth dimension of the input to be the number of samples in the *batch*. We encountered this concept in chapter 4, where we learned how to arrange real-world data into tensors.

BATCHING INPUTS

Any module in nn is written to produce outputs for a *batch* of multiple inputs at the same time. Thus, assuming we need to run nn.Linear on 10 samples, we can create an input tensor of size $B \times N\_in$, where B is the size of the batch and N_in is the number of input features, and run it once through the model. For example,

```
# In[9]:
x = torch.ones(10, 1)
linear_model(x)

# Out[9]:
tensor([[0.6814],
        [0.6814],
        [0.6814],
        [0.6814],
        [0.6814],
        [0.6814],
        [0.6814],
        [0.6814],
        [0.6814],
        [0.6814]], grad_fn=<AddmmBackward>)
```

Let's dig into what's going on here, with figure 6.7 showing a similar situation with batched image data. Our input is $B \times C \times H \times W$ with a batch size of 3 (say, images of a dog, a bird, and then a car), three channel dimensions (red, green, and blue), and an unspecified number of pixels for height and width. As we can see, the output is a tensor of size $B \times N\_out$, where N_out is the number of output features (in this figure, the four output feature values represent classification scores for different categories like "vehicle," "animal," "bird," and "mammal").

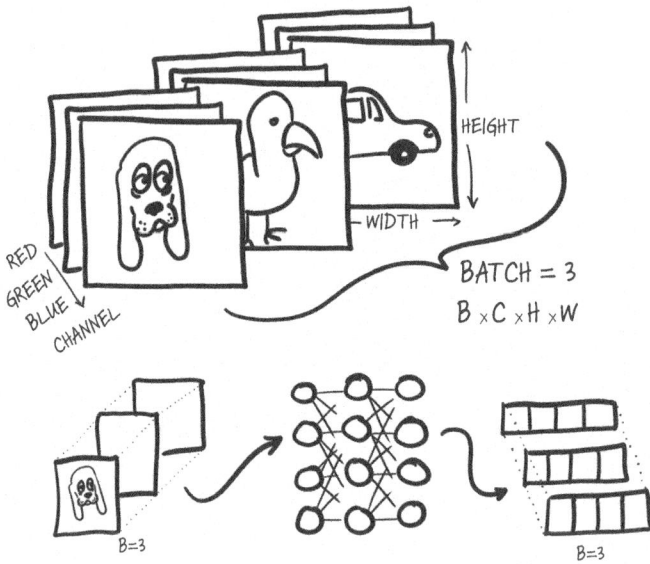

Figure 6.7 Three RGB images batched together and fed into a neural network. The output is a batch of three vectors of size 4.

OPTIMIZING BATCHES

The reason we want to do this batching is multifaceted. One big motivation is to make sure the computation we're asking for is big enough to saturate the computing resources we're using to perform the computation. GPUs, in particular, are highly parallelized, so a single input on a small model will leave most of the computing units idle. By providing batches of inputs, the calculation can be spread across the otherwise idle units, which means the batched results come back just as quickly as a single result would. Another benefit is that some advanced models use statistical information from the entire batch, and those statistics get better with larger batch sizes.

Back to our thermometer data: t_u and t_c were two 1D tensors of size B. Thanks to broadcasting, we could write our linear model as w * x + b, where w and b are two scalar parameters. This method works because we have a single input feature: if we had two, we would need to add an extra dimension to turn that 1D tensor into a matrix with samples in the rows and features in the columns.

That's exactly what we need to do to switch to using nn.Linear. We reshape our B inputs to $B \times N\_in$, where N_in is 1. That is easily done with unsqueeze:

```
# In[2]:
t_c = [0.5,  14.0, 15.0, 28.0, 11.0,  8.0,  3.0, -4.0,  6.0, 13.0, 21.0]
t_u = [35.7, 55.9, 58.2, 81.9, 56.3, 48.9, 33.9, 21.8, 48.4, 60.4, 68.4]
t_c = torch.tensor(t_c).unsqueeze(1)
t_u = torch.tensor(t_u).unsqueeze(1)
```
Adds the extra dimension at axis 1

```
t_u.shape

# Out[2]:
torch.Size([11, 1])
```

We're done; let's update our training code. First, we replace our handmade model with nn.Linear(1,1), and then we need to pass the linear model parameters to the optimizer:

```
# In[10]:
linear_model = nn.Linear(1, 1)       ◁──┐ A redefinition
optimizer = optim.SGD(                   from earlier
    linear_model.parameters(),       ◁──┐ This method retrieves the model
    lr=1e-2)                             parameters. It replaces what we
                                         used as [params] in chapter 5.
```

Earlier, it was our responsibility to create parameters and pass them as the first argument to optim.SGD. Now we can use the parameters method to ask any nn.Module for a list of parameters owned by it or any of its submodules:

```
# In[11]:
linear_model.parameters()

# Out[11]:
<generator object Module.parameters at 0x7f94b4a8a750>

# In[12]:
list(linear_model.parameters())

# Out[12]:
[Parameter containing:
 tensor([[0.7398]], requires_grad=True), Parameter containing:
 tensor([0.7974], requires_grad=True)]
```

This call recurses into submodules defined in the module's init constructor and returns a flat list of all parameters encountered, so that we can conveniently pass it to the optimizer constructor as we did previously.

We can already figure out what happens in the training loop. The optimizer is provided with a list of tensors that were all defined with requires_grad = True. A Parameter, which is just a subclass of a tensor and is specially recognized by nn.Module, is defined as requiring gradients by default since they need to be optimized by gradient descent. When training_loss.backward() is called, grad is accumulated on the leaf nodes of the graph, which are precisely the parameters that were passed to the optimizer.

At this point, the SGD optimizer has everything it needs. When optimizer.step() is called, it will iterate through each Parameter and change it by an amount proportional to what is stored in its grad attribute. Pretty clean design.

Let's take a look at the training loop now:

```
# In[13]:
def training_loop(n_epochs, optimizer, model, loss_fn, t_u_train, t_u_val,
                  t_c_train, t_c_val):
    for epoch in range(1, n_epochs + 1):
        t_p_train = model(t_u_train)              ◁─┐  The model is now
        loss_train = loss_fn(t_p_train, t_c_train)   │  passed in, instead of
                                                     │  the individual params.
        t_p_val = model(t_u_val)                  ◁──┘
        loss_val = loss_fn(t_p_val, t_c_val)

        optimizer.zero_grad()
        loss_train.backward()        ◁───┐  The loss function is also passed
        optimizer.step()                 │  in. We'll use it in a moment.

        if epoch == 1 or epoch % 1000 == 0:
            print(f"Epoch {epoch}, Training loss {loss_train.item():.4f},"
                  f" Validation loss {loss_val.item():.4f}")
```

The model hasn't changed hardly at all, except that now we don't pass params explicitly to model since the model itself holds its parameters internally.

There's one last bit that we can use from torch.nn: the loss. Indeed, nn comes with several common loss functions, among them nn.MSELoss (MSE stands for mean squared error), which is exactly what we defined earlier as our loss_fn. Loss functions in nn are still subclasses of nn.Module, so we will create an instance and call it as a function. In our case, we get rid of the handwritten loss_fn and replace it:

```
# In[15]:
linear_model = nn.Linear(1, 1)
optimizer = optim.SGD(linear_model.parameters(), lr=1e-2)

training_loop(
    n_epochs = 3000,
    optimizer = optimizer,
    model = linear_model,
    loss_fn = nn.MSELoss(),        ◁───┐  We are no longer using our
    t_u_train = t_un_train,            │  handwritten loss function
    t_u_val = t_un_val,                │  from earlier.
    t_c_train = t_c_train,
    t_c_val = t_c_val)

print()
print(linear_model.weight)
print(linear_model.bias)

# Out[15]:
Epoch 1, Training loss 134.9599, Validation loss 183.1707
Epoch 1000, Training loss 4.8053, Validation loss 4.7307
Epoch 2000, Training loss 3.0285, Validation loss 3.0889
Epoch 3000, Training loss 2.8569, Validation loss 3.9105
```

```
Parameter containing:
tensor([[5.4319]], requires_grad=True)
Parameter containing:
tensor([-17.9693], requires_grad=True)
```

Everything else input into our training loop stays the same. Even our results remain the same as before. Of course, getting the same results is expected, as a difference would imply a bug in one of the two implementations.

6.3 Finally, a neural network

It's been a long journey—we've extensively explored these 20-something lines of code required to define and train a model. Hopefully, by now, the magic involved in training has vanished and left room for the mechanics. What we learned so far will allow us to own the code we write instead of merely poking at a black box when things get more complicated.

There's one last step left to take: replacing our linear model with a neural network as our approximating function. We said earlier that using a neural network will not result in a higher-quality model because the process underlying our calibration problem was fundamentally linear. However, it's good to make the leap from a linear to a neural network in a controlled environment so we won't feel lost later.

6.3.1 Replacing the linear model

We are going to keep everything else fixed, including the loss function, and only redefine model. Let's build the simplest possible neural network: a linear module, followed by an activation function, feeding into another linear module. The first linear + activation layer is commonly referred to as a *hidden* layer for historical reasons because its outputs are not observed directly but fed into the output layer.

While the input and output of the model are both size 1 (they have one input and one output feature), the size of the output of the first linear module is usually larger than 1. Recalling our earlier explanation of the role of activations, this setup can lead different units to respond to different ranges of the input, which increases the capacity of our model. The last linear layer will take the output of activations and combine them linearly to produce the output value.

There is no standard way to depict neural networks. Figure 6.8 shows two ways that seem to be somewhat prototypical: the left side shows how our network might be depicted in basic introductions, whereas a style similar to that on the right is often used in the more advanced literature and research papers. It is common to make diagram blocks that roughly correspond to the neural network modules PyTorch offers (though sometimes things like the Tanh activation layer are not explicitly shown). One somewhat subtle difference between the two is that the graph on the left has the inputs and (intermediate) results in the circles as the main elements. On the right, the computational steps are more prominent.

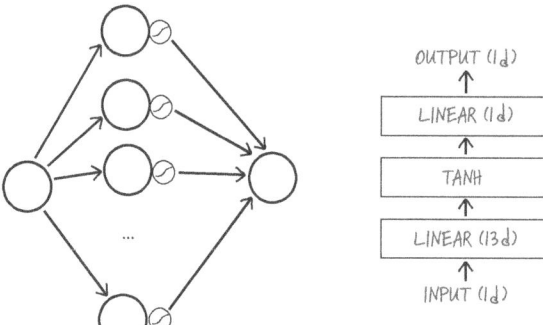

Figure 6.8 Our simplest neural network in two views. Left: beginner's version. Right: higher-level version.

nn provides a simple way to concatenate modules through the nn.Sequential container:

```
# In[16]:
seq_model = nn.Sequential(
            nn.Linear(1, 13),
            nn.Tanh(),
            nn.Linear(13, 1))
seq_model
```

> We chose 13 arbitrarily. We wanted a number that was a different size from the other tensor shapes we have floating around.

> This 13 must match the first size, however.

```
# Out[16]:
Sequential(
  (0): Linear(in_features=1, out_features=13, bias=True)
  (1): Tanh()
  (2): Linear(in_features=13, out_features=1, bias=True)
)
```

The end result is a model that takes the inputs expected by the first module specified as an argument of nn.Sequential, passes intermediate outputs to subsequent modules, and produces the output returned by the last module. The model fans out from 1 input feature to 13 hidden features, passes them through a tanh activation, and linearly combines the resulting 13 numbers into 1 output feature.

6.3.2 Inspecting the parameters

Calling model.parameters() will collect weight and bias from both the first and second linear modules. It's instructive to inspect the parameters in this case by printing their shapes:

```
# In[17]:
[param.shape for param in seq_model.parameters()]

# Out[17]:
[torch.Size([13, 1]), torch.Size([13]), torch.Size([1, 13]), torch.Size([1])]
```

These are the tensors that the optimizer will get. Again, after we call `loss_train`
`.backward()`, all parameters are populated with their grad, and the optimizer then
updates their values accordingly during the `optimizer.step()` call. Not that different
from our previous linear model, eh? After all, they're both differentiable models that
can be trained using gradient descent.

A few notes on parameters of nn.Modules. When inspecting parameters of a model
made up of several submodules, it is handy to be able to identify parameters by name.
There's a method for that, called named_parameters:

```
# In[18]:
for name, param in seq_model.named_parameters():
    print(name, param.shape)

# Out[18]:
0.weight torch.Size([13, 1])
0.bias torch.Size([13])
2.weight torch.Size([1, 13])
2.bias torch.Size([1])
```

> **NOTE** You may have noticed that nn.Tanh is missing from our parameter list
> despite being defined in the model. tanh, like most activation functions, does
> not have any parameters. It is simply a fixed mathematical operation that
> transforms the input in a predetermined way and thus is not tuned during
> training like the linear layers.

The name of each module in Sequential is the ordinal with which the module
appears in the arguments. Interestingly, Sequential also accepts an OrderedDict, in
which we can name each module passed to Sequential:

> **NOTE** Not all versions of Python specify the iteration order for dict, so we're
> using OrderedDict here to ensure the ordering of the layers and emphasize
> that the order of the layers matters.

```
# In[19]:
from collections import OrderedDict

seq_model = nn.Sequential(OrderedDict([
    ('hidden_linear', nn.Linear(1, 8)),
    ('hidden_activation', nn.Tanh()),
    ('output_linear', nn.Linear(8, 1))
]))

seq_model

# Out[19]:
Sequential(
  (hidden_linear): Linear(in_features=1, out_features=8, bias=True)
  (hidden_activation): Tanh()
  (output_linear): Linear(in_features=8, out_features=1, bias=True)
)
```

This step allows us to get more explanatory names for submodules:

```
# In[20]:
for name, param in seq_model.named_parameters():
    print(name, param.shape)

# Out[20]:
hidden_linear.weight torch.Size([8, 1])
hidden_linear.bias torch.Size([8])
output_linear.weight torch.Size([1, 8])
output_linear.bias torch.Size([1])
```

This way is more descriptive, but it does not give us more flexibility in the flow of data through the network, which remains a purely sequential pass-through—the nn.Sequential is very aptly named. To achieve greater control and flexibility over how data is processed—allowing for nonlinear data flows, custom layer interactions, or conditional processing paths—you would need to create custom network architectures by subclassing nn.Module, which will be explored in chapter 8.

We can also access a particular Parameter by using submodules as attributes:

```
# In[21]:
seq_model.output_linear.bias

# Out[21]:
Parameter containing:
tensor([-0.0173], requires_grad=True)
```

Accessing the Parameters is useful for inspecting parameters or their gradients—for instance, to monitor gradients during training, as we did at the beginning of this chapter. Say we want to print out the gradients of weight of the linear portion of the hidden layer. We can run the training loop for the new neural network model and then look at the resulting gradients after the last epoch:

```
# In[22]:
optimizer = optim.SGD(seq_model.parameters(), lr=1e-3)

training_loop(
    n_epochs = 5000,
    optimizer = optimizer,
    model = seq_model,
    loss_fn = nn.MSELoss(),
    t_u_train = t_un_train,
    t_u_val = t_un_val,
    t_c_train = t_c_train,
    t_c_val = t_c_val)

print('output', seq_model(t_un_val))
print('answer', t_c_val)
print('hidden', seq_model.hidden_linear.weight.grad)
```

> We've dropped the learning rate a bit to help with stability.

```
# Out[22]:
Epoch 1, Training loss 182.9724, Validation loss 231.8708
Epoch 1000, Training loss 6.6642, Validation loss 3.7330
Epoch 2000, Training loss 5.1502, Validation loss 0.1406
Epoch 3000, Training loss 2.9653, Validation loss 1.0005
Epoch 4000, Training loss 2.2839, Validation loss 1.6580
Epoch 5000, Training loss 2.1141, Validation loss 2.0215
output tensor([[-1.9930],
        [20.8729]], grad_fn=<AddmmBackward>)
answer tensor([[-4.],
        [21.]])
hidden tensor([[ 0.0272],
        [ 0.0139],
        [ 0.1692],
        [ 0.1735],
        [-0.1697],
        [ 0.1455],
        [-0.0136],
        [-0.0554]])
```

6.3.3 Comparing to the linear model

We can also evaluate the model on all of the data and see how it differs from a line:

```
# In[23]:
from matplotlib import pyplot as plt

t_range = torch.arange(20., 90.).unsqueeze(1)

fig = plt.figure(dpi=600)
plt.xlabel("Fahrenheit")
plt.ylabel("Celsius")
plt.plot(t_u.numpy(), t_c.numpy(), 'o')
plt.plot(t_range.numpy(), seq_model(0.1 * t_range).detach().numpy(), 'c-')
plt.plot(t_u.numpy(), seq_model(0.1 * t_u).detach().numpy(), 'kx')
```

The result is shown in figure 6.9. We can appreciate that the neural network has a tendency to overfit, as we discussed in chapter 5, since it tries to chase the measurements, including the noisy ones. Even our tiny neural network has too many parameters to fit the few measurements we have. It doesn't do a bad job, though, overall.

6.4 Conclusion

We've covered a lot in chapters 5 and 6, although we have been dealing with a very simple problem. We dissected building differentiable models and training them using gradient descent, first using raw autograd and then relying on nn. By now, you should have confidence in your understanding of what's going on behind the scenes. Hopefully, this taste of PyTorch has given you an appetite for more!

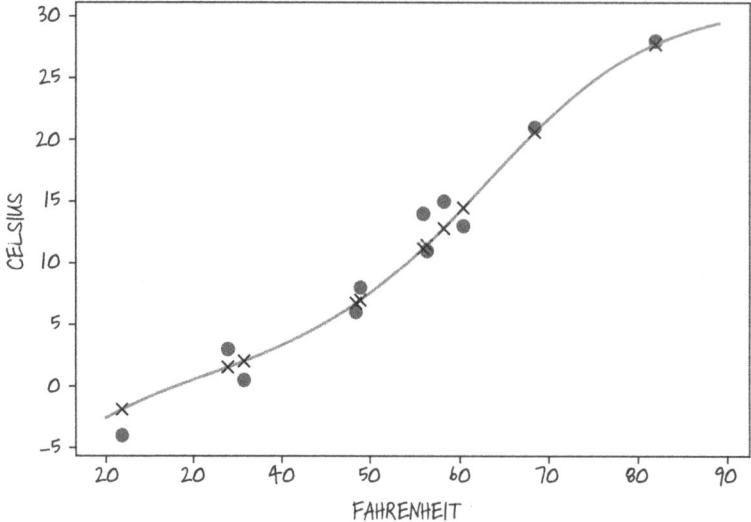

Figure 6.9 The plot of our neural network model, with input data (circles) and model output (Xs). The continuous line shows behavior captured by the neural network between samples.

6.5 Exercises

1 Experiment with the number of hidden neurons in our simple neural network model, as well as the learning rate:
   a What changes result in more linear output from the model?
   b Can you get the model to obviously overfit the data?
2 The third-hardest problem in physics is finding a proper wine to celebrate discoveries. Load the wine data from chapter 4 and create a new model with the appropriate number of input parameters:
   a How long does it take to train compared to the temperature data we have been using?
   b Can you explain what factors contribute to the training times?
   c Can you get the loss to decrease while training on this dataset?
   d How would you go about graphing this dataset?

Summary

- Neural networks can be automatically adapted to specialize themselves on the problem at hand.
- Neural networks allow easy access to the analytical derivatives of the loss with respect to any parameter in the model, which makes evolving the parameters very efficient. Thanks to its automated differentiation engine, PyTorch provides such derivatives effortlessly.

- Combining activation functions with linear transformations makes neural networks capable of approximating highly nonlinear functions, while keeping them simple enough to optimize through gradient-based methods.
- The nn module, together with the tensor standard library, provides all the building blocks for creating neural networks.
- You can inspect the parameters of a neural network using .parameters() and .named_parameters().

Telling birds from airplanes: Learning from images

This chapter covers
- Building a feed-forward neural network
- Loading data using `Datasets` and `DataLoaders`
- Understanding classification loss

The last chapter gave us the opportunity to dive into the inner mechanics of learning through gradient descent and the facilities that PyTorch offers to build and optimize models. We did so using a simple regression model of one input and one output, which allowed us to have everything in plain sight but, admittedly, was only borderline exciting.

In this chapter, we'll keep moving ahead with building our neural network foundations. This time, we'll turn our attention to images. Image recognition is arguably the task that made the world realize the potential of deep learning.

We will approach a simple image recognition problem step by step, building from a simple neural network like the one we defined in the last chapter. This time, instead of a tiny dataset of numbers, we'll use a more extensive dataset of tiny images. Let's download the dataset first and get to work preparing it for use.

7.1 A dataset of tiny images

There is nothing like an intuitive understanding of a subject, and there is nothing to achieve that like working on simple data. One of the most basic datasets for image recognition is the handwritten digit-recognition dataset known as MNIST. Here, we will use another dataset that is similarly simple and a bit more fun. It's called CIFAR-10, and like its sibling CIFAR-100, it has been a computer vision classic for a decade.

CIFAR-10 consists of 60,000 tiny 32 × 32 color (RGB) images, labeled with an integer corresponding to 1 of 10 classes: airplane (0), automobile (1), bird (2), cat (3), deer (4), dog (5), frog (6), horse (7), ship (8), and truck (9).

> **NOTE** The images were collected and labeled by Krizhevsky, Nair, and Hinton of the Canadian Institute for Advanced Research (CIFAR) and were drawn from a larger collection of unlabeled 32 × 32 color images: the "80 million tiny images dataset" from the Computer Science and Artificial Intelligence Laboratory (CSAIL) at the Massachusetts Institute of Technology.

Nowadays, CIFAR-10 is considered too simple for developing or validating new research, but it serves our learning purposes just fine. We will use the `torchvision` module to automatically download the dataset and load it as a collection of PyTorch tensors. Figure 7.1 gives us a taste of CIFAR-10.

Figure 7.1 Image samples from all CIFAR-10 classes

7.1.1 Downloading CIFAR-10

Let's import `torchvision` and use the `datasets` module to download the CIFAR-10 data (code/p1ch7/1_datasets.ipynb).

Listing 7.1 Loading the CIFAR-10 data

```
# In[2]:
from torchvision import datasets
import os
data_path = '../data-unversioned/p1ch7/'
os.makedirs(data_path, exist_ok=True)
cifar10 = datasets.CIFAR10(data_path, train=True, download=True)
cifar10_val = datasets.CIFAR10(data_path, train=False, download=True)
```

Instantiates a dataset for the training data; TorchVision downloads the data if it is not present.

With train=False, we get a dataset for the validation data, again downloading as necessary

The first argument we provide to the CIFAR10 function is the local directory where the data will be downloaded. The second argument specifies whether we're interested in the training set or the validation set. Finally, the third argument determines whether we allow PyTorch to download the data if it is not found in the location specified in the first argument.

Just like CIFAR10, the datasets submodule gives us ready-made access to the most popular computer vision datasets, such as MNIST, Fashion-MNIST, CIFAR-100, SVHN, COCO, and Omniglot. In each case, the dataset is returned as a subclass of torch.utils.data.Dataset. We can see that the method-resolution order of our cifar10 instance includes it as a base class:

```
# In[4]:
type(cifar10).__mro__

# Out[4]:
(torchvision.datasets.cifar.CIFAR10,
 torchvision.datasets.vision.VisionDataset,
 torch.utils.data.dataset.Dataset,
 typing.Generic,
 object)
```

7.1.2 The Dataset class

It's a good time to discover what a subclass of torch.utils.data.Dataset means in practice. Looking at figure 7.2, we see what PyTorch's Dataset is all about. It is an object that should have two methods implemented: __len__ and __getitem__. The former should return the number of items in the dataset, and the latter should return the item, consisting of a sample and its corresponding label (an integer index). We return a sample and label for our image classification example, but getitem could return any data point (with or without corresponding labels, for instance).

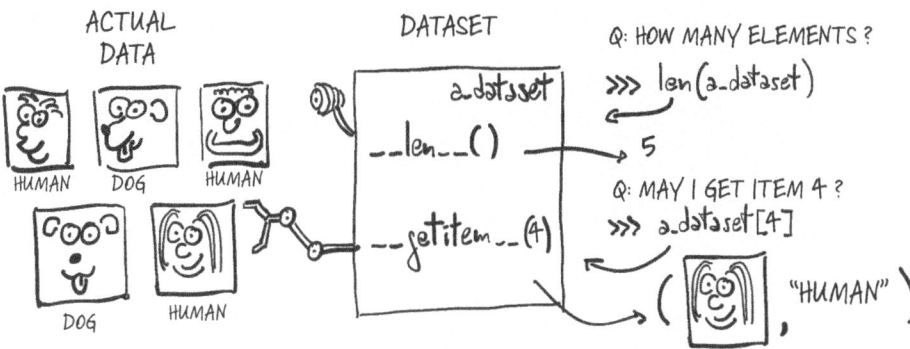

Figure 7.2 Concept of a PyTorch Dataset object. It doesn't necessarily hold the data, but it provides uniform access to it through __len__ and __getitem__.

In practice, when a Python object is equipped with the __len__ method, we can pass it as an argument to the len Python built-in function:

```
# In[5]:
len(cifar10)

# Out[5]:
50000
```

Similarly, since the dataset is equipped with the __getitem__ method, we can use the standard subscript for indexing tuples and lists to access individual items. Here, we get a PIL (Python Imaging Library, the PIL package) image with our desired output—an integer with the value 1, corresponding to "automobile":

```
# In[6]:
img, label = cifar10[99]
img, label, class_names[label]

# Out[6]:
(<PIL.Image.Image image mode=RGB size=32x32>, 1, 'automobile')
```

So, the sample in the CIFAR10 dataset is an instance of an RGB PIL image. We can plot it right away, which produces the output shown in figure 7.3:

```
# In[7]:
plt.imshow(img)
plt.show()
```

It's a red car! (It doesn't translate well to print; you'll have to take our word for it or check it out in the eBook or the Jupyter Notebook.)

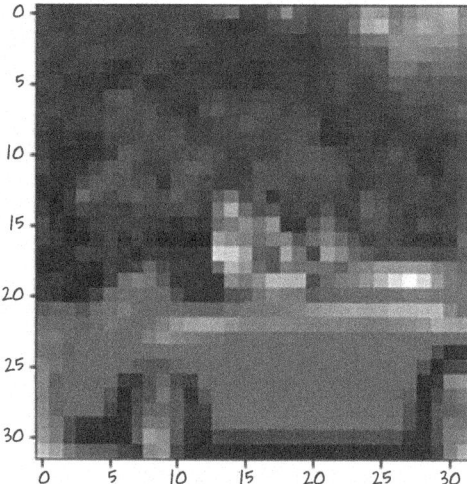

Figure 7.3 The 99th image from the CIFAR-10 dataset: an automobile

7.1.3 Dataset transforms

That's all very nice, but we'll likely need a way to convert the PIL image to a PyTorch tensor before we can do anything with it. That's where torchvision.transforms comes in. We briefly encountered it in chapter 2, where we used transforms to preprocess images. This module defines a set of composable, function-like objects that can be passed as an argument to a torchvision dataset, such as datasets.CIFAR10(…), and that perform transformations on the data after it is loaded but before it is returned by __getitem__. The list of available objects is as follows:

```
# In[8]:
from torchvision import transforms
dir(transforms)

# Out[8]:
['AugMix',
 'AutoAugment',
 'AutoAugmentPolicy',
 'CenterCrop',
 'ColorJitter',
 ...
 'Normalize',
 'PILToTensor',
 'Pad',
 ...
 'RandomChoice',
 'RandomCrop',
 'RandomEqualize',
 ...
]
```

Among those transforms is `ToTensor`, which turns NumPy arrays and PIL images to tensors. It also lays out the dimensions of the output tensor as $C \times H \times W$ (channel, height, width). (Originally, these images are in $H \times W \times C$ format, as shown at https://mng.bz/7QMg.)

Let's try out the `ToTensor` transform. Once instantiated, it can be called like a function with the PIL image as the argument, returning a tensor as output:

```
# In[9]:
from torchvision import transforms

to_tensor = transforms.ToTensor()
img_t = to_tensor(img)
img_t.shape

# Out[9]:
torch.Size([3, 32, 32])
```

The image has been turned into a $3 \times 32 \times 32$ tensor and, therefore, a three-channel (RGB) 32×32 image. Nothing has happened to `label`; it is still an integer.

For convenience, we can also pass the transform directly as an argument to `datasets.CIFAR10`:

```
# In[10]:
tensor_cifar10 = datasets.CIFAR10(data_path, train=True, download=False,
                        transform=transforms.ToTensor())
```

At this point, accessing an element of the dataset will return a tensor, rather than a PIL image:

```
# In[11]:
img_t, _ = tensor_cifar10[99]
type(img_t)

# Out[11]:
torch.Tensor
```

As expected, the shape has the channel as the first dimension, while the scalar type is `float32`:

```
# In[12]:
img_t.shape, img_t.dtype

# Out[12]:
(torch.Size([3, 32, 32]), torch.float32)
```

Whereas the values in the original PIL image ranged from 0 to 255 (8 bits per channel), the `ToTensor` transform turns the data into a 32-bit floating-point per channel, scaling the values down from 0.0 to 1.0. Let's verify that:

```
# In[13]:
img_t.min(), img_t.max()

# Out[13]:
(tensor(0.), tensor(1.))
```

And let's verify that we're getting the same image out:

```
# In[14]:
plt.imshow(img_t.permute(1, 2, 0))       ◁── Changes the order of the
plt.show()                                    axes from C × H × W
                                              to H × W × C
# Out[14]:
<Figure size 432x288 with 1 Axes>
```

As figure 7.4 shows, we get the same output as before. Note that we have to use permute to change the order of the axes from $C \times H \times W$ to $H \times W \times C$ to match what Matplotlib expects.

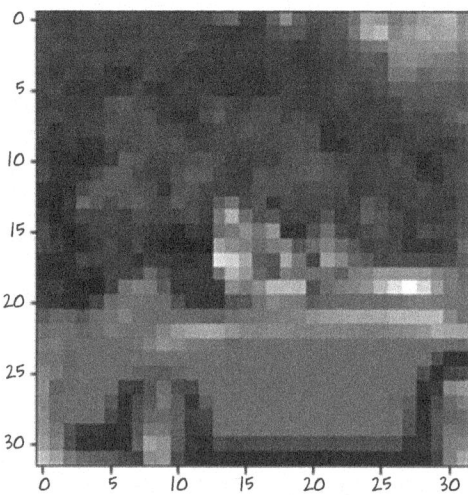

Figure 7.4 We've seen this one already.

7.1.4 Normalizing data

Transforms are really handy because we can chain them using transforms.Compose, and they can handle normalization and data augmentation transparently, directly in the data loader. For instance, it's good practice to normalize the dataset so that each channel has zero mean and unitary standard deviation. We mentioned this in chapter 4, but now, after going through chapter 5, we also have an intuition for why: by choosing activation functions that are linear around 0 plus or minus 1 (or 2), keeping the data in the same range means it's more likely that neurons have nonzero gradients and, hence, will learn sooner. Also, normalizing each channel so that it has the same distribution will ensure that channel information can be mixed and updated through gradient descent using the same learning rate. This situation is like that of section 5.4.4, where we rescaled the weight to be of the same magnitude as the bias in our temperature conversion model.

To make it so that each channel has zero mean and unitary standard deviation, we can compute the mean value and the standard deviation of each channel across the dataset and apply the following transform: v_n[c] = (v[c] - mean[c]) / stdev[c]. This is what transforms.Normalize does. The values of mean and stdev must be computed offline; they are not computed by the transform. Let's compute them for the CIFAR-10 training set.

Since the CIFAR-10 dataset is small, we'll be able to manipulate it entirely in memory. Let's stack all the tensors returned by the dataset along an extra dimension:

```
# In[15]:
imgs = torch.stack([img_t for img_t, _ in tensor_cifar10], dim=3)
imgs.shape

# Out[15]:
torch.Size([3, 32, 32, 50000])
```

Now we can easily compute the mean per channel:

```
# In[16]:
mean = imgs.view(3, -1).mean(dim=1)
mean

# Out[16]:
tensor([0.4914, 0.4822, 0.4465])
```

Recall that view(3, -1) keeps the three channels and merges all the remaining dimensions into one, figuring out the appropriate size. Here, our 3 × 32 × 32 image is transformed into a 3 × 1,024 vector, and then the mean is taken over the 1,024 elements of each channel.

Computing the standard deviation is similar:

```
# In[17]:
std = imgs.view(3, -1).std(dim=1)
std

# Out[17]:
tensor([0.2470, 0.2435, 0.2616])
```

With these numbers in our hands, we can initialize the Normalize transform:

```
# In[18]:
transforms.Normalize(mean=mean, std=std)

# Out[18]:
Normalize(mean=tensor([0.4914, 0.4822, 0.4465]),
➥   std=tensor([0.2470, 0.2435, 0.2616]))
```

and concatenate it after the `ToTensor` transform:

```
# In[19]:
transformed_cifar10 = datasets.CIFAR10(
    data_path, train=True, download=False,
    transform=transforms.Compose([
        transforms.ToTensor(),
        transforms.Normalize(mean=mean, std=std)
    ]))
```

At this point, plotting an image drawn from the dataset won't provide us with a faithful representation of the actual image:

```
# In[21]:
img_t, _ = transformed_cifar10[99]

plt.imshow(img_t.permute(1, 2, 0))
plt.show()
```

The renormalized red car we get is shown in figure 7.5. This result is because normalization has shifted the RGB levels outside the 0.0 to 1.0 range and changed the overall magnitudes of the channels. All of the data is still there; it's just that Matplotlib renders it as black. We'll keep this in mind for the future.

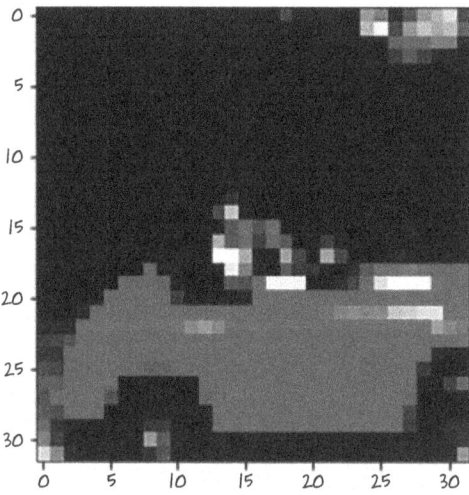

Figure 7.5 Our random CIFAR-10 image after normalization

Still, we have a fancy dataset loaded that contains tens of thousands of images! That's quite convenient because we were going to need something exactly like it.

7.2 Distinguishing birds from airplanes

Jane, our friend at the bird-watching club, has set up a fleet of cameras in the woods south of the airport. The cameras are supposed to save a shot when something enters the frame and upload it to the club's real-time bird-watching blog. The problem is that a lot of planes coming and going from the airport end up triggering the camera, so Jane spends a lot of time deleting pictures of airplanes from the blog. What she needs is an automated system like that shown in figure 7.6. Instead of manually deleting, she needs a neural network—an AI if we're into fancy marketing speak—to throw away the airplanes right away.

Figure 7.6 The problem at hand: we're going to help our friend tell birds from airplanes for her blog, by training a neural network to do the job.

No worries! We'll take care of that, no problem—we just got the perfect dataset for it (what a coincidence, right?). We'll pick out all the birds and airplanes from our CIFAR-10 dataset and build a neural network that can tell birds and airplanes apart.

7.2.1 Building the dataset

The first step is to get the data in the right shape. We could create a Dataset subclass that only includes birds and airplanes. However, the dataset is small, and we only need indexing and len to work on our dataset. It doesn't actually have to be a subclass of torch.utils.data.dataset.Dataset! Well, why not take a shortcut and just filter the data in cifar10 and remap the labels so they are contiguous (code/p1ch7/2_birds_airplanes.ipynb)?

Listing 7.2 Filtering CIFAR-10 to two classes (birds and airplanes)

```
# In[5]:
label_map = {0: 0, 2: 1}
```

```
class_names = ['airplane', 'bird']
cifar2 = [(img, label_map[label])
          for img, label in cifar10
          if label in [0, 2]]
cifar2_val = [(img, label_map[label])
              for img, label in cifar10_val
              if label in [0, 2]]
```

The `cifar2` object satisfies the basic requirements for a `Dataset`—that is, `__len__` and `__getitem__` are defined—so we're going to use that. We should be aware, however, that this is a clever shortcut, and we might wish to implement a proper `Dataset` if we hit limitations with it.

> **NOTE** Here, we built the new dataset manually and also wanted to remap the classes. In some cases, it may be enough to take a subset of the indices of a given dataset. We can accomplish this using the `torch.utils.data.Subset` class. Similarly, we can use `ConcatDataset` to join datasets (of compatible items) into a larger one. For iterable datasets, `ChainDataset` gives a larger, iterable dataset.

We have a dataset! Next, we need a model to feed our data to.

7.2.2 A fully connected model

We learned how to build a neural network in chapter 5. We know that it's a tensor of features in, a tensor of features out. After all, an image is just a set of numbers laid out in a spatial configuration. OK, we don't know how to handle the spatial configuration part just yet, but in theory, if we just take the image pixels and straighten them into a long 1D vector, we could consider those numbers as input features, right? Figure 7.7 illustrates this concept.

Let's try that. How many features per sample? Well, 32 × 32 × 3 is 3,072 input features per sample. Starting from the model we built in chapter 5, our new model would be an `nn.Linear` with 3,072 input features and some number of hidden features, followed by an activation, and then another `nn.Linear` that tapers the network down to an appropriate output number of features (2, for this use case, since we have two classes):

```
# In[6]:
import torch.nn as nn

n_out = 2

model = nn.Sequential(
            nn.Linear(
                3072,          ⟵┘ Input features
                512,           ⟵┐ Hidden layer size
            ),
            nn.Tanh(),
            nn.Linear(
                512,
                n_out,         ⟵── Output classes
            )
        )
```

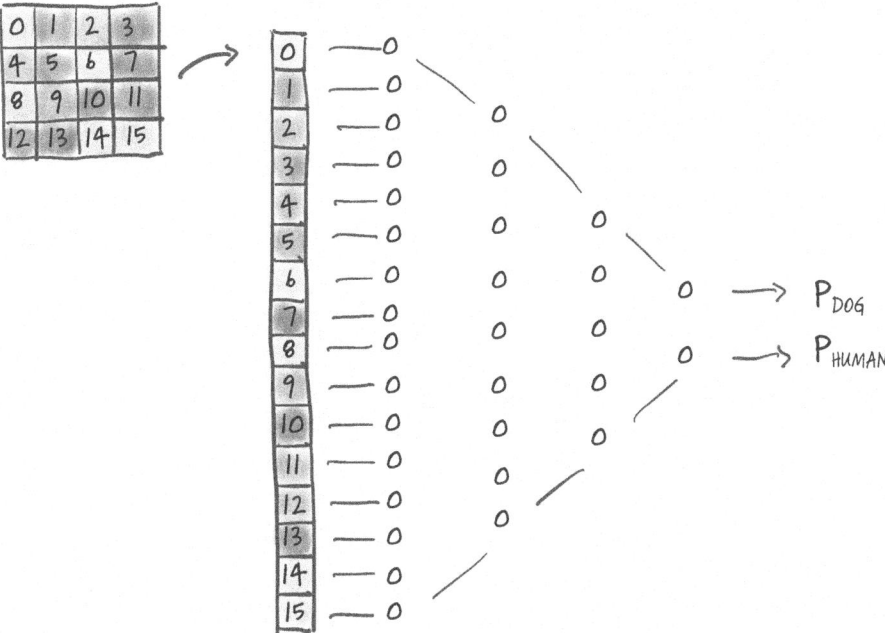

Figure 7.7 Treating our image as a 1D vector of values and training a fully connected classifier on it

We select 512 hidden features somewhat arbitrarily. A neural network needs at least one hidden layer (of activations, so two modules) with a nonlinearity in between to be able to learn arbitrary functions in the way we discussed in section 6.3. Otherwise, it would just be a linear model. The hidden features represent (learned) relations between the inputs encoded through the weight matrix. As such, the model might learn to "compare" vector elements 176 and 208, but it does not a priori focus on them because it is structurally unaware that these are, indeed, (row 5, pixel 16) and (row 6, pixel 16), and thus adjacent.

So, we have a model. Next, we'll discuss what our model output should be.

7.2.3 Output of a classifier

In chapter 6, the network produced the predicted temperature (a number with a quantitative meaning) as output. We could do something similar here: make our network output a single scalar value (so n_out = 1), cast the labels to floats (0.0 for airplane and 1.0 for bird), and use those as a target for MSELoss (the average of squared differences in the batch). Doing so, we would cast the problem into a regression problem. However, looking more closely, we are now dealing with something a bit different in nature.

> **NOTE** Using distance on the "probability" vectors would have already been much better than using MSELoss with the class numbers, which, recalling our

discussion in chapter 4 of types of values, does not make sense for categories and does not work at all in practice. Still, MSELoss is not very well suited to classification problems.

We need to recognize that the output is categorical: it's either a bird or an airplane (or something else if we had all 10 of the original classes). As we learned in chapter 4, when we have to represent a categorical variable, we should switch to a one-hot encoding representation of that variable, such as [1, 0] for airplane or [0, 1] for bird (the order is arbitrary). This method will still work if we have 10 classes, as in the full CIFAR-10 dataset; we'll just have a vector of length 10.

> **NOTE** For the special binary classification case, using two values here is redundant, as one is always 1 minus the other. Indeed, PyTorch lets us output only a single probability using the nn.Sigmoid activation at the end of the model to get a probability and the binary cross-entropy loss function nn.BCELoss. An nn.BCELossWithLogits is also merging these two steps.

In the ideal case, the network would output torch.tensor([1.0, 0.0]) for an airplane and torch.tensor([0.0, 1.0]) for a bird. Practically speaking, since our classifier will not be perfect, we can expect the network to output something in between. The key realization in this case is that we can interpret our output as probabilities: the first entry is the probability of "airplane," and the second is the probability of "bird."

Casting the problem in terms of probabilities imposes a few extra constraints on the outputs of our network:

- Each element of the output must be in the [0.0, 1.0] range. A probability of an outcome cannot be less than 0 or greater than 1.
- The elements of the output must add up to 1.0. We're certain that one of the two outcomes will occur.

It sounds like a tough constraint to enforce in a differentiable way on a vector of numbers. Yet there's a very smart trick that does exactly that, and it's differentiable: it's called *softmax*.

7.2.4 Representing the output as probabilities

Softmax is a function that takes a vector of values and produces another vector of the same dimension, where the values satisfy the constraints we just listed to represent probabilities. The expression for softmax is shown in figure 7.8.

That is, we take the elements of the vector, compute the elementwise exponential, and divide each element by the sum of exponentials. In code, it's something like this:

```
# In[7]:
def softmax(x):
    return torch.exp(x) / torch.exp(x).sum()
```

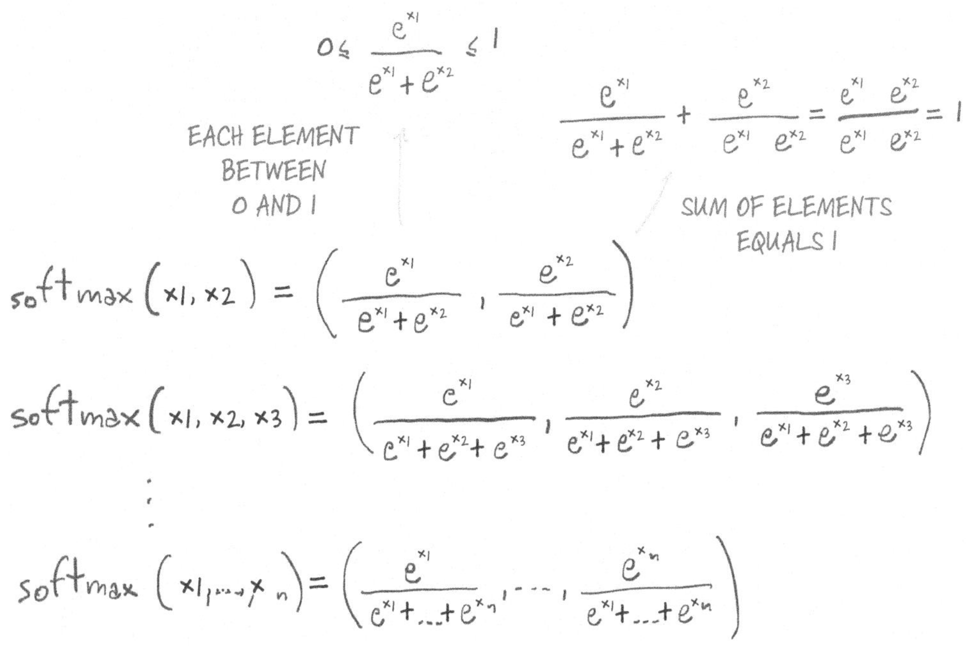

7.2 Distinguishing birds from airplanes

$$0 \leq \frac{e^{x_1}}{e^{x_1}+e^{x_2}} \leq 1$$

EACH ELEMENT BETWEEN 0 AND 1

$$\frac{e^{x_1}}{e^{x_1}+e^{x_2}} + \frac{e^{x_2}}{e^{x_1}+e^{x_2}} = \frac{e^{x_1}}{e^{x_1}} \frac{e^{x_2}}{e^{x_2}} = 1$$

SUM OF ELEMENTS EQUALS 1

$$\text{softmax}(x_1, x_2) = \left(\frac{e^{x_1}}{e^{x_1}+e^{x_2}}, \frac{e^{x_2}}{e^{x_1}+e^{x_2}} \right)$$

$$\text{softmax}(x_1, x_2, x_3) = \left(\frac{e^{x_1}}{e^{x_1}+e^{x_2}+e^{x_3}}, \frac{e^{x_2}}{e^{x_1}+e^{x_2}+e^{x_3}}, \frac{e^{x_3}}{e^{x_1}+e^{x_2}+e^{x_3}} \right)$$

$$\vdots$$

$$\text{softmax}(x_1, \ldots, x_n) = \left(\frac{e^{x_1}}{e^{x_1}+\ldots+e^{x_n}}, \ldots, \frac{e^{x_n}}{e^{x_1}+\ldots+e^{x_n}} \right)$$

Figure 7.8 Handwritten softmax

Let's test it on an input vector:

```
# In[8]:
x = torch.tensor([1.0, 2.0, 3.0])

softmax(x)

# Out[8]:
tensor([0.0900, 0.2447, 0.6652])
```

As expected, it satisfies the constraints on probability:

```
# In[9]:
softmax(x).sum()

# Out[9]:
tensor(1.)
```

Softmax is a monotone function, meaning lower input values will always produce lower output values, preserving the ranking order. However, it's not scale invariant—the ratio between values changes during the transformation. For example, with input vector [1.0, 2.0, 3.0], the ratio between the first and second elements is $1/2 = 0.5$, but after softmax, it becomes approximately $0.090/0.245 = 0.368$. This transformation of ratios doesn't hinder learning since the neural network will automatically adjust its parameters to produce the appropriate logit values needed to generate the desired probability distribution after softmax is applied.

The nn module makes softmax available as a module. Since, as usual, input tensors may have an additional batch zeroth dimension or have dimensions along which they encode probabilities, and others in which they don't, nn.Softmax requires us to specify the dimension along which the softmax function is applied:

```
# In[10]:
softmax = nn.Softmax(dim=1)

x = torch.tensor([[1.0, 2.0, 3.0],
                  [3.0, 2.0, 1.0]])

softmax(x)

# Out[10]:
tensor([[0.0900, 0.2447, 0.6652],
        [0.6652, 0.2447, 0.0900]])
```

In this case, we have two input vectors in two rows (just like when we work with batches), so we initialize nn.Softmax to operate along dimension 1 (apply softmax to each row).

Excellent! We can now add a softmax at the end of our model, and our network will be equipped to produce probabilities:

```
# In[11]:
model = nn.Sequential(
            nn.Linear(3072, 512),
            nn.Tanh(),
            nn.Linear(512, 2),
            nn.Softmax(dim=1))
```

We can try running the model before even training it. Let's do it, just to see what comes out. We first build a batch of one image, our bird (figure 7.9):

```
# In[12]:
img, _ = cifar2[0]

plt.imshow(img.permute(1, 2, 0))
plt.show()
```

We can see the picture has some resemblance to a bird. To call the model, we need to make the input have the right dimensions. We recall that our model expects 3,072 features in the input and that nn works with data organized into batches along the zeroth dimension. So, we need to turn our 3 × 32 × 32 image into a 1D tensor and then add an extra dimension in the zeroth position. We learned how to do this in chapter 3:

```
# In[13]:
img_batch = img.view(-1).unsqueeze(0)
img_batch.shape

# Out[13]:
torch.Size([1, 3072])
```

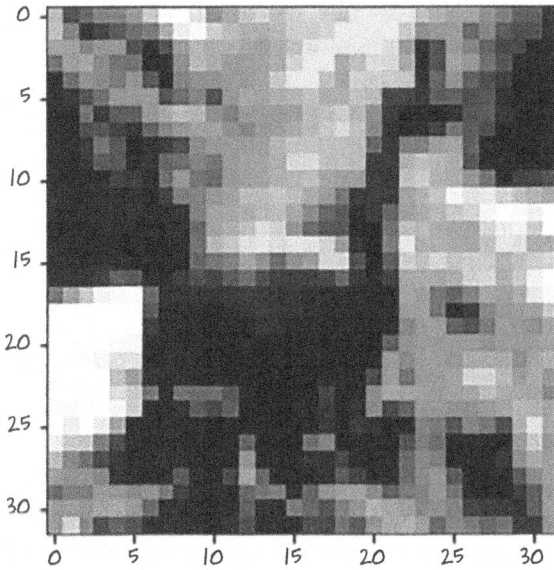

Figure 7.9 A random bird from the CIFAR-10 dataset (after normalization)

Now we're ready to invoke our model:

```
# In[14]:
out = model(img_batch)
out

# Out[14]:
tensor([[0.4784, 0.5216]], grad_fn=<SoftmaxBackward>)
```

So, we got probabilities! Well, we know we shouldn't get too excited: the weights and biases of our linear layers have not been trained at all. Their elements are initialized randomly by PyTorch between –1.0 and 1.0. Interestingly, we also see `grad_fn` for the output, which is the tip of the backward computation graph (it will be used as soon as we need to backpropagate).

> **NOTE** While it is, in principle, possible to say that here the model is uncertain (because it assigns 48% and 52% probabilities to the two classes), typical training results in highly overconfident models. Bayesian neural networks can provide some remedy, but they are beyond the scope of this book.

In addition, while we know which output probability is supposed to be which (recall our `class_names`), our network has no indication of that. Is the first entry "airplane" and the second "bird," or the other way around? The network can't even tell that at this point. It's the loss function that associates a meaning with these two numbers, after backpropagation. If the labels are provided as index 0 for "airplane" and index 1 for "bird," then that's the order the outputs will be induced to take.

Thus, after training, we will be able to get the label as an index by computing the *argmax* of the output probabilities—that is, the index at which we get the maximum probability. Conveniently, when supplied with a dimension, `torch.max` returns the maximum element along that dimension as well as the index at which that value occurs. In our case, we need to take the max along the probability vector (not across batches), therefore, dimension 1:

```
# In[15]:
_, index = torch.max(out, dim=1)

index

# Out[15]:
tensor([1])
```

It says the image is a bird. Pure luck. But we have adapted our model output to the classification task at hand by getting it to output probabilities. We also have now run our model against an input image and verified that our plumbing works. Time to get training. As in the previous two chapters, we need a loss to minimize during training.

A LOSS FOR CLASSIFYING

We just mentioned that the loss is what gives the probabilities returned by the model meaning. In chapters 5 and 6, we used mean square error (MSE) as our loss. We could still use MSE and make our output probabilities converge to [0.0, 1.0] and [1.0, 0.0]. However, thinking about it, we're not really interested in reproducing these values exactly. Looking back at the argmax operation we used to extract the index of the predicted class, what we're really interested in is that the first probability is higher than the second for airplanes, and vice versa for birds. In other words, we want to penalize misclassifications rather than painstakingly penalize everything that doesn't look exactly like a 0.0 or 1.0.

What we need to maximize in this case is the probability associated with the correct class, `out[class_index]`, where `out` is the output of softmax and `class_index` is a vector containing 0 for "airplane" and 1 for "bird" for each sample. This quantity—that is, the probability associated with the correct class—is referred to as the *likelihood* (of our model's parameters, given the data).

> **TIP** For a succinct definition of the terminology, refer to David MacKay's *Information Theory, Inference, and Learning Algorithms* (Cambridge University Press, 2003), section 2.3.

In other words, we want a loss function that is very high when the likelihood is low—so low that the alternatives have a higher probability. Conversely, the loss should be low when the likelihood is higher than the alternatives, and we're not really fixated on driving the probability up to 1.

There's a loss function that behaves that way, and it's called *negative log likelihood* (NLL). It has the expression `NLL = - sum(log(out_i[c_i]))`, where the sum is taken over N samples and `c_i` is the correct class for sample i. Let's take a look at figure 7.10, which shows the NLL as a function of predicted probability.

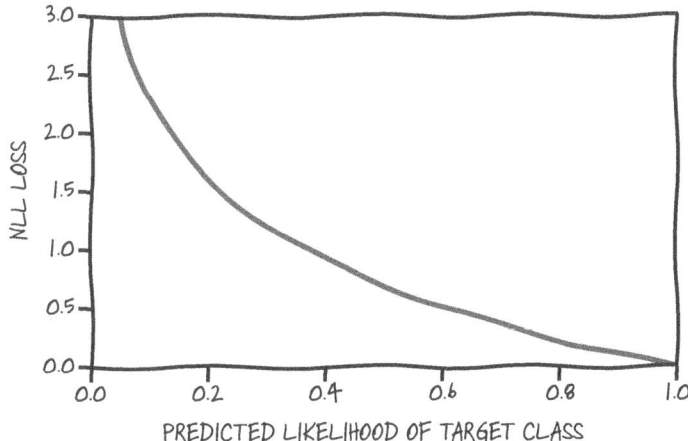

Figure 7.10 The NLL loss as a function of the predicted probabilities

Figure 7.10 shows that when low probabilities are assigned to the data, the NLL grows to infinity, whereas it decreases at a rather shallow rate when probabilities are greater than 0.5. Remember that the NLL takes probabilities as input, so as the likelihood grows, the other probabilities will necessarily decrease.

Summing up, our loss for classification can be computed as follows. For each sample in the batch,

1 Run the forward pass and obtain the output values from the last (linear) layer.
2 Compute their softmax and obtain probabilities.
3 Take the predicted probability corresponding to the correct class (the likelihood of the parameters). We know the correct class because it's a supervised problem—it's our ground truth.
4 Compute its logarithm, slap a minus sign in front of it, and add it to the loss.

So, how do we do this in PyTorch? PyTorch has an `nn.NLLLoss` class. However (gotcha ahead), as opposed to what you might expect, it does not take probabilities but rather takes a tensor of log probabilities as input. It then computes the NLL of our model given the batch of data. There's a good reason behind the input convention: taking the logarithm of a probability is tricky when the probability gets close to zero. The workaround is to use `nn.LogSoftmax` instead of `nn.Softmax`, which takes care to make the calculation numerically stable.

We can now modify our model to use `nn.LogSoftmax` as the output module:

```
# In[16]:
model = nn.Sequential(
            nn.Linear(3072, 512),
            nn.Tanh(),
            nn.Linear(512, 2),
            nn.LogSoftmax(dim=1))
```

Then we instantiate our NLL loss:

```
# In[17]:
loss = nn.NLLLoss()
```

The loss takes the output of `nn.LogSoftmax` for a batch as the first argument and a tensor of class indices (zeros and ones, in our case) as the second argument. We can now test it with our birdie:

```
# In[18]:
img, label = cifar2[0]
out = model(img.view(-1).unsqueeze(0))
loss(out, torch.tensor([label]))

# Out[18]:
tensor(0.5077, grad_fn=<NllLossBackward0>)
```

Continuing our exploration of different loss functions, *cross-entropy loss* is closely related to negative log likelihood. When you apply cross-entropy loss directly to the logits (the outputs of a layer before applying `LogSoftmax`), it yields the same result as applying `NLLLoss` to the output of a `LogSoftmax` layer. Cross-entropy loss internally computes the softmax of the logits before calculating the negative log likelihood, effectively combining the two steps into one operation.

We can observe the advantages of using cross-entropy loss over MSE for classification tasks. As illustrated in figure 7.11, cross-entropy loss maintains a gradient or slope even when the prediction is nearly correct, such as when the correct class is assigned a predicted probability of 99.97%. In contrast, MSE tends to saturate much earlier. This saturation occurs even when predictions are significantly incorrect, which is a critical drawback. The reason behind this behavior is that the slope of MSE is too shallow to effectively counteract the flatness introduced by the softmax function in scenarios of incorrect predictions. This characteristic of MSE makes it unsuitable for handling probabilities in classification tasks, where maintaining a responsive gradient is essential for effective learning and model adjustment.

7.2 Distinguishing birds from airplanes

SUCCESSFUL AND LESS SUCCESSFUL CLASSIFICATION LOSSES

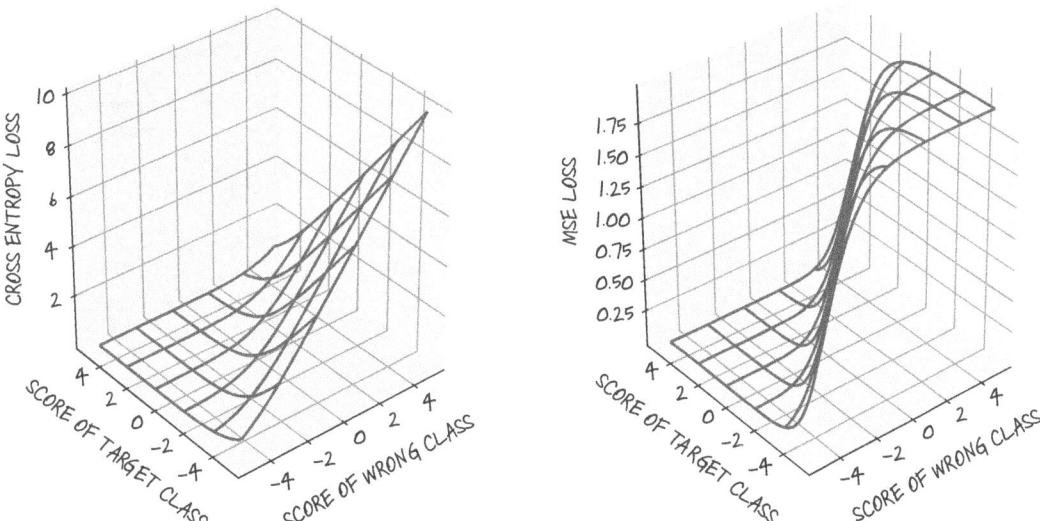

Figure 7.11 The cross-entropy (left) and MSE between predicted probabilities and the target probability vector (right) as functions of the predicted scores—that is, before the (log-) softmax.

7.2.5 Training the classifier

All right! We're ready to bring back the training loop we wrote in chapter 5 and see how it trains (the process is illustrated in figure 7.12). Now we can write our training loop:

```
# In[19]:
import torch
import torch.nn as nn
import torch.optim as optim

model = nn.Sequential(
            nn.Linear(3072, 512),
            nn.Tanh(),
            nn.Linear(512, 2),
            nn.LogSoftmax(dim=1))

learning_rate = 1e-2
optimizer = optim.SGD(model.parameters(), lr=learning_rate)
loss_fn = nn.NLLLoss()
n_epochs = 5

for epoch in range(n_epochs):
    for img, label in cifar2:
        img_tensor = img.view(-1).unsqueeze(0)
        label_tensor = torch.tensor([label])
```

```
out = model(img_tensor)
loss = loss_fn(out, label_tensor)

optimizer.zero_grad()
loss.backward()
optimizer.step()

print("Epoch: %d, Loss: %f" % (epoch, float(loss)))
```

Prints the loss for the last image

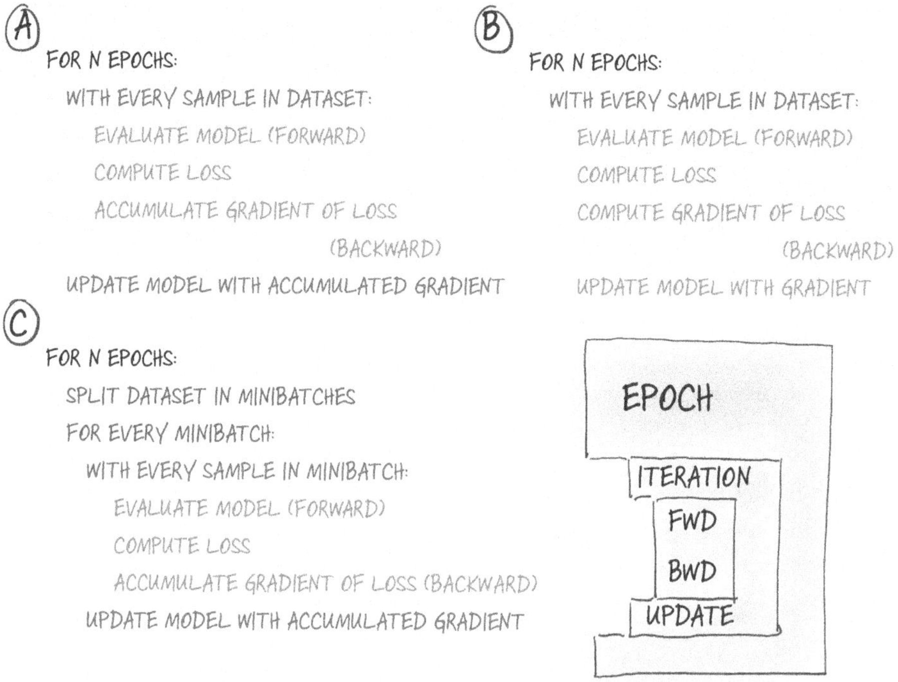

(A)
FOR N EPOCHS:
  WITH EVERY SAMPLE IN DATASET:
    EVALUATE MODEL (FORWARD)
    COMPUTE LOSS
    ACCUMULATE GRADIENT OF LOSS
          (BACKWARD)
  UPDATE MODEL WITH ACCUMULATED GRADIENT

(B)
FOR N EPOCHS:
  WITH EVERY SAMPLE IN DATASET:
    EVALUATE MODEL (FORWARD)
    COMPUTE LOSS
    COMPUTE GRADIENT OF LOSS
          (BACKWARD)
    UPDATE MODEL WITH GRADIENT

(C)
FOR N EPOCHS:
  SPLIT DATASET IN MINIBATCHES
  FOR EVERY MINIBATCH:
    WITH EVERY SAMPLE IN MINIBATCH:
      EVALUATE MODEL (FORWARD)
      COMPUTE LOSS
      ACCUMULATE GRADIENT OF LOSS (BACKWARD)
    UPDATE MODEL WITH ACCUMULATED GRADIENT

EPOCH
  ITERATION
    FWD
    BWD
  UPDATE

Figure 7.12 Training loops: (A) averaging updates over the whole dataset; (B) updating the model at each sample; and (C) averaging updates over minibatches.

You might have noticed that we modified the training loop from before. In chapter 5, we used a single loop that processed the entire dataset and performed forward propagation, backward propagation, and an optimizer step, repeating this process for N epochs (where an epoch covers a full pass through the entire training dataset). A batch is the number of samples processed before the model is updated, so in this case, each epoch we processed only one batch.

However, as we have 10,000 images in our dataset, processing all of them in a single batch would be impractical due to the large batch size. Consequently, we've implemented an inner loop where we evaluate one sample at a time and perform backpropagation for that individual sample.

While in the original training loop, the gradient is accumulated over all samples before being applied, in this new implementation, we apply changes to parameters based on a single sample, which is only a partial estimation of the gradient. However, what is a good direction for reducing the loss based on one sample might not be a good direction for others. By shuffling samples at each epoch and estimating the gradient on one or a few samples at a time, we are effectively introducing randomness in our gradient descent. Remember SGD? It stands for *stochastic gradient descent*, and this is what the *S* is about: working on small batches (aka minibatches) of shuffled data. Following gradients estimated over minibatches, which are poorer approximations of gradients estimated across the whole dataset, actually helps convergence and prevents the optimization process from getting stuck in local minima it encounters along the way. As depicted in figure 7.13, gradients from minibatches are randomly off the ideal trajectory, which is part of the reason why we want to use a reasonably small learning rate. Shuffling the dataset at each epoch helps ensure that the sequence of gradients estimated over minibatches is representative of the gradients computed across the full dataset.

Typically, minibatches are a constant size that we need to set before training, just like the learning rate. These are called *hyperparameters* to distinguish them from the parameters of a model.

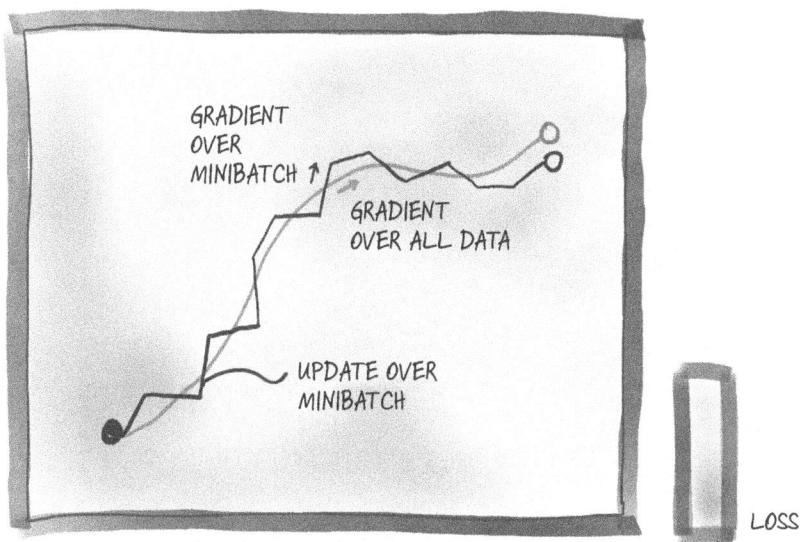

Figure 7.13 Gradient descent averaged over the whole dataset (light path) vs. stochastic gradient descent, where the gradient is estimated on randomly picked minibatches

In our training code, we chose minibatches of size 1 by picking one item at a time from the dataset. The `torch.utils.data` module has a class that helps with shuffling and organizing the data in minibatches, DataLoader, which can help us with larger batch sizes. The job of a data loader is to sample minibatches from a dataset, giving us the flexibility to choose from different sampling strategies. A very common strategy is uniform sampling after shuffling the data at each epoch. Figure 7.14 shows the data loader shuffling the indices it gets from the Dataset.

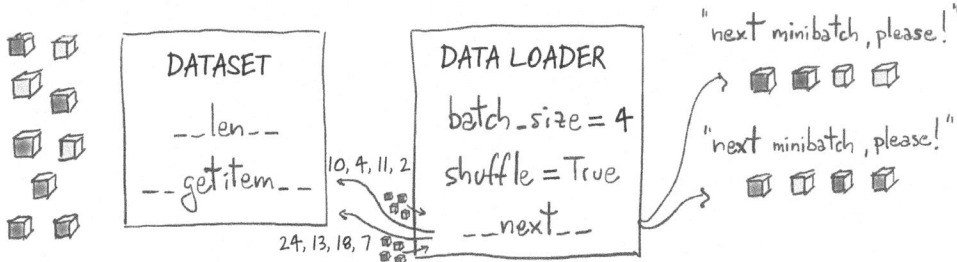

Figure 7.14 A data loader dispensing minibatches by using a dataset to sample individual data items.

Let's see how this is done. At a minimum, the DataLoader constructor takes a Dataset object as input, along with batch_size and a shuffle Boolean that indicates whether the data needs to be shuffled at the beginning of each epoch:

```
# In[20]:
train_loader = torch.utils.data.DataLoader(cifar2, batch_size=64,
                                           shuffle=True)
```

A DataLoader can be iterated over, so we can use it directly in the inner loop of our new training code:

```
# In[21]:
model = nn.Sequential(
            nn.Linear(3072, 512),
            nn.Tanh(),
            nn.Linear(512, 2),
            nn.LogSoftmax(dim=1))

learning_rate = 1e-2
optimizer = optim.SGD(model.parameters(), lr=learning_rate)
loss_fn = nn.NLLLoss()
n_epochs = 100

for epoch in range(n_epochs):
    for imgs, labels in train_loader:
        batch_size = imgs.shape[0]
        img_tensor = imgs.view(batch_size, -1)
        label_tensor = torch.tensor(labels)
        out = model(img_tensor)
        loss = loss_fn(out, label_tensor)
```

```
        optimizer.zero_grad()
        loss.backward()
        optimizer.step()

    print("Epoch: %d, Loss: %f" % (epoch, float(loss)))    ◁─┐
```

Due to the shuffling, this now prints the loss for a random batch—clearly something we want to improve in chapter 8.

At each inner iteration, `imgs` is a tensor of size 64 × 3 × 32 × 32—that is, a minibatch of 64 (32 × 32) RGB images—while `labels` is a tensor of size 64 containing label indices.

Let's run our training:

```
Epoch: 0, Loss: 0.523478
Epoch: 1, Loss: 0.391083
Epoch: 2, Loss: 0.407412
Epoch: 3, Loss: 0.364203
...
Epoch: 96, Loss: 0.019537
Epoch: 97, Loss: 0.008973
Epoch: 98, Loss: 0.002607
Epoch: 99, Loss: 0.026200
```

We see that the loss decreases somehow, but we have no idea whether it's low enough. Since our goal here is to correctly assign classes to images, preferably on an independent dataset, we can compute the accuracy of our model on the validation set in terms of the number of correct classifications over the total:

```
# In[22]:
val_loader = torch.utils.data.DataLoader(cifar2_val, batch_size=64,
                                         shuffle=False)

correct = 0
total = 0

with torch.no_grad():
    for imgs, labels in val_loader:
        batch_size = imgs.shape[0]
        outputs = model(imgs.view(batch_size, -1))
        _, predicted = torch.max(outputs, dim=1)
        total += labels.shape[0]
        correct += int((predicted == labels).sum())

print("Accuracy: %f", correct / total)

Accuracy: 0.811000
```

Not a great performance, but quite a lot better than random. In our defense, our model was quite a shallow classifier; it's a miracle that it worked at all. It did because our dataset is really simple—a lot of the samples in the two classes likely have systematic differences (such as the color of the background) that help the model tell birds from airplanes, based on a few pixels.

We can certainly add some bling to our model by including more layers, which will increase the model's depth and capacity. One rather arbitrary possibility is

```
# In[23]:
model = nn.Sequential(
            nn.Linear(3072, 1024),
            nn.Tanh(),
            nn.Linear(1024, 512),
            nn.Tanh(),
            nn.Linear(512, 128),
            nn.Tanh(),
            nn.Linear(128, 2),
            nn.LogSoftmax(dim=1))
```

Here, we are trying to taper the number of features more gently toward the output, in the hope that intermediate layers will do a better job of squeezing information in increasingly shorter intermediate outputs.

Combining nn.LogSoftmax and nn.NLLLoss is essentially the same as using nn.CrossEntropyLoss. This might seem a bit puzzling due to PyTorch's terminology. Here's what's happening:

- nn.NLLLoss computes the cross-entropy but expects log probabilities as inputs.
- nn.CrossEntropyLoss, on the other hand, works with raw scores (often called *logits*). Technically, nn.NLLLoss measures the cross-entropy between a distribution that concentrates all its mass on the target and the distribution predicted from the log probabilities.

It is quite common to drop the last nn.LogSoftmax layer from the network and just use nn.CrossEntropyLoss as a loss. Let's try that:

```
# In[24]:
model = nn.Sequential(
            nn.Linear(3072, 1024),
            nn.Tanh(),
            nn.Linear(1024, 512),
            nn.Tanh(),
            nn.Linear(512, 128),
            nn.Tanh(),
            nn.Linear(128, 2))

loss_fn = nn.CrossEntropyLoss()
```

Note that the numbers will be *exactly* the same as with nn.LogSoftmax and nn.NLLLoss. It's just more convenient to do it all in one pass, with the only gotcha being that the output of our model will not be interpretable as probabilities (or log probabilities). We'll need to explicitly pass the output through a softmax to obtain those.

Training this larger model and evaluating the accuracy on the validation set gets us 0.813000, a small increase in accuracy, but not much. However, the accuracy on the training set is perfect (1.000000). What is this result telling us? That we are overfitting

7.2 Distinguishing birds from airplanes

our model in both cases. Our fully connected model is finding a way to discriminate between birds and airplanes on the training set by memorizing the training set, but performance on the validation set is not all that great, even if we choose a larger model.

PyTorch offers a quick way to determine how many parameters a model has through the parameters() method of nn.Module (the same method we use to provide the parameters to the optimizer). To find out how many elements are in each tensor instance, we can call the numel method. Summing those gives us our total count. Depending on our use case, counting parameters might require us to check whether a parameter has requires_grad set to True, as well. We might want to differentiate the number of *trainable* parameters from the overall model size. Let's take a look at what we have right now:

```
# In[28]:
numel_list = [p.numel()
              for p in model.parameters()
              if p.requires_grad == True]
sum(numel_list), numel_list

# Out[28]:
(3737474, [3145728, 1024, 524288, 512, 65536, 128, 256, 2])
```

Wow, 3.7 million parameters! That's quite substantial to handle such a small input size, isn't it? Even our initial network was already quite substantial:

```
# In[29]:
numel_list = [p.numel() for p in first_model.parameters()]
sum(numel_list), numel_list

# Out[29]:
(1574402, [1572864, 512, 1024, 2])
```

The number of parameters in our first model is roughly half that in our latest model. From the list of individual parameter sizes, we start having an idea of what's responsible: the first module, which has 1.5 million parameters. In our latest network, we had 1,024 output features, which led the first linear module to have 3 million parameters. This shouldn't be unexpected: we know that a linear layer computes y = weight * x + bias, and if x has length 3,072 (disregarding the batch dimension for simplicity) and y must have length 1,024, then the weight tensor needs to be of size 1,024 × 3,072, and the bias size must be 1,024. And 1,024 * 3,072 + 1,024 = 3,146,752, as shown in the first two parameter values in cell 28 of numel_list. We can verify these quantities directly:

```
# In[30]:
linear = nn.Linear(3072, 1024)

linear.weight.shape, linear.bias.shape

# Out[30]:
(torch.Size([1024, 3072]), torch.Size([1024]))
```

What is this telling us? That our neural network won't scale very well with the number of pixels. What if we had a 1,024 × 1,024 RGB image? That's 3.1 million input values. Even abruptly going to 1,024 hidden features (which is not going to work for our classifier), we would have over 3 *billion* parameters. Using 32-bit floats, we're already at 12 GB of RAM, and we haven't even hit the second layer, much less computed and stored the gradients. That's just not going to fit on most present-day GPUs.

7.2.6 The limits of going fully connected

Let's reason about what using a linear module on a 1D view of our image entails; figure 7.15 visualizes what is going on. It's like taking every single input value—that is, every single component in our RGB image—and computing a linear combination of it with all the other values for every output feature. On one hand, we are allowing for the combination of any pixel with every other pixel in the image being potentially relevant for our task. On the other hand, we aren't utilizing the relative position of neighboring or far-away pixels, since we are treating the image as one big vector of numbers.

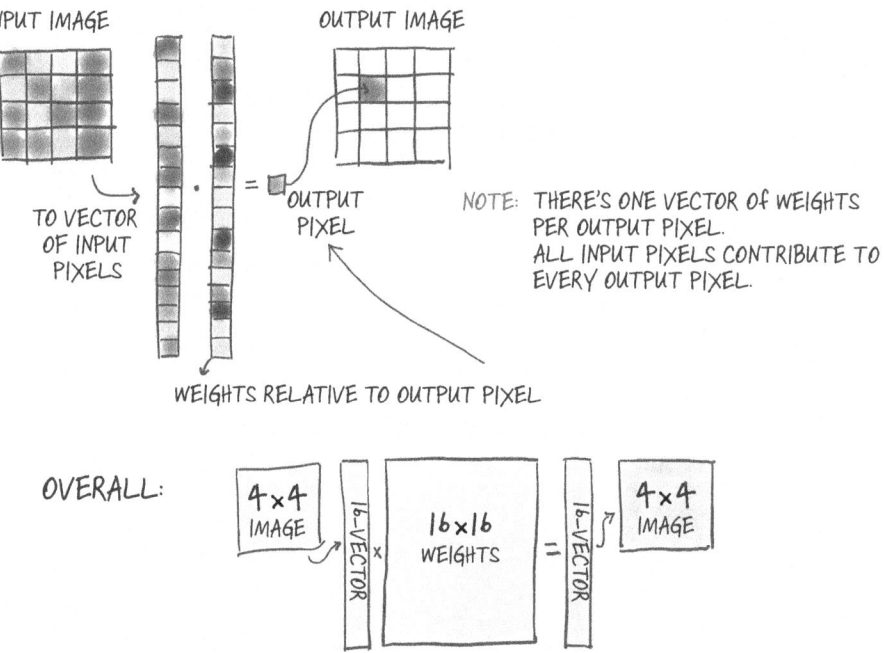

Figure 7.15 Using a fully connected module with an input image. Every input pixel is combined with every other to produce each element in the output.

An airplane flying in the sky captured in a 32 × 32 image will be very roughly similar to a dark, cross-like shape on a blue background. A fully connected network, as in figure 7.15, would need to learn that when pixel [x=0,y=1] is dark, pixel [x=1,y=1] is also dark, and so on, that's a good indication of an airplane. This is illustrated in the top half of figure 7.16. However, shift the same airplane by one pixel or more, as in the bottom half of the figure, and the relationships between pixels will have to be relearned from scratch. This time, an airplane is likely when pixel [x=0,y=2] is dark, pixel [x=1,y=2] is dark, and so on. In more technical terms, a fully connected network is not *translation invariant*. A network that has been trained to recognize an airplane starting at position 4,4 will not be able to recognize the *exact same* airplane starting at position 8,8.

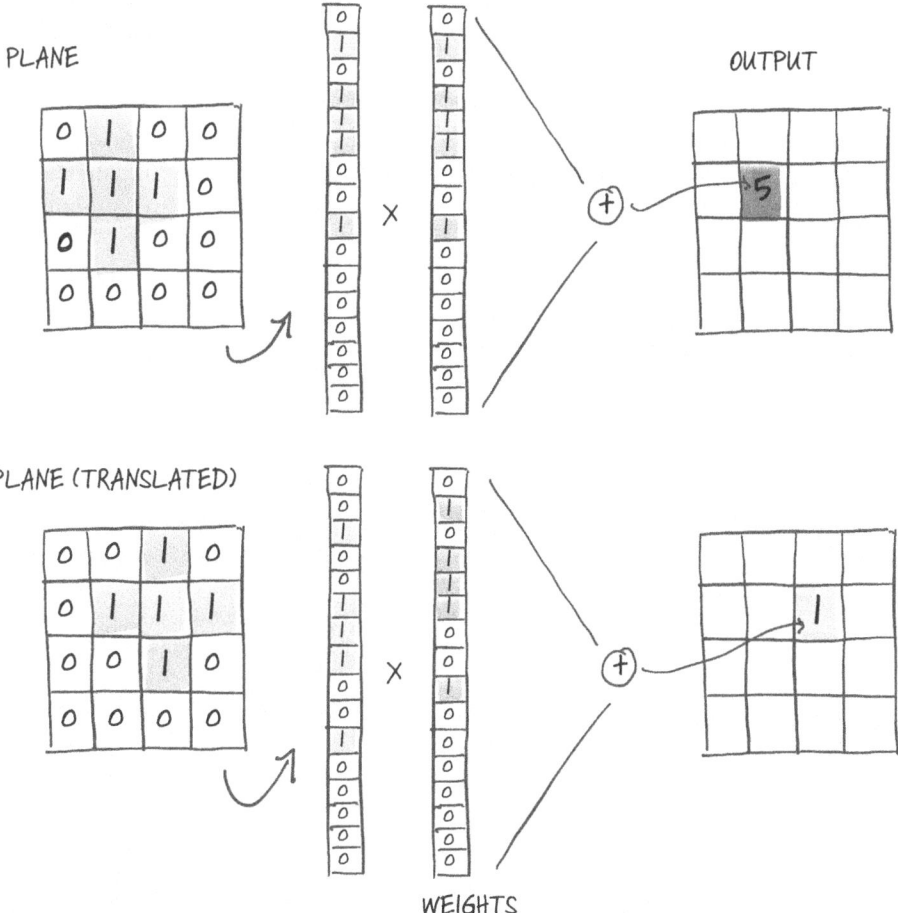

Figure 7.16 Translation invariance, or the lack thereof, with fully connected layers

We would then have to *augment* the dataset—that is, apply random translations to images during training—so the network would have a chance to see airplanes over different portions of the image, and we would need to do this for every image in the dataset (for the record, we could concatenate a transform from `torchvision.transforms` to do this transparently). However, this *data augmentation* strategy comes at a cost: the number of hidden features—that is, of parameters—must be large enough to store the information about all of these translated replicas.

So, at the end of this chapter, we have a dataset, a model, and a training loop, and our model learns. However, due to a mismatch between our problem and our network structure, we end up overfitting our training data, rather than learning the generalized features of what we want the model to detect.

We've created a model that allows for relating every pixel to every other pixel in the image, regardless of their spatial arrangement. We have a reasonable assumption that pixels that are closer together are, in theory, a lot more related, though. We are training a classifier that is not translation-invariant, so we're forced to use a lot of capacity for learning translated replicas if we want to hope to do well on the validation set. There has to be a better way, right?

Of course, most such questions in a book like this are rhetorical. The solution to our current set of problems is to change our model to use convolutional layers. We'll cover what that means in the next chapter.

7.3 Conclusion

In this chapter, we have solved a simple classification problem from dataset, to model, to minimizing an appropriate loss in a training loop. All of these things will be standard tools for your PyTorch toolbelt, and the skills needed to use them will be useful throughout your PyTorch tenure.

We've also found a severe shortcoming of our model: we have been treating 2D images as 1D data. Also, we do not have a natural way to incorporate the translation invariance of our problem. In the next chapter, you'll learn how to exploit the 2D nature of image data to get much better results.

> **NOTE** The same caveat about translation invariance also applies to purely 1D data: an audio classifier should likely produce the same output even if the sound to be classified starts a tenth of a second earlier or later.

We could use what we have learned right away to process data without this translation invariance. For example, using it on tabular data or the time-series data we met in chapter 4, we can probably do great things already. To some extent, it would also be possible to use it on text data that is appropriately represented.

> **NOTE** *Bag-of-words models*, which just average over word embeddings, can be processed with the network design from this chapter. More contemporary models take the positions of the words into account and need more advanced models.

7.4 Exercises

1. Use `torchvision` to implement random cropping of the data:
   a. How are the resulting images different from the uncropped originals?
   b. What happens when you request the same image a second time?
   c. What is the result of training using randomly cropped images?
2. Switch loss functions (perhaps MSE):
   a. Does the training behavior change?
   b. Is it possible to reduce the capacity of the network enough that it stops overfitting?
   c. How does the model perform on the validation set when doing so?

Summary

- Computer vision is one of the most extensive applications of deep learning.
- Several datasets of annotated images are publicly available; many, including `cifar10` can be accessed via `torchvision`.
- `torchvision` contains `transforms`, which are common image transformations that can be used for preparing the data before it is evaluated by deep learning models. We used `transforms` to turn images into tensors and normalize the data.
- `Datasets` and `DataLoaders` provide a simple yet effective abstraction for loading and sampling datasets. They allow you to change the batch size and shuffle the data for each batch, among other utilities.
- For a classification task, the output is categorical, and we can use a one-hot encoding representation to represent the correct output. Applying the softmax function on the output of a network produces values that sum to 1 and satisfy the requirements for being interpreted as probabilities.
- In classification, we get the loss function by using the softmax output as input for a negative log likelihood loss. This combination of softmax and negative log likelihood is known as cross-entropy loss in PyTorch.
- Nothing prevents us from treating images as vectors of pixel values, dealing with them using a fully connected network, just like any other numerical data. However, doing so makes it much harder to take advantage of the spatial relationships in the data.
- You can build models using PyTorch's `nn.Sequential` and `nn.Linear`. In this setup, the first linear layer in the sequence tends to have a significant number of parameters because it deals with the input size. It's a common practice to progressively reduce the number of parameters in the subsequent layers as they approach the output size. This gradual tapering helps optimize the model's architecture.

Using convolutions to generalize

This chapter covers

- Understanding convolution
- Building a convolutional neural network
- Creating custom `nn.Module` subclasses
- The difference between the module and functional APIs
- Design choices for neural networks

In the previous chapter, we built a simple neural network that could fit (or overfit) the data, thanks to the many parameters available for optimization in the linear layers. Our model used fully connected layers, where each neuron connects to every neuron in the previous layer, treating the image as a flattened vector with no spatial structure preserved. However, we had problems with our model in that it was better at memorizing the training set than it was at generalizing the properties of birds and airplanes. Based on our model architecture, we've got a guess as to why that's the case. Due to the fully connected setup needed to detect the various possible translations of the bird or airplane in the image, we have too many parameters (making it easier for the model to memorize the training set) and no position independence (making it harder to generalize). As we discussed in the last chapter, we could augment our training data by using a wide variety of re-cropped images to try to force generalization, but that won't address the issue of having too many parameters.

There is a better way! It consists of replacing the dense, fully connected affine transformation in our neural network unit with a different linear operation: convolution.

8.1 The case for convolutions

Let's get to the bottom of what convolutions are and how we can use them in our neural networks. Yes, yes, we were in the middle of our quest to tell birds from airplanes, and our friend is still waiting for our solution, but this diversion is worth the extra time spent. We'll develop an intuition for this foundational concept in computer vision and then return to our problem equipped with superpowers.

In this section, we'll see how convolutions deliver locality and translation invariance. We'll do so by taking a close look at the formula defining convolutions and applying it using pen and paper—but don't worry, the gist will be in pictures, not formulas.

We said earlier that taking a 1D view of our input image and multiplying it by an `n_output_features` × `n_input_features` weight matrix, as is done in `nn.Linear`, means for each channel in the image, computing a weighted sum of all the pixels multiplied by a set of weights, one per output feature. We also said that, if we want to recognize patterns corresponding to objects, like an airplane in the sky, we will likely need to look at how nearby pixels are arranged, and we will be less interested in how pixels that are far from each other appear in combination. Essentially, it doesn't matter whether our image of a Spitfire has a tree, a cloud, or a kite in the corner or not.

To translate this intuition into mathematical form, we could compute the weighted sum of a pixel with its immediate neighbors, rather than with all other pixels in the image. This would be equivalent to building weight matrices, one per output feature and output pixel location, in which all weights beyond a certain distance from a center pixel are zero. This will still be a weighted sum—that is, a linear operation.

8.1.1 What convolutions do

We identified one more desired property earlier: we would like these localized patterns to have an effect on the output, regardless of their location in the image—that is, to be *translation invariant*. Achieving this goal in a matrix applied to the image-as-a-vector we used in chapter 7 would require implementing a rather complicated pattern of weights (don't worry if it is *too* complicated; it'll get better shortly): most of the weight matrix would be zero (for entries corresponding to input pixels that are too far away from the output pixel to have an influence). For other weights, we would have to find a way to keep entries in sync that correspond to the same relative position of input and output pixels. So, we would need to initialize them to the same values and ensure that all these *tied* weights stayed the same while the network is updated during training. This way, we would ensure that weights operate in neighborhoods to respond to local patterns, and local patterns are identified, no matter where they occur in the image.

Of course, this approach is more than impractical. Fortunately, there is a readily available, local, translation-invariant linear operation on the image: a *convolution*. We can come up with a more compact description of a convolution, but what we are going to describe is exactly what we just delineated—only taken from a different angle.

Convolution, or more precisely, *discrete convolution* (there's an analogous continuous version that we won't go into here), is defined for a 2D image as the scalar product of a weight matrix, the *kernel*, with every neighborhood in the input. Consider a 3 × 3 kernel (in deep learning, we typically use small kernels; we'll see why later on) as a 2D tensor,

```
weight = torch.tensor([[w00, w01, w02],
                       [w10, w11, w12],
                       [w20, w21, w22]])
```

and a 1-channel, MxN image,

```
image = torch.tensor([[i00, i01, i02, i03, ..., i0N],
                      [i10, i11, i12, i13, ..., i1N],
                      [i20, i21, i22, i23, ..., i2N],
                      [i30, i31, i32, i33, ..., i3N],
                      ...
                      [iM0, iM1m iM2, iM3, ..., iMN]])
```

NOTE There is a subtle difference between PyTorch's convolution and mathematics' convolution: one argument's sign is flipped. If we were in a pedantic mood, we could call PyTorch's convolutions *discrete cross-correlations*.

We can compute an element of the output image (without bias) as follows:

```
o11 = i11 * w00 + i12 * w01 + i13 * w02 +
      i21 * w10 + i22 * w11 + i23 * w12 +
      i31 * w20 + i32 * w21 + i33 * w22
```

Figure 8.1 shows this computation in action.

That is, we "translate" the kernel on the i11 location of the input image, and we multiply each weight by the value of the input image at the corresponding location. Thus, the output image is created by translating the kernel on all input locations and performing the weighted sum. For a multichannel image, like our RGB image, the weight matrix would be a 3 × 3 × 3 matrix: one set of weights for every channel, contributing together to the output values.

Note that, just like the elements in the weight matrix of nn.Linear, the weights in the kernel are not known in advance, but they are initialized randomly and updated through backpropagation. The same kernel, and thus each weight in the kernel, is reused across the whole image. Thinking back to autograd, the use of each weight has a history spanning the entire image. Thus, the derivative of the loss with respect to a convolution's weight includes contributions from the entire image.

8.1 The case for convolutions

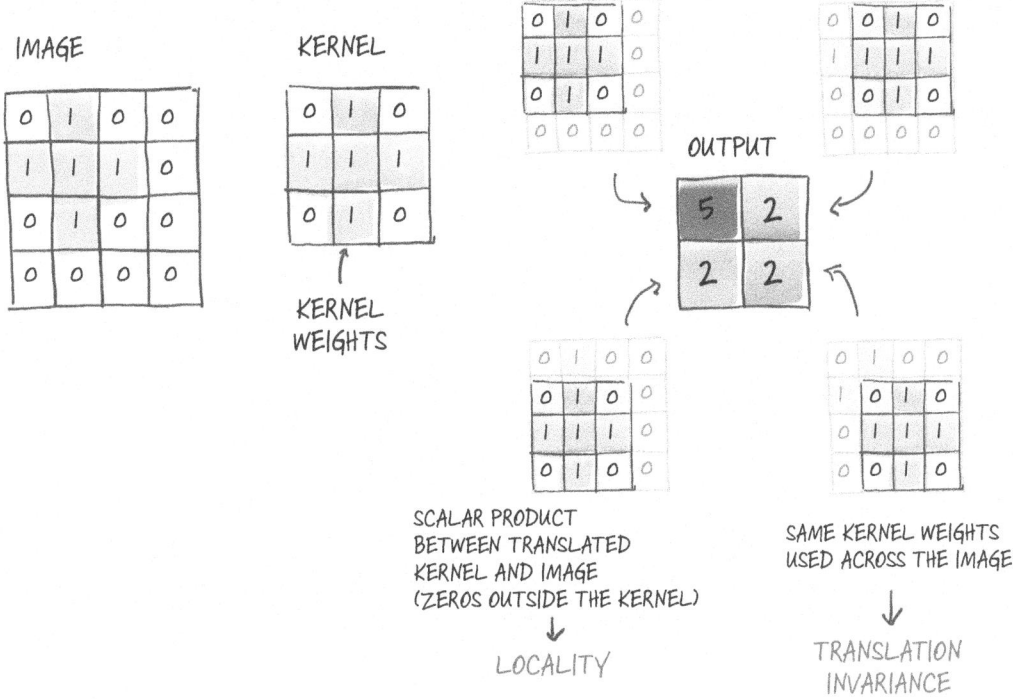

Figure 8.1 Convolution: locality and translation invariance

It's now possible to see the connection to what we were stating earlier: a convolution is equivalent to having multiple linear operations whose weights are zero almost everywhere except around individual pixels and that receive equal updates during training. This process is illustrated in figure 8.2.

Summarizing, by switching to convolutions, we get

- Local operations on neighborhoods
- Translation invariance
- Models with a lot fewer parameters

The key insight underlying the third point is that, with a convolutional layer, the number of parameters depends not on the number of pixels in the image, as was the case in our fully connected model, but rather on the size of the convolution kernel (3×3, 5×5, and so on) and on how many convolution filters (or output channels) we decide to use in our model.

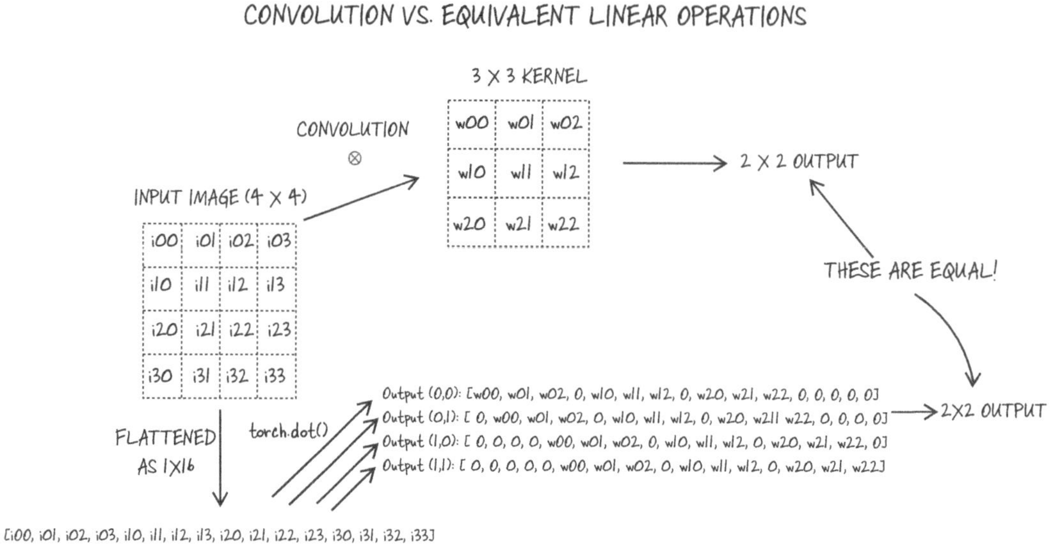

CONVOLUTION VS. EQUIVALENT LINEAR OPERATIONS

Figure 8.2 Convolution and the equivalent linear operations. The linear weights will be sparse (only a few nonzero values) and tied (the same values appear in multiple places).

8.2 Convolutions in action

Well, it looks like we've spent enough time down a rabbit hole! Let's see some PyTorch in action on our birds versus airplanes challenge. The `torch.nn` module provides convolutions for 1, 2, and 3 dimensions: `nn.Conv1d` for time series, `nn.Conv2d` for images, and `nn.Conv3d` for volumes or videos.

For our CIFAR-10 data, we'll resort to `nn.Conv2d`. At a minimum, the arguments we provide to `nn.Conv2d` are the number of input features (or *channels*, since we're dealing with *multichannel* images; that is, more than one value per pixel), the number of output features, and the size of the kernel. For instance, for our first convolutional module, we'll have three input features per pixel (the RGB channels) and an arbitrary number of channels in the output—say, 16. The more channels in the output image, the greater the capacity of the network. We need the channels to be able to detect many different types of features. Also, because we are randomly initializing them, some of the features we'll get, even after training, will turn out to be useless. Let's stick to a kernel size of 3 × 3.

> **NOTE** This is part of the *lottery ticket hypothesis*: that many kernels will be as useful as losing lottery tickets. See Jonathan Frankle and Michael Carbin, "The Lottery Ticket Hypothesis: Finding Sparse, Trainable Neural Networks," 2019, https://arxiv.org/abs/1803.03635.

It is very common to have kernel sizes that are the same in all directions, so PyTorch has a shortcut for this: whenever `kernel_size=3` is specified for a 2D convolution, it means 3 × 3 (provided as a tuple (3, 3) in Python). For a 3D convolution, it means 3 × 3 × 3. The CT scans we will see in part 2 of the book have a different voxel (volumetric pixel) resolution in one of the three axes. In such a case, it makes sense to consider kernels that have a different size for the exceptional dimension. But for now, we stick with having the same size of convolutions across all dimensions:

```
# In[7]:
conv = nn.Conv2d(3, 16, kernel_size=3)
conv

# Out[7]:
Conv2d(3, 16, kernel_size=(3, 3), stride=(1, 1))
```

3 represents the number of input channels (typically for a colored image with red, green, and blue channels). 16 represents the number of output channels. For the last argument kernel_size=3, we could equivalently pass in the tuple that we see in the output: kernel_size=(3, 3).

What do we expect to be the shape of the `conv.weight` tensor?

So, this layer is designed to take input data with 3 channels, apply 16 different 3 × 3 convolutional filters to it, and produce 16 output channels as a result. For a single output pixel value, the kernel considers all 3 input channels, so the weight component for one output pixel (and consequently, for the entire output channel) is of shape in_ch (3) × 3 × 3. Since there are 16 output channels, the complete weight tensor for this layer has a shape of out_ch (16) × in_ch (3) × 3 × 3. In this case, the complete weight tensor is 16 × 3 × 3 × 3. The bias will have size 16 (we haven't talked about bias for a while for simplicity, but just as in the linear module case, it's a constant value we add to each channel of the output image). Let's verify our assumptions:

```
# In[8]:
conv.weight.shape, conv.bias.shape

# Out[8]:
(torch.Size([16, 3, 3, 3]), torch.Size([16]))
```

We can see how convolutions are a convenient choice for learning from images. We have smaller models looking for local patterns whose weights are optimized across the entire image.

A 2D convolution pass produces a 2D image as output, whose pixels are a weighted sum over neighborhoods of the input image. In our case, both the kernel weights and the bias `conv.weight` are initialized randomly, so the output image will not be particularly meaningful. As usual, we need to add the zeroth batch dimension with unsqueeze if we want to call the conv module with one input image, since nn.Conv2d expects a $B \times C \times H \times W$-shaped tensor as input:

```
# In[9]:
img, _ = cifar2[0]
output = conv(img.unsqueeze(0))
img.unsqueeze(0).shape, output.shape

# Out[9]:
(torch.Size([1, 3, 32, 32]), torch.Size([1, 16, 30, 30]))
```

We're curious, so we can display the output, shown in figure 8.3:

```
# In[12]:
# skip definition of helper function plot_images
plot_images(img, output)
```

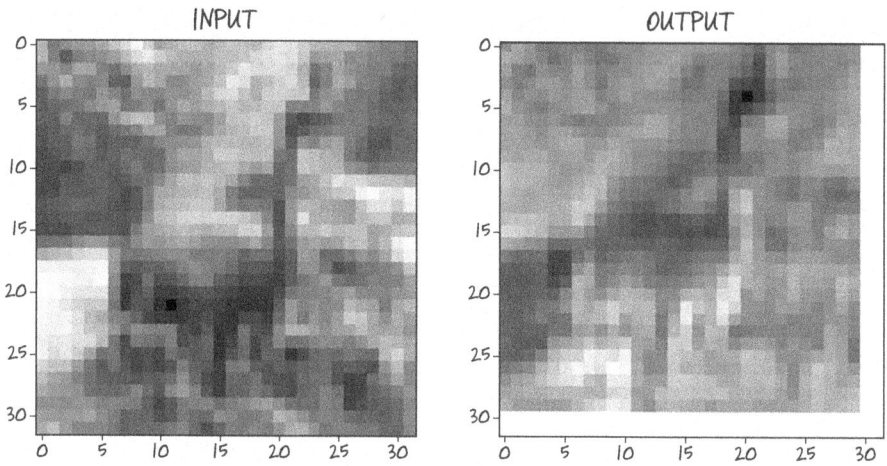

Figure 8.3 Our original bird image on the left and modified image on the right after a random convolution treatment.

Wait a minute. Let's take a look at the size of output: it's torch.Size([1, 16, 30, 30]). Huh, we lost a few pixels in the process. How did that happen?

8.2.1 Padding the boundary

The fact that our output image is smaller than the input is a side effect of deciding what to do at the boundary of the image. Applying a convolution kernel as a weighted sum of pixels in a 3 × 3 neighborhood requires that there are neighbors in all directions. If we are at index (0, 0), we only have pixels to the right of and below us. By default, PyTorch will slide the convolution kernel within the input picture, getting width - kernel_width + 1 horizontal and vertical positions. For odd-sized kernels, this results in images that are one-half the convolution kernel's width (in our case, 3//2 = 1) smaller on each side. This explains why we're missing two pixels in each dimension.

However, PyTorch gives us the possibility of *padding* the image by creating *ghost* pixels around the border that have value zero as far as the convolution is concerned. Figure 8.4 shows padding in action.

In our case, specifying padding=1 when kernel_size=3 means index (0, 0) has an extra set of neighbors above it and to its left, so that an output of the convolution can be computed even in the corner of our original image.

8.2 Convolutions in action 207

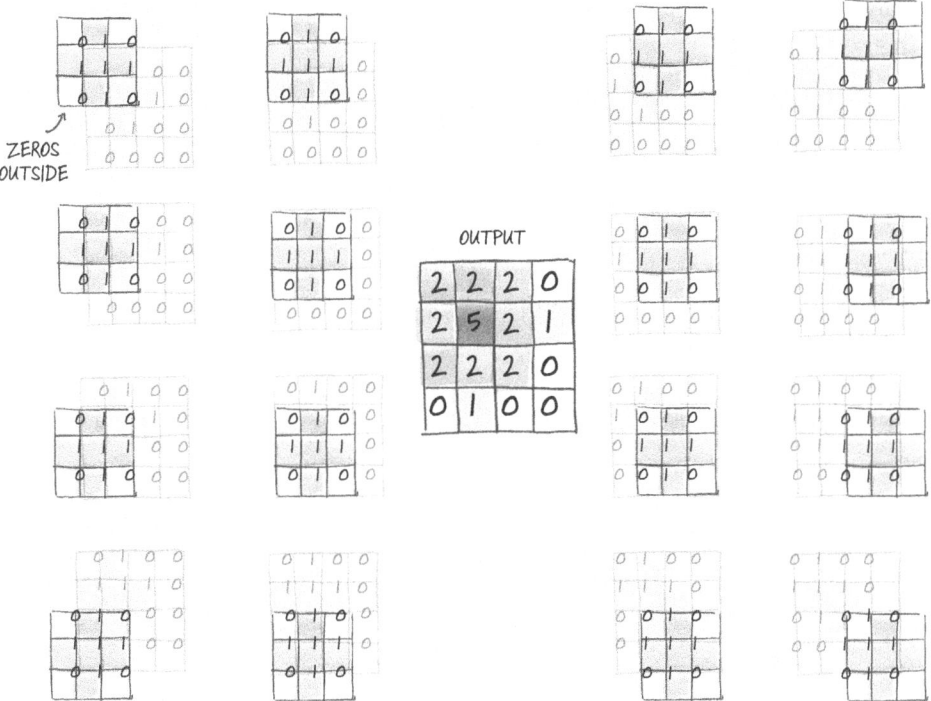

Figure 8.4 padding=1 wraps 0s around all sides of the input to preserve the image size in the output.

NOTE For even-sized kernels, we would need to pad by a different number on the left and right (and top and bottom). PyTorch doesn't offer to do this in the convolution itself, but the function torch.nn.functional.pad can take care of it. But it's best to stay with odd kernel sizes; even-sized kernels are just odd.

The net result is that the output has now the exact same size as the input:

```
# In[13]:
conv = nn.Conv2d(3, 1, kernel_size=3, padding=1)      # Now with padding
output = conv(img.unsqueeze(0))
img.unsqueeze(0).shape, output.shape

# Out[13]:
(torch.Size([1, 3, 32, 32]), torch.Size([1, 1, 32, 32]))
```

Note that the sizes of weight and bias don't change, regardless of whether padding is used.

There are two main reasons to pad convolutions. First, doing so helps us separate the matters of convolution and changing image sizes, so we have one less thing to remember. Second, when we have more elaborate structures such as skip connections (discussed in section 8.5.3) or the U-Nets (covered in chapter 10), we want the tensors

8.2.2 Detecting features with convolutions

We said earlier that `weight` and `bias` are parameters that are learned through backpropagation, exactly as it happens for `weight` and `bias` in `nn.Linear`. However, we can play with convolution by setting weights by hand and see what happens.

Let's first zero out `bias`, just to remove any confounding factors, and then set `weights` to a constant value so that each pixel in the output gets the mean of its neighbors. For each 3 × 3 neighborhood,

```
# In[14]:
with torch.no_grad():
    conv.bias.zero_()

with torch.no_grad():
    conv.weight.fill_(1.0 / 9.0)
```

We could have gone with `conv.weight.one_()`—that would result in each pixel in the output being the *sum* of the pixels in the neighborhood. Not a big difference, except that the values in the output image would have been nine times larger.

Anyway, let's see the effect on our CIFAR image:

```
# In[15]:
output = conv(img.unsqueeze(0))
plot_images(img, output)
```

As we could have predicted, the filter produces a blurred version of the image, as shown in figure 8.5. After all, every pixel of the output is the average of a neighborhood of the input, so pixels in the output are correlated and change more smoothly.

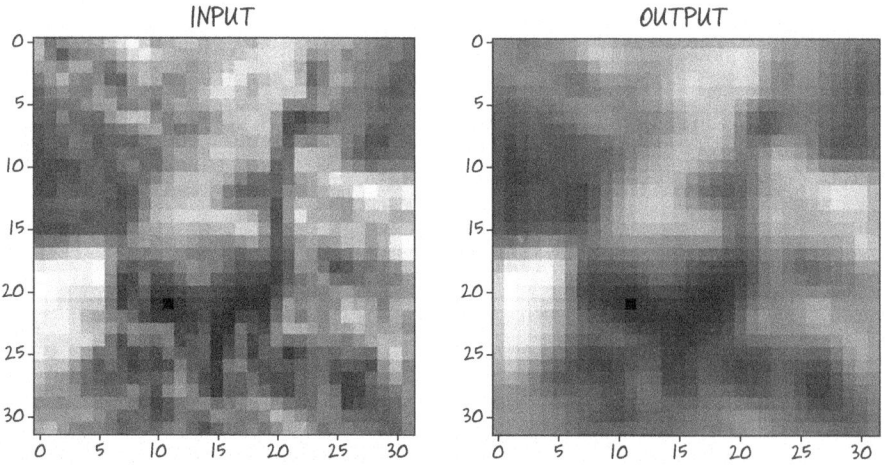

Figure 8.5 Our bird, this time blurred thanks to a constant convolution kernel

Next, let's try something different. The following kernel may look a bit mysterious at first:

```
# In[16]:
conv = nn.Conv2d(3, 1, kernel_size=3, padding=1)

with torch.no_grad():
    conv.weight[:] = torch.tensor([[-1.0, 0.0, 1.0],
                                   [-1.0, 0.0, 1.0],
                                   [-1.0, 0.0, 1.0]])
    conv.bias.zero_()
```

Working out the weighted sum for an arbitrary pixel in position 2,2, as we did earlier for the generic convolution kernel, we get

```
o22 = i13 - i11 +
      i23 - i21 +
      i33 - i31
```

which performs the difference of all pixels on the right of `i22` minus the pixels on the left of `i22`. If the kernel is applied on a vertical boundary between two adjacent regions of different intensity, `o22` will have a high value. If the kernel is applied on a region of uniform intensity, `o22` will be zero. It's an *edge-detection* kernel: the kernel highlights the vertical edge between two horizontally adjacent regions.

Applying the convolution kernel to our image, we see the result shown in figure 8.6. As expected, the convolution kernel, applied to the vertical edges throughout our bird, enhances the vertical edges. We could build lots more elaborate filters, such as for detecting horizontal or diagonal edges, or cross-like or checkerboard patterns, where "detecting" means the output has a high magnitude. In fact, the job of a computer vision expert has historically been to come up with the most effective combination of filters so that certain features are highlighted in images and objects can be recognized (see figure 8.7).

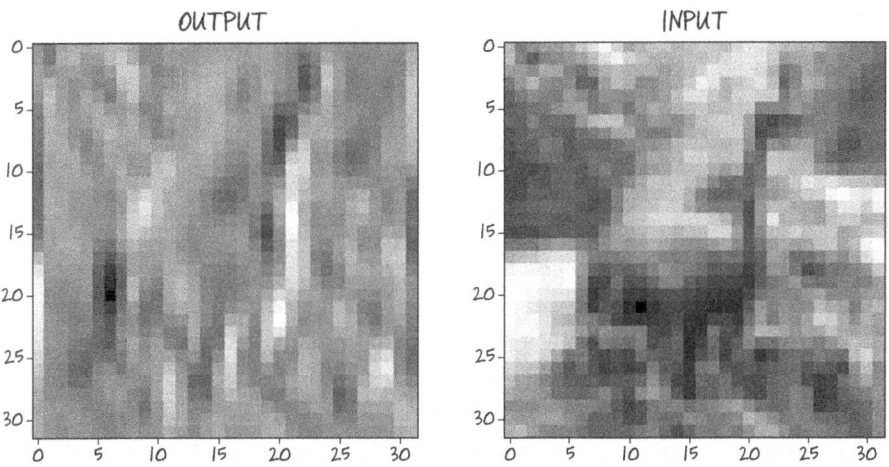

Figure 8.6 **Vertical edges throughout our bird, courtesy of a handcrafted convolution kernel**

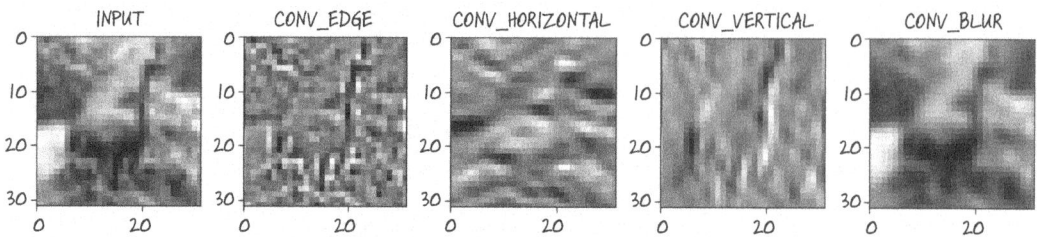

Figure 8.7 Different kernel examples for detecting different features. We have hardcoded these examples for illustration purposes, but, in reality, the model will learn the appropriate kernels for the task at hand.

With deep learning, we let kernels be estimated from data in whatever way the discrimination is most effective: for instance, in terms of minimizing the negative cross-entropy loss between the output and the ground truth that we introduced in section 7.2.5. From this angle, the job of a convolutional neural network is to estimate the kernel of a set of filter banks in successive layers that will transform a multichannel image into another multichannel image, where different channels correspond to different features (such as one channel for the average, another channel for vertical edges, and so on). Figure 8.8 shows how the training automatically learns the kernels.

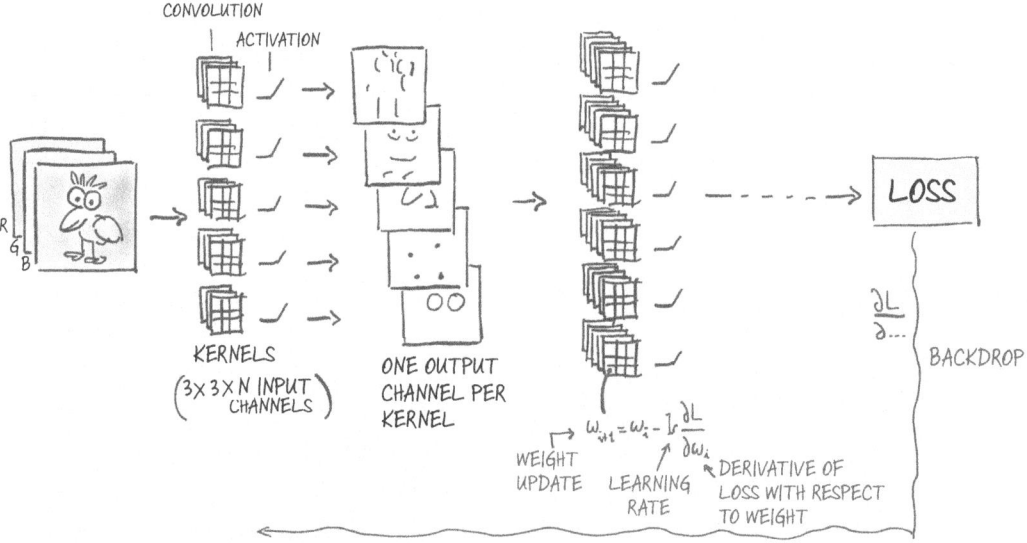

Figure 8.8 The process of learning with convolutions by estimating the gradient at the kernel weights and updating them individually to optimize for the loss

8.2.3 Looking further with depth and pooling

What we've done so far is all well and good, but conceptually, there's an elephant in the room. We got all excited because by moving from fully connected layers to convolutions, we achieve locality and translation invariance. Then we recommended the use of small kernels, like 3×3, or 5×5: that's peak locality, all right. What about the *big picture*? How do we know that all structures in our images are 3 pixels or 5 pixels wide? Well, we don't because they aren't. And if they aren't, how are our networks going to be equipped to see those patterns with a larger scope? We'll really need to think about this issue if we want to solve our birds-versus-airplanes problem effectively—although CIFAR-10 images are small, the objects still have a (wing-)span of several pixels across.

One possibility could be to use large convolution kernels. Well, sure, at the limit, we could get a 32×32 kernel for a 32×32 image, but we would converge to the old fully connected, affine transformation and lose all the nice properties of convolution. Another option, which is used in convolutional neural networks, is stacking one convolution after the other and, at the same time, downsampling the image between successive convolutions. Downsampling, also known as pooling or subsampling, involves reducing the spatial dimensions of the feature maps, typically by taking the maximum or average value over certain regions of the feature map.

FROM LARGE TO SMALL: DOWNSAMPLING

Downsampling can, in principle, occur in different ways. Scaling an image by half is the equivalent of taking four neighboring pixels as input and producing one pixel as output. How we compute the value of the output based on the values of the input is up to us. We could

- *Average the four pixels*—This *average pooling* was a common approach early on but has fallen out of favor somewhat.
- *Take the maximum of the four pixels*—This approach, called *max pooling*, is currently the most commonly used, but it has a downside of discarding the other three-fourths of the data.
- *Perform a strided convolution, where only every Nth pixel is calculated*—A convolution kernel size greater than or equal to 2×2, with stride 2, still incorporates input from all pixels from the previous layer. The literature shows promise for this approach, but it has not yet supplanted max pooling.

We will be focusing on max pooling going forward. Figure 8.9 shows the most common setup of taking non-overlapping 2×2 tiles and taking the maximum over each of them as the new pixel at the reduced scale.

Intuitively, the output images from a convolution layer, especially since they are followed by an activation just like any other linear layer, tend to have a high magnitude where certain features corresponding to the estimated kernel are detected (such as vertical lines). By keeping the highest value in the 2×2 neighborhood as

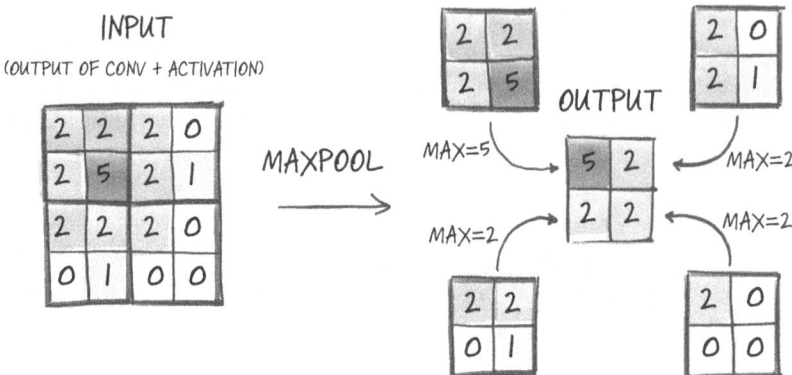

Figure 8.9 Max pooling in detail

the downsampled output, we ensure that the features that are found *survive* the downsampling at the expense of the weaker responses.

Max pooling is provided by the nn.MaxPool2d module (as with convolution, there are versions for 1D and 3D data). It takes as input the size of the neighborhood over which to operate the pooling operation. If we wish to downsample our image by half, we'll want to use a size of 2. Let's verify that it works as expected directly on our input image:

```
# In[21]:
pool = nn.MaxPool2d(2)
output = pool(img.unsqueeze(0))

img.unsqueeze(0).shape, output.shape

# Out[21]:
(torch.Size([1, 3, 32, 32]), torch.Size([1, 3, 16, 16]))
```

COMBINING CONVOLUTIONS AND DOWNSAMPLING FOR GREAT GOOD

Let's now see how combining convolutions and downsampling can help us recognize larger structures. In figure 8.10, we start by applying a set of 3 × 3 kernels on our 8 × 8 image, obtaining a multichannel output image of the same size. Then we scale down the output image by half, obtaining a 4 × 4 image, and apply another set of 3 × 3 kernels to it. This second set of kernels operates on a 3 × 3 neighborhood of something that has been scaled down by half, so it effectively maps back to 8 × 8 neighborhoods of the input. In addition, the second set of kernels takes the output of the first set of kernels (features like averages, edges, and so on) and extracts additional features on top of those.

So, on one hand, the first set of kernels operates on small neighborhoods on first-order, low-level features, while the second set of kernels effectively operates on wider neighborhoods, producing features that are compositions of the previous features.

8.2 Convolutions in action 213

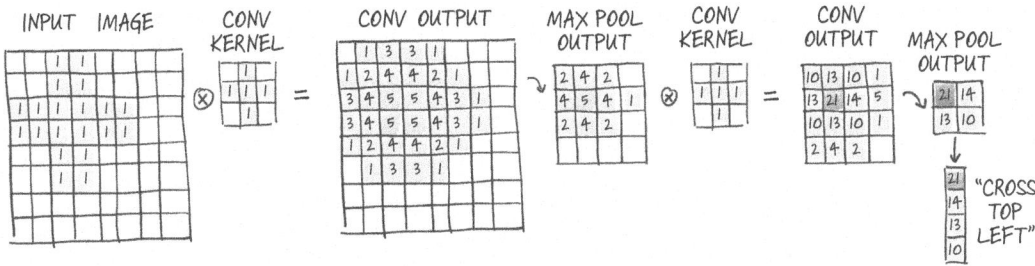

Figure 8.10 More convolutions by hand, showing the effect of stacking convolutions and downsampling: a large cross is highlighted using two small, cross-shaped kernels and max pooling

> **The receptive field of output pixels**
>
> When the second 3 × 3 convolution kernel produces 21 in its conv output in figure 8.10, this is based on the top-left 3 × 3 pixels of the first max pool output. They, in turn, correspond to the 6 × 6 pixels in the top-left corner in the first conv output, which in turn are computed by the first convolution from the top-left 7 × 7 pixels. So the pixel in the second convolution output is influenced by a 7 × 7 input square. The first convolution also uses an implicitly "padded" column and row to produce the output in the corner; otherwise, we would have an 8 × 8 square of input pixels informing a given pixel (away from the boundary) in the second convolution's output. In fancy language, we say that a given output neuron of the 3 × 3 conv, 2 × 2 max pool, 3 × 3 conv construction has a receptive field of 8 × 8.

This very powerful mechanism provides convolutional neural networks with the ability to see into very complex scenes—much more complex than our 32 × 32 images from the CIFAR-10 dataset.

8.2.4 Putting it all together for our network

With these building blocks in our hands, we can now proceed to build our convolutional neural network for detecting birds and airplanes. Let's take our previous fully connected model as a starting point and introduce nn.Conv2d and nn.MaxPool2d as described previously:

```
# In[22]:
model = nn.Sequential(
            nn.Conv2d(3, 16, kernel_size=3, padding=1),
            nn.Tanh(),
            nn.MaxPool2d(2),
            nn.Conv2d(16, 8, kernel_size=3, padding=1),
            nn.Tanh(),
            nn.MaxPool2d(2),
            # ...
            )
```

The first convolution takes us from 3 RGB channels to 16, thereby giving the network a chance to generate 16 independent features that operate to (hopefully) discriminate low-level features of birds and airplanes. Then we apply the Tanh activation function.

> **NOTE** We could also use ReLUs, which we saw in the previous chapter, but we use Tanh to add variety in showing how we can easily utilize other activation functions.

The resulting 16-channel 32 × 32 image is pooled to a 16-channel 16 × 16 image by the first MaxPool2d. At this point, the downsampled image undergoes another convolution that generates an 8-channel 16 × 16 output. With any luck, this output will consist of higher-level features. Again, we apply a Tanh activation and then pool to an 8-channel 8 × 8 output.

Where does this end? After the input image has been reduced to a set of 8 × 8 features, we expect to be able to output some probabilities from the network that we can feed to our negative log likelihood. However, probabilities are a pair of numbers in a 1D vector (one for airplane, one for bird), but here we're still dealing with multichannel 2D features.

Thinking back to the beginning of this chapter, we already know what we need to do: turn the 8-channel 8 × 8 image into a 1D vector and complete our network with a set of fully connected layers:

```
# In[23]:
model = nn.Sequential(
            nn.Conv2d(3, 16, kernel_size=3, padding=1),
            nn.Tanh(),
            nn.MaxPool2d(2),
            nn.Conv2d(16, 8, kernel_size=3, padding=1),
            nn.Tanh(),
            nn.MaxPool2d(2),
            # ...
            nn.Linear(8 * 8 * 8, 32),     ◁─── Warning: Something important is missing here!
            nn.Tanh(),
            nn.Linear(32, 2))
```

This code gives us a neural network as shown in figure 8.11.

Ignore the "something missing" comment for a minute. Let's first notice that the size of the linear layer is dependent on the expected size of the output of MaxPool2d: 8 × 8 × 8 = 512. Let's count the number of parameters for this small model:

```
# In[25]:
numel_list = [p.numel() for p in model.parameters()]
sum(numel_list), numel_list

# Out[25]:
(18090, [432, 16, 1152, 8, 16384, 32, 64, 2])
```

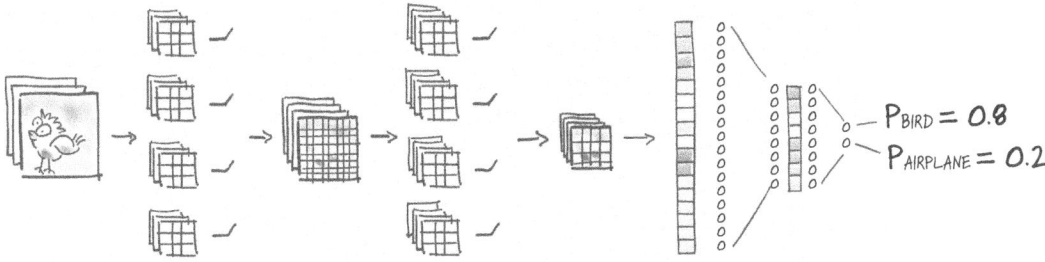

Figure 8.11 Shape of a typical convolutional network, including the one we're building. An image is fed to a series of convolutions and max pooling modules and then straightened into a 1D vector and fed into fully connected modules.

That's very reasonable for a limited dataset of such small images. To increase the capacity of the model, we could increase the number of output channels for the convolution layers (i.e., the number of features each convolution layer generates), which would lead the linear layer to increase its size as well.

We put the "warning" note in the code for a reason. The model has zero chance of running without complaining:

```
# In[26]:
model(img.unsqueeze(0))
```

```
# Out[26]:
...
RuntimeError: mat1 and mat2 shapes cannot be multiplied (64x8 and 512x32)
```

Admittedly, the error message is a bit obscure, but not too much so. We find references to linear in the traceback: looking back at the model, we see that the only module that has to have a 512 × 32 tensor is nn.Linear(512, 32), the first linear module after the last convolution block.

What's missing there is the reshaping step from an 8-channel 8 × 8 image to a 512-element, 1D vector (1D if we ignore the batch dimension, that is). This could be achieved by calling view on the output of the last nn.MaxPool2d, but, unfortunately, we don't have any explicit visibility of the output of each module when we use nn.Sequential. We'll see how to fix this problem in the next section.

8.3 Subclassing nn.Module

At some point in developing neural networks, we will find ourselves in a situation where we want to compute something that the premade modules do not cover. Here, it is something very simple like reshaping. (We could have used nn.Flatten starting from PyTorch 1.3, but we are subclassing nn.Module for educational purposes.) Later in this chapter, we'll use the same technique to implement more complex neural network architectures. In this section, we learn how to make our own nn.Module subclasses that we can then use just like the prebuilt ones or nn.Sequential.

When we want to build models that do more complex things than just applying one layer after another, we need to leave nn.Sequential for something that gives us added flexibility. PyTorch allows us to use any computation in our model by subclassing nn.Module.

In PyTorch, nn.Module is a fundamental building block that can represent both entire networks and individual components within networks. This recursive nature is key to PyTorch's flexibility—any component (like a convolution layer) is itself an nn.Module, and your complete network is also an nn.Module.

To subclass nn.Module, at a minimum we need to define a forward function that takes the inputs to the module and returns the output. This is where we define our module's computation. Additionally, with PyTorch, if we use standard torch operations, autograd will take care of the backward pass automatically; and indeed, an nn.Module never comes with a backward since it is implicitly defined.

Typically, our computation will use other modules—premade like convolutions or customized. To include these *submodules*, we typically define them in the constructor __init__ and assign them to self for use in the forward function. They will, at the same time, hold their parameters throughout the lifetime of our module. Note that you need to call super().__init__() before you can do that (or PyTorch will remind you).

8.3.1 Our network as an nn.Module

Let's write our network as a subclass of nn.Module. To create our network, we'll instantiate all the individual layer modules (nn.Conv2d, nn.Linear, etc.) in the constructor and then specify how data flows through these modules in the forward method:

```
# In[27]:
class Net(nn.Module):
    def __init__(self):
        super().__init__()
        self.conv1 = nn.Conv2d(3, 16, kernel_size=3, padding=1)
        self.act1 = nn.Tanh()
        self.pool1 = nn.MaxPool2d(2)
        self.conv2 = nn.Conv2d(16, 8, kernel_size=3, padding=1)
        self.act2 = nn.Tanh()
        self.pool2 = nn.MaxPool2d(2)
        self.fc1 = nn.Linear(8 * 8 * 8, 32)
        self.act3 = nn.Tanh()
        self.fc2 = nn.Linear(32, 2)

    def forward(self, x):
        out = self.pool1(self.act1(self.conv1(x)))
        out = self.pool2(self.act2(self.conv2(out)))
        out = out.view(-1, 8 * 8 * 8)             ◁── This reshape is what we were missing earlier.
        out = self.act3(self.fc1(out))
        out = self.fc2(out)
        return out
```

The Net class is equivalent to the nn.Sequential model we built earlier in terms of submodules, but by writing the forward function explicitly, we can manipulate the output of self.pool2 directly and call view on it to turn it into a $B \times N$ vector. Note that we leave the batch dimension as –1 in the call to view (which tells PyTorch to automatically infer this dimension's size) because, in principle, we don't know how many samples will be in the batch.

Here we use a subclass of nn.Module to contain our entire model. We could also use subclasses to define new building blocks for more complex networks. Picking up on the diagram style in chapter 6, our network looks like the one shown in figure 8.12. We are making some ad hoc choices about what information to present where.

Recall that the goal of classification networks is typically to compress information in the sense that we start with an image with a sizable number of pixels and compress it into (a vector of probabilities of) classes. Two things about our architecture deserve some commentary with respect to this goal.

First, our goal is reflected by the size of our intermediate values, which are generally shrinking. We reduce the number of channels in the convolutions by reducing the number of pixels through pooling and by having an output dimension lower than the input dimension in the linear layers. This is a common trait of classification networks. However, in many popular architectures like the ResNets, the reduction is achieved by pooling in the spatial resolution (reducing width and height), but the number of channels increases (still resulting in a reduction in total size). It seems that our pattern of fast information reduction works well with networks of limited depth and small images, but for deeper networks, the decrease is typically slower.

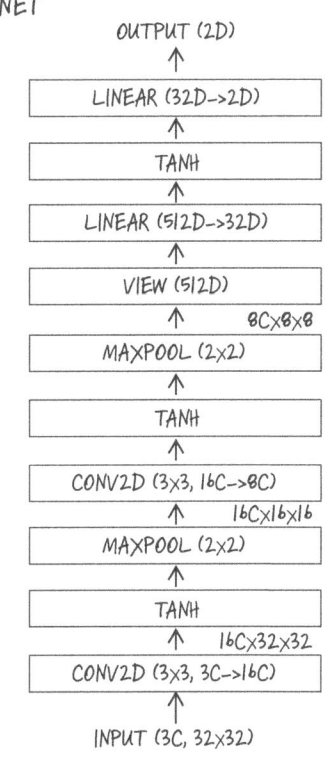

Figure 8.12 Our baseline convolutional network architecture

Second, in one layer, the output size does not decline with regard to input size—the initial convolution. If we consider a single output pixel as a vector of 32 elements (the channels), it is a linear transformation of 27 elements (as a convolution of 3 channels × 3 × 3 kernel size)—only a moderate increase. In ResNet, the initial convolution generates 64 channels from 147 elements (3 channels × 7 × 7 kernel size).

NOTE The dimensions in the pixel-wise linear mapping defined by the first convolution were emphasized by Jeremy Howard in his fast.ai course (https://www.fast.ai).

So, the first layer is exceptional in that it greatly increases the overall dimension (as in channels times pixels) of the data flowing through it, but the mapping for each output pixel considered in isolation still has approximately as many outputs as inputs.

> **NOTE** Outside of and older than deep learning, projecting into high-dimensional space and then doing conceptually simpler (than linear) machine learning is commonly known as the *kernel trick*. The initial increase in the number of channels could be seen as a somewhat similar phenomenon, but striking a different balance between the cleverness of the embedding and the simplicity of the model working on the embedding.

8.3.2 How PyTorch keeps track of parameters and submodules

Interestingly, assigning an instance of nn.Module to an attribute in an nn.Module, as we did in the earlier constructor, automatically registers the module as a submodule.

> **NOTE** The submodules must be top-level *attributes*, not buried inside list or dict instances! Otherwise, the optimizer will not be able to locate the submodules (and, hence, their parameters). For situations where your model requires a list or dict of submodules, PyTorch provides nn.ModuleList and nn.ModuleDict.

We can call arbitrary methods of an nn.Module subclass. For example, for a model where training is substantially different than its use—say, for prediction—it may make sense to have a predict method. Be aware that calling such methods will be similar to calling forward instead of the module itself; some features and mechanisms such as hooks (registered functions in forward and backward) are not executed when using custom methods instead of the standard __call__ to the model.

The following allows Net to have access to the parameters of its submodules without further action by the user:

```
# In[28]:
model = Net()

numel_list = [p.numel() for p in model.parameters()]
sum(numel_list), numel_list

# Out[28]:
(18090, [432, 16, 1152, 8, 16384, 32, 64, 2])
```

Here, the parameters() call delves into all submodules assigned as attributes in the constructor and recursively calls parameters() on them. No matter how nested the submodule, any nn.Module can access the list of all child parameters. By accessing their grad attribute, which has been populated by autograd, the optimizer will know how to change parameters to minimize the loss. We know that story from chapter 5.

We now know how to implement our own modules—and we will need this a lot for part 2.

8.3.3 The functional API

Looking back at the implementation of the Net class and thinking about the utility of registering submodules in the constructor so that we can access their parameters, it appears a bit of a waste that we are also registering submodules that have no parameters, like nn.Tanh and nn.MaxPool2d. Wouldn't it be easier to call these directly in the forward function, just as we called view?

It sure would! And that's why PyTorch has *functional* counterparts for every nn module. By "functional" here we mean "having no internal state"—in other words, "whose output value is solely and fully determined by the value input arguments." Indeed, torch.nn.functional provides many functions that work like the modules we find in nn. But instead of working on the input arguments and stored parameters like the module counterparts, they take inputs and parameters as arguments to the function call. For instance, the functional counterpart of nn.Linear is nn.functional.linear, which is a function that has signature linear(input, weight, bias=None). The weight and bias parameters are arguments to the function, whereas in the module based counterpart that we used earlier, they are stored in the module. Table 8.1 shows some key differences between module-based and functional approaches.

Table 8.1 Comparing module-based and functional APIs in PyTorch

Module-based (nn.Module)	Functional (torch.nn.functional)
Example: nn.Linear(in_features, out_features)	Example: F.linear(input, weight, bias=None)
Has internal state (parameters stored in the module)	No internal state (stateless functions)
Parameters are stored as attributes.	Parameters are passed as arguments.
Parameters are registered and tracked automatically.	Parameters must be managed manually.
Common for layers like nn.Conv2d, nn.Linear	Common for activations like F.relu, F.tanh
Called via layer(input)	Called via F.function(input, other_args)

Back to our model, it makes sense to keep using nn modules for nn.Linear and nn.Conv2d so that Net will be able to manage their Parameters during training. However, we can safely switch to the functional counterparts of pooling and activation, since they have no parameters:

```
# In[29]:
import torch.nn.functional as F

class Net(nn.Module):
    def __init__(self):
        super().__init__()
        self.conv1 = nn.Conv2d(3, 16, kernel_size=3, padding=1)
        self.conv2 = nn.Conv2d(16, 8, kernel_size=3, padding=1)
```

```
        self.fc1 = nn.Linear(8 * 8 * 8, 32)
        self.fc2 = nn.Linear(32, 2)

    def forward(self, x):
        out = F.max_pool2d(torch.tanh(self.conv1(x)), 2)
        out = F.max_pool2d(torch.tanh(self.conv2(out)), 2)
        out = out.view(-1, 8 * 8 * 8)
        out = torch.tanh(self.fc1(out))
        out = self.fc2(out)
        return out
```

This definition is a lot more concise than and fully equivalent to our previous definition of Net in section 8.3.1. It would still make sense to instantiate modules that require several parameters for their initialization in the constructor.

Thus, the functional way also sheds light on what the nn.Module API is all about: a Module is a container for state in the form of Parameters and submodules combined with the instructions to do a forward.

Whether to use the functional or the modular API is a decision based on style and taste. When part of a network is so simple that we want to use nn.Sequential, we're in the modular realm. When we are writing our own forwards, it may be more natural to use the functional interface for things that do not need state in the form of parameters.

So now we can make our own nn.Module if we need to, and we also have the functional API for cases when instantiating and then calling an nn.Module is overkill. This bit has been the last missing piece to understanding how the code organization works in just about any neural network implemented in PyTorch.

Let's double-check that our model runs, and then we'll get to the training loop:

```
# In[30]:
model = Net()
model(img.unsqueeze(0))

# Out[30]:
tensor([[ 0.0190, -0.0683]], grad_fn=<AddmmBackward0>)
```

We got two numbers! Information flows correctly. We might not realize it right now, but in more complex models, getting the size of the first linear layer right is sometimes a source of frustration. We've heard stories of famous practitioners putting in arbitrary numbers and then relying on error messages from PyTorch to backtrack the correct sizes for their linear layers. Lame, eh? Nah, it's all legit!

8.4 Training our convolutional neural network

We're now at the point where we can assemble our complete training loop. We already developed the overall structure in chapter 5, and the training loop looks much like the one from chapter 6, but here we will revisit it to add some details, like some tracking for accuracy. After we run our model, we will also have an appetite for a little more speed, so we will learn how to run our models fast on a GPU. But first, let's look at the training loop.

Recall that the core of our training is two nested loops: an outer one over the *epochs* and an inner one of the `DataLoader` that produces batches from our `Dataset`. In each loop, we then have to

1. Feed the inputs through the model (the forward pass).
2. Compute the loss (also part of the forward pass).
3. Zero any old gradients.
4. Call `loss.backward()` to compute the gradients of the loss with respect to all parameters (the backward pass).
5. Have the optimizer take a step in toward lower loss.

Also, we collect and print some information. Here is our training loop, looking almost as it does in the previous chapter, but it is good to remember what each thing is doing:

```
# In[31]:
import datetime   ◁── Uses the datetime module included in the Python standard library

def training_loop(n_epochs, optimizer, model, loss_fn, train_loader):
    for epoch in range(1, n_epochs + 1):   ◁── Our loop over the epochs, numbered from 1 to n_epochs rather than starting at 0
        start_time = datetime.datetime.now()
        loss_train = 0.0
        for imgs, labels in train_loader:   ◁── Loops over our dataset in the batches the data loader creates for us

            outputs = model(imgs)   ◁── Feeds a batch through our model ...

            loss = loss_fn(outputs, labels)   ◁── ... and computes the loss we wish to minimize

            optimizer.zero_grad()   ◁── After getting rid of the gradients from the last round ...

            loss.backward()   ◁── ... performs the backward step. That is, we compute the gradients of all parameters we want the network to learn.

            optimizer.step()

            loss_train += loss.item()   ◁── Sums the losses we saw over the epoch. Recall that it is important to transform the loss to a Python number with .item(), to escape the gradients.

        end_time = datetime.datetime.now()
        epoch_duration = (end_time - start_time).total_seconds()
        if epoch == 1 or epoch % 10 == 0:
            print('{} Epoch {}, Training loss {:.6f}, Time {:.2f}s'.format(
                datetime.datetime.now(), epoch,
                loss_train / len(train_loader), epoch_duration))
```

Updates the model using the gradients we just computed

Divides by the length of the training data loader to get the average loss per batch. This is a much more intuitive measure than the sum.

We use the `Dataset` from chapter 7; wrap it into a `DataLoader`; instantiate our network, an optimizer, and a loss function as before; and call our training loop.

The substantial changes in our model from the last chapter are that now our model is a custom subclass of `nn.Module` and that we're using convolutions. Let's run training for 100 epochs while printing the loss. Depending on your hardware, this run may take 20 minutes or more to finish:

```
# In[32]:
train_loader = torch.utils.data.DataLoader(cifar2, batch_size=64,
                                           shuffle=True)
```
← The DataLoader batches up the examples of our cifar2 dataset. Shuffling randomizes the order of the examples from the dataset.

```
model = Net()  #
optimizer = optim.SGD(model.parameters(), lr=1e-2)  #
loss_fn = nn.CrossEntropyLoss()  #

training_loop(
    n_epochs = 100,
    optimizer = optimizer,
    model = model,
    loss_fn = loss_fn,
    train_loader = train_loader,
)
```
← Instantiates our network …
… the stochastic gradient descent optimizer we have been working with …
… and the cross-entropy loss we introduced in chapter 7
Calls the training loop we defined earlier

```
# Out[32]:
2025-06-08 14:34:27.755713 Epoch 1, Training loss 0.553273, Time 1.72s
2025-06-08 14:34:39.389411 Epoch 10, Training loss 0.332629, Time 1.30s
2025-06-08 14:34:52.348689 Epoch 20, Training loss 0.283454, Time 1.34s
2025-06-08 14:35:05.399002 Epoch 30, Training loss 0.259716, Time 1.28s
2025-06-08 14:35:18.432120 Epoch 40, Training loss 0.239583, Time 1.26s
2025-06-08 14:35:31.409170 Epoch 50, Training loss 0.220342, Time 1.46s
2025-06-08 14:35:44.441435 Epoch 60, Training loss 0.204420, Time 1.24s
2025-06-08 14:35:57.261905 Epoch 70, Training loss 0.190523, Time 1.29s
2025-06-08 14:36:10.689505 Epoch 80, Training loss 0.175177, Time 1.32s
2025-06-08 14:36:23.668655 Epoch 90, Training loss 0.160240, Time 1.40s
2025-06-08 14:36:36.904013 Epoch 100, Training loss 0.147124, Time 1.20s
```

So now we can train our network. But again, our friend, the bird watcher, will likely not be impressed when we tell her that we trained to very low training loss.

8.4.1 Measuring accuracy

To have a measure that is more interpretable than the loss, we can take a look at our accuracy on the training and validation datasets. We use the same code as in chapter 7:

```
# In[33]:
train_loader = torch.utils.data.DataLoader(cifar2, batch_size=64,
                                           shuffle=False)
val_loader = torch.utils.data.DataLoader(cifar2_val, batch_size=64,
                                         shuffle=False)
```

8.4 Training our convolutional neural network

```
def validate(model, train_loader, val_loader):
    for name, loader in [("train", train_loader), ("val", val_loader)]:
        correct = 0
        total = 0

        with torch.no_grad():
            for imgs, labels in loader:
                outputs = model(imgs)
                _, predicted = torch.max(outputs, dim=1)
                total += labels.shape[0]
                correct += int((predicted == labels).sum())

        print("Accuracy {}: {:.2f}".format(name , correct / total))

validate(model, train_loader, val_loader)

# Out[33]:
Accuracy train: 0.95
Accuracy val: 0.90
```

- We do not want gradients here, as we will not want to update the parameters.
- Gives us the index of the highest value as output
- Comparing the predicted class that had the maximum probability and the ground-truth labels, we first get a Boolean array. Taking the sum gives the number of items in the batch where the prediction and ground truth agree.
- Counts the number of examples, so the total is increased by the batch size

We cast to a Python int—for integer tensors, this is equivalent to using .item(), similar to what we did in the training loop.

This model is quite a lot better than the fully connected model, which achieved only 80% accuracy. We about halved the number of errors on the validation set. Also, we used far fewer parameters, dropping from over 3.7 million in our fully connected model in the last chapter to just 18,090 parameters in our convolutional model (a reduction of more than 99%). This reduction highlights a fundamental concept in deep learning: model architecture matters more than parameter count! Our convolutional model does a better job of generalizing its task of recognizing the subject of images from a new sample, through locality and translation invariance. We could now let it run for more epochs and see what performance we could squeeze out.

8.4.2 Saving and loading our model

Since we're satisfied with our model so far, it would be nice to actually save it, right? It's easy to do. Let's save the model to a file:

```
# In[34]:
torch.save(model.state_dict(), data_path + 'birds_vs_airplanes.pt')
```

The birds_vs_airplanes.pt file now contains all the parameters of model—that is, weights and biases for the two convolution modules and the two linear modules. So, no structure, just the weights. This means when we deploy the model in production for our friend, we'll need to keep the model class handy, create an instance, and then load the parameters back into it:

```
# In[35]:
loaded_model = Net()
loaded_model.load_state_dict(torch.load(data_path
                                        + 'birds_vs_airplanes.pt'))
```

> We will have to make sure we don't change the definition of Net between saving and later loading the model state.

```
# Out[35]:
<All keys matched successfully>
```

We have also included a pretrained model in our code repository, saved to ../data/p1ch8/birds_vs_airplanes.pt.

8.4.3 Training on the GPU

We have a net and can train it! But it would be good to make it a bit faster. It is no surprise that we do so by moving our training onto the GPU. Using the .to method we saw in chapter 3, we can move the tensors we get from the data loader to the GPU, after which our computation will automatically take place there. But we also need to move our parameters to the GPU. Happily, nn.Module implements a .to function that moves all of its parameters to the GPU (or casts the type when you pass a dtype argument).

There is a somewhat subtle difference between Module.to and Tensor.to. In Module.to, the module instance is modified in place. But Tensor.to is out of place (in some ways, computation, just like Tensor.tanh), returning a new tensor. As a concrete example, let's look at the following code:

```
# In[]:
model_a = Net()
model_b = model_a.to("cuda")
print(model_a is model_b)

tensor_a = torch.rand(1)
tensor_b = tensor_a.to("cuda")
print(tensor_a is tensor_b)

# Out[]:
True
False
```

In Python, the is operator checks whether two variables refer to the same object. We can see in the output that model_a and model_b are the same object, but tensor_a and tensor_b are not. One implication of Module.to is that it is good practice to create the Optimizer after moving the parameters to the appropriate device.

It is considered good style to move things to the GPU if one is available. A good pattern is to set a variable device depending on torch.cuda.is_available:

```
# In[36]:
device = (torch.device('cuda') if torch.cuda.is_available()
          else torch.device('cpu'))
print(f"Training on device {device}.")
```

Then we can amend the training loop by moving the tensors we get from the data loader to the GPU by using the Tensor.to method. Note that the code is exactly like our first version at the beginning of this section, except for the two lines moving the inputs to the GPU:

```
# In[37]:
import datetime

def training_loop(n_epochs, optimizer, model, loss_fn, train_loader):
    for epoch in range(1, n_epochs + 1):
        start_time = datetime.datetime.now()
        loss_train = 0.0
        for imgs, labels in train_loader:
            imgs = imgs.to(device=device)
            labels = labels.to(device=device)
            outputs = model(imgs)
            loss = loss_fn(outputs, labels)

            optimizer.zero_grad()
            loss.backward()
            optimizer.step()

            loss_train += loss.item()

        end_time = datetime.datetime.now()
        epoch_duration = (end_time - start_time).total_seconds()
        if epoch == 1 or epoch % 10 == 0:
            print('{} Epoch {}, Training loss {:.6f}, Time {:.2f}s'.format(
                datetime.datetime.now(), epoch,
                loss_train / len(train_loader), epoch_duration))
```

These two lines, which move imgs and labels to the training device, are the only difference from our previous training_loop function.

The same amendment must be made to the validate function. We can then instantiate our model, move it to device, and run it as before:

> **NOTE** There is a pin_memory option for the data loader that will cause the data loader to use memory pinned to the GPU, with the goal of speeding up transfers. Whether we gain something varies, though, so we will not pursue this here.

```
# In[38]:
train_loader = torch.utils.data.DataLoader(cifar2, batch_size=64,
                                           shuffle=True)

model = Net().to(device=device)
```

Moves our model (all parameters) to the GPU. If you forget to move either the model or the inputs to the GPU, you will get errors about tensors not being on the same device because the PyTorch operators do not support mixing GPU and CPU inputs.

```
optimizer = optim.SGD(model.parameters(), lr=1e-2)
loss_fn = nn.CrossEntropyLoss()

training_loop(
    n_epochs = 100,
    optimizer = optimizer,
    model = model,
    loss_fn = loss_fn,
    train_loader = train_loader,
)

# Out[38]:
2025-06-08 14:36:43.831980 Epoch 1, Training loss 0.591598, Time 6.02s
2025-06-08 14:36:47.707613 Epoch 10, Training loss 0.328330, Time 0.40s
2025-06-08 14:36:52.163547 Epoch 20, Training loss 0.289371, Time 0.36s
2025-06-08 14:36:56.326006 Epoch 30, Training loss 0.262738, Time 0.44s
2025-06-08 14:37:00.233507 Epoch 40, Training loss 0.241435, Time 0.50s
2025-06-08 14:37:05.260639 Epoch 50, Training loss 0.227982, Time 0.53s
2025-06-08 14:37:09.706318 Epoch 60, Training loss 0.211528, Time 0.44s
2025-06-08 14:37:14.019777 Epoch 70, Training loss 0.198672, Time 0.51s
2025-06-08 14:37:17.456679 Epoch 80, Training loss 0.186976, Time 0.32s
2025-06-08 14:37:20.734218 Epoch 90, Training loss 0.175323, Time 0.32s
2025-06-08 14:37:24.933440 Epoch 100, Training loss 0.162720, Time 0.42s
```

Even for our small network here, we see a sizable increase in speed. The advantage of computing on GPUs is more visible for larger models.

There is a slight complication when loading network weights: PyTorch will attempt to load the weight to the same device it was saved from—that is, weights on the GPU will be restored to the GPU. As we don't know whether we want the same device, we have two options: we could move the network to the CPU before saving it, or move it back after restoring. It is a bit more concise to instruct PyTorch to override the device information when loading weights. This is done by passing the map_location keyword argument to torch.load:

```
# In[40]:
loaded_model = Net().to(device=device)
loaded_model.load_state_dict(torch.load(data_path
                                        + 'birds_vs_airplanes.pt',
                                        map_location=device))

# Out[40]:
<All keys matched successfully>
```

8.5 Model design

We built our model as a subclass of nn.Module, the de facto standard for all but the simplest models. Then we trained it successfully and saw how to use the GPU to train our models. We've reached the point where we can build a feed-forward convolutional neural network and train it successfully to classify images. The natural question is, what now? What if we are presented with a more complicated problem? Admittedly, our birds-versus-airplanes dataset wasn't that complicated: the images were very small, and the object under investigation was centered and took up most of the viewport.

If we moved to, say, ImageNet, we would find larger, more complex images, where the right answer would depend on multiple visual clues, often hierarchically organized. For instance, when trying to predict whether a dark brick shape is a remote control or a cell phone, the network could be looking for something like a screen.

Plus, images may not be our sole focus in the real world, where we have tabular data, sequences, and text. The promise of neural networks is sufficient flexibility to solve problems on all these kinds of data given the proper architecture (i.e., the interconnection of layers or modules) and the proper loss function.

PyTorch ships with a very comprehensive collection of modules and loss functions to implement state-of-the-art architectures ranging from feed-forward components to long short-term memory (LSTM) modules and transformer networks (two very popular architectures for sequential data). Several models are available through PyTorch Hub or as part of torchvision and other vertical community efforts.

We'll see a few more advanced architectures in part 2, where we'll walk through end-to-end problems while exploring variations on neural network architectures. However, we can build on the knowledge we've accumulated thus far to understand how we can implement almost any architecture thanks to the expressivity of PyTorch. The purpose of this section is precisely to provide conceptual tools that will allow us to read the latest research paper and start implementing it in PyTorch or, since authors often release PyTorch implementations of their papers, to read the implementations without choking on our coffee.

8.5.1 Adding memory capacity: Width

Given our feed-forward architecture, there are a couple of dimensions we'd likely want to explore before getting into further complications. The first dimension is the *width* of the network: the number of neurons per layer, or channels per convolution. We can make a model wider very easily in PyTorch. We just specify a larger number of output channels in the first convolution and increase the subsequent layers accordingly, taking care to change the forward function to reflect the fact that we'll now have a longer vector once we switch to fully connected layers:

```
# In[41]:
class NetWidth(nn.Module):
    def __init__(self):
        super().__init__()
        self.conv1 = nn.Conv2d(3, 32, kernel_size=3, padding=1)
        self.conv2 = nn.Conv2d(32, 16, kernel_size=3, padding=1)
        self.fc1 = nn.Linear(16 * 8 * 8, 32)
        self.fc2 = nn.Linear(32, 2)

    def forward(self, x):
        out = F.max_pool2d(torch.tanh(self.conv1(x)), 2)
        out = F.max_pool2d(torch.tanh(self.conv2(out)), 2)
```

```
out = out.view(-1, 16 * 8 * 8)
out = torch.tanh(self.fc1(out))
out = self.fc2(out)
return out
```

If we want to avoid hardcoding numbers in the definition of the model, we can easily pass a parameter to init and parameterize the width, taking care to also parameterize the call to view in the forward function:

```
# In[42]:
class NetWidth(nn.Module):
    def __init__(self, n_chans1=32):
        super().__init__()
        self.n_chans1 = n_chans1
        self.conv1 = nn.Conv2d(3, n_chans1, kernel_size=3, padding=1)
        self.conv2 = nn.Conv2d(n_chans1, n_chans1 // 2, kernel_size=3,
                               padding=1)
        self.fc1 = nn.Linear(8 * 8 * n_chans1 // 2, 32)
        self.fc2 = nn.Linear(32, 2)

    def forward(self, x):
        out = F.max_pool2d(torch.tanh(self.conv1(x)), 2)
        out = F.max_pool2d(torch.tanh(self.conv2(out)), 2)
        out = out.view(-1, 8 * 8 * self.n_chans1 // 2)
        out = torch.tanh(self.fc1(out))
        out = self.fc2(out)
        return out
```

The numbers specifying channels and features for each layer are directly related to the number of parameters in a model; all other things being equal, they increase the *capacity* of the model. As we did previously, we can look at how many parameters our model has now:

```
# In[45]:
sum(p.numel() for p in model.parameters())

# Out[45]:
38386
```

The greater the capacity, the more variability in the inputs the model will be able to manage, but at the same time, the more likely overfitting will occur since the model can use a greater number of parameters to memorize unessential aspects of the input. We already went into ways to combat overfitting, the best being increasing the sample size or, in the absence of new data, augmenting existing data through artificial modifications of the same data.

There are a few more tricks we can play at the model level (without acting on the data) to control overfitting. Let's review the most common ones.

8.5.2 Helping our model to converge and generalize: Regularization

Training a model involves two critical steps: optimization, when we need the loss to decrease on the training set, and generalization, when the model has to work not only on the training set but also on data it has not seen before, like the validation set. The mathematical tools aimed at easing these two steps are sometimes subsumed under the label *regularization.*

Regularization encompasses the set of techniques that help to prevent overfitting. In this section, we will explore a few such strategies.

KEEPING THE PARAMETERS IN CHECK: WEIGHT PENALTIES

The first way to stabilize generalization is to add a regularization term to the loss. This term is crafted so that the weights of the model tend to be small on their own, limiting how much training makes them grow. In other words, it is a penalty on larger weight values. This makes the loss have a smoother topography, and there's relatively less to gain from fitting individual samples.

The most popular regularization terms of this kind are L2 regularization, which is the sum of squares of all weights in the model, and L1 regularization, which is the sum of the absolute values of all weights in the model.

> **NOTE** We'll focus on L2 regularization here. L1 regularization—popularized in the more general statistics literature by its use in Lasso—has the attractive property of resulting in sparse trained weights. Both of them are scaled by a (small) factor, which is a hyperparameter we set prior to training.

L2 regularization is also referred to as *weight decay*. The reason for this name is that, thinking about Stochastic Gradient Descent (SGD) and backpropagation, the negative gradient of the L2 regularization term with respect to a parameter `w_i` is - 2 * `lambda` * `w_i`, where `lambda` is the aforementioned hyperparameter. So, adding L2 regularization to the loss function is equivalent to decreasing each weight by an amount proportional to its current value during the optimization step (hence, the name *weight decay*). Note that weight decay applies to all parameters of the network, such as biases.

For an intuitive understanding of how this works, imagine the parameters of your neural network are like plants in a garden. Just as in a garden where you do not want one plant to grow too large and overshadow the others, you want to prevent any single weight from becoming too dominant in deciding the neural network output. Luckily, in your toolbox, you have *weight decay*, which acts as the equivalent of pruning shears to trim your flora. The larger the `lambda`, the larger your shears become!

In PyTorch, we could implement regularization pretty easily by adding a term to the loss. After computing the loss, whatever the loss function is, we can iterate the parameters of the model, sum their respective square (for L2) or abs (for L1), and backpropagate:

```
# In[46]:
def training_loop_l2reg(n_epochs, optimizer, model, loss_fn,
                        train_loader):
```

```
for epoch in range(1, n_epochs + 1):
    loss_train = 0.0
    for imgs, labels in train_loader:
        imgs = imgs.to(device=device)
        labels = labels.to(device=device)
        outputs = model(imgs)
        loss = loss_fn(outputs, labels)

        l2_lambda = 0.001
        l2_norm = sum(p.pow(2.0).sum()
                  for p in model.parameters())      ◁─┐ Replaces pow(2.0)
        loss = loss + l2_lambda * l2_norm                with abs() for L1
                                                         regularization
        optimizer.zero_grad()
        loss.backward()
        optimizer.step()

        loss_train += loss.item()
    if epoch == 1 or epoch % 10 == 0:
        print('{} Epoch {}, Training loss {}'.format(
            datetime.datetime.now(), epoch,
            loss_train / len(train_loader)))
```

However, the SGD optimizer in PyTorch already has a `weight_decay` parameter that corresponds to `2 * lambda`, and it directly performs weight decay during the update as described previously. It is fully equivalent to adding the L2 norm of weights to the loss, without the need for accumulating terms in the loss and involving autograd, so usually we should defer to using the Pytorch `weight_decay` parameter to reduce the risk of any implementation mistakes.

NOT RELYING TOO MUCH ON A SINGLE INPUT: DROPOUT

An effective strategy for combating overfitting was originally proposed in 2014 by Nitish Srivastava and coauthors from Geoff Hinton's group in Toronto, in a paper aptly entitled "Dropout: A Simple Way to Prevent Neural Networks from Overfitting" (http://mng.bz/nPMa). Sounds like pretty much exactly what we're looking for, right? The idea behind dropout is indeed simple: zero out a random fraction of outputs from neurons across the network, where the randomization happens at each training iteration.

This procedure effectively generates slightly different models with different neuron topologies at each iteration, giving neurons in the model less chance to coordinate in the memorization process that happens during overfitting. An alternative point of view is that dropout perturbs the features being generated by the model, exerting an effect that is close to data augmentation (applying various transformations or perturbations to the training data), but this time throughout the network.

In PyTorch, we can implement dropout in a model by adding an `nn.Dropout` module between the nonlinear activation function and the linear or convolutional module of the subsequent layer. As an argument, we need to specify the probability with which inputs will be zeroed out. In case of convolutions, we'll use the specialized `nn.Dropout2d` or `nn.Dropout3d`, which zero out entire channels of the input:

```
# In[48]:
class NetDropout(nn.Module):
    def __init__(self, n_chans1=32):
        super().__init__()
        self.n_chans1 = n_chans1
        self.conv1 = nn.Conv2d(3, n_chans1, kernel_size=3, padding=1)
        self.conv1_dropout = nn.Dropout2d(p=0.4)
        self.conv2 = nn.Conv2d(n_chans1, n_chans1 // 2, kernel_size=3,
                               padding=1)
        self.conv2_dropout = nn.Dropout2d(p=0.4)
        self.fc1 = nn.Linear(8 * 8 * n_chans1 // 2, 32)
        self.fc2 = nn.Linear(32, 2)

    def forward(self, x):
        out = F.max_pool2d(torch.tanh(self.conv1(x)), 2)
        out = self.conv1_dropout(out)
        out = F.max_pool2d(torch.tanh(self.conv2(out)), 2)
        out = self.conv2_dropout(out)
        out = out.view(-1, 8 * 8 * self.n_chans1 // 2)
        out = torch.tanh(self.fc1(out))
        out = self.fc2(out)
        return out
```

Note that dropout is normally active during training, while during the evaluation of a trained model in production, dropout is bypassed or, equivalently, assigned a probability equal to zero. This is controlled through the train property of the Dropout module. Recall that PyTorch lets us switch between the two modalities by calling

model.train()

or

model.eval()

on any nn.Module subclass. The call will be automatically replicated on the submodules so that if Dropout is among them, it will behave accordingly in subsequent forward and backward passes. Not putting the model in the eval mode during inference can be a silent failure that will impair the model's performance.

KEEPING ACTIVATIONS IN CHECK: BATCH NORMALIZATION

Dropout was all the rage when, in 2015, another seminal paper was published by Sergey Ioffe and Christian Szegedy from Google, entitled "Batch Normalization: Accelerating Deep Network Training by Reducing Internal Covariate Shift" (https://arxiv.org/abs/1502.03167). The paper describes a technique that had multiple beneficial effects on training, allowing us to increase the learning rate and make training less dependent on initialization and act as a regularizer, thus representing an alternative to dropout.

The main idea behind batch normalization is to rescale the inputs to the activations of the network so that minibatches have a certain desirable distribution. Recalling the mechanics of learning and the role of nonlinear activation functions, this distribution helps avoid the inputs to activation functions being too far into the saturated portion of the function, thereby killing gradients and slowing training (see figure 8.13).

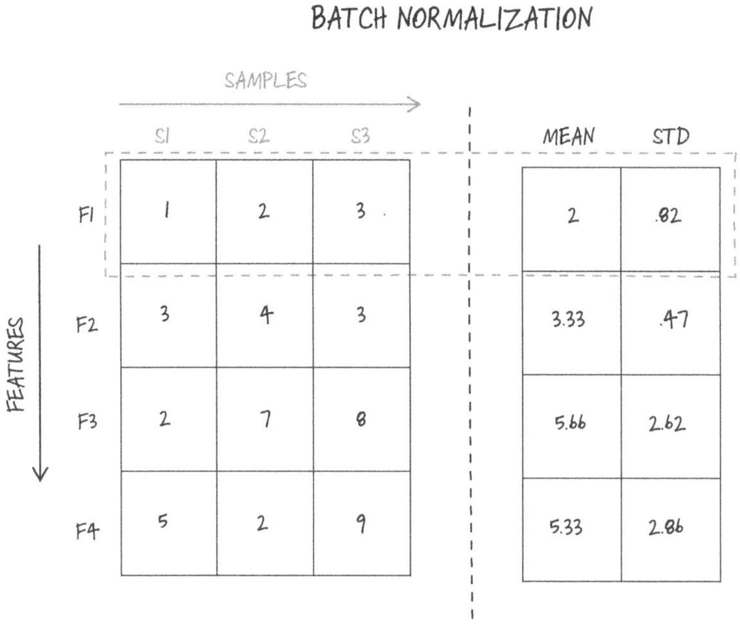

BATCH NORMALIZATION

	S1	S2	S3	MEAN	STD
F1	1	2	3	2	.82
F2	3	4	3	3.33	.47
F3	2	7	8	5.66	2.62
F4	5	2	9	5.33	2.86

Figure 8.13 BatchNorm for three samples with four input features involves calculating the mean and standard deviation for each feature across the samples. The mean and standard deviation are then used to normalize the input features such that each feature has zero mean and unit variance.

In practical terms, batch normalization shifts and scales an intermediate input using the mean and standard deviation collected at that intermediate location over the samples of the minibatch. The regularization effect is a result of the fact that an individual sample and its downstream activations are always seen by the model as shifted and scaled, depending on the statistics across the randomly extracted minibatch. This is in itself a form of *principled* augmentation. The authors of the paper suggest that using batch normalization eliminates or at least alleviates the need for dropout.

Batch normalization in PyTorch is provided through the nn.BatchNorm1D, nn.Batch-Norm2d, and nn.BatchNorm3d modules, depending on the dimensionality of the input. Since the aim of batch normalization is to rescale the inputs of the activations, the natural location is after the linear transformation (convolution, in this case) and the activation, as shown here:

```
# In[50]:
class NetBatchNorm(nn.Module):
    def __init__(self, n_chans1=32):
        super().__init__()
        self.n_chans1 = n_chans1
```

```
        self.conv1 = nn.Conv2d(3, n_chans1, kernel_size=3, padding=1)
        self.conv1_batchnorm = nn.BatchNorm2d(num_features=n_chans1)
        self.conv2 = nn.Conv2d(n_chans1, n_chans1 // 2, kernel_size=3,
                               padding=1)
        self.conv2_batchnorm = nn.BatchNorm2d(num_features=n_chans1 // 2)
        self.fc1 = nn.Linear(8 * 8 * n_chans1 // 2, 32)
        self.fc2 = nn.Linear(32, 2)

    def forward(self, x):
        out = self.conv1_batchnorm(self.conv1(x))
        out = F.max_pool2d(torch.tanh(out), 2)
        out = self.conv2_batchnorm(self.conv2(out))
        out = F.max_pool2d(torch.tanh(out), 2)
        out = out.view(-1, 8 * 8 * self.n_chans1 // 2)
        out = torch.tanh(self.fc1(out))
        out = self.fc2(out)
        return out
```

Just as for dropout, batch normalization needs to behave differently during training and inference. In fact, at inference time, we want to avoid having the output for a specific input depend on the statistics of the other inputs we're presenting to the model. As such, we need a way to still normalize, but this time, fixing the normalization parameters once and for all.

As minibatches are processed, in addition to estimating the mean and standard deviation for the current minibatch, PyTorch also updates the running estimates for the mean and standard deviation that are representative of the whole dataset, as an approximation. This way, when the user specifies

`model.eval()`

and the model contains a batch normalization module, the running estimates are frozen and used for normalization. To unfreeze running estimates and return to using the minibatch statistics, we call `model.train()`, just as we did for dropout.

8.5.3 Going deeper to learn more complex structures: Depth

Earlier, we talked about width as the first dimension to act on to make a model larger and, in a way, more capable. The second fundamental dimension is obviously *depth*. Since this is a deep learning book, depth is something we're supposedly into. After all, deeper models are always better than shallow ones, aren't they? Well, it depends. With depth, the complexity of the function the network is able to approximate generally increases. Regarding computer vision, a shallower network could identify a person's shape in a photo, whereas a deeper network could identify the person, the face on their top half, and the mouth within the face. Depth allows a model to deal with hierarchical information when we need to understand the context to say something about some input.

There's another way to think about depth: increasing depth is related to increasing the length of the sequence of operations that the network will be able to perform when processing input. This view of a deep network that performs sequential operations

SKIP CONNECTIONS

Depth comes with some additional challenges, which prevented deep learning models from reaching 20 or more layers until late 2015. Adding depth to a model generally makes training harder to converge. Let's recall backpropagation and think about it in the context of a very deep network. The derivatives of the loss function with respect to the parameters, especially those in early layers, need to be multiplied by a lot of other numbers originating from the chain of derivative operations between the loss and the parameter. Those numbers being multiplied could be small, generating ever-smaller numbers, or large, swallowing smaller numbers due to floating-point approximation. The bottom line is that a long chain of multiplications will tend to make the contribution of the parameter to the gradient *vanish*, leading to ineffective training of that layer since that parameter and others like it won't be properly updated.

In December 2015, Kaiming He and coauthors presented *residual networks* (ResNets), an architecture that uses a simple trick to allow very deep networks to be successfully trained (https://arxiv.org/abs/1512.03385). That work opened the door to networks ranging from tens of layers to 100 layers in depth, surpassing the then state of the art in computer vision benchmark problems. The trick is the following: using a *skip connection* to short-circuit blocks of layers, as shown in figure 8.14.

A skip connection is nothing but the addition of the input to the output of a block of layers. This is exactly how it is done in PyTorch. Let's add one layer to our simple convolutional model, and for variety, we'll switch from Tanh to ReLU as our activation function. The vanilla module with an extra layer looks like this:

```
# In[52]:
class NetDepth(nn.Module):
    def __init__(self, n_chans1=32):
        super().__init__()
        self.n_chans1 = n_chans1
        self.conv1 = nn.Conv2d(3, n_chans1, kernel_size=3, padding=1)
        self.conv2 = nn.Conv2d(n_chans1, n_chans1 // 2, kernel_size=3,
                               padding=1)
        self.conv3 = nn.Conv2d(n_chans1 // 2, n_chans1 // 2,
                               kernel_size=3, padding=1)
        self.fc1 = nn.Linear(4 * 4 * n_chans1 // 2, 32)
        self.fc2 = nn.Linear(32, 2)

    def forward(self, x):
        out = F.max_pool2d(torch.relu(self.conv1(x)), 2)
        out = F.max_pool2d(torch.relu(self.conv2(out)), 2)
        out = F.max_pool2d(torch.relu(self.conv3(out)), 2)
        out = out.view(-1, 4 * 4 * self.n_chans1 // 2)
        out = torch.relu(self.fc1(out))
        out = self.fc2(out)
        return out
```

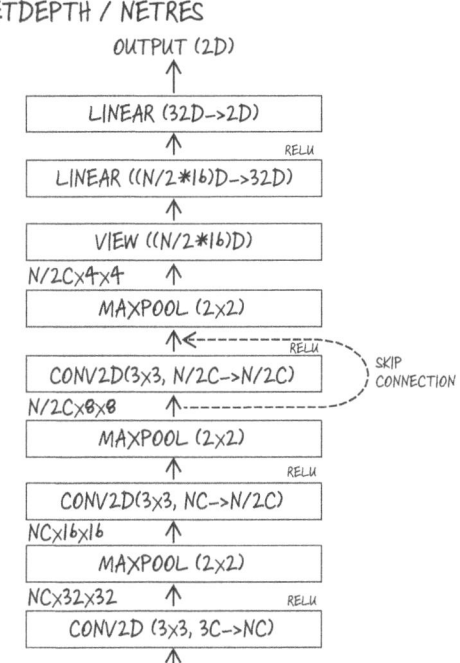

Figure 8.14 The architecture of our network with three convolutional layers. The skip connection is what differentiates NetRes from NetDepth.

Adding a skip connection a la ResNet to this model amounts to adding the output of the second layer in the forward function to the input of the third layer:

```
# In[54]:
class NetRes(nn.Module):
    def __init__(self, n_chans1=32):
        super().__init__()
        self.n_chans1 = n_chans1
        self.conv1 = nn.Conv2d(3, n_chans1, kernel_size=3, padding=1)
        self.conv2 = nn.Conv2d(n_chans1, n_chans1 // 2, kernel_size=3,
                               padding=1)
        self.conv3 = nn.Conv2d(n_chans1 // 2, n_chans1 // 2,
                               kernel_size=3, padding=1)
        self.fc1 = nn.Linear(4 * 4 * n_chans1 // 2, 32)
        self.fc2 = nn.Linear(32, 2)

    def forward(self, x):
        out = F.max_pool2d(torch.relu(self.conv1(x)), 2)
        out = F.max_pool2d(torch.relu(self.conv2(out)), 2)
        out1 = out
        out = F.max_pool2d(torch.relu(self.conv3(out)) + out1, 2)
        out = out.view(-1, 4 * 4 * self.n_chans1 // 2)
        out = torch.relu(self.fc1(out))
        out = self.fc2(out)
        return out
```

In other words, we're using the output of the first activations as inputs to the last, in addition to the standard feed-forward path. This is also referred to as *identity mapping*. So, how does this alleviate the issues with vanishing gradients we mentioned earlier?

Thinking about backpropagation, we can appreciate that a skip connection, or a sequence of skip connections in a deep network, creates a direct path (or a shortcut) from the deeper parameters to the loss. This makes their contribution to the gradient of the loss more direct, as partial derivatives of the loss with respect to those parameters have a chance not to be multiplied by a long chain of other operations.

It has been observed that skip connections have a beneficial effect on convergence, especially in the initial phases of training. Also, the loss landscape of deep residual networks is a lot smoother than feed-forward networks of the same depth and width.

It is worth noting that skip connections were not new to the world when ResNets came along. Highway networks and U-Net made use of skip connections of one form or another. However, the way ResNets used skip connections enabled models of depths greater than 100 to be amenable to training.

Since the advent of ResNets, other architectures have taken skip connections to the next level. One in particular, DenseNet, proposed to connect each layer with several other layers downstream through skip connections, achieving state-of-the-art results with fewer parameters. By now, we know how to implement something like DenseNets: just arithmetically add earlier intermediate outputs to downstream intermediate outputs.

BUILDING VERY DEEP MODELS IN PYTORCH

We talked about exceeding 100 layers in a convolutional neural network. How can we build that network in PyTorch without losing our minds in the process? The standard strategy is to define a building block, such as a (Conv2d, ReLU, Conv2d) + skip connection block, and then build the network dynamically in a for loop. Let's see it done in practice. We will create the network depicted in figure 8.15.

We first create a module subclass whose sole job is to provide the computation for one *block*—that is, one group of convolutions, activation, and skip connection:

```
# In[56]:
class ResBlock(nn.Module):
    def __init__(self, n_chans):
        super(ResBlock, self).__init__()
        self.conv = nn.Conv2d(n_chans, n_chans, kernel_size=3,
                              padding=1, bias=False)
        self.batch_norm = nn.BatchNorm2d(num_features=n_chans)
        torch.nn.init.kaiming_normal_(self.conv.weight,
                                      nonlinearity='relu')
        torch.nn.init.constant_(self.batch_norm.weight, 0.5)
        torch.nn.init.zeros_(self.batch_norm.bias)

    def forward(self, x):
        out = self.conv(x)
        out = self.batch_norm(out)
        out = torch.relu(out)
        return out + x
```

The BatchNorm layer would cancel the effect of bias, so it is customarily left out.

Uses custom initializations. kaiming_normal_ initializes with normal random elements with standard deviation as computed in the ResNet paper (https://arxiv.org/abs/1512.03385). The batch norm is initialized to produce output distributions that initially have 0 mean and 0.5 variance.

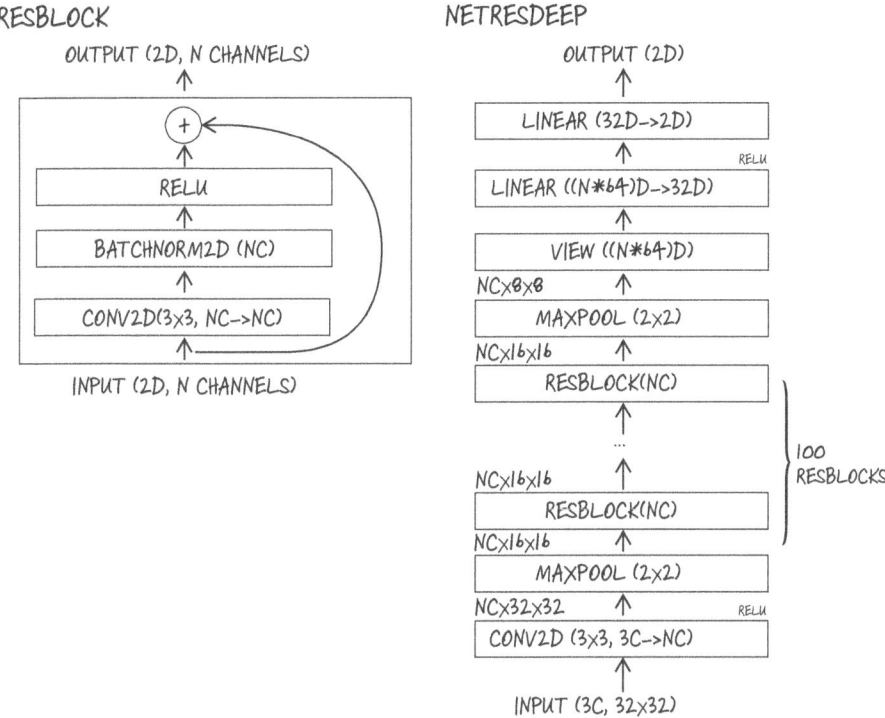

Figure 8.15 Our deep architecture with residual connections. On the left, we define a simplistic residual block. We use it as a building block in our network, as shown on the right.

Since we're planning to generate a deep model, we are including batch normalization in the block, since this will help prevent gradients from vanishing during training. We'd now like to generate a 100-block network. Does this mean we have to prepare for some serious cutting and pasting? Not at all. We already have the ingredients for imagining what this could look like.

First, in __init__, we create nn.Sequential containing a list of ResBlock instances. nn.Sequential will ensure that the output of one block is used as input to the next. It will also ensure that all the parameters in the block are visible to Net. Then, in forward, we just call the sequential to traverse the 100 blocks and generate the output:

```
# In[57]:
class NetResDeep(nn.Module):
    def __init__(self, n_chans1=32, n_blocks=100):
        super().__init__()
        self.n_chans1 = n_chans1
        self.conv1 = nn.Conv2d(3, n_chans1, kernel_size=3, padding=1)
        self.resblocks = nn.Sequential(
            *(n_blocks * [ResBlock(n_chans=n_chans1)]))
        self.fc1 = nn.Linear(8 * 8 * n_chans1, 32)
        self.fc2 = nn.Linear(32, 2)
```

```
def forward(self, x):
    out = F.max_pool2d(torch.relu(self.conv1(x)), 2)
    out = self.resblocks(out)
    out = F.max_pool2d(out, 2)
    out = out.view(-1, 8 * 8 * self.n_chans1)
    out = torch.relu(self.fc1(out))
    out = self.fc2(out)
    return out
```

In the implementation, we parameterize the actual number of layers, which is important for experimentation and reuse. Also, needless to say, backpropagation will work as expected. Unsurprisingly, the network is quite a bit slower to converge. It is also more fragile in convergence. This is why we used more detailed initializations and trained our NetRes with a smaller learning rate than what we used for the other networks. We trained none of the networks to convergence, but we would not have gotten anywhere without these tweaks.

This discussion shouldn't encourage us to seek depth on a dataset of 32 × 32 images, but it clearly demonstrates how this can be achieved on more challenging datasets like ImageNet. It also provides the key elements for understanding existing implementations for models like ResNet, for instance, in torchvision.

INITIALIZATION

Let's briefly comment on the earlier initialization. Initialization is one of the important tricks in training neural networks. Unfortunately, for historical reasons, PyTorch has default weight initializations that are not ideal. People are looking at fixing the situation; if progress is made, it can be tracked on GitHub (https://github.com/pytorch/pytorch/issues/18182). In the meantime, we need to fix the weight initialization ourselves. We found that our model did not converge and looked at what people commonly choose as initialization (a smaller variance in weights and zero mean and unit variance outputs for batch norm), and then we halved the output variance in the batch norm when the network would not converge.

Weight initialization could fill an entire chapter on its own, but we think that would be excessive. In part 2, we'll bump into initialization again and use what arguably could be PyTorch defaults without much explanation.

NOTE Once you've progressed to the point where the details of weight initialization are of specific interest to you—probably not before finishing this book—you might revisit this topic. The seminal paper on the topic is by X. Glorot and Y. Bengio, "Understanding the Difficulty of Training Deep Feedforward Neural Networks" (2010), which introduces PyTorch's *Xavier* initializations (http://mng.bz/vxz7). The ResNet paper (https://arxiv.org/abs/1512.03385) we mentioned expands on the topic, too, giving us the Kaiming initializations used earlier. More recently, H. Zhang et al. have tweaked initialization to the point that they do not need batch norm in their experiments with very deep residual networks (https://arxiv.org/abs/1901.09321).

8.5.4 Comparing the designs from this section

We summarize the effect of each of our design modifications in isolation in figure 8.16. We should not overinterpret any of the specific numbers: our problem setup and experiments are simplistic, and repeating the experiment with different random seeds will probably generate variation at least as large as the differences in validation accuracy. For this demonstration, we left all other things equal, from learning rate to number of epochs to train; in practice, we would try to get the best results by varying those. Also, we would likely want to combine some of the additional design elements.

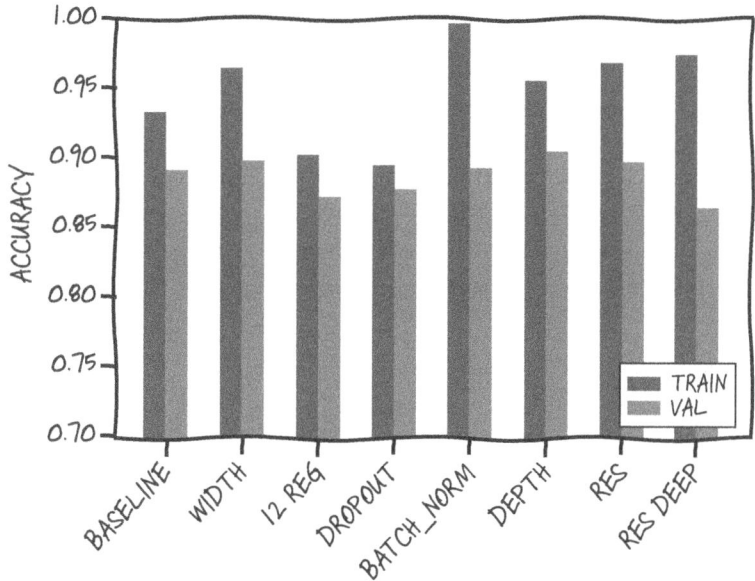

Figure 8.16 The modified networks all perform similarly.

But a qualitative observation may be in order: as we saw in section 5.5.3, when discussing validation and overfitting, the weight decay and dropout regularizations, which have a more rigorous statistical estimation interpretation as regularization than batch norm, have a much narrower gap between the two accuracies. Batch norm, which serves more as a convergence helper, lets us train the network to nearly 100% training accuracy, so we interpret the first two as regularization.

8.5.5 It's already outdated

The curse and blessing of a deep learning practitioner is that neural network architectures evolve at a very rapid pace. This is not to say that what we've seen in this chapter is necessarily old school, but a thorough illustration of the latest and greatest architectures is a matter for another book (and they would cease to be the latest and the greatest pretty quickly anyway). The take-home message is that we should make every effort to proficiently translate the math behind a paper into actual PyTorch code, or at least understand the code that others have written with the same intention. In the last few chapters, you have hopefully gathered quite a few of the fundamental skills to translate ideas into implemented models in PyTorch.

8.6 Conclusion

After quite a lot of work, we now have a model that our fictional friend Jane can use to filter images for her blog. All we have to do is take an incoming image, crop and resize it to 32 × 32, and see what the model has to say about it. Admittedly, we have solved only part of the problem, but it was a journey in itself.

We have solved just part of the problem because there are a few interesting unknowns we would still have to face. One is picking out a bird or airplane from a larger image. Creating bounding boxes around objects in an image is something a model like ours can't do.

Another hurdle concerns what happens when Fred the cat walks in front of the camera. Our model will not refrain from giving its opinion about how bird-like the cat is! It will happily output "airplane" or "bird," perhaps with 0.99 probability. This issue of being very confident about samples that are far from the training distribution is called *overgeneralization*. It's one of the main problems when we take a (presumably good) model to production in those cases where we can't really trust the input (which, sadly, is the majority of real-world cases).

In this chapter, we have built reasonable, working models in PyTorch that can learn from images. We did it in a way that helped us build our intuition around convolutional networks. We also explored ways in which we can make our models wider and deeper, while controlling effects like overfitting. Although we still only scratched the surface, we have taken another significant step forward from the previous chapter. We now have a solid basis for facing the challenges we'll encounter when working on deep learning projects.

Now that we're familiar with PyTorch conventions and common features, we're ready to tackle something bigger. We will use the tools we have learned and build models for real-world applications. Part 2 will provide exposure to generative AI models to learn various architectures and culminate in a project that uses automatic detection of lung cancer; we will go from being familiar with the PyTorch API to being able to implement entire projects using PyTorch.

8.7 Exercises

1 Change our model to use a 5 × 5 kernel with `kernel_size=5` passed to the `nn.Conv2d` constructor:
    a What effect does this change have on the number of parameters in the model?
    b Does the change improve or degrade overfitting?
    c Read https://pytorch.org/docs/stable/nn.html#conv2d.

d Can you describe what `kernel_size=(1,3)` will do?
  e How does the model behave with such a kernel?
2 Can you find an image that contains neither a bird nor an airplane, but that the model claims has one or the other with more than 95% confidence?
  a Can you manually edit a neutral image to make it more airplane-like?
  b Can you manually edit an airplane image to trick the model into reporting a bird?
  c Do these tasks get easier with a network with less capacity? More capacity?

Summary

- Convolution can be used as the linear operation of a feed-forward network dealing with images. Using convolution produces networks with fewer parameters, exploiting locality and featuring translation invariance.
- Stacking multiple convolutions with their activations one after the other, and using max pooling in between, has the effect of applying convolutions to increasingly smaller feature images, thereby effectively accounting for spatial relationships across larger portions of the input image as depth increases.
- Any `nn.Module` subclass can recursively collect and return its and its children's parameters. This technique can be used to count them, feed them into the optimizer, or inspect their values.
- The functional API `torch.nn.functional` provides modules that do not depend on storing internal state. It is used for operations that do not hold parameters and, hence, are not trained.
- Once trained, the parameters of a model can be saved to disk (`torch.save`) and loaded back in (`torch.load`) with one line of code each.
- You can accelerate training by moving training onto the GPU. Using the `.to` method we saw we can move tensors to the GPU and also move the model parameters to the GPU.
- The width and depth of models are two dimensions that can be changed to increase the capacity of a model. Increasing capacity can help a model learn more complex functions, but it can also lead to overfitting.
- Regularization is a set of techniques that help prevent overfitting. In the convolutional neural network example, we applied weight decay, dropout, and batch normalization.
- A skip connection in deep learning is a technique used in architectures like Residual Networks (ResNets) to allow gradients to flow through a shortcut pathway in very deep networks, bypassing one or more layers, which helps in combating the vanishing gradient problem and enables successful training of deeper models.

Part 2

Practical deep learning applications

Part 2 is structured differently than part 1; it's almost a book within a book. Part 2 focuses on practical applications of deep learning, spanning chapters 9 through 17. This section moves beyond foundational concepts to explore how deep learning is used in real-world scenarios, covering a range of tasks and domains.

Chapter 9 introduces text generation with modern language models, providing hands-on experience with generative AI for natural language. Chapter 10 shifts to image generation, exploring an entirely different architecture of models that can create visual content. Chapters 11 through 15 form an extended project on medical image analysis, guiding you through the process of building, training, and evaluating models for early detection of lung cancer using real medical imaging data. These chapters cover data preparation, model development, segmentation and classification, handling imbalanced data, and integrating models into a complete diagnostic pipeline.

Finally, chapters 16 and 17 address advanced topics in scaling and deploying deep learning solutions. Chapter 16 covers distributed training, enabling you to use multiple GPUs or machines for large-scale experiments. Chapter 17 focuses on deployment strategies, including model optimization, quantization, and serving models in production environments.

By the end of part 2 (chapters 9–17), you will have gained hands-on experience with a variety of deep learning applications, from text and image generation to medical imaging, distributed training, and deployment.

How transformers work

This chapter covers
- An explanation of the text generation problem
- An introduction to unsupervised learning
- Learning structure using an attention mechanism
- Building up from simple probabilistic models to deep learning models
- The *transformer* architecture and its variants and applications

While earlier chapters have showcased deep learning's capabilities in regression and classification, the true transformative power of this technology extends far beyond analyzing existing data. Deep learning is now venturing into creative territory—generating entirely new images, composing original text, and even producing realistic videos. These generative capabilities, once considered to be within the exclusive purview of human intelligence, have become central to the current AI revolution, fueling much of the AI boom and enthusiasm we've witnessed in recent years.

The origins of AI-generated content can be traced back to the 1960s, a time when computer scientists were first exploring the idea of machine-generated language.

ELIZA, a computer program developed by Joseph Weizenbaum at MIT, was one of the first programs to use natural language processing (NLP) to simulate a conversation. As such, it is considered one of the first chatbots ever created. One of ELIZA's most famous configurations (DOCTOR) was designed to mimic a Rogerian psychotherapist, a type of therapy that focuses on the patient's feelings and thoughts rather than the therapist's. By recognizing keywords in the patient's responses, ELIZA could generate new questions and maintain a conversation. For example, if the patient said, "I am sad," ELIZA would respond with "Why are you sad?"

The program was a success, and many people were fooled into thinking they were talking to a real person. However, ELIZA was not able to understand the meaning of the conversation. It was simply a clever trick that used a set of fixed rules to generate responses. Consider the previous exchange:

Patient: "I am sad."
ELIZA: "Why are you sad?"

ELIZA would respond with this question regardless of whether the patient had previously explained their feelings. Using pattern matching and a sophisticated set of rule-based statements, ELIZA was able to give the illusion of understanding without actually understanding the context of the conversation. It would take many decades before researchers could devise a viable architecture that accurately captures conversational context, a crucial precondition for generating realistic text. This chapter will focus on this architecture.

A big question remains: How do AIs generate content? With regression and classification, the problems are more defined—you have data and specific targets (labels). However, with generation, the outputs are theoretically infinite. It seems like there's an endless number of ways to rearrange text or brush strokes before you can create something akin to Shakespeare or Monet. It turns out, deep learning models are equipped to handle these challenges thanks to their remarkable ability to discover *latent* structure within data. The term "latent," originating from the Latin word *lateo* meaning "to lie hidden," emphasizes the type of concealed data that humans unconsciously rely on when doing creative work. A significant part of artistic creation, whether it's writing, painting, or making music, involves technical skill and adhering to certain conventions.

This situation presents an interesting paradox: creative mediums follow implicit rules while simultaneously remaining dynamic and constantly evolving. Although these underlying patterns prove difficult to express through explicit programming, deep learning models excel at capturing these hidden conventions by analyzing patterns in existing data and learning to reproduce them. For instance, when dealing with music, we need to understand the structure of melodies, rhythms, and harmonies. Similarly, for a painting, we need to comprehend the arrangement of colors, textures, and forms. Once we've mastered these structures, we can use them to build a probabilistic model that generates new material.

In this chapter, we explore how transformers power text generation. Beginning with a practical example of character-by-character name generation, we'll introduce techniques for handling text data. The chapter progresses to examine the attention mechanism, the cornerstone of transformer technology, before delving into the complete Transformer architecture and its applications in NLP. In this chapter, we will focus on text generation, and in the subsequent chapter, we will look into images.

9.1 A motivating example: Generating names character by character

As we have done in prior chapters, let's start with a problem statement and see how we can use PyTorch to help us solve it. Let's begin by examining the problem of word generation, character by character, and explore how deep learning can generate human names. Eventually, we will work our way up to generating entire paragraphs of text, but let's stick with characters for now to get a better understanding of the techniques involved.

Imagine you've been tasked with creating an algorithm that generates original human names. These names need to be in English, easy to pronounce, and follow familiar naming patterns that people would recognize. The challenge is to create names that feel natural and authentic (similar to names you encounter in daily life) without simply reproducing existing names. How might we approach this problem?

This is a classic example of a problem that can be solved using generative language models. To understand how these models operate, it's important to grasp the concept of *vocabulary* in the language domain. Vocabulary refers to the distinct set of elements that the model can recognize and utilize. Each element is called a *token*, and it is the basic unit that makes up the input and output sequences of the model.

In our problem, the vocabulary comprises all the lowercase letters of the English alphabet (we are ignoring upper cases for our names). Each letter, or token, is assigned a unique integer representation—"a" is represented as 1, "b" as 2, and so on. This method, as shown in figure 9.1, allows us to express any name as a sequence of these integers. For instance, the name "ada" would be represented as the sequence [1, 4, 1].

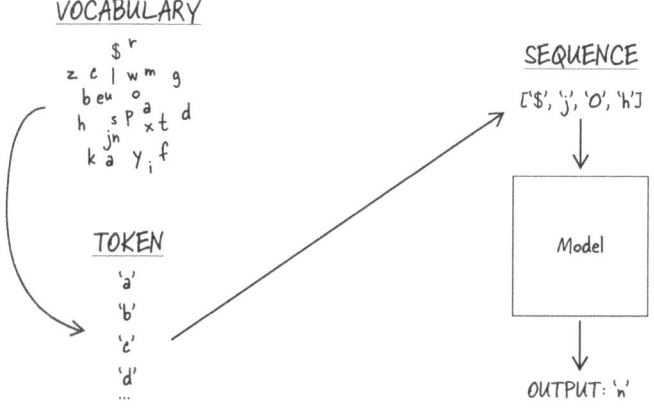

Figure 9.1 General terminology in language models relating to vocabulary, token, and sequence. The $ token is a special token that indicates the start or end of a name.

We can create a mapping from characters to integers, and vice versa, using standard Python dictionaries. Let's open /code/p2ch9/generating_names.ipynb to see how this is done.

Listing 9.1 Setting up vocabulary and character mappings

```
# In[]:
vocab = "$abcdefghijklmnopqrstuvwxyz"
vocab_size = len(vocab)
ch_to_i = {char: i for i, char in enumerate(vocab)}
i_to_ch = {i: char for i, char in enumerate(vocab)}
```

You may have noticed we included an additional character in our vocabulary, $ mapping to 0. This special character indicates the start or end of a name. For example, the name "ada" is represented as the sequence [0, 1, 4, 1, 0], with $ marking both boundaries.

As a crude first step, we could generate names by randomly selecting letters and stringing them together. We can generate a uniform distribution of the letters where each letter appears with equal probability. We will utilize the softmax function to convert the raw scores into probabilities. Recall that softmax is a function that takes a vector of numbers and outputs a probability distribution over the numbers:

```
# In[]:
import torch
import torch.nn as nn
import torch.nn.functional as F
equal_probs = F.softmax(torch.ones(vocab_size), dim=0)   # We are passing a vector of all the same values, so we get a uniform distribution (1/27) over the characters.
for i in range(5):
    generated = ""
    while True:
        random_int = torch.multinomial(equal_probs, 1).item()   # To sample from a probability distribution, we can use torch.multinomial. It takes a tensor of probabilities and returns a single index sampled from the distribution.
        random_char = i_to_ch[random_int]
        if random_char == "$":
            break
        generated += random_char
    print(f"name {i}: {generated}")

# Out[]:
name 0: zrcgahwsalcydnvq
name 1: allatytiyxpckqwbwmeyi
name 2: jrwymeibyroivykbrqqhhbowjpm
name 3: ancvvzdtzhzlweiew
name 4: fvydasrmttj
```

Well, that output is not very good. The names are neither readable nor pronounceable. I won't be naming my child "zrcgahwsalcydnvq" anytime soon—unless I suddenly inherit a tech fortune and need to ensure my offspring stands out at boarding school. We could try to improve this by using a different distribution over the letters.

Some characters, like x or q, are rarely found in names, so treating them all with equal probability doesn't make a lot of sense.

Furthermore, names have an inherent structure in that some characters are more likely to come after another. For example, a followed by n is seen commonly in names like "Hannah," "Morgan," or "Jordan."

9.2 Self-supervised learning

At the core of most NLP models lies the concept of statistical generation. This approach uses probability distributions to predict and generate text sequences. For instance, when modeling names statistically, we calculate the probability of specific letter sequences occurring in order. Take the name "John" as an example: its probability is determined by calculating the likelihood of J appearing as the first letter, followed by o, then h, and finally n in that precise sequence.

To learn such a structure, we could begin by looking at a large list of names and counting the number of times each letter appears after another. We would be learning a probability distribution over the letter pairs. This is called a *bigram* model, where "bi" refers to the fact that we are looking at pairs of letters.

To create such a model, we will need a large list of existing names. It so happens that the official US Social Security administration aggregates the names of all babies born in the US and makes them available for download (https://www.ssa.gov/oact/babynames/names.zip).

We can download the latest list of names from 2022, which is saved to ../data/p2ch9/names_2022.txt, and use it to approximate the probability of each letter appearing in a name:

```
# In[]:
names = []
with open('../data/p2ch9/names_2022.txt', 'r') as file:
    for line in file:
        name, _, _= line.lower().strip().split(',')
        names.append("$" + name + "$")
len(names)

# Out[]:
31915
```

We've collected a list of 31,915 names. Let's see what the distribution of each letter pair is.

Creating a distribution of character pairs requires the construction of a 27 × 27 matrix, as shown in figure 9.2. Each row in this matrix corresponds to the likelihood of different characters appearing after a specific character. For instance, the first row represents the probabilities of all possible characters that could follow $. A particular index in this grid, such as [2, 3] (we are using zero indexing), represents the probability of a character—in this case, c (column 4)—appearing immediately after b (row 3).

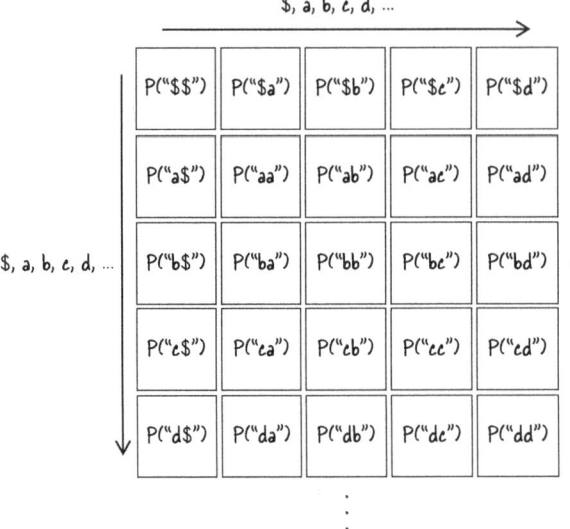

Figure 9.2 Bigram probabilities for the first 5 characters, which can extend up to 27 characters

The bigram model can be created as follows:

```
# In[]:
bigram = torch.zeros((vocab_size, vocab_size))
total = 0
for name in names:
    for ch1, ch2 in zip(name, name[1:]):
        ch1_int = ch_to_i[ch1]
        ch2_int = ch_to_i[ch2]
        bigram[ch1_int][ch2_int] += 1
        total += 1
bigram /= total
```

We are creating a 27 × 27 matrix to store the counts of each character pair.

This code first initializes a zero matrix to store the bigram counts. It then iterates over all names in the dataset, and for each name, it iterates over all pairs of consecutive characters. For each pair of characters, it increments the corresponding count in the bigram matrix and the total count of character pairs. Finally, it normalizes the bigram matrix by the total count of character pairs to get the probabilities.

We can then sample from this distribution to generate names:

```
# In[]:
for i in range(5):
    generated = "$"
    while True:
        bigram_probs = bigram[char_to_index[generated[-1]]]
        sampled_char = index_to_char[
            torch.multinomial(bigram_probs, 1).item()
        ]
        if sampled_char == "$":
            break
```

```
        generated += sampled_char
    print(f"name {i}: {generated[1:]}")

# Out[]:
name 0: liahuli
name 1: deiannnis
name 2: cl
name 3: de
name 4: neynee
```

This result is sort of better. The names are now readable, and some are even pronounceable. However, they are still not very realistic. For example, we see results like cl and de, which do not look like passing names.

Here, it's important to highlight a fundamental paradigm shift. When training models for precision-oriented tasks like classification or regression, we must compare the model's predictions against known "correct" answers or ground truth values for each input. Typically, this ground truth is provided by manually labeled training data, a process known as *supervised* learning due to human involvement. However, in *self-supervised* learning, tasks are structured in a way that allows the ground truth to be inferred from unlabeled data.

Put another way, in all our prior examples during previous chapters, we have depended on training models with data with explicit inputs (x) and targets (y). However, in this example, we do not have any explicit targets. We are learning from the data itself without any labels.

With self-supervised learning, as we get more and more data, we are able to create more sophisticated models. These models can learn about the structure of the data and use this latent information to generate new data. This approach is very powerful as it eliminates the costly and time-consuming process of manual data annotation.

9.2.1 Limits of the bigram model

We computed the probability of the next character given the previous character ($P(c_n|c_{n-1})$) for every character pair. This works since we are only dealing with characters, but even with a small vocabulary of 27 characters, the number of possible character pairs is $27^2 = 729$. We needed to calculate 729 unique probabilities!

This number grows exponentially with the size of the vocabulary. For example, if we were to use a vocabulary of 1,000 characters, the number of possible character pairs would be $1000^2 = 1,000,000$. Most of these probabilities would be 0 since it is likely that some characters never appear after others. This inefficiency in calculating rare or unseen pairs is a problem known as *data sparsity*. We can also see how infeasible this approach would be if our vocabulary consisted of words in the English text, where the vocabulary size is in the hundreds of thousands.

A similar complexity issue arises if we want to capture longer-range dependencies. If you want to capture the probability of the next character given the previous two characters ($P(c_n|c_{n-1}, c_{n-2})$), we would need to calculate $27^3 = 19,683$ probabilities.

This number grows exponentially with the number of characters we want to consider in the range.

To address these challenges, neural networks offer a superior solution. Unlike traditional models, they create dense, continuous representations that effectively capture relationships between characters. This approach allows neural networks to generalize to unseen patterns and handle both sparse data and long-range dependencies efficiently. Most importantly, they maintain a fixed parameter count regardless of vocabulary size or dependency length, making them computationally practical for complex language tasks.

9.3 Generating our training data

Before we start training with neural networks, we need to format the training data we want to feed into our network. Given the unsupervised nature of our task, we do not have explicit input-target pairs included in the data. Instead, we will create input-target pairs by splitting the names into input and target sequences. The input sequence will be the n characters of the name, and the target sequence will be the $n+1^{th}$ character of the name. We will then use these pairs to train our model to predict the next character given the previous characters:

```
# In[]:
example_name = "$ada$"
encode = lambda word: torch.tensor([ch_to_i[c] for c in word])
decode = lambda tensor_i: ''.join(i_to_ch[i.item()] for i in tensor_i)
print(encode(example_name))
print(decode(encode(example_name)))

name_indices = [encode(name) for name in names]
target_indices = [name_index[1:] for name_index in name_indices]

# Out[]:
tensor([0, 1, 4, 1, 0])
$ada$
```

First, we define encode and decode functions to convert the characters to integers and vice versa. We then use these functions to convert the names to integer sequences. We then create the target sequences by shifting the input sequences by one character. For example, the input sequence for the name ada (recall $ is the character boundary) is [0, 1, 4, 1, 0], and the target sequence is [1, 4, 1, 0].

The core idea is that our data will consist of contiguous subsets of the inputs up to an index, and the corresponding target will be the value at that index. For example, for ada:

- First sample:
  - Input: [0] (representing $)
  - Target: [1] (representing a)

- Second sample:
  - Input: [0, 1] (representing $a)
  - Target: [4] (representing d)
- Third sample:
  - Input: [0, 1, 4] (representing $ad)
  - Target: [1] (representing a)
- Fourth sample:
  - Input: [0, 1, 4, 1] (representing $ada)
  - Target: [0] (representing $)

Notice, as shown in figure 9.3, that from our single name, we can generate multiple input-target pairs.

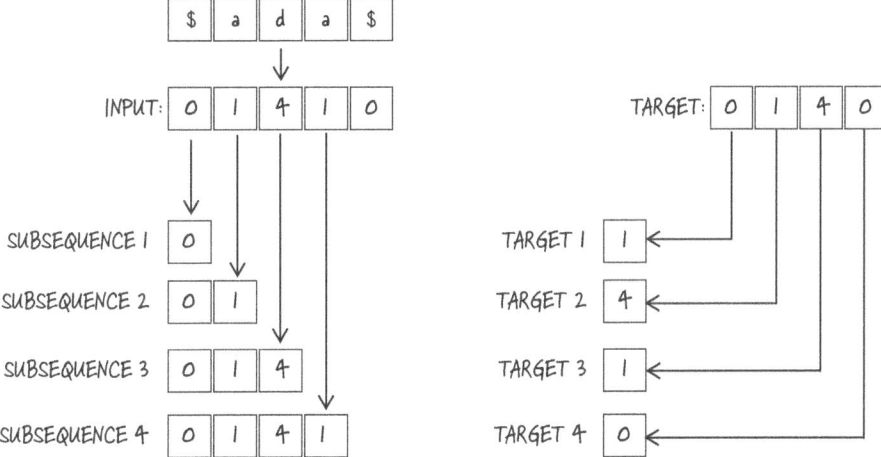

Figure 9.3 Each input has multiple subsequences, and each subsequence has a corresponding target, which is inferred from the data itself.

We will pad the input and target sequences to the same lengths (the length of the longest name, in this case) to facilitate processing for our models. To ensure uniformity in length, we will pad the input sequences with 0 and the target sequences with -1 Later in our loss function, we will specify to ignore the -1 values, which means this target will not be processed:

```
# In[]:
from torch.nn.utils.rnn import pad_sequence
X = pad_sequence(name_indices, batch_first=True, padding_value=0)
max_name_length = max(len(name) for name in names)
target_indices.append(torch.empty((max_name_length),
    dtype=torch.long))
```

This is a trick to pad Y with a tensor for size 11 so that all targets are the same length.

```
Y = pad_sequence(target_indices, batch_first=True, padding_value=-1)[:-1]
print(X[0])
print(Y[0])

# Out[]:
tensor([ 0, 15, 12,  9, 22,  9,  1,  0,  0,  0,  0])
tensor([15, 12,  9, 22,  9,  1,  0, -1, -1, -1, -1])
```

Now, we can define a helper function to create a batch of input-target pairs. This function takes a batch size and returns a batch of input-target pairs. We will use this function to create our training data:

```
# In[]:
def get_batch(batch_size=64):
    random_idx = torch.randint(0, X.size(0), (batch_size,))
    inputs = X[random_idx]
    labels = Y[random_idx]
    return inputs, labels
inputs, labels = get_batch(3)
print(inputs)
print(labels)

# Out[]:
tensor([[ 0,  2, 18,  9, 26,  5, 25,  4,  1,  0,  0],
        [ 0, 21, 26,  9,  1, 19,  0,  0,  0,  0,  0],
        [ 0, 14, 15, 15, 18, 21, 12,  1,  9, 14,  0]])
tensor([[ 2, 18,  9, 26,  5, 25,  4,  1,  0, -1, -1],
        [21, 26,  9,  1, 19,  0, -1, -1, -1, -1, -1],
        [14, 15, 15, 18, 21, 12,  1,  9, 14,  0, -1]])
```

Now we have all our data ready! Let's get to using it.

9.4 Embeddings and linear layers

In chapter 4, we looked at some representations of data, including text data. We saw that text can be represented as text embeddings, where words are mapped to a higher-dimensional space to help facilitate downstream learning. In our problem, we can similarly use embeddings to represent characters. Currently, each character is only represented by a single integer. However, we can transform each character into a vector of numbers. This helps to capture the similarity between characters. For example, the embeddings for vowel characters like "a" and "e" will be more similar in use than the embeddings for "a" and "z" (we will visualize this later).

Luckily, in PyTorch, there is another already-written module that does this for us. The nn.Embedding module takes a tensor of indices and returns a tensor of embeddings. We need to specify the size of the dictionary—in this case, our vocabulary size of 27 characters and the size of the embeddings, which we will set to a constant 3 (the choice to set it to 3 is an arbitrary decision):

9.4 Embeddings and linear layers

```
# In[]:
embedding_dim = 3
embedding = nn.Embedding(vocab_size, embedding_dim)
example_input = torch.tensor([1, 1, 0, 2])
input_embd = embedding(example_input)
print(input_embd.shape)
input_embd

# Out[]:
torch.Size([4, 3])
tensor([[-2.0552, -0.5413, -0.2367],
        [-2.0552, -0.5413, -0.2367],
        [ 0.6718, -0.1038,  2.3367],
        [-0.0655,  1.0041,  2.0066]], grad_fn=<EmbeddingBackward0>)
```

The nn.Embedding module is specifically designed to work with integer indices. It functions as a trainable lookup table that stores embeddings for each of our 27 characters and returns the corresponding row of values for each index, as shown in figure 9.4. These embeddings begin with random initializations and are continuously updated during the training process through backpropagation, allowing the model to learn optimal character representations for our specific task.

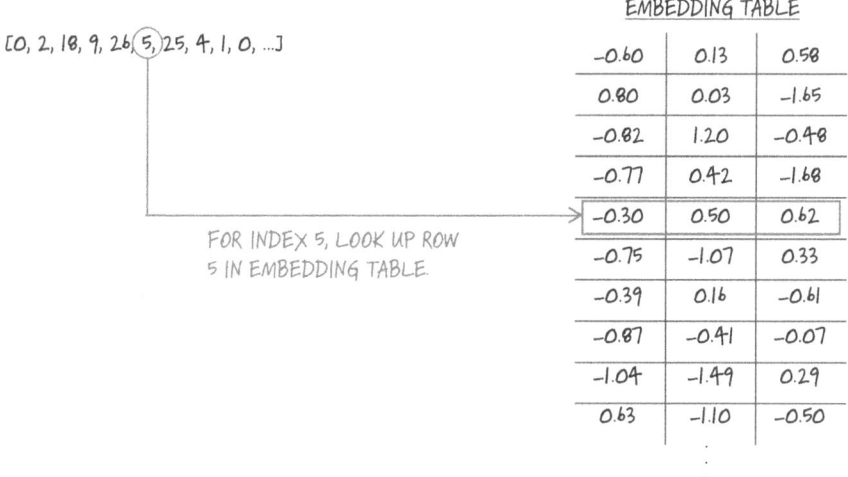

Figure 9.4 The embedding lookup process. Each index is used to look up the corresponding row of values in the embedding tensor.

The input tensor has size 4, and the embedding tensor has size 4 × 3 because the input tensor has 4 indices and the embedding tensor has 4 rows of 3 values each.

Each row of the embedding tensor corresponds to the embedding of the character at the matching index in the input tensor. For instance, the first two rows of the embedding tensor are identical because the first two indices in the input tensor are the same.

Now we can evolve from our prior bigram model into a deep learning model by using embeddings and linear layers. During our new model forward, we are converting each subsequence into a list of embeddings. We then flatten the embeddings and pass them through a linear layer to get the output. We can then use the output to predict the next character. Figure 9.5 shows a diagram of the model:

```
# In[]:
class SequenceMLP(nn.Module):
    def __init__(self, vocab_size, max_sequence_length,
      embedding_dim, hidden_dim=32):
        super().__init__()
        self.vocab_size = vocab_size
        self.max_sequence_length = max_sequence_length
        self.embedding_dim = embedding_dim
        self.embedding = nn.Embedding(vocab_size, embedding_dim)
        self.linear = nn.Linear(embedding_dim * max_sequence_length,
          hidden_dim)
        self.relu = nn.ReLU()
        self.out = nn.Linear(hidden_dim, vocab_size)

    def forward(self, x):
        batch_size, seq_len = x.shape
        sequence_embeddings = torch.zeros(batch_size, seq_len,
          self.max_sequence_length * self.embedding_dim)
        for i in range(seq_len):
            subsequence = torch.zeros(batch_size, self.max_sequence_length,
              dtype=torch.int)
            prefix = x[:, :i+1]
            subsequence[:, :i+1] = prefix
            emb = self.embedding(subsequence)
            sequence_embeddings[:, i, :] = emb.view(
              batch_size, -1)
        x = self.linear(sequence_embeddings)
        x = self.relu(x)
        x = self.out(x)
        return x

embedding_dim = 3
max_sequence_length = X.shape[1]
model = SequenceMLP(vocab_size, max_sequence_length, embedding_dim)
```

> We are iterating over the sequence length and creating a subsequence for each index in the sequence.

> The embeddings representing the subsequence are flattened into a list of values.

> The flattened embeddings are passed through a hidden layer and an output layer to get the output.

The training loop is similar to what we saw in previous chapters. We will not focus on the hyperparameters since our focus is on exploring different architectures rather

9.4 Embeddings and linear layers

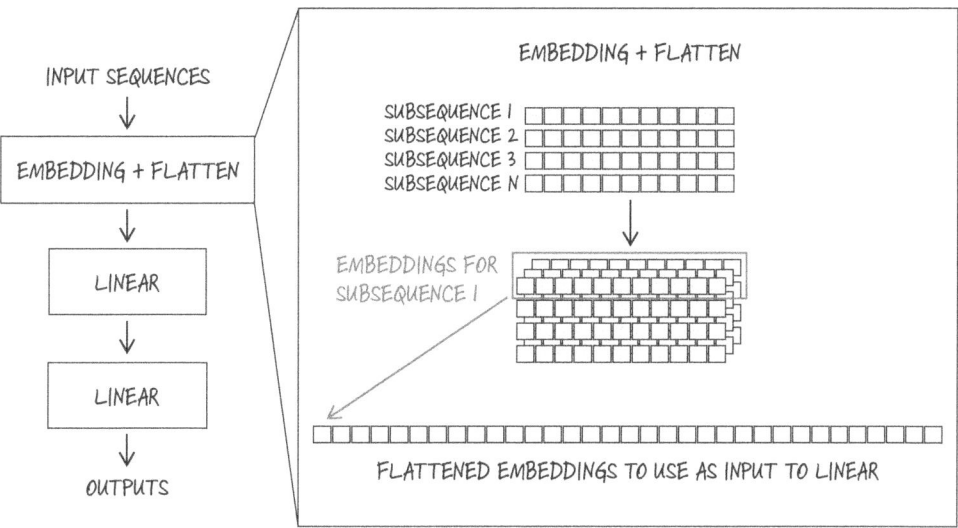

Figure 9.5 Diagram of the model

than a state-of-the-art model. We will use a simple SGD optimizer and the cross-entropy loss function, reporting the loss every 1,000 steps:

```
# In[]:
import torch.optim as optim

def train(model, optimizer, num_steps=10_001, loss_report_interval=1_000):
    losses = []
    for i in range(1, num_steps):
        inputs, labels = get_batch()            # We need to flatten the
        optimizer.zero_grad()                   # logits to a 2D tensor and
        logits = model(inputs)                  # the labels to a 1D tensor.
        loss = F.cross_entropy(logits.view(-1, logits.shape[-1]),
            labels.view(-1), ignore_index=-1)
        losses.append(loss.item())
        if i % loss_report_interval == 0:
            print(f'Average loss at step {i}: {sum(losses[
                -loss_report_interval:]) / loss_report_interval:.4f}')
        loss.backward()
        optimizer.step()

optimizer = optim.SGD(model.parameters(), lr=0.1)
```

One important note about our data organization: each training batch contains multiple names, and each name produces multiple training examples. For every name, we generate several input-target pairs by creating subsequences of increasing length (the inputs) paired with their corresponding next character (the targets). This approach maximizes the learning signal from our limited name dataset. This is different from what we have seen in the past, where the `batch_size` was the number of samples observed.

Now, each sample contains multiple inputs and targets. As a result, in our loss function, we flatten the logits to a 2D tensor, where the second dimension is the 27 characters in consideration, and the targets are a 1D tensor with the correct character. We also specify to ignore the -1 values in the targets to ignore subsequences that are not valid and should not be considered in training.

Finally, we are ready to train:

```
# In[]:
train(model, optimizer)

# Out[]:
Average loss at step 1000: 2.6099
Average loss at step 2000: 2.5163
Average loss at step 3000: 2.4691
Average loss at step 4000: 2.4229
Average loss at step 5000: 2.3910
Average loss at step 6000: 2.3728
Average loss at step 7000: 2.3593
Average loss at step 8000: 2.3517
Average loss at step 9000: 2.3420
Average loss at step 10000: 2.3352
```

To sample from this trained model and generate names, we can utilize the autoregressive character-level generation method. (Autoregressive means the model generates each token in a sequence one at a time, using its previous outputs as input for predicting the next token.) This involves feeding in a $ as the model's starting character. The model, which has been trained to predict the next character based on the previous ones, will generate a prediction.

This predicted character is then appended to the input sequence and fed back into the model, creating a growing input that incorporates each newly generated character. The model continues to predict and generate subsequent characters, creating a sequence, until it reaches the end character $. This autoregressive process allows the model to generate names or any other sequences of characters in a way that is contextually relevant to the preceding characters:

```
# In[]:
def generate_samples(model, num_samples=1, max_len=max_name_length):
    sequences = torch.zeros((num_samples, 1)).int()
    for _ in range(max_len):
        logits = model(sequences)
        logits = logits[:, -1, :]
        probs = F.softmax(logits, dim=-1)
        idx_next = torch.multinomial(probs, num_samples=1)
        sequences = torch.cat((sequences, idx_next), dim=1)
```

```
    for sequence in sequences:
        indices = torch.where(sequence == 0)[0]
        end = indices[1] if len(indices) > 1 else max_len
        sequence = sequence[1:end]
        print(decode(sequence))

generate_samples(model, num_samples=10)

# Out[]:
jatini
tladauh
ceney
aamsse
keisvta
yassi
aenmli
lydude
ikiyo
jayhal
```

The output generation is much better than before. Intuitively, they seem much more name-like and are more realistic in their form and length. We can see that the model is learning the structure of the names and using this latent information to generate new names.

9.4.1 Visualizing embeddings

The effect of training is also evident in our embedding values. As a result of the training process, the embeddings now effectively capture the structural nuances of the characters. Each character is represented by a tensor of size 3, allowing us to visualize them in a 3D space. In our visualization, the first, second, and third values of the tensor correspond to the x, y, and z coordinates, respectively.

In figure 9.6, we can see that the embeddings for the vowels are closer together, and the embeddings for the consonants are closer together, and the special character $ is separated from the rest. This is a result of the model learning the structure of the characters used in the English language and our dataset.

The embedding space is designed to capture as much information about the character as possible, including its meaning, its role within names, and its relationships with other characters. While our example uses just three dimensions for visualization purposes, real-world applications typically employ embeddings with thousands of dimensions to represent the complex linguistic relationships in our language.

We have already come so far, but we can do even better by using a more sophisticated model. Next, we will focus on a model that is designed to dynamically capture the structure of the data and the relationships within our character sequences. This is where attention comes in.

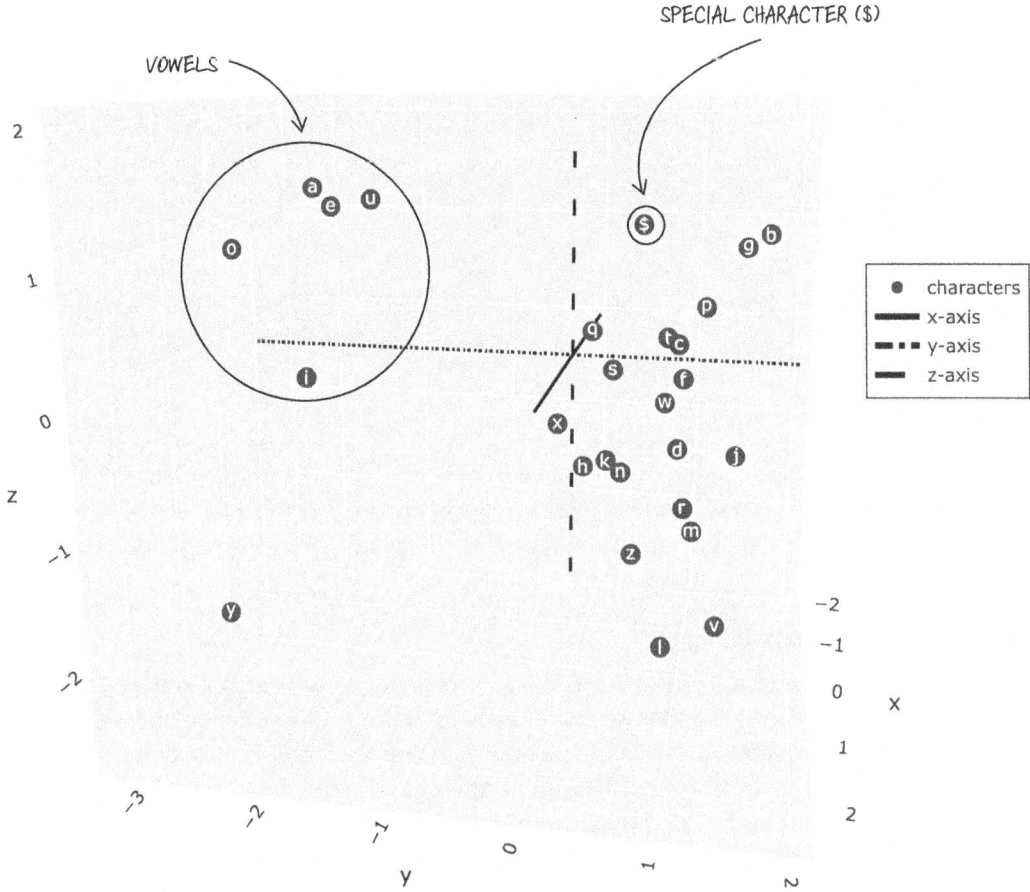

Figure 9.6 Embeddings visualized in 3D space

9.5 Attention

Embeddings do capture semantic and syntactic relationships between characters, but they are static for each character. The same character has the same embedding regardless of its context. In our previous model, the character a would have identical embedding values whether it appears in car, where it's pronounced as in far, or in care, where it has a completely different sound. Even though it's the same letter, its function differs dramatically, which static embeddings cannot capture.

In contrast, the attention mechanism dynamically considers the context of each character, adjusting the model's focus on different parts of the input sequence. This enables the model to weigh the importance of each character based on its surrounding context, thus enhancing the generation of contextually appropriate names.

A real-life analogy for the attention mechanism is the way a spotlight operator works during a theater performance. Imagine the theater stage as the entire sequence, and each character in a name is an actor on this stage. Without attention, the spotlight shines uniformly on the actors, regardless of who is currently speaking or playing the most critical role in a scene, which is akin to traditional embeddings, where each character is given equal importance regardless of context. With the attention mechanism, the spotlight operator (the model) dynamically adjusts the focus and intensity of the light to highlight the actor who is currently speaking or is most relevant to the scene's context.

In practice, attention achieves this focus through three components: the query, the key, and the value. These terms are analogous to those used in information retrieval systems. When you search on Google, the search engine will map your query (search text) against a set of keys (indexed web pages) and return the most relevant values (search results).

To explain these components more concretely:

- *Query*—Represents what we're looking for at each position in the sequence.
- *Key*—Represents what each position contains that might match what we're looking for.
- *Value*—The actual content that gets retrieved when a match is found between a query and key.

Together, these components allow the attention mechanism to determine which parts of the input sequence are most relevant to each position. When the query at one position closely matches the key at another position, the model gives more weight to the corresponding value, effectively focusing on the most important information for generating the next character in our sequence.

We will be looking at a specific type of attention mechanism called *self-attention*, where one sequence attends to itself (as opposed to cross-attention, where attention is based on two sequences). Now let's look at the self-attention mechanism in more detail.

9.5.1 Dot product self-attention

Self-attention is the core mechanism that allows us to capture relationships between different positions in a sequence. Here's how it works:

1 *Inputs*—A self-attention block takes N inputs ($x_1, ..., x_n$), where each input has dimension D. In our character-level model, each input represents a character embedding.

2 *Creating values*—For each position m in the sequence, we transform its embedding into a "value" vector using a learnable linear transformation:

$$v_m = x_m W_v^T + b_v$$

This is simply an nn.Linear layer applied to each position, creating N value vectors of dimension D.

3 *Attention weights*—For each position n, we compute attention weights that determine how much to focus on each position m in the sequence. These weights are normalized to sum to 1.

4 *Weighted Combination*—The output for position n is a weighted sum of all value vectors:

$$sa_n[x_1, \ldots, x_N] = \sum_{m=1}^{N} a[x_m, x_n] v_m$$

where the weights $(a_n[x_m, x_n])$ reflect the importance of each position m to position n. For now, let's assume these weights are given to us—we'll explore exactly how to calculate them in the next section.

This mechanism enables the model to dynamically focus on relevant parts of the input sequence when processing each position. For example, when predicting the next character in a name, the model might give higher weights to positions containing characters that commonly influence what comes next (see figure 9.7).

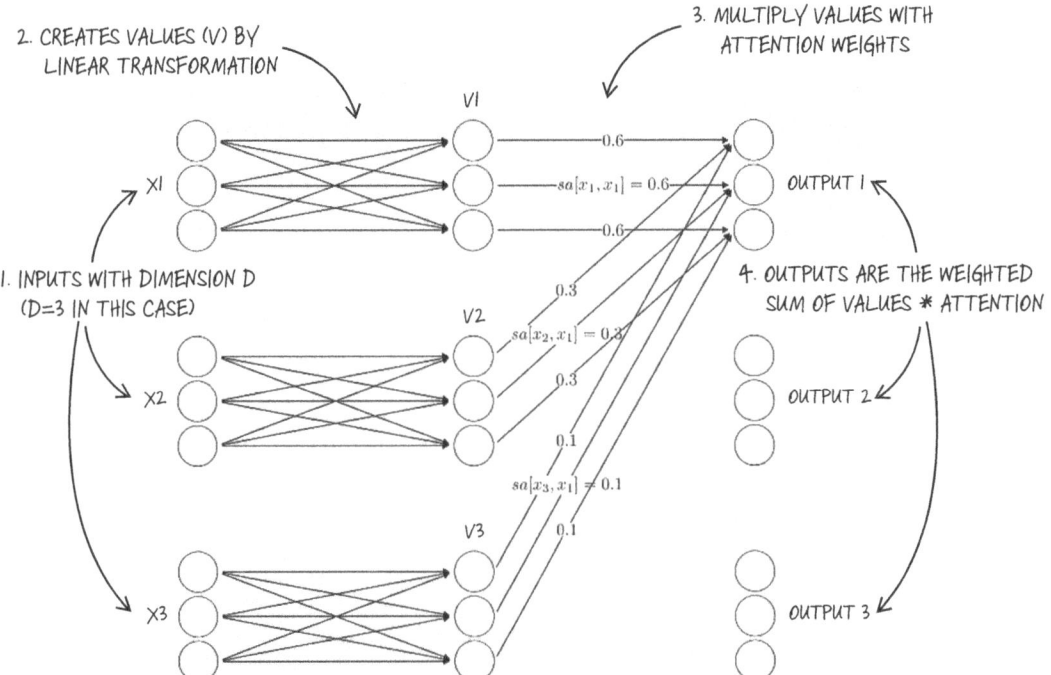

Figure 9.7 Self attention, step-by-step from input to output

An alternative way to think of attention is as *routing* information. It determines which parts of the input data should be focused on at each step of the computation. For example, when processing part of a name, an attention mechanism might route more focus to important characters and less focus on less important characters.

COMPUTING ATTENTION WEIGHTS

The question still remains: How do we compute these magical attention weights $a_n[x_m, x_n]$ we just happen to be using? To compute attention weights, we first compute a set of *query* and *key* vectors. This is performed in a similar fashion to how we computed the *values* but with a different set of weights and biases:

$$q_n = x_n W_q^T + b_q$$

$$k_m = x_m W_k^T + b_k$$

We then compute the attention weights by taking the dot product of the query and key vectors and applying a softmax function to the result:

$$a[x_m, x_n] = \text{softmax}(q_n \cdot k_m^T) = \frac{\exp(q_n \cdot k_m^T)}{\sum_{m=1}^{N} \exp(q_n \cdot k_m^T)}$$

This gives us an attention weight for a particular m and n. The softmax function ensures that the attention weights across all m from $1,...,N$ sum to 1, which is important for the weighted sum to be a proper average.

IMPLEMENTING DOT PRODUCT SELF-ATTENTION

To make this more concrete, let's see the entire dot product self-attention implemented in code (code/p2ch9/attention.ipynb). In this example, our input x has shape [2, 3]; therefore, our query, key, and value matrices each have shape [2, 3], representing two positions with three embedding dimensions each.

Listing 9.2 attention.ipynb

```
# In[]:
torch.manual_seed(0)
x = torch.rand(2, 3)

query = F.linear(x, weight=torch.rand(3, 3),
    bias=torch.rand(3))
key = F.linear(x, weight=torch.rand(3, 3), bias=torch.rand(3))
value = F.linear(x, weight=torch.rand(3, 3), bias=torch.rand(3))

def dot_product_attention_single(q, k, v):
    attn_weights = q @ k.T
```

Uses the F.linear function to perform the linear transformation of the input x into the query, key, and value vectors

The set of dot products over N inputs can be expressed as a matrix multiplication (@), where .T performs matrix transpose to align dimensions properly.

```
            attn_weights = F.softmax(attn_weights, dim=-1)
            output = attn_weights @ v
            return output

dot_product_attention_single(query, key, value)

# Out[]:
tensor([[1.3667, 0.6913, 1.0614],
        [1.3718, 0.6930, 1.0627]])
```

Applies the softmax function to the dot products to get the attention weights. We apply along the -1 dimension since we want the average across the row of values.

Uses the attention weights to compute the weighted sum of the values

The implementation uses matrix multiplication to efficiently compute all dot products between query and key vectors in a single operation. Softmax is then applied to convert these scores into properly normalized attention weights. Finally, these weights are multiplied by the value vectors to produce a weighted sum, with more relevant information contributing more strongly to the output.

9.5.2 Scaled dot product causal self-attention

We now have a new representation of our input that takes into consideration the relationships between all other elements in the sequence, as shown in figure 9.8. In practice, there are three extensions to this form of dot product attention:

- *Batching*—We want to allow batching of inputs, so we need to make sure that the attention weights are computed for each input in the batch.
- *Causal masking*—In some cases, we want to ensure that the attention mechanism does not "look" at future elements in the sequence. This is particularly

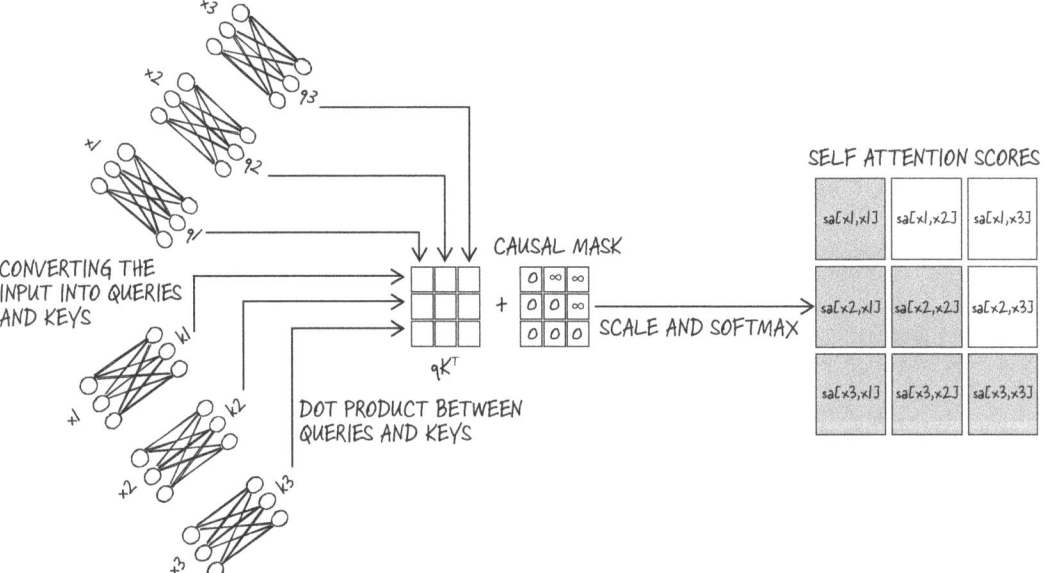

Figure 9.8 Full causal self-attention mechanism

9.5 Attention

useful for autoregressive models, where we want to ensure that the model only attends to previous elements in the sequence.

- *Scaling*—We want to scale the attention weights to ensure that the gradients do not vanish or explode.

Thus, our former implementation can then be adapted to

```
# In[]:
torch.manual_seed(0)
x = torch.rand(1, 2, 3)

query = F.linear(x, weight=torch.rand(3, 3), bias=torch.rand(3))
key = F.linear(x, weight=torch.rand(3, 3), bias=torch.rand(3))
value = F.linear(x, weight=torch.rand(3, 3), bias=torch.rand(3))

def scaled_dot_product_causal_attention(q, k, v):
    attn_weights = q @ k.transpose(1, 2)
    mask = torch.tril(torch.ones(attn_weights.
    shape[1:]), diagonal=0)
    attn_weights = attn_weights.masked_fill(mask == 0, value=float('-inf'))
    attn_weights = attn_weights / torch.sqrt(torch.tensor(
    k.shape[-1]).float())
    attn_weights = F.softmax(attn_weights, dim=-1)
    output = attn_weights @ v
    return output, attn_weights

output, attn_weights = scaled_dot_product_causal_attention(query, key, value)
output

# Out[]:
tensor([[[1.6253, 0.7788, 1.1252],
         [1.3849, 0.6974, 1.0659]]])
```

> In this example, we are using a batch of size 1, so now we have a 3D tensor with dimensions 1 × 2 × 3.

> We scale the attention weights by dividing by the square root of the dimension of the key vectors. This is a common trick to ensure that the gradients do not vanish or explode.

> We create a mask to prevent the model from attending to future tokens. We use the tril function to create a lower triangular matrix of 1s and then fill the upper triangular part with negative infinity. This will ensure that the attention weights are 0 for future tokens.

> We are using the transpose function to swap the last two dimensions of the key tensor to perform the dot product. The first dimension remains as the batch dimension.

Congratulations! You have now implemented a scaled dot product causal attention mechanism. This is the core operation that underpins the functionality of many of the state-of-the-art models. As expected, PyTorch has a built-in function for this that we can use, but give yourself a pat on the back for working through the underlying mechanics. We can verify our implementation is equivalent to the PyTorch implementation F.scaled_dot_product_attention:

```
# In[]:
expected_output = F.scaled_dot_product_attention(
    query, key, value, is_causal=True)
print(torch.allclose(output, expected_output))

# Out[]:
True
```

> We use the torch.allclose function to check if the two tensors are close enough to be considered equal.

NOTE The PyTorch implementation of F.scaled_dot_product_attention is equivalent to our version of scaled_dot_product_attention in the sense that the results are the same. However, it is highly efficient and uses optimized kernels. In production, we should defer to using the official PyTorch implementation.

Now that we have our attention implementation, let's put it into action for a new model. As before, we will use an embedding layer to transform the input sequence into a set of embeddings; however, instead of flattening and concatenating the embeddings together, we will then use the attention mechanism to capture the relationships between these embeddings. Finally, just like the previous model, we are using multiple linear layers to transform the attention outputs into the output:

```
# In[]:
class AttentionMLP(nn.Module):
    def __init__(self, n_embd, vocab_size, block_size, n_hidden=64):
        super().__init__()
        self.tok_embd = nn.Embedding(vocab_size, n_embd)
        self.attn_weights = None

        self.query_proj = nn.Linear(n_embd, n_embd)
        self.key_proj = nn.Linear(n_embd, n_embd)
        self.value_proj = nn.Linear(n_embd, n_embd)

        self.register_buffer("mask", torch.tril(torch.ones(
            (block_size, block_size)), diagonal=0))

        self.mlp = nn.Sequential(
            nn.Linear(n_embd, n_hidden),
            nn.ReLU(),
            nn.Linear(n_hidden, n_embd)
        )

        self.output_proj = nn.Linear(n_embd, vocab_size)

    def forward(self, x):
        x = self.tok_embd(x)
        batch_size, seq_len, embd_dim = x.shape

        q = self.query_proj(x)
        k = self.key_proj(x)
        v = self.value_proj(x)

        attn_weights = q @ k.transpose(1, 2)
        attn_weights = attn_weights.masked_fill(self.mask[
            :seq_len, :seq_len] == 0, value=float('-inf'))
        attn_weights = attn_weights / torch.sqrt(torch.tensor(
            k.shape[-1]).float())
        self.attn_weights = F.softmax(attn_weights, dim=-1)
        x = self.attn_weights @ v
        x = self.mlp(x)
```

```
        x = self.output_proj(x)
        return x

model = AttentionMLP(32, vocab_size, max_name_length)
optimizer = optim.SGD(model.parameters(), lr=0.01)
train(model, optimizer, num_steps=10_001, loss_report_interval=1_000)

# Out[]:
Average loss at step 1000: 2.9688
Average loss at step 2000: 2.6580
Average loss at step 3000: 2.5903
Average loss at step 4000: 2.5739
Average loss at step 5000: 2.5555
Average loss at step 6000: 2.5278
Average loss at step 7000: 2.4915
Average loss at step 8000: 2.4602
Average loss at step 9000: 2.4377
Average loss at step 10000: 2.4284
```

Our train() and generate() functions are the same as before, so we can use them to train and generate samples from our new model. Let's see how our new model performs:

```
# In[]:
generate_samples(model, 10)

# Out[]:
venen
cckaeelr
karori
resedl
wlynhoe
jom
amylas
ryinya
kaihun
ernii
```

We get a performance similar to the previous model, but without having to unroll the embeddings by looping through each subsequence and flattening them. This is because the attention mechanism can capture the relationships between the characters in the sequence and use this information to generate the next character.

As a bonus in our implementation, we are also returning the attention weights, so we can visualize the attention score to see which characters the model is focusing on when generating the next character. Figure 9.9 presents an example using the name "john."

In figure 9.9, the row represents the scale at which each character on the x-axis is attending to each character on the y-axis. For example, in row 3, for character o, it weights the context of itself the highest, followed by $, followed by j. As a result, when

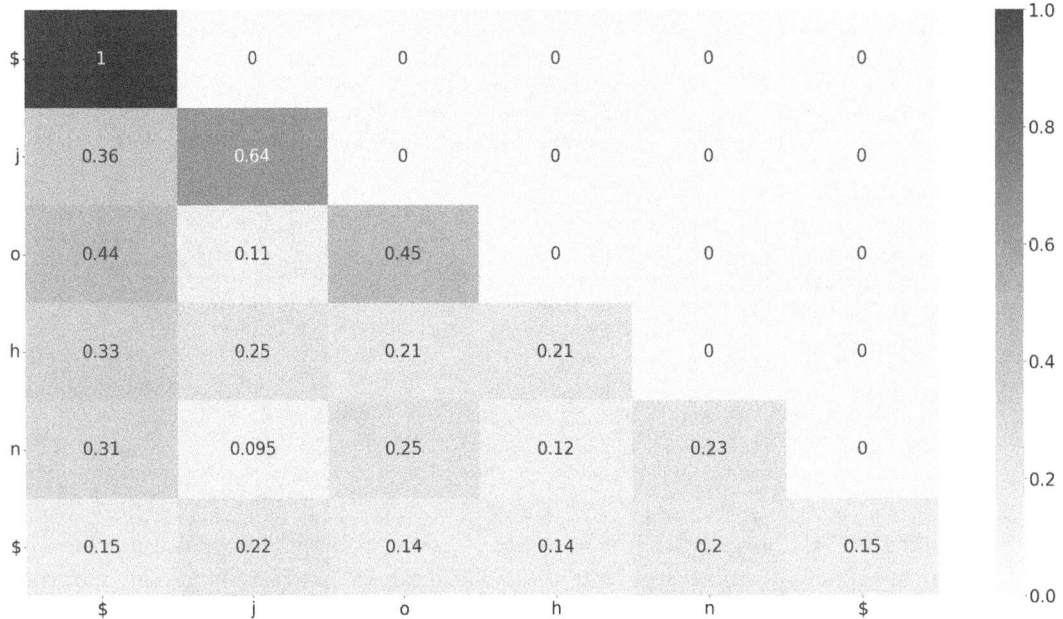

Figure 9.9 Attention weights for the name "john" visualized on a grid. Each row of values sums to 1. The darker the color, the higher the attention weight.

the model is processing the character o in "john," it primarily focuses on the o itself and then considers the start token and the initial j, suggesting the model recognizes that the letter o in this position is strongly influenced by its own identity and the beginning of the name.

Pretty cool, right? This visualization shows how our model pays attention to connections between characters in the sequence. It's like the model is saying, "Hey, I should consider both what's happening now *and* what came before!" By looking at these relationships, it identifies useful patterns that help predict which character should come next. Now that we've got these attention basics down, let's dive into the full Transformer architecture and see what it can really do.

9.6 *Transformers*

The Transformer architecture was popularized in 2017 in the seminal paper "Attention Is All You Need" by Vaswani et al. (https://arxiv.org/pdf/1706.03762.pdf). As the title of the paper suggests, at the core of the Transformer architecture is the attention mechanism that we just implemented in the previous section. The transformer has since become the foundation of many state-of-the-art models in NLP and other fields.

In Vaswani et al.'s paper, the transformer was used for machine translation, translating a sentence from one language to another. The original transformer architecture consists of two main components: the encoder and the decoder. The encoder takes an input sequence and transforms it into a set of representations that captures the relationships between the elements in the sequence. The decoder then takes these representations and generates an output sequence.

We'll begin our exploration with the decoder component rather than the full encoder-decoder architecture because decoder-only transformers have gained tremendous popularity in recent years, powering virtually all leading large language models, such as GPT, Claude, and Llama. This decoder-first approach aligns with the current industry focus, where generative AI applications predominantly utilize decoder architectures for their remarkable text generation capabilities.

9.6.1 The decoder

The transformer decoder is used for tasks such as language generation because the model can generate a sequence of tokens based on an input sequence. The most popular decoder models are the GPT series, which stands for *Generative Pre-Trained Transformer*. These models are the core of OpenAI's ChatGPT and have been widely popular in recent years, fueling the generative AI boom. These models are trained on large amounts of text data and are able to generate text that is contextually relevant and coherent. In chapter 2, we saw how to use GPT-2, a transformer-based language model, to generate text. GPT-style models are considered decoder-only transformers because they only have a decoder component. The decoder architecture is responsible for generating the output sequence.

Let's implement a GPT-style decoder of our own in PyTorch, as shown in figure 9.10. We will be able to build off our existing work as the decoder transformer block looks very similar to the attention multilayer perceptron (MLP) block we previously implemented but with a few more extensions.

There are a few more components that we need to add to the attention MLP block to make it a full transformer decoder block. These include

- *Residual connections*—These are also called *skip connections* and help to combat the problem of vanishing gradients, which is prevalent in deep networks as the gradients get smaller and smaller as they are backpropagated through the network. Residual connections allow the gradients to flow directly through the network, bypassing the layers.
- *Multiheaded attention*—Instead of using a single attention mechanism, the input is processed through multiple parallel attention "heads." Each head has its own set of learned projection parameters (for queries, keys, and values), allowing it to focus on different aspects of the input. For example, with two attention heads, one model might learn to focus on syntactic relationships while another captures semantic associations. The outputs from all heads are then concatenated and passed through a linear layer to produce the final representation. This parallel processing enables the model to capture diverse relationships within the sequence simultaneously.

GPT-STYLE DECODER

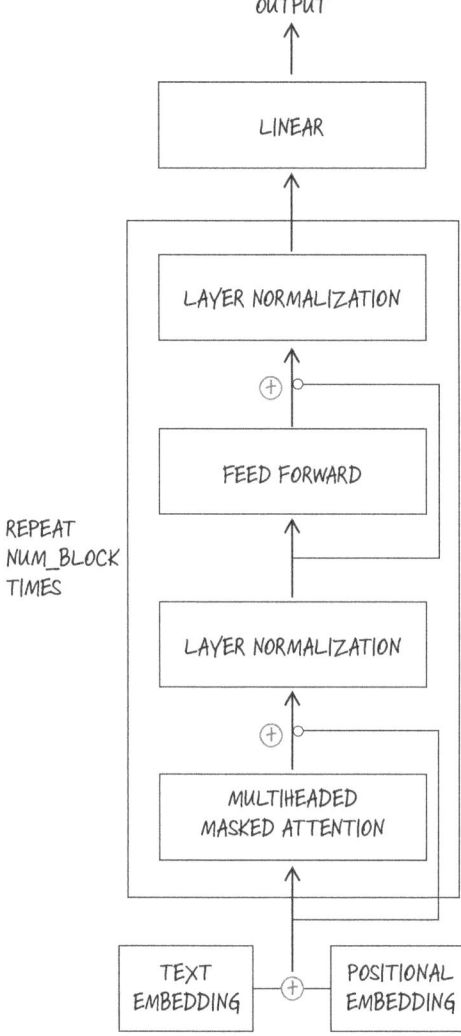

Figure 9.10 GPT-style decoder. The pluses represent residual connections where outputs are summed.

- *Positional embeddings*—Since Transformer architectures process all tokens in parallel rather than sequentially, they have no inherent understanding of token order. Positional embeddings address this by adding position-specific information to each token embedding. These can be learned parameters or fixed sinusoidal functions, and they allow the model to understand the relative or absolute positions of tokens in a sequence. Without positional embeddings, the transformer would treat input sequences as unordered sets of tokens, losing critical syntactic and semantic information that depends on word order.

- *Layer normalization*—Layer normalization is similar to batch normalization, which we saw in chapter 8, but instead of normalizing the inputs across the batch, layer normalization normalizes the inputs across the features. This helps to stabilize the training of the model. See figure 9.11 for the difference between layer normalization and batch normalization.

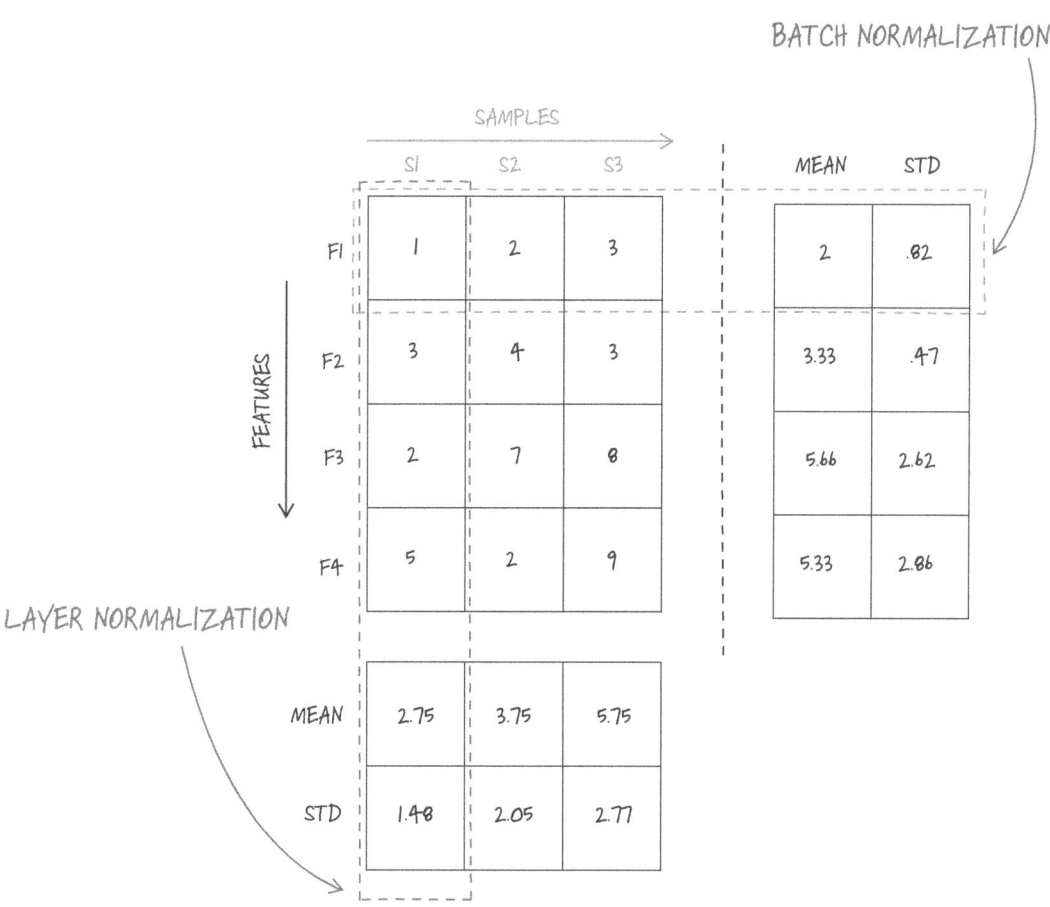

Figure 9.11 Layer normalization compared with batch normalization

We can implement the decoder block as a PyTorch module. For simplicity, instead of our previous implementation of scaled dot product causal attention, we will use the equivalent PyTorch implementation we saw earlier of F.scaled_dot_product_attention:

```python
class TransformerBlock(nn.Module):
    def __init__(self, n_embd, num_heads=4, n_hidden=64):
        super().__init__()
        assert n_embd % num_heads == 0, "Embedding dimension must be
         ↳ divisible by the number of heads"

        self.num_heads = num_heads
        self.head_dim = n_embd // num_heads

        self.query_proj = nn.Linear(n_embd, n_embd)
        self.key_proj = nn.Linear(n_embd, n_embd)
        self.value_proj = nn.Linear(n_embd, n_embd)

        self.mlp = nn.Sequential(
            nn.Linear(n_embd, n_hidden),
            nn.ReLU(),
            nn.Linear(n_hidden, n_embd)
        )

        # Layernorms
        self.norm_1 = nn.LayerNorm(n_embd)
        self.norm_2 = nn.LayerNorm(n_embd)

    def forward(self, x):
        batch_size, sequence_length, _ = x.shape

        q = self.query_proj(x)
        k = self.key_proj(x)
        v = self.value_proj(x)

        # multiheaded attention
        q = q.view(batch_size, sequence_length, self.num_heads,
         ↳ self.head_dim).transpose(1, 2)
        k = k.view(batch_size, sequence_length, self.num_heads,
         ↳ self.head_dim).transpose(1, 2)
        v = v.view(batch_size, sequence_length, self.num_heads,
         ↳ self.head_dim).transpose(1, 2)

        # attention
        attn_weights = F.scaled_dot_product_attention(
         ↳q, k, v, is_causal=True)

        # multiple heads concatenation
        attn_weights = attn_weights.transpose(1, 2).contiguous().view(
         ↳batch_size, sequence_length, -1)

        # norm and residual connections here
        x = self.norm_1(x + attn_weights)
        x = self.norm_2(x + self.mlp(x))
        return x
```

Finally, we can use the transformer block to create the decoder. A decoder takes input embeddings and adds them to a positional encoding. The positional encoding is a set of embeddings that encode the position of each element in the sequence. This is important because the transformer does not have any inherent notion of the position of each element in the sequence. It is passed through a series of multiple transformer blocks and then a linear layer to get the output. We can use the same code again to train and generate samples from our new model:

```
# In[]:
class Transformer(nn.Module):
    def __init__(self, n_embd, vocab_size, block_size, num_blocks=6):
        super().__init__()
        self.char_embedding = nn.Embedding(vocab_size, n_embd)
        self.positional_embedding = nn.Embedding(block_size, n_embd)

        self.transformer_blocks = nn.Sequential(
            *[TransformerBlock(n_embd) for _ in range(num_blocks)]
        )

        self.output_proj = nn.Linear(n_embd, vocab_size)

    def forward(self, x):
        _, seq_len = x.shape

        pos_embd = self.positional_embedding(torch.arange(seq_len))
        char_embd = self.char_embedding(x)
        x = char_embd + pos_embd
        x = self.transformer_blocks(x)
        x = self.output_proj(x)

        return x

n_embd = 64
model = Transformer(n_embd, vocab_size, block_size=max_name_length)
optimizer = optim.SGD(model.parameters(), lr=0.1)
train(model, optimizer, num_steps=10_001, loss_report_interval=1_000)

# Out[]:
Average loss at step 1000: 2.2924
Average loss at step 2000: 2.1520
Average loss at step 3000: 2.0999
Average loss at step 4000: 2.0626
Average loss at step 5000: 2.0346
Average loss at step 6000: 2.0107
Average loss at step 7000: 1.9852
Average loss at step 8000: 1.9629
Average loss at step 9000: 1.9477
Average loss at step 10000: 1.9299
```

The model has become more complex, and, as a result, we see a significant increase in training time compared to our previous models. Fortunately, the loss is orders of magnitude lower than our previous models. Let's see how our official transformer decoder performs with its generations:

```
# In[]:
generate_samples(model, num_samples=10)

# Out[]:
journe
green
huxson
chanie
antura
robinna
bryce
jazleah
daryza
bailanie
```

The names are quite good and unique! The model can generate names that are very similar to the ones in our dataset. This is a testament to the power of the Transformer architecture. We have delivered on our original goal of generating human names without using any human-crafted rules or templates. We have trained a model that is able to generate names that are relevant to our dataset and realistic.

9.7 Other Transformer architectures

The remainder of the chapter will discuss alternative adaptations of the transformer, as well as how we would adapt such a decoder model beyond single-word generation.

9.7.1 The encoder

A transformer encoder, as illustrated in figure 9.12, is very similar to the decoder, but it does not use causal masking. Unlike a decoder, where a mask is used to prevent the model from attending to future tokens, the encoder is allowed to glean information from all words in the sentence. The encoder takes in a sequence of tokens and outputs a new fixed-size vector representation of the sequence.

This output is useful for tasks such as text classification, where we want to classify the input sequence into a category. Some practical applications include sentiment analysis, spam detection, and topic classification. One of the most popular encoder models is BERT, introduced by Google in 2018, which stands for Bidirectional Encoder Representations from Transformers. BERT is pretrained on a large corpus of text and fine-tuned on a large number of tasks.

9.7 Other Transformer architectures

TRANSFORMER ENCODER

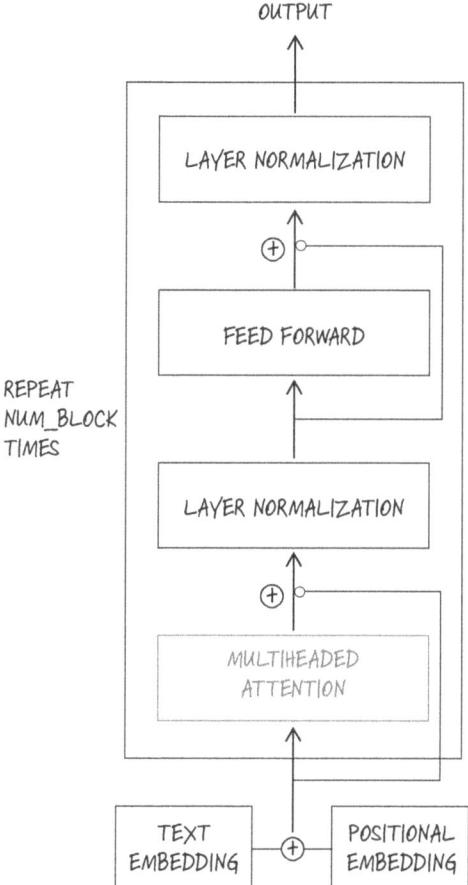

Figure 9.12 Diagram of the transformer encoder. The only changes from the previous GPT-style decoder are the removal of the masking from the multiheaded attention and the linear layer before output.

9.7.2 The encoder-decoder

Putting the encoder and decoder together, we get the full transformer architecture. This concept was originally introduced in the "Attention Is All You Need" paper, as shown in figure 9.13. The encoder takes an input sequence and transforms it into a set of representations that capture the relationships between the elements in the sequence. The decoder then takes these representations and generates an output sequence.

By now, the core operations illustrated in the transformer diagram in figure 9.13 should be familiar to you. We have implemented the feed-forward networks, layer norms, residual connections, and, of course, the multiheaded attention mechanism.

One thing to note in the encoder-decoder transformer is that the encoder output is used for the keys and values in the decoder-encoder attention. This allows the decoder to attend to the encoder output and use this information to generate the output sequence. This capability is especially useful for machine translation—for example,

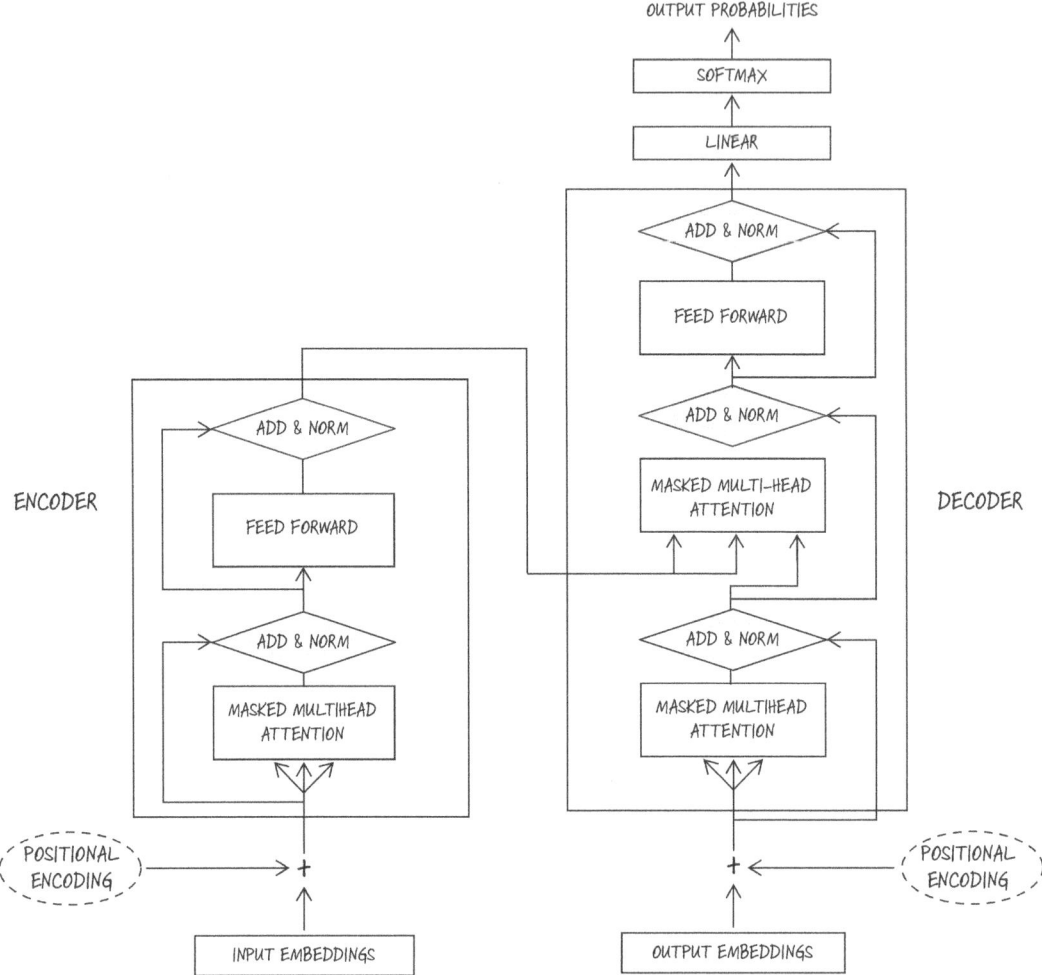

Figure 9.13 Diagram of the Transformer architecture from the original paper "Attention Is All You Need." The encoder is on the left, and the decoder is on the right. The encoder output is fed into the decoder as the key and value for the multi-head attention mechanism.

translating a sentence from one language to another. Different languages have different word orders and grammatical structures, so the encoder is able to capture the relationships between the words in the input sentence while the decoder uses this information to generate the output sentence in the target language.

9.8 Tokenization

The tokens we used in our motivating example were characters. However, in practice, we often use words or subwords as tokens because words are more semantically meaningful than characters. For example, the word "dog" has a specific meaning, whereas the character "d" does not. This is especially important for languages like English, where the meaning of a word can change depending on the order of the characters. For example, "dog" and "god" have very different meanings.

A tokenizer prepares raw text as input to a model. Its objective is to transform raw text into numbers, as a model can only take numbers as input. It does so by splitting the text into tokens and then converting these tokens into numbers.

Our previous version of a tokenizer did this, but it was very naive because we only considered lowercase characters as tokens. In practice, splitting text into smaller chunks is a task that is harder than it looks, and there are many ways of doing so. The tokenizer library from Hugging Face is an open source library dedicated to such a task. We can use a tokenizer to expand to tokenize and train on word-level tokens.

First, we need to pip install tokenizer and then import a few classes to train a tokenizer on a new dataset. For our data, we will be using the text of *The Odyssey*, a classic epic poem by Homer. When using the tokenizer library, the input text will go through the following pipeline: normalization, pretokenization, model, and postprocessing:

```
# In[]:
from tokenizers import Tokenizer
from tokenizers.models import WordLevel
from tokenizers.pre_tokenizers import Whitespace
from tokenizers.trainers import WordLevelTrainer

tokenizer = Tokenizer(WordLevel(unk_token="[UNK]"))
tokenizer.pre_tokenizer = Whitespace()
trainer = WordLevelTrainer(special_tokens=["[UNK]"])
tokenizer.train(["../data/p2ch9/odyssey.txt"], trainer=trainer)

vocab_size = tokenizer.get_vocab_size()
decode = tokenizer.decode
encode = tokenizer.encode
```

- We are using the WordLevel model from the tokenizers library. This model is used to train a tokenizer on a word-level vocabulary. We also specify a special token [UNK] to represent unknown tokens.
- This sets the tokenizer to split the text at any whitespace before any tokenization is done.
- This is necessary to specify the core algorithm used to actually tokenize. In this case, WordLevelTrainer is not doing anything fancy, but other options are available, such as Byte-Pair Encoding, Wordpiece, etc.

Now that the tokenizer has looked through our text, we can get the vocab_size and specify the encode and decode functions. As before, we can construct the dataset necessary to train the model by going through the text and taking subsections with their targets:

```
# In[]:
with open('../data/p2ch9/odyssey.txt', 'r', encoding='utf-8') as f:
    text = f.read()
encoding = tokenizer.encode(text)
sequence_length = 100
X, Y = [], []
for i in range(0, len(encoding.ids) - sequence_length, sequence_length):
    X.append(encoding.ids[i:i+sequence_length])
    Y.append(encoding.ids[i+1:i+sequence_length+1])
```

```
device = torch.device('cuda' if torch.cuda.is_available() else 'cpu')
X = torch.tensor(X).to(device)
Y = torch.tensor(Y).to(device)
```

9.8.1 Generating sentences

We can use the same model architecture we constructed in the decoder section of this chapter to train on this new dataset. Because we wrote the code in such a way that only tokens are considered, it makes no difference to the model whether the tokens are characters or words, which makes it very flexible:

```
# In[]:
n_embd = 64
model = Transformer(n_embd, vocab_size, block_size=sequence_length)
model.to(device)
optimizer = optim.SGD(model.parameters(), lr=0.1)
train(model, optimizer, num_steps=501, loss_report_interval=100)
```

We need to update the `generate_samples` method slightly to format the output correctly, as the tokenizer outputs a list of tokens and we want punctuation to be correctly spaced. We can add a new `format_sequence` method to help massage the output into something more readable before we print it:

```
# In[]:
def generate_samples(model, num_samples=1, max_len=sequence_length):
    sequences = torch.zeros((num_samples, 1)).int().to(device)
    for _ in range(max_len):
        logits = model(sequences)
        logits = logits[:, -1, :]
        probs = F.softmax(logits, dim=-1)
        idx_next = torch.multinomial(probs, num_samples=1)
        sequences = torch.cat((sequences, idx_next), dim=1)

    for sequence in sequences:
        indices = torch.where(sequence == 0)[0]
        end = indices[1] if len(indices) > 1 else max_len
        sequence = sequence[1:end]
        decoded_sequence = decode(sequence.tolist())
        print(format_sequence(decoded_sequence))

def format_sequence(sequence):
    formatted_sequence = ""
    for i, char in enumerate(sequence):
        if char in ",.;:!?":
            formatted_sequence = formatted_sequence.rstrip() + char + " "
        else:
            formatted_sequence += char
    return formatted_sequence.strip()

# Out[]:
day horses and as she were dream to do.  twittering spake Ulysses laid fain.  He
    fear.  Man for their choice,  for t he councils and one Hebe angrily
    πύματον treating which?  61 140 they went - offering in the son of all
```

```
before the island, and saw mother ', would have a set it did a sweet that
we could already, see the Cnossus mortal - rejoinder ahead into your
country to quantity of it, till Ulysses to Troy, nor just in us who was
as he heard his eyelids
```

This generated text may not rise to the level of a new epic, but the influence of *The Odyssey* on our output is unmistakable. References to Ulysses and Troy, along with mentions of other heroes, are scattered throughout the sample. Not bad for just a few minutes of training.

9.9 The Vision Transformer

Lastly, we would be doing a disservice to the reader if we didn't mention the Vision Transformer (ViT; https://arxiv.org/pdf/2010.11929), an entirely new model that applies the Transformer architecture to image data. Here, tokens are neither characters nor words but rather patches of the input image. The ViT model processes these patches in a manner similar to how text tokens are handled in NLP transformers, allowing it to capture visual patterns and relationships.

We used ViT in chapter 2, where we called a pretrained model from torchvision to use for image classification on ImageNet. ViT accomplishes this by using self-attention and multiheaded attention to capture relationships between image patches. When an image is passed through a ViT model, it is first split into a grid of smaller patches, with each being treated as a token. These tokens are then embedded into a high-dimensional space, similar to word embeddings in NLP. In figure 9.14, we can see this process illustrated.

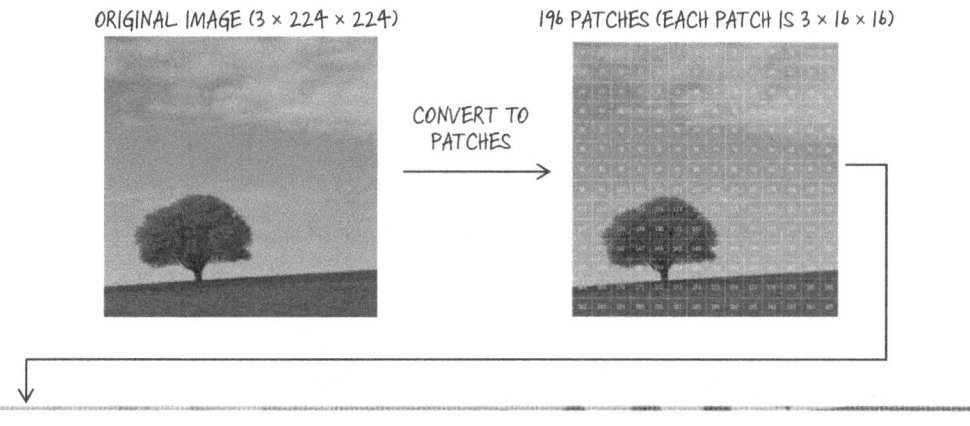

Figure 9.14 Image converted to image patches, which are then flattened and fed into the model

After we have our tokens, ViT prepends a learnable [CLS] token and adds learnable positional embeddings to every token to encode patch locations. The sequence [B,

N+1, D] (representing batch size, number of tokens plus a single [CLS] token, and the embedding dimension) then flows through a stack of transformer encoder blocks. The entire process is shown in figure 9.15.

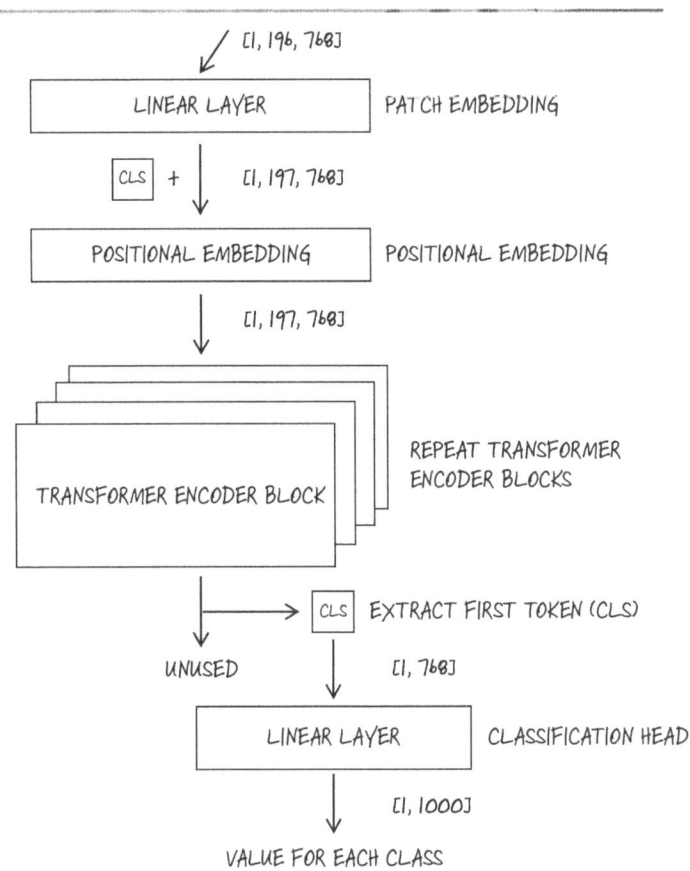

Figure 9.15 Vision Transformer architecture. The image tokens are passed through a patch embedding layer, and then positional information is added before being fed into the transformer encoder blocks. Only one single output [CLS] token is used in the final output head for classification.

We add labels of the example input size beside each arrow in figure 9.15. One interesting thing to note is that the learnable class token we prepended previously is the only output used for classification. The other tokens are discarded because the [CLS] token is designed to aggregate information from all other tokens in the sequence. Self-attention allows the [CLS] token to attend to all other tokens, so it can capture global information about the image.

While the original ViT paper (https://arxiv.org/pdf/2010.11929) focuses on image classification, the ViT architecture has been adapted for a variety of other computer vision tasks, including object detection and image segmentation. In these cases, we may use all the outputs of the transformer encoder blocks, rather than just the [CLS] token. Even diffusion models, which we will see in the next chapter, have adopted Transformer architectures to enhance their performance in generating high-quality images. The important takeaway is that the Transformer architecture is not limited to text data; it can be applied to any type of data that can be represented as a sequence of tokens. The fundamental concepts of attention and self-attention remain the same, regardless of the type of data being processed.

9.10 Conclusion

In this chapter, we made significant progress, moving from generating simple character sequences to crafting entire paragraphs of text and even understanding images. The ability of machines to generate human-like text, long a coveted goal in artificial intelligence and once relegated to science fiction, has become a tangible reality through the Transformer architecture. These models remain at the forefront of cutting-edge research, with ongoing work to enhance their performance, efficiency, and capabilities. With transformers increasingly used for natural language generation and content understanding, it is easier to envision a future in which we can engage in meaningful conversations with systems that appear to think autonomously—or at least convincingly appear to do so. The prospects are both exciting and sobering, and understanding the mechanics behind these technologies is essential for any capable AI practitioner.

9.11 Exercises

1. How could you take into account the relative frequency of names in the names_2022.txt file?
   a. How would this affect the bigram model?
   b. What about the transformer models?
2. Try to modify your self-attention implementation to achieve cross-attention.
3. Read the "Attention Is All You Need" paper (https://arxiv.org/pdf/1706.03762):
   a. Try to implement the encoder-decoder transformer as described in the paper.
   b. Where does the encoder output feed into the decoder?
   c. How does the architecture in the original paper differ from GPT-style decoders?
4. Can you see any potential issues with word-level tokenization?
   a. Look up Byte Pair Encoding (BPE).
   b. How do different methods address the issues with word-level tokenization?
5. Read the Vision Transformer (ViT) paper (https://arxiv.org/pdf/2010.11929):
   a. Load a pretrained ViT from Torchvision and fine-tune it on a small dataset (e.g., CIFAR-10). Report top-1 accuracy and training time.
   b. Change the patch size and/or embedding dimension; observe the effects on accuracy, speed, and memory.

Summary

- In language models, the *vocabulary* consists of all distinct elements recognized by the model. Each element is termed a *token*, which serves as the fundamental unit in forming *sequences* for both input and output processing.
- A key concept underlying most natural language processing (NLP) models is the statistical model of generation, which involves using statistical methods to predict and generate text based on the probability distributions of sequences of words or characters learned from large datasets.
- We crudely estimate the next character in a sequence using a *bigram model*, which considers the probability of a character given the previous character.
- Using deep learning and starting with simple embeddings and linear layers, we can build more sophisticated models that can learn the structure of the data and generate more realistic sequences.
- The attention mechanism enhances model responsiveness to input context by using queries to identify focus areas, keys to assess relevance, and values to integrate relevant information.
- Scaled dot product attention calculates attention scores by taking the dot product of queries and keys, scaling by the dimension of the keys, and applying a softmax function to determine the weights for the values, which are then combined to produce the output. It is provided by the `torch.nn.functional.scaled_dot_product_attention` function in PyTorch.
- The Transformer architecture, introduced in the paper "Attention Is All You Need," uses the attention mechanism to capture relationships between elements in a sequence, enabling the model to generate contextually relevant text.
- The architecture of transformers consists of two main components: the encoder, which transforms input sequences into representations capturing relationships between elements, and the decoder, which generates output sequences based on these representations.
- Decoder-only transformers, such as GPT models, which have exploded in popularity, are used for text generation tasks and are trained on large text corpora to generate coherent and contextually relevant text.
- Tokenizers are used to convert raw text into numerical inputs for models, with the `tokenizer` library from Hugging Face providing a powerful tool for training tokenizers on custom datasets.
- Vision Transformers (ViTs) treat images as sequences of patches and use transformer encoders with a learnable [CLS] token for classification.

Diffusion models for images

This chapter covers

- A walkthrough of generative AI used in image synthesis
- The foundational principles of diffusion models
- Implementing a diffusion model from scratch

Continuing our journey with generative AI, we now turn our attention to image synthesis. In the previous chapter, we explored how transformers can be used for text generation. In this chapter, we will delve into the realm of image generation using deep learning techniques.

At first glance, the task of generating images appears considerably different from generating text. Images consist of pixels, each defined by specific color values, whereas text is composed of a sequence of words, or tokens. In text generation, the relationships between elements are primarily sequential and largely determined by the order of tokens. In contrast, image generation involves spatial dependencies, where context is influenced not only by the proximity of elements but also by their arrangement across the entire image. Applying the methods we learned to probabilistically predict next tokens using previous tokens does not intuitively seem feasible for generating images.

However, the underlying principles of generative AI remain: create a model of the underlying distribution of the data to generate new samples. Despite the differences between text and image generation models, our goal is the same: we want to learn the probability distribution of the training dataset to generate new, plausible samples that could believably belong to the original dataset. Whether it's predicting the next word in a sentence or the color values of a pixel in an image, the fundamental challenge is to capture and reproduce the complex patterns observed in real-world data.

In this chapter, we will first cover some historical background on generative models for images. We will look into how variational autoencoders (VAEs) and generative adversarial networks (GANs) were the earliest successful model architectures for image generation. We will then dive into diffusion models, which have largely outperformed VAEs and GANs on image generation tasks and have become the dominant model. We will look into the basic implementation of a diffusion model to understand the foundational elements of training and sampling from diffusion models and then generate new images from an existing dataset.

10.1 History of VAEs and GANs

VAEs were introduced in late 2013 (https://arxiv.org/abs/1312.6114), featuring a dual-model architecture consisting of a recognition model (also known as the *encoder*) and a generative model (also known as the *decoder*). The encoder's role is to compress an input, such as an image, into a lower-dimensional latent representation. The decoder then attempts to reconstruct the original data from this latent representation. To generate new samples with VAE, we can simply remove the encoder and pass in a sample of noise to the decoder, which will interpret the noise as an "image representation" to decode into a new image.

Another model used in image generation, GANs, was introduced in 2014 and quickly overshadowed VAEs in popularity due to their ability to produce sharper and more realistic images (see figure 10.1). A GAN comprises two components: a generator and a discriminator. The generator creates data from random noise in an attempt to fool the discriminator, which acts as a binary classifier. The discriminator evaluates both real data from the dataset and fake data from the generator, aiming to distinguish between the two. During training, these networks engage in an adversarial process, continuously improving by challenging each other. Once trained, new samples can be generated simply by using the generator to create new data.

GANs remained the preferred architecture for cutting-edge image generation for several years. Although diffusion models were introduced in 2015, they did not

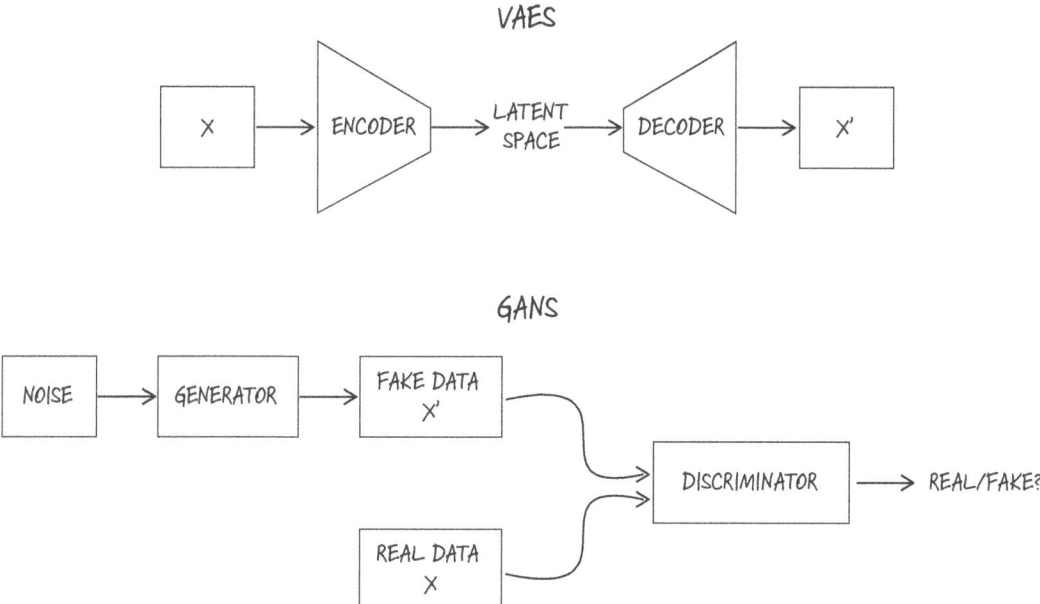

Figure 10.1 Architectural comparison of VAEs and GANs. VAEs utilize latent space to generate new samples, while GANs use a generator/discriminator pair to create new data.

achieve significant popularity or recognition as a viable alternative to GANs until around 2020. As we'll see in the next section, diffusion models take an alternative approach to training.

10.2 Motivator for diffusion models

Diffusion models exploded into popular culture when OpenAI released its DALL-E model, which demonstrated the practicality of diffusion models for commercial use. DALL-E is a generative model that can create images from text descriptions. The model was trained on a large dataset of images and their corresponding captions. Soon, other open source variants of diffusion models like Stable Diffusion were released, which could generate high-resolution images. An example of an image generated by Stable Diffusion XL is shown in figure 10.2.

For the rest of the chapter, we will explore the foundational principles that enable diffusion models to generate such high-quality images.

Figure 10.2 Stable Diffusion XL–generated image with a provided prompt of "Astronaut in a prairie, warm color palette, detailed, 8k"

10.3 Diffusion in detail

Diffusion, commonly understood as the process of spreading something more widely, has specific implications in various fields. In physics, for example, diffusion describes the movement of particles from areas of high concentration to areas of low concentration, much like a drop of milk dispersing evenly throughout a cup of coffee.

In the context of deep learning, diffusion models uniquely adopt this concept. These models are a specialized class of generative models that gradually introduce noise across an image. While in physics, diffusion is irreversible, and the process will naturally increase entropy or randomness—in diffusion models, the noise is reversible by design. The model learns to reverse this noise to reconstruct the original image. The real power of diffusion models lies in their ability to learn how to methodically reverse this noise, gradually reconstructing the image. This process effectively inverts the natural diffusion phenomenon, transforming pixels from apparent randomness into a coherent structure that is representative of an actual image.

The idea can be condensed down to this quote from the original 2015 paper, "Deep Unsupervised Learning Using Nonequilibrium Thermodynamics," by Sohl-Dickstein et al. (https://arxiv.org/pdf/1503.03585):

> The essential idea, inspired by non-equilibrium statistical physics, is to systematically and slowly destroy structure in a data distribution through an iterative forward diffusion process. We then learn a reverse diffusion process that restores structure in data, yielding a highly flexible and tractable generative model of the data.

To further dissect this dense quote, the forward diffusion process slowly breaks down the structure of the data, much like a sandcastle being gradually eroded by waves. Each wave (or iteration in the diffusion process) washes over the sandcastle, smoothing out details and reducing its definition. For this analogy, the sandcastle represents the original data or image, and the waves symbolize the application of noise that incrementally degrades its clarity and structure.

This forward diffusion process is controlled and maintained by a certain schedule, ensuring that the degradation happens slowly and predictably. By understanding and controlling this process, a neural network can then be trained to perform the reverse process, effectively rebuilding the sandcastle. This involves learning to counteract the noise, restoring the original structure and details of the data with each reverse step, and ultimately regenerating the data to its clear and defined original form. Figure 10.3 illustrates the forward and reverse processes of diffusion models.

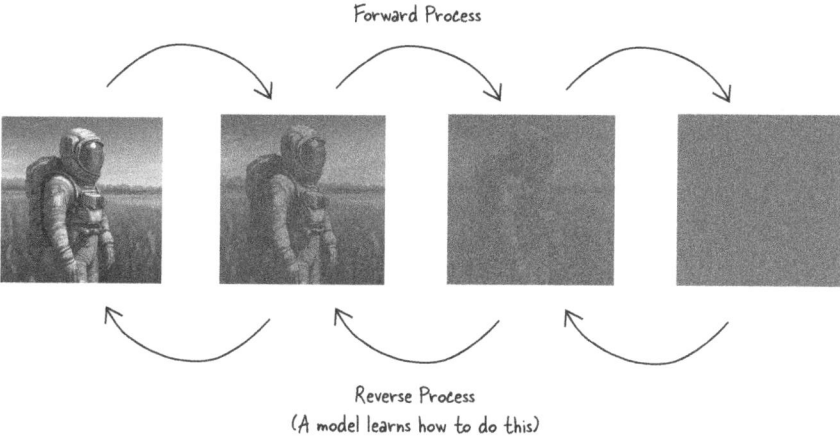

Figure 10.3 Forward and reverse processes of diffusion models on an image

In the next few sections, we will take a deeper look at the mathematical theory underpinning diffusion models and get our hands dirty in implementing one.

10.4 Setting up the data

Diffusion models and their functionality are best understood visualized, so we will start with one of the most basic sets of data to visualize, 2D points. We want to demonstrate diffusion on points with x, y coordinates.

Let's first import all the libraries that we will need to use for our implementation:

```
from PIL import Image, ImageFilter
import numpy as np
import seaborn as sns
import matplotlib.pyplot as plt
import torch
import torch.nn.functional as F
```

We will define two helper methods: one to convert an image to a set of 2D points representing its outline and the other to plot a set of 2D points. The first will be used to generate a custom dataset of 2D points, and the other will be used to help us visualize how our points look through the diffusion process. The full implementation of these methods is omitted in the text for brevity but can be found at /code/p2ch10/forward_diffusion.ipynb:

```
def points_from_img(img_file, min_distance=5):
    ...

def plot_points(all_points, highlight_index=None):
    ...
```

We can use any image for our points_from_img helper method to extract a list of size 2 float tuples. In our example, we are using a PNG of the PyTorch logo as input and outputting a list of points, as shown in figure 10.4. We can then take this list to convert it into a tensor:

```
# In[]:
points = points_from_img("../data/p2ch10/pytorch_logo.png")
for x, y in points[:3]:
    print(f"({x:.3f}, {y:.3f})")
x0 = torch.tensor(points, dtype=torch.float32)
x0.shape

# Out:
(4.310, -479.528)
(0.310, -475.528)
(4.310, -472.528)
torch.Size([3177, 2])
```

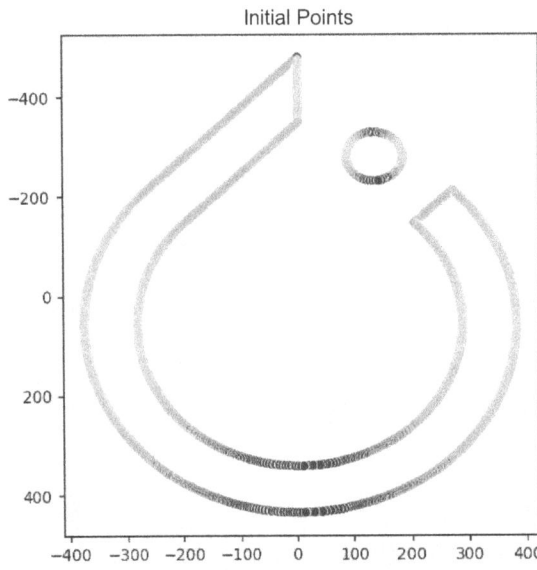

Figure 10.4 PyTorch logo outline created from 2D points

Each item in the points list has the (x,y) coordinates of a point for the outline of the image. Now we can use plot points to visualize what this tensor (aka the list of points) looks like:

```
plot_points(x0, ["Initial points"])
```

We are now ready to use our dataset for the diffusion model. The goal is to gradually add noise to these points until we get a random set of points. Then we can train a neural network to remove the added noise and reconstruct the original image.

10.5 The forward process

The forward process of diffusion models involves progressively destroying all the information in the dataset of 2D points over a series of steps, which we'll call T. The initial set of points, which we'll refer to as x_0, is transformed at each timestep t by a small degree. As a result, the set of points at x_t is slightly different from the set at x_{t-1}. This process is repeated T times, and by the end of the process, the set of points is completely unrecognizable.

A single forward generation step can be expressed mathematically as shown in figure 10.5. We include β_t, a scalar value that controls the amount of noise added at each step. The value of β_t increases at each timestep, following a noise schedule. While β_t increases, the total noise added to the system also accumulates over time. However, the noise schedule ensures that the relative contribution of newly added noise becomes smaller at each step, gradually reducing its overall effect on the process as it progresses.

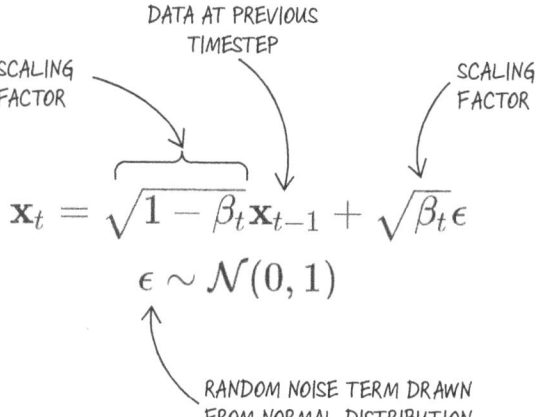

Figure 10.5 The forward diffusion process equation

Different noise schedules may have different values for β_t. It is a critical component of the diffusion process and has been shown to affect the training outcome. (Several different schedules are discussed in Ting Chen's paper, "On the Importance of Noise Scheduling for Diffusion Models," https://arxiv.org/pdf/2301.10972). In our example, we will use a linear schedule that starts with a small value of β_0 and increases linearly to a larger value of β_T. Consequently, the noise added to the image will increase over time, making the image progressively more distorted:

```
# In[]:
def linear_beta_schedule(timesteps, start=0.0001, end=0.02):
    return torch.linspace(start, end, timesteps)
T = 1000
betas = linear_beta_schedule(T)
print(betas[0], betas[10], betas[T-1])

# Out[]:
tensor(1.0000e-04) tensor(0.0003) tensor(0.0200)
```

Now that we have the set of β_t to apply across all the steps, we can implement the forward diffusion equation we presented earlier:

```
def diffuse_points(points, beta):
    new_mean = torch.sqrt(1-beta) * points
    noise = torch.randn(points.shape)
    perturbation = torch.sqrt(beta) * noise
    points = new_mean + perturbation
    return points, noise
```

For every point, we multiply the points by the square root of 1-beta and add the square root of beta times the noise. Let's think about the *why* of what this equation is performing. $\sqrt{1-\beta_t} * x_{t-1}$ is meant to scale down the contribution of the previous image x_{t-1} of its effects on the current image x_t. This term decreases as β_t increases, so the influence of the original image reduces over time. The second part, $\sqrt{\beta_t} * \epsilon$, is the noise that is added to the image. It increases as β_t increases, so we are adding more and more noise to the image.

We generate noise using the convenient torch.randn function, which generates a tensor of random numbers from a normal distribution with a mean of 0 and a standard deviation of 1. The new points are then the sum of the modified points and the noise.

To build a visual intuition, let's apply this function to a single point and see its effects over time:

```
temp_x0 = x0.clone()
index = len(temp_x0) - 1
single_point = temp_x0[index]
all_points = []
for i in range(500):
    if i % 100 == 0:
        temp_x0[index] = single_point
        all_points.append(temp_x0.clone())
    single_point, _ = diffuse_points(single_point, betas[i])

plot_points(all_points, ["T=0", "T=100", "T=200", "T=300", "T=400"],
↪ highlight_index=index)
```

We copy our original points, take the last point, and gradually apply our diffusion process. The resulting plots with the modified points show the point gradually moving, as shown in figure 10.6.

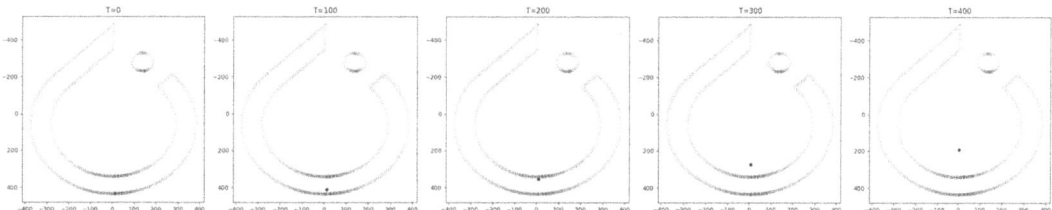

Figure 10.6 PyTorch logo with one point diffused over 500 steps. This is just an example of one point to build intuition, but in reality, all points will undergo this diffusion.

We can see the point incrementally moving away from its original position toward a mean of 0 as the diffusion process progresses. Eventually, the point will be indistinguishable from a random point. This transition becomes even more apparent as we apply the diffusion process to all the points in the dataset, as shown in figure 10.7:

```
x = torch.zeros(T, *x0.shape)
x[0] = x0
for t in range(1, T):
    beta_t = betas[t]
    x_t, noise = diffuse_points(x[t - 1], beta_t)
    x[t] = x_t
plot_points([x[0], x[250], x[500], x[800], x[999]],
    ["T=0", "T=250", "T=500", "T=800", "T=999"])
```

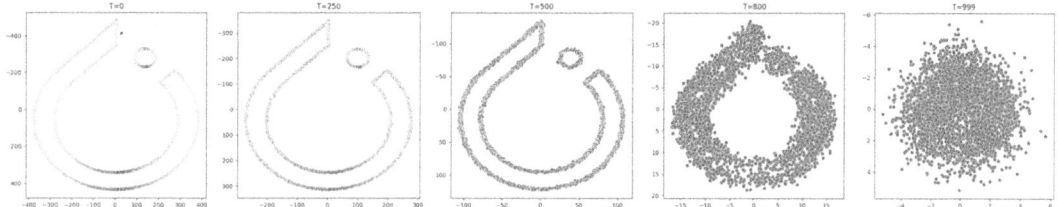

Figure 10.7 PyTorch logo with all points diffused over 1,000 steps

As the points are diffused collectively, they become increasingly random and normally distributed around a 0 mean. Neat!

We have been repeatedly applying the diffusion process, where each step is based on the previous data. It turns out that instead of the cumbersome process of looping over all the timesteps and repeatedly applying the diffusion process, we can compute the entire forward diffusion process in a closed-form equation, as shown in figure 10.8.

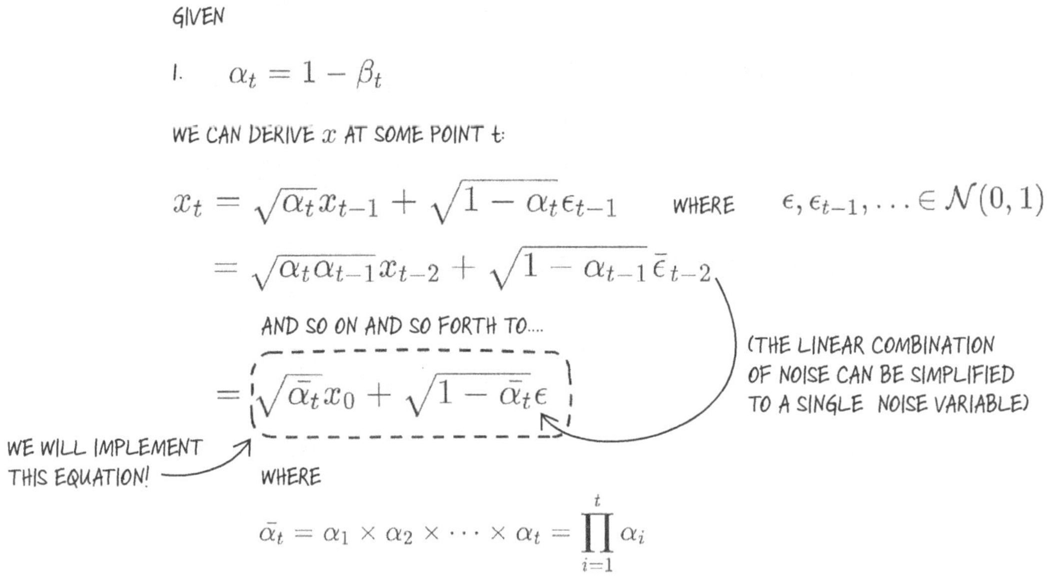

GIVEN

1. $\alpha_t = 1 - \beta_t$

WE CAN DERIVE x AT SOME POINT t:

$$x_t = \sqrt{\alpha_t} x_{t-1} + \sqrt{1 - \alpha_t} \epsilon_{t-1} \quad \text{WHERE} \quad \epsilon, \epsilon_{t-1}, \ldots \in \mathcal{N}(0, 1)$$

$$= \sqrt{\alpha_t \alpha_{t-1}} x_{t-2} + \sqrt{1 - \alpha_{t-1}} \bar{\epsilon}_{t-2}$$

AND SO ON AND SO FORTH TO....

$$= \sqrt{\bar{\alpha}_t} x_0 + \sqrt{1 - \bar{\alpha}_t} \epsilon$$

(THE LINEAR COMBINATION OF NOISE CAN BE SIMPLIFIED TO A SINGLE NOISE VARIABLE)

WE WILL IMPLEMENT THIS EQUATION!

WHERE

$$\bar{\alpha}_t = \alpha_1 \times \alpha_2 \times \cdots \times \alpha_t = \prod_{i=1}^{t} \alpha_i$$

Figure 10.8 Forward diffusion equation in closed form

We end up deriving that x_t can be computed from a particular point at Time x by using the initial point x_0 and a product of alpha values. This allows us to compute the entire forward diffusion process in a single step (no more needing to loop)! We can implement this in PyTorch:

```
alphas = 1. - betas
alphas_cumprod = torch.cumprod(alphas, dim=0)
sqrt_alphas_cumprod = torch.sqrt(alphas_cumprod)
sqrt_one_minus_alphas_cumprod = torch.sqrt(1. - alphas_cumprod)

def reshape_for_x(a, x):
    ones_to_broadcast = len(x.shape) - 1
    # python unpacking performed here
    return a.view(-1, *([1] * ones_to_broadcast)).to(x.device)

device = torch.device("cuda" if torch.cuda.is_available() else "cpu")
def forward_diffusion_sample(x, t):
    x = x.to(device)
    noise = torch.randn_like(x)
    sqrt_alphas_cumprod_t = reshape_for_x(sqrt_alphas_cumprod[t], x)
    sqrt_one_minus_alphas_cumprod_t = reshape_for_x(
       sqrt_one_minus_alphas_cumprod[t], x)
    return sqrt_alphas_cumprod_t * x + sqrt_one_minus_alphas_cumprod_t *
       noise, noise
```

α_t from above, computed from the original β values

$\bar{\alpha}_t$ from above

We use this method to reshape the alpha values (a 1D tensor) to match the shape of the input tensor, which is usually an N-D tensor for images. We do this to apply the values to each point in the image.

The derived final equation for x_t, which depends on x_0 and the product of α_t values.

Now our `forward_diffusion_sample` function takes the original data x_0 and a timepoint t and, using the formula, returns the diffused data and the noise added in a single computation. If we use this on our original set of points, we can see the same pattern of diffusion process as before:

```
example_x0 = x0.clone()
example_timesteps = [0, 250, 500, 800, 999]
sample_points = []
for t in example_timesteps:
    t = torch.tensor(t).expand(example_x0.shape[0])
    new_points, _ = forward_diffusion_sample(example_x0, t)
    sample_points.append(new_points)
plot_points(sample_points, ["T=0", "T=250", "T=500", "T=800", "T=999"])
```

This results in similar-looking plots, as shown in figure 10.3, but done so all with the formulas that we derived, as shown in figure 10.9.

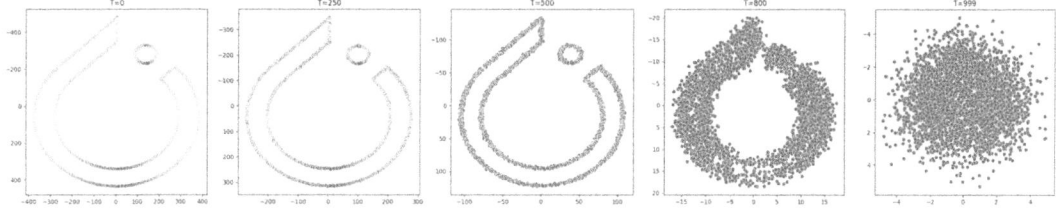

Figure 10.9 PyTorch logo with all points diffused over 1,000 steps using the closed formula

We have successfully implemented the forward diffusion process and can generate the noise for any given timestep. In the next section, we will learn how to train a neural network to reverse this process and generate new images from the noise.

10.6 Training

Now that we have a method to add noise to our data, we can train a neural network to reverse this process by predicting the noise added. The primary objective of the neural network is to learn a function that, given the noisy (diffused) data and a specific timestep, estimates the exact amount of noise introduced at that step.

While this task may seem unrelated to the ultimate goal of generating new images, it is crucial. By learning to predict and remove noise step by step, the model essentially learns how to reverse the process of adding noise. Think of it like uncrumpling a piece of paper—starting with something chaotic and gradually restoring its original form. When we want to sample, we pass in noise (the crumpled paper) and let the model predict the noise added at each step, progressively refining it to reconstruct the original data.

For the model, we will use a simple feedforward neural network. Similar to our input transformation in the last chapter, we will use embeddings to encode the inputs for our points and time. A commonly used embedding function in transformer models is the sinusoidal positional embedding, which became popular when introduced in the original Transformer paper, "Attention Is All You Need" by Vaswani et al. In transformer models, these embeddings are commonly used to inject information about the relative or absolute position of the tokens in the sequence. In our case, we will use these embeddings to inject information about the timestep and coordinates of our 2D points into the neural network. As before, by transforming these inputs into higher-dimensional embeddings, we can better capture complex interactions between the data points and the noise in our model.

First, we will define the class for SinusoidalEmbedding, the implementation here is omitted for brevity, but it can be found in /code/p2ch10/training.ipynb:

```
class SinusoidalEmbedding(nn.Module):
    ...
```

Then we can define our model. Like our transformer models in the previous chapter, we will embed the inputs and pass them through a series of linear layers with ReLU activations. The final layer will output the predicted noise, as shown in figure 10.10. The implementation of this model is provided as follows (training.ipynb):

```
class DenoisingModel(nn.Module):
    def __init__(self):
        super(DenoisingModel, self).__init__()
        self.time_mlp = SinusoidalEmbedding(128)      ◁─┐  We define the
        self.pos1_mlp = SinusoidalEmbedding(128)         │  embeddings for the time
        self.pos2_mlp = SinusoidalEmbedding(128)         │  and the x (pos1_mlp) and
                                                         │  y (pos2_mlp) coordinates
        concat_size = len(self.time_mlp) + \             │  of the points.
            len(self.pos1_mlp) + len(self.pos2_mlp)

        hidden_size = 128
        num_layers = 3
        layers = [nn.Linear(concat_size, hidden_size), nn.ReLU()]
        for _ in range(num_layers):
            layers.extend([nn.Linear(hidden_size, hidden_size), nn.ReLU()])
        layers.append(nn.Linear(hidden_size, 2))       ◁─┐  The last layer in our
        self.joint_mlp = nn.Sequential(*layers)           │  model outputs two
                                                          │  values, which represent
    def forward(self, x, t):                              │  the predicted noise for
        x1_emb = self.pos1_mlp(x[:, 0])                   │  each point.
        x2_emb = self.pos2_mlp(x[:, 1])
        t_emb = self.time_mlp(t)
        x = torch.cat((x1_emb, x2_emb, t_emb), dim=-1)
        x = self.joint_mlp(x)                          ◁─┐  We concatenate the embeddings
        return x                                          │  and pass them through a series of
                                                          │  linear layers and nonlinearity to
                                                          │  predict the noise.
```

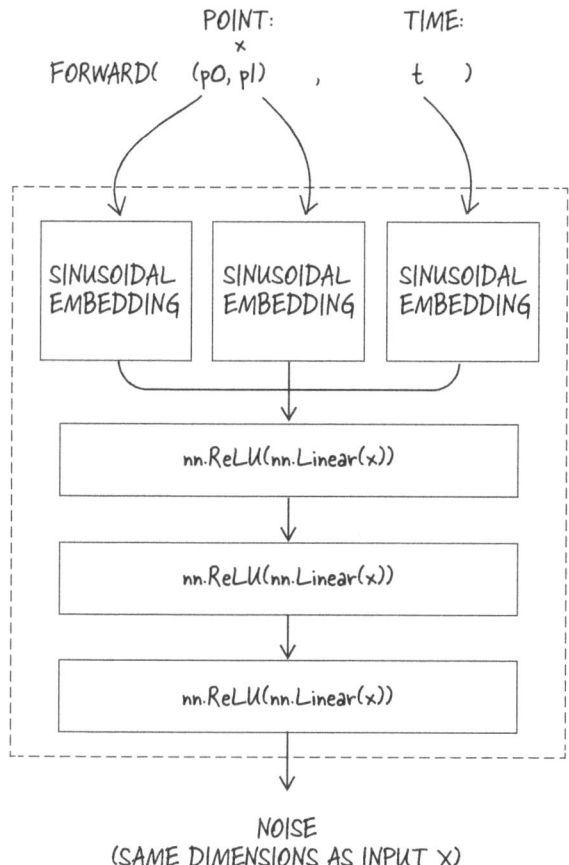

Figure 10.10 Denoising model architecture. The model takes in the time and the x and y coordinates of the points, embeds them, and passes them through a series of linear layers to predict the noise.

10.6.1 Loss

Now that we have a model defined, we have to train it to predict the noise that was previously added to the data. The loss function for this task is the mean squared error between the predicted noise (ϵ_θ) and the actual noise (ϵ):

$$\text{loss} = \left\| \epsilon - \epsilon_\theta \left(\sqrt{\bar{\alpha}_t} x_0 + \sqrt{1 - \bar{\alpha}_t} \epsilon, t \right) \right\|^2$$

The

$$\epsilon_\theta \left(\sqrt{\bar{\alpha}_t} x_0 + \sqrt{1 - \bar{\alpha}_t} \epsilon, t \right)$$

portion should seem familiar as it is just the equation for the forward diffusion process we derived earlier. The loss is determined by taking the mean squared error of the predicted noise and the actual noise. The loss function measures how well the model can predict the noise that was added to the original image through the diffusion process. In the reverse process (generation), the model will start with pure noise and gradually remove it. If the model can accurately predict the noise at each step (this is what we want to achieve with a low loss), it can effectively denoise the image, thus being able to generate good-quality images.

The entire loss equation can be implemented as

```
def get_loss(model, x, t):
    x_noisy, noise = forward_diffusion_sample(x, t)
    noise_pred = model(x_noisy, t)
    return F.mse_loss(noise, noise_pred)
```

We apply the forward diffusion process to the data to get the noisy data and the noise added.

We then pass the noisy data and the timestep to the model to get the noise that the model predicts was added at that timestep.

We use PyTorch's mse_loss to calculate the mean squared error between the predicted noise and the actual noise, as shown in the formula above.

Using this method, we can build a simple training loop as we have done in previous chapters to compute the loss, backpropagate, and update our model parameters:

```
# In[]:
device = "cuda" if torch.cuda.is_available() else "cpu"
model = DenoisingModel().to(device)
optimizer = torch.optim.Adam(model.parameters(), lr=0.001)

x0 = x0.to(device)
def train(model, optimizer, num_epochs):
    model.train()
    for epoch in range(num_epochs):
        t = torch.randint(0, T, (
        ➥x0.shape[0],)).to(device)
        optimizer.zero_grad()
        loss = get_loss(model, x0, t)
        loss.backward()
        optimizer.step()
        print(f"Finished epoch {epoch + 1}/{num_epochs},
        ➥loss: {loss.item():.4f}")

train(model, optimizer, 1)

# Out[]:
Finished epoch 1/1, loss: 0.9687
```

We are testing multiple timesteps at once, so we generate a random timestep for each point in our dataset.

We calculate the loss from our equation and use this loss to backpropagate and update our model parameters.

We define a method train, which takes in the model, optimizer, and number of epochs to train the model. The model is an instance of the DenoisingModel class we defined earlier, and we use an Adam optimizer to update the parameters. During a single epoch, we randomly select a timestep and calculate the loss by comparing the predicted noise to the actual noise. We then backpropagate this loss and update the model parameters using the optimizer. We can also utilize CUDA if it is available on the machine to accelerate the training process. Repeating this process over many iterations, we can train our model to predict the noise that was added to the data:

```
# In[]:
train(model, optimizer, 20000)

# Out[]:
Finished epoch 1/1, loss: 1.0119
...
Finished epoch 19997/20000, loss: 0.6959
Finished epoch 19998/20000, loss: 0.7143
Finished epoch 19999/20000, loss: 0.7026
Finished epoch 20000/20000, loss: 0.7178
```

10.7 Reversing diffusion (how to sample)

We have trained our model. We can now finally use it in our original goal of turning a set of random points into a PyTorch logo! By performing the reverse diffusion process, we can "predict" what the previous points were before the noise was added.

This process is iterative as it requires us to sample from the model at each timestep and gradually reconstruct the original data. Unlike the forward diffusion process, there is no closed-form solution for this reversal. Each step requires us to pass in the previous data and the timestep to the model to predict the noise that was added at that timestep. This iterative process ultimately makes diffusion models slow. That's why modern models like SDXL-Lightning focus on reducing denoising steps to generate images faster. Since a new set of data is required at each step, we have to sample from the model repeatedly over timesteps to perform the reconstruction. This process is similar to how transformers autoregressively generate text, where each token is predicted based on the previously generated tokens in an iterative manner.

The equation to sample the expected data for the previous timestep is

$$x_{t-1} = \text{model expected mean} + \text{standard deviation} \cdot \text{noise}$$

or, in mathematical form,

$$x_{t-1} = \frac{1}{\sqrt{\alpha_t}} \left(x_t - \frac{1 - \alpha_t}{\sqrt{1 - \bar{\alpha}_t}} \epsilon_\theta(x_t, t) \right) + \sigma_t z$$

where

$$\sigma_t^2 = \frac{1 - \bar{\alpha}_{t-1}}{1 - \bar{\alpha}_t} \beta_t$$

and

$$z \sim \mathcal{N}(0, 1)$$

if

$$t > 1 \text{ else } z = 0$$

Recall, we are trying to reconstruct the original data from the noisy data, so we solve for x_{t-1} given x_t and the current timestep t. The left side of the equation is the expected data at the previous timestep, which adds some controlled reintroduction of noise. Our learned denoising model ϵ_θ is used to predict the noise that was added at the current timestep, and we use this to subtract it out of x_t. While subtracting the estimated noise, we add a small amount of noise back in a controlled manner to help explore the variety of possible reconstructions and better capture the complex nature of the data distribution.

> **NOTE** The derivation for this formula is out of scope for the book, but the mathematical derivation can be found in the "Denoising Diffusion Probabilistic Models" paper by Ho et al. (https://arxiv.org/pdf/2006.11239.pdf).

We can implement this equation in PyTorch as follows:

```
alphas_cumprod_prev = F.pad(alphas_cumprod[:-1], (1, 0), value=1.0)
sqrt_recip_alphas = torch.sqrt(1.0 / alphas)
posterior_variance = betas * (1. - alphas_cumprod_prev) /          ◁─┐ σ_t² from the
 (1. - alphas_cumprod)                                                │ previous equation

@torch.no_grad()                                          ◁─┐ Disables gradient
def sample_timestep(model, x, t):                           │ computation, similar to
    betas_t = reshape_for_x(betas[t], x)                    │ torch.no_grad(), but it
    sqrt_one_minus_alphas_cumprod_t = reshape_for_x(        │ decorates a function.
 sqrt_one_minus_alphas_cumprod[t], x)
    sqrt_recip_alphas_t = reshape_for_x(sqrt_recip_alphas[t], x)

    # Call model (current image - noise prediction)
    model_mean = sqrt_recip_alphas_t * (
        x - betas_t * model(x, t) / sqrt_one_minus_alphas_cumprod_t
    )
    posterior_variance_t = reshape_for_x(posterior_variance[t], x)    ◁─┐
                                                                         │ Model mean, the
                                                                         │ first part of the sum
    if t[0] == 0:
        return model_mean
    else:
        noise = torch.randn_like(x)                     ┌─ Standard deviation *
        return model_mean + torch.sqrt(                 │  Noise, the second part
 posterior_variance_t) * noise                    ◁─┘  of the sum
```

With this defined, we can now start at the last timestep and work our way back to the original data. Start with a random set of points and gradually reconstruct the original image:

```
eval_batch_size = 1000
sample = torch.randn(eval_batch_size, 2, device=device)
example_times = [999, 800, 500, 400, 0]
```

10.7 Reversing diffusion (how to sample)

```
example_points = []
for i in range(T-1, -1, -1):
    t = torch.full((eval_batch_size,), i, dtype=torch.long, device=device)
    sample = sample_timestep(sample, t)
    if i in example_times:
        example_points.append(sample.clone())
plot_points(sample, ["Generated Logo"])
```

In the example, we are creating 1,000 random 2D points for `sample`, which is represented as a `1000x2` tensor. We then iterate over all the timesteps in reverse order and apply the `sample_timestep` function we created earlier. We pass in the `t+1` image along with the current timestep to get the `t` image. We then plot the final image to see the reconstructed PyTorch logo, as shown in figure 10.11. We can also see the gradual progression of the image as we move back in time, shown in figure 10.12.

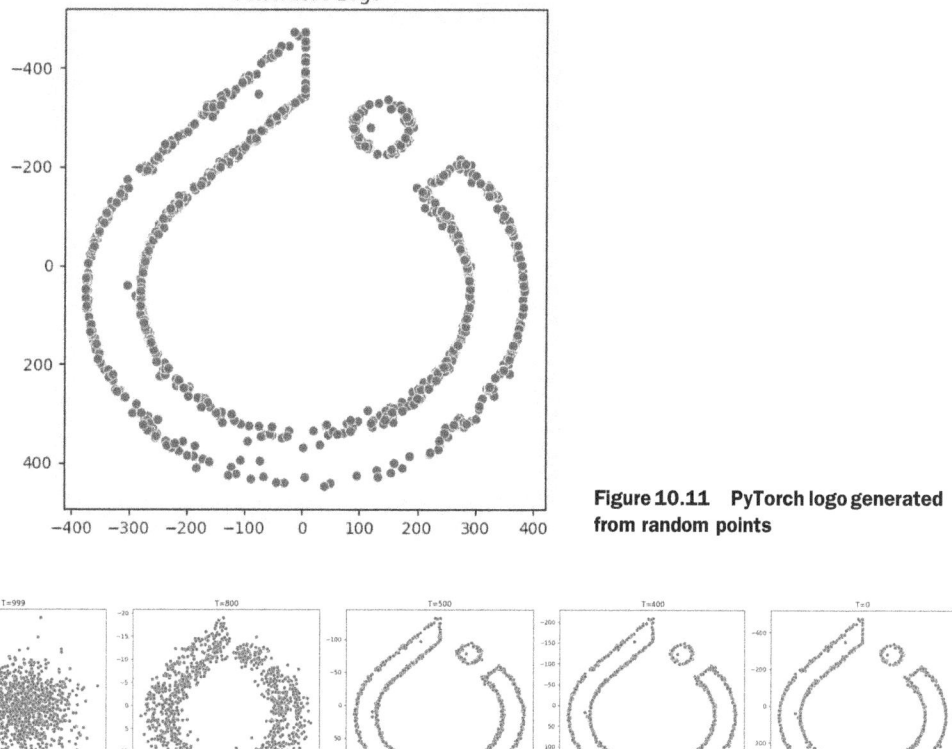

Figure 10.11 PyTorch logo generated from random points

Figure 10.12 PyTorch logo generated from random points at different timesteps.

We have created something from chaos. We started with a random set of points and used a diffusion model to gradually reconstruct the original shape. This is the power of diffusion models in image generation. While this is a simple example, the same principles can be applied to more complex image datasets. The same equations that we used to modify points can be used to modify the RGB values of an image. This underpins the cutting-edge image generation models we have today, like DALL-E and Stable Diffusion.

10.8 Conclusion

The field of image generation has evolved significantly since the inception of generative models. Initially, VAEs and GANs paved the way as pioneering technologies. These models aimed to produce photorealistic images and learn the data's underlying distribution to create diverse synthetic images. While GANs succeeded in generating high-quality images, they struggled with diversity. Then, diffusion models emerged, revolutionizing the landscape with their ability to achieve both remarkable photorealism as well as ability to produce a wide variety of images. Today, diffusion models are recognized as the leading approach for image generation tasks.

In this chapter, we explored building our own diffusion models for image generation. We learned how diffusion models gradually destroy the structure of the data by adding noise and then learn to reverse this process to reconstruct the original data. As a guiding example, we started with a dataset of an image's outline represented as 2D points. We used the PyTorch logo and applied the forward diffusion process to gradually destroy the shape of the logo until it was a random set of points.

To reverse the diffusion process, we trained a neural network that predicted the noise added to the data. We used a simple feedforward neural network to predict the noise and trained it using the mean squared error loss by comparing the predicted noise with the actual noise that was applied. Once our model was trained, we could sample from the diffusion model to generate new images. The sampling equation was derived from the research papers in which the diffusion models were introduced.

Sampling from the model repeatedly over timesteps allowed us to take a set of random points and gradually reconstruct it into the original shape. The same principles can be applied to more complex image datasets, such as the CIFAR-10 dataset, to generate new images. Diffusion models seem to be the future of image generation, and even video generation (after all, videos are just a series of images). Many of the state-of-the-art models for image generation are based on diffusion models, and they continue to push the boundaries of what is possible in generative AI.

10.9 Exercises

1. What are the main differences between VAEs, GANs, and diffusion models for image generation?
2. How does adding noise to 2D points compare to adding noise to an image?
3. We fixed some different parameters, like noise levels and the number of diffusion steps. How does changing this affect the output of a diffusion model?
    a. What are some different schedules that could be used for the noise levels?

4   How is the sampling equation derived from the research papers introducing diffusion models?
5   Look through the Hugging Face diffusers library (https://huggingface.co/docs/diffusers/en/quicktour) and look at the different available diffusion models. Try to use `StableDiffusion` to generate images.

Summary

- In image generation, as in text generation, we are interested in learning the underlying distribution of the data to generate new samples.
- Variational autoencoders (VAEs) and generative adversarial networks (GANs) were the earliest successful model architectures for image generation.
- Diffusion models are a specialized class of generative models that gradually introduce noise across an image and then learn to reverse this noise to reconstruct the image.
- The forward diffusion process slowly breaks down the structure of the data.
- We use a *schedule* to control the amount of noise, or *beta* values, added at each step in the forward diffusion process.
- We can compute the entire forward diffusion process in closed form using the initial data and a cumulative product of beta values.
- *Sinusoidal embeddings* are a commonly used embedding function because they help to preserve spatial information and capture complex interactions between data points.
- We can train a neural network to predict the noise that was added to the data during the forward diffusion process.
- Diffusion models are sampled in an autoregressive format by passing in the previous data and the timestep to predict the noise that needs to be subtracted.
- This diffusion process is the fundamental principle behind the cutting-edge image generation models like DALL-E and Stable Diffusion.

Using PyTorch to fight cancer

This chapter covers

- Breaking a large problem into smaller, easier ones
- Exploring an intricate deep learning problem, and deciding on a structure and approach
- Downloading the training data

We have two main goals for this chapter. We'll start by covering the overall plan for part 2 of the book so that we have a solid idea of the larger scope the following individual chapters will be building toward. In chapter 12, we will begin to build out the data-parsing and data manipulation routines that will produce data to be consumed in chapter 13, while training our first model. To do what's needed for those upcoming chapters well, we'll also use this chapter to cover some of the context in which our project will be operating: we'll go over data formats and data sources and explore the constraints that our problem domain place on us. Get used to performing these tasks, since you'll have to do them for any serious deep learning project.

11.1 Introduction to the use case

Our goal for this part of the book is to give you the tools to deal with situations where things aren't working, which is a far more common state of affairs than previous chapters might have led you to believe. We can't predict every failure case or cover every debugging technique, but, hopefully, we'll give you enough to not feel stuck when you encounter a new roadblock. Similarly, we want to help you avoid situations with your own projects where you have no idea what you could do next when your projects are underperforming. Instead, we hope your ideas list will be so long that the challenge will be to prioritize!

To present these ideas and techniques, we need a context with some nuance and a fair bit of heft to it. We've chosen automatic detection of malignant tumors in the lungs using only a computed tomography (CT) scan of a patient's chest as input. We'll be focusing on the technical challenges rather than the human impact, but make no mistake—even from just an engineering perspective, this will require a more serious, structured approach than what we have needed in the past in order to have the project succeed.

> **NOTE** CT scans are essentially 3D X-rays, represented as a 3D array of single-channel data. We'll cover them in more detail soon.

As you might have guessed, the title of this chapter is more eye-catching and implied hyperbole than anything approaching a serious statement of intent. Let us be precise: our project in this part of the book will take three-dimensional CT scans of human torsos as input and produce as output the location of suspected malignant tumors, if any exist.

Detecting lung cancer early has a huge effect on the survival rate, but it is difficult to do manually, especially in any comprehensive, whole-population sense. Currently, the work of reviewing the data must be performed by highly trained specialists, requires painstaking attention to detail, and is dominated by cases where no cancer exists.

Doing that job well is akin to being placed in front of 100 haystacks and being told, "Determine which of these, if any, contain a needle." Searching this way results in the potential for missed warning signs, particularly in the early stages when the hints are more subtle. The human brain just isn't built well for that kind of monotonous work. And that, of course, is where deep learning comes in.

Automating this process is going to give us experience working in an uncooperative environment where we have to do more work from scratch and there are fewer easy answers to problems that we might run into. Together, we'll get there, though! Once you're finished reading part 2, we think you'll be ready to start working on a real-world, unsolved problem of your own choosing.

We chose this problem of lung tumor detection for a few reasons. The primary reason is that the problem itself is unsolved! This is important because we want to make it clear that you can use PyTorch to tackle cutting-edge projects effectively. We hope that increases your confidence in PyTorch as a framework, as well as in yourself as a problem solver.

Another nice aspect of this problem space is that while it's unsolved, a lot of teams have been paying attention to it recently and have seen promising results. As a result, this challenge is probably right at the edge of our collective ability to solve; we won't be wasting our time on a problem that's actually decades away from reasonable solutions. That attention on the problem has also resulted in a lot of high-quality papers and open source projects, which are great sources of inspiration and ideas. They will be a huge help once we conclude part 2 if you are interested in continuing to improve on the solution we create.

This part of the book will remain focused on the problem of detecting lung tumors, but the skills we'll teach are general. Learning how to investigate, preprocess, and present your data for training is important no matter what project you're working on. While we'll be covering preprocessing in the specific context of lung tumors, the general idea is that *this is what you should be prepared to do* for your project to succeed. Similarly, setting up a training loop, getting the right performance metrics, and tying the project's models together into a final application are all general skills that we'll employ as we go through chapters 11 to 15.

> **NOTE** While the end result of part 2 will work, the output will not be accurate enough to use clinically. We're focusing on using this topic as a motivating example for *teaching PyTorch*, not on employing every last trick to solve the problem.

11.2 Preparing for a large-scale project

This project will build off the foundational skills learned in part 1. In particular, the content covering model construction from chapter 8 will be directly relevant. Repeated convolutional layers followed by a resolution-reducing downsampling layer will still make up the majority of our model. We will use 3D data as input to our model. This is conceptually similar to the 2D image data used in chapters 7 and 8, but we will not be able to rely on all the 2D-specific tools available in the PyTorch ecosystem.

The main differences between the work we did with convolutional models in chapter 8 and what we'll do in part 2 are related to how much effort we put into things outside the model itself. In chapter 8, we used an off-the-shelf dataset and did little data manipulation before feeding the data into a model for classification. Almost all our time and attention were spent building the model itself, whereas now we're not even going to begin designing the first of our two model architectures until chapter 13. That is a direct consequence of having nonstandard data without prebuilt libraries ready to hand us training samples suitable to plug into a model. And, in practice, that will be the case for most real-life projects. We'll have to learn about our data and implement quite a bit ourselves.

Even when that's done, this will not end up being a case where we convert the CT to a tensor, feed it into a neural network, and have the answer pop out the other side. As is common for real-world use cases such as this, a workable approach will be more complicated to account for confounding factors such as limited data availability, finite computational resources, and limitations on our ability to design effective models. Please keep that in mind as we build toward a high-level explanation of our project architecture.

Speaking of finite computational resources, part 2 will require access to a GPU to achieve reasonable training speeds, preferably one with at least 8 GB of RAM. Trying to train the models we will build on CPU could take weeks! (We presume—we haven't tried it, much less timed it.) If you don't have a GPU handy, we provide pretrained models in chapter 15; the nodule analysis script there can probably be run overnight. While we don't want to tie the book to proprietary services if we don't have to, we should note that at the time of writing, Colaboratory (https://colab.research.google.com) provides free GPU instances that might be of use. PyTorch even comes preinstalled! You will also need to have at least 220 GB of free disk space to store the raw training data, cached data, and trained models.

> **NOTE** Many of the code examples presented in part 2 have complicating details omitted. Rather than clutter the examples with logging, error handling, and edge cases, the text of this book contains only code that expresses the core idea under discussion. Full working code samples can be found on the book's website (https://www.manning.com/books/deep-learning-with-pytorch-second-edition) and GitHub (https://github.com/deep-learning-with-pytorch/dlwpt-code).

OK, we've established that this is a hard, multifaceted problem, but what are we going to do about it? Instead of looking at an entire CT scan for signs of tumors or their potential malignancy, we're going to solve a series of simpler problems that will combine to provide the end-to-end result we're interested in. Like a factory assembly line, each step will take raw materials (data) and/or output from previous steps, perform some processing, and hand off the result to the next station down the line.

Not every problem needs to be solved this way, but breaking off chunks of the problem to solve in isolation is often a great way to start. Even if it turns out to be the wrong approach for a given project, it's likely we'll have learned enough while working on the individual chunks that we'll have a good idea how to restructure our approach into something successful.

Before we get into the details of how we'll break down our problem, we need to learn some details about the medical domain. While the code listings will tell you *what* we're doing, learning about radiation oncology will explain *why*. Learning about the problem space is crucial, no matter what the domain is. Deep learning is powerful, but it's not magic, and trying to apply it blindly to nontrivial problems will likely fail. Instead, we have to combine insights into the space with intuition about neural network behavior. From there, disciplined experimentation and refinement should give us enough information to close in on a workable solution.

11.3 What is a CT scan, exactly?

Before we get too far into the project, we need to take a moment to explain what a CT scan is. We will be using data from CT scans extensively as the main data format for our project, so having a working understanding of the data format's strengths, weaknesses, and fundamental nature will be crucial to utilizing it well. The key point we noted earlier is this: CT scans are essentially 3D X-rays, represented as a 3D array of single-channel data. As we might recall from chapter 4, it is like a stacked set of grayscale PNG images.

> **Voxel**
>
> A voxel is the 3D equivalent of the familiar 2D pixel. It encloses a volume of space (hence, *volumetric pixel*), rather than an area, and it is typically arranged in a 3D grid to represent a field of data. Each of those dimensions will have a measurable distance associated with it. Often, voxels are cubic, but, for this chapter, we will be dealing with voxels that are rectangular prisms. A rectangular prism is defined by three dimensions: length, width, and height, each representing a measurable distance along one of the three axes in 3D space. This shape can vary in proportions, unlike a cube, where all sides are equal.

In addition to medical data, we can see similar voxel data in fluid simulations, 3D scene reconstructions from 2D images, light detection and ranging (LIDAR) data for self-driving cars, and many other problem spaces. Those spaces all have their individual quirks and subtleties, and while the APIs that we're going to cover here apply generally, we must also be aware of the nature of the data we're using with those APIs if we want to be effective.

Each voxel of a CT scan has a numeric value that roughly corresponds to the average mass density of the matter contained inside. Most visualizations of that data show high-density material like bones and metal implants as white, low-density air and lung tissue as black, and fat and tissue as various shades of gray. Again, this ends up looking somewhat similar to an X-ray, with some key differences.

The primary difference between CT scans and X-rays is that whereas an X-ray is a projection of 3D intensity (in this case, tissue and bone density) onto a 2D plane, a CT scan retains the third dimension of the data. This allows us to render the data in a variety of ways—for example, as a grayscale solid, which we can see in figure 11.1.

> **NOTE** CT scans actually measure radiodensity, which is a function of both mass density and atomic number of the material under examination. For our purposes, the distinction isn't relevant, since the model will consume and learn from the CT data no matter what the exact units of the input happen to be.

11.3 *What is a CT scan, exactly?*

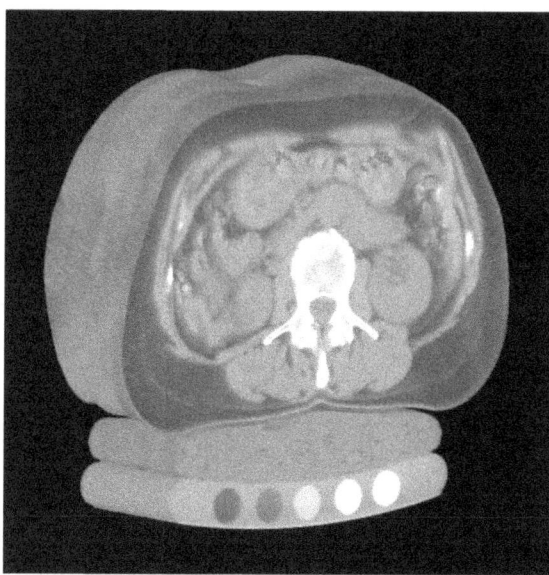

Figure 11.1 A CT scan of a human torso showing, from the top, skin, organs, spine, and patient support bed. Source: http://mng.bz/04r6; Mindways CT Software / CC BY-SA 3.0.

This 3D representation also allows us to "see inside" the subject by hiding tissue types we are not interested in. For example, we can render the data in 3D and restrict visibility to only bone and lung tissue, as in figure 11.2.

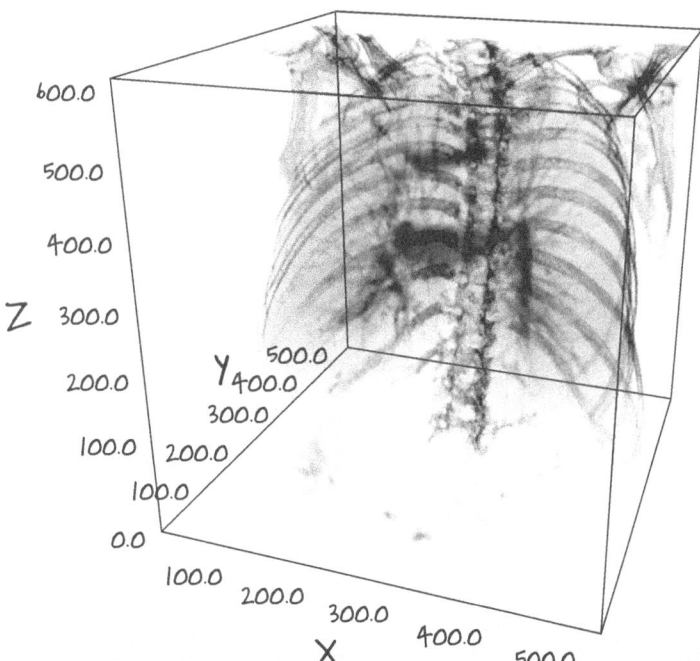

Figure 11.2 A CT scan showing ribs, spine, and lung structures

CT scans are much more difficult to acquire than X-rays because they require a machine like the one shown in figure 11.3, which typically costs upward of a million dollars and requires trained staff to operate. Most hospitals and some well-equipped clinics have a CT scanner, but they aren't nearly as ubiquitous as X-ray machines. This limitation, combined with patient privacy regulations, can make it somewhat difficult to get CT scans unless someone has already done the work of gathering and organizing a collection of them.

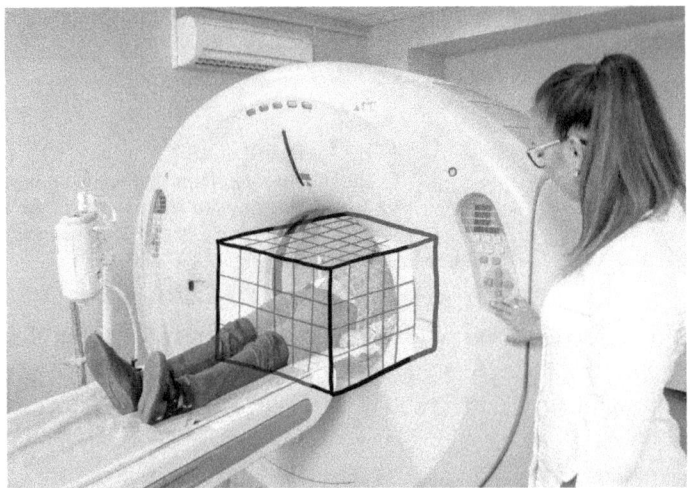

Figure 11.3 A patient inside a CT scanner, with the CT scan's bounding box overlaid. Other than in stock photos, patients don't typically wear street clothes while in the machine.

Figure 11.3 also shows an example bounding box for the area contained in the CT scan. The bed the patient is resting on moves back and forth, allowing the scanner to image multiple slices of the patient and hence fill the bounding box. The scanner's darker, central ring is where the actual imaging equipment is located.

A final difference between a CT scan and an X-ray is that the data is a digital-only format. The raw output of the scanning process doesn't look particularly meaningful to the human eye and must be properly reinterpreted by a computer into something we can understand. The settings of the CT scanner when the scan is taken can have a large effect on the resulting data.

While this information might not seem particularly relevant, we have actually learned something. From figure 11.3, we can see that the patient actually moves along the head-to-foot axis. As a result, the way the CT scanner measures distance along that axis differs from the other two axes, which explains (or at least is a strong hint as to) why our voxels might not be cubic and also ties into how we approach massaging our data in chapter 14. This is a good example of why we need to understand our problem space if we're going to make effective choices about how to solve our problem. When starting to work on your own projects, be sure you do the same investigation into the details of your data.

11.4 The project: An end-to-end detector for lung cancer

Now that we've got our heads wrapped around the basics of CT scans, let's discuss the structure of our project. Most of the bytes on disk will be devoted to storing the CT scans' 3D arrays containing density information, and our models will primarily consume various subslices of those 3D arrays. We're going to use three main steps to go from examining a whole-chest CT scan to giving the patient a lung cancer diagnosis.

Our full, end-to-end solution, shown in figure 11.4, will load CT data files to produce a Ct instance that contains the full 3D scan, combine that with a module that performs *segmentation* (flagging voxels of interest).

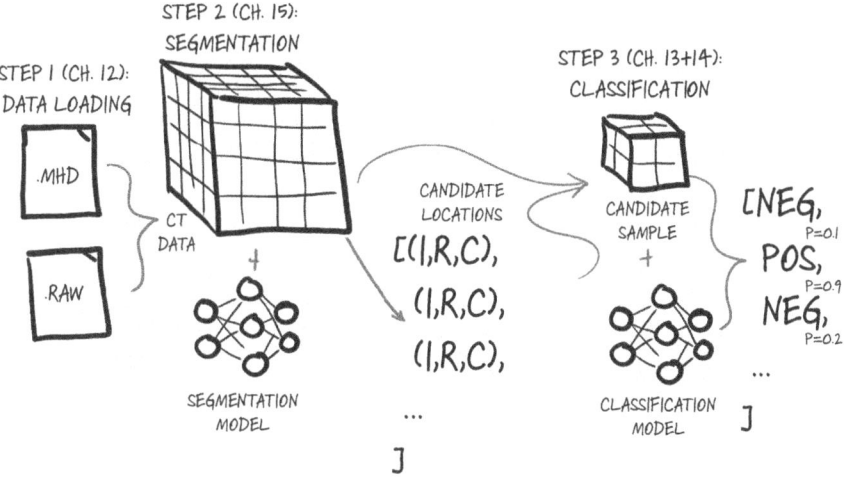

Figure 11.4 The end-to-end process of taking a full-chest CT scan and determining whether the patient has a malignant tumor.

> **Nodules**
>
> A mass of tissue made of proliferating cells in the lung is a tumor. A tumor can be benign, or it can be malignant, in which case it is also referred to as cancer. A small tumor in the lung (just a few millimeters wide) is called a nodule. About 40% of lung nodules turn out to be malignant small cancers. It is very important to catch those as early as possible, which depends on medical imaging of the kind we are looking at here.

The nodule locations are combined back with the CT voxel data to produce nodule candidates, which can then be examined by our nodule classification model to determine whether they are actually nodules in the first place and, eventually, whether they're malignant. This latter task is particularly difficult because malignancy might not be apparent from CT imaging alone, but we'll see how far we get. Last, each of those individual, per-nodule classifications can then be combined into a whole-patient diagnosis.

In more detail, we will do the following:

1 Load our raw CT scan data into a form that we can use with PyTorch. Putting raw data into a form usable by PyTorch will be the first step in any project you face. The process is somewhat less complicated with 2D image data and simpler still with non-image data.
2 Identify the voxels of potential tumors in the lungs using PyTorch to implement a technique known as *segmentation*, which is roughly akin to producing a heatmap of areas that should be fed into our classifier in step 3. This will allow us to focus on potential tumors inside the lungs and ignore huge swaths of uninteresting anatomy (e.g., a person can't have lung cancer in the stomach).

    Generally, being able to focus on a single, small task is best while learning. With experience, there are some situations where more complicated model structures can yield superlative results, but designing those from scratch requires extensive mastery of the basic building blocks first.
3 Classify candidate nodules as actual nodules or non-nodules using 3D convolution. This will be similar in concept to the 2D convolution we covered in chapter 8. The features that determine the nature of a tumor from a candidate structure are local to the tumor in question, so this approach should provide a good balance between limiting input data size and excluding relevant information. Making scope-limiting decisions like this can keep each individual task constrained, which can help limit the amount of things to examine when troubleshooting.

> **On the shoulders of giants**
> We are standing on the shoulders of giants when deciding on this three-step approach. There isn't any particular reason why we should know in advance that this project structure will work well for this problem. Instead, we're relying on others who have actually implemented similar things and reported success when doing so. Expect to have to experiment to find workable approaches when transitioning to a different domain but always try to learn from earlier efforts in the space and from those who have worked in similar areas and have discovered things that might transfer well. Go out there, look for what others have done, and use that as a benchmark. At the same time, avoid getting code and running it blindly because you need to fully understand the code you're running in order to use the results to make progress for yourself.

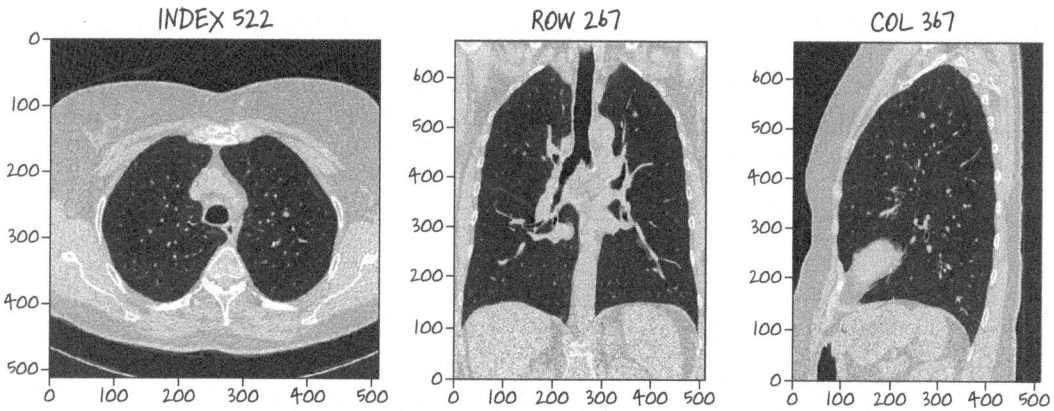

Figure 11.5 A CT scan with approximately 1,000 structures that look like tumors to the untrained eye. Exactly one has been identified as a nodule when reviewed by a human specialist. The rest are normal anatomical structures, such as blood vessels, lesions, and other nonproblematic lumps.

Figure 11.4 only depicts the final path through the system once we've built and trained all the requisite models. The actual work required to train the relevant models will be detailed as we get closer to implementing each step.

Let's recap the steps that we will take:

- *Step 1*—Data loading
- *Step 2*—Segmentation
- *Step 3*—Classification

The data we'll use for training provides human-annotated output for step 3. This allows us to treat step 2 (identifying voxels) as almost a separate project from step 3 (nodule candidate classification). Human experts have annotated the data with nodule locations, so we can work on step 2 or step 3 in whichever order we prefer.

We will first work on step 1, and then jump to step 3 before we come back and implement step 2, since step 3 requires an approach similar to what we used in chapter 8, using multiple convolutional and pooling layers to aggregate spatial information before feeding it into a linear classifier. Once we've got a handle on our classification model, we can start working on step 2. Since segmentation is the more complicated topic, we want to tackle it without having to learn both segmentation and the fundamentals of CT scans and malignant tumors at the same time. Instead, we'll explore the cancer-detection space while working on a more familiar classification problem.

This approach of starting in the middle of the problem and working our way out probably seems odd. Starting at step 1 and working our way forward would make more intuitive sense. However, being able to carve up the problem and work on steps independently is useful, since it can encourage more modular solutions; in addition, it's easier to partition the workload between members of a small team. Also, actual clinical users would likely prefer a system that flags suspicious nodules for review rather than provides a single binary diagnosis. Adapting our modular solution to different use cases will probably be easier than if we'd done a monolithic, from-the-top system.

As we work our way through implementing each step, we'll be going into a fair bit of detail about lung tumors, as well as presenting a lot of fine-grained detail about CT scans. While that might seem off topic for a book that's focused on PyTorch, we're doing so specifically so that you begin to develop an intuition about the problem space and because it's something practitioners do in real life. That clinical information is crucial to have because the space of all possible solutions and approaches is too large to effectively code, train, and evaluate.

If we were working on a different project (say, the one you tackle after finishing this book), we'd still need to do an investigation to understand the data and problem space. Perhaps you're interested in satellite mapping, and your next project needs to consume pictures of our planet taken from orbit. You'd need to ask questions about the wavelengths being collected: Do you get only normal RGB or something more exotic? What about infrared or ultraviolet? In addition, there might be effects on the images based on the time of day or if the imaged location isn't directly under the satellite, skewing the image. Will the image need correction?

Even if your hypothetical *third* project's data type remains the same, it's probable that the domain you'll be working in will change things, possibly drastically. Processing camera output for self-driving cars still involves 2D images, but the complications and caveats are wildly different. For example, it's much less likely that a mapping satellite will need to worry about the sun shining into the camera or getting mud on the lens!

We must be able to use our intuition to guide our investigation into potential optimizations and improvements. That's true of deep learning projects in general, and we'll practice using our intuition as we go through part 2. So, let's do that. Take a quick step back and do a gut check. What does your intuition say about this approach? Does it seem overcomplicated to you?

11.4.1 Why can't we just throw data at a neural network until it works?

After reading the last section, you might be wondering why we have two separate model architectures or why the overall data flow is so complicated. Well, our approach is different from that in chapter 8 for a reason. It's a hard task to automate, and people haven't fully figured it out yet. That difficulty translates to complexity; once we, as a society, have solved this problem definitively, there will probably be an off-the-shelf library package we can grab to have it just work, but we're not there just yet.

Why so difficult, though? Well, for starters, the majority of a CT scan is fundamentally uninteresting with regard to answering the question, "Does this patient have a malignant tumor?" This makes intuitive sense since the vast majority of the patient's body will consist of healthy cells. In the cases where there is a malignant tumor, up to 99.9999% of the voxels in the CT still won't be cancer. That ratio is equivalent to a two-pixel blob of incorrectly tinted color somewhere on a high-definition television, or a single misspelled word out of a shelf of novels.

Can you identify the white dot in the three views of figure 11.5 that has been flagged as a nodule? (The `series_uid` of this sample is `1.3.6.1.4.1.14519.5.2.1.6279.6001.126264578931778258890037 1755354`, which can be useful if you'd like to look at it in detail later.)

If you need a hint, the index, row, and column values can be used to help find the relevant blob of dense tissue. Do you think you could figure out the relevant properties of tumors given only images (and that means *only* the images—no index, row, and column information!) like these? What if you were given the entire 3D scan, not just three slices that intersect the interesting part of the scan?

> **NOTE** Don't fret if you can't locate the tumor! We're trying to illustrate just how subtle this data can be. The fact that it is hard to identify visually is the entire point of this example.

You might have seen elsewhere that end-to-end approaches for detection and classification of objects are very successful in general vision tasks. Torchvision includes end-to-end models like Fast R-CNN/Mask R-CNN, but these are typically trained on hundreds of thousands of images, and those datasets aren't constrained by the number of samples from rare classes.

The project architecture we will use has the benefit of working well with a more modest amount of data. So, while it's certainly theoretically possible to just throw an arbitrarily large amount of data at a neural network until it learns the specifics of the proverbial lost needle, as well as how to ignore the hay, it's going to be practically prohibitive to collect enough data and wait for a long enough time to train the network properly. That isn't the *best* approach since the results are poor, and most readers won't have access to the compute resources to pull it off at all.

To come up with the best solution, we could investigate proven model designs that can better integrate data in an end-to-end manner—for example, Retina U-Net (https://arxiv.org/pdf/1811.08661.pdf) and FishNet (http://mng.bz/K240). These complicated designs are capable of producing high-quality results, but they're not the *best* because understanding the design decisions behind them requires having mastered fundamental concepts first. That makes these advanced models poor candidates to use while teaching those same fundamentals!

That's not to say that our multistep design is the best approach, either, but that's because "best" is only relative to the criteria we chose to evaluate approaches. There are *many* "best" approaches, just as there are many goals we could have in mind as we work on a project. Our self-contained, multistep approach has some disadvantages as well.

Recall the GAN game from chapter 2. There, we had two networks cooperating to produce convincing forgeries of old master artists. The artist would produce a candidate work, and the scholar would critique it, giving the artist feedback on how to improve. Put in technical terms, the structure of the model allowed gradients to backpropagate from the final classifier (fake or real) to the earliest parts of the project (the artist).

Our approach to solving the problem won't use end-to-end gradient backpropagation to directly optimize for our end goal. Instead, we'll optimize discrete chunks of the problem individually, since our segmentation model and classification model won't be trained in tandem with each other. That might limit the top-end effectiveness of our solution, but we feel that it will make for a much better learning experience.

We feel that being able to focus on a single step at a time allows us to zoom in and concentrate on the smaller number of new skills we're learning. Each of our two models will be focused on performing exactly one task. Similar to a human radiologist, as they review slice after slice of CT, the job gets much easier to train for if the scope is well contained. We also want to provide tools that allow for rich manipulation of the data. Being able to zoom in and focus on the details of a particular location will have a huge effect on overall productivity while training the model, compared to having to look at the entire image at once. Our segmentation model is forced to consume the entire image, but we will structure things so that our classification model gets a zoomed-in view of the areas of interest.

Step 3 (classification) will consume data similar to the image in figure 11.6, which shows sequential transverse slices of a tumor. This image is a close-up view of a potentially malignant (or at least indeterminate) tumor as either benign or malignant. While this lump may seem nondescript to an untrained eye (or untrained convolutional network), identifying the warning signs of malignancy in this sample is at least a far more constrained problem than having to consume the entire CT we saw earlier.

> **NOTE** Our code for the next chapter will provide routines to produce zoomed-in nodule images like figure 11.6.

We will perform the step 1 data-loading work in chapter 12, and chapters 13 and 14 will focus on solving the problem of classifying these nodules. After that, we'll back up to work on step 2 (using segmentation to find the candidate tumors) in chapter 15.

> **NOTE** Standard rendering of CTs places the superior at the top of the image (basically, the head goes up), but CTs order their slices such that the first slice is the inferior (toward the feet). So, Matplotlib renders the images upside down unless we take care to flip them. Since that flip doesn't really matter to our model, we won't complicate the code paths between our raw data and the model, but we will add a flip to our rendering code to get the images right-side up.

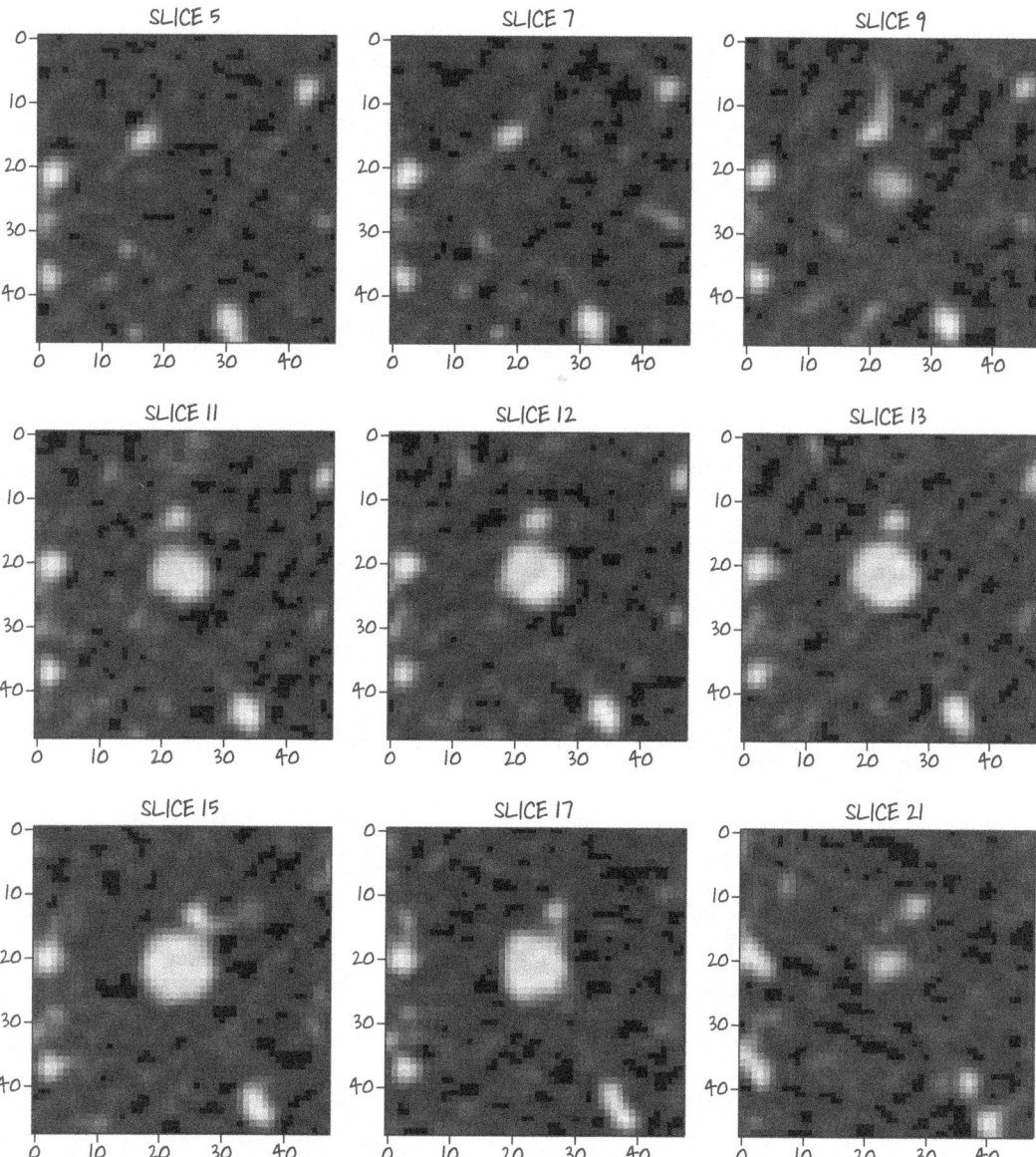

Figure 11.6 A close-up, multislice crop of the tumor from the CT scan in figure 11.5.

WHAT IS A NODULE?

As we've said, to understand our data well enough to use it effectively, we need to learn some specifics about cancer and radiation oncology. One last key thing we need to understand is what a *nodule* is. Simply put, a nodule is any of the myriad lumps and bumps that might appear inside someone's lungs. Some are problematic from a health-of-the-patient perspective; some are not. The precise definition (see Eric J. Olson,

"Lung Nodules: Can They Be Cancerous?" Mayo Clinic, http://mng.bz/yyge) limits the size of a nodule to 3 cm or less, with a larger lump being a *lung mass*. We will use the term *nodule* interchangeably for all such anatomical structures, since it's a somewhat arbitrary cutoff and we're going to deal with lumps on both sides of 3 cm using the same code paths. A nodule can turn out to be benign or a malignant tumor (also referred to as *cancer*). From a radiological perspective, a nodule is really similar to other lumps that have a wide variety of causes: infection, inflammation, blood supply issues, malformed blood vessels, and diseases other than tumors.

The key part is that the cancers that we are trying to detect will *always* be nodules, either suspended in the very nondense tissue of the lung or attached to the lung wall. That means we can limit our classifier to only nodules, rather than have it examine all tissue. Being able to restrict the scope of expected inputs will help our classifier learn the task at hand.

This is another example of how the underlying deep learning techniques we'll use are universal, but they can't be applied blindly—not if we want decent results at least. We'll need to understand the field we're working in to make choices that will serve us well.

In figure 11.7, we can see a stereotypical example of a malignant nodule. The smallest nodules we'll be concerned with are only a few millimeters across, although

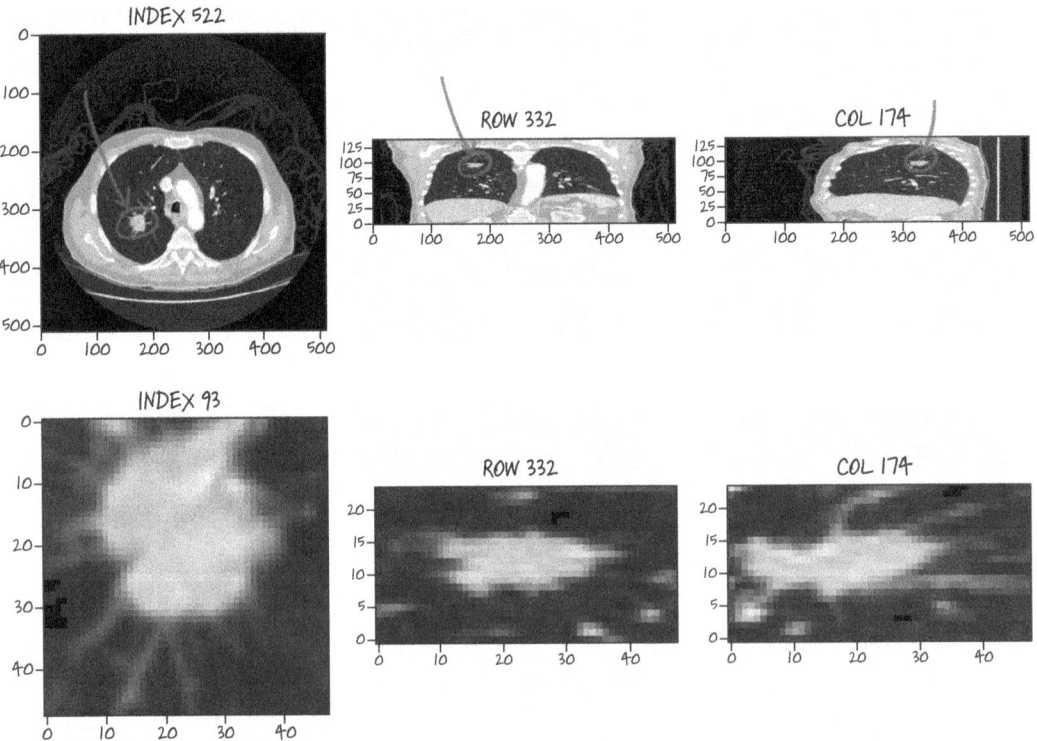

Figure 11.7 A CT scan with a malignant nodule displaying a visual discrepancy from other nodules

the one in figure 11.7 is larger. As we discussed earlier in the chapter, this makes the smallest nodules approximately a million times smaller than the CT scan as a whole. According to the National Cancer Institute's *NCI Dictionary of Cancer Terms* (http://mng.bz/jgBP), more than half of the nodules detected in patients are not malignant.

11.4.2 Our data source: The LUNA Grand Challenge

The CT scans we were just looking at come from the LUNA (LUng Nodule Analysis) Grand Challenge. The LUNA Grand Challenge is the combination of an open dataset with high-quality labels of patient CT scans (many with lung nodules) and a public ranking of classifiers against the data. There is something of a culture of publicly sharing medical datasets for research and analysis; open access to such data allows researchers to use, combine, and perform novel work on this data without having to enter into formal research agreements between institutions (obviously, some data is kept private). The goal of the LUNA Grand Challenge is to encourage improvements in nodule detection by making it easy for teams to compete for high positions on the leaderboard. A project team can test the efficacy of their detection methods against standardized criteria (the dataset provided). To be included in the public ranking, a team must provide a scientific paper describing the project architecture, training methods, and so on. The LUNA Grand Challlenge makes for a great resource to provide further ideas and inspiration for project improvements.

> **NOTE** Many CT scans "in the wild" are incredibly messy, in terms of idiosyncrasies between various scanners and processing programs. For example, some scanners indicate areas of the CT scan that are outside of the scanner's field of view by setting the density of those voxels to something negative. CT scans can also be acquired with a variety of settings on the CT scanner, which can change the resulting image in ways ranging from subtly to wildly different. Although the LUNA data is generally clean, be sure to check your assumptions if you incorporate other data sources.

We will be using the LUNA 2016 dataset. The LUNA site (https://luna16.grand-challenge.org/Description) describes two tracks for the challenge: the first track, "Nodule detection (NDET)," roughly corresponds to our step 1 (segmentation); and the second track, "False positive reduction (FPRED)," is similar to our step 3 (classification). When the site discusses "locations of possible nodules," it is talking about a process similar to what we'll cover in chapter 15.

11.4.3 Downloading the LUNA data

Before we go any further into the nuts and bolts of our project, we'll cover how to get the data we'll be using. It's about 60 GB of data compressed, so depending on your internet connection, it might take a while to download. Once uncompressed, it takes up about 120 GB of space, and we'll need another 100 GB or so of cache space to store smaller chunks of data so that we can access it more quickly than reading in the whole CT. The cache space required is per chapter, but once you're done with a chapter, you can delete the cache to free up space.

Navigate to https://luna16.grand-challenge.org/Download/. You should see two download links to Zenodo data. You will need to download from both of those links.

The data we will be using comes in 10 subsets, aptly named subset0 through subset9. Unzip each of them so you have separate subdirectories like code/data-unversioned/part2/luna/subset0, and so on. On Linux, you'll need the 7z decompression utility (Ubuntu provides this via the p7zip-full package). Windows users can get an extractor from the 7-Zip website (www.7-zip.org). Some decompression utilities will not be able to open the archives; make sure you have the full version of the extractor if you get an error.

In addition, you need the candidates.csv and annotations.csv files. We've included these files on the book's website and in the GitHub repository for convenience, so they should already be present in code/data/part2/luna/*.csv. They can also be downloaded from the same location as the data subsets.

> **NOTE** If you do not have easy access to ~220 GB of free disk space, it's possible to run the examples using only 1 or 2 of the 10 subsets of data. The smaller training set will result in the model performing much more poorly, but that's better than not being able to run the examples at all.

Once you have the candidates file and at least one subset downloaded, uncompressed, and put in the correct location, you should be able to start running the examples in the next chapter.

11.5 Conclusion

We've made major strides toward our project! You might have the feeling that we haven't accomplished much; after all, we haven't implemented a single line of code yet. But keep in mind that you'll need to do research and preparation, as we have here, when you tackle projects on your own.

In this chapter, we set out to do two things:

1 Understand the larger context around our lung-cancer-detection project.
2 Sketch out the direction and structure of our project for part 2.

If you still feel that we haven't made real progress, please recognize that mindset as a trap—understanding the space your project is working in is crucial, and the design work we've done will pay off handsomely as we move forward. We'll see those dividends shortly, once we start implementing our data-loading routines in chapter 12.

Since this chapter has been informational only, without any code, we'll skip the exercises for now.

Summary

- Our approach to detecting cancerous nodules will have three rough steps: data loading, segmentation, and classification.
- Breaking down our project into smaller, semi-independent subprojects makes teaching each subproject easier. Other approaches might make more sense for future projects with different goals than the ones for this book.
- A CT scan is a 3D array of intensity data with approximately 32 million voxels, which is around a million times larger than the nodules we want to recognize. Focusing the model on a crop of the CT scan relevant to the task at hand will make it easier to get reasonable results from training.
- Understanding our data will make it easier to write processing routines for our data that don't distort or destroy important aspects of the data. The array of CT scan data typically will not have cubic voxels; mapping location information in real-world units to array indexes requires conversion. The intensity of a CT scan corresponds roughly to mass density but uses unique units.
- Identifying the key concepts of a project and making sure they are well-represented in our design can be crucial. Most aspects of our project will revolve around nodules, which are small masses in the lungs and can be spotted on a CT along with many other structures that have a similar appearance.
- We are using the LUNA Grand Challenge data to train our model. The LUNA data contains CT scans, as well as human-annotated outputs for classification and grouping. Having high-quality data has a significant effect on a project's success.

Combining data sources into a unified dataset

This chapter covers

- Loading and processing raw data files
- Implementing a Python class to represent our data
- Converting our data into a format usable by PyTorch
- Visualizing the training and validation data

Now that we've discussed the high-level goals for our project, as well as outlined how the data will flow through our system, let's get into the specifics of what we're going to do in this chapter. It's time to implement basic data-loading and data-processing routines for our raw data. The techniques we cover here are foundational and will be applicable to any major project you undertake. To the rare researcher who has all their data well prepared for them in advance: lucky you! The rest of us will be busy writing code for loading and parsing. Figure 12.1 shows the high-level map of our project from chapter 11. We'll focus on step 1, data loading, for the rest of this chapter.

Our goal is to be able to produce a training sample given our inputs of raw CT scan data and a list of annotations for those CTs. This might sound simple, but quite a bit needs to happen before we can load, process, and extract the data we're

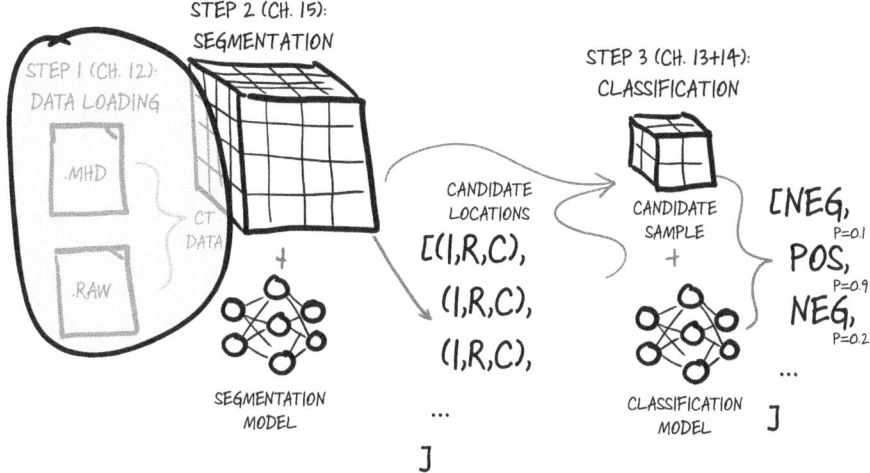

Figure 12.1 Our end-to-end lung-cancer-detection project, with a focus on this chapter's topic: step 1, data loading

interested in. Figure 12.2 shows what we'll need to do to turn our raw data into a training sample. Luckily, we got a head start on *understanding* our data in the last chapter, but we have more work to do on that front.

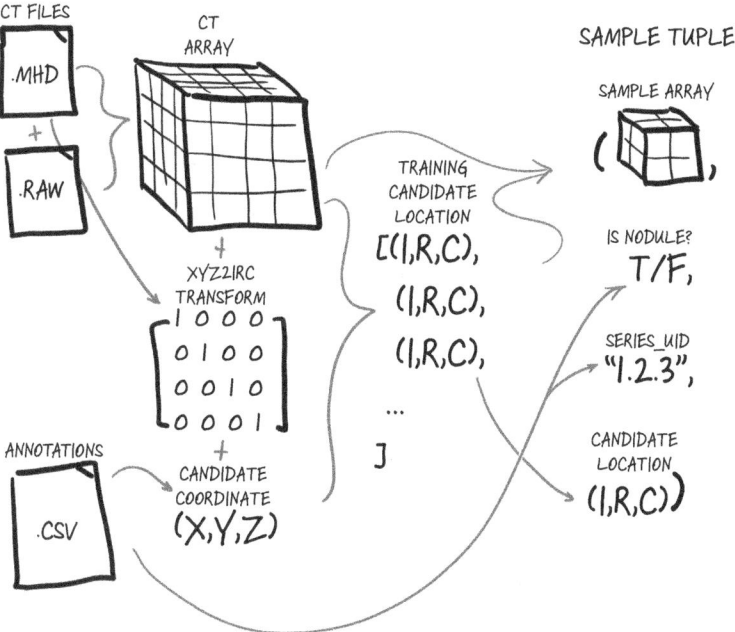

Figure 12.2 The data transforms required to make a sample tuple. These sample tuples will be used as input to our model training routine.

This is a crucial moment, where we start to transform the heavy, unrefined raw data, if not into gold, then at least into material that our neural network will eventually turn into gold. We first explored the mechanics of this transformation of raw data into tensors in chapter 4.

12.1 Raw CT data files

Our raw CT data consists of the majority of the LUNA dataset and is contained within the `subset` directories. Each subset directory contains a number of CT scans, each of which is represented by two files: an .mhd file and a .raw file. The .mhd file contains metadata header information, and the .raw file contains the raw bytes that make up the 3D array. Each file's name starts with a unique identifier called the *series UID* (from the Digital Imaging and Communications in Medicine [DICOM] nomenclature) for the CT scan in question. For example, for series UID 1.2.3, there would be two files: 1.2.3.mhd and 1.2.3.raw.

Our `Ct` class will consume those two files and produce the 3D array tensor, as well as the transformation matrix to convert from the patient coordinate system (which we will discuss in more detail in section 12.4) to the index, row, and column coordinates needed for the 3D array tensor; these coordinates are shown as (I,R,C) in the figures and are denoted with `_irc` variable suffixes in the code. Don't sweat the details of all this right now; just remember that we've got some coordinate system conversion to do before we can apply these coordinates to our CT data.

We will also load the annotation data provided by LUNA, which will give us a list of nodule coordinates, each with a malignancy flag, along with the series UID of the relevant CT scan. By combining the nodule coordinate with coordinate system transformation information, we get the index, row, and column of the voxel at the center of our nodule.

Using the (I,R,C) coordinates, we can crop a small 3D slice of our CT data to use as the input to our model. We will also construct the rest of our training sample tuple, which, altogether, will have the sample array, nodule status flag, series UID, and the index of this sample in the CT list of nodule candidates. This sample tuple is exactly what PyTorch expects from our `Dataset` subclass and represents the last section of our bridge from our original raw data to the standard structure of PyTorch tensors.

Limiting or cropping our data so as not to drown our model in noise is important, as is making sure we're not so aggressive that our signal gets cropped out of our input. We want to make sure the range of our data is well-behaved, especially after normalization. Clamping our data to remove outliers can be useful, especially if our data is prone to extreme outliers.

12.2 Parsing LUNA's annotation data

The first thing we need to do is begin loading our data. When working on a new project, that's often a good place to start. Making sure we know how to work with the raw input is required no matter what and knowing how our data will look after it loads can help inform the structure of our early experiments. We could try loading individual CT scans, but we think it makes sense to parse the CSV files that LUNA provides, which contain information about the points of interest in each CT scan. As we can see in figure 12.3, we expect to get some coordinate information, an indication of whether the coordinate is a nodule, and a unique identifier for the CT scan. Since there are fewer types of information in the CSV files, and they're easier to parse, we're hoping they will give us some clues about what to look for once we start loading CTs.

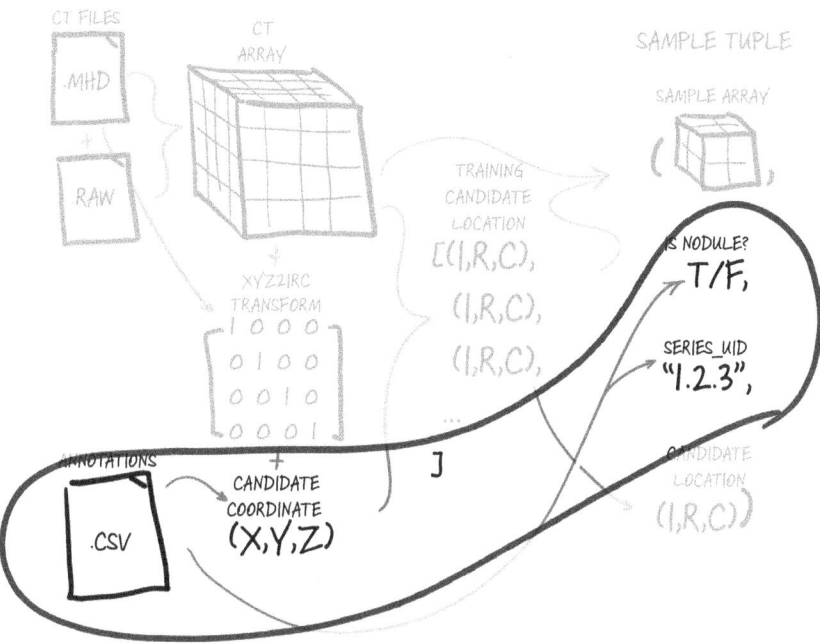

Figure 12.3 The LUNA annotations in candidates.csv contain the CT series, the nodule candidate's position, and a flag indicating whether the candidate is actually a nodule or not.

The candidates.csv file contains information about all lumps that potentially look like nodules, whether those lumps are malignant, benign tumors, or something else altogether. We'll use this as the basis for building a complete list of candidates that can then be split into our training and validation datasets. The following Bash shell session shows what the file contains:

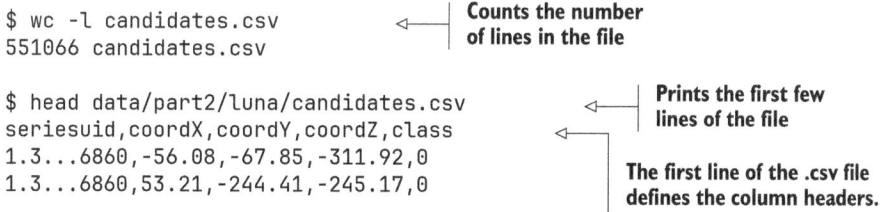

```
1.3...6860,103.66,-121.8,-286.62,0
1.3...6860,-33.66,-72.75,-308.41,0
...

$ grep ',1$' candidates.csv | wc -l
1351
```

◁— Counts the number of lines that end with 1, which indicates it is a nodule

> **NOTE** The values in the `seriesuid` column have been truncated to better fit the printed page.

So we have 551,000 lines, each with a `seriesuid` (which we'll call `series_uid` in the code), some (X,Y,Z) coordinates describing a point in 3D space for the location of the candidate nodule, and a `class` column that corresponds to the nodule status. The `class` column is a Boolean value: 0 for a candidate that is not a nodule (e.g., a blood vessel) and 1 for a candidate that is a nodule, which can be malignant or benign. We have 1,351 candidates flagged as nodules.

The annotations.csv file contains information about some of the candidates that have been flagged as nodules. We are interested in the `diameter_mm` information in particular:

```
$ wc -l annotations.csv
1187 annotations.csv
```
◁— This is a different number than in the candidates.csv file.

```
$ head data/part2/luna/annotations.csv
seriesuid,coordX,coordY,coordZ,diameter_mm
1.3.6...6860,-128.6994211,-175.3192718,-298.3875064,5.651470635
1.3.6...6860,103.7836509,-211.9251487,-227.12125,4.224708481
1.3.6...5208,69.63901724,-140.9445859,876.3744957,5.786347814
1.3.6...0405,-24.0138242,192.1024053,-391.0812764,8.143261683
...
```
◁— The last column is also different.

We have size information for about 1,200 nodules. This is useful, since we can use it to make sure our training and validation data includes a representative spread of nodule sizes. Without this, it's possible that our validation set could end up with only extreme values, making it seem as though our model is underperforming. This principle applies broadly: whether predicting how many views a movie will have, classifying text as spam or not, or detecting words in a long audio file, including diverse data prevents skewed results and ensures the model performs well in real-world scenarios. Having a representative dataset is essential for building a reliable model in any machine learning project.

12.2.1 Training and validation sets

For any standard supervised learning task (classification is the prototypical example), we'll split our data into training and validation sets. We want to make sure both sets are *representative* of the range of real-world input data we're expecting to see and handle normally. If either set is meaningfully different from our real-world use cases, it's pretty likely that our model will behave differently than we expect—all of the training and statistics we collect won't be predictive once we transfer over to production use! We're not trying to make this an exact science, but you should keep an eye out in future projects for hints that you are training and testing on data that doesn't make sense for your operating environment.

Let's get back to our nodules. We're going to sort them by size and take every *N*th one for our validation set. That should give us the representative spread we're looking for. Unfortunately, the location information provided in annotations.csv doesn't always precisely line up with the coordinates in candidates.csv:

```
$ grep 100225287222365663678666836860 annotations.csv
1.3.6...6860,-128.6994211,-175.3192718,-298.3875064,5.651470635
1.3.6...6860,103.7836509,-211.9251487,-227.12125,4.224708481

$ grep '100225287222365663678666836860.*,1$' candidates.csv
1.3.6...6860,104.16480444,-211.685591018,-227.011363746,1
1.3.6...6860,-128.94,-175.04,-297.87,1
```

These two coordinates are very close to each other.

If we truncate the corresponding coordinates from each file, we end up with (-128.70, -175.32, -298.39) versus (-128.94, -175.04, -297.87). Since the nodule in question has a diameter of 5 mm, both points are clearly meant to be the "center" of the nodule, but they don't line up exactly. It would be a perfectly valid response to decide that dealing with this data mismatch isn't worth it and to ignore the file. We are going to do the legwork to make things line up, though, since real-world datasets are often imperfect this way, and this is a good example of the kind of work you will need to do to assemble data from disparate data sources.

12.2.2 Unifying our annotation and candidate data

Now that we know what our raw data files look like, let's build a `getCandidateInfoList` function that will stitch it all together. We'll use a named tuple that is defined at the top of the file to hold the information for each nodule.

Listing 12.1 Getting candidate data (dsets.py)

```python
from collections import namedtuple
# ... line 27
CandidateInfoTuple = namedtuple(
  'CandidateInfoTuple',
  'isNodule_bool, diameter_mm, series_uid, center_xyz',
)
```

These tuples are *not* our training samples, as they're missing the chunks of CT data we need. Instead, these represent a sanitized, cleaned, unified interface to the human-annotated data we're using. It's very important to isolate having to deal with messy data from model training. Otherwise, your training loop can get cluttered quickly because you have to keep dealing with special cases and other distractions in the middle of code that should be focused on training.

TIP Clearly separate the code that's responsible for data sanitization from the rest of your project. Don't be afraid to rewrite your data once and save it to disk if needed.

Our list of candidate information will have the nodule status (what we're going to be training the model to classify), diameter (useful for getting a good spread in training, since large and small nodules will not have the same features), series UID (to locate the correct CT scan), and candidate center (to find the candidate in the larger CT). The function that will build a list of these NoduleInfoTuple instances starts by using an in-memory caching decorator, followed by getting the list of files present on disk:

```
@functools.lru_cache(1)                                     ◁── Standard library in-memory caching
def getCandidateInfoList(require_on_disk=True):             ◁── require_on_disk defaults to screening out series from data subsets that aren't downloaded onto the computer.
    data_directory = Path(f"{mhd_data_folder}")
    mhd_files = list(data_directory.rglob("subset*/*.mhd"))
    if not mhd_files:
        print(f"Warning: No .mhd files found under {data_directory}")
    present_on_disk_set = {path.stem for path in mhd_files}
```

Since parsing some of the data files can be slow, we'll cache the results of this function call in memory. This will come in handy later because we'll be calling this function more often in future chapters. Speeding up our data pipeline by carefully applying in-memory or on-disk caching can result in some pretty impressive gains in training speed. Keep an eye out for these opportunities as you work on your projects.

After we get our candidate series UID, we want to merge in the diameter information from annotations.csv. First, we need to group our annotations by series_uid, as that's the first key we'll use to cross-reference each row from the two files:

```
diameter_dict = {}
with open('data/part2/luna/annotations.csv', "r") as f:
  for row in list(csv.reader(f))[1:]:
    series_uid = row[0]
    annotationCenter_xyz = tuple([float(x) for x in row[1:4]])
    annotationDiameter_mm = float(row[4])

    diameter_dict.setdefault(series_uid, []).append(
      (annotationCenter_xyz, annotationDiameter_mm)
    )
```

Next, we'll build our full list of candidates using the information in the candidates.csv file:

```
candidateInfo_list = []
with open('data/part2/luna/candidates.csv', "r") as f:
  for row in list(csv.reader(f))[1:]:
    series_uid = row[0]

    if series_uid not in present_on_disk_set and require_on_disk:    ◁── If a series_uid isn't present, it's in a subset we don't have on disk, so we should skip it.
      continue
```

12.3 Loading individual CT scans

```
        isNodule_bool = bool(int(row[4]))
        candidateCenter_xyz = tuple([float(x) for x in row[1:4]])

        candidateDiameter_mm = 0.0
        for annotation_tup in diameter_dict.get(series_uid, []):
          annotationCenter_xyz, annotationDiameter_mm = annotation_tup
          for i in range(3):
            delta_mm = abs(candidateCenter_xyz[i] - annotationCenter_xyz[i])
            if delta_mm > annotationDiameter_mm / 4:     ◁─┐
              break
          else:
            candidateDiameter_mm = annotationDiameter_mm
            break

        candidateInfo_list.append(CandidateInfoTuple(
          isNodule_bool,
          candidateDiameter_mm,
          series_uid,
          candidateCenter_xyz,
        ))
```

> Divides the diameter by 2 to get the radius and then divides the radius by another 2 to ensure that the two nodule center points are not too far apart relative to the size of the nodule. (This results in a bounding-box check, not a true distance check.)

For each of the candidate entries for a given series_uid, we loop through the annotations we collected earlier for the same series_uid and see whether the two coordinates are close enough to consider them the same nodule. If they are, great! Now we have the diameter information for that nodule. If we don't find a match, that's fine; we'll just treat the nodule as having a placeholder 0.0 diameter. Since we're only using this information to get a good spread of nodule sizes in our training and validation sets, having placeholder diameter sizes for some nodules shouldn't be a problem, but we should remember we're doing this in case our assumption here is wrong.

That's a lot of somewhat fiddly code just to merge in our nodule diameter. Unfortunately, having to do this kind of manipulation and fuzzy matching can be fairly common, depending on your raw data. Once we get to this point, however, we just need to sort the data and return it:

```
candidateInfo_list.sort(reverse=True)     ◁─┐
return candidateInfo_list
```

> We have all the actual nodule samples starting with the largest first, followed by all of the non-nodule samples (which don't have nodule size information).

The ordering of the tuple members in noduleInfo_list is driven by this sort. We're using this sorting approach to help ensure that when we take a slice of the data, that slice gets a representative chunk of the actual nodules with a good spread of nodule diameters.

12.3 Loading individual CT scans

Next up, we need to be able to take our CT data from a pile of bits on disk and turn it into a Python object from which we can extract 3D nodule density data. We can see this path from the .mhd and .raw files to Ct objects in figure 12.4. Our nodule annotation information acts like a map to the interesting parts of our raw data.

Before we can follow that map to our data of interest, we need to get the data into an addressable form.

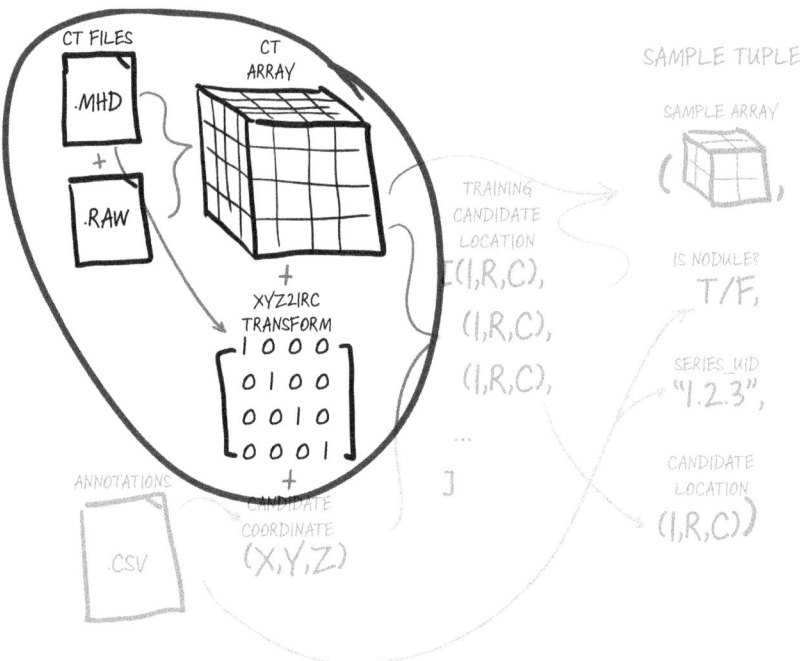

Figure 12.4 Loading a CT scan produces a voxel array and a transformation from patient coordinates to array indices. This process is essential for converting raw data into a structured, machine-readable format suitable for analysis. The .mhd and .raw files provide the raw volumetric data, which is transformed into a 3D voxel array for easy indexing and processing.

The native file format for CT scans is DICOM (www.dicomstandard.org). The first version of the DICOM standard was authored in 1984, and as we might expect from anything computing-related that comes from that time period, it's a bit of a mess (e.g., whole sections that are now retired were devoted to the data link layer protocol to use, since Ethernet hadn't won yet).

> **NOTE** We've done the legwork of finding the right library to parse these raw data files, but for other formats you've never heard of, you'll have to find a parser yourself. We recommend taking the time to do so! The Python ecosystem has parsers for just about every file format under the sun, and your time is almost certainly better spent working on the novel parts of your project than writing parsers for esoteric data formats.

Happily, LUNA has converted the data we're going to be using for this chapter into the MetaIO format, which is quite a bit easier to use. Don't worry if you've never heard of the format before! We can treat the format of the data files as a black box and use an open source SimpleITK library to load them into more familiar NumPy arrays:

```
class Ct:
  def __init__(self, series_uid):
    import SimpleITK as sitk
      mhd_path = glob.glob(
          f'{mhd_data_folder}/{series_uid}.mhd'
      )[0]

    ct_mhd = sitk.ReadImage(mhd_path)
    ct_a = np.array(sitk.GetArrayFromImage(ct_mhd), dtype=np.float32)
```

> We don't care to track which subset a given series_uid is in, so we wildcard the subset.
>
> sitk.ReadImage implicitly consumes the .raw file in addition to the passed-in .mhd file.
>
> Re-creates an np.array since we want to convert the value type to np.float32.

For real projects, you'll want to understand what types of information are contained in your raw data, but it's perfectly fine to rely on third-party code like SimpleITK to parse the bits on disk. Finding the right balance of knowing everything about your inputs versus blindly accepting whatever your data-loading library hands you will probably take some experience. Just remember that we're mostly concerned about *data*, not *bits*. It's the information that matters, not how it's represented.

Being able to uniquely identify a given sample of our data can be useful. For example, clearly communicating which sample is causing a problem or is getting poor classification results can drastically improve our ability to isolate and debug the issue. Depending on the nature of our samples, sometimes that unique identifier is a number or a string, and sometimes it's more complicated, like a tuple.

We identify specific CT scans using the *series instance UID* (series_uid) assigned when the CT scan was created. DICOM makes heavy use of unique identifiers (UIDs) for individual DICOM files, groups of files, courses of treatment, and so on. These identifiers are similar in concept to UUIDs (https://docs.python.org/3/library/uuid.html), but they have a different creation process and are formatted differently. For our purposes, we can treat them as opaque ASCII strings that serve as unique keys to reference the various CT scans. Officially, only the characters 0 through 9 and the period (.) are valid characters in a DICOM UID.

The 10 subsets we discussed earlier have about 90 CT scans each (888 in total), with every CT scan represented as two files: one with a .mhd extension and one with a .raw extension. The data being split between multiple files is hidden behind the sitk routines, however, and is not something we need to be directly concerned with.

At this point, ct_a is a three-dimensional array. All three dimensions are spatial. There is only a single intensity channel, like a grayscale image, so this dimension is omitted from the array.

12.3.1 Hounsfield Units

Recall that earlier, we said that we need to understand our *data*, not the *bits* that store it. Here, we have a perfect example of that in action. Without understanding the nuances of our data's values and range, we'll end up feeding values into our model that will hinder its ability to learn what we want it to.

Continuing under the Ct class `__init__` method, we need to do a bit of cleanup on the ct_a values. CT scan voxels are expressed in Hounsfield units (HU), which are odd units; air is –1,000 HU (close enough to 0 g/cc [grams per cubic centimeter] for our purposes), water is 0 HU (1 g/cc), and bone is at least +1,000 HU (2–3 g/cc).

Some CT scanners use HU values that correspond to negative densities to indicate that those voxels are outside of the CT scanner's field of view. For our purposes, everything outside of the patient should be air, so we discard that field-of-view information by setting a lower bound of the values to –1,000 HU. Similarly, the exact densities of bones, metal implants, and so on are not relevant to our use case, so we cap density at roughly 2 g/cc (1,000 HU), even though that's not biologically accurate in most cases:

```
ct_a.clip(-1000, 1000, ct_a)
```

Values above 0 HU don't scale perfectly with density, but the tumors we're interested in are typically around 1 g/cc (0 HU), so we're going to ignore that HU doesn't map perfectly to common units like grams per cubic centimeter. That's fine, since our model will be trained to consume HU directly.

We want to remove all these outlier values from our data: they aren't directly relevant to our goal, and having those outliers can make the model's job harder. This can happen in many ways, but a common example is when batch normalization (discussed in chapter 8) is fed these outlier values and the statistics about how to best normalize the data are skewed. Always be on the lookout for ways to clean your data.

All the values we've built are now assigned to self:

```
self.series_uid = series_uid
self.hu_a = ct_a
```

It's important to know that our data uses the range of –1,000 to +1,000. If we don't account for the disparity between HU and our additional data, those new channels can easily be overshadowed by the raw HU values. Sometimes, domain-specific knowledge is required to build a good model, understanding what Hounsfield units are and how they relate to the density of the material being scanned is a good illustration of this.

12.4 Locating a nodule using the patient coordinate system

Deep learning models typically need fixed-size inputs (there are exceptions, but they're not relevant right now) due to having a fixed number of input neurons. We need to be able to produce a fixed-size array containing the candidate so that we can use it as input to our classifier. We'd like to train our model using a crop of the CT scan that has a candidate nicely centered, since then our model doesn't have to learn how to notice nodules tucked away in the corner of the input. By reducing the variation in expected inputs, we make the model's job easier.

12.4.1 The patient coordinate system

Unfortunately, all the candidate center data we loaded in section 12.2 is expressed in millimeters, not voxels! We can't just plug locations in millimeters into an array index and expect everything to work out the way we want. As we can see in figure 12.5, we need to transform our coordinates from the millimeter-based coordinate system (X,Y,Z) they're currently expressed in to the voxel-address-based coordinate system (I,R,C) used to take array slices from our CT scan data. This is a classic example of how it's important to handle units consistently!

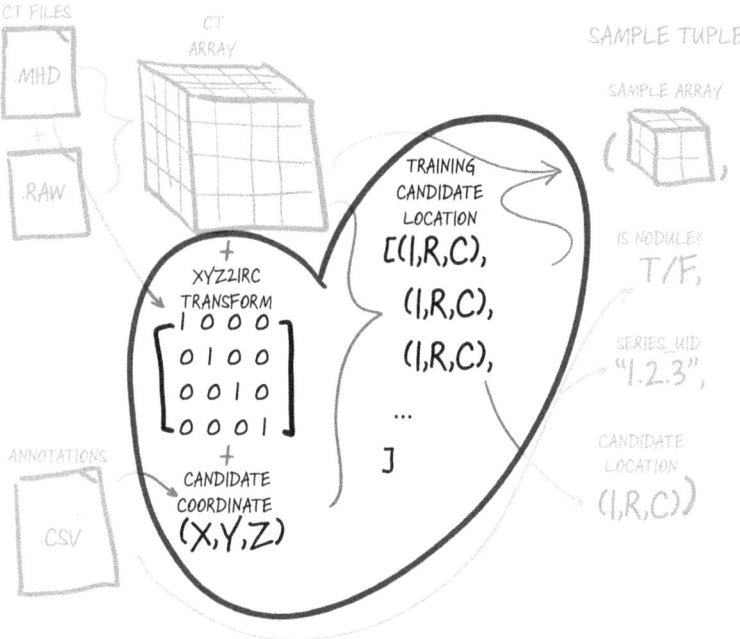

Figure 12.5 Using the transformation information to convert a nodule center coordinate in candidate coordinates (X,Y,Z) to an array index (I,R,C)

As we have mentioned previously, when dealing with CT scans, we refer to the array dimensions as *index*, *row*, and *column* because a separate meaning exists for X, Y, and Z, as illustrated in figure 12.6. The *patient coordinate system* defines positive X to be patient-left (*left*), positive Y to be patient-behind (*posterior*), and positive Z to be toward-patient-head (*superior*). Left-posterior-superior is sometimes abbreviated *LPS*.

The patient coordinate system is measured in millimeters and has an arbitrarily positioned origin that does not correspond to the origin of the CT voxel array, as shown in figure 12.7.

The patient coordinate system is often used to specify the locations of interesting anatomy in a way that is independent of any particular scan. The metadata that defines

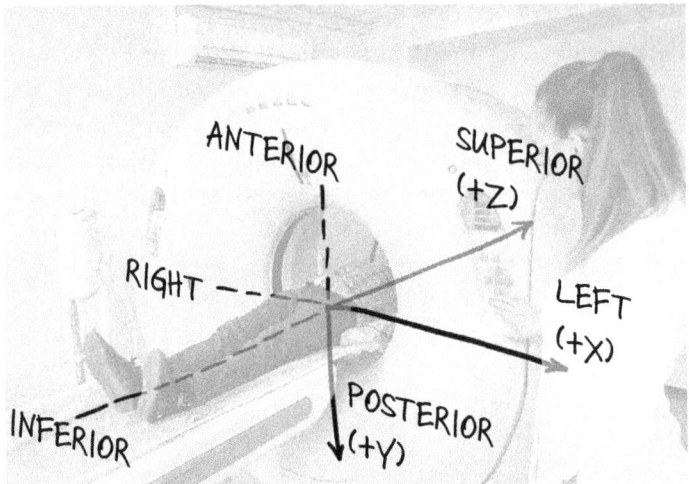

Figure 12.6 Our inappropriately clothed patient demonstrating the axes of the patient coordinate system

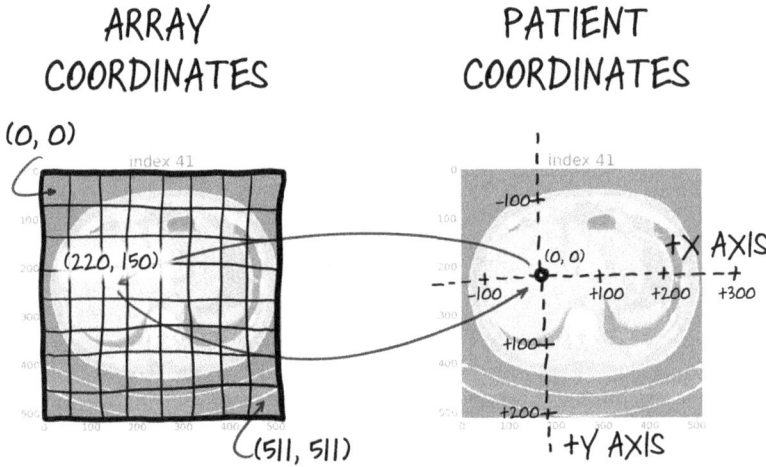

Figure 12.7 Array coordinates (left) and patient coordinates (right) have different origins and scaling.

the relationship between the CT array and the patient coordinate system is stored in the header of DICOM files, and that meta-image format preserves the data in its header as well. This metadata allows us to construct the transformation from (X,Y,Z) to (I,R,C) that we saw in figure 12.5.

12.4.2 CT scan shape and voxel sizes

One of the most common variations between CT scans is the size of the voxels; typically, they are not cubes. Instead, they can be 1.125 mm × 1.125 mm × 2.5 mm or similar. Usually, the row and column dimensions have voxel sizes that are the same, and the index dimension has a larger value, but other ratios can exist.

When plotted using square pixels, the noncubic voxels can end up looking somewhat distorted, similar to the distortion near the north and south poles when using a Mercator projection (https://mng.bz/pZqE) map. That's an imperfect analogy, since in this case the distortion is uniform and linear—the patient looks far more squat or barrel-chested in figure 12.8 than they would in reality. We will need to apply a scaling factor if we want the images to depict realistic proportions.

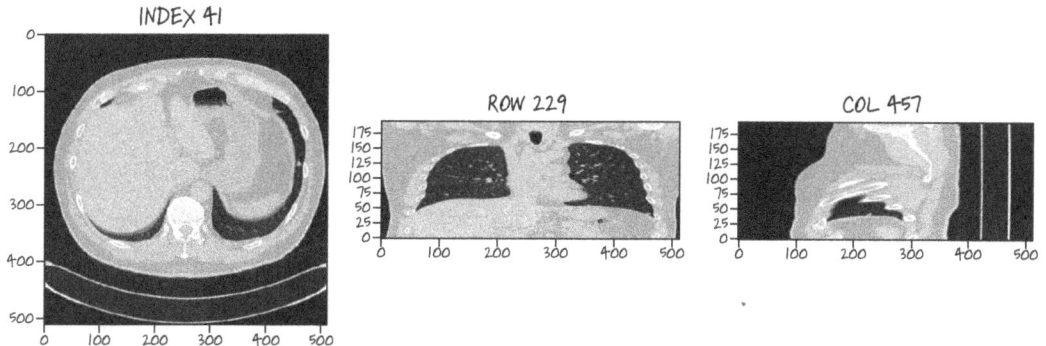

Figure 12.8 A CT scan with noncubic voxels along the index axis. Note how compressed the lungs are from top to bottom.

Knowing these kinds of details can help when trying to interpret our results visually. Without this information, it would be easy to assume that something was wrong with our data loading; we might think the data looked so squat because we were skipping half of the slices by accident, or something along those lines. It can be easy to waste a lot of time debugging something that's been working all along, and being familiar with your data can help prevent that.

CTs are commonly 512 rows by 512 columns, with the index dimension ranging from around 100 total slices up to perhaps 250 slices (250 slices times 2.5 millimeters is typically enough to contain the anatomical region of interest). Each CT specifies the voxel size in millimeters as part of the file metadata.

12.4.3 Converting between millimeters and voxel addresses

We will define some utility code to assist with the conversion between patient coordinates in millimeters (which we will denote in the code with an _xyz suffix on variables and the like) and (I,R,C) array coordinates (which we will denote in code with an _irc suffix).

You might wonder whether the SimpleITK library comes with utility functions to convert these. And indeed, an Image instance does feature two methods—TransformIndexToPhysicalPoint and TransformPhysicalPointToIndex—to do just that (except shuffling from CRI [column,row,index] to IRC). However, we want to be able to do this computation without keeping the Image object around, so we'll perform the math manually here.

Flipping the axes (and potentially a rotation or other transforms) is encoded in a 3 × 3 matrix returned as a tuple from ct_mhd.GetDirections(). To go from voxel indices to coordinates, we need to follow these four steps in order:

1. Flip the coordinates from IRC to CRI to align with XYZ.
2. Scale the indices with the voxel sizes.
3. Matrix-multiply with the directions matrix, using @ in Python.
4. Add the offset for the origin.

To go back from XYZ to IRC, we need to perform the inverse of each step in the reverse order.

We keep the voxel sizes in named tuples, so we convert these into arrays.

Listing 12.2 Converting between patient coordinates (XYZ) and array indices (IRC) (utils.py)

```
IrcTuple = collections.namedtuple('IrcTuple', ['index', 'row', 'col'])
XyzTuple = collections.namedtuple('XyzTuple', ['x', 'y', 'z'])

def irc2xyz(coord_irc, origin_xyz, vxSize_xyz, direction_a):
    cri_a = np.array(coord_irc)[::-1]         ◁── Swaps the order while we convert to a NumPy array
    origin_a = np.array(origin_xyz)
    vxSize_a = np.array(vxSize_xyz)
    coords_xyz = (direction_a @ (cri_a * vxSize_a)) + origin_a   ◁── The bottom three steps of our plan, all in one line
    return XyzTuple(*coords_xyz)

def xyz2irc(coord_xyz, origin_xyz, vxSize_xyz, direction_a):
    origin_a = np.array(origin_xyz)
    vxSize_a = np.array(vxSize_xyz)
    coord_a = np.array(coord_xyz)
    cri_a = ((coord_a - origin_a) @ np.linalg.inv(direction_a)) / vxSize_a   ◁── Inverse of the last three steps
    cri_a = np.round(cri_a)                              ◁── Sneaks in proper rounding before converting to integers
    return IrcTuple(int(cri_a[2]), int(cri_a[1]), int(cri_a[0]))   ◁── Shuffles and converts to integers
```

Phew. If that was a bit heavy, don't worry. Just remember that we need to convert and use the functions as a black box. The metadata we need to convert from patient coordinates (_xyz) to array coordinates (_irc) is contained in the MetaIO file alongside the CT data itself. We pull the voxel sizing and positioning metadata out of the .mhd file at the same time we get the ct_a:

12.4 Locating a nodule using the patient coordinate system

```
class Ct:
  def __init__(self, series_uid):
    import SimpleITK as sitk
    mhd_path = glob.glob(
        f'{mhd_data_folder}/{series_uid}.mhd'
    )[0]

    ct_mhd = sitk.ReadImage(mhd_path)
    # ...
    self.origin_xyz = XyzTuple(*ct_mhd.GetOrigin())
    self.vxSize_xyz = XyzTuple(*ct_mhd.GetSpacing())
    self.direction_a = np.array(ct_mhd.GetDirection()).reshape(3, 3)
```

Converts the directions to an array and reshapes the nine-element array to its proper 3 × 3 matrix shape

These are the inputs we need to pass into our xyz2irc conversion function, in addition to the individual point to convert. With these attributes, our CT object implementation now has all the data needed to convert a candidate center from patient coordinates to array coordinates.

12.4.4 Extracting a nodule from a CT scan

As we mentioned in chapter 11, up to 99.9999% of the voxels in a CT scan of a patient with a lung nodule won't be part of the actual nodule (or cancer, for that matter). Again, that ratio is equivalent to a two-pixel blob of incorrectly tinted color somewhere on a high-definition television or a single misspelled word out of a shelf of novels. Forcing our model to examine such huge swaths of data for the hints of the nodules we want it to focus on is going to work about as well as asking you to find a single misspelled word from a set of novels written in a language you don't know! Have you found a misspelled word in this book yet? ;)

Instead, as we can see in figure 12.9, we will extract an area around each candidate and let the model focus on one candidate at a time. This is akin to letting you read individual paragraphs in that foreign language, which is still not an easy task, but far less daunting! Looking for ways to reduce the scope of the problem for our model can help, especially in the early stages of a project when we're trying to get our first working implementation up and running.

The getRawCandidate function takes the center expressed in the patient coordinate system (X,Y,Z), just as it's specified in the LUNA CSV data, as well as a width in voxels. It returns a cubic chunk of CT, and the center of the candidate is converted to array coordinates:

```
def getRawCandidate(self, center_xyz, width_irc):
  center_irc = xyz2irc(
    center_xyz,
    self.origin_xyz,
    self.vxSize_xyz,
    self.direction_a,
  )

  slice_list = []
  for axis, center_val in enumerate(center_irc):
```

```
    start_ndx = int(round(center_val - width_irc[axis]/2))
    end_ndx = int(start_ndx + width_irc[axis])
    slice_list.append(slice(start_ndx, end_ndx))

ct_chunk = self.hu_a[tuple(slice_list)]

return ct_chunk, center_irc
```

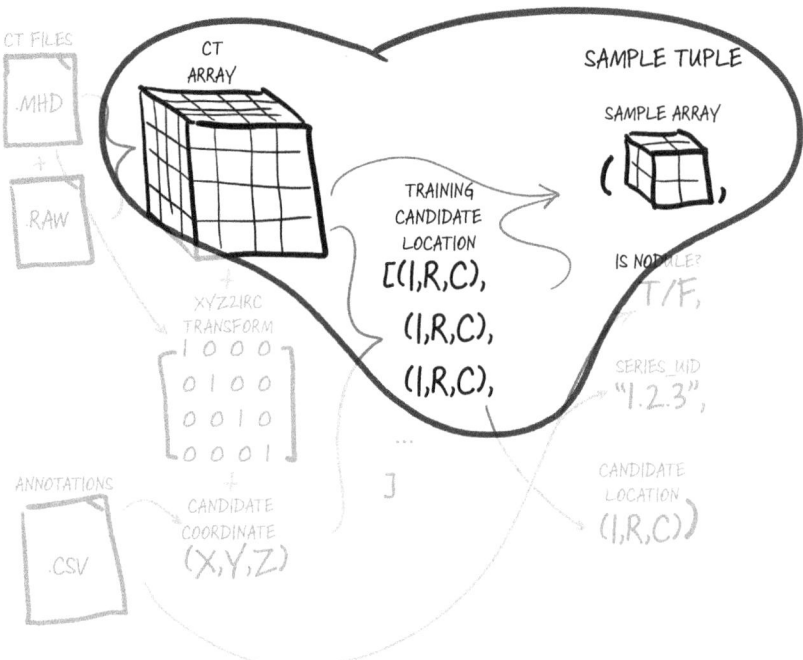

Figure 12.9 Cropping a candidate sample out of the larger CT voxel array using the candidate center's array coordinate information (I,R,C)

The actual implementation will need to deal with situations where the combination of center and width puts the edges of the cropped areas outside of the array. But as noted earlier, we will skip complications that obscure the larger intent of the function.

12.5 Straightforward dataset implementation

We first saw PyTorch Dataset instances in chapter 7, but this will be the first time we've implemented one ourselves. By subclassing Dataset, we will take our arbitrary data and plug it into the rest of the PyTorch ecosystem. Each Ct instance represents hundreds of different samples that we can use to train our model or validate its effectiveness.

Our LunaDataset class will normalize those samples, flattening each CT's nodules into a single collection from which samples can be retrieved without regard for which Ct instance the sample originates from. This flattening is often how we want to process data, though we'll soon see that a simple flattening isn't always enough when class imbalance or other sampling constraints matter.

In terms of implementation, we are going to start with the requirements imposed from subclassing Dataset and work backward. This is different from the datasets we worked with earlier; there, we were using classes provided by external libraries, whereas here we need to implement and instantiate the class ourselves. Once we have done so, we can use it similarly to those earlier examples. Luckily, the implementation of our custom subclass will not be too difficult, as the PyTorch API only requires that any Dataset subclasses we want to implement must provide these two functions:

- An implementation of __len__ that must return a single, constant value representing the length of the dataset (the value ends up being cached in some use cases)
- The __getitem__ method, which takes an index and returns a tuple with sample data to be used for training (or validation, as the case may be)

First, let's see what the function signatures and return values of those functions look like:

```
def __len__(self):
  return len(self.candidateInfo_list)

def __getitem__(self, ndx):
  # ... line 200
  return (
    candidate_t,
    pos_t,
    candidateInfo_tup.series_uid,     ⟵ This is our
    torch.tensor(center_irc),          training sample.
  )
```

Our __len__ implementation is straightforward: we have a list of candidates, each candidate is a sample, and our dataset is as large as the number of samples we have. We don't have to make the implementation as simple as it is here; in later chapters, we'll see this change to something simpler, actually, but the point is, we have options. The only rule is that if __len__ returns a value of N, then __getitem__ needs to return something valid for all inputs 0 to $N-1$.

For __getitem__, we take ndx (typically an integer, given the rule about supporting inputs 0 to $N-1$) and returns a four-item sample tuple as depicted in figure 12.2. This four-item tuple is specific to the dataset we are building, but it will be different for other problems. Building this tuple is a bit more complicated than getting the length of our dataset, however, so let's take a look.

The first part of this method implies that we need to construct self.candidate-Info_list as well as provide the getCtRawNodule function (we will get to those in a moment in sections 12.5.1 and 12.5.2):

```
def __getitem__(self, ndx):
  candidateInfo_tup = self.candidateInfo_list[ndx]
  width_irc = (32, 48, 48)
```

```
candidate_a, center_irc = getCtRawCandidate(     ◁── The return value
    candidateInfo_tup.series_uid,                    candidate_a has shape
    candidateInfo_tup.center_xyz,                    (32,48,48); the axes are
    width_irc,                                       depth, height, and width.
)
```

The next thing we need to do in the `__getitem__` method is to manipulate the data into the proper data types and required array dimensions that will be expected by the downstream code:

```
candidate_t = torch.from_numpy(candidate_a)          │ .unsqueeze(0)
candidate_t = candidate_t.to(torch.float32)          │ adds the Channel
candidate_t = candidate_t.unsqueeze(0)            ◁──┘ dimension.
```

Don't worry too much about exactly why we are manipulating dimensionality for now; the next chapter will contain the code that ends up consuming this output and imposing the constraints we're proactively meeting here. This *will* be something you should expect for every custom `Dataset` you implement. These conversions are a key part of transforming your Wild West data into nice, orderly tensors.

Finally, we need to build our classification tensor:

```
pos_t = torch.tensor([
    not candidateInfo_tup.isNodule_bool,
    candidateInfo_tup.isNodule_bool
  ],
  dtype=torch.long,
)
```

This has two elements, one each for our possible candidate classes (nodule or non-nodule, respectively). We could have a single output for the nodule status (positive or negative), but we are considering these as two classes and `nn.CrossEntropyLoss` expects one output value per class, so that's what we provide here. The exact details of the tensors you construct will change based on the type of project you're working on.

Let's take a look at our final sample tuple (the larger `nodule_t` output isn't particularly readable, so we elide most of it in the listing).

> **Listing 12.3 Inspecting training sample from LunaDataset (p2ch12_explore_data.ipynb)**

```
# In[10]:                                         candidate_t (tensor of
LunaDataset()[0]                                  shape [1, 32, 48, 48] for
                                                  the CT scan data in HU)
# Out[10]:
(tensor([[[[-899., -903., -825., ..., -901., -898., -893.],
           ...,
           [ -92.,  -63.,    4., ...,   63.,   70.,   52.]]]]),
 tensor([0, 1]),                               ◁──┐ pos_t (nodule class,
                                                    non-nodule class)
```

```
'1.3.6...287966244644280690737019247886',
tensor([ 91, 360, 341]))
```
⟵ candidate_tup.series_uid (truncated unique id for the candidate)

⟵ center_irc (center of the candidate in IRC format)

Here we see the four items from our __getitem__ return statement.

12.5.1 Caching candidate arrays with the getCtRawCandidate function

To get decent performance out of LunaDataset, we'll need to invest in some on-disk caching. This will allow us to avoid having to read an entire CT scan from disk for every sample. Doing so would be prohibitively slow! Make sure you're paying attention to bottlenecks in your project and doing what you can to optimize them once they start slowing you down. We're kind of jumping the gun here since we haven't demonstrated that we need caching here. Without caching, the LunaDataset is easily 50 times slower! We'll revisit this in the chapter's exercises.

The function itself is easy. It's a file-cache-backed (https://pypi.python.org/pypi/diskcache) wrapper around the Ct.getRawCandidate method we saw earlier:

```
@functools.lru_cache(1, typed=True)
def getCt(series_uid):
  return Ct(series_uid)

@raw_cache.memoize(typed=True)
def getCtRawCandidate(series_uid, center_xyz, width_irc):
  ct = getCt(series_uid)
  ct_chunk, center_irc = ct.getRawCandidate(center_xyz, width_irc)
  return ct_chunk, center_irc
```

We use a few different caching methods here. First, we're caching the getCt return value in memory so that we can repeatedly ask for the same Ct instance without having to reload all the data from disk. That's a huge speed increase in the case of repeated requests, but we're only keeping one CT in memory, so cache misses will be frequent if we're not careful about the access order.

The getCtRawCandidate function that calls getCt *also* has its outputs cached, so after our cache is populated, getCt won't ever be called. These values are cached to disk using the Python library diskcache. We'll discuss why we have this specific caching setup in chapter 13. For now, it's enough to know that it's much, much faster to read in 2^{15} float32 values from disk than it is to read in 2^{25} int16 values, convert to float32, and then select a 2^{15} length subset. From the second pass through the data forward, I/O times for input should drop to insignificance.

> **NOTE** If the definitions of these functions ever materially change, we will need to remove the cached values from disk. If we don't, the cache will continue to return them, even if now the function will not map the given inputs to the old output. The data is stored in the data-unversioned/cache directory.

12.5.2 Constructing our dataset in LunaDataset.__init__

Just about every project will need to separate samples into a training set and a validation set. We are going to do that here by designating every 10th sample, specified by the val_stride parameter, as a member of the validation set. We will also accept an isValSet_bool parameter and use it to determine whether we should keep only the training data, the validation data, or everything:

```
class LunaDataset(Dataset):
  def __init__(self,
      val_stride=0,
      isValSet_bool=None,
      series_uid=None,
  ):
    self.candidateInfo_list = copy.copy(getCandidateInfoList())

    if series_uid:
      self.candidateInfo_list = [
        x for x in self.candidateInfo_list if x.series_uid == series_uid
      ]
```

Copies the return value so the cached copy won't be affected by altering self.candidateInfo_list

If we pass in a truthy series_uid, the instance will only have nodules from that series. This can be useful for visualization or debugging by making it easier to look at, for instance, a single problematic CT scan.

12.5.3 A training/validation split

We allow for the Dataset to partition out 1/Nth of the data into a subset used for validating the model. How we will handle that subset is based on the value of the isValSet_bool argument:

```
if isValSet_bool:
  assert val_stride > 0, val_stride
  self.candidateInfo_list = self.candidateInfo_list[::val_stride]
  assert self.candidateInfo_list
elif val_stride > 0:
  del self.candidateInfo_list[::val_stride]
  assert self.candidateInfo_list
```

Deletes the validation images (every val_stride-th item in the list) from self.candidateInfo_list. We made a copy earlier so that we don't alter the original list.

As a result, we can create two Dataset instances and be confident that there is strict segregation between our training data and our validation data. Of course, this depends on there being a consistent sorted order to self.candidateInfo_list, which we ensure by having a stable sorted order to the candidate info tuples and by the getCandidateInfoList function sorting the list before returning it.

The other caveat regarding the separation of training and validation data is that, depending on the task at hand, we might need to ensure that data from a single patient is only present either in training or in testing but not both. Here, this is not a problem; otherwise, we would have needed to split the list of patients and CT scans before going to the level of nodules.

Let's take a look at the data using p2ch12_explore_data.ipynb:

```
# In[2]:
from p2ch12.dsets import getCandidateInfoList, getCt, LunaDataset
candidateInfo_list = getCandidateInfoList(require_on_disk=False)
positiveInfo_list = [x for x in candidateInfo_list if x[0]]
diameter_list = [x[1] for x in positiveInfo_list]

# In[4]:
for i in range(0, len(diameter_list), 100):
    print('{:4} {:4.1f} mm'.format(i, diameter_list[i]))

# Out[4]:
   0   32.3 mm
 100   17.7 mm
 200   13.0 mm
 300   10.0 mm
 400    8.2 mm
 500    7.0 mm
 600    6.3 mm
 700    5.7 mm
 800    5.1 mm
 900    4.7 mm
1000    4.0 mm
1100    0.0 mm
1200    0.0 mm
1300    0.0 mm
```

We have a few very large candidates, starting at 32 mm, but they rapidly drop off to half that size. The bulk of the candidates are in the 4 to 10 mm range, and several hundred don't have size information at all. This looks as expected; you might recall that we had more actual nodules than we had diameter annotations. Quick sanity checks on your data can be very helpful; catching a problem or mistaken assumption early may save hours of effort!

The larger takeaway is that our training and validation splits should have a few properties to work well:

- Both sets should include examples of all variations of the expected inputs.
- Neither set should have samples that aren't representative of the expected inputs *unless* they have a specific purpose like training the model to be robust to outliers.
- The training set shouldn't offer unfair hints about the validation set that wouldn't be true for real-world data. (Including the same sample or different samples of the same node in both sets is known as a *leak* in the training set.)

12.5.4 Rendering the data

Again, either use p2ch12_explore_data.ipynb directly or start Jupyter Notebook and enter

```
# In[7]:
from p2ch12.vis import findPositiveSamples, showCandidate
positiveSample_list = findPositiveSamples()

# In[8]:
series_uid = positiveSample_list[11][2]
showCandidate(series_uid)
```

> **TIP** For more information about Jupyter's Matplotlib inline magic (their term, not ours!), see http://mng.bz/rrmD.

This produces images akin to those showing CT and nodule slices earlier in this chapter.

If you're interested, we invite you to edit the implementation of the rendering code in p2ch12/vis.py to match your needs and tastes. The rendering code makes heavy use of Matplotlib (https://matplotlib.org), which is too complex a library for us to attempt to cover here.

Remember that rendering your data is not just about getting nifty-looking pictures. The point is to get an intuitive sense of what your inputs look like. Being able to tell at a glance "This problematic sample is very noisy compared to the rest of my data" or "That's odd; this looks pretty normal" can be useful when investigating issues. Effective rendering also helps foster insights like "Perhaps if I modify things like *so*, I can solve the problem I'm having." That level of familiarity will be necessary as you start tackling harder and harder projects.

> **NOTE** Due to the way each subset has been partitioned, combined with the sorting used when constructing LunaDataset.candidateInfo_list, the ordering of the entries in noduleSample_list is highly dependent on which subsets are present at the time the code is executed. Remember this when trying to find a particular sample a second time, especially after decompressing more subsets.

12.6 Conclusion

In chapter 11, we got our heads wrapped around our data. In this chapter, we got *PyTorch's* head wrapped around our data! By transforming our DICOM-via-meta-image raw data into tensors, we've set the stage to start implementing a model and a training loop, which we'll see in the next chapter.

It's important not to underestimate the impact of the design decisions we've already made: the size of our inputs, the structure of our caching, and how we're partitioning our training and validation sets will all make a difference to the success or failure of our overall project. Don't hesitate to revisit these decisions later, especially once you're working on your own projects.

12.7 Exercises

1 Implement a program that iterates through a `LunaDataset` instance and time how long it takes to do so. In the interest of time, it might make sense to have an option to limit the iterations to the first N=1000 samples:
   a How long does it take to run the first time?
   b How long does it take to run the second time?
   c What does clearing the cache do to the run time?
   d What does using the *last* N=1000 samples do to the first/second run time?
2 Change the `LunaDataset` implementation to randomize the sample list during `__init__`. Clear the cache and run the modified version. What does that do to the run time of the first and second runs?
3 Revert the randomization and comment out the `@functools.lru_cache(1, typed=True)` decorator to `getCt`. Clear the cache and run the modified version. How does the run time change now?

Summary

- Often, the code required to parse and load raw data is nontrivial. For this project, we implement a `Ct` class that loads data from disk and provides access to cropped regions around points of interest.
- Caching can be useful if the parsing and loading routines are expensive. Keep in mind that some caching can be done in memory, and some is best performed on disk. Each can have its place in a data-loading pipeline.
- PyTorch `Dataset` subclasses are used to convert data from its native form into tensors suitable to pass into the model. We can use this functionality to integrate our real-world data with PyTorch APIs.
- Subclasses of `Dataset` need to provide implementations for two methods: `__len__` and `__getitem__`. Other helper methods are allowed but not required.
- Splitting our data into a sensible training set and a validation set requires that we make sure no sample is in both sets. We accomplish this here by using a consistent sort order and taking every tenth sample for our validation set.
- Data visualization is important; being able to investigate data visually can provide important clues about errors or problems. We are using Jupyter Notebooks and Matplotlib to render our data.

Training a classification model to detect suspected tumors

This chapter covers

- Using PyTorch `DataLoader`s to load data
- Implementing a model that performs classification on our CT data
- Setting up the basic skeleton for our application
- Adding logging and displaying metrics during training

In the previous chapters, we set the stage for our cancer-detection project. We covered medical details of lung cancer, took a look at the main data sources we will use for our project, and transformed our raw CT scans into a PyTorch `Dataset` instance. Now that we have a dataset, we can easily consume our training data. So, let's do that!

13.1 A foundational model and training loop

We're going to do two main things in this chapter. We'll start by building the nodule classification model and training loop that will be the foundation that the rest of part 2 uses to explore the larger project. To do that, we'll use the `Ct` and `LunaDataset` classes we implemented in chapter 12 to feed `DataLoader` instances. Those instances, in turn, will feed our classification model with data via training and validation loops.

We'll finish the chapter by using the results from running that training loop to introduce one of the hardest challenges in this part of the book: how to get high-quality results from messy, limited data. In later chapters, we'll explore the specific ways in which our data is limited, as well as mitigate those limitations.

Let's recall our high-level roadmap from chapter 11, shown here in figure 13.1. Right now, we'll work on producing a model capable of performing step 3: classification. As a reminder, we will classify candidates as nodules or non-nodules (we'll build another classifier to attempt to tell malignant nodules from benign ones in chapter 14). That means we're going to assign a single, specific label to each sample that we present to the model. In this case, those labels are *nodule* and *non-nodule*, since each sample represents a single candidate.

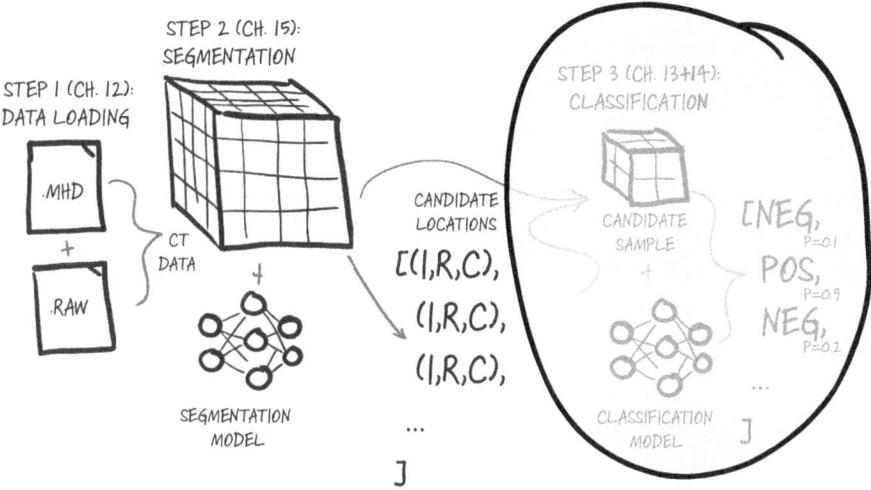

Figure 13.1 Our end-to-end project to detect lung cancer, with a focus on this chapter's topic: step 3, classification

Getting an early end-to-end version of a meaningful part of your project is a great milestone to reach. Having something that works well enough for the results to be evaluated analytically lets you move forward with future changes, confident that you are improving your results with each change—or at least that you're able to set aside any changes and experiments that don't work out! Expect to have to do a lot of experimentation when working on your own projects. Getting the best results will usually require considerable tinkering and tweaking.

But before we can get to the experimental phase, we must lay our foundation. Let's see what our part 2 training loop looks like in figure 13.2; it should seem generally familiar, given that we saw a similar set of core steps in chapter 5. Here, we will also use a validation set to evaluate our training progress, as discussed in section 5.5.3.

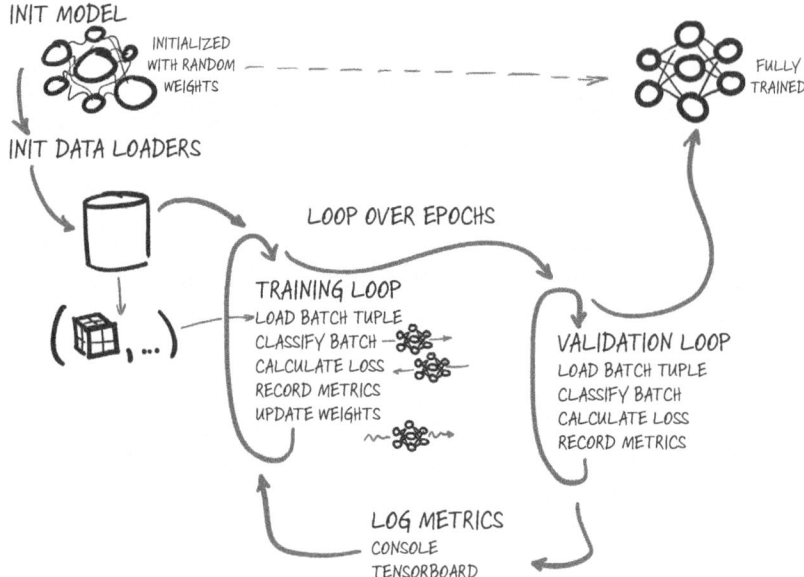

Figure 13.2 The training and validation script we will implement in this chapter

The basic structure of what we're going to implement is as follows:

1 Initialize our model and data loading.
2 Loop over a semi-arbitrarily chosen number of epochs:
   a Loop over each batch of training data returned by LunaDataset:
      i Pass the batch into our classification model to get results.
      ii Calculate our loss based on the difference between our predicted results and our ground-truth data.
      iii Record metrics about our model's performance into a temporary data structure.
      iv Update the model weights via backpropagation of the error.
   b Loop over each batch of validation data (in a manner very similar to the training loop):
      i Load the relevant batch of validation data (again, in the background worker process).
      ii Classify the batch and compute the loss.
      iii Record information about how well the model performed on the validation data.
   c Print out progress and performance information for this epoch.

As we go through the code for the chapter, keep an eye out for two main differences between the code we're producing here and what we used for a training loop in part 1. First, we'll put more structure around our program since the project as a whole is quite a bit more complicated than what we did in earlier chapters. Without that extra structure, the code can get messy quickly. And for this project, we will have our main training application use a number of well-contained functions, and we will further separate code for things like our dataset into self-contained Python modules.

Make sure that for your own projects, you match the level of structure and design to the complexity level of your project. Too little structure, and it will become difficult to perform experiments cleanly, troubleshoot problems, or even describe what you're doing! Conversely, too *much* structure means you're wasting time writing infrastructure that you don't need and most likely slowing yourself down by having to conform to it after all that plumbing is in place. Plus, it can be tempting to spend time on infrastructure as a procrastination tactic, rather than digging into the hard work of making actual progress on your project. Don't fall into that trap!

The other big difference between this chapter's code and our past experimentation is that we will focus on collecting a variety of metrics about how training is progressing. We'll also see how important it is to collect not just metrics, but the *right metrics for the job*. We'll lay the infrastructure for tracking those metrics in this chapter, and we'll exercise that infrastructure by collecting and displaying the loss and percentage of samples correctly classified, both overall and per class. That's enough to get us started, but we'll cover a more realistic set of metrics in chapter 14.

13.2 The main entry point for our application

One of the big structural differences from earlier training work we've done in this book is that part 2 wraps our work in a fully fledged command-line application. It will parse command-line arguments, have a full-featured --help command, and be easy to run in a wide variety of environments. All this will allow us to easily invoke the training routines from both Jupyter and a Bash shell—or any shell, really, but if you're using a non-Bash shell, you already knew that.

Our application's functionality will be implemented via a class so that we can instantiate the application and pass it around if we feel the need. This can make testing, debugging, or invocation from other Python programs easier. We can invoke the application without needing to spin up a second OS-level process. (We won't do explicit unit testing in this book, but the structure we create can be helpful for real projects where that kind of testing is appropriate.)

One way to take advantage of being able to invoke our training by either a function call or an OS-level process is to wrap the function invocations into a Jupyter Notebook so the code can easily be called from either the native CLI or the browser.

Listing 13.1 Helper function to run training scripts from Jupyter (p2_run_everything.ipynb)

```
# In[2]:
def run(app, *argv):
    argv = list(argv)
    argv.insert(0, '--num-workers=4')
    log.info(f"Running: {app}({argv!r}).main()")
```

We assume you have a four-core, eight-thread CPU. Change the 4 if needed.

```
    app_cls = importstr(*app.rsplit('.', 1))
    app_cls(argv).main()                              ◁─── This is a slightly
                                                           cleaner call to
    log.info(f"Finished: {app}.{argv!r}).main()")          __import__.

# In[6]:
run('p2ch13.training.LunaTrainingApp', '--epochs=1')
```

> **NOTE** The training here assumes that you're on a workstation that has a four-core, eight-thread CPU; 16 GB of RAM; and a GPU with 8 GB of RAM. Reduce --batch-size if your GPU has less RAM, and --num-workers if you have fewer CPU cores or less CPU RAM.

Let's get some semistandard boilerplate code out of the way. We'll start at the end of the file with a pretty standard if main stanza that instantiates the application object and invokes the main method.

Listing 13.2 Running the training application from the command line (training.py)

```
if __name__ == '__main__':
    LunaTrainingApp().main()
```

From there, we can jump back to the top of the file and have a look at the application class and the two functions we just called, __init__ and main. We'll want to be able to accept command-line arguments, so we'll use the standard argparse library (https://docs.python.org/3/library/argparse.html) in the application's __init__ function. Note that we can pass in custom arguments to the initializer, should we wish to do so. The main method will be the primary entry point for the core logic of the application:

```
class LunaTrainingApp:
    def __init__(self, sys_argv=None):
        if sys_argv is None:                      ◁─── If the caller doesn't provide
            sys_argv = sys.argv[1:]                    arguments, we get them
                                                       from the command line.
        parser = argparse.ArgumentParser()
        parser.add_argument('--num-workers',
            help='Number of worker processes for background data loading',
            default=8,
            type=int,
        )
        # ... line 63
        self.cli_args = parser.parse_args(sys_argv)
        self.time_str = datetime.datetime.now().strftime(     ◁─── We'll use the
            '%Y-%m-%d_%H.%M.%S')                                   timestamp to help
                                                                   identify training runs.
```

This structure is pretty general and could be reused for future projects. In particular, parsing arguments in __init__ allows us to configure the application separately from invoking it.

We can easily instantiate the application within a notebook for easier testing and experimentation. Our setup enables us to initialize the app directly in a notebook cell, allowing us to later demonstrate the functionality of the methods we define.

Listing 13.3 Running our app with an interactively (sandbox.ipynb)

```
# In[]
import torch
from p2ch13.training import LunaTrainingApp
args = [
    '--num-workers', '1',   # Example: Set number of workers to 1
    '--batch-size', '4',    # Example: Set batch size to 4
    '--epochs', '1',        # Example: Set number of epochs to 1
]
app = LunaTrainingApp(args)
app

# Out[]
2024-11-17 14:29:45,449 INFO     pid:1852 p2ch13.training:085:initModel
sing CUDA; 1 devices.
<p2ch13.training.LunaTrainingApp at 0x27416137700>
```

13.3 Pretraining setup and initialization

Before we can begin iterating over each batch in our epoch, some initialization work needs to happen. After all, we can't train a model if we haven't even instantiated one yet! We need to do two main things, as we can see in figure 13.3. The first, as we just

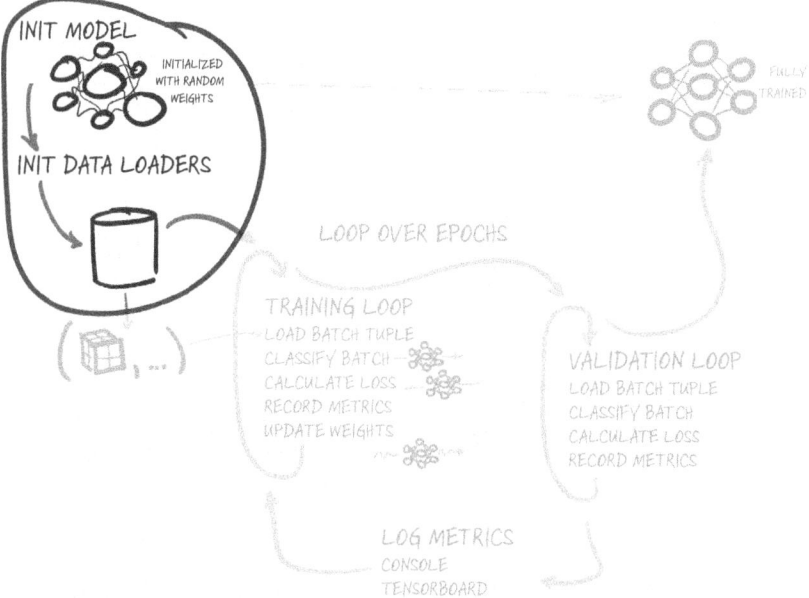

Figure 13.3 The training and validation script we will implement in this chapter, with a focus on the preloop variable initialization

mentioned, is to initialize our model and optimizer, and the second is to initialize our Dataset and DataLoader instances. LunaDataset will define the randomized set of samples that will make up our training epoch, and our DataLoader instance will perform the work of loading the data out of our dataset and providing it to our application.

13.3.1 Initializing the model and optimizer

For this section, we are treating the details of LunaModel as a black box. In section 13.4, we will detail the internal workings. Let's see what our starting point looks like.

Listing 13.4 LunaTrainingApp class initialization

```
class LunaTrainingApp:
  def __init__(self, sys_argv=None):
    # ... line 70
    self.use_cuda = torch.cuda.is_available()
    self.device = torch.device("cuda" if self.use_cuda else "cpu")

    self.model = self.initModel()
    self.optimizer = self.initOptimizer()

  def initModel(self):
    model = LunaModel()
    if self.use_cuda:
      log.info(f"Using CUDA; {torch.cuda.device_count()} devices.")
      if torch.cuda.device_count() > 1:       ◁── Detects multiple GPUs
        model = nn.DataParallel(model)        ◁── Wraps the model to accelerate
      model = model.to(self.device)           ◁──   training across multiple GPUs
    return model                              ◁── Sends model parameters to the GPU

  def initOptimizer(self):
    return SGD(self.model.parameters(), lr=0.001, momentum=0.99)
```

If the system used for training has more than one GPU, we will use the nn.DataParallel class to distribute the work between all the GPUs in the system and then collect and resync parameter updates and so on. This is almost entirely transparent in terms of both the model implementation and the code that uses that model.

> **DataParallel vs. DistributedDataParallel**
>
> We are using DataParallel to handle utilizing multiple GPUs. We chose DataParallel because it's a simple drop-in wrapper around our existing models. It is not the best-performing solution for using multiple GPUs, however, and it is limited to working with the hardware available on a single machine.
>
> PyTorch also provides DistributedDataParallel, which is the recommended wrapper class to use when you need to spread work between more than one GPU or machine. This involves the proper setup and configuration, which are nontrivial. We will cover this API in the distributed training chapter of the book (chapter 16).

Assuming that self.use_cuda is true, the call self.model.to(device) moves the model parameters to the GPU, setting up the various convolutions and other calculations to use the GPU for the heavy numerical lifting. It's important to do so before constructing the optimizer because, otherwise, the optimizer would be left looking at the CPU-based parameter objects rather than those copied to the GPU.

For our optimizer, we'll use basic stochastic gradient descent (https://mng.bz/7Q27) with momentum. Using SGD is generally considered a safe place to start when it comes to picking an optimizer; there are some problems that might not work well with SGD, but they're relatively rare. Similarly, a learning rate of 0.001 and a momentum of 0.99 are standard choices. Empirically, SGD with those values has worked reasonably well for a wide range of projects, and it's easy to try a learning rate of 0.01 or 0.0001 if things aren't working well right out of the box.

That's not to say any of those values are the best for our use case, but trying to find better ones is getting ahead of ourselves. Systematically trying different values for learning rate, momentum, network size, and other similar configuration settings is called a *hyperparameter search*. There are other, more glaring issues we need to address first in the coming chapters. Once we address those, we can begin to fine-tune these values. As we mentioned in the section Testing Other Optimizers in chapter 5, there are also other, more exotic optimizers we might choose. However, other than perhaps swapping torch.optim.SGD for torch.optim.Adam, understanding the trade-offs involved is a topic too advanced for this book.

13.3.2 Care and feeding of data loaders

The LunaDataset class that we built in the last chapter acts as the bridge between whatever Wild West data we have and the somewhat more structured world of tensors that the PyTorch building blocks expect. For example, torch.nn.Conv3d (https://mng.bz/mZWW) expects five-dimensional input: (N, C, D, H, W)—the number of samples, channels per sample, depth, height, and width, respectively. Quite different from the native 3D our CT originally provided!

You may recall the ct_t.unsqueeze(0) call in LunaDataset.__getitem__ from the last chapter; it provides the fourth dimension, a "channel" for our data. Recall from chapter 4 that an RGB image has three channels, one each for red, green, and blue. Astronomical data could have dozens, one each for various slices of the electromagnetic spectrum—gamma rays, X-rays, ultraviolet light, visible light, infrared, microwaves, and/or radio waves. Since CT scans are single-intensity, our channel dimension is only size 1.

Also, recall from part 1 that training on single samples at a time is typically an inefficient use of computing resources because most processing platforms are capable of more parallel calculations than are required by a model to process a single training or validation sample. The solution is to group sample tuples together into a batch tuple, as in figure 13.4, allowing multiple samples to be processed at the same time. The fifth dimension (N) differentiates multiple samples in the same batch.

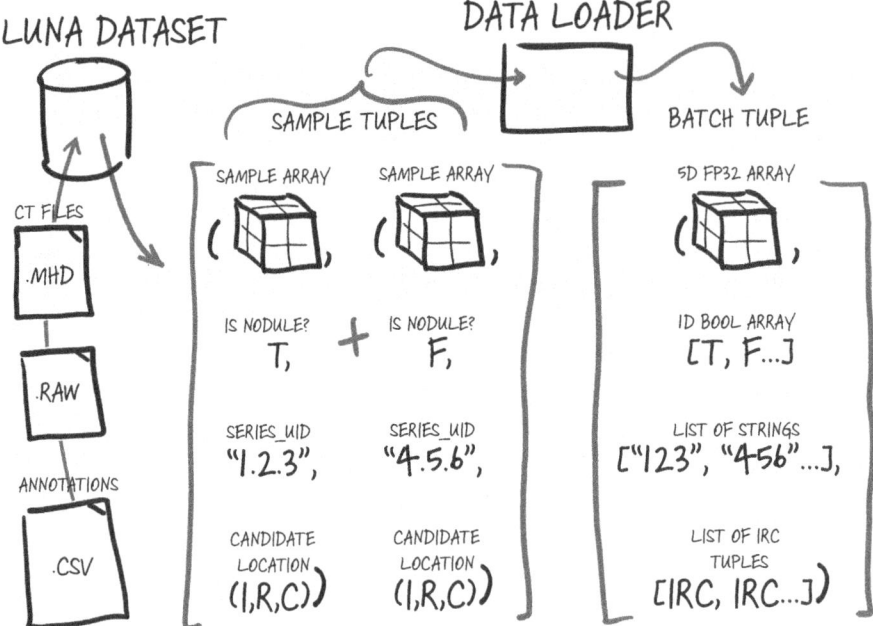

Figure 13.4 Sample tuples being collated into a single batch tuple inside a data loader

Conveniently, we don't have to implement any of this batching; the PyTorch Data-Loader class will handle all the collation work for us. We've already built the bridge from the CT scans to PyTorch tensors with our LunaDataset class, so all that remains to do is to plug our dataset into a data loader:

```
def initTrainDl(self):
  train_ds = LunaDataset(              ◁──── Our custom dataset
    val_stride=10,
    isValSet_bool=False,
  )

  batch_size = self.cli_args.batch_size
  if self.use_cuda:
    batch_size *= torch.cuda.device_count()

  train_dl = DataLoader(               ◁──── A utility class for loading
    train_ds,                                and processing data,
    batch_size=batch_size,                   provided by PyTorch
    num_workers=self.cli_args.num_workers,  ◁──── Batching is done automatically
    pin_memory=self.use_cuda,                     through this argument.
  )                                    ◁──── Pinned memory transfers
                                              data from CPU to GPU
  return train_dl                             more quickly.

# In[]
train_dl = app.initTrainDl()
val_dl = app.initValDl()             ◁──── The validation data loader is
                                            very similar to training.
```

```
data_sample = next(iter(train_dl))
print(data_sample[0].shape)
print(data_sample[1:])
```
❮— The first tensor in the batch is the input data.
Recall the format is (batch_size, number of
channels, depth, height, width).

Remaining 3 items in the batch are the labels,
series_uids, and center coordinates.

```
# Out[]
2024-11-17 14:42:27,055 INFO     pid:1852 p2ch13.dsets:182:__init__ <
↪p2ch13.dsets.LunaDataset object at 0x000002741C890F10>:
↪495958 training samples
2024-11-17 14:42:27,109 INFO     pid:1852 p2ch13.dsets:182:__init__ <
↪p2ch13.dsets.LunaDataset object at 0x00000274161377F0>:
↪55107 validation samples
torch.Size([2, 1, 32, 48, 48])
[tensor([[1, 0],
        [1, 0]]), ['1.3.6.1.4.1.14519.5.2.1.6279.6001.18305615178056746032
↪2586876100', '1.3.6.1.4.1.14519.5.2.1.6279.6001.76545923655035
↪8748053283544075'], tensor([[222, 244,  70],
        [115, 203, 190]])]
```

In addition to batching individual samples, data loaders can also provide parallel loading of data by using separate processes and shared memory. All we need to do is specify num_workers=… when instantiating the data loader, and the rest is taken care of behind the scenes. Each worker process produces complete batches as in figure 13.4. This helps make sure hungry GPUs are well-fed with data. Our validation_ds and validation_dl instances look similar, except for the obvious isValSet_bool=True.

When we iterate, like for batch_tup in self.train_dl:, we won't have to wait for each Ct to be loaded, samples to be taken and batched, and so on. Instead, we'll get the already-loaded batch_tup immediately, and a worker process will be freed up in the background to begin loading another batch to use on a later iteration. Using the data-loading features of PyTorch can help speed up most projects because we can overlap data loading and processing with GPU calculation.

13.4 Our first-pass neural network design

The possible design space for a convolutional neural network capable of detecting tumors is effectively infinite. Luckily, considerable effort has been spent over the past decade or so investigating effective models for image recognition. While these have largely focused on 2D images, the general architecture ideas transfer well to 3D, so there are many tested designs that we can use as a starting point. This helps because although our first network architecture is unlikely to be our best option, right now we are only aiming for "good enough to get us going."

We will base the network design on what we used in chapter 8. We will have to update the model somewhat because our input data is 3D, and we will add some complicating details, but the overall structure shown in figure 13.5 should feel familiar. Similarly, the work we do for this project will be a good base for your future projects, although the further you get from classification or segmentation projects, the more you'll have to adapt this base to fit. Let's dissect this architecture, starting with the four repeated blocks that make up the bulk of the network.

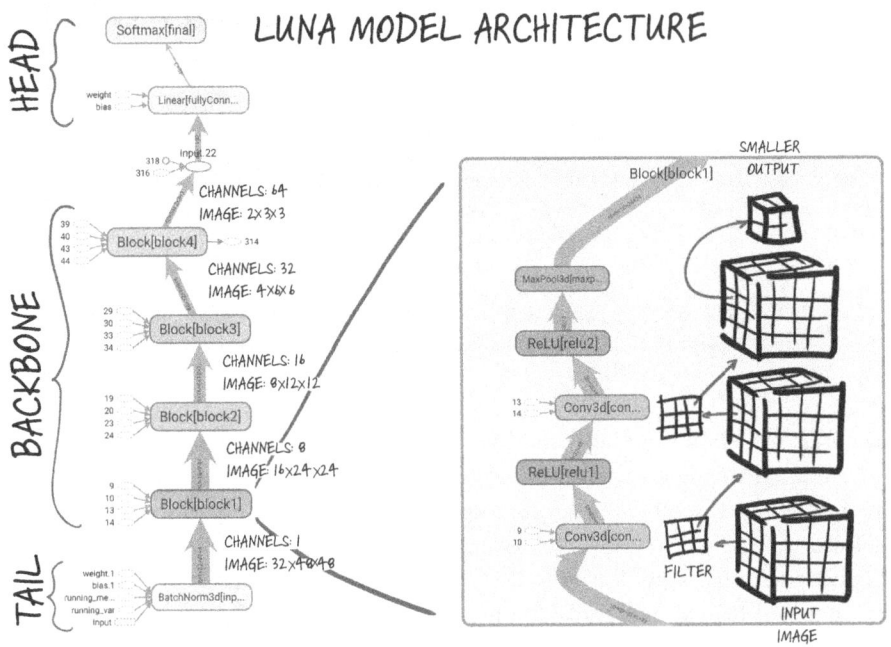

Figure 13.5 The architecture of the `LunaModel` class, consisting of a batch-normalization tail, a four-block backbone, and a head comprised of a linear layer followed by softmax

13.4.1 The core convolutions

Classification models often have a structure that consists of a tail, a backbone (or body), and a head. Unlike the phrase "head to tail," the data flows from tail to head in these models. The *tail* is the first few layers that process the input to the network. These early layers often have a different structure or organization than the rest of the network, as they must adapt the input to the form expected by the backbone. In this case, we utilize a straightforward batch normalization layer. However, it's common for the tail of the network to include convolutional layers as well. These layers are typically employed to reduce the image size while simultaneously learning important features. Since our image size is already compact, additional downsampling is unnecessary here.

Next, the *backbone* of the network typically contains the bulk of the layers, which are usually arranged in a series of *blocks*. Each block has the same (or at least a similar) set of layers, though often the size of the expected input and the number of filters changes from block to block. We will use a block that consists of two 3 × 3 convolutions, each followed by an activation, with a max-pooling operation at the end of the block. We can see this in the expanded view of figure 13.5 labeled Block[block1]. (In the code, these are the LunaBlock class.) These blocks are a design choice by the authors; typically, it is normal to start with an established model architecture for a problem. For the purposes of this book, we are coding these from scratch. The following listing is what the implementation of the block looks like in code.

Listing 13.5 Defining the LunaBlock model (model.py)

```
class LunaBlock(nn.Module):
  def __init__(self, in_channels, conv_channels):
    super().__init__()

    self.conv1 = nn.Conv3d(
      in_channels, conv_channels, kernel_size=3, padding=1, bias=True,
    )
    self.relu1 = nn.ReLU(inplace=True)
    self.conv2 = nn.Conv3d(
      conv_channels, conv_channels, kernel_size=3, padding=1, bias=True,
    )
    self.relu2 = nn.ReLU(inplace=True)

    self.maxpool = nn.MaxPool3d(2, 2)

  def forward(self, input_batch):
    block_out = self.conv1(input_batch)
    block_out = self.relu1(block_out)
    block_out = self.conv2(block_out)
    block_out = self.relu2(block_out)

    return self.maxpool(block_out)
```

Finally, the *head* of the network takes the output from the backbone and converts it into the desired output form. For convolutional networks, this often involves flattening the intermediate output and passing it to a fully connected layer. For some networks, it makes sense to also include a second fully connected layer, although that is usually more appropriate for classification problems in which the imaged objects have more structure (think about cars versus trucks having wheels, lights, a grill, doors, and so on) and for projects with a large number of classes. Since we are only doing binary classification and we don't seem to need the additional complexity, we have only a single flattening layer.

Using a structure like this can be a good first building block for a convolutional network. There are more complicated designs out there, but for many projects, they're overkill in terms of both implementation complexity and computational demands. It's a good idea to start simple and add complexity only when there's a demonstrable need for it.

We can see the convolutions of our block represented in 2D in figure 13.6. Since this illustration is a small portion of a larger image, we omit the padding on the edges of the convolution. (The ReLU activation function is not shown, as applying it does not change the image sizes.)

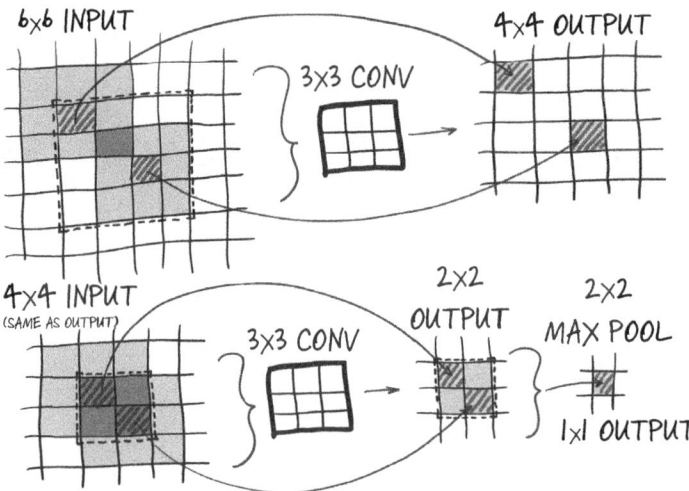

Figure 13.6 The convolutional architecture of a LunaModel block, consisting of two 3 × 3 convolutions followed by a max pool. The final pixel has a receptive field of 6 × 6.

Let's walk through the information flow between our input voxels and a single voxel of output. We want to have a strong sense of how our output will respond when the inputs change. It might be a good idea to review chapter 8, particularly sections 8.1 through 8.3, just to make sure you're 100% solid on the basic mechanics of convolutions.

We're using 3 × 3 × 3 convolutions in our block. A single 3 × 3 × 3 convolution has a receptive field of 3 × 3 × 3. Twenty-seven voxels are fed in, and one comes out.

It gets interesting when we use two 3 × 3 × 3 convolutions stacked back to back. When we stack two 3 × 3 × 3 convolutional layers, the final output voxel (or pixel in the 2D case) can be influenced by input data that extends beyond the immediate 3 × 3 × 3 area. This happens because the output of the first layer becomes the input to the second layer. If an output voxel from the first layer is positioned at the edge of the second layer's 3 × 3 × 3 kernel, it means that some of the initial inputs are outside the direct reach of the second layer's kernel. Together, these layers create an *effective receptive field* of 5 × 5 × 5, acting as a single layer with a larger size. Stacking two 3 × 3 × 3 layers uses fewer parameters than a single 5 × 5 × 5 convolution, making it faster to compute.

We can see this if we go in the backward direction (bottom right to top left) in figure 13.6. (Remember that we're actually working in 3D, despite the 2D figure.) Our 2 × 2 output has a receptive field of 4 × 4, which, in turn, has a receptive field of 6 × 6. For computing receptive fields, each 3 × 3 × 3 convolutional layer adds an additional one-voxel-per-edge border to the receptive field.

The output from our two stacked convolutions is fed into a 2 × 2 × 2 max pool, which reduces the data by selecting the largest value from the 2 x 2 x 2 output. Although some input voxels are discarded, they can still influence the final output because we captured their contributions in the prior convolutions.

Note that while we show the receptive field shrinking with each convolutional layer, we're using *padded* convolutions, which add a virtual one-pixel border around the image. Doing so keeps our input and output image sizes the same.

The nn.ReLU layers are the same as the ones we looked at in chapter 6. Outputs greater than 0.0 will be left unchanged, and outputs less than 0.0 will be clamped to zero.

This block will be repeated multiple times to form our model's backbone.

13.4.2 The full model

Let's take a look at the full model implementation. We'll skip the block definition, since we just saw that in the previous code listing:

```
class LunaModel(nn.Module):
  def __init__(self, in_channels=1, conv_channels=8):
    super().__init__()

    self.tail_batchnorm = nn.BatchNorm3d(1)         # Tail (responsible for initial processing of the input data)

    self.block1 = LunaBlock(in_channels,
      conv_channels)
    self.block2 = LunaBlock(conv_channels,
      * 2)
    self.block3 = LunaBlock(conv_channels * 2,      # Backbone (performs the meat of the work and the main feature extraction)
      conv_channels * 4)
    self.block4 = LunaBlock(conv_channels * 4,
      conv_channels * 8)

    self.head_linear = nn.Linear(1152, 2)           # Head (responsible for producing the final output)
    self.head_softmax = nn.Softmax(dim=1)
```

Here, our tail is relatively simple. We are going to normalize our input using nn.BatchNorm3d, which, as we saw in chapter 8, will shift and scale our input so that it has a mean of 0 and a standard deviation of 1. As a result, the original Hounsfield unit (HU) scale of the input won't be apparent to the rest of the network, as we're working on a different scale.

Our backbone is four repeated blocks, with the block implementation pulled out into the separate nn.Module subclass we saw earlier. Since each block ends with a 2 × 2 × 2 max-pool operation, after four layers, we will have decreased the resolution of the image 16 times in each dimension. Our data is returned in chunks that are 32 × 48 × 48, which will become 2 × 3 × 3 by the end of the backbone.

Finally, our head is just a fully connected layer followed by a call to nn.Softmax. Softmax is a useful function for single-label classification tasks and has a few nice properties: it bounds the output between 0 and 1, it's relatively insensitive to the absolute range of the inputs (only the *relative* values of the inputs matter), and it allows our model to express the degree of certainty it has in an answer.

The function itself is relatively simple. Every value from the input is used to exponentiate e, and the resulting series of values is then divided by the sum of all the results of exponentiation. Here's what it looks like when implemented in a simple fashion as a nonoptimized softmax implementation in pure Python:

```
# In[]
logits = [1, -2, 3]
exp = [math.exp(x) for x in logits]
print(exp)
softmax = [x / sum(exp) for x in exp]
print(softmax)

# Out
[2.718, 0.135, 20.086]
[0.118, 0.006, 0.876]
```

Of course, we use the PyTorch version of nn.Softmax for our model, as it natively understands batches and tensors and will perform autograd quickly and as expected.

COMPLICATION: CONVERTING FROM CONVOLUTION TO LINEAR

Continuing with our model definition, we come to a complication. We can't just feed the output of self.block4 into a fully connected layer, since that output is a per-sample $2 \times 3 \times 3$ image with 64 channels, and fully connected layers expect a 1D vector as input (well, technically they expect a *batch* of 1D vectors, which is a 2D array, but the mismatch remains either way). Let's take a look at the forward method (model.py:50, LunaModel.forward).

Listing 13.6 LunaModel forward pass

```
def forward(self, input_batch):
  bn_output = self.tail_batchnorm(input_batch)

  block_out = self.block1(bn_output)
  block_out = self.block2(block_out)
  block_out = self.block3(block_out)
  block_out = self.block4(block_out)

  conv_flat = block_out.view(          ◁── Keeps the same batch
    block_out.size(0),                       size and flattens
    -1,                                      everything else
  )
  linear_output = self.head_linear(conv_flat)
  return linear_output, self.head_softmax(linear_output)
```

Before we pass data into a fully connected layer, we must flatten it using the view function. Since that operation is stateless (it has no parameters that govern its behavior), we can simply perform the operation in the forward function. This is somewhat similar to the functional interfaces we discussed in chapter 8. Almost every model that uses convolution and produces classifications, regressions, or other non-image outputs will have a similar component in the head of the network.

For the return value of the forward method, we return both the raw *logits* and the softmax-produced probabilities. We first discussed logits in section 7.2.6: they are the numerical values produced by the network prior to being normalized into probabilities by the softmax layer. That might sound a bit complicated, but logits are really just the raw input to the softmax layer. They can have any real-valued input, and the softmax will squash them to the range 0 to 1.

We'll use the logits when we calculate the nn.CrossEntropyLoss during training. (There are numerical stability benefits for doing so. Propagating gradients accurately through an exponential calculated using 32-bit floating-point numbers can be problematic.) We'll use the probabilities for when we want to actually classify the samples. This kind of slight difference between what's used for training and what's used in production is fairly common, especially when the difference between the two outputs is a simple, stateless function like softmax.

INITIALIZATION

Finally, let's talk about initializing our network's parameters. To get well-behaved performance out of our model, the network's weights, biases, and other parameters need to exhibit certain properties. Let's imagine a degenerate case, where all of the network's weights are greater than 1. In that case, repeated multiplication by those weights would result in layer outputs that became very large as data flowed through the layers of the network. Similarly, weights less than 1 would cause all layer outputs to become smaller and vanish. Similar considerations apply to the gradients in the backward pass.

Many normalization techniques can be used to keep layer outputs well behaved, but one of the simplest is to just make sure the network's weights are initialized such that intermediate values and gradients become neither unreasonably small nor unreasonably large. We can treat the following _init_weights function as boilerplate, as the exact details aren't particularly important (model.py:30, LunaModel._init_weights).

Listing 13.7 Kaiming initialization for convolutional and linear layer weights

```
def _init_weights(self):
  for m in self.modules():
    if type(m) in {
        nn.Linear, nn.Conv3d, nn.Conv2d, nn.ConvTranspose2d,
        nn.ConvTranspose3d,
    }:
      nn.init.kaiming_normal_(
          m.weight.data, a=0, mode='fan_out', nonlinearity='relu',
      )
      if m.bias is not None:
        fan_in, fan_out = nn.init._calculate_fan_in_and_fan_out(
            m.weight.data)
        bound = 1 / math.sqrt(fan_out)
        nn.init.normal_(m.bias, -bound, bound)
```

We have completed the setup for our model (sandbox.ipynb). Now we can instantiate it and use it!

> **NOTE** For those interested, see Ye et al.'s paper, "Delving Deep into Rectifiers," which introduced the Kaiming initialization (https://arxiv.org/pdf/1502.01852).

> Listing 13.8 Kaiming initialization for convolutional and linear layer weights

```
# In[]
model = app.model
model

# Out[]
LunaModel(
(tail_batchnorm): BatchNorm3d(1, eps=1e-05, momentum=0.1, affine=True,
➥track_running_stats=True)
(block1): LunaBlock(
...
```

13.5 Training and validating the model

Now it's time to take the various pieces we've been working with and assemble them into something we can actually execute. This training loop should be familiar—we saw loops like figure 13.7 in previous chapters.

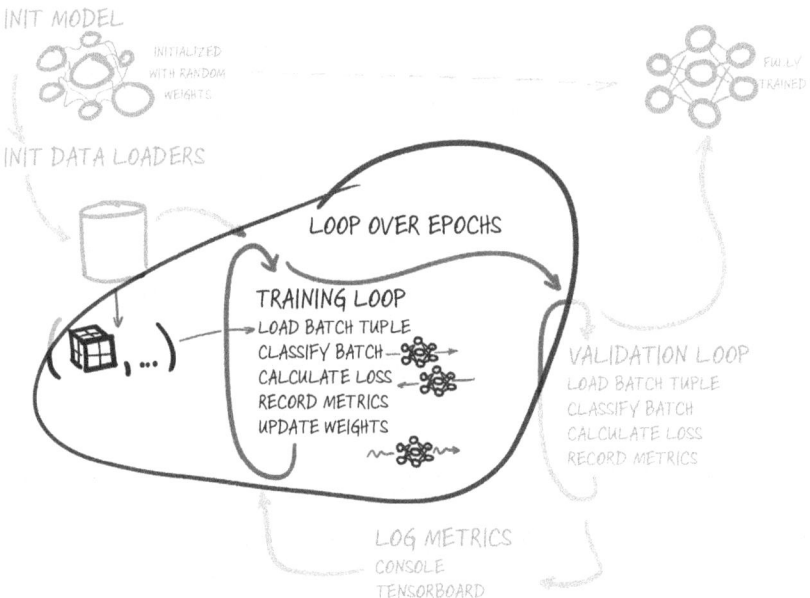

Figure 13.7 The training and validation script we will implement in this chapter, with a focus on the nested loops over each epoch and batches in the epoch.

13.5 Training and validating the model

The code is relatively compact. First, we have the driver code that calls `doTraining` and saves it in our metrics (training.py:143, `LunaTrainingApp.main`).

Listing 13.9 Inspecting the instantiated LunaModel structure in a notebook

```
def main(self):
  # ... line 143
  for epoch_ndx in range(1, self.cli_args.epochs + 1):
    trnMetrics_t = self.doTraining(epoch_ndx, train_dl)
    self.logMetrics(epoch_ndx, 'trn', trnMetrics_t)
```

Then we peek into the `doTraining` implementation (training.py:165, `LunaTraining-App.main`).

Listing 13.10 Main training loop iteration

```
def doTraining(self, epoch_ndx, train_dl):
  self.model.train()
  trnMetrics_g = torch.zeros(                    ◁── Initializes an empty metrics array
    METRICS_SIZE,
    len(train_dl.dataset),
    device=self.device,
  )
  train_progress = tqdm(                         ◁── Sets up our batched iterable to include progress tracking with tqdm
    train_dl,
    desc="E{} Training".format(epoch_ndx),
    total=len(train_dl)
  )
  for batch_ndx, batch_tup in enumerate(train_progress):
    self.optimizer.zero_grad()                   ◁── Frees any leftover gradient tensors

    loss_var = self.computeBatchLoss(            ◁── We'll discuss this method in detail in the next section.
      batch_ndx,
      batch_tup,
      train_dl.batch_size,
      trnMetrics_g
    )

    loss_var.backward()                          ◁── Backpropagation and optimizer step to update the model weights
    self.optimizer.step()

  self.totalTrainingSamples_count += len(train_dl.dataset)

  return trnMetrics_g.to('cpu')
```

The main differences that we see from the training loops in earlier chapters are as follows:

- The `trnMetrics_g` tensor collects detailed per-class metrics during training. For larger projects like ours, this kind of insight can be very nice to have.

- We don't directly iterate over the `train_dl` data loader. We use `tqdm` to provide our processing speed and estimated time of completion. This isn't crucial; it's just a stylistic choice.
- The actual loss computation is pushed into the `computeBatchLoss` method. Again, this isn't strictly necessary, but code reuse is typically a plus.

The purpose of the `trnMetrics_g` tensor is to transport information about how the model is behaving on a per-sample basis from the `computeBatchLoss` function to the `logMetrics` function. Let's take a look at `computeBatchLoss` next. We'll cover `logMetrics` after we're done with the rest of the main training loop.

13.5.1 The computeBatchLoss function

The `computeBatchLoss` function is called by both the training and validation loops. As the name suggests, it computes the loss over a batch of samples. In addition, the function also computes and records per-sample information about the output that the model is producing. This lets us compute things like the percentage of correct answers per class, which allows us to focus on areas where our model is having difficulty.

Of course, the function's core functionality is around feeding the batch into the model and computing the per-batch loss. We're using `CrossEntropyLoss` (https://mng.bz/5v28). Unpacking the batch tuple, moving the tensors to the GPU, and invoking the model should all feel familiar after that earlier training work (training.py:225, `computeBatchLoss`).

Listing 13.11 Computing per-sample cross-entropy loss

```
def computeBatchLoss(self, batch_ndx, batch_tup, batch_size, metrics_g):
    input_t, label_t, _series_list, _center_list = batch_tup

    input_g = input_t.to(self.device, non_blocking=True)
    label_g = label_t.to(self.device, non_blocking=True)

    logits_g, probability_g = self.model(input_g)

    loss_func = nn.CrossEntropyLoss(reduction='none')     # reduction='none' gives the loss per sample.
    loss_g = loss_func(
        logits_g,
        label_g[:,1],                                     # Index of the one-hot-encoded class
    )
    # ... line 238
    return loss_g.mean()                                  # Recombines the loss per sample into a single value
```

Here we are *not* using the default behavior to get a loss value averaged over the batch. Instead, we get a tensor of loss values, one per sample in our batch. This lets us track the individual losses, which means we can aggregate them as we wish (e.g., per class). We'll see that in action in just a moment. For now, we'll return the mean of those per-sample losses, which is equivalent to the batch loss. In situations where you don't want to keep statistics per sample, using the loss averaged over the batch is perfectly fine. Whether that's the case is highly dependent on your project and goals.

Once that's done, we've fulfilled our obligations to the calling function in terms of what's required to do backpropagation and weight updates. As part of our loss function, we also want to record our per-sample statistics for posterity (and later analysis). We'll use the metrics_g parameter passed in to accomplish this (training.py:26).

Listing 13.12 Recording metrics per sample

```
METRICS_LABEL_NDX = 0          These named array
METRICS_PRED_NDX = 1           indexes are declared
METRICS_LOSS_NDX = 2           as constants.
METRICS_SIZE = 3

  # ... line 225
  def computeBatchLoss(self, batch_ndx, batch_tup, batch_size, metrics_g):
    # ... line 238
    start_ndx = batch_ndx * batch_size
    end_ndx = start_ndx + label_t.size(0)

    metrics_g[METRICS_LABEL_NDX, start_ndx:end_ndx] = \
      label_g[:,1].detach()                                We use detach since
    metrics_g[METRICS_PRED_NDX, start_ndx:end_ndx] = \     none of our metrics
      probability_g[:,1].detach()                          need to hold on to
    metrics_g[METRICS_LOSS_NDX, start_ndx:end_ndx] = \     gradients.
      loss_g.detach()

    return loss_g.mean()          Again, this is the loss
                                  over the entire batch.
```

By recording the label, prediction, and loss for each and every training (and later, validation) sample, we have a wealth of detailed information we can use to investigate the behavior of our model. It is very hard to debug neural networks that are not training correctly, so these metrics can be vital for finding issues. For now, we're going to focus on compiling per-class statistics, but we could easily use this information to find the sample that is classified the most incorrectly and start to investigate why. Again, for some projects, this kind of information will be less interesting, but it's good to remember that you have these kinds of options available.

We can test out the computeBatchLoss function by running it on a subset of the data in our sandbox notebook (sandbox.ipynb).

Listing 13.13 Running computeBatchLoss with a progress bar

```
from tqdm import tqdm
device = app.device
train_dl_subset = app.get_dl_subset(train_dl, num_samples=20)
trnMetrics_g = torch.zeros(
    3,
    len(train_dl_subset.dataset),
```

```
        device=device,
    )
    batch_iter = tqdm(train_dl_subset, desc="E{} Training".format(epoch_ndx),
    ↪total=len(train_dl_subset))
    for batch_ndx, batch_tup in enumerate(batch_iter):
        loss_var = app.computeBatchLoss(
            batch_ndx, batch_tup, train_dl_subset.batch_size, trnMetrics_g
        )
```

13.5.2 The validation loop is similar

The validation loop in figure 13.8 looks very similar to training but is somewhat simplified. The key difference is that validation is read-only. Specifically, the loss value returned is not used, and the weights are not updated.

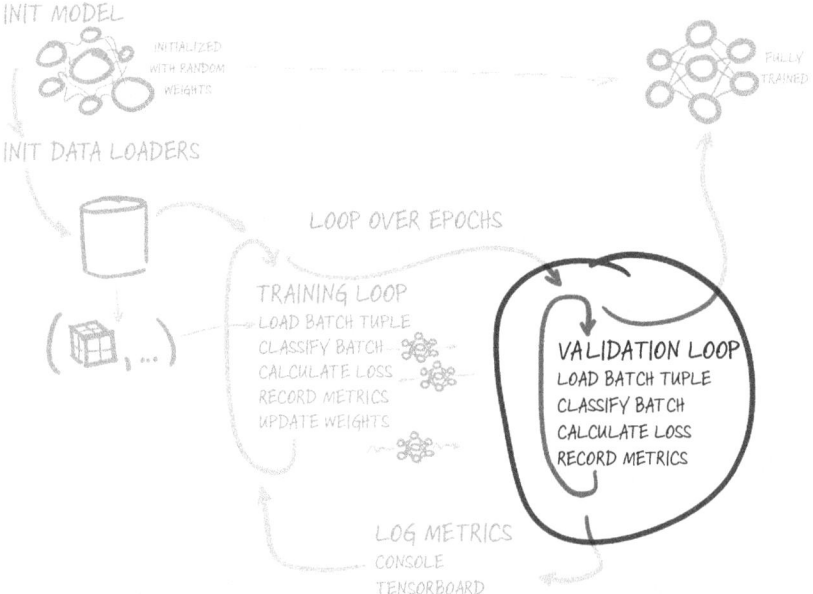

Figure 13.8 The training and validation script we will implement in this chapter, with a focus on the per-epoch validation loop

Nothing about the model should have changed between the start and end of the function call. In addition, it's quite a bit faster due to the with torch.no_grad() context manager explicitly informing PyTorch that no gradients need to be computed (training.py:137, LunaTrainingApp.main).

Listing 13.14 Validation loop using eval() mode and no_grad context

```
def main(self):
    for epoch_ndx in range(1, self.cli_args.epochs + 1):
```

```
# ... line 157
valMetrics_t = self.doValidation(epoch_ndx, val_dl)
self.logMetrics(epoch_ndx, 'val', valMetrics_t)

# ... line 203
def doValidation(self, epoch_ndx, val_dl):
  with torch.no_grad():
    self.model.eval()                          ◁──┐  model.eval() is important
    valMetrics_g = torch.zeros(                    │  and turns off training-
      METRICS_SIZE,                                │  time behavior.
      len(val_dl.dataset),
      device=self.device,
    )

    val_progress = tqdm(
      val_dl,
      desc="E{} Validation".format(epoch_ndx),
      total=len(val_dl)
    )
    for batch_ndx, batch_tup in enumerate(val_progress):
      self.computeBatchLoss(
        batch_ndx, batch_tup, val_dl.batch_size, valMetrics_g)

  return valMetrics_g.to('cpu')
```

Without needing to update network weights (recall that doing so would violate the entire premise of the validation set; something we never want to do!), we don't need to use the loss returned from computeBatchLoss, nor do we need to reference the optimizer. All that's left inside the loop is the call to computeBatchLoss. Note that we are still collecting metrics in valMetrics_g as a side effect of the call, even though we aren't using the overall per-batch loss returned by computeBatchLoss for anything.

13.6 Outputting performance metrics

The last thing we do per epoch is log our performance metrics for this epoch. As shown in figure 13.9, once we've logged metrics, we return to the training loop for the next epoch of training. Logging results and progress as we go is important, since if training goes off the rails ("does not converge" in the parlance of deep learning), we want to notice this is happening and stop spending time training a model that's not making meaningful progress. In less catastrophic cases, it's good to be able to keep an eye on how your model behaves.

Earlier, we were collecting results in trnMetrics_g and valMetrics_g for logging progress per epoch. Each of these two tensors now contains everything we need to compute our percent correct and average loss per class for our training and validation runs. Doing this per epoch is a common choice, though somewhat arbitrary. In future chapters, we'll see how to manipulate the size of our epochs such that we get feedback about training progress at a reasonable rate.

366 CHAPTER 13 *Training a classification model to detect suspected tumors*

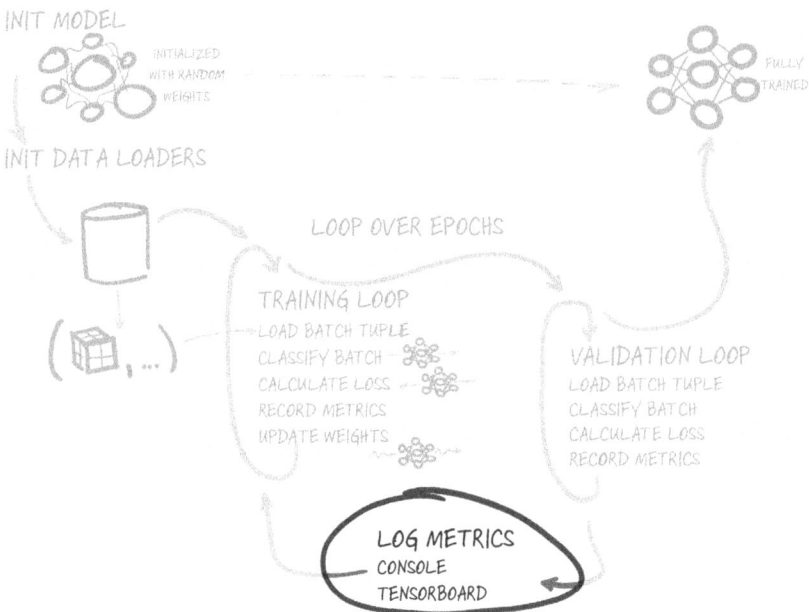

Figure 13.9 The training and validation script we will implement in this chapter, with a focus on the metrics logging at the end of each epoch

13.6.1 The logMetrics function

Let's talk about the high-level structure of the `logMetrics` function. The signature looks like the following code listing (training.py:251, `LunaTrainingApp.logMetrics`).

Listing 13.15 `logMetrics` function signature

```
def logMetrics(
    self,
    epoch_ndx,
    mode_str,
    metrics_t,
    classificationThreshold=0.5,
):
```

We use `epoch_ndx` purely for display while logging our results. The `mode_str` argument tells us whether the metrics are for training or validation.

We consume either `trnMetrics_t` or `valMetrics_t`, which is passed in as the `metrics_t` parameter. Recall that both of those inputs are tensors of floating-point values that we filled with data during `computeBatchLoss` and then transferred back to the CPU right before we returned them from `doTraining` and `doValidation`. Both tensors have three rows and as many columns as we have samples (training samples or validation samples, depending). As a reminder, those three rows correspond to the following constants (training.py:26).

Listing 13.16 Constants for metrics

```
METRICS_LABEL_NDX = 0
METRICS_PRED_NDX = 1
METRICS_LOSS_NDX = 2
```

> **Tensor masking and Boolean indexing**
>
> Masked tensors are a common usage pattern that might be opaque if you have not encountered them before. You may be familiar with the NumPy concept called masked arrays; tensor and array masks behave the same way.
>
> If you aren't familiar with masked arrays, an excellent page in the NumPy documentation (http://mng.bz/XPra) describes the behavior well. PyTorch purposely uses the same syntax and semantics as NumPy.

CONSTRUCTING MASKS

Next, we're going to construct masks that will let us limit our metrics to only the nodule or non-nodule (aka positive or negative) samples. We will also count the total samples per class, as well as the number of samples we classified correctly (training.py:264, LunaTrainingApp.logMetrics).

Listing 13.17 Masking for classification metrics

```
negLabel_mask = metrics_t[METRICS_LABEL_NDX] <= classificationThreshold
negPred_mask = metrics_t[METRICS_PRED_NDX] <= classificationThreshold

posLabel_mask = ~negLabel_mask
posPred_mask = ~negPred_mask
```

All of the values stored in metrics_t[METRICS_LABEL_NDX] belong to the set {0.0, 1.0} since we know that our nodule status labels are simply True or False. By comparing to classificationThreshold, which defaults to 0.5, we get an array of binary values where a True value corresponds to a non-nodule (aka negative) label for the sample in question.

We do a similar comparison to create the negPred_mask, but we must remember that the METRICS_PRED_NDX values are the positive predictions produced by our model and can be any floating-point value between 0.0 and 1.0, inclusive. That doesn't change our comparison, but it does mean the actual value can be close to 0.5. The positive masks are simply the inverse of the negative masks (the inverse can be computed through ~).

> **NOTE** While other projects can utilize similar approaches, it's important to realize that we're taking some shortcuts that are allowed because this is a binary classification problem. If your next project has more than two classes or has samples that belong to multiple classes at the same time, you'll have to use more complicated logic to build similar masks.

Next, we use those masks to compute some per-label statistics and store them in a dictionary, metrics_dict (training.py:270, LunaTrainingApp.logMetrics).

Listing 13.18 Masking for classification metrics

```
neg_count = int(negLabel_mask.sum())                    ◁─── Converts to a normal
pos_count = int(posLabel_mask.sum())                         Python integer

neg_correct = int((negLabel_mask & negPred_mask).sum())
pos_correct = int((posLabel_mask & posPred_mask).sum())

metrics_dict = {}
metrics_dict['loss/all'] = metrics_t[METRICS_LOSS_NDX].mean()
metrics_dict['loss/neg'] = metrics_t[METRICS_LOSS_NDX, negLabel_mask].mean()
metrics_dict['loss/pos'] = metrics_t[METRICS_LOSS_NDX, posLabel_mask].mean()

metrics_dict['correct/all'] = (pos_correct + neg_correct) /
➥ np.float32(metrics_t.shape[1]) * 100
metrics_dict['correct/neg'] = neg_correct / np.float32(neg_count) * 100   ◁───
metrics_dict['correct/pos'] = pos_correct / np.float32(pos_count) * 100
```
Avoids integer division by
converting to np.float32

First, we compute the average loss over the entire epoch. Since the loss is the single metric that is being minimized during training, we always want to be able to keep track of it. Then we limit the loss averaging to only those samples with a negative label using the negLabel_mask we just made. We do the same with the positive loss. Computing a per-class loss like this can be useful if one class is persistently harder to classify than another, since that knowledge can help drive investigation and improvements.

We'll close out the calculations by determining the fraction of samples we classified correctly, as well as the fraction correct from each label. Since we will display these numbers as percentages in a moment, we also multiply the values by 100. Similar to the loss, we can use these numbers to help guide our efforts when making improvements. After the calculations, we then log our results with three calls to log.info (training.py:289, LunaTrainingApp.logMetrics).

Listing 13.19 Training and validation results

```
log.info(
    f"E{epoch_ndx} {mode_str:8} {metrics_dict['loss/all']:.4f} loss, "
    f"{metrics_dict['correct/all']:-5.1f}% correct"
)
log.info(
    f"E{epoch_ndx} {mode_str + '_neg':8} {metrics_dict[
➥ 'loss/neg']:.4f} loss, "
    f"{metrics_dict['correct/neg']:-5.1f}% correct ({
➥ neg_correct} of {neg_count})"
)
```

```
log.info(
  # ... line 319
)
```
◁─┐ The 'pos' logging is similar
   │ to the 'neg' logging earlier.

The first log has values computed from all of our samples and is tagged /all, while the negative (non-nodule) and positive (nodule) values are tagged /neg and /pos, respectively. We don't show the third logging statement for positive values here for brevity; it's identical to the second except for swapping *neg* for *pos* in all cases.

13.7 Running the training script

Now that we've completed the core of the training.py script, we'll start actually running it. This will initialize and train our model and print statistics about how well the training is going. The idea is to get this kicked off to run in the background while we're covering the model implementation in detail. Hopefully, we'll have results to look at once we're done.

We're running this script from the main code directory; it should have subdirectories called p2ch13, util, and so on. The python environment used should have all the libraries listed in requirements.txt installed. Once those libraries are ready, we can run

```
$ python -m p2ch13.training     ◁─┐ The command line for Linux/Bash; Windows users
Starting LunaTrainingApp,         │ will probably need to invoke Python differently,
  Namespace(batch_size=256, channels=8, epochs=20, layers=3, num_workers=8)
<p2ch13.dsets.LunaDataset object at 0x7fa53a128710>: 495958 training samples
<p2ch13.dsets.LunaDataset object at 0x7fa537325198>: 55107 validation samples
Epoch 1 of 20, 1938/216 batches of size 256
E1 Training ----/1938, starting
E1 Training    16/1938, done at 2018-02-28 20:52:54, 0:02:57
...
```

As a reminder, I also provide a Jupyter Notebook that contains invocations of the training application.

We can now run our entire workflow.

Listing 13.20 The run command (code/p2_run_everything.ipynb)

```
# In[5]:
run('p2ch13.prepcache.LunaPrepCacheApp')

# In[6]:
run('p2ch13.training.LunaTrainingApp', '--epochs=1')
```

If the first epoch seems to be taking a very long time (more than 10 or 20 minutes), it might be related to needing to prepare the cached data required by LunaDataset. See section 12.5.1 for details about the caching we are performing. The exercises for chapter 12 included writing a script to prestuff the cache in an efficient manner. We also provide the prepcache.py file to do the same thing; it can be invoked with `python -m p2ch13.prepcache`. Since we repeat our dsets.py files per chapter, the caching will need to be repeated for every chapter. This is somewhat space and time-inefficient, but it means we can keep the code for each chapter much more well-contained. For your future projects, we recommend reusing your cache more heavily.

Once training is underway, we want to make sure we're using the computing resources at hand the way we expect. An easy way to tell whether the bottleneck is data loading or computation is to wait a few moments after the script starts to train (look for output like `E1 Training 16/7750, done at...`) and then check both `top` and `nvidia-smi`:

- If the eight Python worker processes are consuming >80% CPU, the cache probably needs to be prepared (we know this here because I've made sure there aren't CPU bottlenecks in this project's implementation; this won't be generally true).
- If `nvidia-smi` reports that `GPU-Util` is >80%, you're saturating your GPU.

The intent is that the GPU is saturated; we want to use as much of that computing power as we can to complete epochs quickly. A single NVIDIA GTX 1080 Ti should complete an epoch in under 15 minutes. Since our model is relatively simple, it doesn't take a lot of CPU preprocessing for the CPU to be the bottleneck. When working with models with greater depth (or more needed calculations in general), processing each batch will take longer, which will increase the amount of CPU processing we can do before the GPU runs out of work before the next batch of input is ready.

13.7.1 Data needed for training

If the number of samples is less than 495,958 for training or 55,107 for validation, it might make sense to do some double-checking to be sure the full data is present and accounted for. For your future projects, make sure your dataset returns the number of samples that you expect.

First, let's take a look at the basic directory structure of our data-unversioned/part2/luna directory. Our terminal command `ls` will list all the content in the directory with the `-1` flag, which will list each item on a separate line. The `-p` flag will append a / to directories to make them easier to identify:

```
$ ls -1p data-unversioned/part2/luna/
subset0/
subset1/
...
subset9/
```

Next, let's make sure we have one .mhd file and one .raw file for each series UID:

```
$ ls -1p data-unversioned/part2/luna/subset0/
1.3.6.1.4.1.14519.5.2.1.6279.6001.105756658031515062000744821260.mhd
1.3.6.1.4.1.14519.5.2.1.6279.6001.105756658031515062000744821260.raw
1.3.6.1.4.1.14519.5.2.1.6279.6001.108197895896446896160048741492.mhd
1.3.6.1.4.1.14519.5.2.1.6279.6001.108197895896446896160048741492.raw
...
```

We also need to check that we have the overall correct number of files:

```
$ ls -1 data-unversioned/part2/luna/subset?/* | wc -l
1776
$ ls -1 data-unversioned/part2/luna/subset0/* | wc -l
178
...
$ ls -1 data-unversioned/part2/luna/subset9/* | wc -l
176
```

If all of these seem right but things still aren't working, ask on Manning LiveBook (https://livebook.manning.com/book/deep-learning-with-pytorch/chapter-13) and hopefully someone can help get things sorted out.

13.7.2 Interlude: The tqdm function

Working with deep learning involves a lot of waiting. We're talking about real-world, sitting around, glancing at the clock on the wall, a watched pot never boils (but you could fry an egg on the GPU), straight up *boredom*.

The only thing worse than sitting and staring at a blinking cursor that hasn't moved for over an hour is flooding your screen with this:

```
2020-01-01 10:00:00,056 INFO training batch 1234
2020-01-01 10:00:00,067 INFO training batch 1235
2020-01-01 10:00:00,077 INFO training batch 1236
2020-01-01 10:00:00,087 INFO training batch 1237
...etc...
```

At least the quietly blinking cursor doesn't blow out your scrollback buffer!

Fundamentally, while doing all this waiting, we want to answer the question "Do I have time to go refill my water glass?" along with follow-up questions about having time to

- Brew a cup of coffee
- Grab dinner
- Grab dinner in Paris. (If getting dinner in France doesn't involve an airport, feel free to substitute "Paris, Texas" to make the joke work.)

To answer these pressing questions, we're going to use our `tqdm` function (sandbox.ipynb).

Listing 13.21 Example of using tqdm for progress tracking

```
# In[]
from tqdm import tqdm
import time
import random
for _ in tqdm(range(234), desc="Sleeping"):
    time.sleep(random.random())
```

```
# Out[]
Sleeping:  16%|█         | 37/234  [00:22<01:28,  2.22it/s]
Sleeping:  28%|██        | 66/234  [00:38<01:37,  1.72it/s]
Sleeping:  41%|████      | 95/234  [00:54<01:04,  2.17it/s]
Sleeping:  70%|██████    | 163/234 [01:31<00:49,  1.44it/s]
Sleeping:  82%|████████  | 193/234 [01:44<00:16,  2.43it/s]
Sleeping: 100%|██████████| 234/234 [02:08<00:00,  1.83it/s]
```

While the code listing shows multiple outputs to illustrate the progress made of tqdm, by default tqdm provides a dynamic progress bar that updates the text in place during the iteration. The estimate is also quite accurate. Even given the wide variance of random.random(), the function had a pretty decent estimate from early in the loop.

In terms of behavior, tqdm wraps around a loop or iterable and provides dynamic progress bar updates in real time, such as the following log:

```
70%|███████   | 163/234 [01:31<00:49,  1.44it/s]
```

It provides a percentage and visual representation, the number of iterations completed, the total number of iterations, the time elapsed, and an estimate of the time remaining. The 1.44it/s at the end is the rate of iterations per second. This is a great way to keep track of progress in a long-running loop.

Deep learning projects can be very time-intensive. Knowing when something is expected to finish means you can use your time until then wisely, and it can also clue you in that something isn't working properly (or an approach is unworkable) if the expected time to completion is much larger than expected.

13.8 Evaluating the model: Getting 99.7% correct means we're done, right?

Let's take a look at some (abridged) output from our training script. As a reminder, we've run this with the command line python -m p2ch13.training:

```
E1 Training ----/969, starting
...
E1 LunaTrainingApp
E1 trn      2.4576 loss,  99.7% correct
...
E1 val      0.0172 loss,  99.8% correct
...
```

After one epoch of training, both the training and validation sets show at least 99.7% correct results. That's an A+! Time for a round of high-fives, or at least a satisfied nod and smile. We just solved cancer! Right? Well, no.

Let's take a closer look at that epoch 1 output:

```
E1 LunaTrainingApp
E1 trn        2.4576 loss,  99.7% correct,
E1 trn_neg    0.1936 loss,  99.9% correct (494289 of 494743)
E1 trn_pos  924.34 loss,    0.2% correct (3 of 1215)
```

```
...
E1 val       0.0172 loss,  99.8% correct,
E1 val_neg   0.0025 loss, 100.0% correct (494743 of 494743)
E1 val_pos   5.9768 loss,   0.0% correct (0 of 1215)
```

On the validation set, we're getting non-nodules 100% correct, but the actual nodules are 100% wrong. The network is just classifying everything as not-a-nodule! The value 99.7% just means only approximately 0.3% of the samples are nodules.

After 10 epochs, the situation is only marginally better:

```
E10 LunaTrainingApp
E10 trn      0.0024 loss,  99.8% correct
E10 trn_neg  0.0000 loss, 100.0% correct
E10 trn_pos  0.9915 loss,   0.0% correct
E10 val      0.0025 loss,  99.7% correct
E10 val_neg  0.0000 loss, 100.0% correct
E10 val_pos  0.9929 loss,   0.0% correct
```

The classification output remains the same—none of the nodule (aka positive) samples are correctly identified. It's interesting that we're starting to see some decrease in the val_pos loss, while not seeing a corresponding increase in the val_neg loss. This result implies that the network *is* learning something. Unfortunately, it's learning very, very slowly.

Even worse, this particular failure mode is the most dangerous in the real world! We want to avoid the situation where we classify a tumor as an innocuous structure because that would not facilitate a patient getting the evaluation and eventual treatment they might need. It's important to understand the consequences of misclassification for all your projects, as that can have a large effect on how you design, train, and evaluate your model. We'll discuss this more in the next chapter.

Before we get to that, we need to upgrade our tooling to make the results easier to understand. We're sure you love to squint at columns of numbers as much as anyone, but pictures are worth a thousand words. Let's graph some of these metrics.

13.9 *Graphing training metrics with TensorBoard*

We're going to use a tool called TensorBoard as a quick and easy way to get our training metrics out of our training loop and into some pretty graphs. This will allow us to follow the *trends* of those metrics, rather than only look at the instantaneous values per epoch. It gets much, much easier to know whether a value is an outlier or just the latest in a trend when you're looking at a visual representation.

You might be wondering, "Isn't TensorBoard part of the TensorFlow project? Why are we using it with PyTorch?" While TensorBoard originated with TensorFlow, it has become a widely adopted tool across different deep learning frameworks, including PyTorch. The PyTorch and TensorBoard teams have collaborated to provide seamless integration, allowing us to use TensorBoard's capabilities directly within PyTorch. This integration means it's got some easy-to-use PyTorch APIs that let us hook data into it from just about anywhere for quick and easy display. If you stick with deep learning, you'll probably be seeing (and using) a *lot* of TensorBoard.

If you've been running the chapter examples, you should already have some data on disk ready and waiting to be displayed. Let's see how to run TensorBoard and see what it can show us.

13.9.1 Running TensorBoard

By default, our training script will write metrics data to the runs/ subdirectory. If you list the directory content, you might see something like this during your Bash shell session:

```
$ ls -lA runs/p2ch13/
total 24
drwxrwxr-x 2 elis elis 4096 Sep 15 13:22 2020-01-01_12.
↪55.27-trn-dlwpt/
drwxrwxr-x 2 elis elis 4096 Sep 15 13:22 2020-01-01_12.
↪55.27-val-dlwpt/
drwxrwxr-x 2 elis elis 4096 Sep 15 15:14 2020-01-01_13.
↪31.23-trn-dwlpt/
drwxrwxr-x 2 elis elis 4096 Sep 15 15:14 2020-01-01_13.
↪31.23-val-dwlpt/
```

The single-epoch run from earlier

The more recent 10-epoch training run

To get the TensorBord program, use pip install tensorboard. If you have another version of TensorBoard installed already, that's fine. Either make sure the appropriate directory is on your path or invoke it with ../path/to/tensorboard --logdir runs/. It doesn't really matter where you invoke it from, as long as you use the --logdir argument to point it at where your data is stored.

Let's start TensorBoard now:

```
$ tensorboard --logdir runs/

TensorBoard 1.14.0 at http://localhost:6006/ (Press CTRL+C to quit)
```

Once that's done, you should be able to point your browser at http://localhost:6006 and see the main dashboard. Figure 13.10 shows us what that looks like.

NOTE If you're running training on a different computer from your browser, you'll need to replace *localhost* with the appropriate hostname or IP address.

Along the top of the browser window, you should see the orange header. The right side of the header has the typical widgets, such as the settings. The left side of the header has items for the data types we've provided. You should have at least the following:

- Scalars (the default tab)
- Histograms
- Precision-recall curves (shown as PR Curves)

13.9 Graphing training metrics with TensorBoard

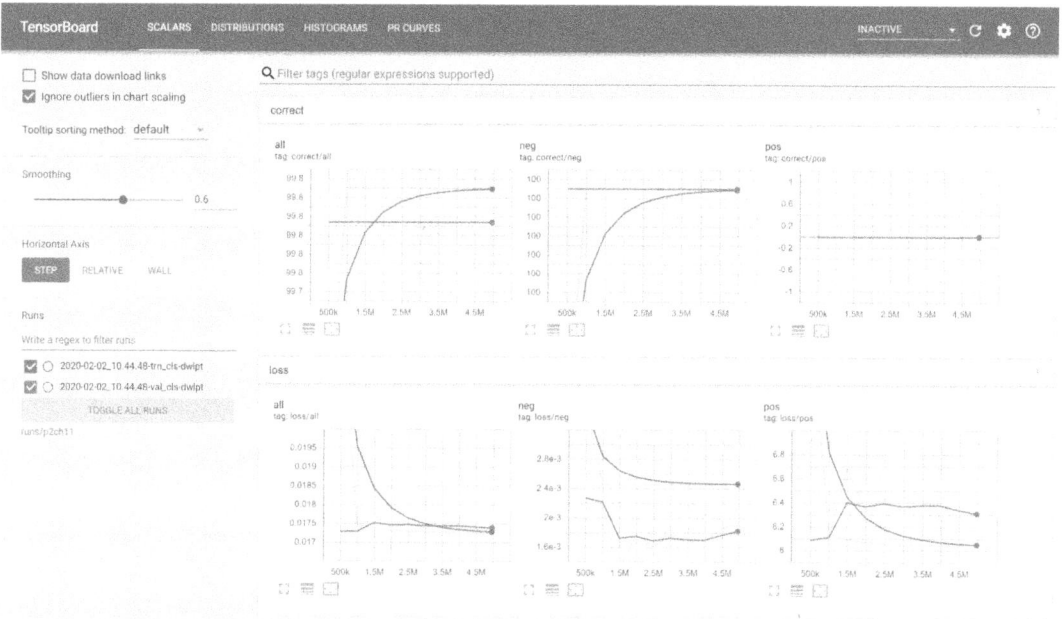

Figure 13.10 The main TensorBoard UI, showing a paired set of training and validation runs

You might see Distributions as the second UI tab (to the right of Scalars in figure 13.10). We won't use or discuss those here. Make sure you've selected Scalars by clicking it.

On the left is a set of controls for display options, as well as a list of runs that are present. The smoothing option can be useful if you have particularly noisy data; it will calm things down so that you can pick out the overall trend—although too strong a smoothing may hide important trends! The original nonsmoothed data will still be visible in the background as a faded line in the same color. Figure 13.11 shows this, although it might be difficult to discern when printed in black and white.

Depending on how many times you've run the training script, you might have multiple runs to select from. With too many runs being rendered, the graphs can get overly noisy, so don't hesitate to deselect runs that aren't of interest at the moment.

If you want to permanently remove a run, the data can be deleted from disk while TensorBoard is running. You can do this to get rid of experiments that crashed, had bugs, didn't converge, or are so old they're no longer interesting. The number of runs can grow pretty quickly, so it can be helpful to prune it often and to rename runs or move runs that are particularly interesting to a more permanent directory so they don't get deleted by accident. To remove both the `train` and `validation` runs, execute

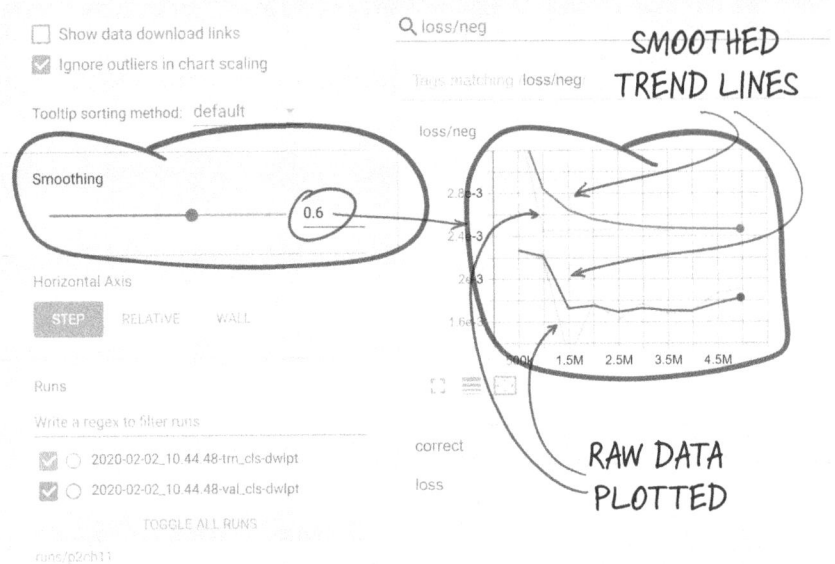

Figure 13.11 The TensorBoard sidebar with Smoothing set to 0.6 and two runs selected for display

the following (after changing the chapter, date, and time to match the run you want to remove):

```
$ rm -rf runs/p2ch13/2020-01-01_12.02.15_*
```

Keep in mind that removing runs will cause the runs that are later in the list to move up, which will result in them being assigned new colors.

OK, let's get to the point of TensorBoard: the pretty graphs! The main part of the screen should be filled with data from gathering training and validation metrics, as shown in figure 13.12.

That's much easier to parse and absorb than E1 trn_pos 924.34 loss, 0.2% correct (3 of 1215)! Take a moment to cross-reference the numbers you get by mousing over the lines with the numbers spit out by training.py during the same training run. You should see a direct correspondence between the Value column of the tooltip and the values printed during training. Once you're comfortable and confident that you understand exactly what TensorBoard is showing you, let's move on and discuss how to get these numbers to appear in the first place.

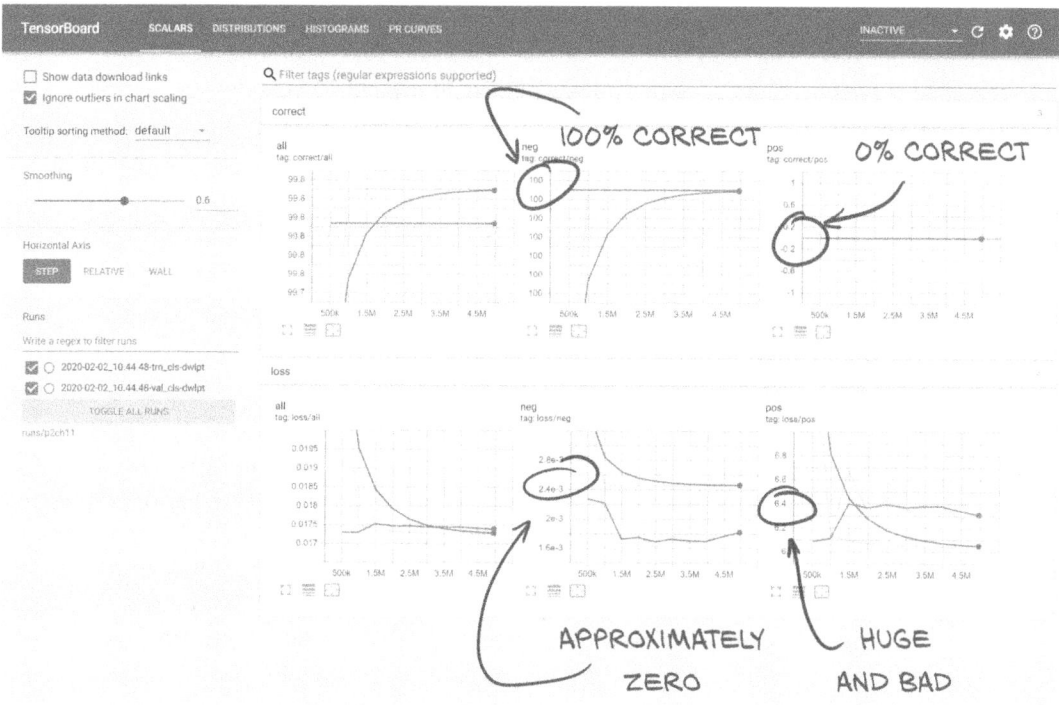

Figure 13.12 The main TensorBoard data display area showing us that our results on actual nodules are downright awful

13.9.2 Adding TensorBoard support to the metrics logging function

We are going to use the torch.utils.tensorboard module to write data in a format that TensorBoard will consume. This will allow us to write metrics for this and any other project quickly and easily. TensorBoard supports a mix of NumPy arrays and PyTorch tensors, but since we don't have any reason to put our data into NumPy arrays, we'll use PyTorch tensors exclusively.

The first thing we need to do is to create our SummaryWriter objects (which we imported from torch.utils.tensorboard). The only parameter we're going to pass in is log_dir, which we will initialize to something like runs/p2ch13/2020-01-01_12 .55.27-trn-dlwpt. We can add a comment argument to our training script to change dlwpt to something more informative; use python -m p2ch13.training --help for more information.

We create two writers, one for the training run and one for the validation run. Those writers will be reused for every epoch. When the SummaryWriter class gets initialized, it also creates the log_dir directories as a side effect. These directories show up in TensorBoard and can clutter the UI with empty runs if the training script crashes before any data gets written, which can be common when you're experimenting with something. To avoid writing too many empty junk runs, we wait to instantiate the `SummaryWriter` objects until we're ready to write data for the first time. This function is called from `logMetrics()` (training.py:127, `initTensorboardWriters`).

Listing 13.22 Initializing TensorBoard writers for training and validation

```
def initTensorboardWriters(self):
  if self.trn_writer is None:
    log_dir = os.path.join('runs', self.cli_args.tb_prefix, self.time_str)

    self.trn_writer = SummaryWriter(
      log_dir=log_dir + '-trn_cls-' + self.cli_args.comment)
    self.val_writer = SummaryWriter(
      log_dir=log_dir + '-val_cls-' + self.cli_args.comment)
```

If you recall, the first epoch is kind of a mess, with the early output in the training loop being essentially random. When we save the metrics from that first batch, those random results end up skewing things a bit. Recall from figure 13.11 that TensorBoard has smoothing to remove noise from the trend lines, which helps somewhat.

Another approach could be to skip metrics entirely for the first epoch's training data, although our model trains quickly enough that it's still useful to see the first epoch's results. Feel free to change this behavior as you see fit; the rest of part 2 will continue with this pattern of including the first, noisy training epoch.

> **TIP** If you end up doing a lot of experiments that result in exceptions or killing the training script relatively quickly, you might be left with a number of junk runs cluttering up your runs/ directory. Don't be afraid to clean those out!

WRITING SCALARS TO TENSORBOARD

Writing scalars is straightforward. We can take the `metrics_dict` we've already constructed and pass in each key/value pair to the `writer.add_scalar` method. The `torch.utils.tensorboard.SummaryWriter` class has the `add_scalar` method (http://mng.bz/RAqj) with the following signature (PyTorch torch/utils/tensorboard/writer.py:267).

Listing 13.23 How to add metrics

```
def add_scalar(self, tag, scalar_value, global_step=None, walltime=None):
  # ...
```

The `tag` parameter tells TensorBoard which graph we're adding values to, and the `scalar_value` parameter is our data point's Y-axis value. The `global_step` parameter acts as the X-axis value.

Recall that we updated the `totalTrainingSamples_count` variable inside the `doTraining` function. We'll use `totalTrainingSamples_count` as the X-axis of our TensorBoard plots by passing it in as the `global_step` parameter (training.py:323, `LunaTrainingApp.logMetrics`).

Listing 13.24 Logging training metrics to TensorBoard

```
for key, value in metrics_dict.items():
    writer.add_scalar(key, value, self.totalTrainingSamples_count)
```

Note that the slashes in our key names (such as 'loss/all') result in TensorBoard grouping the charts by the substring before the '/'.

The documentation suggests that we should be passing in the epoch number as the global_step parameter, but that results in some complications. By using the number of training samples presented to the network, we can do things like change the number of samples per epoch and still be able to compare those future graphs to the ones we're creating now. Saying that a model trains in half the number of epochs is meaningless if each epoch takes four times as long! Keep in mind that this might not be standard practice; expect to see a variety of values used for the global step.

13.10 Why isn't the model learning to detect nodules?

Our model is clearly learning *something*—the loss trend lines are consistent as epochs increase, and the results are repeatable. There is a disconnect, however, between what the model is learning and what we *want* it to learn. What's going on? Let's use a quick metaphor to illustrate the problem.

Imagine that a professor gives students a final exam consisting of 100 True/False questions. The students have access to previous versions of this professor's tests going back 30 years, and every time there are only *one or two* questions with a True answer. The other 98 or 99 are False, every time.

Assuming that the grades aren't on a curve and instead have a typical scale of 90% correct or better being an A, and so on, it is trivial to get an A+: just mark every question as False! Let's imagine that this year, there is only one True answer. A student like the one on the left in figure 13.13, who mindlessly marked every answer as False, would get a 99% on the final but wouldn't really demonstrate that they had learned anything (beyond how to cram from old tests, of course). That's basically what our model is doing right now.

Figure 13.13 A professor giving two students the same grade, despite different levels of knowledge. Question 9 is the only question with an answer of True.

Contrast that with a student like the one on the right, who also got 99% of the questions correct, but did so by answering two questions with True. Intuition tells us that the student on the right in figure 13.13 probably has a much better grasp of the material than the all-False student. Finding the one True question while only getting one answer wrong is pretty difficult! Unfortunately, neither our students' grades nor our model's grading scheme reflects this gut feeling.

We have a similar situation, where 99.7% of the answers to "Is this candidate a nodule?" are "Nope." Our model is taking the easy way out and answering False on every question.

Still, if we look back at our model's numbers more closely, the loss on the training and validation sets *is* decreasing! The fact that we're getting any traction at all on the cancer-detection problem should give us hope. It will be the work of the next chapter to realize this potential. We'll start chapter 14 by introducing some new, relevant terminology, and then we'll come up with a better grading scheme that doesn't lend itself to being gamed quite as easily as what we've done so far.

13.11 Conclusion

We've come a long way this chapter—we now have a model and a training loop, and we are able to consume the data we produced in the last chapter. Our metrics are being logged to the console as well as graphed visually.

While our results aren't usable yet, we're actually closer than it might seem. In chapter 14, we will improve the metrics we're using to track our progress and use them to inform the changes we need to make to get our model producing reasonable results.

13.12 Exercises

1 Implement a program that iterates through a `LunaDataset` instance by wrapping it in a `DataLoader` instance, while timing how long it takes to do so. Compare these times to the times from the exercises in chapter 10. Be aware of the state of the cache when running the script:
    a What impact does setting `num_workers=…` to 0, 1, and 2 have?
    b What are the highest values your machine will support for a given combination of `batch_size=…` and `num_workers=…` without running out of memory?
2 Reverse the sort order of `noduleInfo_list`. How does that change the behavior of the model after one epoch of training?
3 Change `logMetrics` to alter the naming scheme of the runs and keys that are used in TensorBoard:
    a Experiment with different forward-slash placement for keys passed in to `writer.add_scalar`.
    b Have both training and validation runs use the same writer and add the `trn` or `val` string to the name of the key.
    c Customize the naming of the log directory and keys to suit your taste.

Summary

- Data loaders can be used to load data from arbitrary datasets in multiple processes. This allows otherwise-idle CPU resources to be devoted to preparing data to feed to the GPU.
- Data loaders load multiple samples from a dataset and collate them into a batch. PyTorch models expect to process batches of data, not individual samples.
- Data loaders can be used to manipulate arbitrary datasets by changing the relative frequency of individual samples.
- We will use PyTorch's `torch.optim.SGD` (stochastic gradient descent) optimizer with a learning rate of 0.001 and a momentum of 0.99 for the majority of part 2. These values are also reasonable defaults for many deep learning projects.
- Our initial model for classification will be very similar to the model we used in chapter 8. This lets us get started with a model that we have reason to believe will be effective. We can revisit the model design if we think it's the thing preventing our project from performing better.
- The choice of metrics that we monitor during training is important. It is easy to accidentally pick metrics that are misleading about how the model is performing. Using the overall percentage of samples classified correctly is not useful for our data. Chapter 14 will detail how to evaluate and choose better metrics.
- TensorBoard can be used to display a wide range of metrics visually. This makes it much easier to consume certain forms of information (particularly trend data) as they change per epoch of training.

Improving training with metrics and augmentation

This chapter covers
- Defining and computing precision, recall, and true/false positives/negatives
- Using the F1 score versus other quality metrics
- Balancing and augmenting data to reduce overfitting
- Using TensorBoard to graph quality metrics

The close of the last chapter left us in a predicament. While we were able to get the mechanics of our deep learning project in place, none of the results were actually useful; the network simply classified everything as non-nodule! To make matters worse, the results seemed great on the surface, since we were looking at the overall percentage of the training and validation sets that were classified correctly. With our data heavily skewed toward negative samples, blindly calling everything negative is a quick and easy way for our model to score well. Too bad doing so makes the model basically useless!

That means we're still focused on the same part of figure 14.1 as we were in chapter 13. But now we're working on getting our classification model working *well* instead of *just working*. This chapter is all about how to measure, quantify, express, and then improve on how well our model is doing its job.

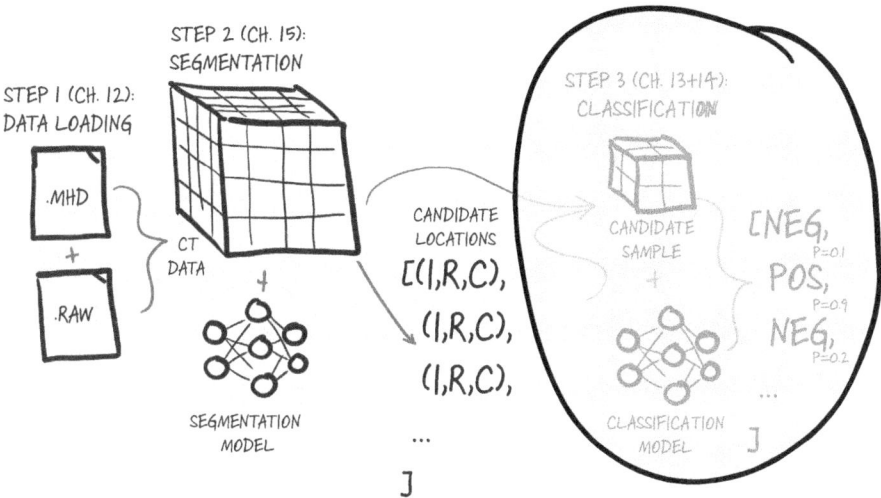

Figure 14.1 Our end-to-end lung cancer detection project, with a focus on this chapter's topic: step 3, classification.

14.1 High-level plan for improvement

While a bit abstract, figure 14.2 shows us how we are going to approach that broad set of topics. Let's walk through this somewhat abstract map of the chapter in detail. We will be dealing with the issues we're facing, like excessive focus on a single, narrow metric, and the resulting behavior being useless in the general sense. To make some of this chapter's concepts a bit more concrete, we'll first employ a metaphor that puts our troubles in more tangible terms—guard dogs (1) and birds and burglars (2), as shown in figure 14.2.

After that, we will develop a graphical language to represent some of the core concepts needed to formally discuss the difficulty with the implementation from the last chapter—ratios: recall and precision (3), as shown in figure 14.2. Once we have those concepts solidified, we'll touch on some math using those concepts that will encapsulate a more robust way of grading our model's performance and condensing it into a single number—new metric: F1 score (4). We will implement the formula for those new metrics and look at how the resulting values change epoch by epoch during training. Finally, we'll make some much-needed changes to our LunaDataset implementation with an aim at improving our training results—balancing (5) and augmentation (6). Then we will see whether those experimental changes have the expected effect on our performance metrics.

By the time we're through with this chapter, our trained model will be performing much better—workin' great! (7), as shown in figure 14.2. While it won't be

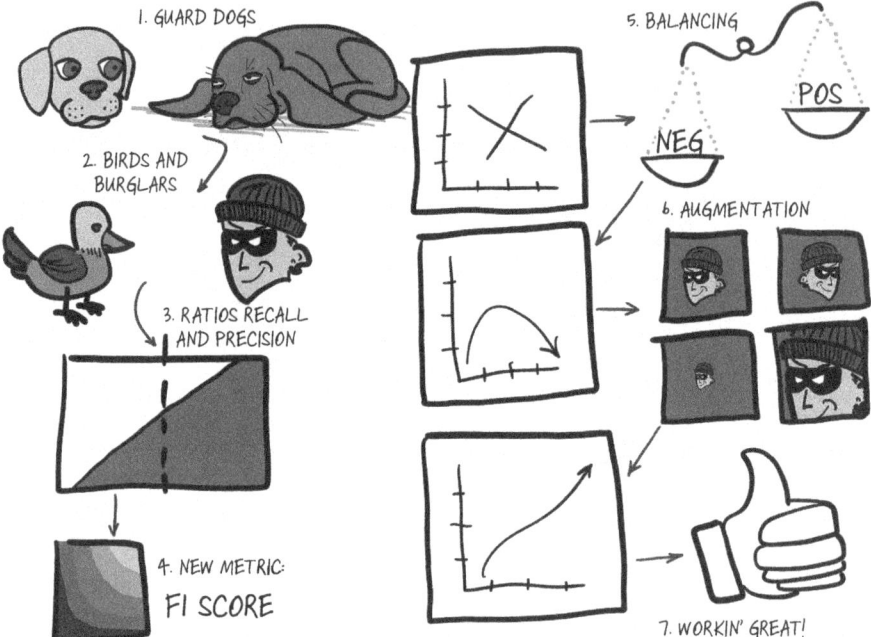

Figure 14.2 The metaphors we'll use to modify the metrics measuring our model to make it magnificent.

ready to drop into clinical use just yet, it will be capable of producing results that are clearly better than random. As a result, we have a workable implementation of step 3 in our overall plan for nodule candidate classification, and once we're finished, we can begin to think about how to incorporate step 2 (segmentation) into the project.

14.2 Good dogs vs. bad guys: False positives and false negatives

To start with a metaphor, instead of models and tumors, we're going to consider the two guard dogs in figure 14.3, both fresh out of obedience school. They both want to alert us to burglars—a rare but serious situation that requires prompt attention.

Unfortunately, while both dogs are good boys, neither is a good *guard* dog. Our terrier (Chirpy) barks at just about everything, while our old hound dog (Dozer) barks almost exclusively at burglars—but only if he happens to be awake when they arrive.

Chirpy *will* alert us to a burglar just about every time. She will also alert us to fire engines, thunderstorms, helicopters, birds, the mail carrier, squirrels, passersby, and so on. If we follow up on every bark, we'll almost never get robbed (only the sneakiest of sneak-thieves can slip past). Perfect! Except that being that diligent means we aren't really saving any work by having a guard dog. Instead, we'll be up every couple

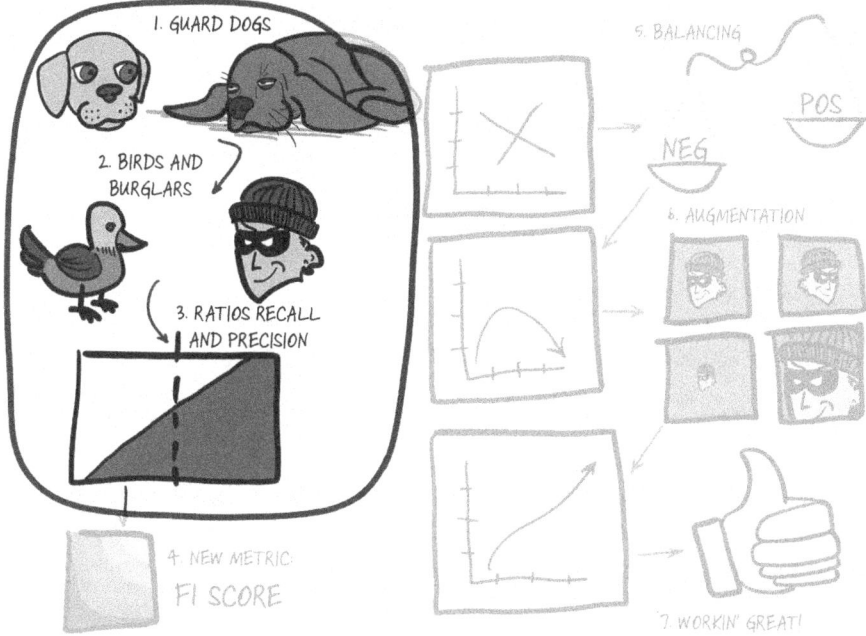

Figure 14.3 The set of topics for this chapter, with a focus on the framing metaphor

of hours, flashlight in hand, due to Chirpy having smelled a cat, heard an owl, or seen a late bus roll by. Chirpy has a problematic number of false positives.

A *false positive* is an event that is classified as of interest or as a member of the desired class (positive as in "Yes, that's the type of thing I'm interested in knowing about") but that in truth is *not* really of interest. For the nodule-detection problem, it's when an uninteresting candidate is flagged as a nodule and, hence, in need of a radiologist's attention. For Chirpy, these would be fire engines, thunderstorms, and so on. We will use an image of a cat as the canonical false positive in the next section and the figures that follow throughout the rest of the chapter.

Contrast false positives with *true positives*: items of interest that are classified correctly. These will be represented in the figures by a human burglar.

Meanwhile, if Dozer barks, call the police, since that means someone has almost certainly broken in, the house is on fire, or Godzilla is attacking. Dozer is a deep sleeper, however, and the sound of an in-progress home invasion isn't likely to rouse him, so we'll still get robbed just about every time someone tries. Again, while it's better than nothing, we're not really ending up with the peace of mind that motivated us to get a dog in the first place. Dozer has a problematic number of false negatives.

A *false negative* is an event that is classified as not of interest or not a member of the desired class (negative as in "No, that's not the type of thing I'm interested in knowing about") but that in truth *is* actually of interest. For the nodule-detection problem, it's when a nodule (i.e., a potential cancer) goes undetected. For Dozer, these would be the robberies that he sleeps through. We'll get a bit creative here and use a picture of a *rodent* burglar for false negatives. They're sneaky!

Contrast false negatives with *true negatives*: uninteresting items that are correctly identified as such. We'll go with a picture of a bird for these.

Just to complete the metaphor, chapter 13's model is basically a Dozer. It classifies most nodules as uninteresting because most nodules in our dataset are not cancerous. However, this leads to a large degree of false negatives. Our focus at the end of the last chapter was on the percentage correct for the overall training and validation sets. Clearly, that wasn't a great way to grade ourselves, and as we can see from each of our dogs' myopic focus on a single metric—like the number of true positives or true negatives—we need a metric with a broader focus to capture our overall performance.

14.3 Graphing the positives and negatives

Let's start developing the visual language we'll use to describe true/false positives/negatives. Please bear with us if our explanation gets repetitive; we want to make sure you develop a solid mental model for the ratios we're going to discuss. Consider figure 14.4, which shows events that might be of interest to one of our guard dogs.

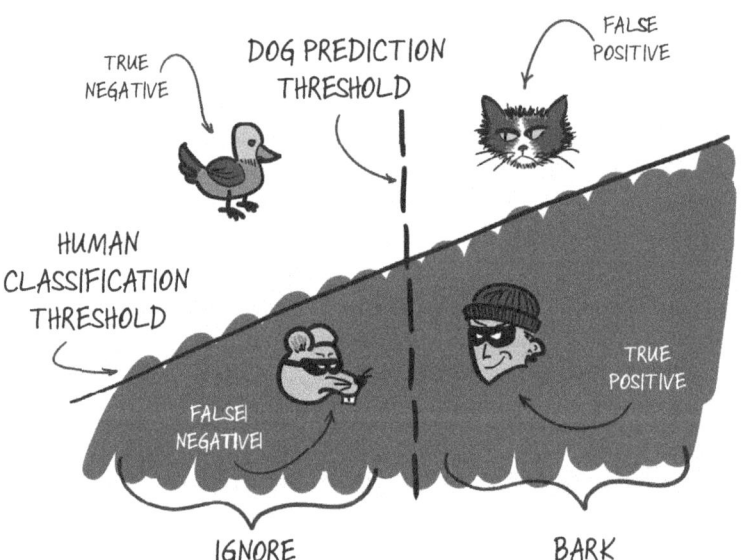

Figure 14.4 Cats, birds, rodents, and robbers make up our four classification quadrants. They are separated by a human label and the dog classification threshold.

We'll use two thresholds shown in figure 14.4. The first is the human-decided dividing line that separates burglars from harmless animals. In concrete terms, this label is given for each training or validation sample. The second is the dog-determined *classification threshold* that determines whether the dog will bark at something. For a deep learning model, this is the predicted value that the model produces when considering a sample.

The combination of these two thresholds divides our events into quadrants: true/false positives/negatives. We will shade the events of concern with a darker background (what with those bad guys sneaking around in the dark all the time).

Of course, reality is far more complicated. There is no platonic ideal of a burglar and no single point relative to the classification threshold at which all burglars will be located. Instead, figure 14.5 shows us that some burglars will be particularly sneaky, and some birds will be particularly annoying. We will also go ahead and enclose our instances in a graph. Our X-axis will remain the bark-worthiness of each event, as determined by one of our guard dogs. The Y-axis represents some vague set of qualities that we as humans are able to perceive, but our dogs cannot.

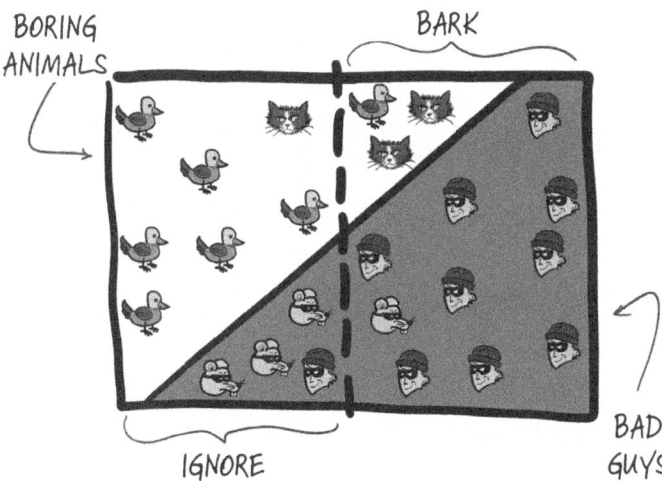

Figure 14.5 Each type of event will have many possible instances that our guard dogs will need to evaluate.

Since our model produces a binary classification, we can think of the prediction threshold as comparing a single-numerical-value output to our classification threshold value. This is why we will require that the classification threshold line be perfectly vertical in figure 14.5.

Each possible burglar is different, so our guard dogs will need to evaluate many different situations, and that means more opportunities to make mistakes. We can see the clear diagonal line that separates the birds from the burglars, but Dozer and Chirpy can only perceive the X-axis here: they have a muddled, overlapped set of events in the middle of our graph. They must pick a vertical bark-worthiness threshold, which means it's impossible for either one of them to do so perfectly. Sometimes the person hauling your appliances to their van is the repair person you hired to fix your washing machine, and sometimes burglars show up in a van that says "Washing Machine Repair" on the side. Expecting a dog to pick up on those nuances is bound to fail.

388 CHAPTER 14 *Improving training with metrics and augmentation*

The actual input data we're going to use has high dimensionality: we need to consider a ton of CT voxel values, along with more abstract things like candidate size, overall location in the lungs, and so on. The job of our model is to map each of these events and respective properties into this rectangle in such a way that we can separate those positive and negative events cleanly using a single vertical line (our classification threshold). This is done by the nn.Linear layers at the end of our model. The position of the vertical line corresponds exactly to the classificationThreshold we saw in section 13.6.1. There, we chose the hardcoded value 0.5 as our threshold.

Note that, in reality, the data presented is not two-dimensional; it goes from very high dimensional after the second-to-last layer, to one-dimensional (here, our X-axis) at the output—just a single scalar per sample (which is then bisected by the classification threshold). Here, we use the second dimension (the Y-axis) to represent per-sample features that our model cannot see or use: things like age or gender of the patient, the location of the nodule candidate in the lung, or even local aspects of the candidate that the model hasn't utilized. It also gives us a convenient way to represent confusion between non-nodule and nodule samples.

The quadrant areas in figure 14.5 and the count of samples contained in each will be the values we use to discuss model performance, since we can use the ratios between these values to construct increasingly complex metrics that we can use to objectively measure how well we are doing. As they say, "the proof is in the proportions." (Okay fine, maybe no one actually says this.) Next, we'll use ratios between these event subsets to start defining better metrics.

14.3.1 Recall is Chirpy's strength

Recall is basically "Make sure you never miss any interesting events!" Formally, *recall* is the ratio of the true positives to all positives (the union of true positives and false negatives). We can see this depicted in figure 14.6.

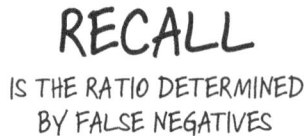

Figure 14.6 Recall is the ratio of the true positives to the union of true positives and false negatives. High recall minimizes false negatives.

NOTE In some contexts, recall is referred to as *sensitivity*.

To improve recall, minimize false negatives. In guard dog terms, that means if you're unsure, bark at it, just in case. Don't let any rodent thieves sneak by on your watch!

Chirpy accomplishes having an incredibly high recall by pushing her classification threshold all the way to the left, such that it encompasses nearly all the positive events in figure 14.7. Note that doing so means her recall value is near 1.0, which means 99% of robbers are barked at. Since that's how Chirpy defines success, in her mind, she's doing a great job. Never mind the huge expanse of false positives!

Figure 14.7 Chirpy's choice of threshold prioritizes minimizing false negatives. Every last rat is barked at . . . and cats and most birds.

14.3.2 Precision is Dozer's forte

Precision is basically "Never bark unless you're sure." To improve precision, minimize false positives. Dozer won't bark at something unless he's certain it's a burglar. More formally, *precision* is the ratio of the true positives to everything detected as positive (union of true positives and false positives), as shown in figure 14.8.

Dozer accomplishes having an incredibly high precision by pushing his classification threshold all the way to the right, such that it excludes as many uninteresting, negative events as he can manage (see figure 14.9). This approach is the opposite of Chirpy's and means Dozer has a precision of nearly 1.0: 99% of the things he barks at are robbers. This also matches his definition of being a good guard dog, even though a large number of events pass undetected.

While neither precision nor recall can be the single metric used to grade our model, they are both useful numbers to have on hand during training. Let's calculate and display these as part of our training program, and then we'll discuss other metrics we can employ.

Figure 14.8 Precision is the ratio of the true positives to the union of true positives and false positives. High precision minimizes false positives.

Figure 14.9 Dozer's choice of threshold prioritizes minimizing false positives. Cats get left alone; only burglars are barked at!

14.3.3 Implementing precision and recall in logMetrics

Both precision and recall are valuable metrics to be able to track during training, since they provide important insight into how the model is behaving. If either drops to zero (as we saw in chapter 13!), it's likely that our model has started to behave in a degenerate manner. We can use the exact details of the behavior to guide where to investigate and experiment with getting training back on track. Let's update the `log-Metrics` function to add precision and recall to the output we see for each epoch, to complement the loss and correctness metrics we already have.

It turns out that we are already computing some of the values we need to calculate precision and recall, even though we had named them differently (training.py:315, `LunaTrainingApp.logMetrics`).

Listing 14.1 Computing counts for true/false positives and negatives

```
neg_count = int(negLabel_mask.sum())
pos_count = int(posLabel_mask.sum())

trueNeg_count = neg_correct = int((negLabel_mask & negPred_mask).sum())
truePos_count = pos_correct = int((posLabel_mask & posPred_mask).sum())

falseNeg_count = pos_count - pos_correct
falsePos_count = neg_count - neg_correct
```

Here, we can see that `neg_correct` is the same thing as `trueNeg_count`! That actually makes sense, since non-nodule is our "negative" value (as in "a negative diagnosis"), and if the classifier gets the prediction correct, then that's a true negative. Similarly, correctly labeled nodule samples are true positives.

We do need to add the variables for our false positive and false negative values. That's straightforward, since we can take the total number of benign labels and subtract the count of the correct ones. What's left is the count of non-nodule samples misclassified *as positive*. Hence, they are false positives. Again, the false negative calculation is of the same form but uses the nodule count.

With those values, we can compute `recall` and `precision` and store them in `metrics_dict` (training.py:333, LunaTrainingApp.logMetrics).

Listing 14.2 Calculating recall and precision from classification counts

```
recall  = metrics_dict['pr/recall'] = \
    truePos_count / np.float32(truePos_count + falseNeg_count)
precision = metrics_dict['pr/precision'] = \
    truePos_count / np.float32(truePos_count + falsePos_count)
```

14.3.4 Our ultimate performance metric: The F1 score

While useful, neither precision nor recall entirely captures what we need to be able to evaluate a model. As we've seen with Chirpy and Dozer, it's possible to game either one individually by manipulating our classification threshold, resulting in a model that scores well on one or the other but does so at the expense of any real-world utility. We need something that combines both of those values in a way that prevents such gamesmanship. As we can see in figure 14.10, it's time to introduce our ultimate metric.

The generally accepted way of combining precision and recall is by using the F1 score (https://en.wikipedia.org/wiki/F-score). As with other metrics, the F1 score ranges between 0 (a classifier with no real-world predictive power) and 1 (a classifier that has perfect predictions). We will update `logMetrics` to include this as well.

Listing 14.3 Calculating F1 score

```
metrics_dict['pr/f1_score'] = \
    2 * (precision * recall) / (precision + recall)
```

392 CHAPTER 14 *Improving training with metrics and augmentation*

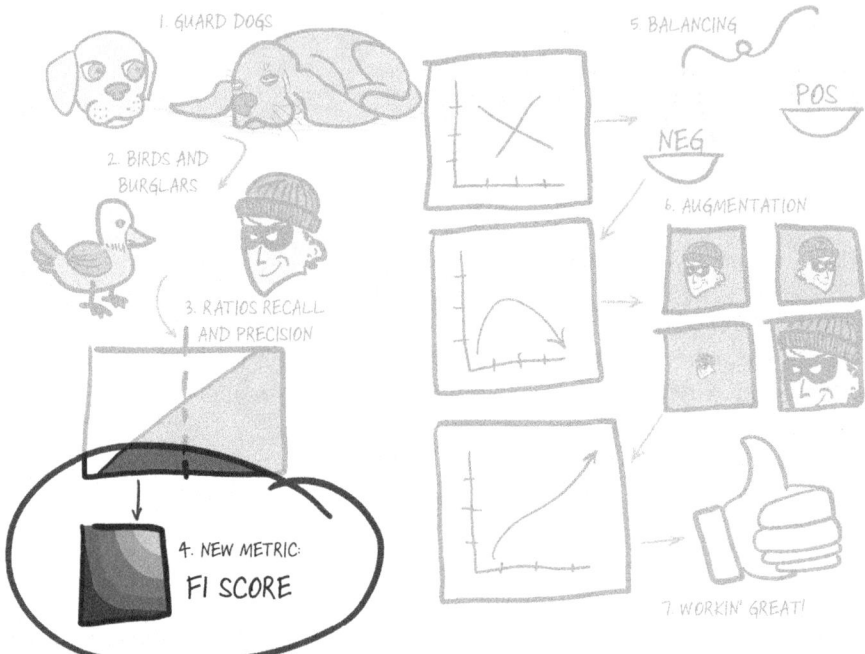

Figure 14.10 The set of topics for this chapter, with a focus on the final **F1 score** metric

At first glance, the F1 score formula might seem more complex than necessary, and it may not be immediately clear how it balances precision and recall. However, this formula has many beneficial properties and often performs better than several simpler alternatives.

One immediate possibility for a scoring function is to average the values for precision and recall together. Unfortunately, this gives both `avg(p=1.0, r=0.0)` and `avg(p=0.5, r=0.5)` the same score of 0.5, and as we discussed earlier, a classifier with either precision or recall of zero is usually worthless. Giving something useless the same nonzero score as something useful disqualifies averaging as a meaningful metric immediately.

Still, let's visually compare averaging versus F1 in figure 14.11. A few things stand out. First, we can see a lack of a curve or elbow in the contour lines for averaging. That's what lets our precision or recall skew to one side or the other! There is always a possible strategy where it makes sense to maximize the score by having 100% recall (the Chirpy approach). That puts a floor on the addition score of 0.5 right out of the gate! Having a quality metric that is trivial to score at least 50% on doesn't feel right.

What we are actually doing here in the left chart of figure 14.11 is taking the *arithmetic mean* (https://en.wikipedia.org/wiki/Arithmetic_mean) of the precision and recall, both of which are *rates* rather than countable scalar values. Taking the arithmetic mean of rates doesn't typically give meaningful results. The F1 score is another

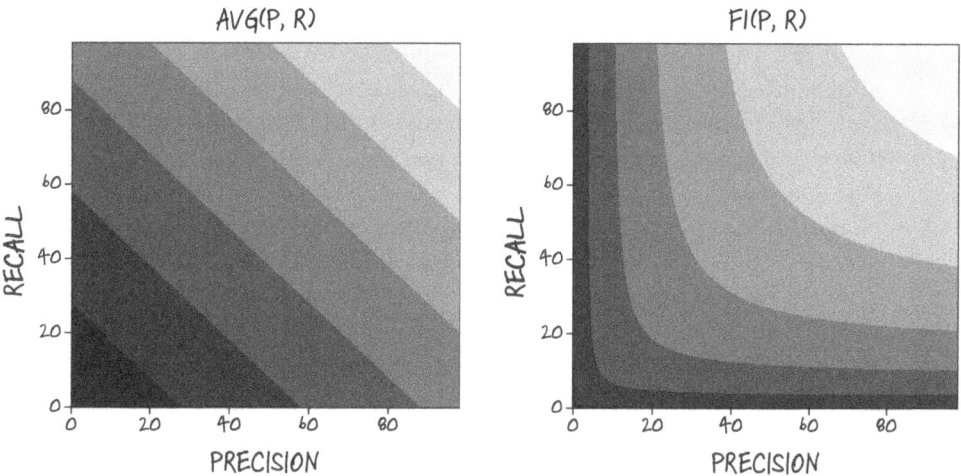

Figure 14.11 Computing the final score with avg(p, r). Lighter values are closer to 1.0 and darker values are closer to 0.0

name for the *harmonic mean* (https://en.wikipedia.org/wiki/Harmonic_mean) of the two rates, which is a more appropriate way of combining those kinds of values.

Contrast that with the F1 score: when recall is high but precision is low, trading off a lot of recall for even a little precision will move the score closer to that balanced sweet spot. There's a nice, deep elbow that is easy to slide into. That encouragement to have balanced precision and recall is what we want from our grading metric.

Let's say we still want a simpler metric, but one that doesn't reward skew at all. To correct for the weakness of addition, we might take the minimum of precision and recall (figure 14.12).

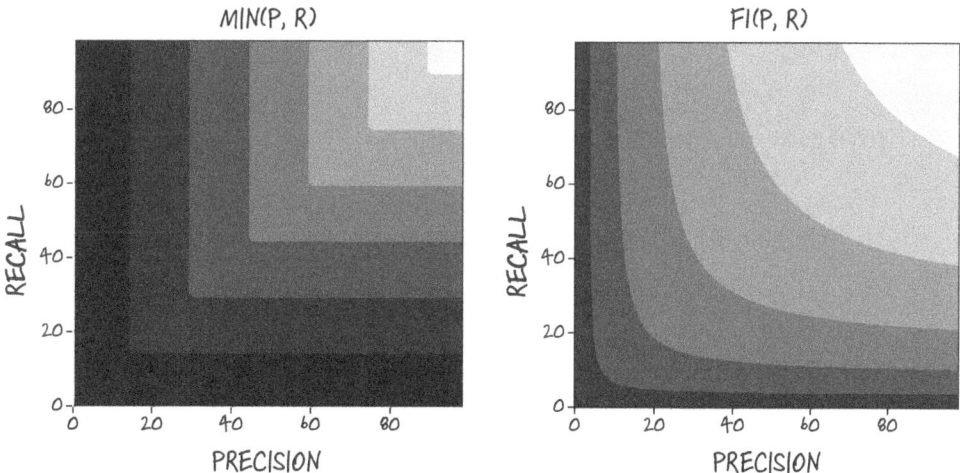

Figure 14.12 Computing the final score with min(p, r)

This computation is nice because if either value is 0, the score is also 0, and the only way to get a score of 1.0 is to have both values be 1.0. However, it still leaves something to be desired, since making a model change that increased the recall from 0.7 to 0.9 while leaving precision constant at 0.5 wouldn't improve the score, nor would dropping recall down to 0.6! Although this metric certainly penalizes for having an imbalance between precision and recall, it isn't capturing a lot of nuance about the two values. As we have seen, it's easy to trade one for the other simply by moving the classification threshold. We'd like our metric to reflect those trades.

We'll have to accept at least a bit more complexity to better meet our goals. We could multiply the two values together, as in figure 14.13. This approach keeps the nice property that if either value is 0, the score is 0, and a score of 1.0 means both inputs are perfect. It also favors a balanced tradeoff between precision and recall at low values, although when it gets closer to perfect results, it becomes more linear. That's not great, since we really need to push both up to have a meaningful improvement at that point.

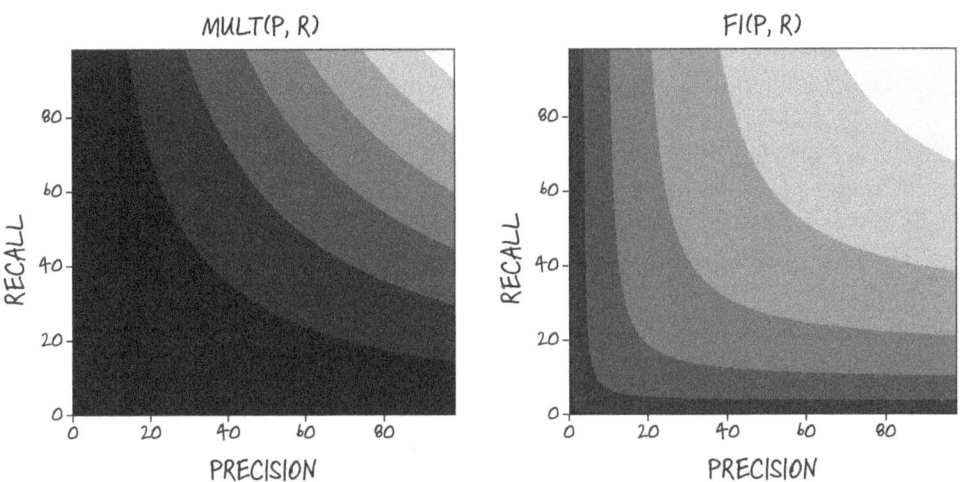

Figure 14.13 Computing the final score with `mult(p, r)`

NOTE We're taking the *geometric mean* (https://en.wikipedia.org/wiki/Geometric_mean) of two rates, which also doesn't produce meaningful results.

There's also the problem of having almost the entire quadrant from (0, 0) to (0.5, 0.5) be very close to zero. As we'll see, having a metric that's sensitive to changes in that region is important, especially in the early stages of our model design.

While using multiplication as our scoring function is feasible (it doesn't have any immediate disqualifications, the way the previous scoring functions did), we will be using the F1 score to evaluate our classification model's performance going forward.

Updating the logging output to include precision, recall, and F1 score

Now that we have our new metrics, adding them to our logging output is pretty straightforward. We'll include precision, recall, and F1 in our main logging statement for each of our training and validation sets (training.py:341, `LunaTrainingApp.logMetrics`).

Listing 14.4 Logging epoch metrics with precision, recall, and F1 score

```
log.info(
    f"E{epoch_ndx} {mode_str:8} {metrics_dict['loss/all']:.4f} loss, "
    f"{metrics_dict['correct/all']:-5.1f}% correct, "
    f"{metrics_dict['pr/precision']:.4f} precision, "         ◁── Format string
    f"{metrics_dict['pr/recall']:.4f} recall, "                    updated
    f"{metrics_dict['pr/f1_score']:.4f} f1 score"
)
```

In addition, we'll include exact values for the count of correctly identified and the total number of samples for each of the negative and positive samples (training.py:353, `LunaTrainingApp.logMetrics`).

Listing 14.5 Logging negative sample accuracy

```
log.info(
    f"E{epoch_ndx} {mode_str + '_neg':8} {"
    ⮡ metrics_dict['loss/neg']:.4f} loss, "
    f"{metrics_dict['correct/neg']:-5.1f}% correct ("
    ⮡ {neg_correct} of {neg_count})"
)
```

The new version of the positive logging statement looks much the same.

14.3.5 How does our model perform with our new metrics?

Now that we've implemented our shiny new metrics, let's take them for a spin; we'll discuss the results after we show the results of the Bash shell session. You might want to read ahead while your system does its number crunching; this could take perhaps half an hour, depending on your system. (If it's taking longer than that, make sure you've run the `prepcache` script.) Exactly how long it takes will depend on your system's CPU, GPU, and disk speeds; our system with an SSD and GTX 1080 Ti took about 20 minutes per full epoch:

```
$ ../.venv/bin/python -m p2ch14.training
Starting LunaTrainingApp...
...
E1 LunaTrainingApp

.../p2ch14/training.py:274: RuntimeWarning:           ◁── The exact count and
⮡ invalid value encountered in double_scalars             line numbers of these
  metrics_dict['pr/f1_score'] = 2 * (precision * recall) /    RuntimeWarning lines
⮡ (precision + recall)                                       might be different
                                                              from run to run.
```

```
E1 trn       0.0025 loss,  99.8% correct, 0.0000 prc, 0.0000 rcl, nan f1
E1 trn_ben   0.0000 loss, 100.0% correct (494735 of 494743)
E1 trn_mal   1.0000 loss,   0.0% correct (0 of 1215)

.../p2ch14/training.py:269: RuntimeWarning:
 invalid value encountered in long_scalars
   precision = metrics_dict['pr/precision'] = truePos_count /
 (truePos_count + falsePos_count)

E1 val       0.0025 loss,  99.8% correct, nan prc, 0.0000 rcl, nan f1
E1 val_ben   0.0000 loss, 100.0% correct (54971 of 54971)
E1 val_mal   1.0000 loss,   0.0% correct (0 of 136)
```

Bummer. We've got some warnings, and given that some of the values we computed were nan, there's probably a division by zero happening somewhere. Let's see what we can figure out.

First, since *none* of the positive samples in the training set are getting classified as positive, that means both precision and recall are zero, which causes our F1 score calculation to divide by zero. Second, for our validation set, truePos_count and falsePos_count, are both zero due to *nothing* being flagged as positive. It follows that the denominator of our precision calculation is also zero; that makes sense, as that's where we're seeing another RuntimeWarning.

A handful of negative training samples are classified as positive (494,735 of 494,743 are classified as negative, so that leaves 8 samples misclassified). While that might seem odd at first, recall that we are collecting our training results *throughout the epoch*, rather than using the model's end-of-epoch state as we do for the validation results. That means the first batch is literally producing random results. A few of the samples from that first batch being flagged as positive isn't surprising.

> **NOTE** Due to both the random initialization of the network weights and the random ordering of the training samples, individual runs will likely exhibit slightly different behavior. Having exactly reproducible behavior can be desirable, but this topic is out of scope for the concepts we're trying to show in part 2 of this book.

Well, that was somewhat painful. Switching to our new metrics resulted in going from A+ to "zero, if you're lucky"—and if we're not lucky, the score is so bad that *it's not even a number*. Ouch. That said, in the long run, this is good for us. We've known that our model's performance was garbage since chapter 13. If our metrics told us anything *but* that, it would point to a fundamental flaw in the metrics!

14.4 What does an ideal dataset look like?

Before we start crying into our cups over the current sorry state of affairs, let's instead think about what we actually want our model to do. Figure 14.14 says that first we need to balance our data so that our model can train properly. Let's build up the logical steps needed to get us there.

14.4 What does an ideal dataset look like?

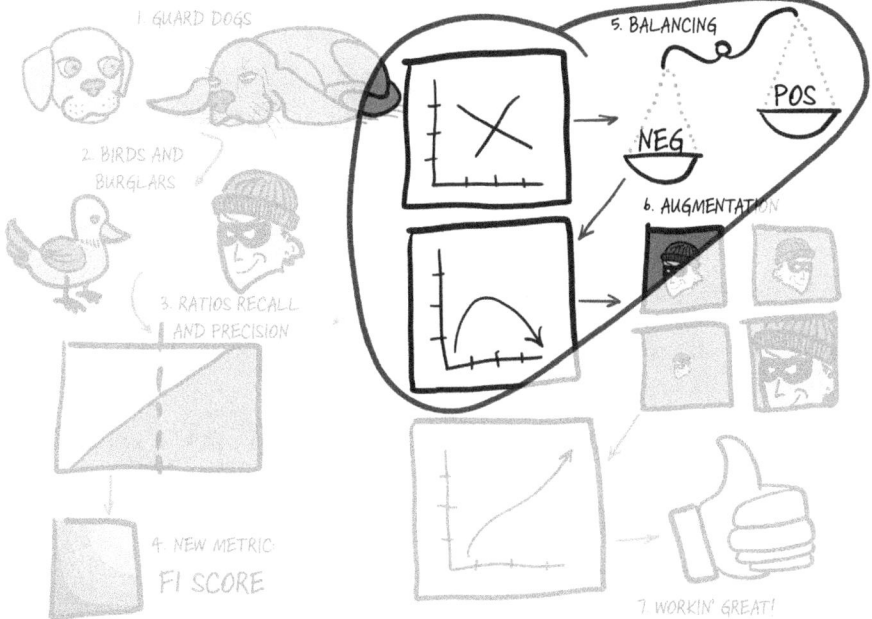

Figure 14.14 The set of topics for this chapter, with a focus on balancing our positive and negative samples

Recall figure 14.5 and the previous discussion of classification thresholds. Getting better results by moving the threshold has limited effectiveness—there's just too much overlap between the positive and negative classes to work with. (Keep in mind that these images are just a representation of the classification space and do not represent ground truth.)

Instead, we want to see an image like figure 14.15. Here, our label threshold is nearly vertical. That's what we want because it means the label threshold and our classification threshold can line up reasonably well. Similarly, most of the samples are concentrated at either end of the diagram. Both things require that our data be easily separable and that our model has the capacity to perform that separation. Our model currently has enough capacity, so that's not the issue. Instead, let's take a look at our data.

Recall that our data is wildly imbalanced. There's a 400:1 ratio of negative samples to positive ones. That's *crushingly* imbalanced! Figure 14.16 shows what that looks like. No wonder our "actually nodule" samples are getting lost in the crowd!

Now, let's be perfectly clear: when we're done, our model will be able to handle this kind of data imbalance just fine. We could probably even train the model all the way there without changing the balancing, assuming we were willing to wait for a gajillion epochs first. (It's not clear whether this is actually true, but it's plausible, and the loss *was* getting better . . .) But we're busy people with things to do, so rather than

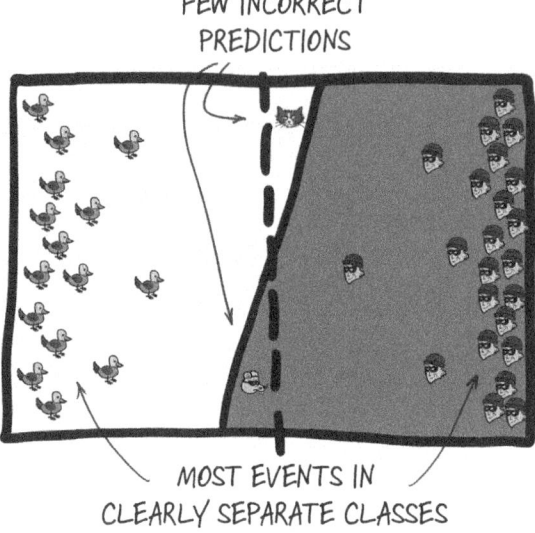

Figure 14.15 A well-trained model can cleanly separate data, making it easy to pick a classification threshold with few tradeoffs.

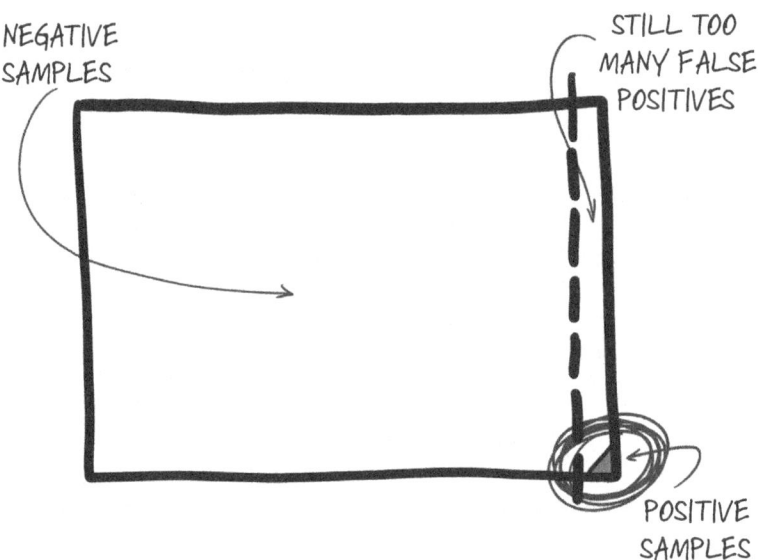

Figure 14.16 An imbalanced dataset that roughly approximates the imbalance in our LUNA classification data

cook our GPU until the heat death of the universe, let's try to make our training data look more ideal by changing the class balance we are training with.

14.4.1 Making the data look less like the actual and more like the "ideal"

The best thing would be to have relatively more positive samples. During the initial epoch of training, when we're going from randomized chaos to something more organized, having so few training samples be positive means they get drowned out.

The process by which this occurs is somewhat subtle. Remember that because our network weights start off as random, the output for each sample is also random (although clamped to the range [0–1]).

> **NOTE** Our loss function is nn.CrossEntropyLoss, which technically operates on the raw logits rather than the class probabilities. For our discussion, we'll ignore that distinction and assume the loss and the label-prediction deltas are the same thing.

The predictions numerically close to the correct label do not result in considerable change to the weights of the network, while predictions that are significantly different from the correct answer are responsible for a much greater change to the weights. Since the output is random when the model is initialized with random weights, we can assume that of our ~500K training samples (495,958, to be exact), we'll have the following groups:

1. 250,000 negative samples will be predicted to be negative (0.0–0.5) and result in at most a small change to the network weights toward predicting negative.
2. 250,000 negative samples will be predicted to be positive (0.5–1.0) and result in a large swing toward the network weights predicting negative.
3. 500 positive samples will be predicted to be negative and result in a swing toward the network weights predicting positive.
4. 500 positive samples will be predicted to be positive and result in almost no change to the network weights.

> **NOTE** Keep in mind that the actual predictions are real numbers between 0.0 and 1.0 inclusive, so these groups won't have strict delineations.

Here's the kicker, though: groups 1 and 4 have close-to-zero effect on training. The only thing that matters is that groups 2 and 3 can counteract each other's pull enough to prevent the network from collapsing to a degenerate "only output one thing" state. Since group 2 is 500 times larger than group 3 and we're using a batch size of 32, roughly 500/32 = 15 batches will go by before seeing a single positive sample. That implies that 14 out of 15 training batches will be 100% negative and will only pull all model weights toward predicting negative. That lopsided pull is what produces the degenerate behavior we've been seeing.

Instead, we'd like to have just as many positive samples as negative ones. For the first part of training, then, half of both labels will be classified incorrectly, meaning that groups 2 and 3 should be roughly equal in size. We also want to make sure we present batches with a mix of negative and positive samples. Balance would result in the tug-of-war evening out, and the mixture of classes per batch will give the model a decent chance of learning to discriminate between the two classes. Since our LUNA data has only a small, fixed number of positive samples, we'll have to settle for taking the positive samples that we have and presenting them repeatedly during training.

> **Discrimination**
>
> Here, we define discrimination as "the ability to separate two classes from each other." Building and training a model that can tell "actually nodule" candidates from normal anatomical structures is the entire point of what we're doing in part 2.
>
> Some other definitions of discrimination are more problematic. While out of the scope for the discussion of our work here, there is a larger issue with models trained from real-world data. If that real-world dataset is collected from sources that have a real-world-discriminatory bias (e.g., racial bias in arrest and conviction rates, or anything collected from social media), and that bias is not corrected for during dataset preparation or training, the resulting model will continue to exhibit the same biases present in the training data. Just as in humans, racism is learned.
>
> As a result, almost any model trained from internet-at-large data sources will be compromised in some fashion, unless extreme care is taken to scrub those biases from the model. Note that like our goal in part 2, this problem is considered unsolved.

Recall our professor from chapter 13, who had a final exam with 99 false answers and 1 true answer. The next semester, after being told, "You should have a more even balance of true and false answers," the professor decided to add a midterm with 99 true answers and 1 false one. "Problem solved!"

Clearly, the actually correct approach is to intermix true and false answers in a way that doesn't allow the students to exploit the larger structure of the tests to answer things correctly. Whereas a student would pick up on a pattern like "Odd questions are true; even questions are false," the batching system used by PyTorch doesn't allow the model to "notice" or utilize that kind of pattern. Our training dataset will need to be updated to alternate between positive and negative samples, as in figure 14.17.

We will not be doing any balancing for validation, however. Our model needs to function well in the real world, and the real world is imbalanced (after all, that's where we got the raw data!). How should we accomplish this balancing? Let's discuss our choices.

SAMPLERS CAN RESHAPE DATASETS

One of the optional arguments to `DataLoader` is `sampler=...`. This argument allows the data loader to override the iteration order native to the dataset passed in and instead shape, limit, or reemphasize the underlying data as desired. This can be incredibly useful when working with a dataset that isn't under your control. Taking a public dataset and reshaping it to meet your needs is far less work than reimplementing that dataset from scratch.

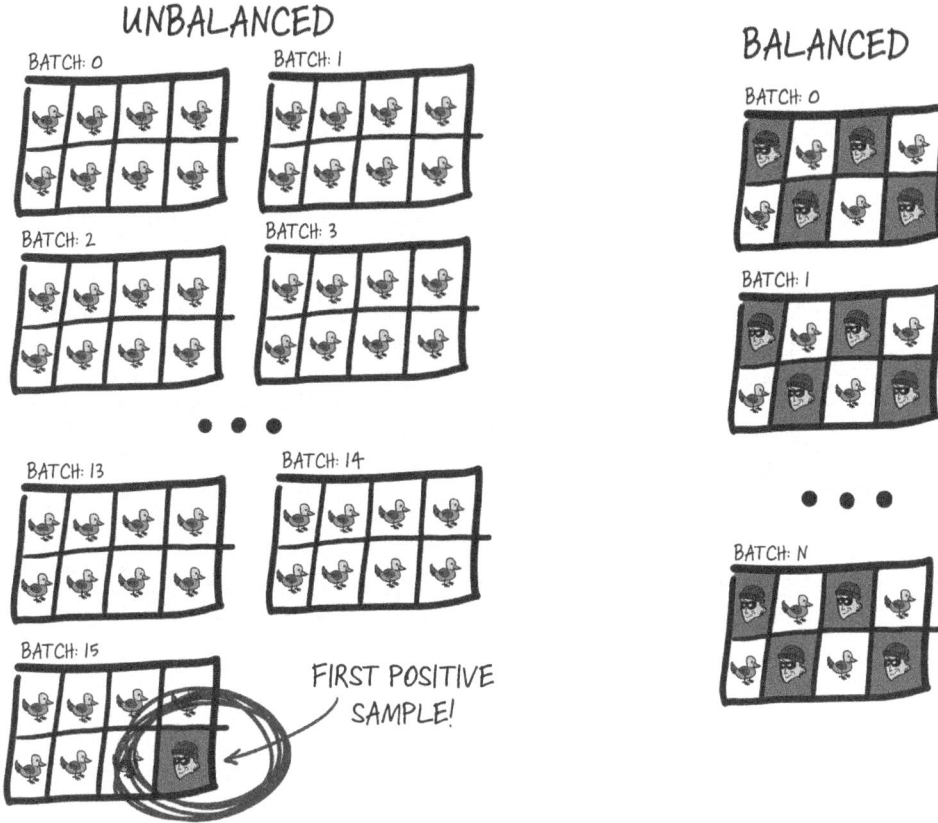

Figure 14.17 Batch after batch of imbalanced data will have nothing but negative events long before the first positive event, while balanced data can alternate every other sample.

The downside is that many of the mutations we could accomplish with samplers require that we break encapsulation of the underlying dataset. For example, let's assume we have a dataset like CIFAR-10 (http://www.cs.toronto.edu/~kriz/cifar.html) that consists of 10 equally weighted classes, and we want to, instead, have 1 class (say, "airplane") make up 50% of all the training images. We could decide to use `WeightedRandomSampler` (https://mng.bz/vZ5m) and weight each of the "airplane" sample indexes higher, but constructing the `weights` argument requires that we know in advance which indexes are airplanes.

As we previously discussed, the `Dataset` API only specifies that subclasses provide `__len__` and `__getitem__`, but there is nothing direct we can use to ask, "Which samples are airplanes?" We'd either have to load up every sample beforehand to inquire about the class of that sample, or we'd have to break encapsulation and hope the information we need is easily obtained from looking at the internal implementation of the `Dataset` subclass.

Since neither of those options is particularly ideal in cases where we have control over the dataset directly, the code for part 2 implements any needed data shaping inside the Dataset subclasses instead of relying on an external sampler.

IMPLEMENTING CLASS BALANCING IN THE DATASET

We are going to directly change our LunaDataset to present a balanced, one-to-one ratio of positive and negative samples for training. We will keep separate lists of negative training samples and positive training samples, and alternate returning samples from each of those two lists. This will prevent the degenerate behavior of the model scoring well by simply answering "false" to every sample presented. In addition, the positive and negative classes will be intermixed so that the weight updates are forced to discriminate between the classes.

Let's add a ratio_int to LunaDataset that will control the label for the Nth sample as well as keep track of our samples separated by label (dsets.py:217, class LunaDataset).

Listing 14.6 Initializing LunaDataset with ratio-based label balancing

```
class LunaDataset(Dataset):
  def __init__(self,
        val_stride=0,
        isValSet_bool=None,
        ratio_int=0,
     ):
    self.ratio_int = ratio_int
    # ... line 228
    self.negative_list = [
      nt for nt in self.candidateInfo_list if not nt.isNodule_bool
    ]
    self.pos_list = [
      nt for nt in self.candidateInfo_list if nt.isNodule_bool
    ]
    # ... line 265

  def shuffleSamples(self):              ◁─── We will call this at the top of each
    if self.ratio_int:                        epoch to randomize the order of
      random.shuffle(self.negative_list)      samples being presented.
      random.shuffle(self.pos_list)
```

With this, we now have dedicated lists for each label. Using these lists, it becomes much easier to return the label we want for a given index into the dataset. To make sure we're getting the indexing right, we should sketch out the ordering we want. Let's assume a ratio_int of 2, meaning a 2:1 ratio of negative to positive samples. That would mean every third index should be positive:

```
DS Index    0 1 2 3 4 5 6 7 8 9 ...
Label       + - - + - - + - - +
Pos Index   0     1     2     3
Neg Index     0 1   2 3   4 5
```

The relationship between the dataset index and the positive index is simple: divide the dataset index by 3 and then round down. The negative index is slightly more complicated because we have to subtract 1 from the dataset index and then subtract the most recent positive index as well. Implemented in our `LunaDataset` class, that looks like the following listing (dsets.py:286, `LunaDataset.__getitem__`).

Listing 14.7 Get balanced positive and negative samples

```
def __getitem__(self, ndx):
  if self.ratio_int:                              ◁── A ratio_int of zero means
    pos_ndx = ndx // (self.ratio_int + 1)              use the native balance.

    if ndx % (self.ratio_int + 1):                ◁── A nonzero remainder means this
      neg_ndx = ndx - 1 - pos_ndx                      should be a negative sample.
      neg_ndx %= len(self.negative_list)
      candidateInfo_tup = self.negative_list[neg_ndx]  ◁── Overflow results
    else:                                                  in wraparound.
      pos_ndx %= len(self.pos_list)
      candidateInfo_tup = self.pos_list[pos_ndx]
```

That can get a little hairy, but if you desk-check it out, it will make sense. Keep in mind that with a low ratio, we'll run out of positive samples before exhausting the dataset. We take care of that by taking the modulus of `pos_ndx` before indexing into `self.pos_list`. While the same kind of index overflow should never happen with `neg_ndx` due to the large number of negative samples, we do the modulus anyway, just in case we later decide to make a change that might cause it to overflow.

We'll also make a change to our dataset's length. Although this isn't strictly necessary, it's nice to speed up individual epochs. We're going to hardcode our `__len__` to be 200,000 (dsets.py:280, `LunaDataset.__len__`).

Listing 14.8 Length of our dataset

```
def __len__(self):
  if self.ratio_int:
    return 200000
  else:
    return len(self.candidateInfo_list)
```

We're no longer tied to a specific number of samples, and presenting a full epoch doesn't really make sense when we would have to repeat positive samples many, many times to present a balanced training set. By picking 200,000 samples, we reduce the time between starting a training run and seeing results (faster feedback is always nice!), and we give ourselves a nice, clean number of samples per epoch. Feel free to adjust the length of an epoch to meet your needs.

For completeness, we also add a command-line parameter (training.py:31, `class LunaTrainingApp`).

Listing 14.9 Adding --balanced command-line argument

```
class LunaTrainingApp:
  def __init__(self, sys_argv=None):
    # ... line 52
    parser.add_argument('--balanced',
      help="Balance the training data to half positive, half negative.",
      action='store_true',
      default=False,
    )
```

Then we pass that parameter into the LunaDataset constructor (training.py:137, Luna-TrainingApp.initTrainDl).

Listing 14.10 LunaDataset constructor with our new argument

```
def initTrainDl(self):
  train_ds = LunaDataset(
    val_stride=10,
    isValSet_bool=False,
    ratio_int=int(self.cli_args.balanced),    ◁── Here, we rely on Python's True being convertible to a 1.
  )
```

We're all set. Let's run it!

14.4.2 Contrasting training with a balanced LunaDataset to previous runs

As a reminder, our unbalanced training run had results like these:

```
$ python -m p2ch14.training
...
E1 LunaTrainingApp
E1 trn      0.0185 loss,  99.7% correct, 0.0000 precision, 0.0000 recall,
➥ nan f1 score
E1 trn_neg  0.0026 loss, 100.0% correct (494717 of 494743)
E1 trn_pos  6.5267 loss,   0.0% correct (0 of 1215)
...
E1 val      0.0173 loss,  99.8% correct, nan precision, 0.0000 recall,
➥ nan f1 score
E1 val_neg  0.0026 loss, 100.0% correct (54971 of 54971)
E1 val_pos  5.9577 loss,   0.0% correct (0 of 136)
```

But when we run with --balanced, we see the following:

```
$ python -m p2ch14.training --balanced
...
E1 LunaTrainingApp
E1 trn      0.1734 loss,  92.8% correct, 0.9363 precision, 0.9194 recall,
➥ 0.9277 f1 score
E1 trn_neg  0.1770 loss,  93.7% correct (93741 of 100000)
E1 trn_pos  0.1698 loss,  91.9% correct (91939 of 100000)
```

```
...
E1 val        0.0564 loss,   98.4% correct, 0.1102 precision, 0.7941 recall,
↳ 0.1935 f1 score
E1 val_neg    0.0542 loss,   98.4% correct (54099 of 54971)
E1 val_pos    0.9549 loss,   79.4% correct (108 of 136)
```

This seems much better! We've given up about 1.6% correct answers on the negative samples (val_neg: 100% → 98.4%) to gain 79% correct positive answers (val_pos: 0% → 79.4%). We're back into a solid B range again! And remember that this is after only the 200,000 training samples presented, not the 500,000+ of the unbalanced dataset, so we got there in less than half the time.

As in chapter 13, however, this result is deceptive due to the extreme class imbalance. Let's do the math. With approximately 400 negative samples for each positive sample, misclassifying just 1% of negatives creates a significant problem:

- *Total negative validation samples*—54,971
- *Total positive validation samples*—136
- *False positives at 1% error rate*—54,971 × 0.01 = ~550 samples
- *Ratio of false positives to total positives*—550 ÷ 136 = ~4:1

This means even with 99% accuracy on negative samples, we'd incorrectly flag about four times as many false positives as there are actual positive samples in the entire dataset! This dramatically reduces the practical utility of the model despite its seemingly high overall accuracy.

Still, it is clearly better than the outright wrong behavior from chapter 13 and much better than a random coin flip. In fact, we've even crossed over into being (almost) legitimately useful in real-world scenarios. Recall our overworked radiologist pouring over each and every speck of a CT: well, now we've got something that can do a reasonable job of screening out 98.4% of the negative samples. That's a huge help, since it translates into about a tenfold increase in productivity for the machine-assisted human.

Of course, there's still that pesky issue of the 20.6% of positive samples that were missed (since we correctly identified 79.4%). Perhaps some additional epochs of training would help. Let's see (and again, expect to spend at least 10 minutes per epoch):

```
$ python -m p2ch14.training --balanced --epochs 20
...
E2 LunaTrainingApp
E2 trn        0.0432 loss,   98.7% correct, 0.9866 precision, 0.9879 recall,
↳ 0.9873 f1 score
E2 trn_ben    0.0545 loss,   98.7% correct (98663 of 100000)
E2 trn_mal    0.0318 loss,   98.8% correct (98790 of 100000)
E2 val        0.0603 loss,   98.5% correct, 0.1271 precision, 0.8456 recall,
↳ 0.2209 f1 score
E2 val_ben    0.0584 loss,   98.6% correct (54181 of 54971)
E2 val_mal    0.8471 loss,   84.6% correct (115 of 136)
...
```

```
E5 trn      0.0578 loss,  98.3% correct, 0.9839 precision, 0.9823 recall,
➥ 0.9831 f1 score
E5 trn_ben  0.0665 loss,  98.4% correct (98388 of 100000)
E5 trn_mal  0.0490 loss,  98.2% correct (98227 of 100000)
E5 val      0.0361 loss,  99.2% correct, 0.2129 precision, 0.8235 recall,
➥ 0.3384 f1 score
E5 val_ben  0.0336 loss,  99.2% correct (54557 of 54971)
E5 val_mal  1.0515 loss,  82.4% correct (112 of 136)...
...
E10 trn      0.0212 loss,  99.5% correct, 0.9942 precision, 0.9953 recall,
➥ 0.9948 f1 score
E10 trn_ben  0.0281 loss,  99.4% correct (99421 of 100000)
E10 trn_mal  0.0142 loss,  99.5% correct (99530 of 100000)
E10 val      0.0457 loss,  99.3% correct, 0.2171 precision, 0.7647 recall,
➥ 0.3382 f1 score
E10 val_ben  0.0407 loss,  99.3% correct (54596 of 54971)
E10 val_mal  2.0594 loss,  76.5% correct (104 of 136)
...
E20 trn      0.0132 loss,  99.7% correct, 0.9964 precision, 0.9974 recall,
➥ 0.9969 f1 score
E20 trn_ben  0.0186 loss,  99.6% correct (99642 of 100000)
E20 trn_mal  0.0079 loss,  99.7% correct (99736 of 100000)
E20 val      0.0200 loss,  99.7% correct, 0.4780 precision, 0.7206 recall,
➥ 0.5748 f1 score
E20 val_ben  0.0133 loss,  99.8% correct (54864 of 54971)
E20 val_mal  2.7101 loss,  72.1% correct (98 of 136)
```

Ugh. That's a lot of text to scroll past to get to the numbers we're interested in. Let's power through and focus on the val_mal XX.X% correct numbers. After epoch 2, we were at 84.6%; on epoch 5, we reached 82.4%; and then by epoch 20 we dropped down to 72.1%—showing a clear downward trend!

> **NOTE** As mentioned earlier, expect each run to have unique behavior due to random initialization of network weights and random selection and ordering of training samples per epoch.

The training set numbers don't appear to have the same problem. After 20 epochs, negative training samples are classified correctly 99.6% of the time, and positive samples are 99.7% correct. Why the big difference?

14.4.3 Recognizing the symptoms of overfitting

What we are seeing are clear signs of overfitting. Let's take a look at the graph of our loss on positive samples in figure 14.18.

Here, we can see that the training loss for our positive samples is nearly zero—each positive training sample gets a nearly perfect prediction. Our validation loss for positive samples is *increasing*, though, and that means our real-world performance is likely getting worse. At this point, it's often best to stop the training script since the model is no longer improving.

14.4 What does an ideal dataset look like?

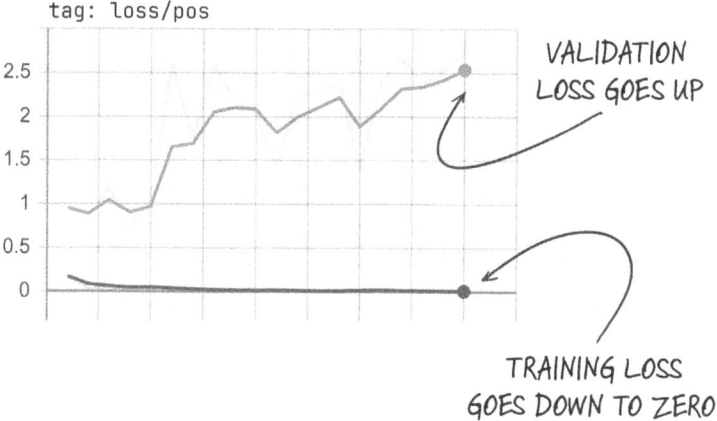

Figure 14.18 Our positive loss shows clear signs of overfitting, as the training and validation losses are trending in different directions.

> **TIP** Generally, if your model's performance is improving on your training set while getting worse on your validation set, the model has started overfitting.

We must take care to examine the right metrics because this trend is only happening on our *positive* loss. If we look at our overall loss, everything seems fine! That's because our validation set is not balanced, so the overall loss is dominated by our negative samples. As shown in figure 14.19, we are not seeing the same divergent behavior for our negative samples. Instead, our negative loss looks great! That's because we have 400 times more negative samples, so it's much, much harder for the model to remember individual details. Our positive training set has only 1,215 samples, though. While we repeat those samples multiple times, that doesn't make them harder to memorize. The model is shifting from generalized principles to essentially memorizing quirks of those 1,215 samples and claiming that anything that's not one of those few samples is negative. This includes both negative training samples and everything in our validation set (both positive and negative).

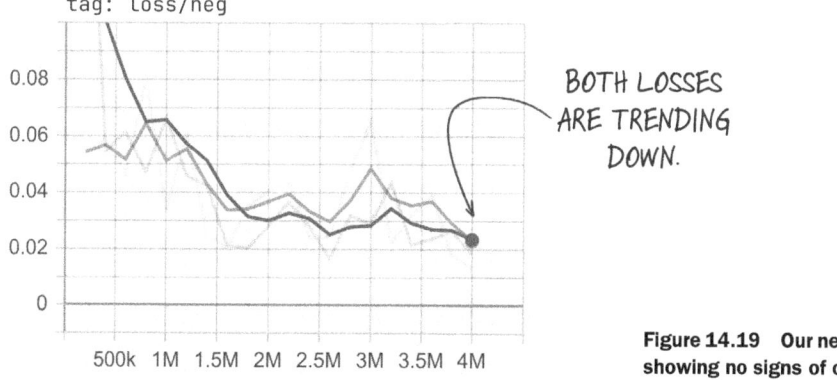

Figure 14.19 Our negative loss is showing no signs of overfitting.

Clearly, some generalization is still going on since we are classifying about 70% of the positive validation set correctly. We just need to change how we're training the model so that our training set and validation set both trend in the right direction.

14.5 Revisiting the problem of overfitting

We touched on the concept of overfitting in chapter 6, and now it's time to take a closer look at how to address this common situation. Our goal with training a model is to teach it to recognize the *general properties* of the classes we are interested in, as expressed in our dataset. Those general properties are present in some or all samples of the class and can be *generalized* and used to predict samples that haven't been trained on. When the model starts to learn *specific properties* of the training set, overfitting occurs, and the model starts to lose the ability to generalize. In case that's a bit too abstract, let's use another analogy.

14.5.1 An overfit face-to-age prediction model

Let's pretend we have a model that takes an image of a human face as input and outputs a predicted age in years. A good model would pick up on age signifiers, such as wrinkles, gray hair, hairstyle, clothing choices, and similar, and use those to build a general model of what different ages look like. When presented with a new picture, it would consider things like "conservative haircut," "reading glasses," and "wrinkles" to conclude "around 65 years old."

An overfit model, by contrast, instead remembers specific people by remembering identifying details. "That haircut and those glasses mean it's Frank. He's 62.8 years old"; "Oh, that scar means it's Harry. He's 39.3"; and so on. When shown a new person, the model won't recognize the person and will have absolutely no idea what age to predict.

Even worse, if shown a picture of Frank Jr. (the spittin' image of his dad, at least when he's wearing his glasses!), the model will say, "I think that's Frank. He's 62.8 years old." Never mind that Junior is 25 years younger!

Overfitting is usually due to having too few training samples when compared to the ability of the model to just memorize the answers. The median human can memorize the birthdays of their immediate family but would have to resort to generalizations when predicting the ages of any group larger than a small village.

Our face-to-age model has the capacity to simply memorize the photos of anyone who doesn't look exactly their age. As we discussed in part 1, model capacity is a somewhat abstract concept, but it is roughly a function of the number of parameters of the model times how efficiently those parameters are used. When a model has a high capacity relative to the amount of data needed to memorize the hard samples from the training set, it's likely that the model will begin to overfit on those more difficult training samples.

14.6 Preventing overfitting with data augmentation

It's time to take our model training from good to great. We need to cover one last step in figure 14.20.

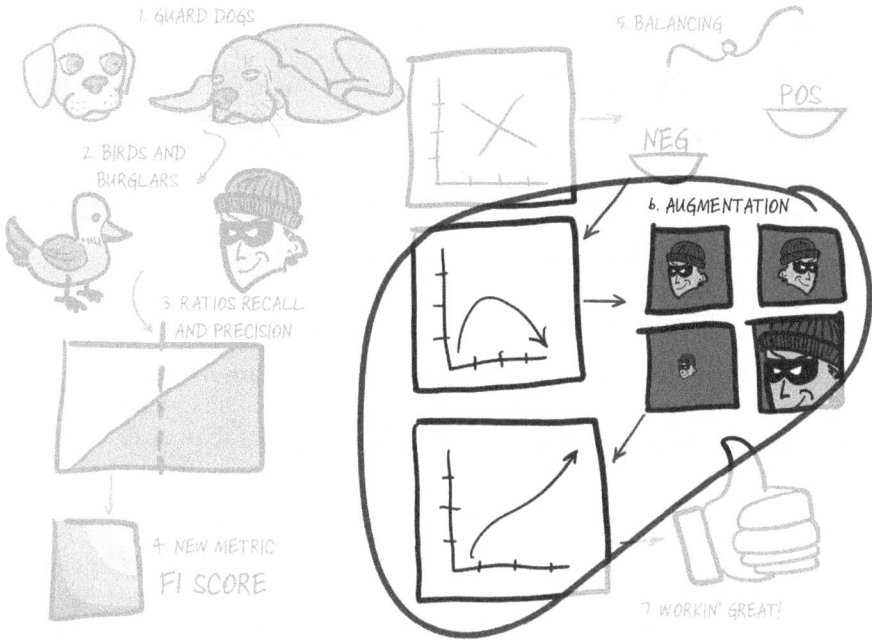

Figure 14.20 The set of topics for this chapter, with a focus on data augmentation

We *augment* a dataset by applying synthetic alterations to individual samples, resulting in a new dataset with an effective size that is larger than the original. The typical goal is for the alterations to result in a synthetic sample that remains representative of the same general class as the source sample, but that cannot be trivially memorized alongside the original. When done properly, this augmentation can increase the training set size beyond what the model is capable of memorizing, resulting in the model being forced to increasingly rely on generalization, which is exactly what we want. Doing so is especially useful when dealing with limited data.

Of course, not all augmentations are equally useful. Going back to our example of a face-to-age prediction model, we could trivially change the red channel of the four corner pixels of each image to a random value (0–255), which would result in a dataset 4 billion times larger than the original. Of course, this wouldn't be particularly useful, since the model can pretty trivially learn to ignore the red dots in the image corners, and the rest of the image remains as easy to memorize as the single, unaugmented original image. Contrast that approach with flipping the image left to right. Doing so would only result in a dataset twice as large as the original, but each image would be quite a bit more useful for training purposes. The general properties of aging are not correlated left to right, so a mirrored image remains representative. Similarly, it's rare for facial pictures to be perfectly symmetrical, so a mirrored version is unlikely to be trivially memorized alongside the original.

14.6.1 Specific data augmentation techniques

We are going to implement five specific types of data augmentation. Our implementation will allow us to experiment with any or all of them, individually or in aggregate. The five techniques are as follows:

- Mirroring the image up-down, left-right, and/or front-back
- Shifting the image around by a few voxels
- Scaling the image up or down
- Rotating the image around the head-foot axis
- Adding noise to the image

NOTE Image augmentation techniques should be chosen based on domain-specific knowledge. For instance, while flipping a face image left-right might be valid, flipping it up-down would create an unnatural, unrealistic training example.

For each technique, we want to make sure our approach maintains the training sample's representative nature, while being different enough that the sample is useful to train with.

We'll define a function getCtAugmentedCandidate that is responsible for taking our standard chunk of CT data with the candidate and modifying it. Our main approach will define an affine transformation matrix (https://mng.bz/4n25) and use it with the PyTorch affine_grid (https://mng.bz/QwN1) and grid_sample (https://mng.bz/X76l) functions to resample our candidate.

We first obtain ct_chunk, either from the cache or directly by loading the CT (something that will come in handy once we are creating our own candidate centers), and then convert it to a tensor (dsets.py:149, def getCtAugmentedCandidate).

Listing 14.11 Loading and converting CT data to tensor format

```
def getCtAugmentedCandidate(
    augmentation_dict,
    series_uid, center_xyz, width_irc,
    use_cache=True):
  if use_cache:
    ct_chunk, center_irc = \
      getCtRawCandidate(series_uid, center_xyz, width_irc)
  else:
    ct = getCt(series_uid)
    ct_chunk, center_irc = ct.getRawCandidate(center_xyz, width_irc)

  ct_t = torch.tensor(ct_chunk).unsqueeze(0).unsqueeze(0).to(torch.float32)
```

14.6 Preventing overfitting with data augmentation

Next is the affine grid and sampling code (dsets.py:162, def `getCtAugmentedCandidate`).

Listing 14.12 Applying affine transformation

```
transform_t = torch.eye(4)
# ...                                      ◁─┐ Modifications to
# ... line 195                                │ transform_tensor will go here.
affine_t = F.affine_grid(
    transform_t[:3].unsqueeze(0).to(torch.float32),
    ct_t.size(),
    align_corners=False,
)

augmented_chunk = F.grid_sample(
    ct_t,
    affine_t,
    padding_mode='border',
    align_corners=False,
).to('cpu')
# ... line 214
return augmented_chunk[0], center_irc
```

Without anything additional, this function won't do much. Let's see what it takes to add in some actual transforms.

> **NOTE** It's important to structure your data pipeline such that your caching steps happen *before* augmentation! Doing otherwise will result in your data being augmented once and then persisted in that state, which defeats the purpose.

MIRRORING

When mirroring a sample, we keep the pixel values exactly the same and only change the orientation of the image. Since there's no strong correlation between tumor growth and left-right or front-back, we should be able to flip those without changing the representative nature of the sample. The index-axis (referred to as *Z* in patient coordinates) corresponds to the direction of gravity in an upright human, so there's a possibility of a difference in the top and bottom of a tumor. We are going to assume it's fine, since quick visual investigation doesn't show any gross bias. Were we working toward a clinically relevant project, we'd need to confirm that assumption with an expert (dsets.py:165, def `getCtAugmentedCandidate`).

Listing 14.13 Flipping images to augment

```
for i in range(3):
    if 'flip' in augmentation_dict:
        if random.random() > 0.5:
            transform_t[i,i] *= -1
```

The `grid_sample` function maps the range [–1, 1] to the extents of both the old and new tensors (the rescaling happens implicitly if the sizes are different). This range mapping means that to mirror the data, all we need to do is multiply the relevant element of the transformation matrix by –1.

SHIFTING BY A RANDOM OFFSET

Shifting the nodule candidate around shouldn't make a huge difference, since convolutions are translation independent, although this will make our model more robust to imperfectly centered nodules. What will make a more significant difference is that the offset might not be an integer number of voxels; instead, the data will be resampled using trilinear interpolation, which can introduce some slight blurring. Voxels at the edge of the sample will be repeated, which can be seen as a smeared, streaky section along the border (dsets.py:165, def getCtAugmentedCandidate).

> **Listing 14.14 Applying random spatial offsets for translation invariance**

```
for i in range(3):
  # ... line 170
  if 'offset' in augmentation_dict:
    offset_float = augmentation_dict['offset']
    random_float = (random.random() * 2 - 1)
    transform_t[i,3] = offset_float * random_float
```

Note that our 'offset' parameter is the maximum offset expressed in the same scale as the [–1, 1] range the grid sample function expects.

SCALING

Scaling the image slightly is very similar to mirroring and shifting. Doing so can also result in the same repeated edge voxels we just mentioned when discussing shifting the sample (dsets.py:165, def getCtAugmentedCandidate).

> **Listing 14.15 Applying random scaling transformations**

```
for i in range(3):
  # ... line 175
  if 'scale' in augmentation_dict:
    scale_float = augmentation_dict['scale']
    random_float = (random.random() * 2 - 1)
    transform_t[i,i] *= 1.0 + scale_float * random_float
```

Since random_float is converted to be in the range [–1, 1], it doesn't actually matter if we add scale_float * random_float to or subtract it from 1.0.

ROTATING

Rotation is the first augmentation technique we're going to use where we have to carefully consider our data to ensure that we don't break our sample with a conversion that causes it to no longer be representative. Recall that our CT slices have uniform spacing along the rows and columns (X- and Y-axes), but in the index (or Z) direction, the voxels are noncubic. Consequently, we can't treat those axes as interchangeable.

One option is to resample our data so that our resolution along the index-axis is the same as along the other two, but that's not a true solution because the data along that axis would be very blurry and smeared. Even if we interpolate more voxels, the fidelity of the data would remain poor. Instead, we'll treat that axis as special and confine our rotations to the X-Y plane (dsets.py:181, def `getCtAugmentedCandidate`).

Listing 14.16 Rotating an image

```
if 'rotate' in augmentation_dict:
  angle_rad = random.random() * math.pi * 2
  s = math.sin(angle_rad)
  c = math.cos(angle_rad)

  rotation_t = torch.tensor([
    [c, -s, 0, 0],
    [s, c, 0, 0],
    [0, 0, 1, 0],
    [0, 0, 0, 1],
  ])

  transform_t @= rotation_t
```

NOISE

Our final augmentation technique is different from the others in that it is actively destructive to our sample in a way that flipping or rotating the sample is not. If we add too much noise to the sample, it will swamp the real data and make it effectively impossible to classify. While shifting and scaling the sample would do something similar if we used extreme input values, we've chosen values that will only affect the edge of the sample. Noise will affect the entire image (dsets.py:208, def `getCtAugmented-Candidate`).

Listing 14.17 Adding random Gaussian noise

```
if 'noise' in augmentation_dict:
  noise_t = torch.randn_like(augmented_chunk)
  noise_t *= augmentation_dict['noise']

  augmented_chunk += noise_t
```

The other augmentation types have increased the effective size of our dataset. Noise makes our model's job *harder*. We'll revisit this once we see some training results.

EXAMINING AUGMENTED CANDIDATES

We can see the result of our efforts in figure 14.21. The upper-left image shows an unaugmented positive candidate, and the next five show the effect of each augmentation type in isolation. Finally, the bottom row shows the combined result three times.

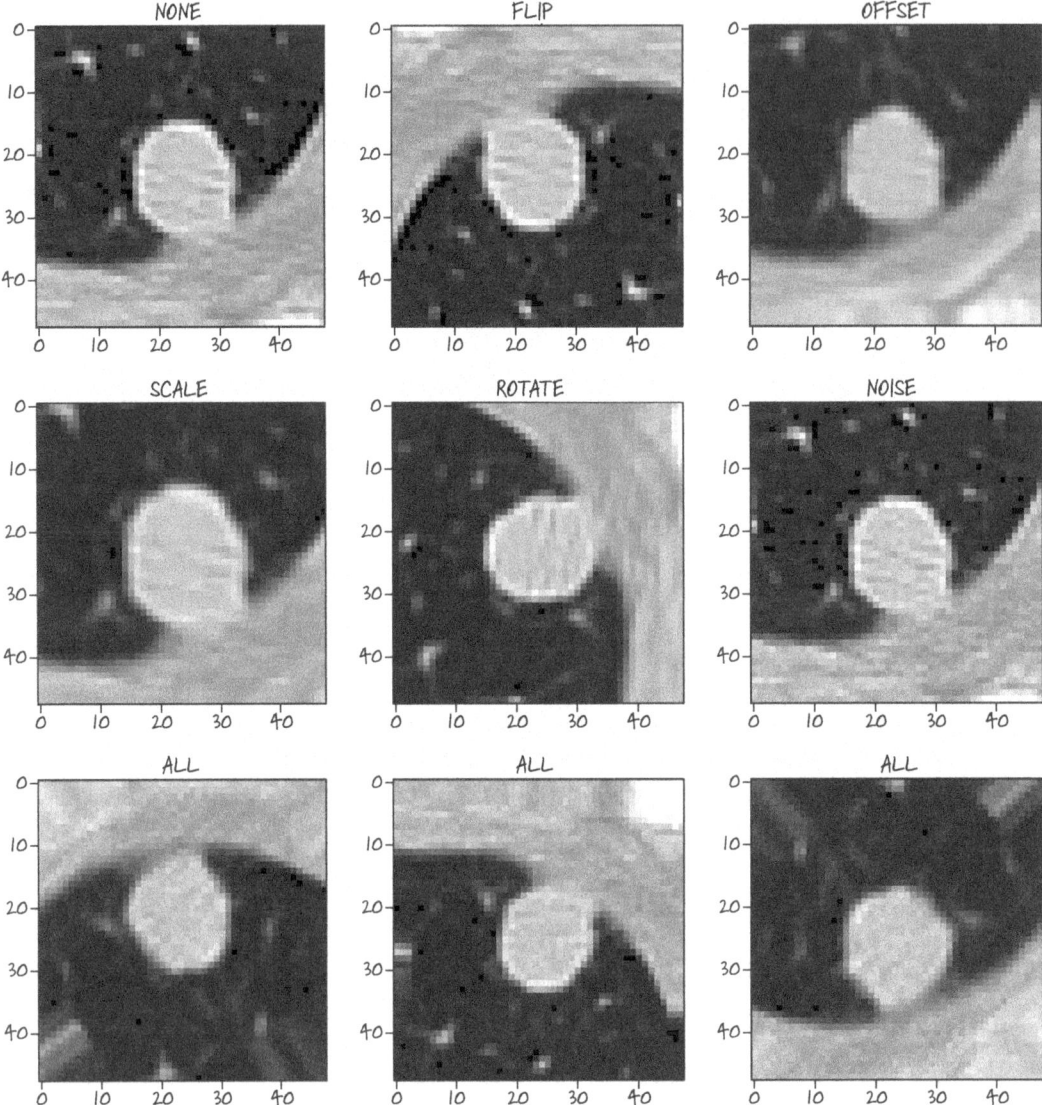

Figure 14.21 Various augmentation types performed on a positive nodule sample

Since each __getitem__ call to the augmenting dataset reapplies the augmentations randomly, each image on the bottom row looks different. This also means it's nearly impossible to generate an image exactly like this again! It's also important to remember that sometimes the 'flip' augmentation will result in *no* flip. Returning always-flipped images is just as limiting as not flipping in the first place. Now let's see whether any of this makes a difference.

14.6.2 Seeing the improvement from data augmentation

We are going to train additional models, one per augmentation type discussed in the last section, with an additional model training run that combines all of the augmentation types. Once they're finished, we'll take a look at our numbers in TensorBoard.

To be able to turn our new augmentation types on and off, we need to expose the construction of augmentation_dict to our command-line interface. Arguments to our program will be added by parser.add_argument calls (not shown, but similar to the ones our program already has), which will then be fed into code that actually constructs augmentation_dict (training.py:105, LunaTrainingApp.__init__).

Listing 14.18 Setting all our augmentation configurations from command-line arguments

```
self.augmentation_dict = {}
if self.cli_args.augmented or self.cli_args.augment_flip:
  self.augmentation_dict['flip'] = True
if self.cli_args.augmented or self.cli_args.augment_offset:
  self.augmentation_dict['offset'] = 0.1
if self.cli_args.augmented or self.cli_args.augment_scale:
  self.augmentation_dict['scale'] = 0.2
if self.cli_args.augmented or self.cli_args.augment_rotate:
  self.augmentation_dict['rotate'] = True
if self.cli_args.augmented or self.cli_args.augment_noise:
  self.augmentation_dict['noise'] = 25.0
```

⟵ These values were empirically chosen to have a reasonable effect, but better values probably exist.

Now that we have those command-line arguments ready, you can either run the following commands or revisit p2_run_everything.ipynb and run cells 8 through 16. Either way you run it, expect these to take a significant time to finish:

```
$ .venv/bin/python -m p2ch14.prepcache

$ .venv/bin/python -m p2ch14.training --epochs 20 \
    --balanced sanity-bal

$ .venv/bin/python -m p2ch14.training --epochs 10 \
    --balanced --augment-flip   sanity-bal-flip

$ .venv/bin/python -m p2ch14.training --epochs 10 \
    --balanced --augment-shift  sanity-bal-shift

$ .venv/bin/python -m p2ch14.training --epochs 10 \
    --balanced --augment-scale  sanity-bal-scale

$ .venv/bin/python -m p2ch14.training --epochs 10 \
    --balanced --augment-rotate sanity-bal-rotate

$ .venv/bin/python -m p2ch14.training --epochs 10 \
    --balanced --augment-noise  sanity-bal-noise

$ .venv/bin/python -m p2ch14.training --epochs 20 \
    --balanced --augmented sanity-bal-aug
```

⟵ You only need to prep the cache once per chapter.

⟵ You might have this run from earlier in the chapter; in that case, there's no need to rerun it!

416 CHAPTER 14 *Improving training with metrics and augmentation*

While that's running, we can start TensorBoard. Let's direct it to show only these runs by changing the logdir parameter like so: `../path/to/tensorboard --logdir runs/p2ch14`.

Depending on the hardware you have at your disposal, the training might take a long time. Feel free to skip the flip, shift, and scale training jobs and reduce the first and last runs to 11 epochs if you need to move things along more quickly. We chose 20 runs because that helps them stand out from the other runs, but 11 should work as well.

If you let everything run to completion, your TensorBoard should have data similar to that shown in figure 14.22. We're going to deselect everything except the validation data to reduce clutter. When you're looking at your data live, you can also change the smoothing value, which can help clarify the trend lines. Take a quick look at the figure, and then we'll go over it in some detail.

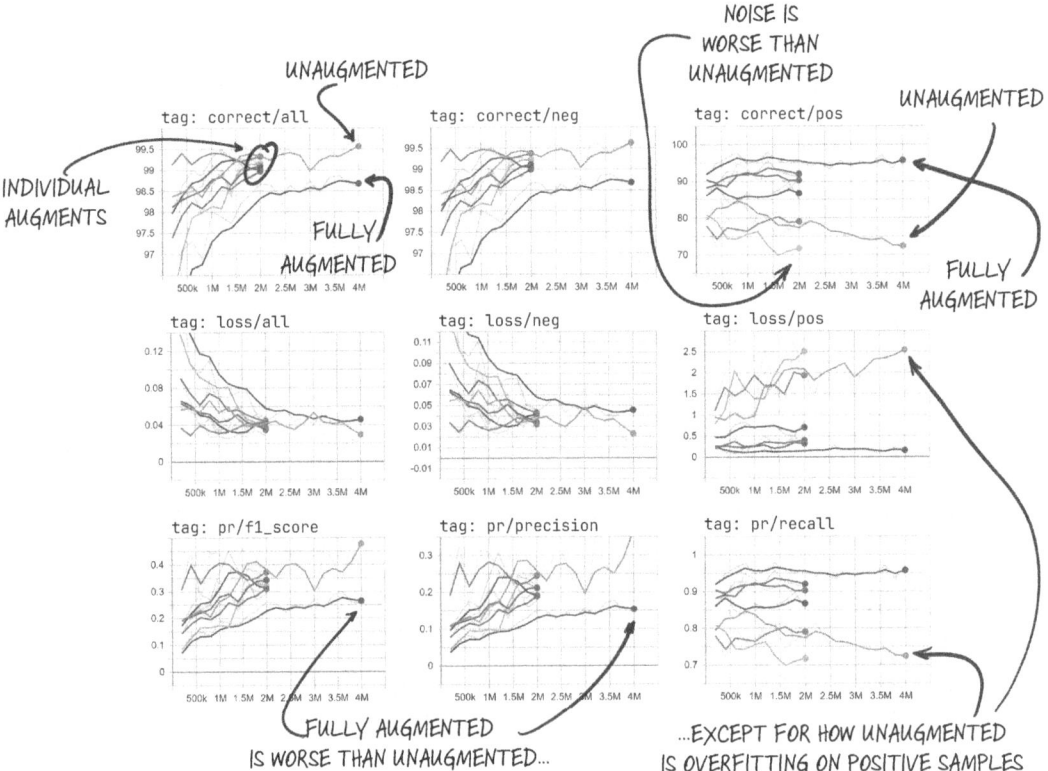

Figure 14.22 Percentage correctly classified, loss, F1 score, precision, and recall for the validation set from networks trained with a variety of augmentation schemes

The first thing to notice in the upper-left graph (tag: correct/all) in figure 14.22 is that the individual augmentation types are something of a jumble. Our unaugmented and fully augmented runs are on opposite sides of that jumble. That means when combined, our augmentation is more than the sum of its parts. Also of interest is that our fully augmented run gets many more wrong answers. While that's bad generally, if we look at the right column of images (which focus on the positive candidate samples we actually care about—the ones that are really nodules), we see that our fully augmented model is *much* better at finding the positive candidate samples. The recall for the fully augmented model is great! It's also much better at not overfitting. As we saw earlier, our unaugmented model gets worse over time.

One interesting thing to note is that the noise-augmented model is *worse* at identifying nodules than the unaugmented model. This makes sense if we remember that we said noise makes the model's job harder.

Another interesting thing to see in the live data (it's somewhat lost in the jumble here) is that the rotation-augmented model is nearly as good as the fully augmented model when it comes to recall, and it has much better precision. Since our F1 score is precision-limited (due to the higher number of negative samples), the rotation-augmented model also has a better F1 score.

We'll stick with the fully augmented model going forward, since our use case requires high recall. The F1 score will still be used to determine which epoch to save as the best. In a real-world project, we might want to devote extra time to investigating whether a different combination of augmentation types and parameter values could yield better results.

14.7 Conclusion

We spent a lot of time and energy in this chapter reformulating how we think about our model's performance. It's easy to be misled by poor methods of evaluation, and it's crucial to have a strong intuitive understanding of the factors that feed into evaluating a model well. Once those fundamentals are internalized, it's much easier to spot when we're being led astray.

We've also learned about how to deal with data sources that aren't sufficiently populated. Being able to synthesize representative training samples is incredibly useful. Situations where we have too much training data are rare indeed!

Now that we have a classifier that is performing reasonably, we'll turn our attention to automatically finding candidate nodules to classify. Chapter 15 will start there.

14.8 Exercises

1 The F1 score can be generalized to support values other than 1:
   a Read https://en.wikipedia.org/wiki/F-score and implement F2 and F0.5 scores.
   b Determine which of F1, F2, and F0.5 makes the most sense for this project. Track that value, and compare and contrast it with the F1 score. (Yep, that's a hint it's not the F1 score!)

2 Implement a `WeightedRandomSampler` approach to balancing the positive and negative training samples for `LunaDataset` with `ratio_int` set to 0:
   a How did you get the required information about the class of each sample?
   b Which approach was easier? Which resulted in more readable code?
3 Experiment with different class-balancing schemes:
   a What ratio results in the best score after two epochs? After 20?
   b What if the ratio is a function of `epoch_ndx`?
4 Experiment with different data augmentation approaches:
   a Can any of the existing approaches be made more aggressive (noise, offset, etc.)?
   b Does the inclusion of noise augmentation help or hinder your training results? Are there other values that change this result?
   c Research data augmentation that other projects have used. Are any applicable here? Implement "mixup" augmentation for positive nodule candidates. Does it help?
5 Change the initial normalization from `nn.BatchNorm` to something custom, and retrain the model:
   a Can you get better results using fixed normalization?
   b What normalization offset and scale make sense?
   c Do nonlinear normalizations like square roots help?
6 What other kinds of data can TensorBoard display besides those we've covered here?
   a Can you have it display information about the weights of your network?
   b What about intermediate results from running your model on a particular sample? Does having the backbone of the model wrapped in an instance of `nn.Sequential` help or hinder this effort?

Summary

- A binary label and a binary classification threshold combine to partition the dataset into four quadrants: true positives, true negatives, false negatives, and false positives. These four quantities provide the basis for our improved performance metrics.
- *Recall* is the ability of a model to maximize true positives. Selecting every single item guarantees perfect recall (because all the correct answers are included) but also exhibits poor precision.
- *Precision* is the ability of a model to minimize false positives. Selecting nothing guarantees perfect precision (because no incorrect answers are included) but also exhibits poor recall.
- The *F1 score* combines precision and recall into a single metric that describes model performance. The formula is: F1 = 2 * (precision * recall) / (precision + recall). We use the F1 score to determine what effect changes to training or the model have on our performance.

- Unbalanced data, such as datasets with far more negative than positive samples, can lead to degenerate behavior where the model predicts only the majority class. This results in poor performance on minority classes and requires balancing or other techniques to address.
- Balancing the training set to have an equal number of positive and negative samples during training can result in better model performance (defined as having a positive, increasing F1 score).
- Overfitting occurs when a model performs well on the training data but poorly on unseen data, indicating that it has memorized the training examples rather than learning generalizable patterns. Signs of overfitting include a large gap between training and validation performance metrics, such as accuracy or F1 score.
- Data augmentation takes existing organic data samples and modifies them such that the resulting augmented sample is nontrivially different from the original, but it remains representative of samples of the same class. This allows additional training without overfitting in situations where data is limited.
- Common data augmentation strategies include changes in orientation, mirroring, rescaling, shifting by an offset, and adding noise. Depending on the project, other, more specific strategies may also be relevant.

15
Using segmentation to find suspected nodules

This chapter covers
- Modifying the data to be used for a 2D segmentation problem
- Performing segmentation with Segment Anything
- Understanding mask prediction using Segformer
- Fine-tuning a segmentation model

In the last four chapters, we have accomplished a lot. We've learned about CT scans and lung tumors, datasets and data loaders, and metrics and monitoring. We have also applied many of the things we learned in part 1, and we have a working classifier that determines whether CT scan candidates are nodules or not nodules.

However, we are still operating in a somewhat artificial environment since we require hand-annotated nodule candidate information (our annotations.csv and candidates.csv files) to load the candidates into our classifier. How can we automatically determine which parts of a CT scan are nodule candidates? This is the question we will address in this chapter.

As we explained at the start, our project uses multiple steps to solve the problem of locating possible nodules and identifying them as nodules or non-nodules. This is a common approach among practitioners, while in deep learning research, there is a tendency to demonstrate the ability of individual models to solve complex problems in an end-to-end fashion. The multistage project design we use in this book gives us a good excuse to introduce new concepts step by step.

In this chapter, we will focus on a different problem than in previous chapters. For educational and demonstration purposes, you can consider this chapter as a stand-alone section. We introduce a new model, a new dataset, and a new training loop. Our approach will involve using popular open-source models and learning how to fine-tune one for our specific use case. We'll use popular open source models and learn to fine-tune them for our use case. While prior chapters provide helpful context, they aren't required to follow along. This chapter is also valuable for understanding the end-to-end pipeline. Let's dive in!

15.1 Utilizing a second model in our project

In the previous two chapters, we worked on step 3 of our plan, shown in figure 15.1: classification. In this chapter, we'll go back to step 2 (figure 15.1). We need to find a way to tell our classifier where to look. To do this, we are going to take raw CT scans to identify anything that might be a nodule. To find these possible nodules, we have to flag voxels that look like they might be part of a nodule, a process known as *segmentation*.

> **NOTE** We expect to mark quite a few things that are not nodules; thus, we used the classification step to reduce the number of these.

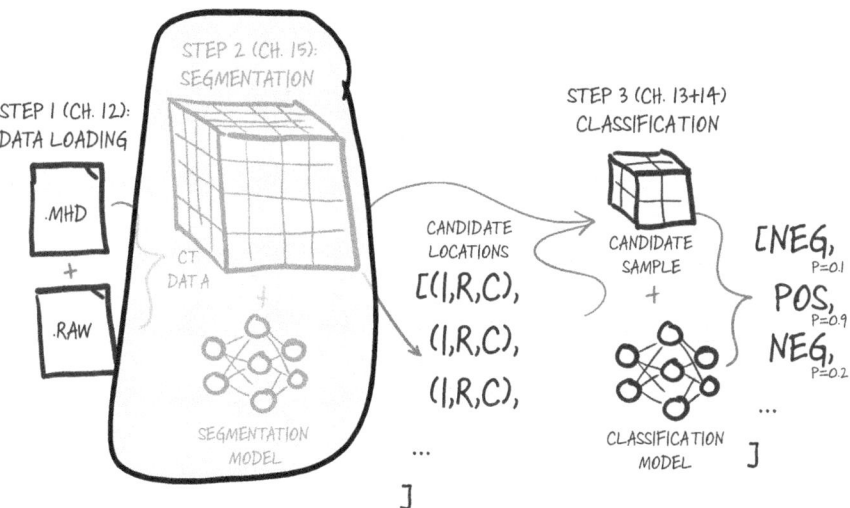

Figure 15.1 Our end-to-end lung cancer detection project, with a focus on this chapter's topic: step 2, segmentation.

For our data, we will be operating on 2D slices of our CT scan. This allows for easier demonstration and gives us the ability to better visualize the results of our segmentation. We could operate on the 3D version of our data, but that is harder to interpret and visualize.

Breaking down figure 15.2 into steps, our plan for this chapter is as follows:

1 *Segmentation*—First, we will learn how segmentation works with the Segment Anything model, including what the new model components are and what happens to them as we go through the segmentation process. This is step 1 in the figure.

2 *Update*—To implement segmentation, we need to change our existing code base in three main places, shown in the substeps on the right side of the figure. The code will be structurally very similar to what we developed for classification, but will differ in detail:

   a *Utilize an open source model (step 2A)*—We will download and integrate the Segment Anything model. Our model in chapter 14 outputs a simple true/false classification; our model in this chapter will instead output an entire image.

   b *Change the dataset (step 2B)*—We need to change our dataset to not only deliver bits of the CT but also provide masks (outlines) for the nodules. The classification dataset consisted of 3D crops around nodule candidates, but we'll need to collect both full CT slices and 2D crops for segmentation training and validation.

   c *Adapt the training loop (step 2C)*—We need to bring in a new model, fine-tune it with our data, and output segmentations.

3 *Results*—Finally, we'll see the fruits of our efforts when we look at the quantitative segmentation results.

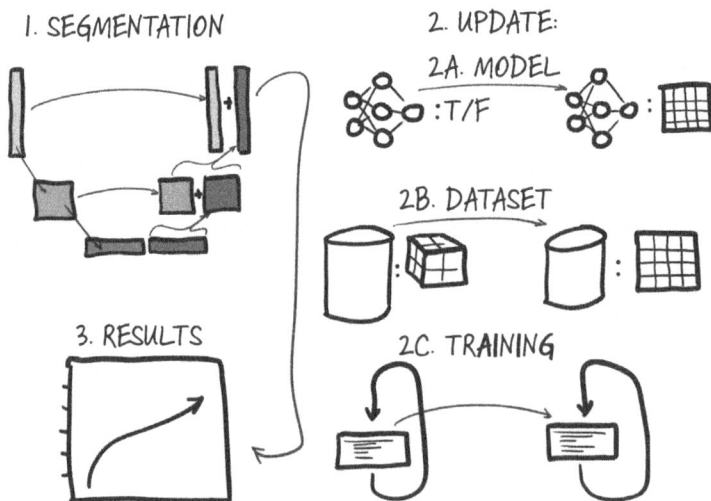

Figure 15.2 The new model architecture for segmentation, along with the model, dataset, and training loop updates we will implement.

15.2 Various types of segmentation

To begin, let's explore the various types of segmentation. For this project, we will focus on *semantic segmentation*, which is the act of classifying individual pixels in an image using labels just like those we've seen for our classification tasks, for example, "bear," "cat," "dog," and so on. If done properly, this will result in distinct chunks or regions that signify things like "all of these pixels are part of a cat." This takes the form of a label mask or heatmap that identifies areas of interest. We will have a simple binary label: true values will correspond to nodule candidates, and false values mean uninteresting healthy tissue. This partially meets our need to find nodule candidates that we will later feed into our classification network.

Before we get into the details, we should briefly discuss other approaches we could take to finding our nodule candidates. For example, *instance segmentation* labels individual objects of interest with distinct labels. In a medical image with multiple tumors, instance segmentation would label each tumor separately, distinguishing between "tumor1" and "tumor2." While this can be beneficial for certain applications, it is often more complex and computationally intensive than semantic segmentation, which focuses on classifying pixels without differentiating between instances of the same class.

Another approach to these kinds of tasks is *object detection*, which locates an item of interest in an image and puts a bounding box around the item. While useful for identifying the presence of certain features, it lacks the pixel-level precision required for detailed medical analysis. Given the need for precision and efficiency for our project, we will focus on semantic segmentation for these reasons.

15.3 Semantic segmentation: Per-pixel classification

Often, segmentation is used to answer questions of the form "Where is a cat in this picture?" Obviously, most pictures of a cat, like figure 15.3, have a lot of noncat in

Figure 15.3 Classification results in one or more binary flags, while segmentation produces a mask or heatmap.

them; there's the table or wall in the background, the keyboard the cat is sitting on—that kind of thing. Being able to say, "This pixel is part of the cat, and this other pixel is part of the wall," requires fundamentally different model output and a different internal structure from the classification models we've worked with thus far. Classification can tell us whether a cat is present, while segmentation will tell us where we can find it.

If your project requires differentiating between a near cat and a far cat, or a cat on the left versus a cat on the right, then segmentation is probably the right approach. The image-consuming classification models that we've implemented so far can be thought of as funnels or magnifying glasses that take a large bunch of pixels and focus them down into a single "point" (or, more accurately, a single set of class predictions), as shown in figure 15.4. Classification models provide answers of the form "Yes, this huge pile of pixels has a cat in it, somewhere" or "No, no cats here." This is great when you don't care where the cat is, just that there is (or isn't) one in the image.

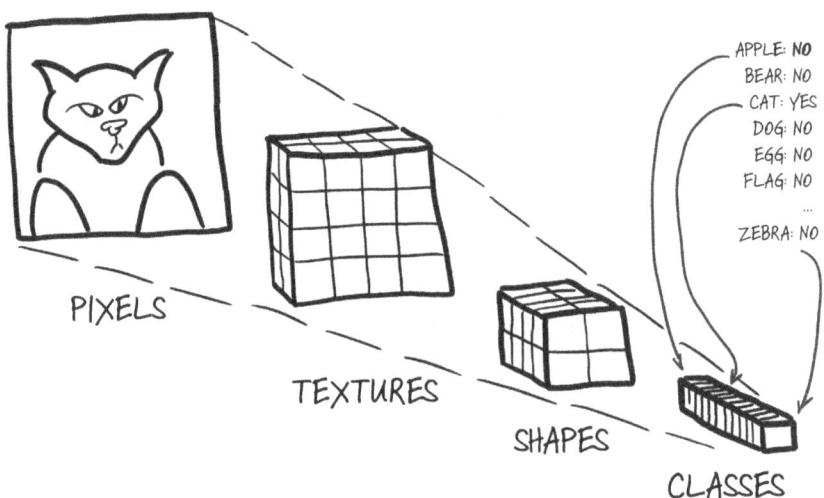

Figure 15.4 **The magnifying glass model structure for classification.**

Repeated layers of convolution and downsampling mean the model starts by consuming raw pixels to produce specific, detailed detectors for things like texture and color, and then builds up higher-level conceptual feature detectors for parts like eyes, ears, mouth, and nose that finally result in "cat" versus "dog." Due to the increasing receptive field of the convolutions after each downsampling layer, those higher-level detectors can use information from an increasingly large area of the input image.

However, segmentation requires producing an image-like output, and ending up with a single classification-like list of binary flags won't suffice. We will be introducing a new model to handle this. Its architecture is designed to handle segmentation tasks by leveraging advanced techniques such as attention mechanisms and transformer-based models (which we covered in chapter 9). This allows it to efficiently process and segment images by focusing on relevant parts of the image without losing spatial information.

15.3.1 The Segment Anything model (SAM)

The new model we will be using for this semantic segmentation problem is called the *Segment Anything model* (SAM; see https://arxiv.org/pdf/2304.02643). It was released and open sourced in 2023 by Meta AI. The model is based on a Transformer architecture and is trained on a large dataset of images and their corresponding segmentation masks. It can handle a wide range of objects and is capable of generalizing well to new images.

Using Segment Anything, you can upload an image and

- Create segmentation masks for all objects within the image.
- Accept prompts using points, boxes, or masks.
- Handle a diverse array of objects and generalize effectively to new images.

When this model was released, it generated a lot of excitement due to its potential applications in a wide range of fields, including autonomous driving, robotics, image editing (background or object removal), annotation assistants, and more. Much like how PyTorch marked a pivotal shift in the deep learning landscape, Segment Anything is poised to have a similar transformative effect on the field of image segmentation. Foundational models have been successfully utilized in natural language processing (NLP), starting with BERT in 2018 and continuing with large language models like ChatGPT. However, computer vision has struggled to find an equally versatile architecture that could be applied to a broad spectrum of tasks. While previous models were effective in specific areas, they often required extensive retraining to adapt to new or diverse tasks. Thus, SAM is the first model to demonstrate the potential to serve as a foundational model for image segmentation.

Segment Anything's impact lies in its ability to perform `zero-shot segmentation`, meaning it can segment objects in images without needing additional training or fine-tuning on specific datasets. This represents a significant advancement over previous segmentation models, which typically required task-specific training data to achieve optimal performance.

This approach draws inspiration from earlier natural language processing models, which, once trained on extensive datasets, could be prompted to perform a wide range of tasks. The creators identified a suitable task, model, and dataset, training it on 11 million images and 1.1 billion masks. In this chapter, we will use this versatile model to segment nodules in our CT scans. Let's first explore the model architecture, and then we'll walk through an example of how to use it.

15.4 SAM architecture

SAM utilizes a transformer-based architecture that is split into three main components, as shown in figure 15.5:

1 *Image encoder*—This component is responsible for extracting features from the input image. It uses a Vision Transformer (ViT) architecture (see https://arxiv.org/pdf/2010.11929), which divides the image into patches and processes them using self-attention mechanisms to capture both local and global information between the patches.
2 *Prompt encoder*—This component encodes the prompts provided to the model, such as points, boxes (sparse prompts), and masks (dense prompts). Much like how images are represented as a series of numbers to the model, these prompts are similarly encoded into a numerical representation to prompt the model. It uses a combination of convolutional neural networks (CNNs) and transformers to process the prompts and generate embeddings that can be processed downstream.
3 *Mask decoder*—This component takes the features from the image encoder and the embeddings from the prompt encoder to generate the final segmentation

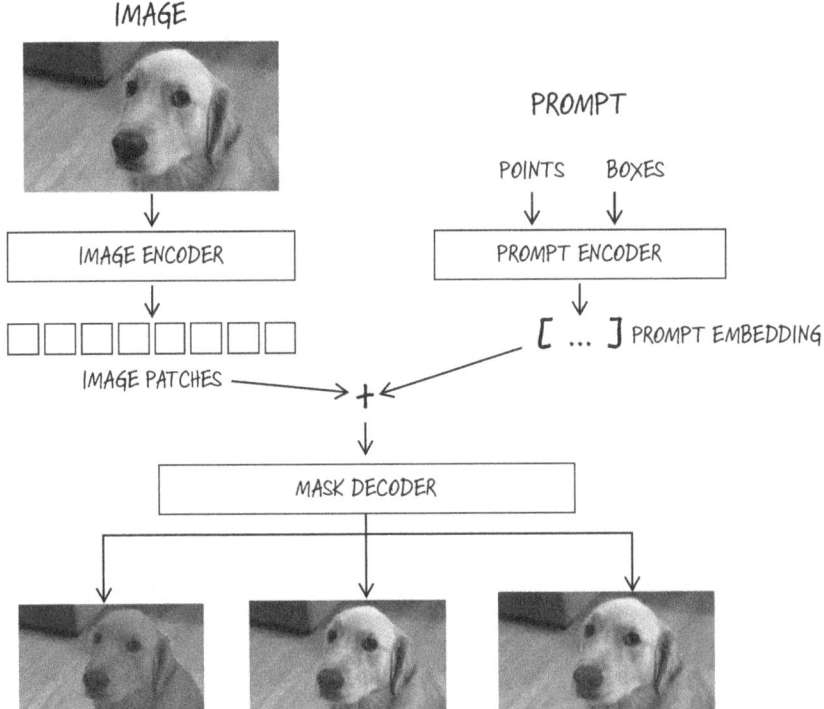

Figure 15.5   SAM Architecture at a high level. Some portions not used in this chapter are omitted for simplicity.

mask. This design draws inspiration from transformer decoder architecture to combine the information and perform self-attention and cross-attention on the image features and prompt embeddings. The mask decoder is responsible for producing the final segmentation mask, which indicates the regions of interest in the image.

To handle ambiguity for multiple output masks for a single prompt, the model will output three different masks of varying sizes as well as its confidence score. The three masks are usually nested masks, and the model outputs the whole, part, and subpart. For example, for the dog image in figure 15.5, SAM's output masks cover the whole dog, the nose of the dog, and a subsection of the nose.

The SAM implementation lives at https://github.com/facebookresearch/segment-anything. While we will be using an already-trained version of the model, the repository also provides code for training the model from scratch. Oftentimes, it will be helpful to reference the code while reading the paper to truly understand the model architecture and how it works. While we won't be implementing such a model from scratch in this chapter, we suggest taking some time to inspect the code and, based on the knowledge you have built up until this point, identify the building blocks of the architecture as they are reflected in the code. When using open source models, it is also important to consider the licenses attached to such models.

> **Licenses**
>
> While it's less of an issue for personal projects, it's important to be aware of the license terms attached to open source software you use for a project. Segment Anything uses the Apache 2.0 license, which is a permissive open source license that allows for significant freedom in using the software, but it still places requirements on users, such as providing proper attribution and including a copy of the license in any distributions of the code.
>
> Additionally, authors retain copyright even if they publish their work in a public forum (yes, even on GitHub), and if they do not include a license, that does *not* mean the work is in the public domain. Quite the opposite! It means you don't have *any* license to use the code, any more than you'd have the right to wholesale copy a book you borrowed from the library. Licenses for the model code may also be different than those for the pretrained weights, so you may have to look out for that.

Now that we have found a model that fits the bill for our problem, we need to adapt it so that it works well for our needs. In general, it's a good idea to keep an eye out for situations where we can use something off the shelf. It's important to have a sense of what models exist, how they're implemented and trained, and whether any parts can be scavenged and applied to the project we're working on at any given moment. While that broader knowledge is something that comes with time and experience, it's a good idea to start building that toolbox now.

15.4.1 Trying out an off-the-shelf model for our project

There is no better way to understand how the model works than to try it out for a test run so let's go through an example. The creators of the model have done most of the hard work and trained the model already, providing the weights for open source use. In previous chapters, we loaded a pretrained model using the Hugging Face `transformers` library, which contains various open source models. In this chapter, we will install a model directly from a source repository.

Let's open the `1_segment_example.ipynb` notebook and see how we can accomplish this. We can install Segment Anything from the repository on GitHub (https://github.com/facebookresearch/segment-anything) via `pip install` (1_segment_example.ipynb).

> **Listing 15.1 Installing Segment Anything from GitHub**

```
pip install git+https://github.com/facebookresearch/segment-anything.git
```

We then need to import the libraries we will use for this demonstration:

```
import matplotlib.pyplot as plt
import numpy as np
import torch
from PIL import Image
from p2ch15.utils import get_sam_model
```

We will load a particular checkpoint of the model, which contains the pretrained weights. Segment Anything comes with 3 variants of varying sizes ("huge", "large", and "base"); by default, we will load the middle-sized model. We already implemented a helper method called `get_sam_model()` which contains the URLs to download the weights and save it to a local `.pth` file.

We will also set the device to use a GPU if available; otherwise, we will use the CPU:

```
from segment_anything import SamAutomaticMaskGenerator, sam_model_registry
device = torch.device("cuda" if torch.cuda.is_available() else "cpu")

model_config, model_weights_path = get_sam_model()
sam = sam_model_registry[model_config](checkpoint=model_weights_path)
sam.to(device)
mask_generator = SamAutomaticMaskGenerator(sam)
```

The `SamAutomaticMaskGenerator` abstraction is a convenient method from the Segment Anything library that facilitates the generation of masks from the model. It takes care of the preprocessing and postprocessing steps required to generate the masks.

Next, we will load the astronaut picture from chapter 10 as our example to the segment:

```
image_path = "data/p2ch10/astronaut.png"
image = Image.open(image_path).convert("RGB")
```

Now we can feed this into our mask generation pipeline and generate all the masks:

```
# In[]
image_array = np.array(image)
masks = mask_generator.generate(image_array)
print(len(masks))
print(masks[0]["segmentation"].shape)
print(masks[0]["predicted_iou"])

# Out[]
79
(1024, 1024)
1.033138632774353
```

> IoU stands for intersection over union (https://en.wikipedia.org/wiki/Jaccard_index), which should be a value between 0 and 1. However, the model is simply predicting a confidence score, not the actual IoU, which allows it to be over 1 (it's very confident!).

The model has generated 79 masks for the image, each with the same dimensions as the original image. These masks are binary arrays where each element represents a pixel in the image: True indicates the pixel belongs to the object, while False indicates it does not. The scores tensor contains confidence scores for each mask, reflecting the model's certainty about the segmentation.

The masks are created based on the features extracted from the image, as shown in figure 15.6. For instance, plotting one of the masks would reveal the outline of the astronaut:

```
def plot_mask(mask):
    int_mask = mask.astype(int)
    plt.imshow(int_mask, cmap='gray', interpolation='nearest')
    plt.axis('off')
    plt.show()
plot_mask(masks[3]["segmentation"])
```

Figure 15.6 Mask of the original astronaut image. The white pixels represent the True values in the mask while the black pixels represent the False values.

We can also plot all the masks together to see how they cover the image (figure 15.7):

```
plot_image_with_masks(image, masks["masks"])
```

What a vibrant segmented astronaut! We've created masks for the entire image, but we can achieve even more precise segmentation by directly querying the model.

Figure 15.7 Multiple masks overlayed on the astronaut image

15.5 Using the SAM model directly

Previously, we used the `SamAutomaticMaskGenerator` utility to create a mask generator that generates all the masks for the image. However, in our case, we want to single out the nodules that are present in the CT scans. To do this, we will need to provide the model with some indication of where we should be segmenting.

Instead of using a `SamAutomaticMaskGenerator`, we can use portions by directly importing parts of the model, which are provided by the Segment Anything library. This will also be important later when we want to fine-tune the model for our own uses.

As mentioned earlier, SAM can take a point prompt, a box prompt, or a mask prompt in its input; next, we will show how to use the point prompt on the model. First, we will load the model, omitting various code pieces such as imports and utility functions (2_point_prompt.ipynb).

Listing 15.2 Loading SAM

```
from segment_anything import SamPredictor, sam_model_registry
model_config, model_weights_path = get_sam_model()

sam = sam_model_registry[model_config](checkpoint=model_weights_path)
sam.to(device)
predictor = SamPredictor(sam)
```

Next, we need to provide an input point that indicates the area of interest for the model. As shown in figure 15.5, this point is encoded by the prompt encoder into an embedding representation. At the same time, the image is divided into patches. These two intermediate representations—embeddings and patches—are then combined and passed into the model. This preprocessing step is separate from the model execution,

15.5 Using the SAM model directly

allowing for flexible and efficient preprocessing. This time, let's use our dog picture from chapter 2 and point (320, 260) as our input point:

```
image_path = "data/p1ch2/bobby.jpg"
image = Image.open(image_path).convert("RGB")
input_points = [[(320, 260)]]

input_points = np.array([[(320, 260)]])
predictor.set_image(np.array(image))
masks, _, _ = predictor.predict(input_points, point_labels=np.array([1]))
```

This produces a similar output of masks as our original method. We obtain three masks of different sizes (full, part, and subpart), which are based on our input point. We can visualize these masks by plotting the image with the input point:

```
plot_mask_with_point(masks[0], input_points[0])
```

The model can process multiple input prompts, which is why we use a nested list for our points. In this example, we are only using a single prompt, hence the [0] indexing. The mask for the dog's nose, generated using the provided point, is shown in figure 15.8.

Figure 15.8 Mask with a point prompt included

How nosey! We have successfully used the Segment Anything model off the shelf. But we aren't in the business of segmenting dogs and noses. Instead, we aim to apply what we've seen so far to our nodule segmentation problem, which belongs to a completely different domain: medical imaging.

> **General-purpose models vs. medical imaging domains**
>
> There are a number of clever and innovative ways to actually solve the segmentation in medical imaging, and we in no way suggest that this is the only approach that will ever work. It's important to note the domain gap between "natural" images, like regular photographs, and medical images.
>
> Segment Anything was designed for general-purpose image segmentation, and it's not obvious that it will perform equally well on medical images. In fact, researchers have explored this challenge, with some adapting SAM specifically for medical imaging tasks (e.g., https://arxiv.org/html/2304.14660v6).

(continued)
We do feel that this approach is one of the simplest that gets the job done to the level we need for our project in this book. We'd rather keep things simple so that we can explore concepts; the clever stuff can come later, once you've mastered the basics.

Now, equipped with our segmenting tools, we can focus on our original goal: segmenting nodules.

15.6 Updating the dataset for segmentation

Our source data for this chapter remains unchanged: we're consuming CT scans and annotation data about them. But our model expects input and will produce output of a different form than we had previously. Our previous dataset produced 3D data, but we need to produce 2D data now. Figure 15.9 provides an overview of where we are in our journey.

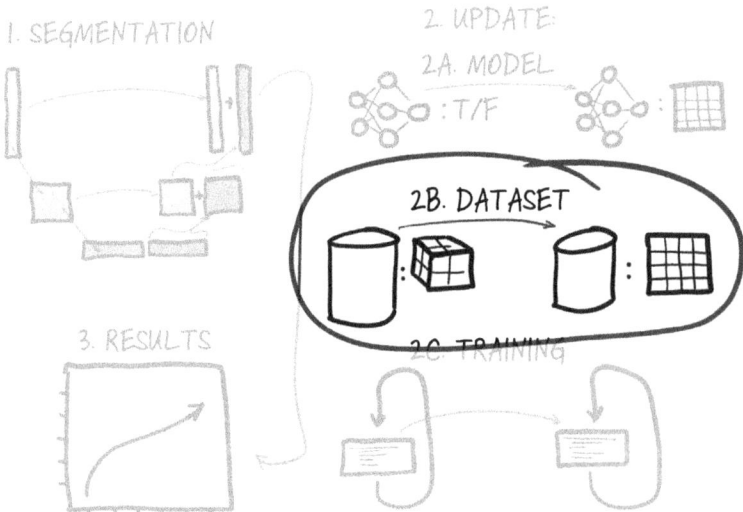

Figure 15.9 The outline of this chapter, with a focus on the changes needed for our segmentation dataset

15.6.1 Working around SAM's limitation on 2D data

The first issue is that our raw data consists of volumetric 3D images, while our model is designed for 2D image processing. SAM is specifically built for 2D images and cannot directly handle 3D volumetric data. To adapt SAM for our segmentation task, we need to extract 2D slices from the 3D CT scans and input them into the model individually.

15.6 Updating the dataset for segmentation

This approach isn't without tradeoffs. Since CT slices are often thicker than the resolution in rows and columns, we do get a somewhat wider view than it seems at first, and this should be enough, considering that nodules typically span a limited number of slices. Another aspect relevant for both the current and fully 3D approaches is that we are now ignoring the exact slice thickness. This is something our model will eventually have to learn to be robust against, by being presented with data with different slice spacings.

In any case, we will be working with 2D images of our CT scans, which is a common approach in medical imaging. By treating each slice as a separate image, we can use the capabilities of SAM to segment nodules that we want. Our goal is, given a 2D image of a CT scan slice, we want to automatically segment out the areas of interest for our classification model. Figure 15.10 shows an example.

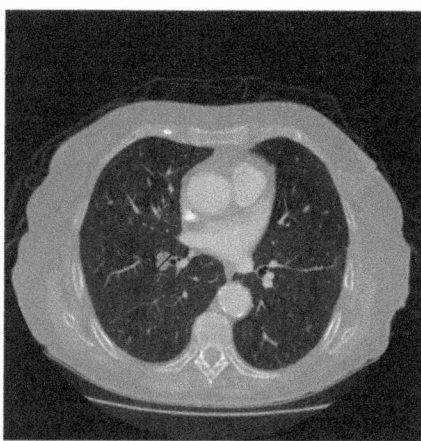

Figure 15.10 Lung CT scan slice with segmentation mask over nodule

To collect our images, we will treat each slice as a distinct spatial position, as illustrated in figure 15.11. It provides a top-down view of a skull, progressing through the brain,

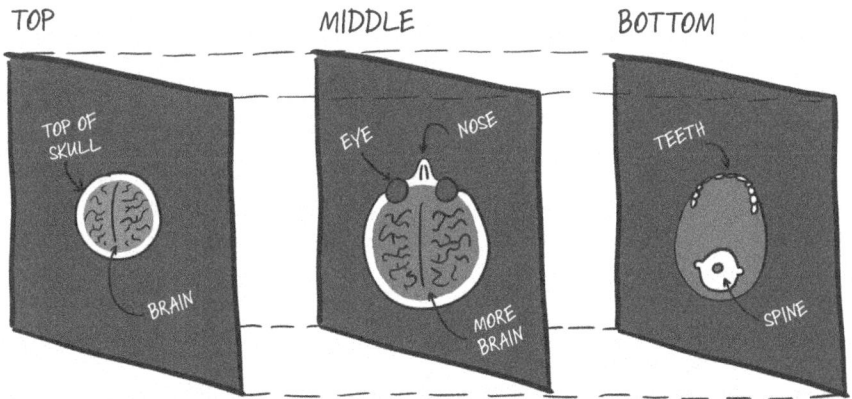

Figure 15.11 Each slice of a CT scan represents a different position in space

eyes, and teeth from the top to the middle and bottom. In a similar manner, we will examine the CT scans of our lungs.

To fine-tune our SAM model, we need to collect images of the CT scan slices, along with the corresponding masks of interest. By using these images, we can further train the model's ability to accurately segment the desired nodules. Let's start constructing our segmentation dataset.

15.6.2 Building the segmentation dataset

The first thing we need to address is that we have a mismatch between our human-labeled training data and the actual output we want to get from our model. We have annotated points, but we want a mask that indicates whether any given pixel in the image is part of a nodule. We'll have to build that mask ourselves using our base SAM and the point provided in the original dataset.

We will use the previous LunaDataset that we used in previous chapters with some minor modifications. First, let's create a helper method that can get a slice of the CT scan data using the candidate info series UID and the xyz coordinates (dsets.py:113, Ct.getSingleSlice).

Listing 15.3 Extracting a single 2D slice from 3D CT scan data

```
center_irc = xyz2irc(
    center_xyz,              ◁──  center_xyz is retrieved from the
    self.origin_xyz,                candidateInfo_tup as we've seen previously:
    self.vxSize_xyz,                as returned by getCandidateInfoList.
    self.direction_a,
)
center_val = int(round(center_irc[axis]))      ◁──  Gets the center voxel
                                                    index of where to select
if axis == 0:                                       the slice from
    ct_slice = self.hu_a[center_val, :, :]     ◁──
elif axis == 1:                                     Indexes the slice out of
    ct_slice = self.hu_a[:, center_val, :]          the 3D data so that we
elif axis == 2:                                     get our 2D data to use
    ct_slice = self.hu_a[:, :, center_val]
else:
    raise ValueError("Invalid axis value. Must be 0, 1, or 2.")

return ct_slice, center_irc
```

We first grab the center point and then use that point to index into our CT scan data to get the slice. Then we can return all the relevant information from our Dataset subclass (dsets.py:211, Ct._get_single_item).

Listing 15.4 Retrieving CT slice and metadata from dataset

```
candidateInfo_tup = self.candidateInfo_list[ndx]
ct_slice, center_irc = getCtSlice(
    candidateInfo_tup.series_uid,
```

15.6 Updating the dataset for segmentation

```
            candidateInfo_tup.center_xyz,
)
ct_slice_tensor = torch.from_numpy(ct_slice).to(torch.float32)
pos_t = torch.tensor([
        not candidateInfo_tup.isNodule_bool,
        candidateInfo_tup.isNodule_bool
    ],
    dtype=torch.long,
)
return ct_slice_tensor, pos_t, candidateInfo_tup.series_uid,
↳ torch.tensor(center_irc)
```

When we retrieve from the dataset, we can inspect the shape of the slice to ensure it is 2D and confirm the other information is correct (3_segment_ct_slice.ipynb).

Listing 15.5 Verifying our CT slice dimensions

```
# In[]
dataset = LunaDataset(sortby_str="label_and_size")
ct_slice, nodule_class, series_uid, center_irc = dataset[3]
ct_slice.shape

# Out[]
torch.Size([512, 512])
```

For visualization, we can plot the slice along with the point that is attached to the candidate nodule:

```
plot_single_slice(ct_slice, center_irc)
```

Figure 15.12 provides an example of a lung CT scan slice, highlighting the nodule.

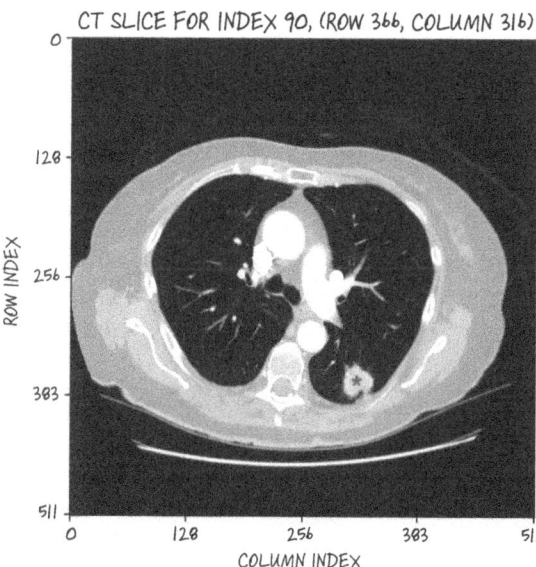

Figure 15.12 Lung CT scan slice with the nodule marked with a star.

In earlier chapters, we cached chunks of CT centered around nodule candidates, since we didn't want to have to read and parse all of a CT's data every time we wanted a small chunk of the CT. We'll want to do the same thing with our new ct_slice (dsets.py:151).

Listing 15.6 How to cache CT slices

```
@raw_cache.memoize(typed=True)
def getCtSlice(series_uid, center_xyz):
    ct = getCt(series_uid)
    ct_slice, center_irc = ct.getSingleSlice(center_xyz)
    return ct_slice, center_irc
```

The prepcache script precomputes and saves all these values for us, helping keep training quick. Now that we have our slices, we can begin to construct our fine-tuning dataset.

15.6.3 Training a model to flag potential candidates

Before we can begin training, we need both 2D images and their corresponding segmentation masks. While we already have the 2D images from the previous section, we still need to generate the masks. We can use the pretrained SAM we saw earlier to create these masks.

In our case, achieving pixel-perfect masks is not our primary concern. Instead, we aim to accurately identify the correct masks from the scans. The classification model we developed in the previous chapter is tasked with determining whether a candidate is a nodule. Our goal in segmentation is to extract all potential candidates from the vast pool of possibilities.

To generate the masks, we will use the same SamPredictor and class we used earlier. We will provide the model with the 2D CT scan slices and the corresponding points. The model will then generate the masks, which we will use as the ground truth for our fine-tuning dataset.

PREPARING OUR CT IMAGES AND MASKS

To recap, our fine-tuning dataset will need two sets of images: CT scan slices and the masks of the nodules that we are interested in segmenting out. With these two images, you can train a variety of segmentation and object detection models like U-Net, Mask R-CNN, DeepLab, and YOLO, among others. We will be using SegFormer, which is a transformer-based model that is lightweight and efficient for semantic segmentation tasks. We will look into this model later in greater detail.

The SAM-generated masks give us a cheap, high-quality training set, which would be really expensive to annotate manually. We use this dataset to fine-tune the much lighter SegFormer model so that it can segment CT slices automatically, without any prompt.

We have a lot of flexibility in organizing our dataset for fine-tuning. One option is to maintain a single large folder containing pairs of images. Ultimately, the organization method we choose is not critical, as long as it is clear and comprehensible to us—or to others, should we decide to share our dataset! In our approach, we will use two separate folders: one for the CT scans and another for the masks. Additionally, we will include a metadata file that provides detailed information about the images and masks, as shown in figure 15.13 (4_create_dataset.ipynb).

Listing 15.7 Setting up directory structure for our new dataset

```
fine_tuning_dir = "data-unversioned/part2/fine-tuning/dataset"
ct_folder = f"{fine_tuning_dir}/ct"
mask_folder = f"{fine_tuning_dir}/mask"
```

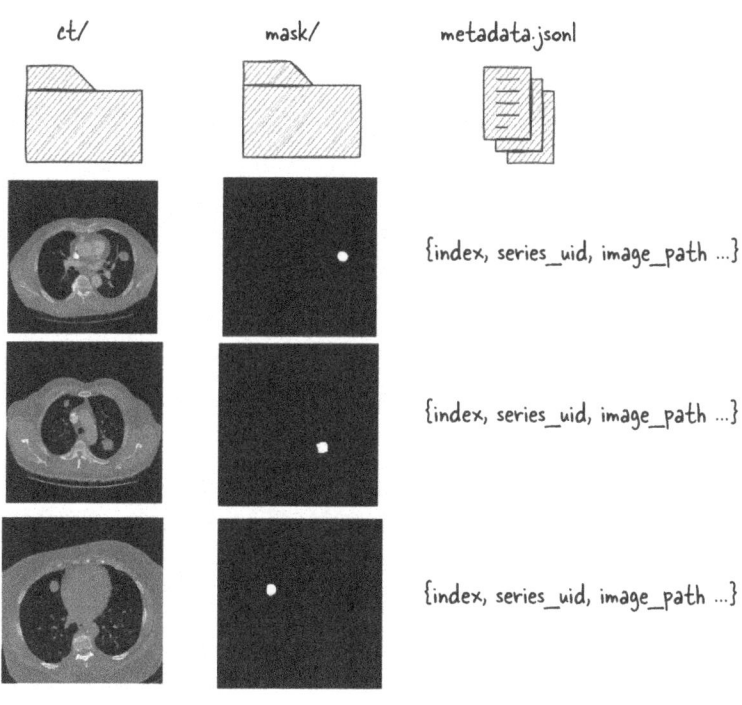

Figure 15.13 Our dataset structure with CT scans and masks

We will create a helper method to automatically generate these folders and populate them with the images, masks, and metadata. This process will utilize data from the LunaDataset we previously developed:

```
def generate_ct_images_and_masks(original_ct_data, max_dataset_size=500,
    recompute=False):
    ...
    for ct_slice, _, series_uid, center_irc in original_ct_data:
        ...
```

We created a `generate_ct_images_and_masks` method that takes in a dataset, which we will pass in as the LUNADataset. We also check whether the images and masks have already been created, in which case we will skip a particular instance.

To create the CT scan images, we convert the tensor into a NumPy array and rearrange the dimensions from channels, height, width (C, H, W) to the format recognized by the PIL image library, which is height, width, channels (H, W, C):

```
ct_filepath = os.path.join(ct_folder, filename)
ct_image_array = np.transpose(scaled_ct_slice.numpy(), (1, 2, 0))
ct_image = Image.fromarray(ct_image_array, mode="RGB")
...
ct_image.save(ct_filepath)
```

For generating the mask images, we use SAM, providing an input point as a prompt. This process yields a 2D array of boolean values (True and False) representing the mask, which we then save as an image:

```
mask_filepath = os.path.join(mask_folder, filename)
x, y = center_irc[2], center_irc[1]
input_points = [[x, y]]

predictor = SamPredictor(sam)
predictor.set_image(ct_image_array)
masks, _, _ = predictor.predict(point_coords=np.array(input_points),
    point_labels=np.array([1]), multimask_output=False)

mask_image_array = masks[0]
mask_image = Image.fromarray(mask_image_array)
mask_image.save(mask_filepath)
```

Finally, we store metadata in a dictionary including the series UID, IRC point, and paths to the images and masks. This metadata is serialized into a file called metadata.jsonl. With this setup, constructing our FineTuning dataset becomes straightforward, as we can load the metadata from the file and implement the `__getitem__` method efficiently.

This may take a few minutes to run as we generate all the images and masks. For convenience, we have publicly uploaded the data to Hugging Face at https://mng.bz/gmGZ, which you can download using the huggingface_hub library:

```
if not os.path.exists(fine_tuning_dir):
    from huggingface_hub import snapshot_download
    repo_id = "H-Huang/LUNA16_segmentation_data"
    snapshot_download(repo_id=repo_id, local_dir=fine_tuning_dir,
        repo_type="dataset")
```

Now that we have our images and masks, we can create our FineTuning dataset class. This class will load the metadata and provide access to the images and masks for training:

```
class FineTuning(dataset):
    ...
    def __getitem__(self, index):
        metadata = self.metadata_list[index]
        ct_image_path = f"{self.fine_tuning_dir}/{metadata['ct_file_name']}"
        mask_image_path = f"{self.fine_tuning_dir}/{metadata['mask_file_name']}"
        series_uid = metadata["series_uid"]
        center_irc = metadata["center_irc"]

        return {
            "series_uid": series_uid,
            "center_irc": torch.tensor(center_irc),
            "ct_image_path": ct_image_path,
            "mask_image_path": mask_image_path,
        }

fine_tuning_data = FineTuning()
```

15.7 Updating our training for fine-tuning

We have a model. We have data. Naturally, the next step, as outlined in step 2C of figure 15.14, is to train our new model using this data.

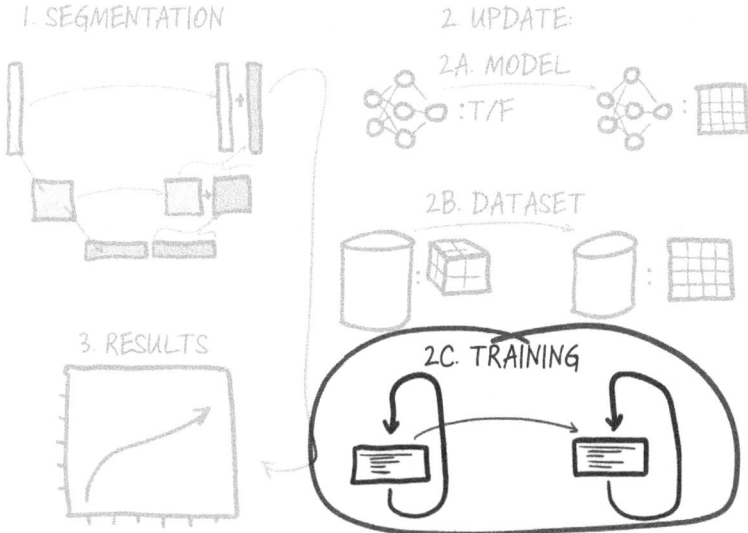

Figure 15.14 The outline of this chapter, with a focus on the changes needed for our training loop

To be more precise about the process of training our model, we will introduce two different concepts that we will need to implement:

- We need to instantiate the new model (unsurprisingly).
- We will also look at a different optimizer; we'll stick with a popular one and use AdamW.

15.7.1 How to fine-tune a model

We want our model to automatically segment nodules of interest so that we can use the model on unseen images and detect areas to pass into our classification model from the previous chapters. Previously, with Segment Anything, we needed to pass in a point prompt to segment the image. However, we want to automate this process and segment the image without any additional input. To do this, we will need to fine-tune the model on our dataset of CT scan slices and masks.

We briefly mentioned that we will be training a different model called a Seg-Former. SegFormer was introduced in Xie et al.'s paper "SegFormer: Simple and Efficient Design for Semantic Segmentation with Transformers" (https://arxiv.org/abs/2105.15203). It is designed for semantic segmentation and can be fine-tuned on specific datasets to optimize performance for particular tasks, such as medical imaging or autonomous driving.

Fine-tuning is a process in machine learning where a pretrained model is further trained on a new dataset to adapt it to a specific task or domain. This approach uses the knowledge the model has already acquired from a large, general dataset and refines it to improve performance on a more specific task. We start with a pretrained model, which has already learned a wide range of features from a large dataset, and then we continue training it on our specific dataset. This allows the model to adapt to the new task while retaining the knowledge it has already acquired.

Because SegFormer is lightweight, it can be trained on a single GPU, making it accessible for us to use for our CT images and masks. Let's see how we can implement this in our code.

SETTING UP THE MODEL

First, we need to set up our datasets and dataloaders. We will use the FineTuning-Dataset class we created earlier to load our images and masks. We will also create a data loader to iterate over the dataset during training (5_fine_tuning.ipynb).

Listing 15.8 Creating training and validation dataloaders

```
from p2ch15.utils import FineTuningDataset
train_dataset = FineTuningDataset(split="train")
val_dataset = FineTuningDataset(split="val")
train_dataloader = DataLoader(train_dataset, batch_size=8, shuffle=True)
val_dataloader = DataLoader(val_dataset, batch_size=8)
```

The model we will use is called SegFormerForSemanticSegmentation and is part of the transformers library. This model is designed for semantic segmentation tasks and can be fine-tuned on our dataset. We will use the nvidia/mit-b0 model as our base model, which is a lightweight version of SegFormer:

```
# In[]:
from transformers import SegformerForSemanticSegmentation
```

```
id2label = {"0": "background", "1": "nodule"}
label2id = {v: k for k, v in id2label.items()}

model = SegformerForSemanticSegmentation.from_pretrained(
    "nvidia/mit-b0",
    num_labels=2,
    id2label=id2label,
    label2id=label2id,
)
model.to(device)

# Out[]:
Some weights of SegformerForSemanticSegmentation were not initialized from
↪the model checkpoint at nvidia/mit-b0 and are newly initialized:
↪['decode_head.batch_norm.bias', 'decode_head.batch_norm.
↪num_batches_tracked', 'decode_head.batch_norm.running_mean',
↪ 'decode_head.batch_norm.running_var', ...]
You should probably TRAIN this model on a down-stream task to be able to
↪use it for predictions and inference.
```

You may have noticed the output message that some weights were not initialized from the model checkpoint. This is expected as we are fine-tuning the model on our dataset, and these weights will be updated during training. Figure 15.15 provides an overview of the SegFormer architecture.

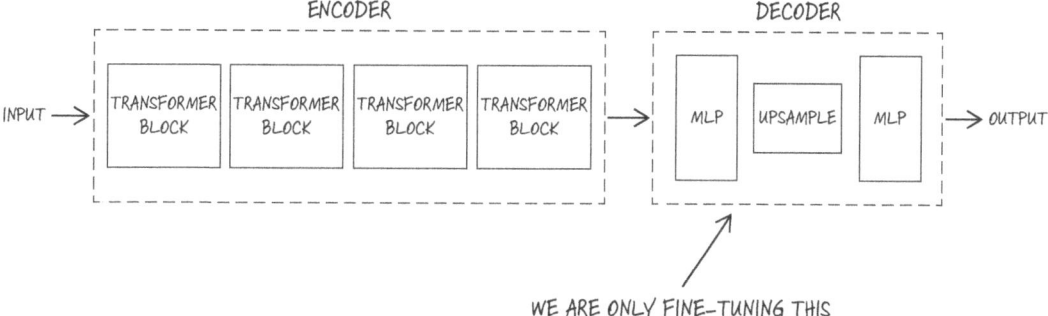

Figure 15.15 The SegFormer architecture. We are only fine-tuning the decoder portion.

We will also need to set up our optimizer and learning rate scheduler:

```
optimizer = torch.optim.AdamW(model.parameters(), lr=0.00006)
```

15.7.2 Using the AdamW optimizer

We will use the AdamW optimizer, which is a variant of the Adam optimizer that includes weight decay. The Adam optimizer (https://arxiv.org/abs/1412.6980) is an alternative to using SGD when training our models. Adam maintains a separate learning rate for each parameter and automatically updates that learning rate as training progresses. Due to these automatic updates, we typically won't need to specify a non-default learning rate when using Adam, since it will quickly determine a reasonable learning rate by itself.

Here's how we instantiate AdamW in code:

```
optimizer = torch.optim.AdamW(model.parameters(), lr=0.00006)
```

It's generally accepted that Adam is a reasonable optimizer to start most projects with (see http://cs231n.github.io/neural-networks-3). Other optimizers' configurations can outperform Adam (e.g., stochastic gradient descent with Nesterov momentum), but finding the correct hyperparameters for a given project can be difficult and time-consuming, and most of the time is overkill or overengineering.

There have been a large number of variations on Adam—AdaMax, RAdam, Ranger, and so on, each with its own strengths and weaknesses. Delving into the details of those is outside the scope of this book, but we think that it's important to know that those alternatives exist. We'll use AdamW in this chapter, as it is what is used in the original paper for SegFormer, and we will use the same learning rate as the paper.

15.7.3 Designing our training loop

The inputs to our model are the CT scan images and masks, but the model requires these images and masks to be in a specific format. Specifically, for the Segformer, the transformer library includes `SegformerImageProcessor` class to preprocess our images and masks. This class will take care of resizing, normalizing, and converting the images and masks into the format expected by the model:

```
image_processor = SegformerImageProcessor()
def encode_inputs_for_model(image_paths, masks_paths=[]):
    images = [Image.open(path) for path in image_paths]
    masks = [Image.open(path) for path in masks_paths] or None
    encoded_inputs = image_processor(images, masks, return_tensors="pt")
    return encoded_inputs["pixel_values"].to(device), encoded_inputs[
    ⇒"labels"].to(device)
```

We can now create our training loop. We will iterate over the data loader and pass the images and masks to the model. We will also compute the loss and update the model weights:

```
num_epochs = 20
for epoch in range(num_epochs):
```

```
        model.train()
        print("Epoch:", epoch)

            total_train_loss = 0
        num_train_batches = 0
        for idx, batch in enumerate(tqdm(train_dataloader)):
            pixel_values, labels = encode_inputs_for_model(batch[
            ➥"ct_image_path"], batch["mask_image_path"])
            outputs = model(pixel_values=pixel_values, labels=labels)
            loss = outputs.loss

            optimizer.zero_grad()
            loss.backward()
            optimizer.step()
            total_train_loss += loss.item()
            num_train_batches += 1
```

This will train our model for 20 epochs. We get a running total of the loss and the number of batches to compute the average loss at the end of each epoch. We will also evaluate the model on the validation set after each epoch:

```
model.eval()
total_val_loss = 0
num_val_batches = 0
with torch.no_grad():
    for batch in val_dataloader:
        pixel_values, labels = encode_inputs_for_model(batch[
        ➥"ct_image_path"], batch["mask_image_path"])
        outputs = model(pixel_values=pixel_values, labels=labels)
        val_loss = outputs.loss
        total_val_loss += val_loss.item()
        num_val_batches += 1

average_train_loss = total_train_loss / num_train_batches
average_val_loss = total_val_loss / num_val_batches
print(f"Training Loss: {average_train_loss:.4f}, Validation Loss: {
➥average_val_loss:.4f}")
```

The validation code closely resembles the training loop, with a few key differences: the model is set to `eval()` mode, and gradient computation is disabled using `with torch.no_grad()`. These settings ensure that no gradients are calculated during validation, which optimizes performance and memory usage.

Because we have written the losses to TensorBoard, we can visualize the loss over time, as shown in figure 15.16. As the model trains, we observe a steady decrease in both training loss and validation loss, indicating that the model is likely learning to generalize well to unseen data.

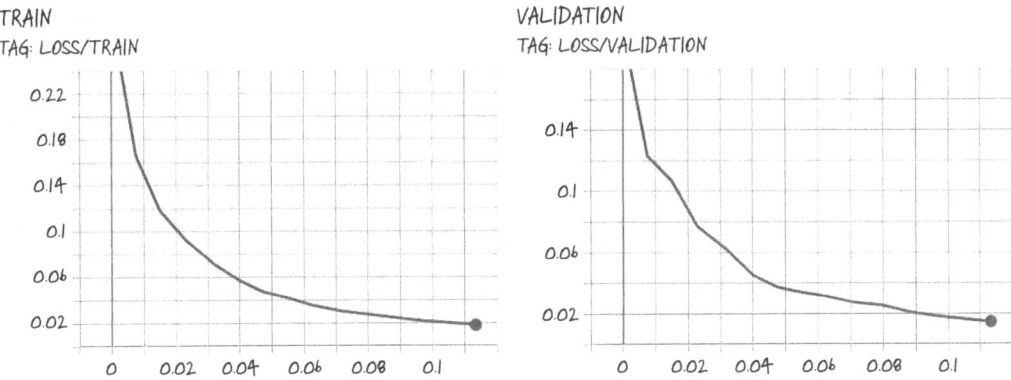

Figure 15.16 Training and validation losses graphed in TensorBoard

15.7.4 Saving our model

PyTorch makes it pretty easy to save our model to disk. Under the hood, torch.save uses the standard Python pickle library, which means we could pass our model instance in directly, and it would save properly. That's not considered the ideal way to persist our model, however, since we lose some flexibility.

Instead, we will save only the *parameters* of our model. Doing this allows us to load those parameters into any model that expects parameters of the same shape, even if the class doesn't match the model those parameters were saved under. The save-parameters-only approach allows us to reuse and remix our models in more ways than saving the entire model.

We can get at our model's parameters using the model.state_dict() function (5_fine_tuning.ipynb).

Listing 15.9 Saving model parameters to disk

```
torch.save(model.state_dict(), "p2ch15/segformer_epoch_20.pt")
```

The model.state_dict() function returns a Python dictionary object that maps each layer to its parameter tensor. This includes weights and biases for each layer in the model.

> **TIP** You can save more than just the model's parameters. The torch.save() function can handle an arbitrary dictionary of keys and objects, allowing you to include additional information such as the optimizer state, timestamps, and the number of training steps completed. This can be invaluable for seamlessly resuming training and tracking experiment progress, especially if your access to computing resources is intermittent. Details on loading a model and optimizer to restart training can be found in the official documentation (https://mng.bz/eBqw).

Loading a model is just as easy as saving it. We instantiate our model as usual and then load the parameters from the file we saved them to:

```
model = SegformerForSemanticSegmentation.from_pretrained(
    "nvidia/mit-b0",
    num_labels=2,
    id2label=id2label,
    label2id=label2id,
)
state_dict = torch.load("p2ch15/segformer_epoch_20.pt")
model.load_state_dict(state_dict)
model.to(device)
```

When you call `torch.load("p2ch15/segformer_epoch_20.pt")`, you are loading the saved state dictionary from the file segformer_epoch_20.pt. Finally, model.to(device) moves the model to the specified device (e.g., CPU or GPU), ensuring that it is ready for further computation.

15.8 Inference and results

Now that the model is trained, it can be used to segment nodules from unseen CT scans. By passing CT scan slices to the model, it generates the corresponding masks, which can then be visualized to evaluate its performance.

To demonstrate how the model generates masks, we'll use specific points from our dataset. A helper method can be defined to perform inference and produce the masks:

```
def inference(model, image_path, mask_image_path, show_plot=False):
    model.eval()
    image = Image.open(image_path)
    mask_image = Image.open(mask_image_path)
    pixel_values = image_processor(images=image, return_tensors="pt").
    pixel_values.to(device)
    with torch.no_grad():
        outputs = model(pixel_values=pixel_values)
    predicted_segmentation_map = image_processor.
    post_process_semantic_segmentation(outputs,
     target_sizes=[(512, 512)])[0]
    if show_plot:
        plot_image_and_masks(image, mask_image,
         predicted_segmentation_map.cpu().numpy())
    return predicted_segmentation_map
```

By providing the image and mask paths to the `inference` method, the model generates the masks. We can also visualize the images and masks to see how well the model is performing (figure 15.17).

Congratulations! Our model is able to segment out nodules from the CT scans.

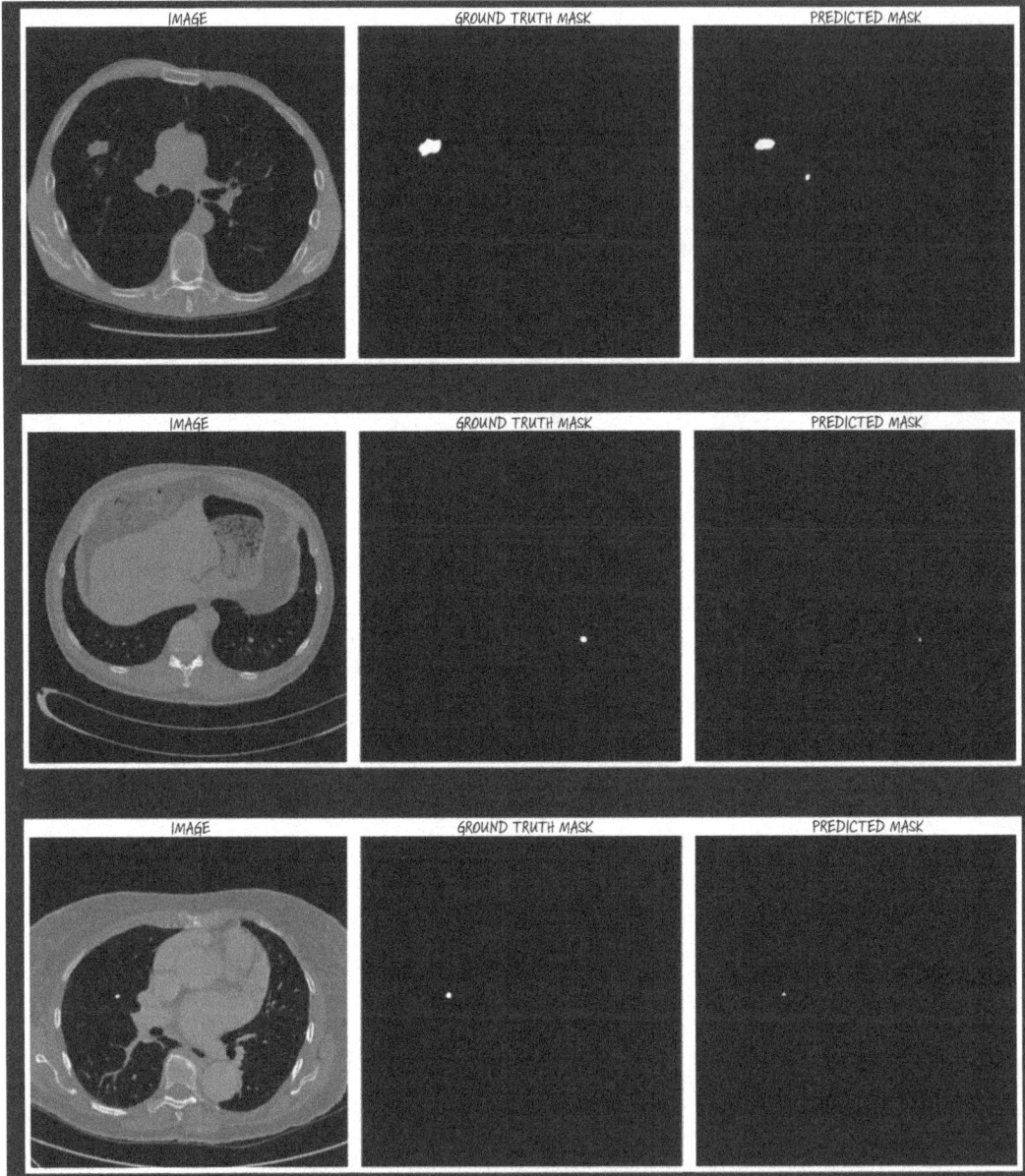

Figure 15.17   CT images (left) with the ground truth mask (middle) and the model predictions (right)

15.9 Conclusion

In this chapter, we explored techniques for pixel-to-pixel-level segmentation, focusing on the Segment Anything model (SAM) and its application to medical imaging tasks. We introduced SAM, a foundational computer vision model designed for versatile segmentation tasks, and demonstrated its capabilities in generating segmentation masks with promptable inputs. Specifically, we demonstrated how SAM can be employed to generate masks for candidate nodules by simply inputting a CT image and a reference point.

Building on this foundation, we proceeded to create a new dataset comprising images and their corresponding masks, which served as a resource for showing how to tackle segmentation problems. This provided a practical framework for experimentation and analysis, for which we could train our own model.

Finally, we fine-tuned the SegFormer model to segment nodules in CT scans. We designed a training loop that processed images and masks. We measured the training and validation losses in TensorBoard, saved the model's parameters for flexibility in reuse, and demonstrated how to load these parameters for inference. Finally, we used the trained model to generate and visualize segmentation masks on unseen CT scans, confirming its effectiveness in identifying nodules.

15.10 Exercises

1. Fine-tune the SegFormer model on a new dataset of your choice:
   a. What changes did you make to the dataset preparation process?
   b. How did the model's performance change after fine-tuning?
2. Experiment with different optimizers, such as AdamW and SGD, for training the SegFormer model:
   a. How do the training dynamics and final performance compare between the optimizers?
   b. What effect does the learning rate have on the training process?
3. Change the segmentation `Dataset` implementation to have a three-way split for training, validation, and test sets:
   a. What fraction of the data did you use for the test set?
   b. Does performance on the test set and the validation set seem consistent with each other?
   c. What additional metadata could be useful for tracking experiment progress?
4. Implement a pipeline that uses segmentation followed by classification to detect nodules:
   a. How does the segmentation output affect the classification results?
   b. What are the benefits and challenges of this approach?
5. Can you find additional sources of data to use beyond just the LUNA (or LIDC) data?

Summary

- Segmentation flags individual pixels or voxels for membership in a class. This is in contrast to classification, which operates at the level of the entire image.
- Different types of segmentation include semantic segmentation, which classifies pixels into categories; instance segmentation, which labels individual objects; and object detection, which identifies objects with bounding boxes.
- The Segment Anything model (SAM) represents a significant advancement in foundational segmentation models. It allows promptable points to be used to guide the model in its segmentation task.
- SAM consists of three main components: an image encoder that processes the input image, a prompt encoder that encodes user-provided prompts (e.g., points, boxes, masks), and a lightweight mask decoder that combines the encoded image and prompt information to generate segmentation masks.
- Using segmentation followed by classification, we can implement detection with relatively modest data and computation requirements.
- We can adapt a model to a new task by fine-tuning it on a new dataset.
- The Adam optimizer family is a popular choice for training models, as it automatically adjusts the learning rate for each parameter.
- The SegFormer is a transformer-based model designed for semantic segmentation.
- We can download pretrained models and available datasets from Hugging Face.
- TensorBoard can display 2D images generated during training and will save a history of how those models changed over the training run. This can be used to visually track changes to model output as training progresses.
- Model parameters can be saved to disk and loaded back to reconstitute a model that was saved earlier. The exact model implementation can change as long as there is a 1:1 mapping between old and new parameters.

Training models on multiple GPUs

This chapter covers
- Distributed training concepts
- PyTorch's distributed package (`torch.distributed`)
- Different forms of parallelism

In previous chapters, we have been mostly focused on training models on a single GPU. But, as models grow larger and datasets grow bigger, training on a single GPU becomes infeasible. Model sizes have exploded over the last several years with the popularity of large language models. In case the naming wasn't clear, large language models are, in fact, quite large. For example, Meta's open LLaMA 3.1 model has 7-billion-, 80-billion-, and 405-billion-parameter variants. The 405-billion-parameter variant requires about 800 GB of memory just to run inference (this is without optimizations such as quantization).

> **NOTE** Readers should check the official licensing on models depending on how they want to use them.

To address this, we will explore how to use PyTorch's distributed subpackage for training models across multiple GPUs, covering distributed training concepts and various forms of parallelism.

16.1 Introduction to parallel programming

Parallel programming is the process of breaking down a problem into smaller tasks that can be executed simultaneously. This is done to improve performance and efficiency.

Imagine you're assembling a large jigsaw puzzle. If you work on it alone, it might take a long time to complete. However, if you have several friends helping you, each person can focus on a different section of the puzzle: one person works on the sky, another on the trees, and someone else on the buildings. By working on these sections simultaneously, the puzzle comes together much faster. In machine learning, parallel programming allows the same model to process different parts of the data at the same time, accelerating the training process.

Consider the following toy code example (1_motivator.py):

Listing 16.1 Sequential execution timing example

```
# In[]
def some_work(x):
    time.sleep(0.5)
    return x

start_time = time.time()
results_sequential = sum([some_work(i) for i in range(10)])
sequential_time = time.time() - start_time

print(results_sequential)
print(f"Sequential Time: {sequential_time:.2f} seconds")

# Out[]
45
Sequential Time: 5.04 seconds
```

In this example, we have a function that performs some work and takes 0.5 seconds to complete. We then call this function 10 times in a loop. The total time taken to complete the loop is around 5 seconds.

In the next example, we will use the concurrent.futures module to parallelize the work.

Listing 16.2 Multithreaded execution timing

```
# In[]
start_time = time.time()
with concurrent.futures.ThreadPoolExecutor() as executor:
    results_multithreaded = sum(list(executor.map(some_work, range(10))))
multithreaded_time = time.time() - start_time

print(results_multithreaded)
print(f"Multithreaded Time: {multithreaded_time:.2f} seconds")
```

```
# Out[]
45
Multithreaded Time: 0.51 seconds
```

We create multiple threads that can run concurrently. The total time taken to complete the loop is around 0.5 seconds. This is a significant speedup compared to the sequential version.

> **On threads and processes**
>
> For those unfamiliar with the difference between threads and processes, a thread is a lightweight process that can be executed concurrently with other threads. Threads share the same memory space, which makes them faster to create and switch between.
>
> Processes, on the other hand, have their own memory space and are more heavyweight. Processes are slower to create and switch between, but they are typically used for distributed training due to their isolation, which results in less complexity when dealing with the underlying accelerators such as GPUs.

16.1.1 Distributed computing terminology

With distributed training, we will be dealing with multiple GPUs, either within a single machine or across multiple machines. This requires a different set of terminology and concepts. The terminology that `torch.distributed` uses is based on the terminology used in the MPI (Message Passing Interface) standard. We can see these concepts illustrated in figure 16.1.

> **NOTE** The MPI standard defines the syntax and semantics of library routines that can be used to implement parallel programs in C and C++.

Some of the key terms we will reference throughout the rest of the chapter include

- *World size*—The entire distributed system is referred to as the "world." The world size is the total number of processes in the distributed system. Generally, we restrict our device management to one GPU per process, so the world size is equal to the number of GPUs we are using. Each process has a unique rank within the world. In figure 16.1, the world size of the single GPU training is 1, the world size of the single machine training is 4, and the world size of the multimachine training is 8.
- *Rank*—The rank is a unique identifier assigned to each process in a distributed system. It is an integer value that ranges from 0 to world size 1. The rank is used to identify the process participating in the distributed system.
- *Process group*—A process group is a collection of processes that can communicate with each other. In PyTorch, a process group is created when we call `torch.distributed.init_process_group`. The process group is used to manage the communication between processes.

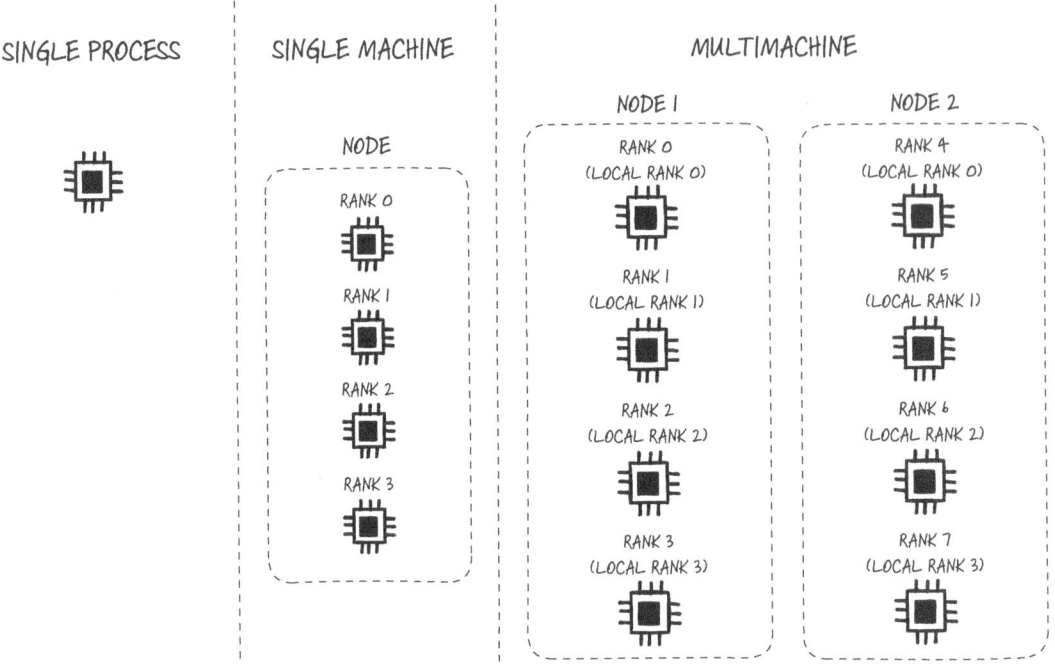

Figure 16.1 Single GPU training (left) vs. multi-GPU training (center) vs. training with multiple machines and multiple GPUs (right)

- *Node*—The term *node* refers to a single machine in a distributed system. A node can be a physical machine or a virtual machine. In the context of deep learning, a node typically refers to a machine with one or more GPUs.
- *Global rank versus local rank*—When dealing with multiple machines, we need to differentiate between the global rank and the local rank. The global rank is the rank of the process in the entire distributed system. The local rank is the rank of the process within a single node. In figure 16.1, for multimachine training, the local rank of each machine goes up to 4 since each machine has four GPUs, while the global rank goes up to 8.
- *SPMD (Single Program Multiple Data)*—SPMD is a programming model where the same program is executed by multiple processes, each with its own data. In the context of deep learning, each process runs the same model on different parts of the data. When we consider executing our script from listing 16.1, each process is running the same logic and operations. However, there could be cases where each process is running a different operation.

In this chapter, we will concentrate on training models using multiple GPUs within a single machine. We'll be using the term *rank*, which applies to both local and global contexts in this scenario. While training models across multiple machines involves a

16.1 Introduction to parallel programming

different setup and initialization process, since machines need to communicate over the network, the underlying concepts and training script are largely similar.

16.1.2 Hardware requirements

Typically, when utilizing distributed training, you will need multiple GPUs. We understand that not everyone has access to multiple GPUs, so we will provide examples that can be run on a single machine using purely CPUs.

While we may not achieve great speed-ups when using CPUs, the code will still work, and you can experiment with the concepts. If you have access to multiple GPUs, you can run the code on those GPUs to see the training speedup in action.

PyTorch's distributed APIs have limited support on Windows. We recommend using Linux or macOS for distributed training. If you are using Windows, you can use Windows Subsystem for Linux (WSL).

NOTE Using VS Code with WSL to run the code is straightforward and explained here: https://mng.bz/dWqX.

16.1.3 Initializing a distributed program

There are a couple of changes that need to be made when converting a single-GPU program to a distributed program. Before we can start utilizing multiple GPUs, we need to initialize the distributed program. As shown in figure 16.2, this involves

1. Creating multiple processes
2. Bootstrapping communication and ensuring that all processes can communicate with each other
3. Updating the training logic of the original program

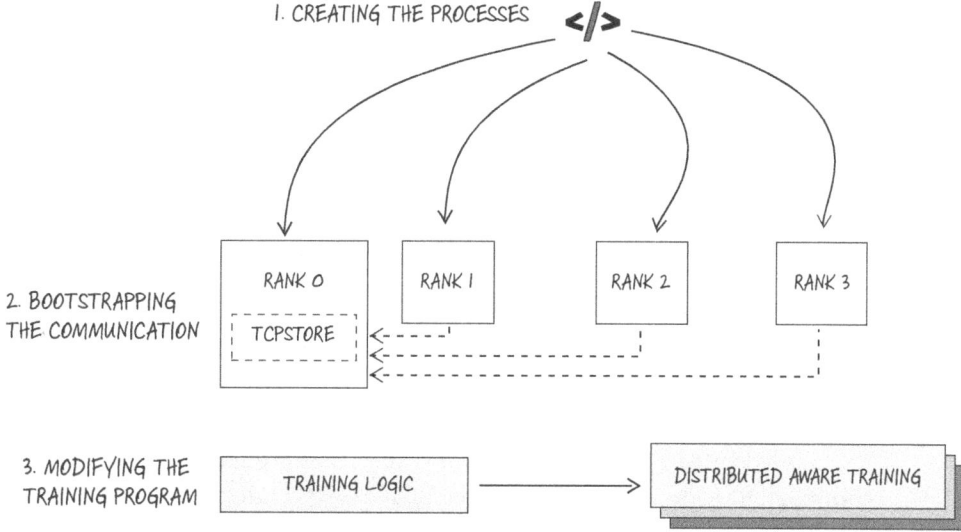

Figure 16.2 Steps required to convert a single-GPU program to a distributed program

For step 1, we can use the `torch.multiprocessing` module to create multiple processes. This module provides a simple way to create and manage multiple processes. The `torch.multiprocessing.spawn` function is used to create multiple processes and run the same function in each process. The `spawn` method takes the function to run, the arguments to pass to the function, and the number of processes to create (2_initialization.py).

> Listing 16.3 Spawning multiple processes with `torch.multiprocessing`

```python
import torch.multiprocessing as mp

if __name__ == "__main__":
    num_processes = 4
    mp.spawn(init_process_with_store, args=(num_processes,), nprocs=num_processes)
```

For each process spawned, it runs the `init_process_with_store` function, which passes in the process index (0, 1, 2, or 3) as the first argument and the argument we provided `num_processes` as the second argument.

Now, for step 2, we need to bootstrap communication and ensure that all processes can communicate with each other. PyTorch provides a `torch.distributed` package that allows us to initialize and manage distributed programs (2_initialization.py).

> Listing 16.4 Initializing a process group

```python
import torch.distributed as dist
import os
os.environ["MASTER_ADDR"] = "localhost"
os.environ["MASTER_PORT"] = "12355"

def init_process_with_store(rank, world_size, backend="gloo"):
    store = dist.TCPStore(
        host_name=os.environ["MASTER_ADDR"],
        port=int(os.environ["MASTER_PORT"]),
        world_size=world_size,
        is_master=rank == 0
    )
    dist.init_process_group(backend, store=store, rank=rank, world_size=world_size)
```

The first step is to initialize the distributed program using a `TCPStore` to bootstrap communication. The `TCPStore` is a simple key-value store that allows us to share information between processes. We need to set the `MASTER_ADDR` and `MASTER_PORT` environment variables to specify the address and port of the master process, which holds the `TCPStore`. We use the `os` module to set these environment variables.

We should also mention that providing the `store` argument to `init_process_group` is optional. If we don't provide a store, PyTorch will create a default store for us. As we can see in the `init_process` example method in the same file, we don't explicitly create a store, and the initialization works just the same.

There is also a convenient utility provided in the torch package, which comes pre-installed with PyTorch. This utility is called torchrun (https://pytorch.org/docs/stable/elastic/run.html), which is a command-line utility that helps us launch distributed training jobs. It takes care of the initialization and communication for us. We can use this utility to launch our distributed training jobs without having to write the initialization code ourselves. With torchrun, we can omit setting the environment variables for bootstrapping and avoid using mp.spawn to create multiple processes. With torchrun, our initialization setup becomes very minimal as we read from the environment variables set by torchrun and call init_process_group directly (3_torchrun.py).

Listing 16.5 Using torchrun

```
# torchrun --nproc-per-node=4 3_torchrun.py
import torch.distributed as dist
import os

def main():
    rank = int(os.environ["RANK"])
    world_size = int(os.environ["WORLD_SIZE"])
    print(f"{rank=} initializing")
    dist.init_process_group(backend="gloo", rank=rank, world_size=world_size)

if __name__ == "__main__":
    main()
```

The command to use torchrun, which will create four processes and run the same script in each one. It also populates the "RANK" and "WORLD_SIZE" environment variables, among others.

We will describe step 3 (modifying the training program) of figure 16.2 in more detail later. Now that our initialization is set up, we are going to use it and dive into a short segue on collective communication.

16.2 Collective communication

In the previous section, we spent a lot of time getting to the stage where we could call torch.distributed.init_process_group(), but what is this actually doing? This function is used to initialize the distributed process group. It sets up the communication between processes and allows them to communicate with each other. This is at the core of distributed training because it is essential for processes to be able to communicate tensor data to each other efficiently.

With distributed training, we are often communicating model gradients, model parameters, and other tensor data between processes. Ensuring performant communication between processes is crucial for efficient distributed training. The more time we spend communicating, the less time we have for computation and training!

There are multiple backends that we can use. The most common backends are gloo and nccl. The gloo backend is CPU-based and is used for distributed training on CPUs, which is why we used it for our examples. The nccl backend is a GPU-based backend that is used for distributed training on GPUs. The mpi backend is a standard backend that is used for distributed training on multiple machines.

NOTE gloo supports GPU tensors for some collective operations but does so by first copying tensors from GPU to CPU memory, performing the communication, and then copying the results back to GPU—introducing overhead that reduces performance compared to native GPU communication.

With these backends, we utilize the collective communication operations built into `torch.distributed`. Let's take a look at a few important collective communication operations:

- *Broadcast*—Broadcast is like a radio station transmitting a message to all listeners. It sends data from one process to all other processes in the group. The data originating from the source process is copied by all other processes. In figure 16.3, we can see that the data (`tensor_0`) is sent from rank 0 and results in all other processes (including rank 0 itself) with the data.
- *Allreduce*—Allreduce is like a group of people, each contributing ingredients to make a shared dish. Each person (process) adds their ingredients (data), and the final dish (result) is distributed back to everyone. This operation combines data from all processes, performs a specified reduction operation (like sum or max), and then shares the result with all processes. In figure 16.3, we can see that each rank has some data (t0, t1, t2, or t3) and as a result of the allreduce operation, all processes end up with the sum of all the data.

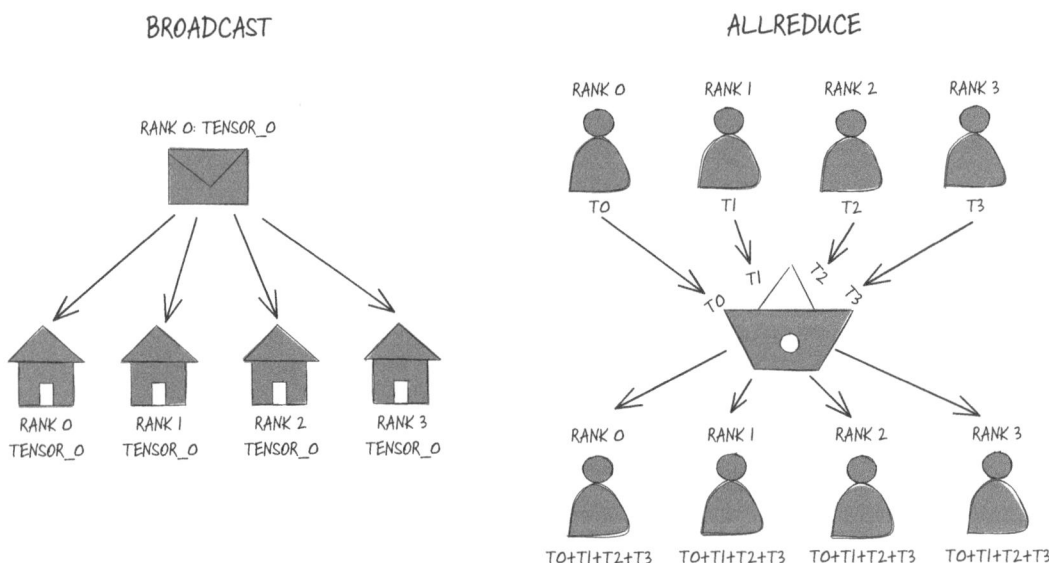

Figure 16.3 Illustration of the broadcast (left) and allreduce (right) collective communication operations

This is just a sample of the collectives available. There are a whole bunch of other collectives that describe different ways in which tensor data is exchanged between

16.2 Collective communication

processes. A good visual resource is shown in this tutorial on the PyTorch website: https://mng.bz/rZqZ. With these collectives, we can imagine all the different kinds of ways we can potentially perform parallelism between processes.

To wrap this all together, we can try running an example script, which demonstrates broadcast and allreduce in action and the result on the tensors (4_collectives.py).

Listing 16.6 PyTorch's broadcast and all_reduce operations

```
import torch.distributed as dist
...
def perform_broadcast(rank):
    if rank == 0:
        tensor = torch.tensor([123.0])
    else:
        tensor = torch.zeros(1)
    dist.broadcast(tensor, src=0)

def perform_all_reduce(rank):
    tensor = torch.tensor([float(rank)])
    dist.all_reduce(tensor, op=dist.ReduceOp.SUM)
...

# Out[]
Process 1 performing broadcast
Process 2 performing broadcast
Process 0 performing broadcast
Process 2 has tensor tensor([0.])
Process 1 has tensor tensor([0.])
Process 0 has tensor tensor([123.])
Process 0 received tensor: tensor([123.])
Process 1 received tensor: tensor([123.])
Process 2 received tensor: tensor([123.])
Process 0 performing all_reduce
Process 2 performing all_reduce
Process 1 performing all_reduce
Process 0 has tensor tensor([0.])
Process 1 has tensor tensor([1.])
Process 2 has tensor tensor([2.])
Process 0 received tensor: tensor([3.])
Process 2 received tensor: tensor([3.])
Process 1 received tensor: tensor([3.])
```

Rank 0 broadcasts tensor 123 to rank 1 and rank 2.

Each rank broadcasts its rank value, so the resulting sum is 0+1+2.

We can see that the broadcast operation sends the tensor from rank 0 to all other processes. The allreduce operation sums the tensor across all processes and sends the result (3.0) back to all processes. It's important to note that the output order on your machine might vary due to the nondeterministic nature of multiprocessing. We add synchronization points (via barrier collectives) to make the output readable, but this is omitted from the previous code for clarity.

With collective communication in our toolbox, we can begin to implement many of the distributed parallelisms that are commonly used to train deep learning models.

16.3 Introduction to parallelisms

The forward pass of a neural network is an "embarrassingly parallel" problem, meaning it can be easily parallelized across multiple GPUs. Each input is processed with the same weights but without needing results from other inputs, so GPUs can compute their portions independently and without talking to each other. Therefore, by duplicating the model across several devices, each GPU can independently process a portion of the data.

For example, if we have two GPUs and are initially training on a single GPU with a batch size of 20, we can divide the data into two equal parts. Each GPU would then handle a batch size of 10, performing the forward pass on its respective portion of the data. This approach allows each device to work independently, maximizing computational efficiency. Figure 16.4 shows this in action. The forward pass is performed independently on each device.

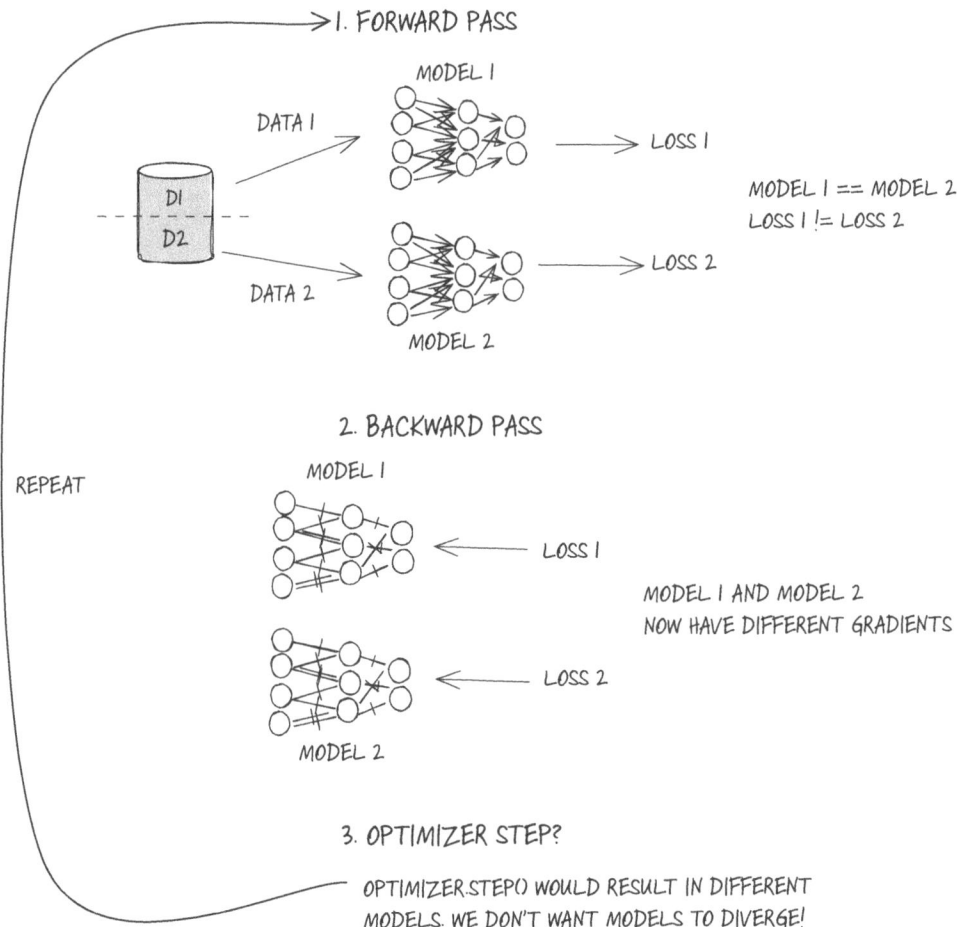

Figure 16.4 The distributed training steps—forward pass (1), backward pass (2), and update (3) parameters—but missing a critical step since models have different gradients

After the initial forward pass, each model produces a loss value. These losses differ because each model processes a distinct shard of the data. (In the context of distributed training, a *shard* refers to a subset of the entire dataset distributed across multiple computing units.)

Similarly, the backward pass can be executed independently. Each model calculates its own gradients based on the loss it computed earlier. Although the model parameters are identical, the gradient tensors differ because they are derived from different data shards.

At this point, we encounter a natural challenge: updating the parameters. If we were to call `optimizer.step()` on each model as we would in single-device training, we would update the parameters using different gradients. This would cause the models to diverge, resulting in two entirely separate models instead of a unified one trained across multiple devices.

To address this, we need to add an additional step to the training process. After the backward pass and before the optimizer step, we must aggregate the gradients from all devices. This step, often referred to as *gradient reduction* in distributed training, ensures that all devices have synchronized gradients before updating the parameters. This synchronization is crucial for training a single model across multiple devices.

This is where the collective communication operations we learned are essential. We can use the `allreduce` operation to average the gradients across all devices. Once the gradients are synchronized, we can proceed with `optimizer.step()` to update the parameters as usual. This ensures that the models remain consistent and don't drift away from each other. Let's explore how to implement the data parallel approach in PyTorch.

16.4 Data parallelism

As previously mentioned, we clone the model across multiple devices and divide the data so that each device processes a separate portion. To ensure consistency before updating the parameters, we must synchronize the model gradients across all devices using collective communication, as shown in figure 16.5.

Let's look at the following listing to see how this would be implemented in practice (5_ddp_from_scratch.py).

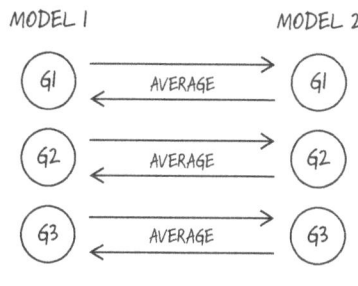

Figure 16.5 Our updated training steps to include a synchronization step

460   CHAPTER 16 *Training models on multiple GPUs*

Listing 16.7 Simple example of gradient synchronization

```
input_data = torch.randn(3) + rank      ◁─── Forward through the model

output = model(input_data)              │ We are using dummy data (rand) and adding rank
loss = output.mean()                    │ ensures that each process has different data.

                                        │ Performs backward pass
opt.zero_grad()                         ◁─┘
loss.backward()                         ◁─── loss.backward() is the same
                                             as in single process training.

for param in model.parameters():                                     │ all_reduce the
    dist.all_reduce(param.grad.data, op=dist.ReduceOp.SUM)           │ model gradients
    param.grad.data /= world_size       ◁───
                                             After all_reduce, which is performing
opt.step()                              ◁─┐  a sum, we divide by the world size to
                                             compute the average.

                                             Updates parameters; opt.step() is the
                                             same as in single process training.
```

In the previous code, we first perform the forward pass and compute the loss. Then we call `loss.backward()` to compute the gradients. After that, we use `dist.all_reduce` to synchronize the gradients across all devices. Finally, we call `opt.step()` to update the parameters.

While our implementation illustrates the basic concept of data parallelism, it is not optimized for performance. In reality, PyTorch provides a more efficient and robust implementation through the `torch.nn.parallel.DistributedDataParallel` (DDP) module. DDP uses optimized communication patterns to minimize the overhead of gradient synchronization, making it a more scalable solution for distributed training. By wrapping our model with DDP, we can easily enable data parallelism and let PyTorch handle the underlying complexities, including gradient synchronization (6_ddp.py).

Listing 16.8 Wrapping a model using `DistributedDataParallel`

```
from torch.nn.parallel import DistributedDataParallel as DDP
model = SimpleModel().to(device)
model = DDP(model)                      ◁─── We only need to wrap our model with
                                             DDP and use it as we would normally in
                                             the single process training.
```

An important aspect we overlooked in our basic implementation is data loading. In real-world scenarios, it's crucial to properly shard the dataset during iteration. PyTorch addresses this with the `DistributedSampler`, which limits data loading to specific subsets. This ensures that the data loader does not repeat dataset entries and that each epoch is processed collectively across all devices (6_ddp.py).

Listing 16.9 Creating a data loader with `DistributedSampler`

```
def get_data_loader(batch_size, rank, world_size):
    transform = transforms.Compose([transforms.ToTensor()])
    dataset = datasets.MNIST(root='../data/
     p2ch16', train=True, download=True, transform=transform)
    sampler = DistributedSampler(dataset,
        num_replicas=world_size, rank=rank)
    loader = DataLoader(dataset, batch_size=batch_size,
        sampler=sampler)
    return loader
```

> `DistributedSampler` needs the rank and world_size to determine which subset of the data this rank will handle.
>
> This sampler is passed in the DataLoader.

The remaining example for training an MNIST detection model using DDP can be seen in 6_ddp.py.

16.5 Model parallelism

Data parallel works great, but there is one caveat. What if our model is too large to fit on a single GPU? Data parallel is dependent on replicating the model across multiple devices so that each device can operate on a piece of data. In essence, for data parallel, we are trading memory for compute to make the training faster. If we have a model that is too large to fit on a single device, we cannot solely rely on data parallelism.

In this case, we need to use model parallelism. Model parallelism is the process of splitting the model across multiple devices. Each device will hold a part of the model and perform the forward and backward pass for that part of the model.

The forward pass for a model distributed across multiple devices is similar to that on a single GPU, with the addition of extra communication. Once a model partition completes processing a data batch, its intermediate output, known as the *activations*, must be communicated to the next device sequentially. Essentially, you can envision the model as being divided into three separate models that interact with each other to produce the same output as the original model. As illustrated in figure 16.6, a batch is

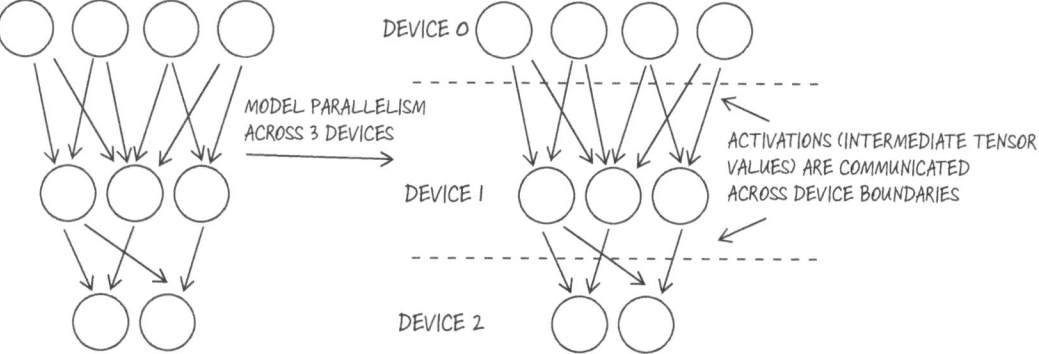

Figure 16.6 A model adapted to run on multiple devices. The direction of the arrow indicates the flow of a batch through the model.

processed by device 0, generating an output that is then passed to device 1. Device 1 processes this output and forwards it to device 2, continuing the sequence.

In our code example, we use simple linear models to represent the model partitions across three devices. Each device processes its segment of the model and transmits the activations to the next device using peer-to-peer (P2P) operations. These operations are similar to the collective communication methods we discussed earlier but are specifically used between two processes. In torch.distributed, the available P2P operations are send() and recv(). Both functions require a tensor and the source and destination ranks for communication. In our example, we utilize these operations to perform the transmission of activations (7_model_parallel.py).

Listing 16.10 Implementing model parallelism using send and recv

```
...
    if rank == 0:                                         ← The setup is omitted.
        model_part1 = nn.Linear(1, 2)                     ← Each rank has a chunk of the model.
        input_batch = torch.tensor([[1.0]])
        part1_activations = model_part1(input_batch)
        print(f"Process {rank} activations from part 1: {part1_activations}")
        dist.send(part1_activations, dst=1)
    elif rank == 1:
        model_part2 = nn.Linear(2, 3)
        part1_activations = torch.zeros(2)
        dist.recv(part1_activations, src=0)               ← Peer-to-peer ops (P2P) are used to send and receive the activation tensors across model partitions.
        part2_activations = model_part2(part1_activations)
        dist.send(part2_activations, dst=2)
        print(f"Process {rank} activations from part 2: {part2_activations}")
    elif rank == 2:
        model_part3 = nn.Linear(3, 1)
        part2_activations = torch.zeros(3)
        dist.recv(part2_activations, src=1)
        part3_output = model_part3(part2_activations)
        print(f"Process {rank} output from part 3: {part3_output}")
```

We can see how model parallelism enables the distribution of a model across multiple devices while maintaining the same output as the original, single-device model. This approach allows us to train larger models that would otherwise exceed the capacity of a single device. During training, the backward pass is also necessary. The process is similar to the forward pass: each device computes the gradients by calling .backward() on its portion of the loss and then communicates these gradients to the other devices to ensure proper updates across the entire model.

16.5.1 Pipeline parallelism

The model parallelism we've described is functional but somewhat simplistic. While one device processes the forward pass, the other devices remain idle, leading to inefficiencies as not all devices can be utilized simultaneously. We can enhance this setup by implementing pipeline parallelism.

Pipeline parallelism involves dividing the model into multiple segments, referred to as *stages*, which are then distributed across different devices. However, unlike the basic model parallelism approach, it also divides the input into smaller units called *microbatches*. This allows one stage to compute a microbatch while another stage processes a different microbatch, ensuring better computational overlap.

Consider figure 16.7, where we have three devices. In the pipeline parallelism approach, we would split the model into three stages, each assigned to a respective device. The input data is divided into microbatches, allowing each device to process its designated stage of the model concurrently.

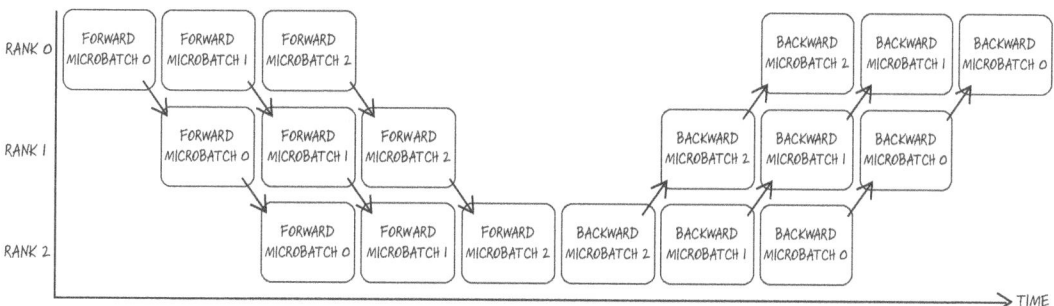

Figure 16.7 Pipeline parallelism with three microbatches involves processing each microbatch and then communicating it to the next device, as indicated by the arrows. This approach enables concurrent processing across devices.

Pipeline parallelism is used in both training and inference for large language models. It excels in models that have many repeated blocks, and large language models fit this characteristic as they repeat transformer layers across their architecture.

However, pipeline parallelism also introduces challenges, such as managing the communication overhead between devices and ensuring that the stages are balanced computationally to prevent bottlenecks and stragglers. Pipeline parallelism requires a degree of manual tuning and understanding of the model architecture to maximize its benefits while minimizing its drawbacks.

Pipeline parallelism is implemented as part of the torch.distributed.pipelining subpackage, which offers utilities for model splitting, schedule definition, and schedule execution.

The following listing demonstrates how to set up pipeline parallelism using PyTorch's built-in utilities. First, we define an example model that includes a split_spec attribute. This attribute indicates where to split the model for pipeline parallelism with SplitPoint.BEGINNING indicating that the split should occur before the specified layer.

Listing 16.11 Model with split points (8_pp.py)

```python
class SimpleMLP(nn.Module):
    def __init__(self, hidden_size=512, n_layers=4):
        super().__init__()
        self.layers = nn.ModuleList([
            nn.Linear(hidden_size, hidden_size) for _ in range(n_layers)
        ])
        self.split_spec = {
            f"layers.{i}": SplitPoint.BEGINNING for i in range(1, n_layers)
        }

    def forward(self, x):
        for layer in self.layers:
            x = torch.relu(layer(x))
        return x
```

Once we have the model defined, we set up the pipeline stages for each rank which will contain a portion of the model. Since we have already defined the `split_spec`, we can conveniently use the `pipeline` API to partition the model automatically based on these split points.

Listing 16.12 Building a pipeline stage

```python
pipe = pipeline(model, mb_args=(x_mb,), split_spec=model.split_spec)
stage = pipe.build_stage(rank, device)
```

Finally, we define a schedule for the pipeline execution. The schedule determines how microbatches are processed across the different stages. In this example, we use the simple GPipe schedule which is a straightforward approach to pipeline execution. GPipe executes all the forwards of the microbatches first, followed by all the backwards.

Listing 16.13 Executing a pipeline schedule

```python
if rank == 0:
    schedule.step(x)
elif rank == world_size - 1:
    output = schedule.step(target=target, losses=losses)
else:
    # Middle ranks just forward/backward
    schedule.step()
```

The example can be run across multiple processes using `torchrun` as described earlier. You can see `code/p2ch16/8_pp.py` for the complete example of pipeline parallelism.

16.5.2 Tensor parallelism

Tensor parallelism is another form of model parallelism used to distribute the computation of neural network models by splitting the model's parameters, or tensors, across multiple devices. Similar to how pipeline parallelism divides the model into stages at the module level, tensor parallelism focuses on splitting within the modules themselves.

As illustrated in figure 16.8, tensor parallelism divides a model's parameters into smaller segments, allowing each linear layer to distribute its weights and biases across two devices. This setup enables each device to independently perform matrix multiplication with the input tensor. However, additional communication is required to exchange intermediate results between devices. This communication ensures that each device has the necessary data to complete the computation, allowing the model to produce the correct output shape as if it were running on a single device. In tensor parallelism, model weights can be split either row-wise (dimension 0) or column-wise (dimension 1) to minimize communication time and accelerate training. While the detailed reasoning behind these strategies is beyond the scope of this book, they are thoroughly discussed in the original paper introducing tensor parallelism (https://arxiv.org/pdf/1909.08053).

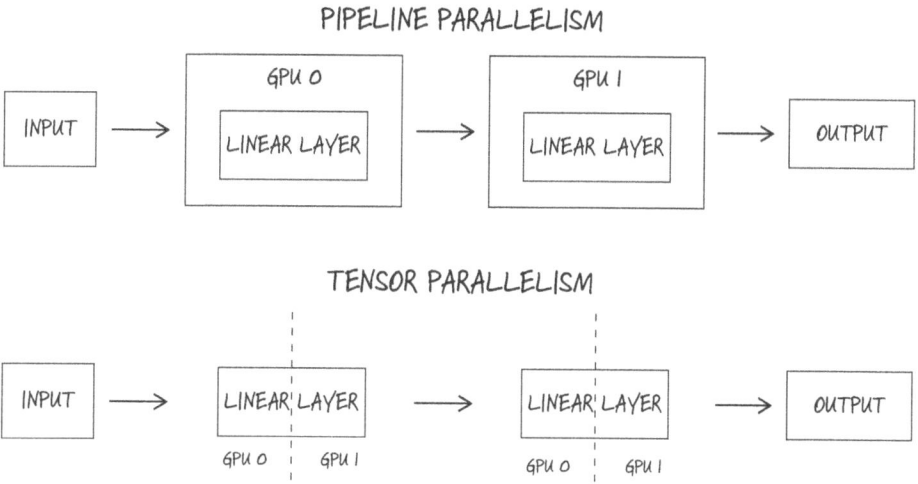

Figure 16.8 Pipeline parallelism (top) compared to tensor parallelism (bottom). Pipeline parallelism splits at the module granularity, while tensor parallelism splits at the module parameter (tensor) granularity.

16.5.3 Deciding between pipeline and tensor parallelism

So, how does one decide between using pipeline parallelism and tensor parallelism? The answer, unfortunately, is that it depends largely on the model's architecture.

For models that are skinnier and deeper, characterized by having many layers with relatively fewer parameters per layer, pipeline parallelism is often more suitable. This approach allows the model to be divided into sequential stages, with each stage processed on a different device. This setup efficiently utilizes the available hardware by keeping all devices busy with different parts of the model.

On the other hand, models that are wider and shallower—those with fewer layers but each layer containing a large number of parameters—are typically better suited for tensor parallelism. In these cases, the computational load of each layer is significant, and distributing the parameters across multiple devices can help manage this load effectively.

Additionally, if a model layer is so large that it cannot fit into the memory of a single device, tensor parallelism becomes necessary. By splitting the layer's parameters across multiple devices, tensor parallelism enables the model to fit within the available memory constraints, ensuring that training or inference can proceed without running into memory limitations.

16.6 *n-dimensional parallelism*

We've described data parallelism and model parallelism, but these strategies are not mutually exclusive. In fact, they are often combined to enable training of larger models and to improve efficiency. This is where n-dimensional parallelism comes into play.

The term *n-dimensional* is used because, in practice, multiple forms of parallelism are layered together for greater efficiency. For example, tensor parallelism involves significant communication overhead, so it's typically used within a single host to take advantage of fast GPU interconnects. In contrast, pipeline parallelism requires less communication and is better suited for distributing work across multiple hosts.

When we reach the point of training large-scale models, it's common to require hundreds or even thousands of GPUs to achieve reasonable training times. Relying on a single type of parallelism, such as data parallelism, can quickly become a bottleneck as collective operations like allreduce become inefficient at scale. By combining different parallelism strategies, we can tune the system for optimal performance, much like tuning hyperparameters such as learning rate or batch size. For example, LLaMA 3 was trained using 4D parallelism, combining data parallelism, tensor parallelism, pipeline parallelism, and context parallelism.

> **NOTE** Distributed training is very important for large language models, and the LLaMA paper describes it in great detail (https://arxiv.org/pdf/2407.21783).

Describing n-dimensional parallelism can be challenging. Managing communication across all devices in a single process group is already challenging, but things become even more intricate when we need to coordinate communication among only specific subsets of devices. Fortunately, `torch.distributed` provides an abstraction called `DeviceMesh`, which allows us to define a mesh of devices and specify custom communication patterns between them. Under the hood, this creates multiple process groups, making it particularly useful for n-dimensional parallelism.

Suppose we want to design a distributed architecture with two replicas of a model, where each replica is further partitioned across multiple GPUs using model parallelism. In this setup, input data flows through the model along the row dimension, while the model replicas are synchronized along the column dimension. Figure 16.9 illustrates how this configuration can be represented using a device mesh.

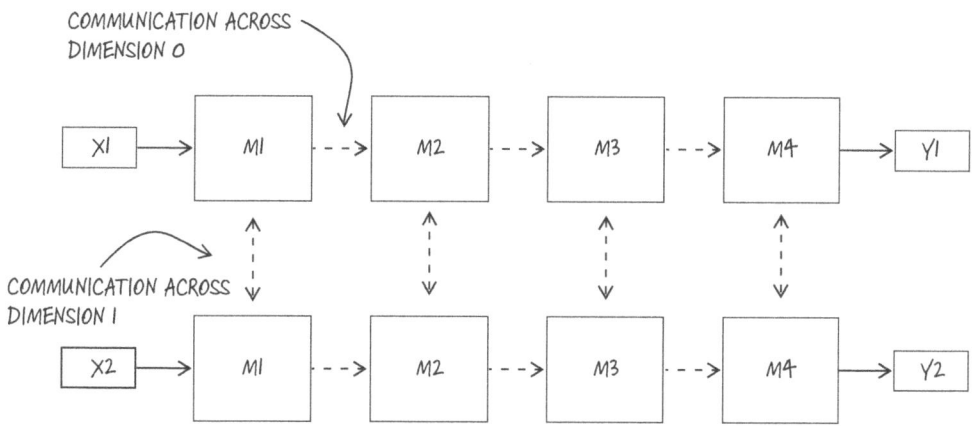

Figure 16.9 Visualization of a 2 × 4 device mesh, where the rows represent model replicas and the columns represent model partitions. The dashed arrows represent how each device is communicating.

To define this device mesh in code, we can use the following initialization (device_mesh.py):

```
from torch.distributed.device_mesh import init_device_mesh

mesh_2d = init_device_mesh(
    "cpu", (2, 4), mesh_dim_names=("replicate", "model_parallel")
)
```

Creates a 2D device mesh with 2 rows and 4 columns. The first argument specifies the device type, the second defines the shape of the mesh, and the third assigns names to the mesh dimensions (we can set these to be any string).

When a 2 × 4 device mesh is created, it internally generates six distinct process groups. Along the row dimension, there are two process groups with ranks [0, 1, 2, 3] and [4, 5, 6, 7]. Along the column dimension, there are four process groups with ranks [0, 4], [1, 5], [2, 6], and [3, 7]. To synchronize model weights, we utilize the process groups in the column dimension. This can be achieved by indexing into the device mesh using the name "replicate" (device_mesh.py).

Listing 16.14 Synchronizing model parameters

```
replica_mesh = mesh_2d["replicate"]
replica_group = replica_mesh.get_group()    ◁── Selects the group from the mesh
def sync_model(replica_mesh):
```

```
    print(f"Mesh {replica_mesh} averaging model parameters")
    for p in model_part.parameters():
        dist.all_reduce(p, group=replica_group)     ◁──┐  Uses this group to
        p.data /= replica_mesh.size()                  │  perform communication
```

After synchronization, the model parameters are consistent across all replicas. Similarly, when processing inputs through each replica, we can use the process groups defined by the column dimension of the device mesh to coordinate communication (device_mesh.py):

```
model_parallel_mesh = mesh_2d["model_parallel"]
forward_pass(model_part, model_parallel_mesh)   ◁──
```
forward_pass implements the logic to perform the forward pass across the model partitions.

With device mesh, it is much easier to express parallelisms and wrangle your process groups!

16.7 Fully sharded data parallelism

Finally, it's essential to highlight one of the most significant distributed APIs: Fully Sharded Data Parallel (FSDP). FSDP combines the strengths of both data parallelism and model parallelism, enabling you to shard both the model and the data across multiple devices. This hybrid approach allows for efficient scaling and resource utilization when training large models.

FSDP was first introduced in 2021 as part of a blog post in Facebook AI Research (https://mng.bz/xZqY). At its core, FSDP applies a process called full parameter sharding, where each device only stores and computes with a subset of the model's parameters, gradients, and optimizers necessary for local computations. A notable implementation of this approach is ZeRO-3 (https://arxiv.org/pdf/2101.06840), popularized by Microsoft, which has demonstrated the effectiveness of full parameter sharding in reducing replication and improving training efficiency.

Similar to tensor parallelism, FSDP shards module parameters across devices, as shown in figure 16.9. When computation is required to process an input, an `all_gather` operation is used to temporarily collect the necessary weights on each device, allowing the forward pass to proceed. Once the computation is complete, the extra weights can be released, returning the parameters to their sharded state. During the backward pass, a similar pattern occurs: gradients are accumulated using `all_gather`, and then distributed back to devices with a `reduce_scatter` operation. These communications are designed to overlap with computation, which helps improve overall performance and minimize communication overhead.

To initialize a model with FSDP, you need to specify which components to shard and across how many devices the sharding will occur. The `torch.distributed.fsdp` package provides a `fully_shard` method that accepts the module you want to shard and an optional device mesh parameter to define the specific devices across which the sharding will be distributed (fsdp_example.py):

16.7 Fully sharded data parallelism

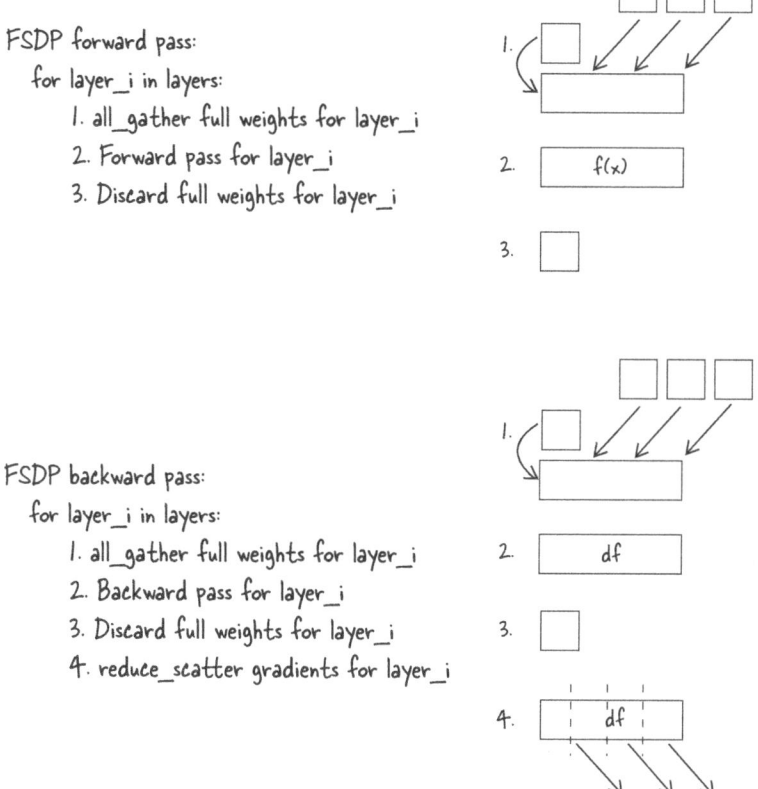

FSDP forward pass:
    for layer_i in layers:
        1. all_gather full weights for layer_i
        2. Forward pass for layer_i
        3. Discard full weights for layer_i

FSDP backward pass:
    for layer_i in layers:
        1. all_gather full weights for layer_i
        2. Backward pass for layer_i
        3. Discard full weights for layer_i
        4. reduce_scatter gradients for layer_i

Figure 16.10 Pseudocode for FSDP implementation

Listing 16.15 Using fully sharded data parallel

```
from torch.distributed.fsdp import fully_shard

model = SimpleModel()

mesh = init_device_mesh(device, (2,))
print(mesh)
for module in model.modules():
    if isinstance(module, nn.Linear):
        fully_shard(module, mesh=mesh)
fully_shard(model, mesh=mesh)
```

To use FSDP, you need to call `fully_shard` multiple times, once over the linear layers since we are sharding the linear layers and once over the entire root model.

FSDP is generally the recommended approach when your model is too large to fit on a single GPU and Distributed Data Parallel (DDP) is not possible. FSDP has demonstrated strong scalability, with successful training runs on up to 512 GPUs, sufficient for most production workloads. However, if communication overhead from `all_gather` or `reduce_scatter` operations becomes a bottleneck at very large scales, it may be necessary to turn to additional forms of parallelism.

16.8 Large language model–specific parallelisms

Large language models (LLMs) have unique characteristics that can be leveraged for more efficient usage of GPUs. Given that transformers and LLMs have become the dominant architecture for many natural language processing tasks, it would be good to highlight the few parallelism strategies that are relevant for these models. These include context parallelism and expert parallelism.

16.8.1 Context parallelism

Context parallelism targets training on long sequences by splitting the sequence length across ranks so each rank owns a contiguous block of tokens. Each rank processes the queries for its own block while coordinating with others to respect causal masking across block boundaries. This trades a few synchronization rounds for lower per-rank memory and better throughput on fast intra-node links.

During training on long sequences, attention compute and activation memory grow roughly with the square of the sequence length L ($O(L^2)$). Sharding by sequence reduces each rank's activation footprint and peak memory from temporary tensors while preserving autoregressive constraints via masking across partition boundaries. This saves memory at the expense of extra synchronization between ranks, which is typically acceptable on fast intra-node interconnects.

Context parallelism is well suited to long-context training where activations are the bottleneck, especially on clusters with fast intra-node interconnects where the additional communication rounds are affordable relative to the saved memory.

16.8.2 Expert Parallelism

A common architecture in LLMs is the Mixture of Experts (MoE) model. In this setup, the feedforward network is replaced with multiple expert networks, where different parts of the model (experts) are specialized for different tasks or types of data. Expert parallelism distributes these experts across devices so each device hosts a subset of experts.

Mixture of experts uses sparse computation: for each token, only a few experts (top-1 or top-2) run. A lightweight router scores experts and picks the top-k per token, with an auxiliary loss to keep load balanced. As a result, expert parallelism relies on all-to-all communication to gather the selected tokens for each expert and scatter back the outputs. This pattern is well-suited for models with many experts, enabling scaling to larger model sizes without a proportional increase in computation or memory per device.

16.9 Tying all parallelisms together

Throughout this chapter, we examined a range of parallelism strategies and how to implement them using PyTorch APIs. While each approach is effective on its own, combining multiple strategies in a real training environment introduces new challenges, such as managing checkpointing, parallelisms composing with each other, and resource utilization. These complexities often require careful engineering, especially when saving and loading model checkpoints or coordinating communication across devices. Real-world systems must address these issues to get the full benefits of distributed training.

To address these challenges and provide a practical reference, the PyTorch team created TorchTitan, a repository that demonstrates distributed training using only native PyTorch APIs. TorchTitan offers a clean and minimal codebase for training large language models, including ready-to-use configurations for LLaMA, DeepSeekV3, and some Hugging Face models. It also integrates necessary components like tokenizers, making it easy to launch a distributed training job to train a large language model from scratch with a single command.

You can find the TorchTitan repository at https://github.com/pytorch/torchtitan. For a deeper dive into the design and experiments behind TorchTitan, refer to the accompanying paper (https://arxiv.org/pdf/2410.06511).

16.10 Conclusion

In this chapter, we explored the landscape of PyTorch's distributed APIs. We covered the fundamentals of distributed training and demonstrated how to use PyTorch's distributed package to train models across multiple GPUs. Along the way, we discussed key concepts in parallel programming and strategies for leveraging multiple hardware resources efficiently. We also examined the process of initializing distributed training scripts.

We looked into collective communication and its role in synchronizing gradients across devices, highlighting why distributed training is essential for scaling up to larger models and datasets. Throughout the chapter, we introduced various forms of parallelism, including data parallelism and model parallelism, as well as advanced techniques like pipeline parallelism, tensor parallelism, and fully sharded data parallelism. We showed how to implement these strategies using `DeviceMesh` and n-dimensional parallelism. Finally, we brought these concepts together by introducing a practical, end-to-end example using TorchTitan.

16.11 Exercises

1. How could you improve the data-parallel implementation from scratch? Look up bucketing, which is explained in the DDP internal design documentation (https://mng.bz/AGn7).
2. Implement a different model parallelism example with varying inputs and output tensors:
   a. What challenges do you encounter with data transfer and synchronization?

3. Read through the pipeline parallelism documentation (https://mng.bz/Z9Ba) and implement GPipe.
4. Create a 3D device mesh on your own.
5. Research fully sharded data parallelism (FSDP) in PyTorch. What are its advantages over traditional data parallelism, and in what scenarios is it most beneficial?
6. Using TorchTitan, run a distributed training job for LLaMA3 8B. What configuration steps are required, and how does the code differ from standard single-GPU training?

Summary

- Distributed training enables scaling deep learning models across multiple GPUs or machines, allowing for efficient handling of large datasets and complex models.
- Parallel programming concepts help break down computations so they can be performed simultaneously, improving training speed and hardware utilization.
- Rank is the unique identifier for each process in a distributed setup, while world size is the total number of participating processes.
- Setting up distributed training involves initializing process groups and launching multiple processes, often using tools like `torchrun`.
- Collective communication operations, such as broadcast and allreduce, are essential for synchronizing data (like gradients) across devices to ensure consistent model updates.
- Data parallelism replicates the model on each device and splits the data, requiring gradient synchronization to maintain consistency across replicas.
- Model parallelism divides the model itself across devices, enabling training of models too large for a single GPU by splitting computations and parameters.
- Pipeline parallelism splits the model into sequential stages, allowing different microbatches to be processed concurrently and improving throughput.
- Tensor parallelism partitions individual layers or tensors across devices, supporting efficient training of very large or wide models.
- n-dimensional parallelism combines multiple parallelism strategies, such as data, model, pipeline, and tensor parallelism, to maximize scalability and efficiency for large-scale training.
- The `DeviceMesh` abstraction in PyTorch helps manage complex communication patterns and process groups, making it easier to implement advanced parallelism strategies.
- Fully sharded data parallelism is a hybrid approach that shards both the model and data across devices, optimizing memory and compute usage.
- Context parallelism and expert parallelism are specialized parallelism techniques for scaling large language models.

- Practical distributed training can be explored using repositories like Torch-Titan, which demonstrate modern techniques and best practices in a minimal codebase.
- Choosing and combining the right parallelism strategies is crucial for scaling deep learning to modern model and dataset sizes, and PyTorch provides robust tools to support these approaches.

Deploying to production

This chapter covers

- Options for deploying PyTorch models
- Deploying models with web frameworks and APIs
- Optimizing inference performance
- Exporting models for various deployment targets
- Running exported and natively implemented models from C++

In part 1 of this book, we learned a lot about models, and part 2 left us with a detailed path for creating good models for a particular problem. Now that we have these great models, we need to take them where they can be useful. Maintaining infrastructure for executing inference of deep learning models at scale can be effective from an architectural as well as cost standpoint. While PyTorch started as a research-focused framework, it has undergone significant evolution, incorporating production-oriented features that make it an ideal end-to-end platform for both research and large-scale production.

What deploying to production means will vary with the use case:

- For our demonstration, we will prototype using Gradio (https://www.gradio.app/), a framework designed to enable users to quickly build a demo or web application for their machine learning models. Gradio offers a simple interface for users to interact with the model and share it with others, making it easy to test and showcase its capabilities without requiring frontend skills.

NOTE Streamlit (https://streamlit.io/) is a similar library to Gradio that also deserves a shoutout.

- One of the most intuitive ways to deploy the models we've developed is by setting up a network service that provides access to them. This can be achieved using any popular Python web framework, such as FastAPI (https://fastapi.tiangolo.com/). FastAPI is widely favored for its ease of use and high performance. It also automatically generates interactive API documentation and offers robust support for data validation and serialization, making it a great choice for building reliable and scalable APIs efficiently.
- We can export our model to a well-standardized format that allows us to ship it using optimized model processors, specialized hardware, or cloud services. For PyTorch models, the Open Neural Network Exchange (ONNX) format fills this role.
- We may wish to integrate our models into larger applications or applications without Python. For this, it would be handy if we were not limited to Python. Thus, we will explore using PyTorch models from C++.
- Finally, for some tasks, it may be nice to run our model on mobile devices. Users may prefer running on their models locally on a mobile device versus having their confidential data, such as images, sent to a cloud service. Luckily for us, PyTorch has built tools for mobile support recently, and we will discuss that.

Throughout this chapter, we'll implement practical examples using both custom models and popular pretrained ones, showcasing deployment strategies that balance performance, accessibility, or resource efficiency.

17.1 Serving PyTorch models

So, we've got a supercool model and want to share it quickly with our coworkers or friends. We'll start with one of the easiest ways to prototype and share your models publicly. Staying true to our hands-on approach, we'll start with the simplest possible server. Once we have something basic that works, we'll examine its limitations and work on addressing them. Let's get started by setting up a server that listens on the network. (To play it safe, do not do this on an untrusted network.)

17.1.1 Our model served by Gradio

Gradio is a Python library that allows us to quickly create a web-based interface for our machine learning models. It provides an easy way to showcase and test models without the need for extensive web development knowledge. Gradio is particularly useful for creating interactive demos and sharing them with others. Gradio can be installed using pip:

```
pip install --upgrade gradio
```

Our UI interface can be created by defining a function that takes inputs and returns outputs. Gradio will automatically generate the UI components based on the input and output types specified in the function signature. For example, if we have a function that takes a string input and returns a string output, Gradio will create a text input box and a text output box for us (gradio_hello_world.py).

Listing 17.1 Creating a simple Gradio interface with text input and output

```
import gradio as gr

def hello_world(name):
    return "Hello, " + name + "!"

demo = gr.Interface(
    fn=hello_world,
    inputs=["text"],
    outputs=["text"],
    flagging_mode="auto",
)

demo.launch()
```

Your application can be started with

```
gradio gradio_hello_world.py
```

This will automatically watch for changes to your Python file and reload the server. The application will run at port 7860 and can be accessed on any web browser at http://localhost:7860.

To make it more interesting, we can use a pretrained model to generate images. For this, we will use the `diffusers` library, which provides a simple interface for working with diffusion models. We will use a version of the Stable Diffusion model we saw earlier in chapter 10 to generate images based on text prompts. To do so, we need to wrap the model in a function that takes a text prompt as input and returns the generated image (gradio_server.py).

Listing 17.2 Loading a Stable Diffusion model for image generation

```
image_generator = None
def load_image_generator():
    global image_generator
    if image_generator is None:
        model_id = "stable-diffusion-v1-5/stable-diffusion-v1-5"
        pipeline = DiffusionPipeline.from_pretrained(model_id,
  torch_dtype=torch.bfloat16)
        device = "cuda" if torch.cuda.is_available() else "cpu"
        pipeline.to(device)

        pipeline.enable_vae_tiling()
        pipeline.enable_sequential_cpu_offload()

        image_generator = pipeline
    return image_generator

def generate_image(prompt):
    image_generator = load_image_generator()
    image = image_generator(prompt).images[0]
    return image

demo = gr.Interface(
    fn=generate_image,
    inputs=gr.Textbox(label="Prompt"),
    outputs=gr.Image(type="pil", label="Generated Image"),
    flagging_mode="auto",
)

demo.launch()
```

Launching the server is similar to before: we can run the script with gradio gradio_server.py. We can even update demo.launch() to demo.launch(share=True) to create a public link that anyone can use to access the application. This is a great way to quickly share our model with others without needing to set up any infrastructure. Figure 17.1 provides an example.

Although an easy way to quickly prototype and share our models, it is not suitable for production use cases. Gradio is great for demos and testing, but it is not designed for high-performance or scalable applications. Let's learn how to set up a more robust server that can handle multiple requests and provide better performance.

17.1.2 Our model behind a FastAPI server

FastAPI is a popular Python framework crafted for building server-side APIs. It can be installed using pip:

```
pip install "fastapi[standard]"
```

> **TIP** You might want to run FastAPI from a Python virtual environment.

Figure 17.1 Image generation example with Gradio

You can create an API by decorating the function with the @app.get or @app.post decorators, depending on whether you want to create a GET or POST endpoint. For example, if we wanted to serve a GPT model that generates text for us, we could use the following (fastapi_hello_world.py):

```
from fastapi import FastAPI

app = FastAPI()

@app.get("/")
async def read_root():
    return "Hello world"
```

The server can be started with the command

```
fastapi dev fastapi_hello_world.py
```

When started, the application will run at http://127.0.0.1:8000 and expose one route, /, which returns the "Hello World" string. This URL is a local address (http) that our computer uses to access the API running on our machine (127.0.0.1 is the IP address for localhost). The port number 8000 specifies which service on our machine we want to connect to.

FastAPI also includes a helpful interactive documentation page at http://127.0.0.1:8000/docs, which we can use to manually query our API. Additionally, because we started the server in development mode, FastAPI will automatically reload the server when we make changes to the code.

At this point, we can augment our web server by loading a previously saved model and expose it through a POST route. For this example, we'll use a text-to-text generation model from the Hugging Face transformers library:

`pip install -U transformers`

We'll use FastAPI's built-in capabilities to define the data structure for our input. Specifically, we'll define a Pydantic model to represent the input data that the user will provide (fastapi_server.py).

> **NOTE** Pydantic is a Python library that provides runtime type checking and validation for data models (https://docs.pydantic.dev/latest/).

Listing 17.3 Defining a FastAPI app

```
from fastapi import FastAPI
from pydantic import BaseModel
# Define a Pydantic model for the input data
class TextInput(BaseModel):
    text: str

app = FastAPI()
```

Instead of the /hello route, we will now define a /generate route. This route will accept a string input (the beginning of a sentence) via a POST request. The server will process this input and return a JSON response containing the predicted continuation of the sentence.

To access the input data, FastAPI automatically parses the incoming JSON request body into a Pydantic model, which we define to match the expected structure of the input. The process of handling the model is similar to using Gradio. We load the model architecture and its pretrained weights from the library. If a GPU is available, we can transfer the model to the GPU for faster processing by calling .to('cuda') on the model. Additionally, we set the model to evaluation mode using model.eval() and wrap the inference code in a torch.no_grad() block to disable gradient calculations, optimizing performance and reducing memory usage during inference (fastapi_server.py).

Listing 17.4 Serving SmolLM2 for text generation

```
...
from transformers import AutoModelForCausalLM, AutoTokenizer

model = None
tokenizer = None
def get_model_and_tokenizer(device):
    global model, tokenizer
    checkpoint = "HuggingFaceTB/SmolLM2-360M-Instruct"
```

We are using this particular model since it is relatively small, but this can be any other supported model from Hugging Face.

```
        if model is None:
            model = AutoModelForCausalLM.from_pretrained(checkpoint)
            model = model.to(device)
            model.eval()
        if tokenizer is None:
            tokenizer = AutoTokenizer.from_pretrained(checkpoint)
        print(f"Memory footprint: {model.get_memory_footprint() / 1e6:.2f} MB")
        return model, tokenizer

    @app.post("/generate")
    def generate_text(input_txt: TextInput =
      TextInput(text="What is PyTorch and why is it cool?")):
        device = torch.device("cuda" if torch.cuda.is_available() else "cpu")
        model, tokenizer = get_model_and_tokenizer(device)
        messages = [{"role": "user", "content": input_txt.text}]
        input_text=tokenizer.apply_chat_template(messages, tokenize=False)
        print(f"Input text: {input_text}")
        inputs = tokenizer.encode(input_text, return_tensors="pt").to(device)
        with torch.no_grad():
            outputs = model.generate(inputs, max_new_tokens=256, do_sample=True,
         temperature=0.7)
        generated_text = tokenizer.decode(outputs[0])
        return generated_text
```

- Sets up our model, loads the weights, and moves to evaluation mode
- Although model.generate() handles this, it is good practice to explicitly turn autograd off for inference.
- Returns the entirety of the text (including the input) as the response

Run the server as follows:

```
fastapi dev fastapi_server.py
```

As a client, we can go to the FastAPI documentation page at http://127.0.0.1:8000/docs and manually interact with our API. We can also use curl in the terminal to send a POST request, which is a type of HTTP request that submits data to a server. In this case, we're sending the request to the /generate endpoint, which is a specific URL path on our API that handles text generation. The JSON payload is the data we're sending with the request, and it contains the input text we want the API to process. For example, we can run the following command in a terminal:

```
curl -X 'POST' \
  'http://127.0.0.1:8000/generate' \
  -H 'accept: application/json' \
  -H 'Content-Type: application/json' \
  -d '{
  "text": "What is PyTorch and why is it cool?"
}'
```

The API should give you an answer about what PyTorch is and, hopefully, the references it makes are understandable at this point in the book! Clearly, our server takes inputs, runs them through our model, and returns the outputs. So are we done? Not quite. Let's look at what we can improve on.

17.1.3 *What we want from deployment*

Let's collect some things we want for serving models. First, we want to support *modern protocols and their features*. Old-school HTTP is deeply serial, which means when a client wants to send several requests in the same connection, the next requests will only be sent after the previous request has been answered—not very efficient if you want to handle multiple requests at a time. FastAPI allows you to define asynchronous endpoints using `async def`, which enables the server to handle multiple requests concurrently. This means that while one request is waiting for an I/O operation (like a database query or an external API call), the server can process other requests.

Asynchronous programming can sound scary and often is shrouded in complex terminology. However, at its core, it's about enabling functions to wait for computation results or events without blocking other tasks. These asynchronous functions are sometimes referred to as *generators* or, more broadly, *coroutines*.

To adapt our endpoints to be asynchronous with FastAPI, we simply need to modify the function definition to add `async`:

```
async def generate_text(...)
```

The beauty of using FastAPI lies in its ability to handle the underlying implementation details, allowing us to focus on writing our code.

However, the main bottleneck in our API endpoint is our model inference time. When using GPUs, it is often much more efficient to *batch requests* than to process them one by one or fire them in parallel. This is due to a GPU's parallel computation abilities. So, next, we have the task of collecting requests from several connections, assembling them into a batch to run on the GPU, and then getting the results back to the respective requesters. This sounds elaborate and (again, when we write this) seems not to be done very often in simple tutorials. That is reason enough for us to do it properly here!

We want to serve several things in *parallel*. Even with asynchronous serving, we need our model to run efficiently on a second thread. This means we want to escape the (in)famous Python global interpreter lock (GIL) with our model.

To reduce latency, we will also be streaming the response token by token back to the client. This is a common practice in modern APIs, especially for text generation tasks. By streaming the response, we can provide a more interactive experience for users, allowing them to see the generated text as it is being produced rather than waiting for the entire response to be generated before displaying it. This can be particularly useful for applications where real-time feedback is important, such as chatbots or interactive writing assistants.

One last thing: when serving our API, ensuring safety is crucial. We want to protect against overflows and resource exhaustion. With fixed-size input text, we are generally in a good position, as it's challenging to cause issues in PyTorch with fixed-size inputs. While decoding images and similar tasks can be more complex, our focus on text simplifies this aspect. We won't delve into internet security, as it's a vast field beyond our scope. It's worth mentioning that neural networks can be vulnerable to input manipulation, leading to incorrect or unexpected outputs (known as *adversarial examples*). Since these concepts are out of the scope of this book, we'll set them aside for now.

Enough talk. Let's improve our server.

17.1.4 Request batching and streaming responses

To do request batching, we have to decouple the request handling from running the model. Figure 17.2 shows the flow of the data.

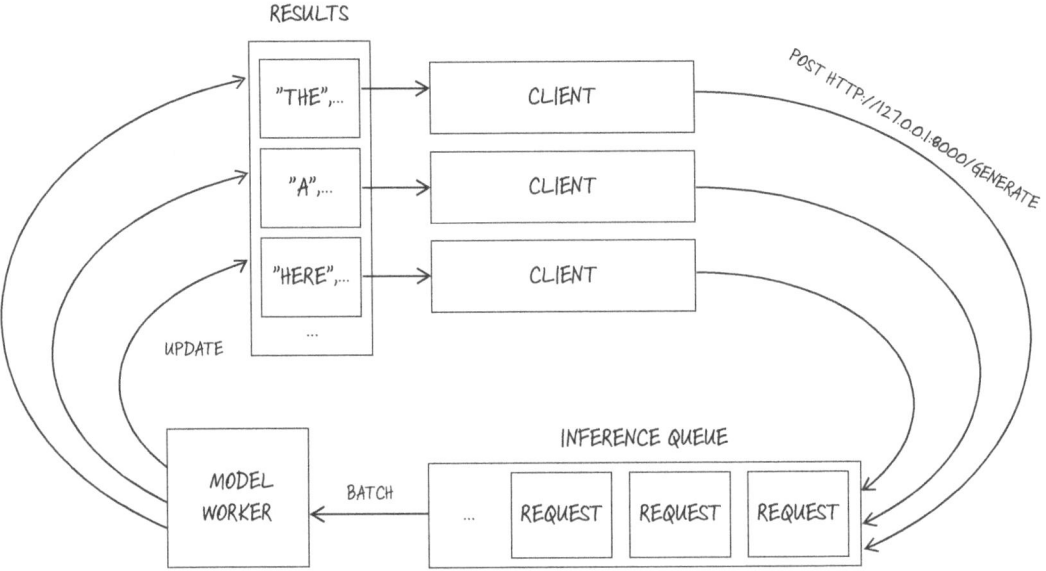

Figure 17.2 Dataflow with request batching and streaming

At the top of figure 17.2, clients initiate requests that populate a queue with work items. Once the queue reaches a full batch or the oldest request has waited for a predetermined maximum time, a model worker retrieves and processes the batch collectively.

This model worker operates on a background thread, enabling the API to continue handling incoming requests concurrently with the model's execution. This design requires additional logic to handle the lifecycle of the queue and the model worker.

Additionally, the API offers a streaming response for each work item, delivering generated tokens to the client as they become available. This approach enhances responsiveness and is implemented through an asynchronous generator that yields tokens one by one.

As an analogy, imagine a busy restaurant where customers place their orders, and each order is written on a ticket and added to a queue in the kitchen. Once there are enough tickets or one has been waiting too long, the chefs start cooking the orders in batches. The chefs work in the background, allowing the waitstaff to keep taking new orders without delay. As each dish is ready, it's immediately served to the customers, similar to how the API sends parts of the response as soon as they're available. This way, customers get their food dish by dish, keeping them happy and engaged.

IMPLEMENTATION

For the implementation, first, we will set up the FastAPI server as we have done before, but this time we will use the lifespan event to start a model worker thread. When the server starts, it creates a background worker thread that runs the model_worker function. The worker thread is set as a daemon, so it will be terminated when the main thread exits. The shutdown_event is used to gracefully terminate the worker thread when the server shuts down (fastapi_enhanced_server.py).

Listing 17.5 Setting up FastAPI with a background worker thread

```
shutdown_event = Event()
@asynccontextmanager
async def lifespan(app: FastAPI) -> AsyncGenerator[None, None]:
  worker_thread = Thread(target=model_worker, daemon=True)
  worker_thread.start()
  yield
  shutdown_event.set()

class TextInput(BaseModel):
  text: str

app = FastAPI(lifespan=lifespan)
```

We also set up the data structures for managing requests and responses, which will be used by both our worker thread and our server:

```
inference_queue = queue.Queue()
results = {}
results_lock = Lock()
```

The inference_queue is a thread-safe queue that holds incoming requests. The results dictionary stores the results of processed requests, and the results_lock is used to synchronize access to this dictionary.

The model_worker function is responsible for processing requests from the inference_queue. This function runs in a continuous loop, checking for new requests and processing them in batches. A lot of the logic is shared with the single request processing we did before, but it is now adapted to deal with multiple requests at once:

```
def model_worker() -> None:
  device = torch.device("cuda" if torch.cuda.is_available() else "cpu")
  model, tokenizer = get_model_and_tokenizer(device)
```

```
while not shutdown_event.is_set():
  try:
    batch = get_batch_from_queue()
    if shutdown_event.is_set() or not batch:
        continue

    formatted_text = []
    for request_id, prompt in batch:
        text = [{"role": "user", "content": prompt}]
        results[request_id] = queue.Queue()
        formatted_text.append(tokenizer.apply_chat_template(text,
  tokenize=False))
  ...
```

Token-by-token generation is also similarly done with the `generate` method of the model. The `generate` method is called with `batch_tokens` and `batch_attention_mask` that we previously generated from our tokenizer. The generated tokens are yielded one by one as they are produced:

```
for _ in range(MAX_TOKENS):
    if not active_requests:
        break  # All requests are done

    with torch.no_grad():
        outputs = model.generate(
            batch_tokens,
            attention_mask=batch_attention_mask,
            max_new_tokens=1,
            pad_token_id=tokenizer.pad_token_id,
        )
    generated_token_ids = [output[-1:] for output in outputs]

    for idx in list(active_requests):
        request_id, _ = batch[idx]
        new_token_id = generated_token_ids[idx]
        new_token = tokenizer.decode(new_token_id)

    ...

    with results_lock:
        if request_id in results:
            results[request_id].put(new_token)
```

By setting the token generation to `max_new_tokens=1`, we ensure that the model generates one token at a time. We then put this token in the results dictionary or the corresponding request ID. This repeats over and over until we have generated the maximum number of tokens or all requests are done.

> **NOTE** The `results_lock` is used to synchronize access to the results dictionary, ensuring that multiple threads can safely read and write to it without causing data corruption.

Finally, when streaming the results back to the client, we can use FastAPI's StreamingResponse class. This allows us to send a stream of data back to the client as it becomes available, rather than waiting for the entire response to be generated before sending it:

```
@app.post("/generate")
async def generate_text(input_txt: TextInput) -> StreamingResponse:
    request_id = str(uuid.uuid4())
    inference_queue.put((request_id, input_txt.text))
    print(f"Received - Request ID: {request_id}, Prompt: {input_txt.text}")
    return StreamingResponse(stream_results(request_id), media_type="text/plain")
```

This implementation depends on the `stream_results` function, which is an asynchronous generator that yields tokens one by one as they are produced. That method will read from the results queue and yield tokens as they become available. This allows us to stream the response back to the client in real time.

We can see our server in action by running the following command:

```
`fastapi dev fastapi_enhanced_server.py`
```

And then we can test it with the following `curl` command:

```
curl -X 'POST' \
  'http://127.0.0.1:8000/generate' \
  -H 'accept: application/json' \
  -H 'Content-Type: application/json' \
  -N \
  -d '{
  "text": "What is PyTorch and why is it cool?"
}'
```

You'll notice that the response looks as if it is being "typed" out in real time, rather than being sent all at once, much like how we see in ChatGPT and other AI assistants. This provides a much more interactive experience for users (or developers building off of your API).

The same applies to batches of multiple requests. We can send multiple requests to the server, and it will process them in batches. For example, we can create a command with multiple prompts and use `curl` to send them all at once:

```
echo "What is the capital of US?" > input1.txt
echo "What is the capital of France?" > input2.txt
echo "What is the capital of UK?" > input3.txt
for i in {1..3}; do
  cat input$i.txt | xargs -I {} curl -s -X POST \
    http://localhost:8000/generate \
    -H 'accept: application/json' \
    -H 'Content-Type: application/json' \
    -N \
    -d '{"text": "{}"}' >> input$i.txt &
done
wait
```

Alternatively, you can open up multiple terminal windows and run the `curl` command in each one; this would achieve the same effect. You'll notice that the `curl` requests will be processed in parallel and finish at different times.

We've come quite far! Let's take a moment to appreciate our handiwork. We have created a web server that can handle multiple requests at once, process them in batches, and stream the results back to the client as they become available. This is a great way to showcase our models and make them accessible to others through a convenient API.

Are we done? Of course not! We can still improve our server and make it even more efficient. In the next section, we'll explore how to make our PyTorch models run faster using PyTorch-native technologies.

17.1.5 How to make PyTorch models even faster

The deep learning community has increasingly adopted PyTorch as the primary framework, not only for research but also for production. In response, the PyTorch team has integrated performance optimizations directly into the framework.

USING TORCH.COMPILE

`torch.compile` was released as part of PyTorch 2.0 and made a big splash. It is a significant technological leap because it addresses the challenge of optimizing PyTorch code for faster execution without requiring significant code changes.

Python is an interpreted language, meaning its code is executed by an interpreter rather than being compiled into machine code beforehand. PyTorch, being a Python library, inherits this limitation. However, a compiler is often useful because it can transform high-level code into more optimized machine code, which can lead to significant performance improvements.

`torch.compile` gets around this limitation by doing just-in-time (JIT) compilation, which analyzes the PyTorch code during execution and generates optimizations, such as

- *Kernel fusion*—Combining multiple operations into a single kernel to reduce overhead and improve performance. For example, pointwise operations, such as `torch.cos()` and `relu()`, involve a sequence of read and comparison operations, often limited by memory bandwidth. Instead of invoking multiple separate kernels for operations like cosine, fusing these operations can reduce overhead and improve efficiency.
- *Operator reordering*—Rearranging operations to improve memory access patterns and reduce cache misses. For example, consider two operations: a matrix multiplication followed by an element-wise addition. If the addition can be reordered to occur during the matrix multiplication (e.g., by modifying the kernel), it can reduce intermediate memory usage and improve cache efficiency.

Using `torch.compile` is simple, as you just need to wrap an existing model. For example, when we load the model in our server:

```
model = AutoModelForCausalLM.from_pretrained(checkpoint)
model = model.to(device)
model = torch.compile(model)
```
← New line to compile the model

← It is best practice to move the model to the device before compiling it. This ensures that the compiled model is optimized for the specific hardware it will run on.

And voila! Depending on the model, we can see speedups of anywhere from 20% to 200% during Inference.

> **NOTE** The speed up is dependent on the underlying hardware and model architecture. In some rare cases, there may even be a slowdown, so this solution is not always a silver bullet.

Later in this chapter, we'll dive deeper into some of the magic behind the torch.compile technology and see how that entire technology stack also enables other features of PyTorch.

ADD QUANTIZATION

When we wish to reduce the memory and compute footprint of our models, the first thing to look at is streamlining the model itself—that is, computing the same or very similar mappings from inputs to outputs with fewer parameters and operations. This is often called *distillation*. The details of distillation vary: sometimes we try to shrink each weight by eliminating small or irrelevant weights; in other examples, we combine several layers of a net into one (DistilBERT) or even train a fully different, simpler model to reproduce the larger model's outputs (OpenNMT's original CTranslate). We mention this because these modifications are likely to be the first step in getting models to run faster.

Another approach is to reduce the footprint of each parameter and operation: instead of expending the usual 32-bit per parameter in the form of a float, we convert our model to work with integers (a typical choice is 8-bit). This is called *quantization*.

> **NOTE** In contrast to quantization, (partially) moving to 16-bit floating-point for training is usually called *reduced* or (if some bits stay 32-bit) *mixed-precision* training.

PyTorch does offer quantized tensors for this purpose. They are exposed as a set of scalar types similar to torch.float, torch.double, and torch.long (as we saw in section 3.5). The most common quantized tensor scalar types are torch.quint8 and torch.qint8, representing numbers as unsigned and signed 8-bit integers, respectively. PyTorch uses a separate scalar type here to use the dispatch mechanism we briefly looked at in section 3.11.

Quantization is generally described in two flavors: quantization-aware training and post-training quantization. Quantization-aware training incorporates quantization directly into the training process itself, while post-training quantization is applied to existing models after they've completed training. For our demonstration, we'll use post-training quantization since we're working with a pretrained model that we want to optimize without retraining. First, let's learn a little about the size of our model before quantization. We crafted a helpful utility method named get_serialized_model_size_in_mb. This function serializes the model to a byte buffer and checks the size of that buffer to calculate the memory footprint of the model (quantization_example.ipynb).

Listing 17.6 Measuring a model size

```
# In[]
model = AutoModelForCausalLM.from_pretrained(checkpoint)
size_before_quantization = get_serialized_model_size_in_mb(model)    ◁─── Gets the serialized size of the model in megabytes
print(f"Serialized model size before quantization:
    {size_before_quantization:.2f} MB")

# Out[]
Serialized model size before quantization: 6528.52 MB
```

We can apply quantization by converting the model to a lower-precision data type, such as bfloat16. This process is straightforward—simply calling the .to(torch.bfloat16) method on the model automatically converts all parameters and buffers from their original 32-bit floating-point format to the more memory-efficient 16-bit brain floating-point format (quantization_example.ipynb):

```
model = model.to(torch.bfloat16)
size_after_quantization = get_serialized_model_size_in_mb(model)
print(f"Serialized model size after quantization1:
    {size_after_quantization:.2f} MB")
```

PyTorch supports various data types for quantization, which can be found in the torch.dtype module (https://mng.bz/Rw9O), including torch.int8 for 8-bit signed integer representation. It might seem surprising that using 8-bit integers instead of 32-bit floating points works at all, and typically, there is a slight degradation in results, but not much. Two things seem to contribute: if we consider rounding errors as essentially random and convolutions and linear layers as weighted averages, we may expect rounding errors to typically cancel.

While quantization effectively reduces model size and accelerates inference, it's important to note that we cannot simply convert an entire model to int8 with a single .to(torch.int8) call. Different module types have varying levels of quantization support—linear layers typically work well with int8 quantization, but other operations like normalization layers or complex activation functions may require floating-point precision or special handling. Furthermore, quantization introduces precision tradeoffs that affect certain operations more significantly than others, potentially affecting model accuracy. In the next example, we will implement a custom quantization function that specifically targets linear layers in the model and quantizes their weights to int8 format while keeping the rest of the model in bfloat16 (quantization_example.ipynb).

Listing 17.7 Custom `int8` quantization function for linear layers

```
...
def quantize_linear_layers_to_int8(model):
    for _, module in model.named_modules():
        if isinstance(module, torch.nn.Linear):
            weight = module.weight.data
            w_int8, scale = int8_symmetric_quantize(weight)
            module.register_buffer('weight_int8', w_int8)
            module.register_buffer('weight_scale', scale)
            delattr(module, 'weight')

            def new_forward(self, x):
                dequantized_weight = self.weight_int8.to(x.dtype) * self.weight_scale
                return torch.nn.functional.linear(x, dequantized_weight, self.bias)
            import types
            module.forward = types.MethodType(new_forward, module)
    return model

model = AutoModelForCausalLM.from_pretrained(checkpoint)
model = model.to(torch.bfloat16)
model = quantize_linear_layers_to_int8(model)
size_after_quantization2 = get_serialized_model_size_in_mb(model)
print(f"Serialized model size after quantization2:
    {size_after_quantization2:.2f} MB")

# Out[]
Serialized model size after quantization2: 1825.69 MB
```

- Stores the int8 weights and scale directly in the module
- Removes the original weight to save space
- Creates a new forward method that uses the quantized weights

Very cool. We've successfully reduced the model size from 6.5 GB to 1.8 GB—that is over a 70% reduction in size! This is a significant improvement, but we don't write this manually for our models. As expected, PyTorch has built-in support for quantization that can handle this process automatically. The `torch.quantization` module provides a comprehensive framework for quantizing models, including support for various quantization schemes and techniques (quantization_example.ipynb).

Listing 17.8 Applying dynamic quantization using a PyTorch API

```
model = AutoModelForCausalLM.from_pretrained(checkpoint)
quantized_model = torch.quantization.quantize_dynamic(
    model,
    {torch.nn.Linear},
    dtype=torch.qint8
)
```

Only quantizes linear layers

Quantization remains a hot research topic in PyTorch, with teams constantly pushing the boundaries of what's possible. It's wild to think that researchers are now experimenting with 1-bit quantization for massive language models—literally representing weights with just 0s and 1s (see https://arxiv.org/html/2402.17764v1)! We can expect further improvements and changes to the quantization APIs in future releases of PyTorch. For deeper insights into PyTorch quantization capabilities, techniques, and best practices, visit the official documentation at https://pytorch.org/docs/stable/quantization.html.

EXISTING TECHNOLOGIES

We've built a server that effectively supports several features and optimizations for our LLM. While there are many additional features we could implement, it's often better to leverage existing technologies rather than reinvent the wheel. Here are a few notable ones worth looking out for:

- *vLLM*—A tool designed to run LLMs very efficiently, especially when serving many users at once (https://github.com/vllm-project/vllm).
- *LitServe*—A flexible serving engine for AI models built on FastAPI. Features like batching, streaming, and GPU autoscaling eliminate the need to rebuild a FastAPI server per model (https://github.com/Lightning-AI/LitServe).

17.2 Exporting models

So far, we have executed our models directly using abstractions provided by PyTorch. This is great for quick iteration and development, but when we want to deploy our models in production, we often may need to export them to a different format or framework. This is especially true if we want to run our models on different hardware or in a different programming language other than Python. In Python, we have the GIL, which is a global lock that prevents multiple threads from executing Python bytecode at once. This is great for single-threaded applications, but it can be a bottleneck for multithreaded applications. (However, with no-GIL Python (https://peps.python.org/pep-0703/), this may be a thing of the past!) Or we might want to run on embedded systems where installing the entire Python stack is too expensive or unavailable. This is when we export our model.

Exporting a model involves converting it into a format that can be used across different environments and platforms. This process typically results in a standardized representation, which allows the model to be interpreted by various systems. While this doesn't directly translate the model into low-level hardware instructions, it prepares the model for further optimization and execution on specific hardware. This is similar to how a compiler translates high-level code into an intermediate form before it is further compiled into machine code.

We have a couple of options to explore:

- Transitioning to specialized frameworks beyond PyTorch
- Utilizing PyTorch's built-in tools for model export

Let's take a look at each of these options.

17.2.1 Interoperability beyond PyTorch with ONNX

In some cases, we may need to step outside the PyTorch ecosystem with our model—for example, to run on embedded hardware with a specialized model deployment pipeline. For this purpose, Open Neural Network Exchange provides an interoperational format for neural networks and machine learning models (https://onnx.ai). Once exported, the model can be executed using any ONNX-compatible runtime, such as ONNX Runtime, provided that the operations in use in our model are supported by the ONNX standard and the target runtime. It is, for example, quite a bit faster on the Raspberry Pi than running PyTorch directly. Beyond traditional hardware, a lot of specialized AI accelerator hardware supports ONNX (https://onnx.ai/supported-tools.html#deployModel).

> **NOTE** The ONNX Runtime code is available at https://github.com/microsoft/onnxruntime. However, make sure to review the privacy statement. If you build ONNX Runtime from source, the resulting package will not include any telemetry or data-sharing features.

In a way, a deep learning model is a program with a very specific instruction set, made of granular operations like matrix multiplication, convolution, relu, tanh, and so on. As such, if we can serialize the computation, we can re-execute it in another runtime that understands its low-level operations. ONNX is a standardization of a format describing those operations and their parameters.

Most of the modern deep learning frameworks support serialization of their computations to ONNX, and some of them can load an ONNX file and execute it (although this is not the case for PyTorch). Some low-footprint ("edge") devices accept an ONNX file as input and generate low-level instructions for the specific device. And some cloud computing providers now make it possible to upload an ONNX file and see it exposed through a REST endpoint.

To export a model to ONNX, we need to run a model with a dummy input; the values of the input tensors don't really matter; what matters is that they are the correct shape and type. By invoking the torch.onnx.export function, PyTorch will *trace* the computations performed by the model and serialize them into an ONNX file with the provided name (onnx_example.ipynb):

```
onnx_model_path = "simple_model.onnx"
dummy_input = torch.randn(1, 10)
torch.onnx.export(              ◁─┐ Exports the model
    model,                          to ONNX format
    dummy_input,
    onnx_model_path
)
```

The resulting ONNX file can now be run in a runtime, compiled to an edge device, or uploaded to a cloud service. It can be used from Python after installing onnxruntime or onnxruntime-gpu (for those with a GPU device) and getting a batch as a NumPy array (onnx_example.ipynb):

```
import onnxruntime
sess = onnxruntime.InferenceSession("simple_model.onnx")
batch = dummy_input.numpy()
input_name = sess.get_inputs()[0].name
pred_onnx, = sess.run(None, {input_name: batch})
```

The ONNX runtime API uses sessions to load models and calls the run method with a set of named inputs.

17.2.2 PyTorch's own export: torch.export

As we mentioned earlier, PyTorch has its own tools for exporting models. The primary purpose of exporting a PyTorch model to the ONNX format is interoperability with other frameworks and runtimes. If you need better cross-framework compatibility, ONNX is the way to go; however, torch.export is a great option for PyTorch users who want to optimize their models for deployment without leaving the PyTorch ecosystem.

PyTorch's torch.export takes a torch.nn.Module and produces a traced graph. This graph is a representation of the model's computation graph, which outlines the sequence of operations and data flow within the model. It captures how inputs are transformed through various layers to produce outputs. The traced graph is described in an ahead-of-time (AOT) compiled manner.

The traced graph in PyTorch can be likened to a flowchart that maps out the logical sequence of operations within a model. Just as a flowchart visually represents the steps and decision points in a process, the traced graph delineates the path data takes as it moves through the model's layers and operations. Each node in the traced graph corresponds to a specific operation or transformation, similar to how each symbol in a flowchart represents a particular action or decision.

Tracing a model looks very similar to ONNX exporting. It shouldn't be surprising, then, that you can also export a PyTorch model to ONNX using this PyTorch's export technology. The only line you need to add is dynamo=True to the export call (onnx_example.ipynb):

```
torch.onnx.export(
    model,
    dummy_input,
    onnx_model_path,
    dynamo=True,
)
```

Adds a line to use TorchDynamo to export the model

For using torch.export directly, we similarly need to pass in an example input into the model to trace the model (torch_export_example.py):

```
from torch.export import export
dummy_input = torch.randn(2, 10)
exported_program = export(model, args=(dummy_input,))
```

Both this and the ONNX example with dynamo=True under the hood utilize Torch-Dynamo, a PyTorch tool that captures and optimizes computation graphs at runtime. Making its debut in PyTorch 2.0, TorchDynamo was a step function forward in the PyTorch compilers ecosystem since it allows for dynamic tracing of models, enabling a user experience that was previously difficult to achieve with static tracing methods. TorchDynamo (also just called Dynamo) achieved this by intercepting the Python bytecode execution and capturing the operations performed, without requiring users to make any changes to the underlying code.

TorchDynamo is a tracer, which means that given a function and an example input, it records a linear sequence of instructions into a graph. This is an FX graph (see the torch.fx documentation at https://docs.pytorch.org/docs/main/fx.html). We won't dive into all the details, but you can think of it as a container that holds functions and their parameters. These containers are later used down the road for compilation optimizations or exporting to other formats. Let's take a look at what this representation looks like (torch_export_example.ipynb).

Listing 17.9 Examining exported program graph representation

```
# In[]
print(exported_program)

# Out[]
ExportedProgram:
  class GraphModule(torch.nn.Module):
    def forward(self, p_fc1_weight: "f32[5, 10]", p_fc1_bias: "f32[5]",
      p_fc2_weight: "f32[2, 5]", p_fc2_bias: "f32[2]", x: "f32[2, 10]"):
      # File: .py:10 in forward, code: x = self.fc1(x)
      linear: "f32[2, 5]" = torch.ops.aten.linear.default(x, p_fc1_weight,
    p_fc1_bias);
        x = p_fc1_weight = p_fc1_bias = None

      # File: .py:11 in forward, code: x = self.relu(x)
      relu: "f32[2, 5]" = torch.ops.aten.relu.default(linear);  linear = None

      # File: .py:12 in forward, code: x = self.fc2(x)
      linear_1: "f32[2, 2]" = torch.ops.aten.linear.default(relu,
    p_fc2_weight, p_fc2_bias);
        relu = p_fc2_weight = p_fc2_bias = None
      return (linear_1,)
```

You'll notice that the model still includes a forward method, but the parameters are now passed in as arguments. This change occurs because the parameters are no longer embedded within the model itself; instead, they are part of the computation graph. The original nn.Linear and nn.ReLU layers are transformed into torch.ops.aten operations, which provide a lower-level representation of these computations. Additionally, the operations are annotated with notations like f32[2, 5], which specify the data type and shape of the tensors involved.

The underlying graph module is still a torch.nn.Module though, which means it can even be called like a normal PyTorch model (torch_export_example.ipynb):

```
exported_program.module()(dummy_input)          ◁—┤ Calling an exported program's
                                                   module still works!
```

Now we can use AOTInductor (AOTI), PyTorch's ahead-of-time compiler, to run inference:

```
import os
output_path = torch._inductor.aoti_compile_and_package(
    exported_program,
    package_path=os.path.join(os.getcwd(), "model.pt2"),
)
```

The torch._inductor.aoti_compile_and_package function compiles the model and packages it into a file that can be loaded later. This is similar to how we would save a PyTorch model using torch.save, but it also includes the compiled code:

```
model = torch._inductor.aoti_load_package(os.path.join(os.getcwd(), "model.pt2"))
model(dummy_input)
```

Now we can call it. Running the model with torch._inductor.aoti_load_package loads the compiled model and allows us to run it with our previous input. This can be thought of as the torch.load equivalent for the compiled model, similar to how we would load a saved PyTorch model. One caveat is that the shapes of the input tensors must match the shapes used during the export process (because the compiled model is optimized for those specific shapes and may not work correctly with different shapes).

> **TIP** You can run the exported PyTorch model without keeping the source. However, we always want to establish a workflow where we automatically go from source model to the installed JITed model for deployment. If we do not, we will find ourselves in a situation where we would like to tweak something with the model but have lost the ability to modify and regenerate.

At this point, we've thrown a lot of new terminology at you, so it would be a good time to recap the workflow of what we just did. As we can see from figure 17.3, we start with our user model code, which is a PyTorch model defined as a subclass of torch.nn.Module. We then export this model to an ONNX file or a PyTorch export file using torch.onnx.export or torch.export, respectively. This export process captures the computation graph of the model and saves it in a particular format. This exported program can be saved and loaded much like a regular PyTorch model, but it is now in a format that can be optimized and executed more efficiently. We pass this into a compiler, which optimizes the graph and generates low-level code for the target hardware. This compiled code is then executed on the target hardware, which can be a CPU, GPU, or specialized accelerator. The execution process involves loading the compiled code and running it with the input data, producing the final output.

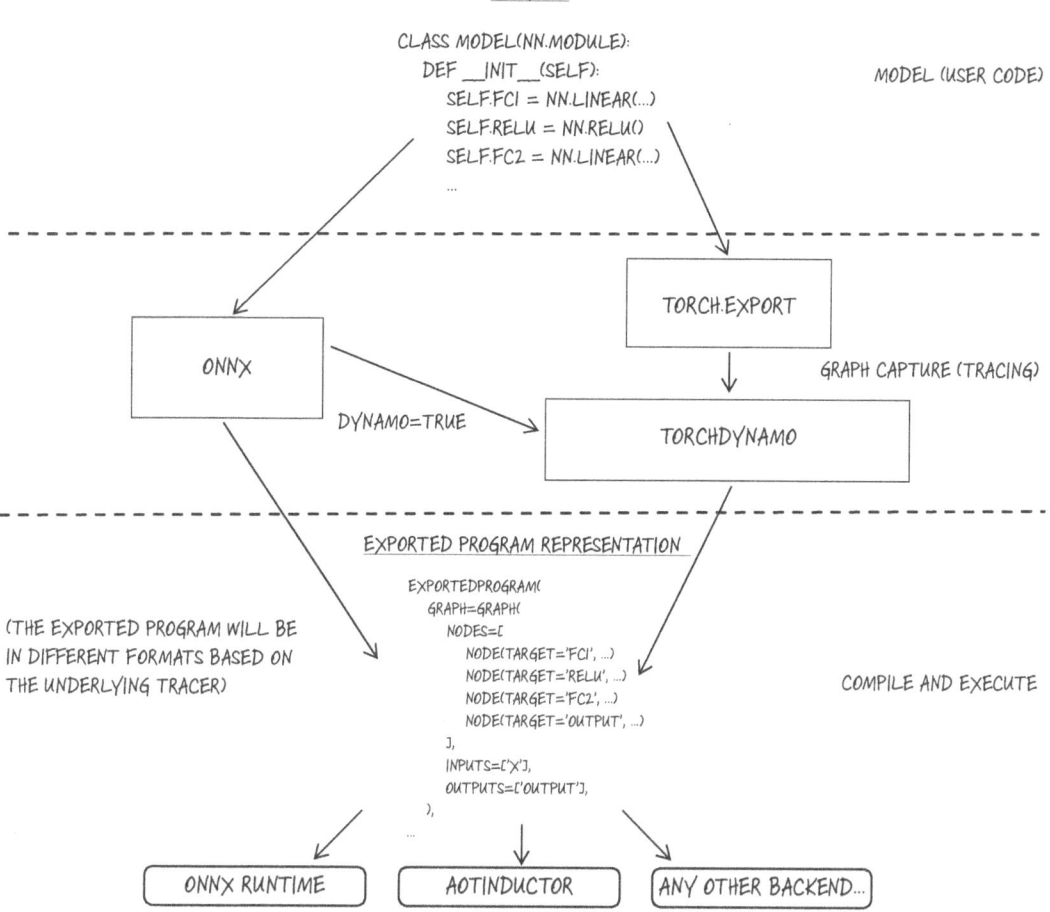

Figure 17.3 From user model code to exported model to execution

17.3 Expanding on torch.compile

The entire flow we discussed from user model code to exported model to execution is logically very similar to what is happening in torch.compile. We briefly discussed torch.compile in our previous section on improving model performance for our batched server. Considering that the PyTorch compiler has heavy investment and active contributions from the PyTorch team, we thought it would be a good idea to take a closer look at it.

So, what are the differences between torch.export and torch.compile, and when should you choose one or the other? First, we need to take a look at what it means for full graph capture and disjoint graphs.

17.3.1 Full graph capture vs. disjoint graphs

torch.export relies on full graph capture, which means it captures the entire computation graph of the model, including all operations and their dependencies. This allows for a complete representation of the model's behavior; the drawback is that it cannot handle certain behavior, such as dynamic control flow or operations that depend on the input data. As a result, if your model has any dynamic behavior, such as conditional statements or loops that depend on the input data, torch.export may not be able to capture it correctly. For example, in the following listing, we have a model that performs a different forward depending on the input value (compile_example.ipynb).

Listing 17.10 A model with dynamic conditional control flow

```python
import torch
import torch.nn as nn
device = torch.device("cuda" if torch.cuda.is_available() else "cpu")
class ConditionalModel(nn.Module):
    def __init__(self):
        super(ConditionalModel, self).__init__()
        self.fc1 = nn.Linear(10, 5)
        self.relu = nn.ReLU()
        self.fc2 = nn.Linear(10, 3)
    def forward(self, x):
        if x.sum() > 0:
            x = self.fc1(x)
        else:
            x = self.fc2(x)
        x = self.relu(x)
        return x
model = ConditionalModel()
model = model.to(device)
model.eval()
```

Then, our torch.export function will error when it tries to trace the model:

```
# In[]
example_input = torch.randn(5, 10)
torch.export.export(model, (example_input,))

# Out[]
from user code:
   File "/var/...py", line 13, in forward        ◁── Conditional portion that is not supported by torch.export.
     if x.sum() > 0:
UserError: Dynamic control flow is not supported at the moment.
```

The error occurs because the torch.export function expects a static computation graph, and the conditional statement introduces dynamic behavior that cannot be captured in a static graph. If it were to assume the example input was passed in, it would only capture one path through the graph, which would not represent the full behavior of the model.

`torch.compile` adopts a more adaptive strategy by breaking the graph into smaller pieces when it encounters operations that cannot be compiled. This approach enables dynamic behavior and allows for more efficient execution. While graph breaks may suffer some performance cost, the tradeoff allows it to handle models with dynamic control flow, such as the one we just defined. When we use `torch.compile`, it will capture the entire computation graph, including all possible paths through the graph, and optimize it for execution.

> **History and motivations behind torch.compile**
>
> TensorFlow was once the leading deep learning framework, relying on a graph computation model where the entire graph was defined before execution. This approach optimized performance but complicated debugging and development.
>
> PyTorch emerged as a more user-friendly alternative, offering step-by-step model execution, known as *eager mode*. This mode allowed simplified debugging through print statements and Python debuggers, making PyTorch more accessible and eventually the preferred framework. Although TensorFlow 2.0 later adopted eager mode, PyTorch had already become the go-to choice for deep learning.
>
> However, the need for performance optimizations and deployment in production environments still spurred the use of graph-based execution. PyTorch addressed the need for performance optimization with the JIT (just-in-time) compiler, which allowed models defined in eager mode to be compiled into static graphs for better performance. Initially, this was done using `torch.jit.trace`, which captured computation graphs by tracing operations performed on sample inputs. These graphs were represented using an intermediate representation called TorchScript. However, `torch.jit.trace` had limitations, particularly with handling dynamic control flow and operations that depended on input data.
>
> The next attempt at making this execution model more convenient was `torch.jit.script`. This technique allowed users to write their models in a more Pythonic way, using standard Python constructs like loops and conditionals. The JIT compiler would then analyze the code and generate a static graph representation. It was a significant improvement over `torch.jit.trace`, but it tried to reimplement all of Python as a static language. As a result, encountering an unimplemented Python feature would lead to a run-time error, which was not ideal for users. In practice, this led to `torch.jit.script` being only able to support a subset of models or otherwise requiring an extensive rework for the model.
>
> When `torch.compile` was introduced, it added a dynamic graph capture functionality through TorchDynamo (also called Dynamo). This allowed users to write their models in eager mode and still compile. If Dynamo encountered unrecognizable control paths, it split the graph and fell back to regular Python. This avoided errors and allowed disjoint graphs to be captured. This flexibility marked a significant departure from earlier deep learning frameworks, which often required manual graph construction and rigid model definitions. By providing a more adaptive and user-friendly compilation process, `torch.compile` has greatly simplified the development of neural networks and empowered researchers to focus on innovation rather than infrastructure.

> **(continued)**
> Nowadays, you may still see references to `torch.jit.trace`, `torch.jit.script`, and TorchScript; however, these are not being actively developed and are in maintenance mode. Instead, you should focus on `torch.export` and `torch.compile` as the primary tools for model optimization and deployment.

The same model we exported can be compiled with `torch.compile` without any issues (compile.ipynb):

```
compiled_model = torch.compile(model)
compiled_model
```

Calling the compiled model is similar to calling a regular PyTorch model, and it will execute the dynamic control flow correctly. We can compare the noncompiled with the compiled output and see that they are the same:

```
input_data = torch.randn(5, 10).to(device)
output_original = model(input_data)
print("Output from original model:", output_original)
output_compiled = compiled_model(input_data)
print("Output from compiled model:", output_compiled)
```

When you use `torch.compile` and execute the compiled model's forward, the process involves several steps to optimize and run the model efficiently. Initially, the system checks whether the current function should be skipped, such as when dealing with non-PyTorch operations. If the code has been compiled before, it attempts to reuse the cached version. If not, it performs an analysis of the model's operations to create a `torch.fx` (FX) graph, which is a representation of the computation that can be optimized. This FX graph is then compiled using a specified backend to enhance performance. If the analysis doesn't cover the entire function, additional functions are generated to handle the remaining parts. Finally, new bytecode is created to execute the optimized FX graph, manage any necessary state, and perform side effects, ensuring the model runs efficiently.

The default backend for `torch.compile` is TorchInductor, which lowers computation graphs to efficient low-level code that can be executed on various hardware architectures, such as CPUs and GPUs. It generates or calls existing optimized kernels using technologies like OpenMP (for CPUs) or Triton (for GPUs; https://github.com/triton-lang/triton).

However, if you wish to employ a different optimization strategy or target a specific hardware architecture, you can specify an alternative backend. Many hardware vendors and frameworks offer their own backends for `torch.compile`. For guidance on developing your own backend, you can refer to the example available at https://mng.bz/269m.

In essence, rather than relying on `torch.export`, we can utilize similar technology to compile the model directly within the PyTorch framework. This approach

17.4 Understanding execution with torch.profiler

allows us to benefit from optimizations while maintaining our original user code within PyTorch.

While the `torch.export` and `torch.compile` technologies offer powerful optimization capabilities, they can sometimes feel like black boxes. To truly understand what's happening during model execution and identify performance bottlenecks, we need more visibility into the running code. This is where `torch.profiler` comes in handy.

PyTorch comes with a built-in profiler that allows us to analyze the performance of our models during training and inference. The profiler captures various metrics, such as execution time, memory usage, and the number of operations performed, which can help us identify bottlenecks and optimize our models.

As part of our example, we will be using a simple model with multiple feed-forward layers. We'll run the model with a dummy input and use the profiler to capture the execution details (profiler_example.ipynb).

Listing 17.11 Using PyTorch profiler to capture model performance metrics

```
from torch.profiler import profile, ProfilerActivity

def run_model(model, input_data, device="cpu", warmup_iters=5):
    ....
    activities = [ProfilerActivity.CPU]
    if device == "cuda":
        activities.append(ProfilerActivity.CUDA)
    with profile(
        activities=activities,
    ) as prof:
        output = model(input_data)

    display = prof.key_averages().table(sort_by="cpu_time_total", row_limit=10)
    ...

print(run_model(model, input_data))
```

This code creates a profiling context that captures computational activities on either CPU or CPU+GPU (depending on the device parameter). After performing warmup iterations (not shown), the profiler monitors the model's forward pass, collecting detailed timing information about operations executed during inference. Once profiling completes, we can generate a performance summary table showing the top 10 most time-consuming operations sorted by CPU execution time:

Name	Self CPU %	...	# of Calls
aten::linear	0.79%	...	20
aten::addmm	65.43%	...	20

```
       aten::copy_        18.10%    ...       20
        aten::relu         1.27%    ...       10
   aten::clamp_min        11.68%    ...       10
           aten::t         1.45%    ...       20
   aten::transpose         0.38%    ...       20
               ...           ...    ...      ...
------------------     ---------    ---  ---------
Self CPU time total: 19.152ms
```

This is useful for a high-level overview of the model's performance, but it doesn't provide detailed information about the execution flow or the underlying operations. For that, we can use `torch.profiler` to generate a trace of the execution:

```
prof.export_chrome_trace("trace.json")
```

This code generates a trace file in JSON format, which visualizes the execution flow, including the time spent on each operation and the dependencies between them. You can examine these traces by opening up the Chrome web browser and going to chrome://tracing (or the newer https://ui.perfetto.dev/).

In the trace visualization, as shown in figure 17.4, the display is divided into two main sections. The upper portion illustrates the CPU execution timeline, where each row represents an individual operation in chronological order. You can observe how CPU operations initiate corresponding tasks on the GPU stream. The lower section displays the GPU execution timeline, showing how operations are processed by the GPU hardware. By incorporating `record_function()` decorators in our model's forward method, we've enhanced the trace with custom labels like "Layer 1 Forward" and "Layer 2 Forward," making it easy to identify which operations correspond to specific layers in our neural network architecture.

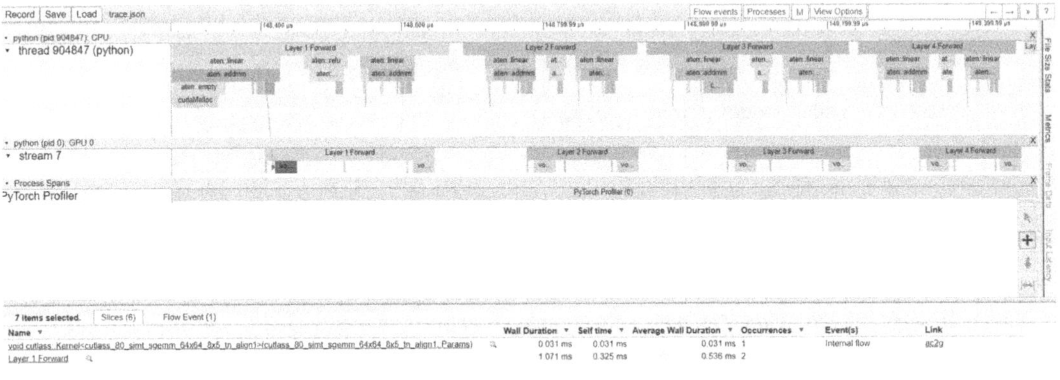

Figure 17.4 Trace of the model execution

When we compile the model, as shown in figure 17.5, we see that the trace is quite different: the forwards are fused together, and the operations are under a "Compiled

Region" umbrella. This also leads to fused GPU operations, like custom kernels for the linear layers, which are optimized for performance.

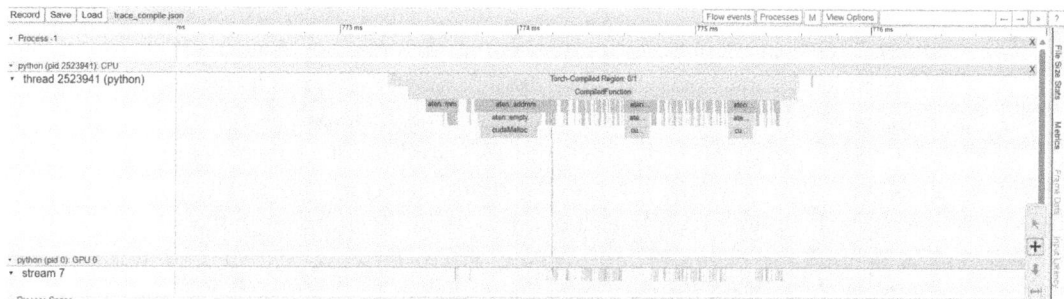

Figure 17.5 Trace of the model execution after compilation

17.5 Using PyTorch outside of Python

So far, we've shown how to use PyTorch in Python and how to optimize models for efficiency, serve them, and export them to other formats. However, there are times when we want to use PyTorch models outside of Python, such as in C++ applications or on mobile devices. In these cases, we can use other offerings from PyTorch's Ecosystems, which enable us to run PyTorch models in other languages and environments.

Specifically, we will be covering LibTorch (https://docs.pytorch.org/cppdocs/installing.html) for C++ and ExecuTorch (https://mng.bz/15Kn) for mobile.

17.5.1 LibTorch: PyTorch in C++

LibTorch is the C++ distribution of PyTorch that provides direct access to PyTorch's functionality without Python. Many components of PyTorch are actually written in C++, with Python bindings providing the familiar interface most users interact with. LibTorch gives you direct access to these underlying C++ components.

The C++ API is deliberately designed to mirror the Python API, making the transition easier for PyTorch developers:

```
// Python
model = torch.nn.Linear(10, 5)
input = torch.randn(1, 10)
output = model(input)

// Equivalent C++
auto model = torch::nn::Linear(10, 5);
auto input = torch::randn({1, 10});
auto output = model->forward(input);
```

Still, since Python is the de facto language used by the deep learning community, the C++ API is not as feature-rich as the Python API, and some features are available only in Python (e.g., some distributed training APIs). Python remains the preferred option for most PyTorch development, so the recommendation is to use LibTorch only when integrating PyTorch into a C++ application or deploying in environments where Python is not well-suited.

One of the pain points of using C++ is that it is just not as easy to get started, so stick with us as we slog through the setup. The good news is that once you have it set up, running PyTorch models in C++ is quite straightforward.

We will be using CMake to build our C++ application, so make sure you have it installed and set up. CMake is a build system that helps manage the compilation of C++ projects, including handling dependencies and generating build files for different platforms. It can be installed using your system's package manager or downloaded from the CMake website (https://cmake.org/download/):

```
brew install cmake (mac)
apt install cmake (ubuntu)
```

Next, you will need to have LibTorch. Since we have already downloaded PyTorch using pip, we can also find the LibTorch binaries already included in the PyTorch installation directory. However, if you want to download it separately, you can find the latest version of LibTorch from the PyTorch website (https://pytorch.org/get-started/locally/).

We will point cmake to where the necessary CMake configuration files are for LibTorch. This is done by setting the CMAKE_PREFIX_PATH environment variable to the path where LibTorch is installed. We can generate a build folder and run CMake to configure the project. Keeping build files separate from source files helps maintain a clean project structure. It allows you to easily clean up build artifacts by simply deleting the build directory:

```
cmake -B build -S . -DCMAKE_PREFIX_PATH=
⇒ $(python3 -c 'import torch;print(torch.utils.cmake_prefix_path)')
```

We can now build the project using CMake. This will compile the C++ code and link it with the LibTorch library:

```
cmake --build build --config Release
```

Now we can run the compiled C++ application. The executable will be located in the build directory, and you can run it from there:

```
./build/example
```

The first part of our example shows the basic usage of LibTorch to create a simple linear model and run inference on it. The C++ code mirrors the Python code we used earlier, demonstrating how similar the APIs are between the two languages.

The second part of our example demonstrates how to create and train a simple neural network. This code defines a Net class that inherits from torch::nn::Module,

17.5 Using PyTorch outside of Python

which is the C++ equivalent of Python's `torch.nn.Module`. The network architecture is a simple feed-forward neural network designed for MNIST digit classification, with

- An input layer accepting flattened 28 × 28 images (784 features)
- One hidden layer with 128 neurons and ReLU activation
- An output layer with 10 neurons (one per digit) and log-softmax activation

The training looks similar to what we did in Python as well (example.cpp).

Listing 17.12 Training in C++ with LibTorch

```
void model_train_example() {
  auto model = std::make_shared<Net>();                              // Creates a model instance
  torch::optim::SGD optimizer(model->parameters(), /*lr=*/0.01);     // and an SGD optimizer

  // Create fake data
  auto x = torch::randn({64, 784});
  auto y = torch::randint(0, 10, {64});

  model->train();
  for (size_t epoch = 0; epoch < 3; ++epoch) {                       // Trains the model for 3
    auto prediction = model->forward(x);                             // epochs using the standard
    auto loss = torch::nll_loss(prediction, y);                      // training loop
    optimizer.zero_grad();
    loss.backward();
    optimizer.step();

    std::cout << "Epoch: " << epoch << " | Loss: " << loss.item<float>()
              << std::endl;
  }

  // Inference
  model->eval();                                                     // Performs inference
  torch::NoGradGuard no_grad;                                        // with the trained
  auto test_input = torch::randn({1, 784});                          // model
  auto output = model->forward(test_input);
  auto predicted = output.argmax(1);

  std::cout << "Prediction: " << predicted.item<int64_t>() << std::endl;
}
```

Lastly, in the final example, we use the ahead-of-time (AOT) inductor feature to compile our PyTorch model and save it to a file, which can then be loaded and executed in C++ applications without requiring the original Python code:

```
torch::inductor::AOTIModelPackageLoader loader("./llm.pt2");
std::vector<torch::Tensor> outputs = loader.run(inputs);
```

17.6 Going mobile: ExecuTorch

As the last variant of deploying a model, we will discuss deployment to mobile devices. In the rapidly evolving landscape of machine learning, the ability to deploy models on a wide range of devices, including those with constrained resources, is becoming increasingly important. Executorch is a PyTorch ecosystem solution designed to address this challenge by enabling PyTorch operations to run efficiently on devices that traditionally do not support a large number of operations.

These devices, such as mobile phones and embedded systems, often lack the computational power and resources to support the full suite of PyTorch operations, which number in the thousands. ExecuTorch bridges this gap by optimizing the execution of PyTorch models on such devices, ensuring that they can still perform complex computations effectively.

The ExecuTorch workflow involves two main stages:

1. The first step in using ExecuTorch is to capture the computational graph of the model using `torch.export`.
2. Once the graph is captured, ExecuTorch provides a runtime environment tailored for constrained devices. On server-class hardware, this role is typically fulfilled by an inference server. However, ExecuTorch adapts this concept to suit the limitations and requirements of mobile and embedded devices.

Capturing this graph is similar to what we did earlier with `torch.export`, but with an additional step to convert the exported program into ExecuTorch's Edge IR format. This format is specifically designed for efficient execution on mobile devices.

Listing 17.13 Model export to ExecuTorch

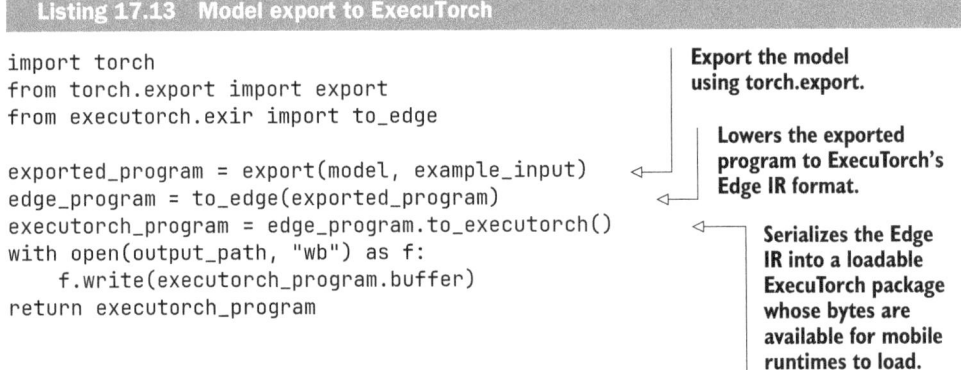

```
import torch
from torch.export import export
from executorch.exir import to_edge

exported_program = export(model, example_input)
edge_program = to_edge(exported_program)
executorch_program = edge_program.to_executorch()
with open(output_path, "wb") as f:
    f.write(executorch_program.buffer)
return executorch_program
```

- Export the model using torch.export.
- Lowers the exported program to ExecuTorch's Edge IR format.
- Serializes the Edge IR into a loadable ExecuTorch package whose bytes are available for mobile runtimes to load.

Next, we can load this package and use it in our mobile application. We will show this in Python for ease of demonstration, but the same principles apply when using it in mobile environments.

Listing 17.14 Running inference with an ExecuTorch model

```
from executorch.extension.pybindings.portable_lib import _load_for_executorch

executorch_module = _load_for_executorch(model_path)
outputs = executorch_module.forward([input_data])
```

In theory, LibTorch and C++ with PyTorch can be compiled for both Android and iOS platforms. On Android, we can access these components from an app written in Java using the Android Java Native Interface (JNI). Similarly, on iOS, we can use Objective-C++ to bridge between Swift/Objective-C and C++ code.

However, in many cases, we only need a few specific functions from PyTorch—such as loading a JIT-compiled model, converting inputs into tensors and IValues, running them through the model, and retrieving the results. To simplify this process and avoid the complexity of using JNI on Android or Objective-C++ on iOS, Executorch makes it easier to run PyTorch models on mobile devices.

Setting up mobile development requires a few additional steps compared to C++ development, and these steps are independent of the deep learning aspects. As such, we'll leave the details of mobile setup as an exercise for the reader to explore on their own. However, you can find the official instructions for setting up Executorch for Android and iOS in the PyTorch documentation at https://mng.bz/Pw0v.

17.7 Conclusion

This concludes our tour of PyTorch deployment options, covering everything from quick prototypes with Gradio to production APIs with FastAPI, model optimization techniques, cross-platform compatibility with ONNX, C++ integration via LibTorch, and mobile deployment with ExecuTorch. The PyTorch ecosystem continues to evolve rapidly, with tools like `torch.compile` and `torch.export` making deployment increasingly accessible.

While some aspects of PyTorch deployment are still maturing, the foundational technologies are strong and growing stronger. You now have a good framework to deploy your models wherever they're needed—whether as web services, in C++ applications, on mobile devices, or optimized for specialized hardware.

Hopefully, we've delivered on the promise of this book: providing you with a working knowledge of deep learning fundamentals and making you comfortable with the PyTorch library. We hope you've enjoyed reading as much as we've enjoyed writing (more, actually; writing books is hard!).

17.8 Exercises

As we close out *Deep Learning with PyTorch*, we have one final exercise for you:

1 Pick a project that sounds exciting to you. Kaggle is a great place to start looking. Dive in.

You have acquired the skills and learned the tools you need to succeed. We can't wait to hear what you do next!

Summary

- We can create interactive demos for PyTorch models using Gradio, which provides an easy way to showcase models without extensive web development knowledge.
- FastAPI enables us to build high-performance REST APIs for serving PyTorch models with built-in validation and asynchronous support.
- Request batching and streaming responses help utilize GPU resources efficiently and provide better user experiences for tasks like text generation.
- `torch.export` enables optimization of models for deployment within the PyTorch ecosystem, with AOT compilation for improved performance.
- To deploy models beyond the PyTorch ecosystem, ONNX provides a standardized format for cross-framework and cross-hardware compatibility.
- *Quantization* in PyTorch models is a technique that reduces the model size and computational requirements by converting the weights and activations from higher precision (such as 32-bit floating point) to lower precision (such as 8-bit integer).
- Using `torch.compile` can significantly improve inference performance without requiring code changes, through optimizations like kernel fusion.
- The PyTorch profiler helps identify performance bottlenecks by visualizing execution flow, operation timing, and resource usage.
- LibTorch allows direct use of PyTorch models in C++ applications, with an API designed to mirror the Python interface for easier transition.
- ExecuTorch enables efficient deployment of PyTorch models on mobile and embedded devices with limited computational resources.

index

Symbols

@app.get decorator 478
@app.post decorator 478

Numerics

2D data, working around SAM's limitation on 432–434
3D images, volumetric data 77–78
   loading specialized format 78
7z decompression utility 318

A

activation functions 148, 152
   adding nonlinearity with 150–152
   choosing best 153–154
activations, defined 462
AdamW optimizer 442
advanced indexing 87
adversarial examples 482
AI (artificial intelligence), defined 4
AlexNet 22–23
allgather operation 470
allreduce operation 459
annotations, parsing LUNA's annotation data 323–327
AOT (ahead-of-time) 492
architectures, transformers
   encoder 274
   encoder-decoder 275–276
argmax 186
argparse library 348
argument unpacking 127
arithmetic mean 393
artificial neurons 148–156
   activation functions 152
   adding nonlinearity with activation functions 150–152
   choosing best activation function 153–154
   composing multilayer networks 149
   error function 150
   learning 155–156
ASCII (American Standard Code for Information Interchange) 97
attention 260–268
   dot product self-attention 261–264
   scaled dot product causal self-attention 264–268
attributes 157, 218
augmentation, overfitting 408–417
   face-to-age prediction model 408
   improvement from 415–417
   preventing with data augmentation 409–417
   specific techniques 410–414
autograd 10, 128–144
   computing gradients automatically 128–132
   nits of 142–144
   optimizers 132–136
   switching off 142–144
   training, validation, and overfitting 136–141
   training sets 142
average pooling 211

B

backbone, defined 354–355
batching inputs 159
batch normalization 27, 231–233
bias 148, 157, 219
bigram model 249
   limits of 251–252
BLAS and LAPACK operations 54
BLIP (Bootstrapping Language-Image Pre-training) 35–37
blocks, defined 354–355
BPE (Byte Pair Encoding) 100, 281
broadcasting 47–49

C

cancer detection
  lung cancer detection 309–318
  preparing for large-scale project 304–306
  training classification model to detect suspected tumors, exercises 380–381
causal self-attention 264–268
ChainDataset 180
chain rule 128
channels, defined 204
characters, one-hot-encoding 97–101
ChatGPT 4
CIFAR-10 dataset 300
  downloading 171–172
CIFAR (Canadian Institute for Advanced Research) 171
classification models
  designing neural networks 353–360
  evaluating model 372–373
  foundational model and training loop 344–347
  training
    graphing training metrics with TensorBoard 373–379
    pretraining setup and initialization 350–353
    training and validating 360–365
    training scripts 369–372
    training to detect suspected tumors, exercises 380–381
classification problems 110
classification threshold 387
class of image 19
CNNs (convolutional neural networks), training 221–226
  measuring accuracy 222–223
  saving and loading models 223–224
  training on GPUs 224–226
Colaboratory 305
collective communication 455–457
color channels 74
combining data sources into unified datasets
  dataset implementation 336–342
  loading individual CT scans 328–330
  parsing LUNA's annotation data 323–327
Comparison ops 54
computation graph 129
ConcatDataset 180
contiguous tensors 62–63
convex functions 113
conv module 205
convolutions 201–241
  converting from to linear 358–359
  core 354–357
  detecting features with 208–210
  in action 204–215
  model design 227–240
  overview of 201–203
  padding 206–208
  subclassing nn.Module 215–220
coroutines 481
Creation ops 54
cross-entropy loss 188
CSAIL (Computer Science and Artificial Intelligence Laboratory) 171
CT (computed tomography) scans 303
  extracting nodules from 335–336
  loading individual 328–330
  overview of 306–309
  raw data files 322–327
  shape and voxel sizes 333
CT images, preparing 436–438
Ct instance 336–337, 339
curl command 485–486

D

data, tabular 89
  categorizing 85–86
  loading wine data tensor 80–82
  one-hot encoding 83–85
  representing scores 83
  thresholds 87–89
  using real-world dataset 79–80
data augmentation 139, 198
data loaders, care and feeding of 351–353
data representation, using tensors, representing text 96–104
Dataset class 12, 172–173, 180, 337–338
Dataset instance 350
Dataset instances 336, 340
Dataset object 192
datasets
  combining data sources into unified datasets 323–330, 336–342
  images 171–178
  splitting 139–141
  transforms 174–176
  unified 320–343
  updating for segmentation 432–438
data sources, combining into unified datasets
  loading individual CT scans 328–330
  parsing LUNA's annotation data 323–327
data sparsity 251
data tensor 85, 87
data types, tensor element types 51–53
DDP (Distributed Data Parallel) 470
  module 460
decoder 269–274, 284
deep learning
  competitive landscape 9–10
  defined 4–5
  hardware and software requirements 13–15
  loss functions 112–114
  machine learning vs. 5–7
  pretrained networks, Model Zoo 34–37
  PyTorch supporting projects 10–13
  transformers 268–274

deep neural networks, defined 5
dense tensors 68
depth 211–238
　combining convolutions and downsampling 212–213
　downsampling 211–212
DeviceMesh 466
DICOM (Digital Imaging and Communications in Medicine) 78, 328
differentiable functions 153
diffusers library 476
diffusion models 283–301
　forward process 289–293
　motivator for 285
　overview of 286–287
　reversing diffusion 297–300
　setting up data 287–289
　training 293–297
discrete
　convolution 202
　cross-correlations 202
diskcache library 339
dispatching mechanism 67
distillation, defined 487
distinguishing birds from airplanes 179–198
　building dataset 179–180
　fully connected model 180–181
　limits of going fully connected 196–198
　loss for classifying 186–188
　output of classifier 181–182
　representing output as probabilities 182–188
　training classifier 189–196
distributed computing, terminology 451–453
DistributedSampler 460
dot product self-attention 261–264
　computing attention weights 263
　implementing 263–264
downsampling 211–212
　combining convolutions and 212–213
dropout 27, 230–231

E

eager mode 497
edge-detection kernel 209
elements, tensor element types 51–53
embeddings 99, 254–259
　text 101–103
　text as blueprint 104
　visualizing 259
encoder 284
　transformers 274
EncoderBlock module 25
encoder-decoder, transformers 275–276
epochs 121
execution
　with torch.profiler 499–501
ExecuTorch 504–506
exporting models 490–494
　interoperability beyond PyTorch with ONNX 491–492
　torch.export 492–494

F

F1 score, updating logging output to include 395
false positives and false negatives 384–386
FastAPI 477–480, 506
features, detecting with convolutions 208–210
fine-tuning 104
　updating training for 439–445
FineTuning dataset 438, 440
FishNet 313
floating-point numbers 40–42
forward
　pass 23
　process 289–293
FSDP (Fully Sharded Data Parallel) 468–470, 472
functional API 219–220

G

GANs (generative adversarial networks) 284–285

generalization 200–240
　convolutions, overview of 201–203
generalized tensors 67–68
generators 481
geometric mean 394
ghost pixels 206
GIL (global interpreter lock) 481
gloo backend 455
GPT2 library 34
GPT (Generative Pre-Trained Transformer) 269
GPUs (graphics processing units) 8, 42
　moving tensors to 64–66
　training models on multiple 450–468
　training on 224–226
gradient descent 116–127
　applying derivatives to model 120
　computing derivatives 118–120
　decreasing loss 117–118
　defining gradient function 120–121
　iterating to fit model 121–124
　normalizing inputs 124–126
　optimizers 133–135
　visualizing data 127
gradient reduction 459
gradients 109
　computing automatically 128–132
Gradio 476–477, 506

H

Hardtanh function 152, 154
harmonic mean 393
HDF5 (Hierarchical Data Format), serializing tensors to with h5py 68–69
hidden layers 163
Hounsfield Units 330, 357
huggingface_hub library 438
hyperparameters 191
　search 351
　tuning 123

I

identity mapping 236
ILSVRC (ImageNet Large Scale Visual Recognition Challenge) 19
image encoder 35
images 73–77, 170–199
    adding color channels 74
    changing layout 75–76
    datasets 171–178
    distinguishing birds from airplanes 179–198
    loading image files 74–75
    normalizing data 76–77
    recognizing subjects of 18–28
indexing, tensors 46–47
Indexing ops 54
inference, defined 26
initialization
    of models and optimizers 350–351
    of neural networks 359–360
in-place operations 57
instance segmentation 423
interoperability, NumPy 66–67

J

JIT (just-in-time) compiler 486, 497
JNI (Java Native Interface) 505
joining ops 54
Jupyter Notebooks 14–15

K

kernel fusion 486
kernels 14, 202
kernel trick 218
key vectors 263

L

labels, overview 18–20
layer normalization 269
layers 24
learning 106–145
    gradient descent 116–127
    loss functions 112–114
    models 107–109
    neural networks 155–156
    parameter estimation 109–112
learning mechanics, autograd 128–144
    computing gradients automatically 128–132
    nits of 142–144
    optimizers 132–136
    switching off 142–144
    training, validation, and overfitting 136–141
    training sets 142
LibTorch 501–503, 506
LIDAR (light detection and ranging) 306
lifespan event 483
linear layers 254–259
    converting from convolution to 358–359
    visualizing embeddings 259
linear models 111–112
    comparing to 167
    replacing 163–164
lists, Python lists to PyTorch tensors 42–43
LitServe 490
LLMs (large language models) 470
loading models 223–224
logistic function 152
logits 194, 359
logMetrics, implementing precision and recall in 390–391
LogSoftmax 188
loss
    diffusion models 295–297
    evaluating training loss 137
    for classifying 186–188
loss functions 7, 12, 112–114
    PyTorch 113–114
loss tensor 129
lottery ticket hypothesis 204
LSTM (long short-term memory) 227
LunaDataset 383, 418, 434
lung cancer detection 309–318
    downloading LUNA data 318
    LUNA Grand Challenge 317
    nodules 316–317

M

machine learning, deep learning vs. 5–7
masks, constructing 367–369
Math ops 54
Matplotlib library 342
max pooling 211
mean square error (MSE) 186
mean square loss 114
medical imaging, segmentation, inference and results 445
metadata, tensor metadata 57–63
    contiguous tensors 62–63
    transposing in higher dimensions 61–62
    transposing without copying 60–61
    views of another tensor's storage 58–59
metrics
    F1 score, updating logging output to include 395
    false positives and false negatives 384–386
    graphing positives and negatives 386–396
    overfitting 408–417
microbatches 463
minibatch 133
mirroring 411–412
mixed-precision training 487
MLP (multilayer perceptron) 269
mobile deployment, ExecuTorch 504–505
modalities 35
model design 227–240
    depth 233–238
    regularization 229–233
    width 227–228
model function 136
model parallelism 461–466
models 107–109
    initializing 350–351
    saving and loading 223–224
    training classification models, pretraining setup and initialization 350–353
models module 23
Model Zoo 34–37

modules 24, 157
MoE (Mixture of experts) 470
mpi backend 455
MPS (Metal Performance Shaders) 64
MSELoss 181
multichannel images 204
multidimensional arrays 41–46
  constructing 43
  essence of 44–46
  from Python lists to PyTorch tensors 42–43
multiheaded attention 269
multilayer networks 149
multiple GPUs, training models on
  fully sharded data parallelism 468–470
  large language model specific parallelisms 470
mutating ops 54

N

named tensors 48–51
names, generating character by character 247–249
nccl backend 455
NCI Dictionary of Cancer Terms 317
n-dimensional parallelism 466–468
networks, as nn.Module 216–218
neural networks 146–169
  artificial neurons 148–156
  comparing to linear model 167
  designing 353–360
  inspecting parameters 164–166
  nn module 157–163
  replacing linear model 163–164
NLL (negative log likelihood) 187
NLP (natural language processing) 96, 246, 425
nn module 184, 219
  linear model
    batching inputs 159
    optimizing batches 160–163

nodules 309
  locating using patient coordinate system 330–336
  segmentation, updating training for fine-tuning 439–445
noise 413
nonlinear functions 153
nonlinearity 150–152
Normalize transform 177
normalizing data 76–77, 177–178
normalizing inputs 124–126
notebook cells, defined 14–15
numbers, converting text to 97
NumPy, interoperability 66–67

O

one-hot encoding 83–85
  characters 97–101
  whole words 99–101
ONNX (Open Neural Network Exchange) 475, 491–492
operator reordering 486
optimizers 132–136
  gradient descent optimizers 133–135
  initializing 350–351
  testing other optimizers 135–136
optimizing batches 160–163
optim module 134, 145
Other operations 54
overfitting 136–141, 408–417
  face-to-age prediction model 408
  preventing with data augmentation 409–417
  specific techniques 411–414
overtraining 122–124

P

P2P (peer-to-peer) operations 462
padded convolutions 206–208, 357
Parallelism 54
parallelism 458–459
  context 470
  data 459–461

exercises 471–472
expert 470
large language model specific 470
strategies 471
parallel programming 450–455
  distributed computing terminology 451–453
  hardware requirements 453
  initializing distributed program 453–455
parameter estimation 109–112
  choosing linear models 111–112
  gathering data 110–111
  regression problems 110
  visualizing data 111
parameters
  inspecting 164–166
  keeping track of 218
params tensor 129
parsing LUNA's annotation data 323–327
  unifying annotation and candidate data 325–327
patient coordinate system 330–336
  converting between millimeters and voxel addresses 333–335
  overview of 331–332
penalization terms 139
performance metrics, outputting 365–369
permute method 75
per-pixel classification 423–425
  Segment Anything model (SAM) 425
pickle library 444
PIL (Python Imaging Library) 173
pipe 31
pipeline API 464
pipeline parallelism 463–464
  deciding between 465–466
pip install tokenizer 277
points tensor 46, 58–60, 65
Pointwise ops 54
pooling 211–213
positional embeddings 269
POST endpoint 478
precision 389–391

predict method 218
prepcache script 395, 436
preprocess function 25
pretrained networks 17–38
   BLIP 35–37
   generating and editing
      images 29–34
   Model Zoo 34–37
   recognizing subjects of
      images 18–28
pretraining setup and
   initialization 350–353
   care and feeding of data
      loaders 351–353
   initializing model and
      optimizer 350–351
Project Gutenberg 97
PyTorch
   deep learning projects,
      supporting 10–13
   expectations 7–10
   hardware and software
      requirements 13–15
   loss functions 113–114
   outputting performance
      metrics 365–369
   reasons for using 8–10
   representing text 96–104
   serving models 475–490
   tensors, from Python lists
      to 42–43
   training classification models
      graphing training metrics
         with TensorBoard
         373–379
   use case 303–304

Q

quantization 487–490, 506
quantized tensors 68
query vectors 263

R

Random sampling 54
rank, defined 451
raw CT data files 322
real-world data representation,
   volumetric data 77–78
recall 388–391
Reduction ops 54

regression problems 110
regularization 139, 229–233
   batch normalization 231–233
   dropout 230–231
   weight penalties 229–230
ReLU (rectified linear
   unit) 152, 214
representing
   characters, one-hot-
      encoding 97–101
   text 96–104
   text embeddings 101–103
   text embeddings as
      blueprint 104
   words, one-hot-encoding
      whole 99–101
residual connections 269
ResNets (residual networks) 234
results dictionary 483
Retina U-Net 313
reversing diffusion 297–300
RNNs (recurrent neural
   networks) 96
rotating 412–413
routing information 263

S

SAM (Segment Anything
   model) 425, 447
   using directly 430–432
saving models 223–224
scaled dot product causal self-
   attention 264–268
scaling 412
scripts, training 369–372
segmentation 309–310, 420–448
   exercises 447
   inference and results 445
   updating dataset for 432–438
   updating training for fine-
      tuning 439–445
   using SAM model
      directly 430–432
self-attention 261–264
   computing attention
      weights 263
   implementing dot product
      self-attention 263–264
self-supervised learning 249–252
   limits of bigram model
      251–252

SentencePiece library 101
Serialization 54
serializing tensors, overview
   of 68–69
serving PyTorch models
   475–490
   deployment 481–482
   FastAPI 477–480
   Gradio 476–477
   optimizing performance
      486–490
   request batching and stream-
      ing responses 482–486
SGD (Stochastic Gradient
   Descent) 133, 191, 229,
   351
shard, defined 459
sharded data parallelism
   468–470
shifting by random offset 412
show method 26
shuffle Boolean 192
Sigmoid function 152
SimpleITK library 329, 334
singleton dimension 85
Sinusoidal positional
   embedding 294
sitk routines 329
skip connections 234–236, 269
slicing ops 54
softmax 182
Softplus function 152
sort function 28
spawn method 454
Spectral ops 54
SPMD (Single Program Multiple Data) 451
stages, defined 463
step method 133
storage 55–57
   indexing into 55–56
   modifying stored values 57
strided tensors 68
subclassing nn.Module 215–220
   functional API 219–220
   keeping track of parameters
      and submodules 218
   network as nn.Module
      216–218
submodules 216
subword-nmt library 101
SummaryWriter class 377–378

T

tabular data 79–89
  categorizing 85–86
  loading wine data tensor 80–82
  one-hot encoding 83–85
  representing scores 83
  thresholds 87–89
  using real-world dataset 79–80
tail, defined 354
tanh activation 164
Tanh activation function 214
Tanh function 152, 156
tanh function 149
target tensor 83, 87
TCPStore 454
tensor
  API 53–57
  storage 55–57
  See also specific tensors
TensorBoard, graphing training metrics with 373–379
Tensor data type 8
tensor parallelism 465–466
  deciding between 465–466
tensors 7, 39–71
  as floating-point numbers 40–42
  broadcasting 47–48
  device attribute 65–66
  generalized 67–68
  images 73–77
  indexing 46–47
  moving to GPU 64–66
  multidimensional arrays 42–46
  named 48–51
  representing tabular data 79–89
  representing text 96–104
  serializing 68–69
  tensor element types 51–53
  tensor metadata 57–63
  time series 89–96
  volumetric data 77–78
test set 142
text, representing 96–104
  converting text to numbers 97
  one-hot-encoding characters 97–101

one-hot-encoding whole words 99–101
text embeddings 101–103
text embeddings as blueprint 104
text decoder 35
t function 60
time series 89–96
  adding time dimension 89–91
  ready for training 94–96
  shaping data by time period 91–93
tokenization 277–279
  generating sentences 278–279
tokenizer library 277
tokens 247, 280–281
torch
  library 15
  module 10, 53, 132, 454
  operations 216, 493
  package 455
torch.compile 13, 495–499, 506
  full graph capture vs. disjoint graphs 495–499
torch.fx (FX) graph 498
TorchInductor 494, 498
torchrun utility 455
TorchTitan 471
torchvision 18, 25, 171, 174
torch_xla package 64
ToTensor transform 175, 178
TPUs (tensor processing units) 64
trainable parameters 195
trained model, overview 13
training
  classification models
    foundational model and training loop 344–347
    graphing training metrics with TensorBoard 373–379
    main entry point for application 347–349
    pretraining setup and initialization 350–353
    training and validating 360–365
    training scripts 369–372
  convolutional neural networks 221–226
    measuring accuracy 222–223

saving and loading models 223–224
training on GPUs 224–226
diffusion models 293–297
  loss 295–297
evaluating training loss 137
graphing training metrics with TensorBoard 373–379
improving, high-level plan for 383–384
improving with metrics and augmentation, exercises 417–418
outputting performance metrics 365–369
pretraining setup and initialization
  care and feeding of data loaders 351–353
  initializing model and optimizer 350–351
training/validation split 340–341
See also training models
training data, generating 252–254
training iterations 121
training loop 121–122
training models
  collective communication 455–457
  on multiple GPUs 449–473
    fully sharded data parallelism 468–470
    large language model specific parallelisms 470
    model parallelism 461–466
    n-dimensional parallelism 466–468
    parallel programming 450–455
    parallelism strategies 471–472
training scripts 369–372
training sets 136, 142, 323–327
transformers 96, 245–282
  architectures 274–276
  attention 260–268
  decoder 269–274
  embeddings and linear layers 254–259
  exercises 281

transformers *(continued)*
  generating names character by character 247–249
  generating training data 252–254
  self-supervised learning 249–252
  tokenization 277–279
  Vision Transformer 279–281
transformers library 440, 479
transformers package 34
translation invariant 197, 201
transpose function 53
transposing tensors 60–62
true negatives 386
true positives 385
tumor detection, training classification model
  evaluating model 372–373
  graphing training metrics with TensorBoard 373–379
  outputting performance metrics 365–369
  to detect suspected tumors, exercises 380–381

U

uint8 52
unboxed C numeric types 44
underfitting, defined 137

unified datasets 320–343
  combining data sources into, parsing LUNA's annotation data 323–327
  locating nodules using patient coordinate system 330–336
updating training for finetuning, setting up model 440–441

V

VAEs (variational autoencoders) 31, 284–285
validation 136–141
  classification models 360–365
  evaluating training loss 137
  generalizing to validation set 138–139
  splitting dataset 139–141
  training/validation split 340–341
validation sets 136, 323–327
view function 359
views of another tensor's storage 58–59
visualizing
  data 111–127
  embeddings 259

ViT (Vision Transformer) 23, 279–281
vLLM 490
volumetric data 77–78
volumetric pixel 205, 306
  addresses 333–335
  sizes 333
voxel (volumetric pixel) 205

W

weight
  decay 229–230
  matrix 202
  penalties 229–230
  tensor 195, 205
WeightedRandomSampler 418
weights 109, 148
  computing attention weights 263
world size 451
WSL (Windows Subsystem for Linux) 453

X

xyz2irc conversion function 335

Z

zero-shot segmentation 425